Using this guide

Call first! Not [...] ear!), but because eve [...] have changed since [...]

Info Lines & [...] r website, www.damr [...] groups as well as servic [...] with a limo.

Accommodations Most accommodations (especially B&Bs) require advance reservations. It's a good idea to request a brochure ahead of time, and to be clear about deposit and cancellation policies when making reservations.

Bars & Nightclubs Many codes apply only a few nights a week, especially when we've noted "theme nights." You should call the bar to verify what is scheduled for which nights. Bars coded BW (beer/wine) might not serve both.

Restaurants All restaurants listed are gay-friendly; those with mostly gay/lesbian clientele are coded MW.

Cafes are casual hangouts serving coffee and pastries, but not full menus.

Entertainment & Recreation Something touristy, maybe a little kitschy, unusual, or commonly overlooked, that even your friends who've lived there all their lives won't mind doing with you.

Publications If you want to know what's new, get one when you get to town. They're usually free and distributed in many of the locations we list. Your best bet, however, is to go right to the local LGBT or alternative bookstore to get the latest issue and/or lowdown.

Gyms are workout facilities, not bathhouses. They're mostly straight, unless coded MW or MO.

Men's Clubs include sex clubs, bathhouses, playspaces, and sex-oriented groups.

Men's Services are mostly telephone-dating services.

Cruisy Areas In many cities, you're more likely to meet vice cops than partners at public grounds. Try the local bar or bathhouse instead if you're bent on picking up. To avoid entrapment, read the notice about "Cruisy Areas," page 4.

Unconfirmed means we've called, several times, but no one answered. The phone still works but everything else may be different. Definitely call first.

Events Calendar Lists those "can't-miss" events for the upcoming year — from circuit parties to bear jamborees to street fairs and festivals.

Tour Operators A brief description of what kinds of tours the tour operator offers.

As Damron has done since 1964, we reward the best letters (those packed with new info of openings and closings we haven't already found) with a **FREE COPY** of next year's edition.

Table of Contents

Table of Contents

Who we are

In 1964, a businessman published a book of all the gay bars he knew from his constant travels across the United States. This book could fit comfortably in the palm of your hand. Despite its small size, it was an impressive accomplishment. Each one of the listings he had visited himself. Every last copy of that book he sold himself. The name of this pioneering businessman—Bob Damron.

Fifty years later, his little book, the *Damron Men's Travel Guide* (originally *Bob Damron's Address Book*), is still a bestseller. And it has remained the model for the countless gay travel guides to follow in its wake. Today, Damron's list of titles includes: the *Damron Women's Traveller* print guide for lesbians; *Gay Scout* and *Gurl Scout* iPhone applications; the *Damron Men's Travel Guide* for Android, and a series of *Damron City Guide* applications, also available for Android.

How we maintain the accuracy of our listings

Our editors contact every single listing in our database annually, usually by phone or email. They also receive updated information directly from business owners and you, our readers. If you send in new, verifiably correct information, Damron will send you a free copy of the next edition as our way of saying a very sincere "thank you" for your help.

PLEASE READ THIS NOTICE ABOUT "CRUISY AREAS"

Certain locations are categorized as "Cruisy Areas." These areas include but are not limited to parks, rest stops, and beaches. Information regarding these areas is furnished to Damron by various sources and, due to time and other constraints, Damron is unable to investigate these areas. Areas marked as "AYOR" (At Your Own Risk) may involve risk and the reader should proceed with caution. However, the absence of an AYOR rating does not guarantee the safety or security of any area. Therefore, Damron makes no warranty or representation as to the safety, security, or status of those areas marked as cruisy areas. Damron urges readers to avoid sexual activity within Cruisy Areas.

BEWARE — MOST POLICE DEPARTMENTS IN THE USA HAVE COPIES OF THE MEN'S TRAVEL GUIDE.

Publisher	**Damron Company**
President & Editor-in-Chief	**Gina M. Gatta**
Managing Editor & Art Director	**Erika O'Connor**
Design Consultant	**Mary Burroughs**

Board of Directors
   Gina M. Gatta, Edward Gatta, Jr., Louise Mock

In Memory of Bob Damron and Dan Delbex

How to Contact Us

Mail: PO Box 422458, San Francisco, CA 94142-2458
Web: www.damron.com
Phone: 415/255-0404 & 800/462-6654
         [9am-5pm (PST) Mon-Fri]
Fax: 415/703-9049

IT'S SO MIAMI

MAR	APR	MAY	JUL	OCT	NOV	2017
Winter Party	Miami Beach Gay Pride	Aqua Girl	Miami Beach Bruthaz Conference	Orgullo	White Party	World Outgames
	Miami Gay & Lesbian Film Festival	Sizzle Miami				

LGBT VISITOR CENTER - 1130 WASHINGTON AVENUE, MIAMI BEACH

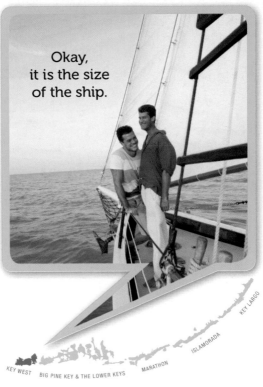

Okay,
it is the size
of the ship.

KEY WEST BIG PINE KEY & THE LOWER KEYS MARATHON ISLAMORADA KEY LARGO

With everything from authentic coastal
sailing ships to gay tours, water sports, drag
shows and even clothing-optional resorts,
no other gay destination measures up to
fabulous Key West.
fla-keys.com/gaykeywest 1.888.294.4603

The Florida Keys
Key West
Close To Perfect - Far From Normal

WARNING
HOT GUYS!
Meet hot guys wherever you're traveling...
FREE
To Set up a Mailbox
To Listen to Personal Ads
To Reply to Personal Ads
USE FREE CODE:
Damron
Call 24/7 to get your local number
1-888-MegaMates™
MegaMatesMen.com
1-888-634-2628
24/7 Friendly Customer Care 1(888) 634.2628 18+ ©2014 PC LLC

MAGNITUDE

FOLSOM STREET FAIR

the official saturday night dance event
of folsom street fair®

folsomstreetfair.com/magnitude

REAL BAD™ XXVI
A GRGR/WEST PRODUCTION

FOLSOM WEEKEND | SAN FRANCISCO
SUNDAY ■ SEPTEMBER 21, 2014 ■ 7PM - 4AM

BE BAD... DO GOOD
realbad.org
100% OF GENERAL ADMISSION TICKET SALES BENEFIT LGBT & HIV/AIDS CHARITIES
PHOTO: MICHAEL SMITH • GRAPHIC DESIGN: KENSHI@KENSHIWESTOVER.com

do you speak
SONOMA?

{ **Sonomads:** *n.* People who embrace the wanderlust of Sonoma Wine Country.

Speak a little Sonoma and you'll feel like a local.

Because you're more than a visitor, you're a new friend.

Learn by immersion and win a savory Sonoma County experience!

1-800-576-6662
SonomaCounty.com/gay

SONOMA
COUNTY
CALIFORNIA

frameline

SAN FRANCISCO INTERNATIONAL LGBT FILM FESTIVAL
JUNE 19 - 29, 2014 & **JUNE 18 - 28, 2015**

The world's first & largest queer film festival
(and so much more)

EXHIBITION

FILMMAKER SUPPORT

DISTRIBUTION

 frameline  @framelinefest

frameline.org

USA

Statewide

■PUBLICATIONS

➤**Ambush Mag** 504/522-8049
LGBT newspaper for the Gulf South (TX through FL)

Anniston

■CRUISY AREAS

Cheaha Park [AYOR] Cheaha Scenic Dr
early evenings, head toward the walking trail (beware of cops!)

Auburn

■ACCOMMODATIONS

Black Bear Camp Men's Retreat
[MO,R,SW,N,NS,WI,WC,GO] 10565 US Hwy
280 W, Waverly 334/887-5152 *hot tub, kitchen*

■CRUISY AREAS

Rest Area [AYOR] Hwy 280 (30 miles E
of Alexander City & 5 miles W of
Auburn) *evenings*

Birmingham

■ACCOMMODATIONS

Hampton Inn [GF,WI,WC] 2021 Park Pl
N (at 21st St N) 205/322-2100 *also restaurant & lounge*

■BARS

The Garage Cafe [GF,F,E] 2304 10th
Terrace S (at 23rd St S) 205/322-3220
11am-close, from 3pm Sun-Mon, great sandwiches, live music

Our Place [M,NH,V,GO] 205/715-0077
4pm-midnight, till 2am Fri-Sat

Wine Loft [GF] 2200 1st Ave N
205/323-8228 *5pm-close, clsd Sun-Mon, wine bar, light food served*

■NIGHTCLUBS

Al's on 7th [MW,NH,D,DS,18+,PC] 2627
7th Ave S (at 27th St) 205/321-2812
theme nights

The Quest Club [M,K,D,DS,PC,WC,$] 416
24th St S (at 5th Ave S)
205/251-4313 *24hrs, [19+] Wed-Sun, patio*

Steel Urban Lounge [GF,D] 2300 1st
Ave N (at 23rd St) 205/324-0666
6pm-close, from 8pm wknds, upscale lounge

■CAFES

Chez Lulu [E] 1909 Cahaba Rd
205/870-7011 *lunch & dinner Tue-Sun, Sun brunch, clsd Mon, plenty veggie, also bakery*

■RESTAURANTS

Bottega Cafe & Restaurant [WC]
2240 Highland Ave S (btwn 22nd &
23rd) 205/939-1000 *5:30pm-10pm, clsd Sun, full bar*

The Bottletree 3719 3rd Ave S (at 37th
St S) 205/533-6288 *3pm-close, from
11am wknds, vegetarian/ vegan, also bar,
live music venue*

Highlands Bar & Grill [WC] 2011 11th
Ave S (at 20th St) 205/939-1400
5:30pm-10pm, clsd Sun-Mon

John's City Diner [WC] 112 21st St N
(btwn 1st & 2nd Ave N)
205/322-6014 *lunch weekdays &
dinner Mon-Sat, clsd Sun, full bar*

Rojo 2921 Highland Ave S (at 30th St)
205/328-4733 *11am-10pm, clsd Mon,
wknd brunch, Latin & American cuisine*

Silvertron Cafe 3813 Clairmont Ave S
(at 39th St S) 205/591-3707 *11am-
9pm, from 8am Sat, also full bar, more
gay Mon*

Taj India 2226 Highland Ave S
205/939-3805 *lunch & dinner, Indian,
plenty veggie*

■ENTERTAINMENT & RECREATION

Terrific New Theatre 2821 2nd Ave S
(in Dr Pepper Design Complex)
205/328-0868

■MEN'S SERVICES

➤**MegaMates** 205/595-3388 *Call to
hook up with HOT local men. FREE to
listen & respond to ads. Use FREE code
DAMRON. MegaMates.com.*

Alabama • *USA*

■EROTICA

Alabama Adult Books 801 3rd Ave N (at 8th) **205/322-7323** *super-arcade*

Birmingham Adult Books 7610 1st Ave N (at 76th St) **205/836-1580** *booths*

Pleasure Books 7606 1st Ave N (at 76th St N) **205/836-7379** *arcade, booths*

■CRUISY AREAS

Cahaba River Rd Park [AYOR] at Jefferson/ Shelby county line (on Hwy 280 E, exit before Cahaba River bridge & turn left) *follow trail; noon & late afternoon popular*

Dothan

■NIGHTCLUBS

Dothan Dance Club [GF,DS,MR,C,PC,GO] 2563 Ross Clark Circle (at Hwy 52 West) **334/792-5166** *11pm Fri, from 6pm Sat-Sun, clsd Mon-Th*

Geneva

■ACCOMMODATIONS

Spring Creek Campground & Resort [MO,SW,N,WI,GO] 163 Campground Rd (at Spring Creek Rd) **334/723-5749** *cabins, tent & RV sites, some theme wknds w/ DJ, day passes*

Huntsville

■BARS

Partners [MW,D,F,E,K,WC,GO] **256/539-0975** *5pm-2am, from 6pm Sat, from 2pm Sun*

■CRUISY AREAS

Monte Sano Scenic Overlook [AYOR] Governors Dr (on left before Monte Sano Blvd)

Mobile

■INFO LINES & SERVICES

Pink Triangle AA Group **251/479-9994** (AA#), **251/438-7080** (church) *7pm Tue, Th & Sat, call for locations*

■ACCOMMODATIONS

Berney Fly B&B [GF,SW,NS,WI,WC] 1118 Government St **251/405-0949** *Victorian B&B, full brkfst, near downtown*

■BARS

Flipside Bar & Patio [MW,NH,NS] 54 S Conception St **251/431-8869** *open 4pm*

Gabriel's Downtown [MW,K,V,PC] 55 S Joachim St (off Government) **251/432-4900** *7pm-close, patio*

Midtown Pub [MW,NH,D,F,K] 153 S Florida St (at Emogene) **251/450-1555** *noon-2am*

■NIGHTCLUBS

B-Bob's Downtown [M,D,B,DS,P,WC] 213 Conti St (at Joachim) **251/433-2262** *6pm-close, from 7pm Sat, 2-level multi-venue club, home den of Gulf Coast Bears, also gift shop*

■RESTAURANTS

True Midtown Kitchen 1104 Dauphin St **251/434-2002** *lunch & dinner, brunch only Sun, full bar, soul food*

Montgomery

■ACCOMMODATIONS

The Lattice Inn [GS,SW,WI,WC,GO] 1414 S Hull St (at Clanton) **334/262-3388**

■NIGHTCLUBS

Club 322 [MW,D,DS] 322 N Lawrence St **334/263-4322** *8pm-close, clsd Mon*

■MEN'S SERVICES

▶**MegaMates** **334/414-9500** *Call to hook up with HOT local men. FREE to listen & respond to ads. Use FREE code DAMRON. MegaMates.com.*

■CRUISY AREAS

Woodmere Park [AYOR] Woodmere Blvd (at Eastern)

Anchorage • Alaska

Steele

■ACCOMMODATIONS
Bluff Creek Falls [M,SW,PC,WI,GO]
1125 Loop Rd 256/538-0678,
205/515-7882 *secluded campground
w/ waterfalls, bluffs, 50 minutes from
Birmingham*

Tuscaloosa

■NIGHTCLUBS
Icon [M,D,DS] 516 Greensboro Ave
9pm-2am, clsd Sun-Mon

■MEN'S SERVICES
▶**MegaMates** 205/535-3200 *Call to
hook up with HOT local men. FREE to
listen & respond to ads. Use FREE code
DAMRON. MegaMates.com.*

■CRUISY AREAS
Bowers Park [AYOR] *from McFarland
Blvd turn E onto 37th St, then turn N
onto Bowers Park Dr*

Jack Warner Pkwy Parks [AYOR] *along
Black Warrior River formerly River Rd
Parks, check out 4th park near boat
ramp*

ALASKA

Statewide

■ENTERTAINMENT &
RECREATION
Out in Alaska [★] PO Box 82096,
Fairbanks 99708 877/374-9958,
907/374-9958 *adventure travel
throughout Alaska for LGBT travelers*

Anchorage

■INFO LINES & SERVICES
AA Gay/ Lesbian 336 E 5th Ave (at
Community Center) 907/929-4528
6pm Mon

Gay/ Lesbian Helpline 1300 East St
907/258-4777, 888/901-9876
(outside Anchorage) *6pm-11pm*

Identity, Inc 336 E 5th Ave
907/929-4528 *community center,
newsletter*

■ACCOMMODATIONS
A Wildflower Inn B&B [GS,NS,WI,GO]
1239 I St (at 13th) 907/274-1239,
877/693-1239 *convenient, downtown
location*

Alaska Heavenly Lodge [GF,NS] 34950
Blakely Rd (at Mile 49 Sterling Hwy),
Cooper Landing 907/595-2012,
866/595-2012 *hot tub, cedar sauna*

Alaska's North Country Castle B&B
[GF,NS] 14600 Joanne Cir
907/345-7296 *ocean & mtn views, full
brkfst*

Anchorage Jewel Lake B&B
[GS,NS,WI,GO] 8125 Jewel Lake Rd
907/245-7321, 877/245-7321 *full
brkfst, kids ok*

Arctic Fox Inn [GS,GO] 327 E 2nd Ct
907/272-4818, 877/693-1239 *also
apts*

City Garden B&B [GS,NS,WI,GO] 1352
W 10th Ave (at N St) 907/276-8686
*beautiful views of Mt McKinley, 10-
minute walk to downtown area*

Copper Whale Inn [GS,WI,NS,WC,GO]
440 L St (at 5th Ave) 907/258-7999,
866/258-7999 *downtown*

Eagle Nest Guest House [MO,WI,GO]
25411 Crystal Creek Dr 907/903-1828

Gallery B&B [GS,WC,GO] 1229 G St (at
12th) 907/274-2567 *lesbian-owned*

Inlet Tower Hotel & Suites
[GS,WI,WC] 1200 L St (at 12th)
907/276-0110, 800/544-0786 *also
bar & restaurant*

Renfro's Lakeside Retreat [GF,WI,GO]
27177 Seward Hwy, Seward
907/288-5059, 877/288-5059 *log
cabins on Kenai Lake, seasonal*

■BARS
Bernie's Bungalow Lounge [GF,F] 626
D St (at W 5th Ave) 907/276-8808
cocktail lounge, patio, food served

Kodiak Bar [MW,D,F] 225 E 5th Ave
(btwn Cordova & Barrow)
907/258-5233, 907/865-8978 *3pm-
2:30am, till 5am Fri-Sat*

Mad Myrna's [MW,NH,D,F,K,DS] 530 E
5th Ave (at Fairbanks) 907/276-9762
4pm-2:30am, till 3am Fri-Sat

Damron Men's Travel Guide 2014   www.damron.com **19**

Alaska • *USA*

Raven [MW,NH,WC] 708 E 4th Ave **907/276-9672** *1pm-2:30am, till 3am wknds*

■RESTAURANTS

Bear Tooth Theatre Pub & Grill 1230 W 27th Ave **907/276-4200** *movie theater, pub & grill all in one*

China Lights 12110 Business Blvd, Eagle River **907/694-8080** *11:30am-10pm, till 10:30pm wknds*

Club Paris 417 W 5th Ave **907/277-6332** *11am-midnight, from 4pm Sun, perhaps the finest restaurant in town*

Garcia's 11901 Business Blvd #104 (next to Safeway), Eagle River **907/694-8600** *11am-midnight, from noon wknds, Mexican*

Ginger 425 W 5th Ave (at D St) **907/929-3680** *lunch Mon-Fri, dinner nightly, bar from 3pm, Pacific Rim/ Asian*

Marx Brothers Cafe 627 W 3rd Ave **907/278-2133** *5:30pm-10pm, clsd Sun-Mon, great food & views*

Simon & Seafort's 420 L St (btwn 4th & 5th) **907/274-3502** *lunch weekdays, dinner nightly, great view, full bar*

Snow City Cafe [★BW,WI] 1034 W 4th Ave (at L St) **907/272-2489** *7am-3pm, till 4pm wknds*

■ENTERTAINMENT & RECREATION

Out North Contemporary Art House 3800 DeBarr Rd **907/279-3800** *community-based & visiting-artist exhibits, screenings & performances*

■BOOKSTORES

Title Wave Books 1360 W Northern Lights Blvd **907/278-9283, 888/598-9283** *10am-8pm, till 9pm Fri-Sat, 11am-7pm Sun, LGBT section*

■PUBLICATIONS

Anchorage Press **907/561-7737** *alternative paper*

■EROTICA

Le Shop 305 W Diamond Blvd (at C St) **907/522-1987** *8am-1am*

Fairbanks

■ACCOMMODATIONS

All Seasons B&B Inn [GF,NS,WI,WC] 763 7th Ave (at Barnette St) **907/451-6649, 888/451-6649** *full brkfst*

Billie's Backpackers Hostel [GF,F] 2895 Mack Blvd **907/479-2034, 907/799-6120**

■CAFES

Hot Licks Ice Cream 3453 College Rd **907/479-7813** *seasonal*

Haines

■ACCOMMODATIONS

The Guardhouse Boarding House [MW,NS,WI,GO] 15 Fort Seward Dr **907/766-2566, 866/290-7445** *in former jail of Fort William H. Seward*

Homer

■ACCOMMODATIONS

Sadie Cove Wilderness Lodge [GF,NS] Kachemak Bay State Park **907/235-2350, 888/283-7234** *tree planted for every guest to offset carbon emission, 3 full meals a day*

■CAFES

Spit Sister Cafe [GS,WI] Homer Spit Rd (at Harbor View Boardwalk #5) **907/235-4921 (summer), 907/299-6868/ 6767 (winter)** *5am-4pm*

■ENTERTAINMENT & RECREATION

Alaska Fantastic Fishing Charters **800/478-7777** *deluxe cabin cruiser for big-game fishing (halibut)*

Juneau

■ACCOMMODATIONS

Pearson's Pond Luxury Suites & Adventure Spa [GF,NS,WI] 4541 Sawa Circle **907/789-3772, 888/658-6328** *B&B resort & spa*

The Silverbow Inn [GF,NS,WI] 120 Second St **907/586-4146, 800/586-4146**

■RESTAURANTS

Hangar on the Wharf 2 Marine Way Ste 106 **907/586-5018** *lunch & dinner, full bar, great fish & chips*

■CRUISY AREAS

Cope Park [AYOR] *mornings & afternoons (summers)*

Ketchikan

■ACCOMMODATIONS

Anchor Inn by the Sea [GF,NS,WI] 4672 S Tongass Hwy **907/247-7117, 800/928-3308**

■ENTERTAINMENT & RECREATION

Southeast Sea Kayaks [GF] 3 Salmon Landing **907/225-1258, 800/287-1607**

McCarthy

■ACCOMMODATIONS

McCarthy Lodge & Ma Johnson's Hotel [GF,F,NS] **907/554-4402** *inside Wrangell St Elias nat'l park*

Palmer

■ACCOMMODATIONS

Alaska Garden Gate B&B [GS,NS,WI,GO] 950 S Trunk Rd **907/746-2333** *full brkfst, hot tub, lesbian-owned*

Seward

■ENTERTAINMENT & RECREATION

Puffin Fishing Charters [GS] PO Box 606, 99664 **907/224-4653, 800/978-3346** *day fishing trips*

Sitka

■CAFES

Backdoor Cafe 104 Barracks St (behind Old Harbor Books on Lincoln St, no street sign) **907/747-8856** *6:30am-5pm, till 2pm Sat, clsd Sun*

■ENTERTAINMENT & RECREATION

Esther G Sea Taxi 215 Shotgun Alley **907/738-6481, 907/747-6481** *marine wildlife tours, transportation service*

ARIZONA

Bisbee

■ACCOMMODATIONS

Casa de San Pedro B&B [GF,SW,NS,WI,WC,GO] 8933 S Yell Ln (at Hwy 92 & Palominas Rd), Hereford **520/366-1300, 888/257-2050** *full brkfst*

Copper Queen Hotel [GF,SW,WC] 11 Howell Ave **520/432-2216** *restored historic landmark, restaurant*

David's Oasis Camping Resort [MW,21+,SW,WI,GO] 5311 W Double Adobe Rd, McNeal **520/979-6650**

Doublejack Guesthouse [M,NS,WI] **520/559-6708**

Eldorado Suites [GF,NS,WI] 55 OK St **520/432-6679**

Sleepy Dog Guest House [GF,NS,WI] 212A Opera Dr **520/432-3057, 520/234-8166 (cell)** *reclaimed miner's cabin*

■BARS

St Elmo's [GF,E] 36 Brewery Ave **520/432-5578** *10am-2am, live bands Fri-Sat*

Bullhead City

includes Laughlin, Nevada

■CRUISY AREAS

Adult Theater Hwy 95 (S of town) *bookstores w/ arcade*

Karen's Adult Bookstore Hwy 95 (near Mohave Jct, S of town)

Flagstaff

■ACCOMMODATIONS

Abineau Lodge [GS,NS,WI,GO] 1080 Mountainaire Rd **928/525-6212, 888/715-6386**

The Historic Hotel Monte Vista [GF,E,NS] 100 N San Francisco St (at Aspen) **928/779-6971, 800/545-3068** *full bar*

Inn at 410 [GF,WI,WC,GO] 410 N Leroux St **928/774-0088, 800/774-2008**

Motel in the Pines [GF,WC] 80 W Pinewood Blvd (exit 322), Pinewood **928/286-9699, 800/574-5080** *20 miles from Flagstaff*

Starlight Pines B&B [GS,NS,WI,GO] 3380 E Lockett Rd (at Fanning) **928/527-1912, 800/752-1912** *full brkfst*

■BARS

Charly's Pub & Grill [GF,F,E,WC] 23 N Leroux St (at Weatherford Hotel) **928/779-1919** *8am-2am*

Monte Vista Lounge [GF,D,E,K] 100 N San Francisco St (at Hotel Monte Vista) **928/774-2403** *noon-2am, from 11am Fri-Sun*

■CAFES

Macy's European Coffee House [F] 14 S Beaver St **928/774-2243** *6am-8pm, vegetarian/ vegan bakey*

■RESTAURANTS

Cafe Olé [BW,WC] 119 S San Francisco St (at Butler) **928/774-8272** *lunch & dinner, clsd Sun, Mexican*

Granny's Closet 218 S Milton Rd **928/774-8331** *lunch & dinner, also sports bar*

Pasto [BW,WC] 19 E Aspen (at San Francisco) **928/779-1937** *lunch & dinner, clsd Sun*

■CRUISY AREAS

Rest Area [AYOR] off I-40 (17 miles W of Flagstaff)

Thorpe Park [AYOR]

Golden Valley

■EROTICA

Pleasure Palace Adult Bookstore 4150 US Hwy 68 (at Houck Rd) **928/565-5600**

Grand Canyon

■ACCOMMODATIONS

Grand Canyon Lodge North [GF,F] end of Hwy 67, North Rim **877/386-4383** *at the North Rim of the Grand Canyon*

Grand Canyon Lodges [GF,F] **928/638-2631** *the only "in-park" lodging at the South Rim*

Jerome

■ACCOMMODATIONS

The Cottage Inn Jerome [GS,GO] **928/634-0701, 928/649-6759** *full brkfst*

Mile High Grill & Inn [GF,GO] 309 Main St **928/634-5094** *cool hotel, also restaurant*

■RESTAURANTS

Quince Grill & Cantina [WC] 363 S Main St **928/634-7087** *8am-5pm, 7am-9pm Th-Sun*

Kingman

■ACCOMMODATIONS

Kings Inn Best Western [GF,F,SW,WI,WC] 2930 E Andy Devine Ave **928/753-6101, 800/750-6101**

Lake Havasu City

■INFO LINES & SERVICES

Lake Havasu City AA 877/652-9005

■ACCOMMODATIONS

Nautical Inn [GF,SW,WI] 1000 McCulloch Blvd N **928/855-2141, 800/892-2141**

Lake Powell

■ACCOMMODATIONS

Dreamkatchers Lake Powell B&B [GS,WI,GO] 435/675-5828

Phoenix

see also Scottsdale & Tempe

■INFO LINES & SERVICES

1 Voice LGBT Community Center 4442 North 7th Ave **602/712-0111** *noon-7pm, clsd Sun*

Lambda Phoenix Center 2622 N 16th St (at Virginia Ave) **602/635-2090** *space for many 12-step programs*

■ACCOMMODATIONS

Arizona Royal Villa Complex [MO,SW,N,NS,WI,GO] 4312 N 12th St **602/266-6883, 888/266-6884** *hot tub*

Arizona Sunburst Inn [MO,R,SW,N,NS,WI,GO] 6245 N 12th Pl (at Rose Ln) 602/274-1474, 800/974-1474 *hot tub*

Clarendon Hotel & Suites [GS,SW,WI,WC,GO] 401 W Clarendon Ave (at 3rd Ave) 602/252-7363

FireSky Resort & Spa [GF,SW,WI,WC] 4925 N Scottsdale Rd, Scottsdale 480/945-7666, 800/528-7867

Hotel San Carlos [GF,F,SW,WI] 202 N Central Ave 602/253-4121, 866/253-4121 *boutique hotel, rooftop pool, restaurant*

Maricopa Manor B&B Inn [GS,SW,WI,WC,GO] 15 W Pasadena Ave 602/274-6302, 800/292-6403

Orange Blossom Hacienda [GF,SW,WI,GO] 3914 E Sunnydale Dr (btwn Recker & Hunt Hwy), Gilbert 480/755-4346, 877/589-8465

The Saguaro [GF,SW,NS] 4000 N Drinkwater Blvd 480/308-1100 *hip boutique hotel*

Scottsdale Thunderbird Suites [GF,SW,NS,WI,WC] 7515 E Butherus Dr (at Scottsdale Rd), Scottsdale 480/951-4000, 800/951-1288

ZenYard [GS,SW,NS,WI,GO] 830 E Maryland Ave 602/845-0830, 866/594-0242

■BARS

Anvil [M,D,L,S] 2303 E Indian School Rd 602/956-2885 *1pm-2am*

Apollo's [M,D,NH,E,K,S,WI] 5749 N 7th St (S of Bethany Home) 602/277-9373 *11am-2am*

Bar 1 [★M,NH,K,WI] 3702 N 16th St (at E Clarendon) 602/266-9001 *10am-2am*

BS West [MW,D,K,S,WC] 7125 E 5th Ave (in the Kiva Center), Scottsdale 480/945-9028 *2pm-2am*

The Bunkhouse Saloon [M,NH,K] 4428 N 7th Ave (at Indian School) 602/200-9154 *8am-2am, from 10am Sun, patio*

Cash Inn Country [W,D,CW,K,WI,WC] 2140 E McDowell Rd (at 22nd St) 602/244-9943 *2pm-close, from noon wknds*

Charlie's [★M,D,CW,DS,WC] 727 W Camelback Rd (at 7th Ave) 602/265-0224 *2pm-2am, noon-4am Fri-Sat*

Club 24 [M,D,WC] 2424 E Thomas Rd (at 24th St) 602/682-5088 *3pm-2am Wed-Sun*

Cruisin' 7th [M,DS,K,TG,WC] 3702 N 7th St (near Indian School) 602/212-9888 *6am-2am, from 10am Sun, hustlers*

Dick's Cabaret [M,D,S,18+] 3432 E Illini (off University) 602/274-3425 *7pm-1am, till 3am Fri-Sat, "all male nude review," no alcohol*

Ice Pics [MW,V] 3108 E McDowell Rd (at 32nd St) 602/267-8707 *10am-2am, from 2pm Sun*

Kobalt [MW,K,E] 3110 N Central Ave 602/264-5307 *11am-2am*

Nu Towne Saloon [★M,NH,WC] 5002 E Van Buren (at 48th St) 602/267-9959 *noon-2am, patio, cruisy*

Oz [MW,NH,V,WI,WC] 1804 W Bethany Home Rd (at 19th) 602/242-5114 *6am-2am*

Plazma [MW,NH,K,V] 1560 E Osborn Rd (at N 16th St) 602/266-0477 *2pm-close, from noon wknds*

Rainbow Cactus [MW,NH] 15615 N Cave Creek Rd (btwn Greenway Pkwy & Greenway Rd) 602/867-2463 *3pm-2am*

The Rock/ La Roca [MW,NH,E,DS,TG,K] 4129 N 7th Ave (at Indian School) 602/248-8559 *2pm-2am, from 11am wknds*

Roscoe's on 7th [MW,F] 4531 N 7th St (at Minnezona) 602/285-0833 *2pm-2am, from 10am wknds, sports bar*

Stacy's @Melrose [★MW,D] 4343 N 7th Ave (at Campbell) 602/264-1700 *4pm-2am*

Zorfs [M,NH,DS,F,K,S,GO] 1028 E Indian School Rd (at N 10th Pl) 602/277-7729 *2pm-2am, from 10am Sun*

■NIGHTCLUBS

Bar Smith [GS,D,F] 602/229-1265 *9pm-2am, till 3am Sat, clsd Sun*

Club Zarape [M,DS,MR-L] 1730 McDowell Rd 602/253-0689 *9:30pm-close Fri-Sat, Latino drag bar*

Arizona • *USA*

Karamba [★M,D,MR-L,DS,WC] 1724 E McDowell (at 16th St) **602/254-0231** *9pm-close, clsd Mon-Wed, Latin wknds*

■CAFES

Copper Star Coffee [WI] 4220 N 7th Ave (at Indian School) **602/266-2136** *6am-9pm, till 11pm Fri-Sat, coffee in a converted gas station*

■RESTAURANTS

DeFalco's Italian Deli 2334 N Scottsdale Rd **480/990-8660**

Alexi's [WC] 3550 N Central Ave #120 (in Valley Bank Bldg) **602/279-0982** *lunch Mon-Fri, dinner nightly, clsd Sun, int'l, full bar, patio*

AZ/88 7553 E Scottsdale Mall, Scottsdale **480/994-5576** *11:30am-1am, bar popular w/ gay men Fri-Sat evenings*

Barrio Cafe [E,GO] 2814 N 16th St **602/636-0240** *lunch Tue-Fri, dinner Tue-Sun, Sun brunch, clsd Mon, Mexican, live music*

Coronado Cafe 2201 N 7th St **602/258-5149** *lunch Mon-Sat, dinner Tue-Sat, clsd Sun*

Dottie's True Blue Cafe [GO] 4151 N Marshall Way, Scottsdale **480/874-0303** *7:30am-3pm, clsd Mon, great brkfst*

Durant's 2611 N Central Ave **602/264-5967** *lunch Mon-Fri, dinner nightly*

FEZ 3815 N Central Ave (S of Clarendon) **602/287-8700** *11am-midnight, from 8:30am wknds, Moroccan influence, full bar, patio*

Green 2240 N Scottsdale Rd #8, Tempe **480/941-9003** *11am-9pm, clsd Sun, vegetarian/ vegan*

Harley's Bistro [MW] 4221 N 7th Ave (N of Indian School) **602/234-0333** *lunch Tue-Fri, dinner nightly, clsd Mon, Italian*

Los Dos Molinos 8684 S Central Ave **602/243-9113** *lunch & dinner, clsd Sun-Mon, Mexican*

MacAlpines's Soda Fountain 2303 N 7th St **602/262-5545** *11am-7pm, till 8pm Fri-Sat, great milkshakes*

Malee's 7131 E Main, Scottsdale **480/947-6042** *lunch & dinner, Thai, full bar*

Mi Patio 3347 N 7th Ave **602/277-4831** *10am-10pm, Mexican*

Persian Garden Cafe [WI] 1335 W Thomas Rd (at N 15th Ave) **602/263-1915** *lunch & dinner, dinner only Sat, clsd Sun-Mon, plenty vegan*

Portland's 105 W Portland St (at Central Ave) **602/795-7480** *lunch Tue-Fri, dinner Mon-Sat, clsd Sun, also wine bar*

Rose & Crown 628 E Adams St **602/256-0223** *11am-2am, British pub*

Switch [WI] 2603 N Central Ave **602/264-2295** *11am-midnight, from 10am wknds, full bar*

Ticoz [WI] 5114 N 7th St (N of Camelback) **602/200-0160** *11am-midnight, Latin cuisine, full bar*

Vincent on Camelback [WC] 3930 E Camelback Rd (at 40th St) **602/224-0225** *dinner Mon-Sat, clsd Sun, Southwestern*

■ENTERTAINMENT & RECREATION

Soul Invictus 1022 NW Grand Ave (near W Van Buren St) **602/214-4344** *queer-friendly art gallery & cabaret*

Stray Cat Theatre 132 E 6th St (at Performing Arts Ctr), Tempe **480/634-6435** *off-the-beaten-path productions*

■BOOKSTORES

Changing Hands 6428 S McClintock Dr, Tempe **480/730-0205** *new & used, LGBT section*

■RETAIL SHOPS

Off Chute Too 4111 N 7th Ave (at Indian School Rd) **602/274-1429** *9am-9pm, till 10pm Fri-Sat, 10am-6pm Sun, LGBT gift shop in Melrose District*

■PUBLICATIONS

Desert Knight News 877/356-0690

Echo Magazine 602/266-0550, 888/324-6624 *bi-weekly LGBT news-magazine*

Ion Arizona Magazine
602/308-4662 *entertainment guide for the AZ gay community*

'N Touch Magazine 602/373-9490
LGBT newsmagazine

■GYMS & HEALTH CLUBS
Pulse Fitness 18221 N Pima Rd #H-130, Scottsdale **480/907-5900**

■MEN'S CLUBS
Chute [B,L,V,18+] 1440 E Indian School Rd 602/234-1654 *24hrs, private rooms, gym, steam room*

Flex Complex [SW,PC] 1517 S Black Canyon Hwy (btwn 19th Ave & I-17) 602/271-9011 *24hrs*

■MEN'S SERVICES
➤**MegaMates** 602/993-4567 *Call to hook up with HOT local men. FREE to listen & respond to ads. Use FREE code DAMRON. MegaMates.com.*

■EROTICA
Adult Shoppe 111 S 24th St (at Jefferson) 602/306-1130 *24hrs; several locations*

Castle Megastore 300 E Camelback (at Central) 602/266-3348 *11am-11pm, till 2am Fri-Sat*

Fascinations 10242 N 19th Ave #1-7 602/943-5859 *many locations*

International Bookstore 3640 E Thomas Rd (at 36th St) 602/955-2000

Modern World 1812 E Apache (at McClintock Dr), Tempe 480/967-9052 *24hrs*

Pleasure World/ Book Cellar 4029 E Washington (at 40th St) 602/275-0015

Zorba's Adult Book Shop 2924 N Scottsdale Rd (N of Thomas), Scottsdale 480/941-9891 *24hrs, video rentals & arcade*

■CRUISY AREAS
Dreamy Draw Park [AYOR] Squaw Peak Pkwy (Hwy 51) (off Northern) *go E along the driveway to the back—popular w/ 9-5ers; be alert—major crackdown on cruising in Phoenix!*

Papago Park [AYOR] Galvin Pkwy (btwn McDowell Rd & Van Buren St) *be alert—major crackdown on cruising in Phoenix!*

Washington Park [AYOR] 21st Ave (at Glendale) *nights; be alert—major crackdown on cruising in Phoenix!*

Prescott

■ACCOMMODATIONS
The Motor Lodge [GF,WI,GO] 503 S Montezuma St (at Leroux) 928/717-0157

■CRUISY AREAS
Heritage Park [AYOR] Willow Creek Rd (3 miles S of Hwy 89)

Sedona

■ACCOMMODATIONS
Apple Orchard Inn [GF,SW,NS,WC] 656 Jordan Rd 928/282-5328, 800/663-6968 *full brkfst*

El Portal Sedona [GF,NS,F,WI,WC] 95 Portal Ln 928/203-9405, 800/313-0017

The Lodge at Sedona—A Luxury B&B Inn [GS,SW,NS,WI] 125 Kallof Pl 928/204-1942, 800/619-4467

Sedona Rouge Hotel & Spa [GF,SW,NS,WI,WC] 2250 W Hwy 89-A 928/203-4111, 866/312-4111 *restaurant & bar*

Southwest Inn at Sedona [GF,SW,NS,WI] 3250 W Hwy 89-A 928/282-3344, 800/483-7422

■CAFES
Old Town Red Rooster Cafe 901 N Main St, Cottonwood 928/649-8100 *10am-4pm, 8am-2pm Sun*

■RESTAURANTS
Judi's 40 Soldiers Pass Rd 928/282-4449 *lunch & dinner, clsd Sun, full bar*

■RETAIL SHOPS
Sedona Green Gallery & Gifts 273 N Hwy 89A #K (btwn Jordan & Mesquite) 928/239-5353 *10-15% discount to self-identifying gay & lesbian customers*

Arizona • *USA*

Tucson

■INFO LINES & SERVICES

AA Gay/ Lesbian 3269 N Mountain Ave 520/624-4183 *many mtgs*

Wingspan, Southern Arizona's LGBT Community Center 430 E 7th St 520/624-1779, 800/553-9387 *11am-2pm, resources, youth support (3pm-8pm Mon-Fri)*

■ACCOMMODATIONS

Armory Park Guesthouse [GF,GO] 219 S 5th Ave 520/206-9252

Catalina Park Inn [GS,NS,WI,GO] 309 E 1st St (at 5th Ave) 520/792-4541, 800/792-4885

Desert Trails B&B [GF,GS,NW,NS] 12851 E Speedway Blvd 520/885-7295, 877/758-3284 *adobe hacienda on 3 acres bordering Saguaro Nat'l Park*

Hotel Congress [GS,F,E,WI] 311 E Congress St 520/622-8848, 800/722-8848 *cafe, full bar & club*

La Casita Del Sol [GS,NS,WI,GO] 407 N Meyer Ave (btwn Church Ave & Franklin Ave) 520/623-8882 *1880s adobe guesthouse*

Natural B&B & Retreat [GS,NS,WI,GO] 520/881-4582, 888/295-8500 *nonallergenic, full brkfst, massage available*

Royal Elizabeth B&B Inn [GS,SW,NS,WI,GO] 204 S Scott Ave (at Broadway) 520/670-9022, 877/670-9022 *historic 1878 downtown mansion*

■BARS

Club Congress/ The Tap Room [GF,NH,D,E,K] 311 E Congress (at Hotel Congress) 520/622-8848 *11am-2am, dance club from 9pm*

IBT's (It's About Time) [MW,D,K,S,WC] 616 N 4th Ave (at University) 520/882-3053 *noon-2am*

New Moon [MW,D,F,K,WI] 915 W Prince Rd (at Fairview) 520/293-7339 *4pm-close, clsd Mon*

Woody's [M,K,V,WC] 3710 N Oracle Rd (at W Thurber Rd) 520/292-6702 *11am-2am*

■CAFES

Revolutionary Grounds [F,WI] 606 N 4th Ave (at E 5th St) 520/620-1770 *8am-8pm, from 9am Sun, also leftist bookstore*

■RESTAURANTS

Blue Willow 2616 N Campbell Ave (at Grant) 520/327-7577 *7am-9pm, from 8am wknds, brkfst served all day*

Cafe Poca Cosa 110 E Pennington St 520/622-6400 *11am-9pm, till 10pm Fri-Sat, clsd Sun-Mon, Mexican-influenced bistro, patio*

The Grill on Congress 100 E Congress St (at Scott) 520/623-7621 *24hrs, full bar*

■ENTERTAINMENT & RECREATION

The Loft Cinema [F,BW] 3233 E Speedway Blvd 520/795-0844, 520/322-5638 *Tucson's independent art house*

■BOOKSTORES

Antigone Books [WC] 411 N 4th Ave (at 7th St) 520/792-3715 *10am-7pm, till 9pm Fri-Sat, 11am-5pm Sun, LGBT*

■MEN'S SERVICES

▶**MegaMates** 520/791-2345 *Call to hook up with HOT local men. FREE to listen & respond to ads. Use FREE code DAMRON. MegaMates.com.*

■EROTICA

The Bookstore Southwest 5754 E Speedway Blvd 520/790-1550

Caesar's Adult Shop 2540 N Oracle Rd (btwn Glen & Grant) 520/622-9479

Continental Book Shop 2655 N Campbell Ave (at Grant) 520/327-8402 *private rooms, arcade*

Hydra 145 E Congress (at 6th) 520/791-3711 *vinyl, leather, toys, shoes*

■CRUISY AREAS

Tanque Verde Falls/ Reddington Pass *upper Tanque Verde Falls, clothing-optional, gay area is beyond straight area*

ARKANSAS

Batesville

■ CRUISY AREAS

Riverside Park [AYOR]

Crosses

■ CAFES

Crosses Grocery & Cafe [★GO] 4223 Hwy 16 (E of Elkins, outside Fayetteville) **479/643-3307** 6am-8:30pm, on the Pig Trail

Eureka Springs

■ ACCOMMODATIONS

A Byrds Eye View [GS,NS,WI,GO] 36 N Main (at Douglas) **479/253-0200, 888/210-8401** in heart of downtown, porch

The Grand TreeHouse Resort [GS,WI,GO] 350 W Van Buren (at Pivot Rock Rd) **479/253-8733**

Heart of the Hills Inn [GS,NS,GO] 5 Summit St (on Historic Loop) **479/253-7468, 800/253-7468**

Lookout Lodge [GF,NS,WI] 3098 E Van Buren **479/253-9335, 877/253-9335**

Magnetic Valley Resort [M,SW,WI,GO] 597 Magnetic Rd (at Passion Play Rd) **479/244-6821, 888/210-8401**

Mount Victoria [GF,WI] 28 Fairmount St **479/253-7979, 888/408-7979** full brkfst & dinner

Out on Main [GS,NS,WI,GO] 269 N Main St (at Magnetic Rd) **479/253-8449** 3-room cottage, full kitchen

Palace Hotel & Bath House [GF,NS,WI] 135 Spring St **479/253-7474, 866/946-0572** historic bathhouse open to all

Pond Mountain Lodge & Resort [GS,SW,NS,WC,GO] **479/253-5877, 800/583-8043** mtntop inn on 150 acres

Red Bud Manor Inn [GF,WI,WO] 7 Kingshighway **479/253-9649, 866/253-9649**

Roadrunner Inn [GF,R,NS,WI] 3034 Mundell Rd **479/253-8166, 888/253-8166** guestrooms & log cabins, lake views

Texaco Bungalow [GS,GO] 77 Mountain St **888/253-8093**

■ BARS

Chelsea's Corner Cafe [GF,E,D,WI] 10 Mountain St (at Center St) **479/253-6723** 11am-2am, till 10pm Sun, patio

Eureka Live [GS,D,F,K] 35 N Main **479/253-7020** 11am-1:30am, clsd Mon-Tue

Henri's Just One More [GS,NH,F,E,WI] 19 1/2 Spring St **479/253-5795** noon-2am, clsd Tue, gay night Wed from 5pm

Pied Piper Pub & Inn [GF,F,V] 82 Armstrong (at Main St) **479/363-9976, 866/363-9976** noon-midnight, also restaurant & hotel

■ CAFES

Mud Street Cafe 22G S Main St **479/253-6732** 8am-3pm, clsd Tue-Wed

■ RESTAURANTS

Autumn Breeze [NS] 190 Huntsville Rd (1/2 mile off Hwy 62) **479/253-7734** 5pm-9pm, clsd Sun, hrs vary in winter

Caribe Restaurant & Cantina 309 W Van Buren **479/253-8102** 4pm-9pm, clsd Tue, from noon wknds, also bar

Cottage Inn 450 Hwy 62 W **479/253-5282** 5pm-9pm, clsd Mon-Wed, Mediterranean, full bar

Ermilio's 26 White St **479/253-8806** 5pm-9pm, Italian, full bar

Gaskins Cabin Steak House [GS,BW,R] 2883 Hwy 23 N (Hwy 187) **479/253-5466** 5pm-9pm, till 8pm Sun, clsd Mon-Tue

■ ENTERTAINMENT &
RECREATION

Diversity Pride Events 479/
253-2555 *seasonal & holiday events*

Fayetteville

■ INFO LINES & SERVICES

AA Gay/ Lesbian 568 W Sycamore
479/443-6366 (AA#)

■ ACCOMMODATIONS

Hilton Garden Inn Bentonville
[GF,SW,WI,WC] 2204 SE Walton Blvd
(Exit 85, off I-540), Bentonville
479/464-7300, 877/782-9444

■ NIGHTCLUBS

Club Push [MW,D,K,DS,18+] 21 N Block
Ave 479/443-4600 *9pm-2am, clsd
Sun-Tue*

Speakeasy [M,D,WC] 509 W Spring St
(at West St) 479/443-3279 *5pm-2am,
clsd Sun-Tue*

■ CAFES

The Common Grounds 412 W Dickson
St (at West) 479/442-3515 *7am-
midnight, full bar, also restaurant*

■ RESTAURANTS

Bordinos 310 W Dickson St
479/527-6795 *dinner nightly, lunch
Tue-Fri, clsd Sun, full bar*

Hugo's 25 1/2 N Block Ave
479/521-7585 *11am-10pm, clsd Sun*

■ BOOKSTORES

Hastings Bookstore 2999 N College
Ave (Fiesta Square Shopping Center)
479/521-0244 *9am-10pm, till 11pm
Fri-Sat, 9am-11pm Sun*

■ CRUISY AREAS

Flat Rock Beach [AYOR] 10 miles W of
town *nude beach*

Fort Smith

■ BARS

Kinkead's [GS,NH,D,DS,K,WI,GO] 1004
1/2 Garrison Ave 479/226-3144 *5pm-
2am, from 7pm Fri-Sat, clsd Mon*

Helena

■ ACCOMMODATIONS

The Edwardian Inn [GF,NS,WI] 317
Biscoe 870/338-9155,
800/598-4749 *60 miles from
Memphis*

Hot Springs

■ ACCOMMODATIONS

The B Inn [GS,WI,GO] 316 Park Ave (at
Cental Ave) 501/547-7172

Park Hotel of Hot Springs [GS,WI] 211
Fountain St (at Central Ave)
501/624-5323, 800/895-7275

The Rose Cottage [GF] 218 Court St
(at Exchange St) 501/623-6449

■ CRUISY AREAS

Degray Lake [AYOR] lakeside area
afternoon in the woods

Rest Area [AYOR] off Hwy 70 (btwn Hot
Springs & I-30)

Jonesboro

■ CRUISY AREAS

Craighead Forest Park [AYOR]
seasonal (beware of cops!)

Little Rock

■ ACCOMMODATIONS

Legacy Hotel & Suites [★GF,WI,WC]
625 W Capitol Ave (at Gaines)
501/374-0100, 888/456-3669 *nat'l
historic property in downtown area*

■ BARS

Discovery [GS,D,DS,S,V,PC,WC] 1021
Jessie Rd (btwn Cantrell & Riverfront)
501/664-4784 *9pm-5am Sat only*

Miss Kitty's [MW,K] 307 W 7th St (at
Center St) 501/374-4699 *9pm-2am
Fri-Sat*

Trax [M,NH,CW,B,L,OC,WI,WC] 415 Main
St, North Little Rock 501/244-0444
5pm-2am, also restaurant

Triniti Nightclub
[MW,D,DS,S,V,18+,PC,WC] 1021 Jessie Rd
(btwn Cantrell & Riverfront)
501/664-2744 *9pm-5am Fri only*

■RESTAURANTS

Bossa Nova 2701 Kavanaugh Blvd (at Ash St) **501/614-6682** *lunch & dinner, Sun brunch, clsd Mon, Brazilian, plenty veggie*

Juanita's [E,R] 614 President Clinton (at River Market) **501/372-1228** *11am-close, clsd Sun, Mexican, also live music*

La Hacienda 3024 Cantrell Rd **501/661-0600** *lunch & dinner, Mexican*

Lilly's Dim Sum, Then Some/ B-Side [GO] 11121 N Rodney Parham Rd **501/716-2700** *11am-9pm, till 10pm Fri-Sat, clsd Sun, contemporary Asian, plenty veggie, lesbian-owned*

Vino's Pizza [BW] 923 W 7th St (at Chester) **501/375-8466** *11am-close*

■ENTERTAINMENT & RECREATION

The Weekend Theater [GO] 1001 W 7th St (at Chester) **501/374-3761** *plays & musicals on wknds*

■BOOKSTORES

Wordsworth Books & Co 5920 R St **501/663-9198** *9am-7pm, till 6pm Fri-Sat, noon-5pm Sun, independent*

■RETAIL SHOPS

A Twisted Gift Shop 1007 W 7th St (at Chester) **501/376-7723** *noon-midnight, gift shop*

Inz & Outz [WC] 6115 W Markham #103 **501/296-9484** *10am-8pm, noon-6pm Sun, pride items, books*

■EROTICA

Adult Video 2923 W 65th St (off I-30 W) **501/562-4282** *24hrs, arcade*

Cupids 3920 W 65th St (off I-30, exit 135) **501/565-2020** *24hrs, arcade*

■CRUISY AREAS

Reservoir Park [AYOR] Cantrell Rd (2 miles E of I-430, exit 9)

Texarkana

■BARS

The Chute [MW,D,K,DS] 714 Laurel St **870/772-6900** *7pm-2am Th-Sat*

Amador City

■ACCOMMODATIONS

Imperial Hotel [GF,NS] 14202 Hwy 49 (at Water St) **209/267-9172** *B&B, brick Victorian hotel, full brkfst, restaurant & bar*

Anaheim

see Orange County

■MEN'S SERVICES

➤**MegaMates** 714/905-0050 *Call to hook up with HOT local men. FREE to listen & respond to ads. Use FREE code DAMRON. MegaMates.com.*

Angeles Nat'l Forest

■CRUISY AREAS

Beach in the Upper Big Tujunga Canyon (UBTC) [AYOR] Hwy 2, exit Angeles Crest Hwy, head N, turn left to UBTC Rd, turn right (btwn marker 4.5 & 4.8) *little nude beach along creek*

Arcata

■INFO LINES & SERVICES

Queer Humboldt PO Box 45, 95518-0045 **707/834-4839** *"Humboldt County's online resource for the LGBT community," includes links & events calendar, check out www.queerhumboldt.org*

■BARS

The Alibi [MW,NH,F,E,YC] 744 9th St **707/822-3731** *cocktail lounge w/ live music, also restaurant (8am-midnight)*

■CAFES

Cafe Mokka [E] 495 J St (at 5th) **707/822-2228** *from noon, coffee & soups (bread bowls), live music, also Finnish sauna & hot tubs*

North Coast Co-op [WI] 811 I St **707/822-5947** *6am-9pm*

■RESTAURANTS

Wildflower Bakery & Cafe [★BW] 1604 G St **707/822-0360** *8am-8pm, till 9pm Th-Sat, vegetarian*

California • *USA*

■BOOKSTORES
Northtown Books 957 H St
707/822-2834 *10am-7pm, till 9pm
Fri-Sat, noon-5pm Sun, LGBT section*

■EROTICA
Pleasure Center 1731 G St #D
707/826-1708

■CRUISY AREAS
Aldergrove Marsh [AYOR] Alder Grove
Rd (off West End Rd) *parking lot on left
after Ericson Way*

Azalea State Reserve [AYOR] along
Mad River (on N Bank Rd) *6 miles N of
Arcata*

Bakersfield

■INFO LINES & SERVICES
Gay AA 1001 34th St **661/322-4025**
(AA#), **661/324-0371** (Alano Club #)
7:30pm Mon

■ACCOMMODATIONS
The Padre Hotel [GS] 702 18th St
661/427-4900 *sleek hotel with nightclubs, bar, cafe, and fine dining room*

■BARS
The Mint [GS,A,E] 1207 19th St (at M)
661/325-4048 *6am-2am, live music*

■NIGHTCLUBS
The Casablanca Club
[GS,NH,D,E,C,DS,V,WC] 1825 N St (at 19th
St) **661/324-0661** *9pm-2am, clsd
Mon-Wed*

■EROTICA
Cinema 19 [★] 1224 19th St (btwn L &
M Sts, across from The Mint)
661/323-7711 *cruisy, arcade & theater*

Deja Vu 1524 Golden State Ave (at
Chester Ave) **661/322-7300** *noon-
2am, arcade*

■CRUISY AREAS
Gordon's Ferry [AYOR] Round
Mountain Rd (at China Grade Loop),
Oildale

Yokuts Park [AYOR] W of Hwy 99 (at
Beach Park) *take W Truxtun Ave to
Empire Dr entrance*

Berkeley
see East Bay

Big Bear Lake

■ACCOMMODATIONS
Alpine Retreats [GS,NS,GO] 433
Edgemoor (at Big Bear Blvd)
909/725-4192, 909/878-4155
(reservations) *3 cottages*

Grey Squirrel Resort [GS,SW,WI,GO]
39372 Big Bear Blvd **909/866-4335,
800/381-5569**

Knickerbocker Mansion Country Inn
[GS,NS,WI,WC,GO] 869 Knickerbocker Rd
909/878-9190, 877/423-1180 *full
brkfst*

Rainbow View Lodge [GS,NS] 2726
View Dr (at Hilltop), Running Springs
909/867-1810

Big Sur

■ACCOMMODATIONS
Eagle's Nest [GF,WI,NS,GO] 46274
Pfeiffer Ridge **831/667-2587,
888/742-9321** *deck w/ views of
Pfeiffer Ridge & ocean, full kitchen*

Lucia Lodge [GF,NS,WI] 62400 Hwy 1
831/688-4884, 866/424-4787
*oceanview cabins, also restaurant &
lounge*

Cambria

■ACCOMMODATIONS
El Colobri [GF,WI] 5620 Moonstone
Beach Dr **805/924-3003**

Sea Otter Inn [GF,SW,NS,WI,WC] 6656
Moonstone Beach Dr **805/927-5888,
800/966-6490**

■BARS
Mozzi's Saloon [GF,E] 2262 Main St
805/927-4767 *1pm-2am, from 11am
Sat-Sun, cowboy bar*

■CRUISY AREAS
Fiscalini Ranch Preserve

Moonstone Beach Boardwalk

Carmel
see also Monterey

■ACCOMMODATIONS
Best Western Carmel Mission Inn
[GF,SW,NS] 3665 Rio Rd
831/624-1841, 800/348-9090 *pets
ok, also restaurant & lounge*

Cypress Inn [GF,WI] Lincoln & 7th **831/624-3871, 800/443-7443** *pets very welcome, owned by Doris Day. also restaurant & lounge*

■RESTAURANTS

Flaherty's Seafood Grill & Oyster Bar [WC] 6th Ave (btwn Dolores and San Carlos) **831/625-1500** *open daily 11am*

Rio Grill 101 Crossroads Blvd **831/625-5436** *lunch & dinner, full bar*

■CRUISY AREAS

Garland Ranch Regional Park [AYOR] Rte G16 (9 miles E of Carmel), Carmel Valley

Garrapata State Beach [AYOR] 10 miles S of crossroads (on right side of Hwy 1) *nude sunbathing*

Chico

■INFO LINES & SERVICES

Stonewall Alliance Center 358 E 6th St (at Flume) **530/893-3336** *HIV testing & counseling, recorded info, meetings*

■CRUISY AREAS

Deer Pens [AYOR] 8th & Forest Sts

Chino

■RESTAURANTS

Riverside Grill 5258 Riverside Dr (at Central) **909/627-4144** *8am-9pm*

Chula Vista

see also San Diego

■MEN'S SERVICES

►**MegaMates** 619/734-1110 *Call to hook up with HOT local men. FREE to listen & respond to ads. Use FREE code DAMRON. MegaMates.com.*

Clearlake

includes major towns of Lake County

■ACCOMMODATIONS

Blue Fish Cove Resort [GF,SW] 10573 E Hwy 20, Clearlake Oaks **707/998-1769** *lakeside resort cottages, boat facilities & rentals*

Edgewater Resort [SW,NS,WI,GO] 6420 Soda Bay Rd (at Hohape Rd), Kelseyville **707/279-0208, 800/396-6224**

Featherbed Railroad B&B [GF,SW,WI] 2870 Lakeshore Blvd, Nice **707/274-8378**

Sea Breeze Resort [GS,SW,NS,WI,WC,GO] 9595 Harbor Dr, Glenhaven **707/998-3327** *lakefront cottages*

Cloverdale

see also Healdsburg

■ACCOMMODATIONS

Vintage Towers B&B [GF,WI] 302 N Main St (at 3rd) **707/894-4535, 888/886-9377** *Queen Anne mansion, full brkfst*

■RESTAURANTS

Hamburger Ranch & Bar-B-Que [BW] 31195 N Redwood Hwy **707/894-5616** *7am-9pm, patio*

Concord

see East Bay

■MEN'S SERVICES

►**MegaMates** 925/695-1100 *Call to hook up with HOT local men. FREE to listen & respond to ads. Use FREE code DAMRON. MegaMates.com.*

Costa Mesa

see Orange County

Cupertino

■ACCOMMODATIONS

Cypress Hotel [GF,SW,WI,NS] 10050 S De Anza Blvd **408/253-8900, 800/499-1408**

■CRUISY AREAS

Stevens Creek Canyon Park [AYOR] Foothill Blvd *at first road, turn left below the dam, go down, then go up to the top parking area on the right*

Davis

see also Sacramento

California • USA

■INFO LINES & SERVICES

LGBT Resource Center [WI,WC]
University House Annex
530/752-2452 9am-5pm, clsd wknds,
info, referrals, meetings, library

■CAFES

Mishka's Cafe [★] 610 2nd St
530/759-0811 7:30am-11pm

■BOOKSTORES

The Avid Reader 617 2nd St
530/758-4040 10am-10pm

■MEN'S SERVICES

➤**MegaMates** 530/760-1011 Call to
hook up with HOT local men. FREE to
listen & respond to ads. Use FREE code
DAMRON. MegaMates.com.

East Bay

includes major cities of Alameda
and Contra Costa Counties:
**Alameda, Antioch, Berkeley,
Concord, Danville, Fremont,
Hayward, Lafayette, Newark,
Oakland, Pleasant Hill, Richmond,
San Leandro, Walnut Creek**

■INFO LINES & SERVICES

East Bay AA 510/839-8900 variety
of LGBT-friendly mtgs

Lighthouse Community Center 1217
A St (near 2nd St), Hayward
510/881-8167 LGBT support groups &
social events

Pacific Center for Human Growth
[WC] 2712 Telegraph Ave (at Derby),
Berkeley 510/548-8283 10am-10pm
Mon-Fri

**Rainbow Community Center of
Contra Costa County** 3024 Willow
Pass Rd #500 (btwn Parkside &
Esperanza), Concord 925/692-0090
10am-5pm Mon-Fri

■ACCOMMODATIONS

Hotel Durant [GS,F,NS,WI] 2600 Durant
Ave, Berkeley 510/845-8981,
800/238-7268

Washington Inn [GF,NS,WC] 495 10th
St (at Broadway), Oakland
510/452-1776 historic boutique hotel,
also restaurant

Waterfront Hotel [GF,SW,NS,WI,WC] 10
Washington St, Oakland
510/836-3800, 888/842-5333

■BARS

The Alley [GS,P] 3325 Grand Ave (btwn
Lake Park & Elwood Aves), Oakland
510/444-8505 4pm-2am, camptastic
sing-along piano bar from 9pm, more
gay Th, also restaurant

Bench & Bar [★,M,D,K,DS,P,S,YC,WC]
510 17th St, Oakland 510/444-2266
4pm-2am

Cafe Van Kleef [GF,E,$] 1621 Telegraph
Ave (at Broadway), Oakland
510/763-7711 4pm-2am, clsd Sun,
eclectic crowd & live-music scene—from
cabaret to blue grass to jazz

Club 21 [M,D,MR-L] 2111 Franklin St (at
21st St), Oakland 510/268-9425
theme nights

The New Easy [GF,NH,F] 3255
Lakeshore Ave, Oakland 510/338-4911
3:30pm-2am, from 2pm Sat, cool lounge

White Horse [MW,D,K,WC] 6551
Telegraph Ave (at 66th), Oakland
510/652-3820 3pm-2am, from 1pm
wknds, popular wknds (also Sun beer
bust)

World Famous Turf Club
[MW,D,K,DS,WI,WC] 22519 Main St (at A
St), Hayward 510/881-9877 4pm-
2am, from noon Sat-Sun, sports bar,
huge patio, BBQs, live music, 2 blks from
BART

■NIGHTCLUBS

Club 1220 [MW,D,CW,K,WI,WC] 1220
Pine St (at Civic Dr), Walnut Creek
925/938-4550 4pm-2am, theme
nights

■CAFES

The Actual Cafe [F] 6334 San Pablo
Ave (at Alcatraz), Oakland
510/653-8386 7am-9pm, till 10pm
wknds, food served, events

Au Coquelet Cafe [BW,WI] 2000
University Ave, Berkeley
510/845-0433 6am-2am

Bittersweet 5427 College Ave (in
Rockridge District), Oakland
510/654-7159 9am-7pm, till 9pm Fri-
Sat

Caffe Strada [★WC] 2300 College Ave (btwn Way & Durant), Berkeley **510/843-5282** *6am-midnight, students, great patio*

Cole Coffee 6255 College Ave (btwn 62nd & 63rd Sts), Oakland **510/985-1958** *7am-7pm, hip hide-away in lovely Rockridge*

Raw Energy [GO] 2050 Addison St (btwn Shattuck & Milvia), Berkeley **510/665-9464** *7:30am-7pm, 11am-4pm Sat, clsd Sun, organic juice cafe*

■**RESTAURANTS**

Arizmendi Bakery & Pizzeria 4301 San Pablo Ave (at 43rd St), Emeryville **510/547-0550** *7am-7pm, till 3pm Mon, clsd Sun, excellent pastries, breads & pizzas*

Banh Cuon Tay Hu [TG,BW] 344-B 12th St (at Webster), Oakland **510/836-6388** *10am-9pm, till 8pm Sun, clsd Mon*

Cactus Taqueria 5642 College Ave (at Shafter, in Rockridge), Oakland **510/658-6180** *11am-10pm, till 9pm Sun*

César [★] 4039 Piedmont, Oakland **510/883-0222** *noon-11pm, Spanish tapas, full bar till midnight*

Connie's Cantina [★] 3340 Grand Ave (btwn Lake Park Ave & Mandana Blvd), Oakland **510/839-4986** *10:30am-9pm, clsd Sun, delicious homemade Mexican food, plenty veggie, patio*

Dopo [★] 4293 Piedmont Ave (btwn Glenwood & Echo), Oakland **510/652-3676** *lunch Mon-Th, dinner nightly, clsd Sun, Italian, worth the wait*

Le Cheval [★BW,WC] 1007 Clay St, Oakland **510/763-8495** *11am-9:30pm, from 5pm Sun, Vietnamese,*

Lois the Pie Queen [★WC] 851 60th St (off Martin Luther King Jr Hwy), Oakland **510/658-5616** *8am-2pm, 7am-3pm wknds, Southern homecooking & killer desserts*

Mama's Royal Cafe [★BW,WC] 4012 Broadway (at 40th), Oakland **510/547-7600** *7am-2:30pm, from 8am wknds, come early for excellent wknd brunch*

Rockridge Cafe [★] 5492 College Ave (at Forest), Oakland **510/653-1567** *7:30am-3pm, great brkfsts, plenty veggie*

Zachary's Chicago Pizza [★BW] 5801 College Ave, Oakland **510/655-6385** *11am-10pm, pizza that is worth the crowds & the long wait!*

■**ENTERTAINMENT & RECREATION**

Oakland East Bay Gay Men's Chorus 800/706-2389

■**BOOKSTORES**

Black Oak Books 2618 San Pablo Ave, Berkeley **510/486-0698** *11am-7pm*

Diesel, A Bookstore 5433 College Avenue, Oakland **510/653-9965** *10am-9pm, till 10pm Fri-Sat, till 6pm Sun, independent*

Laurel Book Store [WC,GO] 4100 MacArthur Blvd (at 39th Ave, 2 blks from High St), Oakland **510/531-2073** *10am-7pm, till 6pm Sat, 11am-5pm, general, LGBT section, readings, lesbian-owned*

Pendragon Books 5560 College Ave (at Oceanview), Oakland **510/652-6259** *9am-10pm, from 10am Sun, used books, great to browse while waiting for a table in Rockridge*

■**RETAIL SHOPS**

Collectors Realm 3 2566 Telegraph Ave (btwn Parker & Dwight), Berkeley **510/540-1182** *2pm-8pm, from noon wknds, vintage gay porn*

■**MEN'S CLUBS**

Steamworks [★WI,PC] 2107 4th St (at Addison), Berkeley **510/845-8992** *24hrs, call for recorded info*

■**EROTICA**

Golden Gate Books/ El Cerrito Secrets 10601 San Pablo Ave (at Moeser Ln), El Cerrito **510/528-1569** *8am-1am, arcade*

Good Vibrations [★WC] 2504 San Pablo Ave (at Dwight Wy), Berkeley **510/841-8987** *10am-9pm, till 10pm Fri-Sat*

Good Vibrations [★] 3219 Lakeshore Ave, Oakland **510/788-2389** *10am-9pm*

California • USA

Not Too Naughty 15670 E 14th St, San Leandro 510/278-4944 *arcade*

■CRUISY AREAS

Aquatic Park [AYOR] Bolivar Dr (off I-80, at Ashby Ave exit), Berkeley

Bushrod Park [AYOR] Shattuck Ave (btwn 59th & 60th Sts), Oakland *near tennis courts*

Central Park (aka Lake Elizabeth) [AYOR] Paseo Padre Ave & Stevenson Blvd, Fremont *trails right of lake & parking lot*

Heather Farm Park [AYOR] Ygnacio Valley Rd, Walnut Creek *take Ygnacio Valley Rd for 2 miles E of Hwy 680, turn right into park on San Carlos Rd*

Hillcrest Park [AYOR] off Larkspur Dr, Antioch *take Hillcrest exit off Hwy 4, take left off Hillcrest Rd onto Larkspur Rd, park is on right after 6 blocks*

Keller Beach [AYOR] Miller-Knox Regional Park, Richmond *take Garrard Blvd exit of Hwy 580 after tunnel on Dornan Dr*

Lake Temescal Park [AYOR] Broadway Ave (at State Hwy 13), Oakland *afternoons*

Oyster Bay Park [AYOR] btwn San Leandro Marina & Oakland Airport (along the bay), San Leandro *take Doolittle to Williams, go W toward bay & make right when Williams ends*

El Cajon

■MEN'S SERVICES

➤MegaMates 619/387-0383 *Call to hook up with HOT local men. FREE to listen & respond to ads. Use FREE code DAMRON. MegaMates.com.*

Elk

■RESTAURANTS

Queenie's Roadhouse Cafe [GO] 6061 S Hwy 1 707/877-3285 *8am-3pm, clsd Tue-Wed, fabulous all-day brkfsts*

Escondido

■MEN'S SERVICES

➤MegaMates 760/708-0800 *Call to hook up with HOT local men. FREE to listen & respond to ads. Use FREE code DAMRON. MegaMates.com.*

Eureka

■ACCOMMODATIONS

Abigail's Elegant Victorian Mansion [GF,NS] 1406 C St (at 14th St) 707/444-3144 *1878 nat'l historic landmark, sauna*

Carter House Inns [GF,NS,WC] 301 L St 707/444-8062, 800/404-1390 *enclave of 4 unique inns, full brkfst, restaurant, wine shop*

Trinidad Bay B&B [GF,NS,WI,GO] 560 Edwards St (at Trinity), Trinidad 707/677-0840 *full brkfst*

■BARS

Lost Coast Brewery [GF,F,BW,WI,WC] 617 4th St (btwn G & H Sts) 707/445-4480 *11am-1am, kitchen open till midnight*

The Shanty [GS,NH,GO] 213 3rd St (at C St) 707/444-2053 *noon-2am*

■NIGHTCLUBS

Where's Queer Bill [MW,D,TG] 707/832-4785 *monthly queer events, wheresqueerbill.com*

■CAFES

The Boathouse Espresso Bar & Eatery [WI,WC,GO] 1125 King Salmon Ave 707/441-1454 *6pm-2am, from 8pm wknds*

North Coast Co-op 25 4th St (at B St) 707/443-6027 *6am-9pm, co-op store w/ bakery, deli & espresso cafe*

Ramone's Cafe & Bakery 209 E St (Old Town) 707/445-2923 *7am-6pm*

■RESTAURANTS

Chalet House of Omelettes [WC] 1935 5th St (at U St) 707/442-0333 *6am-3pm, brkfst & lunch*

Folie Douce [BW,R,WC] 1551 G St, Arcata 707/822-1042 *dinner only, clsd Sun-Mon, bistro*

■BOOKSTORES

Booklegger [WC] 402 2nd St (at E St) 707/445-1344 *10am-5:30pm, 11am-4pm Sun*

■EROTICA

Good Relations [WC] 223 2nd St 707/441-9570, 888/485-5063 *queer-owned/ run*

■ CRUISY AREAS

Hilfiker Reserve [AYOR] off Hilfiker Ln *last parking lot & wood trails*

Fort Bragg

■ ACCOMMODATIONS

The Cleone Gardens Inn [GF,NS,WI,WC] 24600 N Hwy 1 707/964-2788, 800/400-2189 (N CA only) *country garden retreat on 2.5 acres, cottages, hot tub*

The Weller House Inn [GF,NS,WI] 524 Stewart St (at Pine) 707/964-4415, 877/893-5537 *1886 Victorian, full brkfst*

■ RESTAURANTS

Cowlick's 250B N Main St 707/962-9271 *delicious homemade ice cream, including mushroom ice cream (in-season)—it's actually quite good!*

Purple Rose [WC] 24300 N Hwy 1 707/964-6507 *5pm-9pm, clsd Sun-Mon, Mexican*

■ ENTERTAINMENT & RECREATION

Skunk Train California Western foot of Laurel St 707/964-6371, 866/457-5865

Fremont

see East Bay

■ MEN'S SERVICES

➤**MegaMates** 510/401-0101 *Call to hook up with HOT local men. FREE to listen & respond to ads. Use FREE code DAMRON. MegaMates.com.*

Fresno

■ INFO LINES & SERVICES

Community Link 559/266-5465 *LGBT support, also publishes Newslink*

Fresno AA 559/221-6907 *call or check website (www.fresnoaa.org) for meetings*

■ ACCOMMODATIONS

The San Joaquin Hotel [GF,SW,WI,WC] 1309 W Shaw Ave (at Fruit) 559/225-1309, 800/775-1309

■ BARS

The Phoenix [M,NH,CW,B,L,MR,V,OC] 4538 E Belmont Ave (at Maple) 559/252-2899 *4pm-2am, patio, popular beer busts & other events*

Red Lantern [M,NH,CW,MR-L,WI,WC] 4618 E Belmont Ave (at Maple) 559/251-5898 *2pm-2am, Latin night Sat very popular, patio*

■ NIGHTCLUBS

Club Legends [MW,D,DS] 3075 N Maroa Ave 559/222-2271 *7pm-2am,from 9pm Sat, from 4pm Sun*

North Tower Circle [MW,D,DS] 2777 N Maroa Ave (at E Princeton Ave) 559/229-4188 *8pm-2am*

■ RESTAURANTS

Don Pepe's 4582 N Blackstone Ave (at Gettysburg) 559/224-1431 *9am-9pm, Mexican*

Irene's Cafe [BW] 747 E Olive Ave (in Tower District) 559/237-9919 *8am-9pm, some veggie, good hamburgers*

Sequoia Brewing Company [E] 777 E Olive Ave (in Tower District) 559/264-5521 *11am-10pm, till midnight Fri-Sat, till 9pm Sun, micro-brewery w/ restaurant, live music*

Veni Vidi Vici [E,R] 1116 N Fulton (S of Olive Ave, in Tower District) 559/266-5510 *California fine dining, nightclub later*

■ MEN'S CLUBS

The Bunker [MO,PC] 2592 S Railroad Ave (at E Jensen) 559/486-3100 *10am-10pm, till 11pm wknds, clsd Mon*

■ MEN'S SERVICES

➤**MegaMates** 559/261-2221 *Call to hook up with HOT local men. FREE to listen & respond to ads. Use FREE code DAMRON. MegaMates.com.*

■ EROTICA

Suzie's Adult Superstores 1267 N Blackstone Ave 559/497-9613 *24hrs*

Wildcat Book Store 1535 Fresno St (at G St) 559/237-4525 *video arcade*

California • *USA*

■CRUISY AREAS
LA-SF Time Out [AYOR] US 99 (at Kingsburg, S of Fresno) *go to cheap motel next to rest area; rest stop activity discouraged*

Garden Grove
see Orange County

■MEN'S SERVICES
➤**MegaMates** 714/467-9991 *Call to hook up with HOT local men. FREE to listen & respond to ads. Use FREE code DAMRON. MegaMates.com.*

Gaviota

■CRUISY AREAS
Vista Point [AYOR] Hwy 101 S (1/2 S of Gaviota Beach) *parking lot & nearby woods*

Grass Valley
see also Nevada City

Gualala

■ACCOMMODATIONS
Breakers Inn [GS] 39300 S Hwy 1 707/884-3200

North Coast Country Inn [GF,NS] 34591 S Hwy 1 707/884-4537 *hot tub*

■BOOKSTORES
The Four-Eyed Frog 39138 Ocean Dr (in Cypress Village) 707/884-1333

Half Moon Bay

■ACCOMMODATIONS
Mill Rose Inn [GF,NS,WI] 615 Mill St 650/726-8750, 800/900-7673 *classic European elegance by the sea, full brkfst, hot tub*

■RESTAURANTS
Moss Beach Distillery [★WC] 140 Beach Wy (at Ocean) 650/728-5595 *lunch & dinner, Sun brunch, steak & seafood, patio, even own ghost*

Pasta Moon [E,WC] 315 Main St (at Mill) 650/726-5125 *lunch & dinner, Italian, full bar*

Hayward
see East Bay

■MEN'S SERVICES
➤**MegaMates** 510/342-2122 *Call to hook up with HOT local men. FREE to listen & respond to ads. Use FREE code DAMRON. MegaMates.com.*

Healdsburg
see also Russian River & Sonoma County

Hemet

■CRUISY AREAS
Gibbel Park [AYOR] 2500 W Florida Ave (at Kirby, enter here) *very discreet*

Huntington Beach
see Orange County

Idyllwild

■ACCOMMODATIONS
The Heritage House Inn [GF] 25880 Cedar St 951/659-5150, 877/659-4789 *inn & cabins*

The Rainbow Inn [GS,NS,WI,GO] 54420 S Circle Dr 951/659-0111 *full brkfst, patio, also conference center*

Strawberry Creek Inn B&B [GF,NS,WC,GO] 26370 Hwy 243 (at S Cir Dr) 951/659-3202, 800/262-8969 *relaxing getaway w/ sundeck, garden & hammocks*

■RESTAURANTS
Cafe Aroma [E] 54750 North Circle 951/659-5212 *7am-10pm, great ambience & food*

Irvine
see Orange County

Joshua Tree Nat'l Park

■ACCOMMODATIONS
The Desert Lily [GF,WI] PO Box 139, 92252-0800 760/366-4676, 877/887-7370 *artist-owned adobe-style B&B on 5 acres; closed July-Aug*

Desert Wonderland & The Tile House [GS,GO] 805/452-4898 *in high desert near Joshua Tree Nat'l Park*

Joshua Tree Highlands Houses
[GS,NS,WI,WC,GO] 760/366-3636
private, fully equipped rentals

Kate's Lazy Desert [GF,NS,WI] 58380
Botkin Rd, Landers 845/688-7200
*love shack owned by Kate Pierson of the
B-52s*

Sacred Sands [GS,NS,WI,GO] HC1 Box
1071 A, 63155 Quail Springs Rd (at
Desert Shadows), Joshua Tree
760/424-6407

Spin & Margie's Desert Hideaway
[GF] 64491 29 Palms Hwy
760/366-9124 *hacienda-style B&B,
suites w/ private patios*

Starland Retreat [M,N,18+] Yucca
Valley 760/364-2069

■**RESTAURANTS**

The Crossroads Cafe & Tavern 61715
29 Palms Hwy 760/366-5414 *7am-
8pm, till 9pm Fri-Sat, clsd Wed*

Kernville

■**ACCOMMODATIONS**

Riverview Lodge [GS,NS,GO] 2 Sirretta
St 760/376-6019 *resort on Kern River*

La Mirada

■**RESTAURANTS**

Mexico 1900 11531 La Mirada blvd
562/941-2016 *lunch & dinner,
Mexican*

Laguna Beach

see Orange County

Lake Tahoe

see also Lake Tahoe, Nevada

■**ACCOMMODATIONS**

Alpine Inn & Spa [GS,SW] 920
Stateline Ave (Lake Ave/ Hwy 50), South
Lake Tahoe 530/544-3340,
800/826-8885

Black Bear Inn [GS,NS,WI,GO]
530/544-4451, 877/232-7466 *full
brkfst, hot tub, fireplaces*

The Cedar House Sport Hotel
[GF,WI] 10918 Brockway Rd, Truckee
530/582-5655, 866/582-5655

Spruce Grove Cabins [GF,NS] 3599-
3605 Spruce Ave, South Lake Tahoe
530/544-0549, 800/777-0914

Tahoe Valley Lodge [GF,SW,NS,WI]
2241 Lake Tahoe Blvd (at Tahoe Keys
Blvd), South Lake Tahoe
530/541-0353, 800/669-7544
motel

■**RESTAURANTS**

Driftwood Cafe [WC] 1001 Heavenly
Vlg Way #1A 530/544-6545 *7am-
3pm, homecooking*

Passaretti's [BW] 1181 Emerald Bay Rd/
Hwy 50, South Lake Tahoe
530/541-3433 *11am-9pm, Italian*

■**CRUISY AREAS**

El Dorado Beach [AYOR] btwn Rufus
Allen Blvd & Lakeview, South Lake Tahoe

Private Beach [AYOR] off Pine St (near
Park), South Lake Tahoe *private beach
behind resorts*

Lancaster

includes Palmdale

Livermore

see East Bay

Lodi

■**EROTICA**

Intimates & Adult Superstore [AYOR]
203 N Houston Ln 209/369-6191
also arcade

Long Beach

■**INFO LINES & SERVICES**

AA Gay/ Lesbian 2017 E 4th St (at
Cherry, at Gay & Lesbian Center)
562/434-4455 *7pm Mon [MW] & 7pm
Fri [M]*

**The Gay & Lesbian Center of
Greater Long Beach** 2017 E 4th St (at
Cherry) 562/434-4455 *9am-9pm, by
appt Sat, activities & support groups, HIV
testing*

California • *USA*

■ACCOMMODATIONS

Beachrunners' Inn [GS,NS] 231 Kennebec Ave (at Junipero & Broadway) 562/856-0202, 866/221-0001 *B&B, near beach, hot tub*

Dockside Boat & Bed [GF] Dock 5, Rainbow Harbor (at Pine Ave Pier) 562/436-3111 *spend the night on a yacht, views of Queen Mary*

Hotel Current [GS,SW,WI,WC] 5325 E Pacific Coast Hwy 562/597-1341, 800/990-9991

Hotel Maya [GS] 700 Queensway Dr 562/435-7676

Queen Mary [GF,NS,WC] 1126 Queens Hwy 877/342-0742 *historic ocean liner*

The Varden Hotel [GS,WI,NS,WC] 335 Pacific Ave (at 3rd St) 562/432-8950, 877/382-7336

■BARS

The Brit [M,NH,WC] 1744 E Broadway (at Cherry) 562/432-9742 *10am-2am, patio*

The Broadway [MW,NH,K,WC] 1100 E Broadway (at Cerritos) 562/432-3646 *10am-2am, [K] Fri-Sat*

The Crest [M] 5935 Cherry Ave (at South) 562/423-6650 *2pm-2am, from noon wknds*

The Falcon [M,NH,WC] 1435 E Broadway (at Falcon) 562/432-4146 *8am-2am, from 7am wknds*

Flux [MW,NH,WI] 17817 Lakewood Blvd (at Artesia), Bellflower 562/633-6394 *noon-2am, patio, theme nights*

Liquid Lounge [GS,NH,F,E,K,GO] 3522 E Anaheim St 562/494-7564 *11am-1am, till 2am Fri-Sat, [K] Fri-Sat, patio*

Mineshaft [★M,B] 1720 E Broadway (btwn Gaviota & Hermosa) 562/436-2433 *11am-2am*

Paradise Piano Bar & Restaurant [MW,NH,F,E,P] 1800 E Broadway Blvd (at Hermosa) 562/590-8773 *3pm-1am, from 10am Sat-Sun, live entertainment*

Pistons [M,B,L] 2020 E Artesia (at Cherry) 562/422-1928 *2pm-2am patio*

Que Será [GS,D,A,E] 1923 E 7th St (at Cherry) 562/599-6170 *9pm-2am Tue, from 5pm Wed-Sat, from 3pm Sun, clsd Mon, theme nights, [$] after 9pm*

Silver Fox [M,K,V,WC] 411 Redondo (at 4th) 562/439-6343 *4pm-2am, from noon wknds, popular happy hour, [K] Wed & Sun*

Sweetwater Saloon [M,NH,WC] 1201 E Broadway (at Orange) 562/432-7044 *10am-2am, popular days, cruisy*

■NIGHTCLUBS

The Basement Lounge [GS,D,E] 149 Linden Ave (at E Broadway) 562/901-9090 *also restaurant*

Club Ripples [★M,D,MR,F,E,K,DS,S,V,YC] 5101 E Ocean (at Granada) 562/433-0357 *noon-2am, patio, theme nights, T-dance Sun, Bear Bar every 2nd Sat*

Executive Suite [★MW,D,E,WC] 3428 E Pacific Coast Hwy (at Redondo) 562/597-3884 *1pm-2am, from noon wknds*

The Powder Room [W,D,E] 525 E Broadway (at Bliss 525) 562/495-7252

■CAFES

Hot Java [WI] 2101 E Broadway Ave 562/433-0688 *6am-11pm, till midnight Fri-Sat, also soups, sandwiches, salads*

The Library [WI] 3418 E Broadway 562/433-2393 *6am-midnight, till 1am Fri-Sat, from 7am wknds*

■RESTAURANTS

212 Degrees Bistro 2708 E 4th St 562/439-8822 *8am-2pm, clsd Mon, Mexican-inspired*

Cafe Sevilla 140 Pine St 562/495-1111 *dinner only, Sun brunch, Spanish, also music & dancing*

Hamburger Mary's [WI] 740 E Broadway (at Alamitos) 562/436-7900 *11am-2am, full bar w/ theme nights*

Omelette Inn 318 Pine Ave 562/437-5625 *7am-4pm*

Open Sesame 5215 E 2nd St 562/621-1698 *lunch & dinner, Middle Eastern*

Original Park Pantry [WC] 2104 E Broadway (at Junipero) **562/434-0451** *6am-10pm, till 11pm Fri-Sat, int'l*

Two Umbrellas Cafe [GO] 1538 E Broadway (btwn Gaviota & Falcon) **562/495-2323** *8am-2pm, clsd Mon*

Utopia 445 E 1st St **562/432-6888** *lunch Mon-Fri, dinner nightly, clsd Sun, seafood, California cuisine, plenty veggie*

■BOOKSTORES

Open 2226 E 4th St (btwn Cherry & Junipero, in heart of Retro Row) **562/499-6736** *11am-7pm, till 8pm Sat, till 6pm Sun, clsd Mon, general; also films, art & events*

■RETAIL SHOPS

Hot Stuff [GO] 2121 E Broadway (at Junipero) **562/433-0692** *noon-8pm, 10am-6pm Sat-Sun, cards, gifts, and adult novelties, serving community since 1980*

■MEN'S CLUBS

1350 Club [18+] 510 W Anaheim St (at Neptune), Wilmington **310/830-4784** *24hrs*

■MEN'S SERVICES

▶**MegaMates** **562/485-4008** *Call to hook up with HOT local men. FREE to listen & respond to ads. Use FREE code DAMRON. MegaMates.com.*

■EROTICA

The Crypt on Broadway 1712 E Broadway (btwn Cherry & Falcon) **562/983-6560** *10am-midnight, leather, toys*

The RubberTree 5018 E 2nd St (at Granada) **562/434-0027** *gifts for lovers, women-owned*

■CRUISY AREAS

Please Note: All cruisy areas for Long Beach have been removed by request of various LGBT community organizations.

LOS ANGELES

Los Angeles is divided into 8 geographical areas:
LA—Overview
LA—West Hollywood
LA—Hollywood
LA—West LA & Santa Monica
LA—Silverlake
LA—Midtown
LA—Valley
LA—East LA & South Central

LA—Overview

■INFO LINES & SERVICES

Alcoholics Anonymous 323/936-4343 & 735-2089 (en español), 800/923-8722 *call or check web (www.lacoaa.org) for meetings*

Crystal Meth Anonymous 877/262-6691 *call or check website (www.crystalmeth.org) for meetings in LA County*

LA Gay & Lesbian Center 1625 N Schrader Blvd (McDonald/Wright Building) 323/993-7400 *9am-9pm, till 1pm Sat, clsd Sun, wide variety of services*

LA Gay & Lesbian Center's Village at Ed Gould Plaza 1125 N McCadden Pl (at Santa Monica) 323/860-7302 *9am-9pm, clsd Sun, cybercenter, cafe, theaters, library*

■ENTERTAINMENT & RECREATION

Bikes and Hikes LA 8743 Santa Monica Blvd 323/796-8555, 888/836-3710 *bike/hike tour company*

The Celebration Theatre 7051 Santa Monica Blvd (at La Brea) 323/957-1884 *LGBT theater, call for more info*

The Ellen DeGeneres Show *you know you want to dance w/ Ellen! check out ellen.warnerbros.com for tickets*

The Gay Mafia Comedy Group [MW,GO] *improv/ sketch comedy*

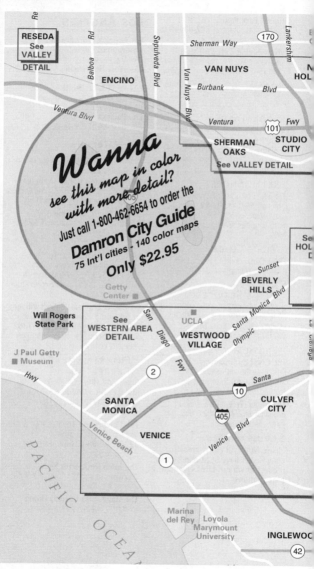

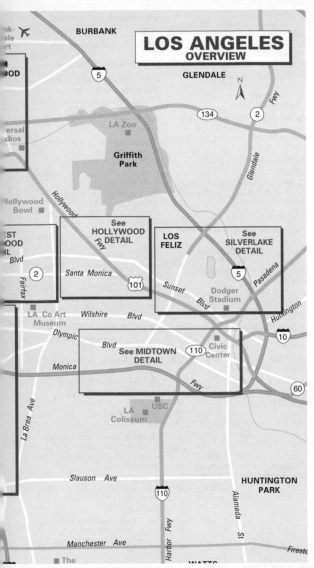

LOS ANGELES
OVERVIEW

BURBANK

GLENDALE

N

LA Zoo

Griffith
Park

Hollywood Bowl

See HOLLYWOOD DETAIL

LOS FELIZ

See SILVERLAKE DETAIL

Santa Monica

Sunset Blvd

Dodger Stadium

Pasadena

Blvd

Fairfax

LA Co Art Museum

Wilshire Blvd

Olympic

Blvd

See MIDTOWN DETAIL

Civic Center

Monica

Fwy

LA Coliseum

USC

Slauson Ave

HUNTINGTON PARK

Manchester Ave

The

WATTS

Alameda St

Firesto

California • *USA*

The Getty Center 1200 Getty Center Dr, Brentwood **310/440-7300** *10am-6pm, till 9pm Fri-Sat, clsd Mon, LA's shining city on a hill & world-class museum; of course, it's still in LA so you'll need to make reservations for parking (!)*

Griffith Observatory enter on N Vermont St (in Griffith Park) **213/473-0800** *noon-10pm, from 10am wknds, clsd Mon*

Highways 1651 18th St (at the 18th Street Arts Center), Santa Monica **310/315-1459** *"full-service performance center"*

IMRU Gay Radio KPFK LA 90.7 FM *7pm Mon*

Outfest **213/480-7088** *annual LGBT film festival each July (see listing in Film Festival Calendar)*

■PUBLICATIONS

Adelante Magazine 323/256-6639 *bilingual LGBT magazine*

Essential Gay & Lesbian Directory 310/841-2800, 866/718-GAYS *business directory serving the LGBT community*

Frontiers Magazine 323/930-3220 *huge LGBT newsmagazine w/ listings for everything*

➤**Gloss Magazine** 415/552-5070 *CA arts/ entertainment magazine, bi-weekly*

➤**Odyssey Magazine** 323/874-8788 *dish on LA's club scene*

■CRUISY AREAS

Beach in the Upper Big Tujunga Canyon (UBTC) [AYOR] Hwy 2, exit Angeles Crest Hwy, head N, turn left to UBTC Rd, turn right (btwn marker 4.5 & 4.8), Angeles Nat'l Forest *little nude beach along creek*

The Usual Suspects: Griffith Park, Elysian Park, Echo Park, Santa Fe Dam Regional Park, Whitsett Park [AYOR] *don't bother: LAPD & the rangers are waiting for you*

LA—West Hollywood

■INFO LINES & SERVICES

➤**Visit West Hollywood** 8687 Melrose Ave, Ste M38 (at San Vicente) **800/368-6020, 310/289-2525**

■ACCOMMODATIONS

Andaz West Hollywood [GS,SW,NS,WI,WC] 8401 Sunset Blvd (at Kings Rd) **323/656-1234, 800/233-1234** *on the Sunset Strip, rooftop pool*

Chamberlain [★GS,SW,WC] 1000 Westmount Dr (near Holloway) **310/657-7400, 800/201-9652** *boutique hotel, rooftop pool, restaurant & lounge*

The Elan Hotel Los Angeles [GS,NS,WI,WC,GO] 8435 Beverly Blvd (at Croft) **323/658-6663, 866/203-2212** *hip & trendy, fitness room*

The Grafton on Sunset [GS,SW,WC] 8462 W Sunset Blvd (at La Cienega) **323/654-4600, 800/821-3660** *sundeck, panoramic views, located in heart of Sunset Strip*

Holloway Motel [GS,NS] 8465 Santa Monica Blvd (at La Cienega) **323/654-2454, 888/654-6400** *centrally located*

Hotel Le Petit [GF,SW,WC] 8822 Cynthia St (at Larrabee) **310/854-1114** *all-suite hotel*

Le Parc Suite Hotel [GF,F,SW,WC] 733 N West Knoll Dr (at Melrose) **310/855-8888, 800/578-4837**

The London West Hollywood [GF,SW,WI] 1020 N San Vicente Blvd **866/282-4560** *luxury hotel including dining in Gordon Ramsay's restaurant*

Mondrian [GF] 8440 Sunset Blvd **323/650-8999, 800/697-1791** *home of trendy Skybar & Asia de Cuba restaurant*

Ramada Plaza Hotel—West Hollywood [GF,F,SW,WC] 8585 Santa Monica Blvd (at La Cienega) **310/652-6400**

San Vicente Inn-Resort [M,SW,N,GO] 845 N San Vicente Blvd (at Santa Monica) **310/854-6915** *hot tub, steam room, cruisy*

WEST
HOLLYWOOD

Whether spending your days lounging next to a rooftop hotel pool, strolling through the chic fashion and design district or living it up at one of the famous LGBT nightlife venues of Santa Monica Boulevard, West Hollywood offers unmatched style and excitement. Best of all, at just 1.9 square miles in size, West Hollywood has been named California's most walkable city!

www.gogaywesthollywood.com

weho
visit west hollywood

California • *USA*

SLS Hotel [GF] 465 S La Cienega Blvd (at San Vicente) **310/247-0400**

Sunset Marquis Hotel & Villas [GS,SW,WI,WC] 1200 Alta Loma Rd (1/2 block S of Sunset Blvd) **310/657-1333** *full brkfst, sauna, hot tub*

■BARS

The Abbey [★MW,F,WC] 692 N Robertson Blvd (at Santa Monica) **310/289-8410** *8am-2am, also restaurant, patio*

Comedy Store [GF] 8433 Sunset Blvd (at La Cienega) **323/650-6268** *8pm-2am, legendary stand-up club*

Fiesta Cantina [MW,F] 8865 Santa Monica Blvd (at San Vicente) **310/652-8865** *noon-2am, raucous Mexican restaurant & bar*

Fubar [★MO,D,K,S] 7994 Santa Monica Blvd (at Crescent Hts) **323/654-0396** *4pm-2am, theme nights*

Gold Coast [★M,NH,WC] 8228 Santa Monica Blvd (at La Jolla) **323/656-4879** *11am-2am, from 10am wknds*

Gym Sports Bar [GS,NH,WC] 8737 Santa Monica Blvd (at Hancock) **310/659-2004** *4pm-2am, from noon wknds*

Here Lounge [MW,P] 696 N Robertson Blvd (at Santa Monica) **310/360-8455** *4pm-2am*

Improv [GF,F] 8162 Melrose Ave (at Crescent Heights) **323/651-2583** *stand-up comedy, also restaurant*

Micky's [★M,D,F,V,YC,GO] 8857 Santa Monica Blvd (at San Vicente) **310/657-1176** *noon-2am, after-hours wknds, patio*

Mother Lode [★M,NH,K,WC] 8944 Santa Monica Blvd (at Robertson) **310/659-9700** *3pm-2am, beer bust Sun*

Revolver Video Bar [★M] 8851 Santa Monica Blvd (at Larrabee St) **310/694-0430** *4pm-2am, from noon wknds, a WeHo institution*

Trunks [M,NH,V,YC] 8809 Santa Monica Blvd (at Larrabee) **310/652-1015** *1pm-2am*

■NIGHTCLUBS

Club Papi Los Angeles [M,D,MR-L] 652 N La Peer Dr **323/692-9573** *9pm-4am, monthly party, call for dates*

Eleven Restaurant & Nightclub 8811 Santa Monica Blvd (at Larrabee St) **310/855-0800** *lunch & dinner, more gay for the bar atmosphere till 2am*

The Factory [★M,D,V,$] 652 N La Peer Dr (at Santa Monica) **310/659-4551** *check www.factorynightclub.com for events*

Plaza [M,D,MR-L,DS,$] 739 N La Brea Ave (at Melrose) **323/939-0703** *9pm-2am, from 8pm Fri-Sat, clsd Tue, shows nightly at 10:15pm & midnight*

Rage [★M,D,F,DS,V,18+,YC,WC] 8911 Santa Monica Blvd (at San Vicente) **310/652-7055** *noon-2am*

Ultra Suede [GS,D,A,E] 661 N Robertson Blvd (at Santa Monica) **310/659-4551** *10pm-2am Wed-Sat, theme nights*

■CAFES

Champagne French Bakery & Cafe [F] 8917-9 Santa Monica Blvd **310/657-4051** *6:30am-9pm, till 11pm Fri-Sat, coffees & pastries as well as brkfst, lunch & dinner, some outdoor seating*

Grind House Cafe [WI] 1051 N Havenhurst Dr **323/650-7717** *6:30am-10pm, coffeehouse*

Urth Caffe [F] 8565 Melrose Ave (btwn Robertson & La Cienega) **310/659-0628** *6:30am-midnight, organic coffees, teas & treats, plenty veggie & vegan, patio*

■RESTAURANTS

AOC 8022 W Third St (at Crescent Heights Blvd) **323/653-6359** *dinner nightly, wine bar, eclectic, upscale*

Basix Cafe 8333 Santa Monica Blvd (at Flores) **323/848-2460** *7am-11pm, outdoor seating*

The Bayou [GO] 8939 Santa Monica Blvd (at Robertson) **310/273-3303**

Bite [BW,WC] 8807 Santa Monica Blvd (at San Vicente) **310/659-3663** *11:30am-11:30pm, plenty veggie*

The source to gay nightlife, music, photos and beauty.

ODYSSEY

odysseymagazine.net

California • *USA*

Bossa Nova [BW,WC] 685 N Robertson Blvd (at Santa Monica) **310/657-5070** *11am-midnight, Brazilian, patio*

Cafe La Boheme [WC] 8400 Santa Monica Blvd (btwn Benecia Ave & Fox Hills Dr) **323/848-2360** *5pm-10pm Fri-Sat, till 11pm Sun-Th, eclectic Californian, full bar, patio*

Canter's Deli [WC] 419 N Fairfax (btwn Melrose & Beverly) **323/651-2030** *24hrs, hip after-hours, Jewish/ American, full bar*

Falcon [GS] 7213 Sunset Blvd (btwn Poinsettia & Formosa) **323/850-5350** *dinner Wed-Sat, California/ cont'l fusion*

Hamburger Mary's Bar & Grill [MW,TG,E,K,DS,S,V,GO] 8288 Santa Monica Blvd **323/654-3800** *11am-1am, till 2am Fri-Sat*

Hedley's 640 N Robertson Blvd **310/659-2009** *lunch & dinner, also wknd brunch, clsd Sun night & Mon*

The Hudson 1114 N Crescent Heights Blvd **323/654-6686** *4pm-2am, from 10am Sat-Sun*

Il Piccolino Trattoria [WC] 350 N Robertson Blvd (btwn Melrose & Beverly) **310/659-2220** *lunch & dinner, clsd Sun, patio*

Joey's Cafe 8301 Santa Monica Blvd **323/822-0671** *8am-10pm, a little bit coffeehouse, a little bit diner, popular at lunch*

Kokomo Cafe [WC] 7385 Beverly Blvd (between La Brea Ave & Fairfax Ave) **323/933-0773** *8am-4pm, diner*

Koo Koo Roo [BW,WC] 8520 Santa Monica Blvd (at La Cienega Blvd) **310/657-3300** *11am-11pm, till 10pm Sun, lots of healthy chicken dishes*

Lola's 945 N Fairfax Ave (at Santa Monica) **323/654-5652** *5:30pm-2am, great martinis*

Louise's Trattoria [BW] 7505 Melrose Ave (at Gardner) **323/651-3880** *11am-10pm, Italian, great foccacia bread, patio*

Lucques [WC] 8474 Melrose Ave (at La Cienega) **323/655-6277** *lunch Tue-Sat, dinner nightly, French, full bar, patio*

Marix Tex Mex [MW,WC] 1108 N Flores (btwn La Cienega & Fairfax) **323/656-8800** *11am-11pm, from 11am wknds, great margaritas, patio*

Nyala 1076 S Fairfax (at Whitworth Dr) **323/936-5918** *many Ethiopian, Nigerian & other African restaurants to choose from on this block*

Real Food Daily [★BW,WC] 414 N La Cienega (btwn Beverly & Melrose) **310/289-9910** *11:30am-10pm, till 11pm Fri-Sat, Sun brunch 10am-3pm, organic vegan, patio*

St Felix 8945 Santa Monica Blvd (at Hilldale) **310/275-4428** *4pm-2am, small plates*

Tart 115 S Fairfax Ave (at Farmer's Daughter Hotel) **323/937-3930, 800/334-1658** *7am-midnight, Southern*

Taste 8454 Melrose Ave (at La Cienega) **323/852-6888** *lunch & dinner, wknd brunch, upscale eclectic, full bar*

Versailles 1415 S La Cienega (at W Pico) **310/289-0392** *lunch & dinner, Cuban*

■ BOOKSTORES

Book Soup 8818 W Sunset Blvd (at Larrabee) **310/659-3110** *9am-10pm, till 7pm Sun, LGBT section*

■ RETAIL SHOPS

665 Leather 8722 Santa Monica Blvd (at Huntley Dr) **310/854-7276** *noon-8pm, till 10pm Fri-Sat, custom leather & neoprene, also accessories & toys*

Marginalized Tattoo [GO] 4228 Melrose Ave (at Vermont) **213/422-4801** *featuring Dave Davenport (aka "Dogspunk"), named best gay tattoo artist by Frontiers*

■ GYMS & HEALTH CLUBS

24 Hour Fitness 8612 Santa Monica Blvd, West Hollywood **310/652-7440** *recently renovated, tres gay*

The Fitness Factory [★] 650 N La Peer Dr (at Santa Monica) **310/358-1838** *6am-9pm, till 8pm Fri, 7am-5pm Sat, 8am-1pm Sun*

■ MEN'S CLUBS

Melrose Spa [★18+,PC] 7269 Melrose Ave (at Poinsettia) 323/937-2122 24hrs

Slammer [18+,PC] 3688 Beverly Blvd (2 blocks E of Vermont) 213/388-8040 8pm-4am, from 2pm wknds

■ MEN'S SERVICES

➤**MegaMates** 323/648-3999 *Call to hook up with HOT local men. FREE to listen & respond to ads. Use FREE code DAMRON. MegaMates.com.*

■ EROTICA

Chi Chi LaRue's 8932 Santa Monica Blvd (at San Vicente) 323/337-9555 10am-midnight, till 2am Th-Sun

Circus of Books 8230 Santa Monica Blvd (at La Jolla) 323/656-6533 6am-2am

The New Unicorn Bookstore 8940 Santa Monica Blvd (at Robertson Blvd) 310/652-6253

Pleasure Chest 7733 Santa Monica Blvd (at Genesee), N Hollywood 323/650-1022 10am-midnight, till 1am Th-Sat

Studs Theatre 7734 Santa Monica Blvd (at the Legendary Pussycat Theatre) 9am-3am, till 5am Fri-Sat

LA—Hollywood

■ ACCOMMODATIONS

Hilton Garden Inn [GF,F,SW,WI,WC] 2005 N Highland (at Franklin) 323/876-8600 exercise room, jacuzzi

Hollywood Hotel – The Hotel of Hollywood [GF,SW,NS,WI,WC] 1160 N Vermont Ave (at Santa Monica) 323/315-1800, 800/800-9733

The Redbury [GS,WI] 1717 Vine St (at Hollywood) 323/962-1717, 877/962-1717 spacious flats, restaurant & bar

■ BARS

Boardner's [GS,D,F,K] 1652 N Cherokee Ave 323/462-9621 4pm-2am, "a Hollywood legend & best-kept secret since 1942", theme nights

Faultline [★M,B,L,V,WC] 4216 Melrose Ave (at Vermont) 323/660-0889 5pm-2am, from 2pm wknds, clsd Mon-Tue, patio

■ NIGHTCLUBS

Arena/ Circus Disco [★M,D,MR-L,S,V] 6655 Santa Monica Blvd (at Seward, Circus behind Arena) 323/810-6993 9pm-2am Tue-Wed & Fri-Sat, theme nights

Avalon [GS,D,$] 1735 Vine St (at Hollywood Blvd) 323/462-8900 one of LA's best dance music clubs, call for events

Club Tranzit [TG] 1775 N Ivar (at Joseph's Cafe), Hollywood 818/660-9472 10pm Th only

Mr Black LA [MW,D] 1737 N Vine St (at Hollywood Blvd, at Bardot) 323/462-8900 Tue only

Tempo [M,D,MR-L,E,S] 5520 Santa Monica Blvd (at Western) 323/466-1094 9pm-2am, 7pm-3am Th-Sat, from 2pm Sun, live bands Sat, beer bust Sun

TigerHeat [GS,D,TG,E,DS,V,18+,$] 1735 Vine (at Avalon) 323/467-4571 9:30pm-3am Th only

■ RESTAURANTS

101 Coffee Shop 6145 Franklin Ave 323/467-1175 7am-3am, diner

La Poubelle [WC] 5907 Franklin Ave (at Bronson) 323/465-0807 5:30pm-midnight, French/ Italian, full bar

Lucy's Cafe El Adobe 5536 Melrose Ave (near Gower St) 323/462-9421 11:30am-11pm, clsd Sun, Mexican, patio

Musso & Frank Grill 6667 Hollywood Blvd (near Las Palmas) 323/467-5123 11am-11pm, clsd Sun-Mon, the grand-dame diner/ steak house of Hollywood: great pancakes, potpies & martinis!

Off Vine [BW] 6263 Leland Wy (at Vine) 323/962-1900 lunch & dinner, wknd brunch

Prado [WC] 244 N Larchmont Blvd (at Beverly) 323/467-3871 lunch & dinner, dinner only Sun, Caribbean

Quality [WC] 8030 W 3rd St (at Laurel) 323/658-5959 8am-3:30pm, home-style brkfst

California • *USA*

Rockwell Table & Stage 1714 N Vermont Ave (at Prospect, enter in alley) 323/669-1550 *11am-midnight, brunch wknds*

Roscoe's House of Chicken & Waffles 1514 N Gower (at Sunset) 323/466-7453 *8:30am-midnight, till 4am Fri-Sat*

■BOOKSTORES

Skylight Books [★] 1818 N Vermont Ave (at Melbourne Ave) 323/660-1175 *10am-10pm, way cool independent in Los Feliz, great fiction & alt-lit sections*

■GYMS & HEALTH CLUBS

Gold's Gym [GF] 1016 N Cole Ave (near Santa Monica & Vine) 323/462-7012 *5am-midnight, 7am-9pm Sat-Sun*

■MEN'S CLUBS

Flex [SW] 4424 Melrose Ave (btwn Normandie & Vermont) 323/663-7786 *24hrs, patio, steam*

➤The North Hollywood Spa [V] 5636 Vineland (at Burbank) 818/760-6969, 800/772-2582 *24hrs, no membership required*

The Zone [PC] 1037 N Sycamore Ave (at Santa Monica) 323/472-6495 *8pm-dawn, from 2pm Sun*

■EROTICA

X Spot 6775 Santa Monica Blvd (at Highland) 323/463-0295 *24hrs*

LA—West LA & Santa Monica

■ACCOMMODATIONS

Casa Malibu [GF,F,WI] 22752 Pacific Coast Hwy, Malibu 310/456-2219

The Georgian Hotel [GF,F,WI,WC] 1415 Ocean Ave (btwn Santa Monica & Broadway), Santa Monica 310/395-9945, 800/538-8147

Hotel Angeleno [GS,SW,NS,WI] 170 N Church Ln (at Hwy 405) 310/476-6411, 866/264-3536 *boutique hotel w/ landmark circular shape, gym*

Hotel Erwin [GS] 1697 Pacific Ave (at Venice Way), Venice Beach 310/452-1111, 800/786-7789

Hotel Palomar [GS,SW,WC] 310/475-8711, 800/472-8556

The Inn at Venice Beach [GF,WI,WC] 327 Washington Blvd (at Via Dolce), Marina Del Rey 310/821-2557, 800/828-0688 *European-style inn*

The Linnington [MW,GO] 310/422-8825 *B&B, jacuzzi, lesbian-owned*

The Malibu Beach Inn [GF,F,WI] 22878 Pacific Coast Hwy, Malibu 310/456-6444 *balconies with views of the Pacific Ocean*

Shutters on the Beach [GF,SW,WI] 1 Pico Blvd, Santa Monica 310/458-0030, 800/334-9000

W Los Angeles [GF,F,SW] 930 Hilgard Ave (at Le Conte) 310/208-8765, 800/421-2317 *suites, gym, day spa*

■BARS

The Dolphin [MW,NH,K,WC] 1995 Artesia Blvd (at Green Ln), Redondo Beach 310/318-3339 *7pm-2am, patio, [D] Tue & Fri-Sat, [K] Sun, Tue & Th*

Roosterfish [★M,NH] 1302 Abbot Kinney Blvd (at Cadiz), Venice 310/392-2123 *11am-2am, patio*

■CAFES

The Novel Cafe 2507 Main St, Santa Monica 310/396-7700 *7am-1am, from 8am Sat, 8am-midnight Sun, also used bookstore*

■RESTAURANTS

12 Washington 12 Washington Blvd (at Pacific), Marina Del Rey 310/822-5566 *5pm-10pm, till 11pm Fri-Sun, cont'l*

Axe 1009 Abbot Kinney, Venice 310/664-9787 *lunch & dinner, clsd Mon, healthy, plenty veggie*

Baja Cantina 311 Washington Blvd (at Sanborn), Marina Del Rey 310/821-2252 *10:30am-1am, also brunch wknds, full bar*

Border Grill [★] 1445 4th St (at Broadway), Santa Monica 310/451-1655 *lunch & dinner from famous "Two Hot Tamales" chefs, Mexican*

California • *USA*

Cantalini's Salerno Beach Restaurant [★E,BW] 193 Culver Blvd (at Vista del Mar), Playa del Rey **310/821-0018** *lunch Mon-Fri, dinner nightly, Italian, homemade pastas, live music Sun nights*

Cora's Coffee Shoppe 1802 Ocean Ave (N of Pico Blvd), Santa Monica **310/451-9562** *7am-3pm, from 7am wknds, clsd Mon, organic*

Drago [WC] 410 N Canon, Beverly Hills **310/786-8283** *lunch Mon-Sat, dinner nightly, Sicilian Italian*

Gjelina [BW] 1429 Abbot Kinney Blvd, Venice **310/450-1429** *pizzas & small plates*

Golden Bull 170 W Channel Rd (at Pacific Coast Hwy), Santa Monica **310/230-0402** *4:30pm-10pm, till 11pm wknds, Sun brunch, American, full bar*

Hamburger Habit [★] 11223 National Blvd (at Sepulveda) **310/478-5000** *10am-11pm, till midnight Fri-Sat*

Joe's 1023 Abbot Kinney Blvd, Venice **310/399-5811** *lunch Tue-Fri, dinner nightly, wknd brunch, clsd Mon, French/ Californian*

Real Food Daily [BW,WC] 514 Santa Monica Blvd (btwn 5th & 6th), Santa Monica **310/451-7544** *11:30am-10pm, organic vegan*

Seed Bistro 11917 Wilshire Blvd **310/477-7070** *lunch Mon-Fri, dinner nightly, clsd Sun, vegan*

Wokcano 1413 5th St, Santa Monica **310/458-3080** *11am-12:30am, till 1:30am Fri-Sat, sushi bar & Chinese cafe*

ENTERTAINMENT & RECREATION

Muscle Beach Ocean Front Walk, Venice Beach *LOTS to see at this popular Venice Boardwalk beach!*

Santa Monica Pier Ocean Ave (at Colorado Ave), Santa Monica

Will Rogers State Beach Pacific Coast Hwy (at Temescal Canyon Rd) *gay beach*

BOOKSTORES

Diesel, A Bookstore 23410 Civic Center Way, Malibu **310/456-9961** *10am-7pm, till 9pm Fri-Sat, till 6pm Sun, independent*

MEN'S CLUBS

Roman Holiday 12814 Venice Blvd (at Beethoven) **310/391-0200** *24hrs*

MEN'S SERVICES

►**MegaMates** 310/883-2299 *Call to hook up with HOT local men. FREE to listen & respond to ads. Use FREE code DAMRON. MegaMates.com.*

EROTICA

Pleasure Island 18426 Hawthorne Blvd (btwn Artesia & 190th), Torrance **310/793-9477** *11am-midnight, till 2am Fri-Sat*

LA—Silverlake

BARS

4100 Bar [GS,NH] 4100 Sunset Blvd (at Manzanita) **323/666-4460** *8pm-2am*

AKBar [★GS,NH,D,WC] 4356 W Sunset Blvd (at Fountain) **323/665-6810** *7pm-2am, hip Silverlake hangout*

Cavern Club Theater 1920 Hyperion Ave (at Casita Del Campo) **323/969-2530, 323/662-4255** *wide variety of shows, Wed-Sat nights*

Cha Cha Lounge [GF,NH,GO] 2375 Glendale Blvd (at Silverlake) **323/660-7595** *5pm-2am, hipster lounge*

Club Nur [★MW,D] 2810 Hyperion Ave (at Rowena, at MJ's) **323/660-1503** *Th only, Middle Eastern night*

Eagle LA [★M,L,WC] 4219 Santa Monica Blvd (at Hoover) **323/669-9472** *4pm-2am, from 2pm wknds, uniform bar*

Good Luck Bar [GF] 1514 Hillhurst Ave (nr Hollywood Blvd) **323/666-3524** *7pm-2am, from 8pm wknds, stylish dive bar*

Little Joy [GS,NH,MR-L] 1477 W Sunset Blvd (at Portia) **213/250-3417** *6pm-2am, from 1pm wknds*

[WC] 2810 Hyperion
323/660-1503 4pm-
Fri- Sun, theme nights

ounge [GS,E,DS] 2906
(at Silver Lake Blvd)
-9636 3pm-2am, rock 'n' roll
g shows wknds

■NIGHTCLUBS

Club Called Rhonda [GS,D]
213/482-2313 monthly party, "house,
disco, & polysexual hard partying," check
www.rhondasays.net for info

The Echo [GS,D,E] 1822 W Sunset Blvd
(at Glendale Blvd) 213/413-8200

Full Frontal Disco [GS,D,TG] 4356 W
Sunset Blvd (at Fountain)
213/626-2285 last Sun only, 70s-80s
disco party

■RESTAURANTS

Casita Del Campo [★] 1920 Hyperion
Ave 323/662-4255 11am-midnight,
till 2am Fri-Sat, Mexican, patio

Cha Cha Cha [MW,WC] 656 N Virgil
Ave (at Melrose) 323/664-7723 lunch
& dinner, Caribbean, plenty veggie

Cliff's Edge 3626 Sunset Blvd (at
Griffith Park Blvd) 323/666-6116
dinner only, wknd brunch, plenty veggie,
romantic, outdoor seating

El Conquistador [BW] 3701 W Sunset
Blvd (at Lucille) 323/666-5136 lunch
Tue-Sun, dinner nightly, Mexican, patio

The Good Microbrew & Grill 3725
Sunset Blvd (at Lucille) 323/660-3645
11am-10pm, till 11pm Fri, 9am-10pm
wknds, plenty veggie

Home 1760 Hillhurst Ave, Los Feliz
323/669-0211 9am-10pm, patio

The Kitchen 4348 Fountain Ave
(at Sunset Blvd) 323/664-3663 5pm-
1am, from 11am Sat, til 10pm Sun, cozy
diner

Michelangelo Pizzeria Ristorante
1742 Rowena 323/660-4843 lunch &
dinner

Square One Dining 4854 Fountain Ave
(at Vermont Ave) 323/661-1109 8am-
pm, great brkfst

Vermont Restaurant & Bar [GO] 1714
N Vermont Ave 323/661-6163 lunch
Mon-Fri, dinner nightly, clsd Sun

■RETAIL SHOPS

Rough Trade Gear 3915 Sunset Blvd
323/660-7956 noon-10pm, 10am-
midnight Fri-Sat, till 8pm Sun

Syren 2809 1/2 W Sunset Blvd
213/289-0334 noon-10pm, clsd Mon,
leather & latex

■EROTICA

Circus of Books 4001 Sunset Blvd (at
Sanborn) 323/666-1304 6am-2am

Romantix Adult Superstore 3147 N
San Fernando Rd 323/258-2867
24hrs

LA—Midtown

■ACCOMMODATIONS

Luxe City Center [GS] 1020 S Figueroa
St 213/748-1291
2 other LA locations

O Hotel [GS,F,WI] 819 S Flower St
213/623-9904

The Standard, Downtown LA
[GS,SW,F,WI] 550 S Flower St
213/892-8080

■BARS

Cafe Club Fais Do-Do [GF,F,E] 5257 W
Adams Blvd (btwn Fairfax & La Brea)
323/931-4636 8pm-2am, live music,
also Cajun restaurant

■NIGHTCLUBS

Bordello [GF,C,F] 901 E 1st St (at S
Vignes St) 213/687-3766 burlesque
shows, also restaurant

Coco Bongo [W,D,MR-L,DS,S,18+] 3311
S Main St 818/233-5322 9pm-2am,
clsd Mon-Wed

Critter Control [MW,D,A,DS,TG] queer
dance parties in downtown LA

Jewel's Catch One Disco [GS,D,A,WC]
4067 W Pico Blvd (at Norton)
323/734-8849 (hotline),
323/737-1159 call for hours, clsd
Wed-Th, theme nights

California • *USA*

Mustache Mondays [MW,D,TG,A] 336 S Hill St (at W 4th St, at La Cita bar) 213/687-7111 *9pm Mon only, queer fashionistas*

■RESTAURANTS

Bar & Kitchen LA 819 S Flower St (at O Hotel) 213/784-3048 *traditional american cuisine with local Californian farm to table influences*

Border Grill Downtown [E,WC] 445 S Figueroa St (at 5th St) 213/486-5171 *lunch & dinner, late-night cocktails*

Cassell's 3266 W 6th St (at Vermont) 213/480-5000 *10:30am-4pm, clsd Sun, great burgers*

Doughboys Cafe 8136 W 3rd St 323/852-1020 *7am-10pm*

■MEN'S CLUBS

Klyt [MR-L] 132 E 4th St 213/972-9145 *24hrs, steam room & dry sauna*

Midtowne Spa—Los Angeles [SW] 615 S Kohler (at Central) 213/680-1838 *24hrs*

LA—Valley

includes San Fernando & San Gabriel Valleys

■BARS

The Bullet [M,L,WC] 10522 Burbank Blvd (at Cahuenga), North Hollywood 818/762-8890 *noon-2am, patio*

Cobra [★M,D,MR-L,WC] 10937 Burbank Blvd (1 block E of Vineland), North Hollywood 818/760-9798 *9pm-2am, till 3am fri-Sat, clsd Sun-Wed*

■NIGHTCLUBS

C Frenz [★MW,NH,D,MR,K,C,S,WC,GO] 7026 Reseda Blvd (at Sherman Way), Reseda 818/996-2976 *3pm-2am, till 3am Sat, patio, theme nights, beer bust Sun*

Club Coco Bongo [MW,D,MR-L,DS,S,18+] 19655 Sherman Wy (at Corbin Ave), Reseda 818/233-5322 *9pm-2am, clsd Mon-Wed*

Oil Can Harry's [M, Ventura Blvd (at Tujur Studio City 818/760-9 2am, from 9pm Fri, from 8 Sun-Mon & Wed, dance less Th, classic disco Sat*

Rain [GS,D] 12215 Ventura Blvd, City 818/755-9596 *9pm-2am Fr.*

■CAFES

Aroma 4360 Tujunga Ave, Studio City 818/508-0677 *6am-11pm, from 7am Sun, coffeehouse w/ small bookstore*

■RESTAURANTS

Firefly Studio City 11720 Ventura Blvd, Studio City 818/762-1833 *5pm-2am, till midnight Sun, great beer braised mussels, full bar*

■MEN'S CLUBS

Eros Station 15164 Oxnard St (rear entrance), Van Nuys 818/994-6200 *2pm-2am Sat, till 1am Suns*

➤The North Hollywood Spa [V] 5636 Vineland (at Burbank) 818/760-6969, 800/772-2582 *24hrs, no membership required*

Roman Holiday [MO] 14435 Victory Blvd, Van Nuys 818/780-1320 *open 24hrs*

■MEN'S SERVICES

➤MegaMates 818/996-7000 *Call to hook up with HOT local men. FREE to listen & respond to ads. Use FREE code DAMRON. MegaMates.com.*

■EROTICA

Diamond Adult World 6406 Van Nuys Blvd (at Victory), Van Nuys 818/997-3665 *24hrs*

Eros Station 15164 Oxnard St, Van Nuys 818/994-6100 *am-1am, videos & toys*

Romantix Adult verstore 21625 Sherman Wy (at yon), Canoga Park 818/992-9801

■CRUISY AS

Chatsworth South [AYOR] 22360 Devonshire S atsworth *parking lot & nearby w*

LA—East LA & South Central

■BARS

Chico Bar [★M,D,MR-L,S] 2915 W Beverly Blvd (at Garfield), Montebello **323/721-3403** *9pm-2am, theme nights*

Manhattan Beach

see also LA—West LA & Santa Monica

■ACCOMMODATIONS

Sea View Inn at the Beach [GF,SW,NS,WI] 3400 Highland Ave **310/545-1504**

■RESTAURANTS

The Local Yolk [WI,WC] 3414 Highland Ave (at Rosecranz) **310/546-4407** *6:30am-2pm*

Marin County

includes Corte Madera, Mill Valley, San Anselmo, San Rafael, Sausalito, Tiburon

■INFO LINES & SERVICES

AA Gay/ Lesbian 415/499-0400 *check www.aasf.org for meeting times*

Spectrum LGBT Center of the North Bay [WC] 30 N San Pedro Rd # 160, San Rafael **415/472-1945** *drop-in hours: 11am-5pm Mon-Fri*

■ACCOMMODATIONS

Acqua Hotel [GF,NS,WI,WC] 555 Redwood Hwy, Mill Valley **415/380-0400, 888/662-9555**

Casa Madrona Hotel & Spa [GF,F] 801 Bridgeway, Sausalito **415/332-0502, 800/288-0502** *overlooks SF skyline*

Larkspur Hotel [GF,SW,NS,WI] 160 Shoreline Hwy, Mill Valley **415/332-5700, 866/823-4669**

The Lodge at Tiburon [GF,SW,NS,WI] 1651 Tiburon Blvd, Tiburon **415/435-3133, 800/762-7770** *also restaurant & bar*

Waters Edge Hotel [GS,NS,WI,WC] 25 Main St, Tiburon **415/789-5999**

■RESTAURANTS

Guaymas 5 Main St (at ferry dock), Tiburon **415/435-6300** *gourmet Mexican, great views of the Bay*

Terrapin Crossroads 100 Yacht Club Dr, San Rafael **415/524-2773** *4pm-10pm, from 11am wknds, clsd Mon*

■ENTERTAINMENT & RECREATION

Black Sand Beach heading to San Francisco: take last exit before Golden Gate Bridge, go right on Outlook Rd, look for dirt parking lot, Golden Gate Nat'l Rec Area *popular nude beach, look for trail*

■BOOKSTORES

Book Passage [★] 51 Tamal Vista Blvd, Corte Madera **415/927-0960, 800/999-7909** *9am-9pm, beloved independent which draws the biggest names to read*

■RETAIL SHOPS

Cowgirl Creamery 80 4th St (at Tomales Bay Foods), Pt Reyes Station **415/663-9335** *10am-6pm Wed-Sun, handmade cheeses, picnic lunches to go*

Mendocino

■ACCOMMODATIONS

Agate Cove Inn [GF,NS] 11201 N Lansing St **707/937-0551, 800/527-3111** *full brkfst, fireplaces*

The Alegria Quartet & Oceanfront Inn Cottages [GF,NS,WI] 44781 Main St **707/937-5150, 800/780-7905** *in the village, ocean views*

Blair House & Cottage [GF,NS] 45110 Little Lake St (at Ford St) **707/937-1800, 800/699-9296** *in former "home" of Jessica Fletcher of Murder, She Wrote*

Brewery Gulch Inn [GS,NS,WI] 9401 N Hwy 1 **707/937-4752, 800/578-4454** *oceanview B&B made of eco-salvaged redwood*

Dennen's Victorian Farmhouse [GF,NS,WI] 7001 N Hwy 1 (at Hwy 128) **707/937-0697, 800/264-4723** *full brkfst*

California • *USA*

Glendeven Inn [GF,NS,WI] 8205 N Hwy 1 (1.7 miles S of Mendocino), Little River 707/937-0083, 800/822-4536 *full brkfst & wine bar, farmhouse on the coast*

Hill House Inn [GS] 10701 Palette Dr 707/937-0554, 800/422-0554 *also restaurant*

The Inn at Schoolhouse Creek [GS,WI,WC] 7051 N Hwy 1, Little River 707/937-5525, 800/731-5525 *B&B w/ cottages & suites, full brkfst*

John Dougherty House [GF,NS,GO] 571 Ukiah St (at Kasten St) 707/937-5266, 800/486-2104

Little River Inn Resort & Spa [GF,F,NS,WI] 7901 N Hwy 1, Little River 707/937-5942, 888/466-5683 *resort w/ spectacular ocean views*

MacCallum House Inn [GS,NS,WI,WC] 45020 Albion St (at Lansing) 707/937-0289, 800/609-0492 *also restaurant & Grey Whale bar & cafe*

Orr Hot Springs [GF,R,SW,N] 13201 Orr Springs Rd, Ukiah 707/462-6277 *mineral hot springs, hostel-style cabins, private cottages & campsites, clothing-optional, no food provided*

Packard House [GF,NS,WI,GO] 45170 Little Lake St (at Kasten St) 707/937-2677, 888/453-2677 *full brkfst*

Sea Gull Inn [GF,NS,WI,WC] 44960 Albion St 707/937-5204, 888/937-5204

Stanford Inn by the Sea [GF,SW,NS,WI,WC] 44850 Comptche-Ukiah Rd (at Coast Hwy 1) 707/937-5615, 800/331-8884 *full brkfst, fireplaces*

Stevenswood Resort & Spa [GS,WI,WC,GO] 8211 N Hwy 1 707/937-2810, 800/421-2810

■RESTAURANTS

Cafe Beaujolais [R,WC] 961 Ukiah St 707/937-5614 *lunch & dinner*

■BOOKSTORES

Gallery Bookshop Main & Kasten St S 707/937-2665 *9:30am-6pm, independent*

Menlo Park
see Palo Alto

Mill Valley
see Marin County

Modesto
see also Stockton

■ACCOMMODATIONS

Rodeway Inn [GF,SW,WI] 936 McHenry Ave (at Roseburg Ave) 209/523-7701

■BARS

Brave Bull [MW,D,MR-L,E,K,S] 701 S 9th St 209/529-6712 *7pm-2am, clsd Mon, [K] Wed, Latin Night Th [DS,S]*

Tiki Lounge [MW,NH,D,MR,TG,K] 932 McHenry Ave (at Roseburg Ave) 209/577-9969 *5:30pm-2am*

■CAFES

Deva Cafe [F,E,WC] 1202 J St 209/572-3382 *7am-3pm, 8am-noon Sun, patio*

Queen Bean 1126 14th St 209/521-8000 *7am-8pm, till 11pm wknds*

■RESTAURANTS

Minnie's Restaurant 107 McHenry Ave 209/524-4621 *lunch Tue-Fri, dinner Tue-Sun, clsd Mon, full bar*

■RETAIL SHOPS

Mystical Body 121 McHenry Ave 209/527-1163 *noon-8pm, clsd Sun-Mon, body piercing*

■EROTICA

L'Amour Shoppe 1507-B 9th St 209/521-7987

Liberty Adult Book Store 1030 Kansas Ave 209/524-7603

Suzie's Adult Superstores 115 McHenry Ave (at Needham) 209/529-5546 *8am-midnight, arcade*

■CRUISY AREAS

McHenry Ave Recreation Area [AYOR] River Rd (N of Modesto) *go N on McHenry to River Rd & turn left*

Tuolumne River Regional Park [AYOR] S Santa Cruz Ave *parking lot & nearby woods*

Monterey

■ ACCOMMODATIONS

Asilomar Conference Grounds
[GF,F,SW,NS,WI] 800 Asilomar Blvd,
Pacific Grove 831/372-8016,
888/635-5310 *Arts & Crafts-style
buildings designed by Julia Morgan*

Gosby House Inn [GF,NS,WC] 643
Lighthouse Ave (at 18th), Pacific Grove
831/375-1287, 800/527-8828

Monterey Fireside Lodge [GF,NS,WI]
1131 10th St 831/373-4172,
800/722-2624

The Monterey Hotel [GF,WI] 406
Alvarado St 831/375-3184,
800/966-6490

■ NIGHTCLUBS

Franco's Club [MW,D,MR-L] 10639
Merritt St, Castroville 831/633-2090
10pm-2am Sat only

■ RESTAURANTS

Old Fisherman's Grotto 39
Fisherman's Wharf #1 831/375-4604
11am-10pm

Tarpy's Roadhouse 2999 Monterey
Salinas Hwy (at Canyon Dr)
831/647-1444 *lunch & dinner, Sun
brunch, patios & gardens, full bar*

■ ENTERTAINMENT & RECREATION

Ag Venture Tours [GF] PO Box 2634,
93942 831/761-8463

Morro Bay

see San Luis Obispo

Mountain View

■ MEN'S SERVICES

➤**MegaMates** 650/210-4300 *Call to
hook up with HOT local men. FREE to
listen & respond to ads. Use FREE code
DAMRON. MegaMates.com.*

Napa Valley

■ ACCOMMODATIONS

Beazley House B&B Inn [GF,NS,WI,WC]
1910 First St, Napa 707/257-1649,
800/559-1649 *historic inn, full brkfst,
pet-friendly*

Brannan Cottage Inn [GF,NS,WI] 109
Wapoo Ave (at Lincoln Ave), Calistoga
707/942-4200 *B&B in Victorian
cottage, full brkfst*

The Chablis Inn [GF,SW,NS,WC] 3360
Solano Ave (Redwood Rd at Hwy 29),
Napa 707/257-1944, 800/443-3490
stylish motel

The Chanric Inn [GS,SW,NS,WI,GO]
1805 Foothill Blvd, Calistoga
707/942-4535, 877/281-3671 *full
brkfst*

Chateau de Vie [GS,SW,WI,NS,GO] 3250
Hwy 128, Calistoga 707/942-6446,
877/558-2513 *chateau w/ gardens,
full brkfst, hot tub*

The Inn on First [GS,WI,GO] 1938 1st
St, Napa 707/253-1331,
866/253-1331

Luxe Calistoga [GF,NS] 1139 Lincoln
Ave (at Myrtle), Calistoga
707/942-9797 *on historic main street*

Meadowlark Country House
[GS,SW,N,NS,WI,GO] 601 Petrified Forest
Rd, Calistoga 707/942-5651,
800/942-5651 *clothing-optional
mineral pool, sauna & hot tub*

Napa River Inn [GF,WI] 500 Main St (at
5th), Napa 707/251-8500,
877/251-8500 *luxury boutique hotel
w/ spa, located in historic Napa Mill*

Yountville Inn [GF,SW,NS] 6462
Washington St, Yountville
707/944-5600, 888/366-8166
*alongside Hopper Creek, spa, private
patios*

■ RESTAURANTS

Barolo Italian Kitchen & Cocktails
[WI,WC,GO] 1457 Lincoln Ave, Calistoga
707/942-9900 *dinner only, Southern
Italian cuisine*

Brannan's [GO] 1374 Lincoln Ave (at
Washington), Calistoga 707/942-2233
*lunch & dinner, brunch wknds, full bar,
live jazz wknds*

Cindy's Backstreet Kitchen 1327
Railroad Ave, St Helena 707/963-1200
11:30am-9:30pm

Redd [R] 6480 Washington St,
Yountville 707/944-2222 *lunch Mon-
Sat, dinner nightly, Sun brunch,
American*

California • *USA*

SolBar 755 Silverado Trail (at the Solage Hotel), Calistoga **707/226-0850** *soul-food*

Tra Vigne [R] 1050 Charter Oak Ave (Hwy 29), St Helena **707/963-4444** *11:30am-10pm, also wine bar*

■ ENTERTAINMENT & RECREATION

Cameo Cinema 1340 Main St, St Helena **707/963-9779** *Cameo exists to entertain, inspire, educate and connect the community through the "art of storytelling"*

Harbin Hot Springs [★GF] 18424 Harbin Springs Rd, Middletown **707/987-2477, 800/622-2477 (CA only)** *retreat & workshop center, massage, some sundecks clothing-optional*

Lavender Hill Spa 1015 Foothill Blvd (at Lincoln Ave), Calistoga **707/942-4495, 800/528-4772** *9am-9pm*

■ BOOKSTORES

Copperfield's Books 1330 Lincoln Ave, Calistoga **707/942-1616** *9am-7pm, till 9pm Fri-Sat, 10am- 6pm Sun*

■ MEN'S SERVICES

➤**MegaMates 707/266-2021** *Call to hook up with HOT local men. FREE to listen & respond to ads. Use FREE code DAMRON. MegaMates.com.*

■ CRUISY AREAS

Red Rock Beach [AYOR] Stinson Beach *nude beach 1 mile S of Stinson Beach, off Hwy 1*

Vista Point [AYOR] Rte 12/121 bridge over Napa River, Napa *parking lot & nearby woods N of bridge on E side*

Nevada City

■ ACCOMMODATIONS

The Flume's End B&B [GS] 317 S Pine St **530/265-9665** *creekside Victorian, full brkfst*

■ CAFES

Java John's 306 Broad St **530/265-3653** *6:30am-5pm*

■ RESTAURANTS

Friar Tuck's [E,WC] 111 N Pine St (at Commercial) **530/265-9093** *dinner from 5pm, American/ fondue, full bar*

■ CRUISY AREAS

Hoyt's Crossing [AYOR] Hwy 49 *take to Hoyt Trail & follow till crosses Yuba River, near upstream end of Miner's Tunnel, nude sunbathing*

Newport Beach

see Orange County

Oakland

see East Bay

Oceanside

■ MEN'S SERVICES

➤**MegaMates 760/405-4005** *Call to hook up with HOT local men. FREE to listen & respond to ads. Use FREE code DAMRON. MegaMates.com.*

Orange County

includes Anaheim, Costa Mesa, Garden Grove, Huntington Beach, Irvine, Laguna Beach, Newport Beach, Santa Ana

■ INFO LINES & SERVICES

AA Gay/ Lesbian Laguna Beach **714/556-4555 (AA#)** *call or visit www.oc-aa.org for meeting times*

The Center Orange County 1605 N Spurgeon St, Santa Ana **714/953-5428** *9am-5pm Mon-Fri or by appt or event*

■ ACCOMMODATIONS

Best Western Plus Plus Laguna Brisas Spa Hotel [GS,SW,NS,WI,WC] 1600 S Coast Hwy (at Bluebird), Laguna Beach **949/497-7272, 888/296-6834** *resort hotel*

Casa Laguna Inn & Spa [GF,SW,WI,NS,GO] 2510 S Coast Hwy, Laguna Beach **949/494-2996, 800/233-0449** *inn & cottages over-looking the Pacific*

Fairfield Inn Placentia [GF,SW,WI,WC] 710 W Kimberly Ave, Placentia **714/996-4410, 800/308-5286**

Holiday Inn & Suites Anaheim
[GF,SW,WI,WC] 1240 S Walnut, Anaheim
714/535-0300, 800/308-5312 *walk to Disneyland, also restaurant*

The Hotel Hanford [GF,SW,WI,WC]
3131 S Bristol St (at Baker St), Costa
Mesa **714/557-3000, 877/426-3673**

Laguna Cliffs Inn [GF,SW,NS,WI,WC]
475 N Coast Hwy, Laguna Beach
949/497-6645, 800/297-0007 *hot tub, easy beach access*

The St Regis Monarch Beach
[GF,F,SW,NS,WI,WC] One Monarch Beach
Resort, Dana Point **949/234-3426**

Surf & Sand Resort [GF,F,SW,WI]
949/497-4477, 888/869-7569

■BARS

Club Bounce [MW,D,E,K] 1460 S Coast
Hwy, Laguna Beach **949/494-0056**
2pm-2am, upstairs dance bar Fri-Sat

Frat House [★MW,D,MR,DS,S,YC,WC]
8112 Garden Grove Blvd (at Beach Blvd),
Garden Grove **714/373-3728** *3pm-2am*

Ibiza Bar & Nightclub [GF,NH,D,WC]
18528 Beach Blvd **714/963-7744**
noon-2am, from 4pm Mon, from 2pm Sun

Tin Lizzie Saloon [M,NH,WC] 752 St
Clair (at Bristol), Costa Mesa
714/966-2029 *11:30am-2am*

Velvet Lounge [MW,D,F,K] 416 W 4th
St, Santa Ana **714/232-8727**
11:30am-2am

■NIGHTCLUBS

Bravo [GS,D,A,MR-L,F,DS,S] 1490 S
Anaheim Blvd, Anaheim
714/533-2291 *Latin music Wed & Fri-Sat, more gay Th & Sat night, goth & electronica Sun*

Club Lucky Presents [★M,D,E,S,18+,$]
949/551-2998 *check www.clubluckypresents.com for weekly parties in OC*

El Calor [GF,D,MR-L,DS] 2916 W Lincoln
Ave (at E Beach Blvd), Anaheim
714/527-8873 *8pm-2am, Latin music, also restaurant*

Lions Den [MW,D,K,DS,YC] 719 W 19th
St (at Pomona Ave), Costa Mesa
949/645-3830 *9pm-2am, clsd Mon, only gay Fri for Fiesta Latino*

■CAFES

Avanti Cafe [F,BW] 259 E 17th St (at
Westminster), Costa Mesa
949/548-2224 *11am-10pm, till 8pm Sun, brkfst, lunch & dinner, veggie & vegan*

The Koffee Klatch [WI] 1440 S Coast
Hwy (btwn Bristol & Pacific Coast
Hwy), Laguna Beach **949/376-6867**
7am-11pm, till midnight Fri-Sat

Zinc Cafe [BW,WC] 350 Ocean Ave (at
Broadway), Laguna Beach
949/494-6302 *7am-4pm, also market till 6pm, patio*

■RESTAURANTS

Cafe Zoolu [BW,WC] 860 Glenneyre St,
Laguna Beach **949/494-6825** *5pm-10pm, clsd Mon*

The Cottage 308 N Coast Hwy (at
Aster), Laguna Beach **949/494-3023**
brkfst, lunch & dinner, homestyle cooking, some veggie

Dizz's As Is 2794 S Coast Hwy (at Nyes
Pl), Laguna Beach **949/494-5250**
open 5:30pm clsd Mon, full bar, patio

Madison Square & Garden Cafe 320
N Coast Hwy, Laguna Beach
949/494-0137 *8am-3pm, clsd Tue, dog-friendly*

Nirvana Grille 303 Broadway St,
Laguna Beach **949/497-0027** *dinner nightly, seasonal rooftop deck*

Three Seventy Common 370
Glenneyre St, Laguna Beach
949/494-8686 *dinner only, upscale American bistro & martini bar*

■ENTERTAINMENT & RECREATION

San Onofre State Beach on I-5, S of
San Clemente (exit at Basilone Rd),
Laguna Beach

West St Beach Laguna Beach

■MEN'S SERVICES

▶**MegaMates** **714/594-0400** *Call to hook up with HOT local men. FREE to listen & respond to ads. Use FREE code DAMRON. MegaMates.com.*

California • *USA*

■EROTICA

A-Z Bookstore 8192 Garden Grove Blvd (at Beach), Garden Grove **714/534-9349**

Garden of Eden 12061 Garden Grove Blvd, Garden Grove **714/534-9805** *24hrs*

Pink Kitty [GO] 17955 Sky Park Cir, Ste A, Irvine **949/660-4990** *10am-6pm*

■CRUISY AREAS

Calafia State Beach [AYOR] to the left, off the fwy (from Hwy 5 S), San Clemente

Eisenhower Park [AYOR] Orange

Fairview Park [AYOR] Costa Mesa

Fullerton Dam [AYOR] on Harbor Blvd, Fullerton *park*

Heisler Park [AYOR] N side of park, Laguna Beach *also take path to the ocean, then climb over the rocks to the right; beware cops (!)*

Santiago Park [AYOR] off I-5 (at Main St), Santa Ana *parking lot & nearby woods, early evenings*

William Mason Regional Park [AYOR] Culver St & University Ave, Irvine

Oroville

■CAFES

Mug Shots [WI,GO] 2040 Montgomery St **530/538-8342** *6am-6pm, 8am-3pm Sun*

Oxnard

■MEN'S SERVICES

►**MegaMates 805/200-0299** *Call to hook up with HOT local men. FREE to listen & respond to ads. Use FREE code DAMRON. MegaMates.com.*

■CRUISY AREAS

Oxnard Shores Beach [AYOR] 5th St (past Harbor Blvd) *head to sand dunes*

Pacifica

■CRUISY AREAS

Grey Whale Cove Beach [AYOR] Hwy 1 *3 miles S of Pacifica on Devil's Slide, large parking lot on left, nude beach*

San Pedro Mountain Park [AYOR] Linda Mar & Odstaad Dr

Palm Springs

■INFO LINES & SERVICES

AA Gay/ Lesbian 760/324-4880 (AA#) *call for meeting schedule*

The Center 611 S Palm Canyon #201 **760/416-7790** *programs & services, 12-step meetings*

■ACCOMMODATIONS

Ace Hotel Palm Springs [GS,SW,F,WI] 701 E Palm Canyon Dr **760/325-9900**

All Worlds Resort [★M,SW,N,WI,GO] 526 S Warm Sands Dr (at Ramon) **760/323-7505** *4 hot properties, rooms for all budgets*

The Bearfoot Inn [MO,B,N,WI] 888 N Indian Canyon Dr (at El Alameda) **760/699-7641**

Caliente Tropics Resort [GS,F,SW,NS,WC,GO] 411 E Palm Canyon Dr **760/327-1391, 888/277-0999** *pet-friendly motor hotel, jacuzzi*

Calla Lily Inn [GF,SW,NS,WI] 350 S Belardo Rd (at Baristo) **760/323-3654, 888/888-5787** *"a tranquil oasis"*

Calmada Boutique Hotel [GS,SW,WI] 3569 Calmada Rd, Pioneertown **760/228-3141** *resort 30 min from Palm Springs*

Canyon Club Hotel [M,SW,N,WI,GO] 960 N Palm Canyon Dr (btwn Tachevah & El Alameda) **760/778-8042, 877/258-2887** *clothing-optional, kitchens, hot tub & patios*

Casa Ocotillo [★M,SW,NS,V,N,WI,GO] 240 E Ocotillo Ave **760/327-6110, 800/996-4108** *intimate & elegant resort-style accommodations in a 1934 Mexican hacienda—"the ultimate get-away for the discriminating traveler"*

►**CCBC Resort Hotel** [★M,SW,N,WC,GO] 68300 Gay Resort Dr (btwn Melrose & Palo Verde), Cathedral City **760/324-1350, 800/472-0836** *mention Damron for 25% off (holidays not included), JocKuzzi Spa, steam room, saltwater pool, waterfall & cave, jail & dungeon*

Chaps Inn [M,SW,WI,WC,GO] 312 E Camino Monte Vista **760/327-8222, 800/445-8916** *catering to leather & bears mostly*

California • *USA*

Desert Eclipse Resort
[M,SW,N,WI,WC,GO] 537 Grenfall Rd (at Ramon) 760/325-0655, 800/798-0655

Desert Paradise Resort Hotel
[M,SW,N,NS,WI,GO] 615 Warm Sands Dr (at Parocela) 760/320-5650, 800/342-7635

The East Canyon Hotel & Spa
[M,SW,N,WI,GO] 288 E Camino Monte Vista 760/320-1928, 877/324-6835 *boutique hotel, day spa*

El Mirasol Villas [M,SW,N,NS,WI,GO] 525 Warm Sands Dr (at Ramon) 760/327-5913, 800/327-2985

Escape [M,SW,N,NS,WI,GO] 641 E San Lorenzo Rd (at Random) 760/325-5269, 800/621-6973 *hot tub*

The Hacienda at Warm Sands
[★M,V,SW,N,NS,WI,WC,GO] 586 Warm Sands Dr (at Parocela) 760/327-8111, 800/359-2007 *brkfst & catered lunch*

Helios Resort [★M,SW,N,NS,WI,WC,GO] 280 East Mel Ave 877/435-4677 *resort, hot tub*

The Horizon Hotel [GF,SW,WI] 1050 E Palm Canyon Dr 760/323-1858, 800/377-7855

Hotel Zoso [GF,SW,WI] 150 S Indian Canyon Dr 760/325-9676 *4-acre resort, restaurant & bar, spa*

INNdulge Palm Springs
[M,SW,N,NS,WI,GO] 601 Grenfall Rd (at Parocela) 760/327-1408, 800/833-5675 *hot tub*

La Dolce Vita Resort
[M,SW,N,NS,WI,WC,GO] 1491 S Via Soledad (at Sonora & S Palm Canyon) 760/325-2686, 877/644-4111 *full brkfst, jacuzzi*

Pura Vida Resorts [M,SW,WI,WC,GO] 589 S Grenfall Rd (at Parocela) 760/832-6438, 877/786-0519

Rendezvous [GF,SW,WI] 1420 N Indian Canyon Dr 760/320-1178, 800/485-2808 *'50s chic*

Ruby Montana's Coral Sands Inn
[GS,SW,WI,WC,GO] 210 W Stevens Rd (at N Palm Canyon) 760/325-4900, 866/820-8302 *resort, kitschy 1950s chic*

The Saguaro [GF,F,SW] 1800 East Palm Canyon Dr 760/323-1711 *hip boutique hotel*

Santiago Resort [M,SW,N,NS,WI,GO] 650 San Lorenzo Rd (at Mesquite) 760/322-1300, 800/710-7729 *brkfst & lunch included*

The Skylark [GS,SW,WI,GO] 1466 N Palm Canyon Dr (at Monte Vista) 760/322-2267, 800/793-0063

Tortuga del Sol [M,SW,N,NS,WI,GO] 715 San Lorenzo 760/416-3111, 888/541-3777 *resort, jacuzzi*

Triangle Inn Palm Springs
[★M,SW,N,GO] 555 San Lorenzo Rd (at Random Rd) 760/322-7993, 800/732-7555 *hot tub, 2 sundecks*

Warm Sands Villas [M,SW,N,NS,WI] 555 Warm Sands Dr (at Ramon) 760/323-3005, 800/357-5695 *hot tub*

■BARS

The Barracks [M,L] 67-625 E Palm Canyon (at Canyon Plaza), Cathedral City 760/321-9688 *2pm-2am*

DiGS [MW,NH,CW,K] 36-737 Cathedral Canyon Dr (at 111), Cathedral City 760/321-0031 *2pm-2am, from 10am Sun, patio*

Georgie's Alibi [M,NH,F,V] 369 N Palm Canyon 760/325-5533 *11am-close, from 10am Sun*

Hunter's Video Bar [★M,D,V] 302 E Arenas Rd (at Calle Encilia) 760/323-0700 *10am-2am, go-go boys Fri, theme nights*

Score [M,NH,V] 301 E Arenas Rd 760/327-0753 *6am-2am*

SpurLine [M,NH,K,V] 200 S Indian Canyon Dr (at Arenas) 760/778-4326 *noon-2am, from 2pm Mon-Tue, lounge*

Streetbar [★M,NH,E,K,WC] 224 E Arenas Rd (at Indian) 760/320-1266 *10am-2am, patio*

Studio One 11 [M,D,S,K] 67-555 E Palm Canyon Dr (at E Eagle Canyon Way), Cathedral City 760/328-2900 *3pm-2am*

Tool Shed [M,NH,L] 600 E Sunny Dunes Rd (at Palm Canyon) 760/320-3299 *10am-2am, from 8am wknds, cruise bar*

Toucan's Tiki Lounge [MW,D,E,DS,S] 2100 N Palm Canyon Dr (at Via Escuela) 760/416-7584 noon-2am, [E] Mon, [DS] Wed & Sun, go-go dancers wknds

■CAFES

Palm Springs Koffi [★WI,GO] 515 N Palm Canyon Dr (at Alejo) 760/416-2244 5:30am-8pm

■RESTAURANTS

Azul 369 N Palm Canyon Dr 760/325-5533 11am-2am, tapas lounge, full bar upstairs

Billy Reed's [WC] 1800 N Palm Canyon Dr (at Vista Chino) 760/325-1946 7am-9pm, till 10pm Fri-Sat

Blue Coyote Grill 445 N Palm Canyon Dr 760/327-1196 11am 10pm, till 11pm Fri-Sat, Southwestern

Bongo Johnny's 214 E Arenas Rd 760/866-1905 8am-10pm, till 11pm Fri-Sat, burgers & sandwiches

Cafe Palette [E,GO] 315 E Arenas 760/322-9264 11am-10pm, also delivers

The Chop House [R] 262 S Palm Canyon Dr 760/320-4500 from 5pm, fine steaks and chops

Copley's 621 N Palm Canyon Dr (btwn E Tamarisk Rd & E Granvia Valmonte) 760/327-9555 6pm-10pm, contemporary American, full bar

The Crazy Coconut Bar & Grill [K] 166 N Palm Canyon Dr 760/327-8175 11am-10pm, till Th-Sat, burgers & fries

Davey's Hideaway [P] 292 E Palm Canyon Dr 760/320-4480 from 5pm, steak, seafood & pasta, patio, full bar

El Gallito [BW] 68820 Grove St (at Palm Canyon), Cathedral City 760/328-7794 10am-9pm, homemade Mexican

Hamburger Mary's 415 N Palm Canyon Dr 760/778-6279 11am-close, full bar

Jake's 664 N Palm Canyon Dr 760/327-4400 lunch & dinner, wknd brunch, clsd Sun night & Mon, American bistro

Las Casuelas 368 N Palm Canyon Dr (btwn Amado & Alejo) 760/325-3213 11am-10pm, Mexican

Matchbox 155 S Palm Canyon Dr (in Mercado Plaza, 2nd level) 760/778-6000 4pm-11pm, till 1am Fri-Sat pizza

Nature's Health Food & Cafe 555 S Sunrise Way #301 760/323-9487 8am-7pm, 9am-5pm wknds, vegan/vegetarian

Peppers Thai Cuisine 396 N Palm Canyon Dr 760/322-1259 lunch & dinner

Pinocchio in the Desert 134 E Tahquitz Canyon Way 760/322-3776 7:30am-2pm, outdoor seating

Pomme Frite 256 S Palm Canyon Dr 760/778-3727 dinner nightly, lunch wknds, clsd Tue, Belgian beer & French food

Rio Azul 350 S Indian Canyon Dr 760/992-5641 dinner nightly, open for lunch wknds, Mexican

Shame on the Moon [R,WC] 69-950 Frank Sinatra Dr (at Hwy 111), Rancho Mirage 760/324-5515 5pm-9:30pm, cont'l, full bar, patio

Sherman's Deli & Bakery [★] 401 E Tahquitz Canyon Wy 760/325-1199 7am-9pm, kosher-style deli

Spencer's Restaurant [R] 701 W Baristo Rd 760/327-3446 9am-2:30pm & 5pm-10pm, Sun brunch, upscale contemporary

Tootie's Texas Barbeque 68-703 Perez Rd, Cathedral City 760/202-6963 11am-8pm, clsd wknds, the name says it all

Towne Center Cafe 44491 Town Center Wy, Palm Desert 760/346-2120 6am-9pm, Greek diner

Trio 707 N Palm Canyon Dr 760/864-8746 dinner nightly, also lounge

Wang's in the Desert 424 S Indian Canyon Dr (at E Saturnino Rd) 760/325-9264 from 5:30pm, Chinese, full bar

Zin American Bistro 198 S Palm Canyon (at Arenas) 760/322-6300 lunch & dinner

California • *USA*

■ BOOKSTORES

Q Trading Company 606 E Sunny Dunes Rd (at Indian Canyon) 760/416-7150, 800/756-2290 *10am-6pm, LGBT, also cards, gifts, videos*

■ RETAIL SHOPS

Bear Wear Etc 319 E Arenas Rd 760/323-8940 *11am-6pm, till 10pm Th-Sat, noon-6pm Sun, men's clothing, leather & resort wear*

GayMartUSA 305 E Arenas Rd (at Indian Canyon) 760/416-6436 *10am-midnight*

Mischief 210 E Arenas Rd (at Indian Canyon) 760/322-8555

Off Ramp Leathers 650 E Sunny Dunes Rd #3 760/778-2798 *custom motorcycle leathers*

■ PUBLICATIONS

Desert Daily Guide/ DDG Media Group 760/320-3237 *LGBT weekly*

Odyssey Magazine 323/874-8788 *dish on LA. & Palm Springs' club scene*

■ GYMS & HEALTH CLUBS

WorkOUT Gym [GO] 2100 N Palm Canyon Dr #C100 760/325-4600

World Gym Palm Springs [★M,WC,GO] 1751 N Sunrise Way (at Vista Chino) 760/327-7100 *5am-10pm, 6am-8pm wknds, day passes available, steam & sauna, club-quality sound system*

■ MEN'S SERVICES

➤**MegaMates** 760/406-8222 *Call to hook up with HOT local men. FREE to listen & respond to ads. Use FREE code DAMRON. MegaMates.com.*

■ EROTICA

Gear Leather & Fetish 650 E Sunny Dunes #1 (at S Calle Palo Fierro) 760/322-3363 *noon-7pm, till 9pm Fri-Sat*

Hidden Joy Book Shop 68-424 Commercial (at Cathedral Canyon), Cathedral City 760/328-1694 *24hrs, arcade*

Perez Images 68-366 Perez Rd, Cathedral City 760/321-1033 *24hrs*

■ CRUISY AREAS

Cahuilla Hills Park [AYOR] Palm Desert

Palmdale

see Lancaster

Palo Alto

■ ACCOMMODATIONS

Creekside Inn [GS,SW,NS,WI,WC] 3400 El Camino Real (at Page Mill Rd) 650/493-2411, 800/492-7335 *restaurant & lounge*

Hotel Avante [GS,SW,NS,WI] 860 E El Camino Real, Mountain View 650/940-1000, 800/538-1600

■ BOOKSTORES

Books Inc 855 El Camino Real 650/321-0600 *9am-8pm*

■ MEN'S SERVICES

➤**MegaMates** 650/223-0505 *Call to hook up with HOT local men. FREE to listen & respond to ads. Use FREE code DAMRON. MegaMates.com.*

Pasadena

■ BARS

The 35er [GS,NH,F] 626 /356-9315 *3pm-1am, from 12:30pm Fri-Sun*

The Boulevard Bar [M,NH,K,P] 3199 E Foothill Blvd (at Sierra Madre Villa) 626/356-9304 *4pm-2am, from 3pm Fri-Sun*

■ RESTAURANTS

Kings Row 20 E Colorado Blvd 626/793-3010 *4pm-midnight, till 2am wknds, gastropub*

Lanna Thai [WC] 400 S Arroyo Pkwy 626/577-6599 *11am-10:30pm, Thai, full bar*

■ ENTERTAINMENT & RECREATION

The Huntington 1151 Oxford Rd, San Marino 626/405-2100 *art collection, botanical gardens*

■ MEN'S SERVICES

➤**MegaMates** 626/720-2999 *Call to hook up with HOT local men. FREE to listen & respond to ads. Use FREE code DAMRON. MegaMates.com.*

■EROTICA

Romantix Adult Superstore 45 E Colorado Blvd (at Raymond) **626/683-9468**

Paso Robles

■ACCOMMODATIONS

Asuncion Ridge Vineyards & Inn [GF,WI,GO] **805/461-0675**

Hotel Cheval [GF,WI] 1021 Pine St **805/226-9995, 866/522-6999**

■ENTERTAINMENT & RECREATION

River Oaks Hot Springs Spa 800 Clubhouse Dr **805/238-4600** *9am-9pm, clsd Mon*

Petaluma

■RESTAURANTS

Brixx [★E] 16 Kentucky St (in Lanmart Bldg) **707/766-8162** *dinner from 4pm, handmade pizzas, paninis*

■BOOKSTORES

Copperfield's Books 140 Kentucky St (btwn Western & Washington, downtown) **707/762-0563** *9am-9pm, 10am-6pm Sun*

■CRUISY AREAS

Lucchesi Park [AYOR]

Placerville

■ACCOMMODATIONS

Albert Shafsky House B&B [GF,NS,WI,GO] 2942 Coloma St (at Spring St/ Hwy 49) **530/642-2776, 877/262-4667** *full brkfst, lesbian-owned*

Rancho Cicada Retreat [M,SW,N,GO] 10001 Bell Rd, Plymouth **209/245-4841, 877/553-9481** *riverside retreat, campsites, tents & cabins*

■CRUISY AREAS

Lumsden Park [AYOR] Wiltse Rd *parking lots & woods*

Pleasant Hill

see East Bay

Point Reyes

■CRUISY AREAS

Hagmire Pond [AYOR] Hwy 1 (at milepost 20.53) *nude sunbathing & woods; walk right across meadow & look for pond on the right, walk up hill to right of pond*

Pomona

■BARS

Alibi East & Back Alley Bar [M,D,K] 225 S San Antonio Ave (at 2nd) **909/623-9422** *noon-2am, till 3am Fri, smoking patio*

The Hookup [MW,F,K,V,WC,GO] 1047 E 2nd St (at Pico) **909/620-2844** *noon-2am, beer bust Sun*

■NIGHTCLUBS

340 [MW,D,F,DS] 340 S Thomas St **909/865-9340** *7pm--2am , clsd Mon-Wed*

Redding

■NIGHTCLUBS

Club 501 [MW,D,YC] 1244 California St (at Center & Division, enter rear) **530/243-7869** *6pm-2am, from 3pm Th-Sun*

■EROTICA

Secrets, Hilltop Books 2131 Hilltop Dr **530/223-2675**

■CRUISY AREAS

Clear Creek Rd [AYOR] 13 miles W of Hwy 273 (4 miles W of old 99) *nude beach, summers*

Redlands

■CRUISY AREAS

Ford Park [AYOR] Ford St (at Parkford Dr) *take I-10 E & exit at Ford St, turn right & first street you come to (Prospect) turn right again; park begins where street stops; take sidewalk adjacent to tennis court that goes up hill*

Sylvan Park [AYOR] 601 N University St (exit 10 E at University St) *make left when going under bridge; weekdays only*

California • *USA*

Redondo Beach

see also Los Angeles—West LA & Santa Monica

■ACCOMMODATIONS

Best Western Sunrise Hotel
[GF,F,SW,WI] 400 N Harbor Dr
310/376-0746, 800/334-7384 *hot tub, kids ok*

Riverside

see also San Bernardino

■NIGHTCLUBS

Menagerie [MW,D,K,DS,WC] 3581
University Ave (at Orange)
951/788-8000 *4pm-2am*

VIP Nightclub & Restaurant
[MW,D,F,K,DS,18+] 3673 Merrill Ave (at
Magnolia) 951/784-2370 *5pm-2am*

■MEN'S SERVICES

➤**MegaMates** 951/530-9991 *Call to hook up with HOT local men. FREE to listen & respond to ads. Use FREE code DAMRON. MegaMates.com.*

■CRUISY AREAS

Fairmount Park [AYOR] off Rte 60 (at
Market St exit)

Riverton

■CRUISY AREAS

Bull Creek Rd [AYOR] off Hwy 50 *trail along river*

Russian River

includes Cazadero, Forestville, Guerneville, Monte Rio, Occidental & Sebastopol

■INFO LINES & SERVICES

AA Meetings in Sonoma County
707/544-1300 (AA#),
800/224-1300 *call for meeting times*

Russian River Chamber of Commerce & Visitors Center 16209
First St (on the plaza), Guerneville
707/869-9000 *10am-5pm, till 4pm Sun*

➤**Sonoma County Tourism Bureau**
800/576-6662 *see ad in front color section*

■ACCOMMODATIONS

Applewood Inn [GF,F,SW,NS,WI,WC,GO]
13555 Hwy 116 (at Mays Canyon),
Guerneville 707/869-9093,
800/555-8509

boon hotel & spa [GS,SW,NS,WI,GO]
14711 Armstrong Woods Rd, Guerneville
707/869-2721

Fern Grove Cottages [GF,SW,NS,WI]
16650 River Rd, Guerneville
888/243-2674

Guerneville Lodge [GS,NS,WI] 15905
River Rd (at Hwy 116), Guerneville
707/869-0102 *camping*

Highland Dell Resort [GF,F,WI] 21050
River Blvd (at Bohemian Hwy), Monte
Rio 707/865-2300

➤**Highlands Resort** [MW,SW,N] 14000
Woodland Dr, Guerneville
707/869-0333 *country retreat on 4 wooded acres, hot tub*

Inn at Occidental [GF,NS,WC] 3657
Church St, Occidental 707/874-1047,
800/522-6324

r3 Hotel [MW,E,F,V,SW,N,WC,GO] 16390
4th St (at Mill), Guerneville
707/869-8399 *bar & restaurant*

Rio Villa Beach Resort [GF,NS,WI,GO]
20292 Hwy 116 (at Bohemian Hwy),
Monte Rio 707/865-1143,
877/746-8455

Village Inn & Restaurant
[GS,NS,WC,WI,GO] 20822 River Blvd,
Monte Rio 707/865-2304 *historic inn w/ restaurant & full bar*

West Sonoma Inn & Spa
[GS,SW,NS,WI,WC] 14100 Brookside Ln
(at Main St), Guerneville
707/869-2470, 800/551-1881 *6-acre resort*

The Woods Resort
[★M,SW,N,NS,WI,WC,GO] 16484 4th St
(at Mill St), Guerneville 707/869-0600,
877/887-9218 *cottages, guest cabins & suites*

■BARS

Mc T's Bullpen [GS,NH,K,E,WI,WC]
16246 First St (at Church), Guerneville
707/869-3377 *10am-2am, sports bar, patio*

Rainbow Cattle Co [★GS,NH] 16220 Main St (at Armstrong Woods Rd), Guerneville 707/869-0206 *6am-2am, DJ Bruce Sat*

Whitetail Winebar [GO] 16230 Main St, Guerneville 707/604-7449 *4pm-10pm, 3pm-11pm Fri-Sat, till 9pm Sun, clsd Tue*

■CAFES

Coffee Bazaar [★WI] 14045 Armstrong Woods Rd (at River Rd), Guerneville 707/869-9706 *6am-8pm, soups, salads & sandwiches*

Coffee Catz [E,WI,WC] 6761 Sebastopol Ave (at Hwy 116), Sebastopol 707/829-6600 *7am-6pm, till 8pm Th, till 10pm Wed & Fri-Sat*

Roasters Espresso Bar [E,WI] 6656 Front St (Hwy 116), Forestville 707/887-1632 *6am-6pm, from 7am Sat-Sun*

■RESTAURANTS

Aioli [BW] 6536 Front St, Forestville 707/887-2476 *9am-5pm, from 10am Sat, gourmet deli, outdoor seating*

boon eat + drink [BW] 16248 Main St (at Hwy 116), Guerneville 707/869-0780 *lunch & dinner, clsd Tue-Wed, American*

Cape Fear Cafe [WC] 25191 Main St, Duncans Mills 707/865-9246 *9am-2:30pm & 5pm-9pm (clsd Wed & Th off-season)*

Chef Patrick [BW,WC] 16337 Main St (at Hwy 116), Guerneville 707/869-9161 *dinner nightly*

Farmhouse Inn Restaurant [BW] 7871 River Rd, Forestville 707/887-3300, 800/464-6642 *dinner, clsd Tue-Wed*

Garden Grill 17132 Hwy 116, Guerneville 707/869-3922 *8am-8pm, great burgers & sandwiches, some veggie, patio*

California • *USA*

Main Street Station [C,BW] 16280 Main St (at Church St), Guerneville **707/869-0501** *11am-7pm, Italian restaurant & pizzeria*

River Inn Grill [★WC] 16141 Main St, Guerneville **707/869-0481** *8am-3pm, local favorite*

Tahoe Chinese Restaurant 6492 Mirabel Rd, Forestville **707/887-9772** *lunch & dinner Mon-Fri, dinner only Sat-Sun*

Underwood Bar & Bistro 9113 Graton Rd, Graton **707/823-7023** *lunch & dinner, clsd Mon*

Willow Wood Market Cafe [★] 9020 Graton Rd, Graton **707/823-0233** *8am-9pm, from 9am Sat, brunch 9am-3pm Sun*

■ENTERTAINMENT & RECREATION

The Nude Beach [AYOR] on Russian River at Wohler Bridge, Guerneville

Pegasus Theater Co [WC] 4444 Wood Rd (at Rio Nido Lodge, at Canyon Two Rd) **707/583-2343** *classic to contemporary plays*

■BOOKSTORES

River Reader [WC] 16355 Main St (at Mill), Guerneville **707/869-2240** *10am-6pm, extended summer hours*

■RETAIL SHOPS

Bruce's Barber Shop 16190 Main St #C (in the Russian River Realty Bldg), Guerneville *11am-5pm, 9am-2pm Sat, clsd Sun-Mon*

Sonoma Nesting Company [GO] 16151 Main St, Guerneville **707/869-3434** *antiques & home decorating*

■CRUISY AREAS

Steelhead Beach Regional Park [AYOR] 9000 River Rd, Forestville *beach & woods*

Sacramento

■INFO LINES & SERVICES

Gay AA 916/454-1100 *24hr helpline*

Sacramento Gay & Lesbian Center 1927 L St **916/442-0185** *noon-6pm Mon-Fri*

■ACCOMMODATIONS

Citizen Hotel [GF,NS,WI,WC] 926 J Street **916/447-2700**

Governors Inn [GF,SW,NS,WI] 210 Richards Blvd (at I-5) **916/448-7224, 800/999-6689** *internet, hot tub, exercise room*

The Greens Hotel [GS,SW,WI,WC] 1700 Del Paso Blvd (at Arden) **707/365-5905**

Inn & Spa at Parkside [GS,WI,WC,GO] 2116 6th St (at U St) **916/658-1818, 800/995-7275** *full brkfst, jacuzzi, also full-service spa*

■BARS

The Bolt [M,NH,B,L] 2560 Boxwood St (at El Camino) **916/649-8420** *5pm-2am, from 2pm wknds, patio, volleyball in summer*

The Depot [★M,NH,TG,E,S,V,WC] 2001 K St **916/441-6823** *4pm-2am, till 4am Fri-Sat, from noon wknds*

Dive Bar [★GS] 1016 K St **916/737-5999** *4pm-2am, super cool water tank*

The Mercantile Saloon [★M,NH,WC] 1928 L St (at 20th St) **916/447-0792** *10am-2am*

■NIGHTCLUBS

Badlands [M,D,S,V] 2003 K St **916/448-8790** *6pm-2am, from 2pm Fri-Sat, from 4pm Sun*

Club Papi Sacramento [M,D,MR-L] 2000 K St (at 20th) **415/675-9763** *monthly party from 9pm-3am., call for dates*

For more resources and the latest updates

DAMRON Online
www.damron.com
the first name and the last word in gay travel guides

➤**Faces** [★MW,D,K] 2000 K St (at 20th St) **916/448-7798** *4pm-2am, 3 bars w/ various theme nights, patio; see color on on next page*

Head Hunters Video Lounge & Grill [MW,E,F] 1930 K St (at 20th St) **916/492-2922** *dinner Tue-Sun, Sun brunch, bar open till 2am*

■CAFES

Mondo Bizarro [E,WI] 1827 I St **916/443-6133** *7am-7pm, from 8am Sun*

N Street Cafe [WI,WC] 2022 N Street **916/491-4008** *6am-6pm, 8am-3pm Sat-Sun*

■RESTAURANTS

Chops 1117 11th St (at L St, across from State Capitol Building) **916/447-8900** *lunch Mon-Fri, dinner nightly, steak & seafood, full bar*

Ernesto's 1901 16th St **916/441-5850** *Mexican*

Hads Steak & Seafood [GO] 1925 J St **916/446-3118**

Hamburger Patties [K,DS,WC] 1630 J St (at 17th) **916/441-4340** *11am-10pm, from 10am wknds, full bar*

Hot Rod's Burgers 2007 K St **916/443-7637** *11am-2am, till 3am Fri-Sat*

Ink Eats & Drinks 2730 N St (at 28th) **916/456-2800** *lunch, dinner, late-night brkfst, wknd brunch, full bar, DJ wknds*

Jack's Urban Eats 1230 20th St (at Capitol Ave) **916/444-0307** *11am-8pm, till 9pm Wed-Sat*

Paesanos 1806 Capitol Ave (at 18th) **916/447-8646** *11:30am-9:30pm, from noon wknds, Italian, funky artwork, patio, full bar; also 8519 Bond Rd, 916/690-8646*

Pizza Rock [★] 1020 K St **916/737-5777** *11am-10pm, till midnight Wed-Th, till 3am Fri-Sat*

Rick's Dessert Diner 2322 K St (btwn 23rd & 24th) **916/444-0969** *10am-midnight, till 1am wknds, from noon Sun*

Thai Palace 3262 J St (33rd St) **916/447-5353** *lunch & dinner*

Zócalo 1801 Capitol Ave (at 18th St) **916/441-0303** *11am-10pm, Mexican, full bar*

■ENTERTAINMENT & RECREATION

Lavender Library, Archives & Cultural Exchange of Sacramento 1414 21st St **916/492-0558** *4:30pm-8pm Th-Fri, noon-6pm wknds, clsd Mon-Wed*

■PUBLICATIONS

➤**Gloss Magazine** 415/552-5070 *CA arts/ entertainment magazine, bi-weekly*

Outword Magazine 916/329-9280 *statewide LGBT newspaper*

■MEN'S CLUBS

Folsom Park Sauna [MO,$] 9261 Folsom Blvd #400 **916/363-1247** *10am-10pm*

The Sacs4men Men's Club near Watt & Elkhorn, Rio Linda **916/879-4611, 916/410-6550 (info line)** *call for info & location; also over night room rentals*

■MEN'S SERVICES

➤**MegaMates** 916/340-1414 *Call to hook up with HOT local men. FREE to listen & respond to ads. Use FREE code DAMRON. MegaMates.com.*

■EROTICA

G Spot [★GO] 2009 K St (at 20th) **916/441-3200**

Goldie's I 201 N 12th St (at North B St) **916/447-5860**

Kiss-N-Tell 4201 Sunrise Blvd (at Fair Oaks) **916/966-5477** *clean, well-lighted erotica store; also 2401 Arden Wy, 916/920-5477*

L'Amour Shoppe 2531 Broadway (at 26th) **916/736-3467**

2 LEVELS   3 DANCE FLOORS

2000 K ST.

California • *USA*

■ CRUISY AREAS
American River Access [AYOR] off La Rivera Dr, near Howe Ave & Watt Ave

Beach & levee on American River [AYOR] at end of N 10th St, off Richards Blvd

San Bernardino
see also Riverside

■ INFO LINES & SERVICES
AA Gay/ Lesbian 897 Via Lata, Colton **909/825-4700** *call or visit www.inlandempireaa.org for times*

■ MEN'S SERVICES
►**MegaMates 909/663-0300** *Call to hook up with HOT local men. FREE to listen & respond to ads. Use FREE code DAMRON. MegaMates.com.*

■ EROTICA
Bearfacts Book Store 1434 E Baseline St **909/885-9176** *24hrs, arcade*

Le Sex Shoppe 304 W Highland Ave **909/881-3583** *arcade*

■ CRUISY AREAS
Cajon Pass [AYOR] Cajon Pass (off Rte 138, W of I-15, in San Bernardino Nat'l Forest), Cajon Junction *parking lot & nearby woods*

San Clemente
see Orange County

San Diego

■ INFO LINES & SERVICES
Live & Let Live Alano Club 1730 Monroe Ave **619/298-8008** *10:30am-10pm, from 8:30am wknds, see www.lllac.org for meetings*

San Diego LGBT Community Center 3909 Centre St (at University) **619/692-2077** *9am-10pm, till 7pm Sat, clsd Sun*

■ ACCOMMODATIONS
Balboa Park Inn [GF,NS] 3402 Park Blvd (at Upas) **619/298-0823,** **800/938-8181**

Beach Area B&B/ Elsbree House [GF,NS] 5054 Narragansett Ave (at Sunset Cliffs Blvd) **619/226-4133,** **800/607-4133** *B&B & 3-bdrm condo near beach*

The Bristol Hotel [GS,WI,WC] 1055 First Ave **619/232-6141, 800/662-4477** *restaurant & bar, great collection of pop art*

Handlery Hotel & Resort [GF,SW,NS,WI,WC] 950 Hotel Circle N **619/298-0511, 800/676-6567**

Inn at the Park [GF,WI] 525 Spruce St (btwn 5th & 6th) **619/291-0999, 877/499-7163** *1926 hotel, bar [P] & 2 restaurants, popular Fri happy hour*

Keating House [GF,NS,WI,GO] 2331 2nd Ave (at Juniper) **619/239-8585, 800/995-8644** *Victorian B&B, full brkfst*

Kings Inn Hotel [GS,SW,WI,NS,WC] 1333 Hotel Circle S (Bachman St) **619/297-2231, 800/785-4647**

Lafayette Hotel & Suites [GF,F,SW,NS,WI,WC] 2223 El Cajon Blvd (btwn Louisiana & Mississippi) **619/296-2101, 800/468-3531** *also restaurant*

Ocean Inn [GF,WI,WC] 1444 N Hwy 101, Encinitas **760/436-1988, 800/546-1598** *30 min from downtown San Diego*

The Sofia Hotel [GS,WC] 150 W Broadway **619/234-9200, 800/826-0009**

Sunburst Court Inn [GS,NS,WI,GO] 4086 Alabama St (at Polk) **619/294-9665, 866/217-5490** *all-suite inn*

■ BARS
Bourbon Street [★M,E,V] 4612 Park Blvd (at Adams) **619/291-4043** *4pm-2am, front bar, lounge & patio*

The Brass Rail [MW,D,WC] 3796 5th Ave (at Robinson) **619/298-2233** *7pm-2am, from 2pm Fri-Sun, clsd Tue, theme nights, Latin night Sat*

The Caliph [M,E,K,P,OC,WC] 3100 5th Ave (at Redwood) **619/298-9495** *11am-2am, from noon wknds, piano bar*

Cheers [M,NH] 1839 Adams Ave (at Park) **619/298-3269** *11am-2am, patio*

El Camino [GF,D,F,YC] 2400 India St (at Kalmia, in Little Italy) **619/685-3881** *dinner nightly, Sun brunch, kitschy Mexican, live music, full bar*

Fiesta Cantina [F] 142 University Ave **619/298-2500** *noon-2am, from 10am wknds*

Flicks [★M,K,V,YC] 1017 University Ave (at 10th Ave) **619/297-2056** *2pm-2am*

Gossip Grill [W,F,WC,GO] 1440 University Ave (at Normal) **619/260-8023** *2pm-close, also restaurant*

The Hole [M,NH,L] 2820 Lytton St (at Rosecrans) **619/226-9019** *4pm-close, from noon wknds, tropical patio*

Kickers [★MW,D,CW,WC] 308 University Ave (at 3rd Ave, at Urban Mo's) **619/491-0400** *Th only, also dance lessons*

The Loft [M,NH,WC] 3610 5th Ave (at Brookes) **619/296-6407** *11am-2am*

No 1 Fifth Ave (no sign) [M,NH,V] 3845 5th Ave (at University) **619/299-1911** *noon-2am, patio*

Pecs [M,NH,B,L,WC] 2046 University Ave (at Alabama) **619/296-0889** *noon-2am, from 10am Sun, patio, cruisy*

Redwing Bar & Grill [M,NH] 4012 30th St (at Lincoln, North Park) **619/281-8700** *11am-2am, patio*

San Diego Eagle [M,NH,L,WC] 3040 North Park Wy (at 30th) **619/295-8072** *4pm-2am, from 2pm Fri-Sun*

SRO Lounge [M,NH,TG,OC] 1807 5th Ave (btwn Elm & Fir) **619/232-1886** *10am-2am, cocktail lounge*

■NIGHTCLUBS

Bear Night [M,D,B] 3811 Park Blvd (btwn University & Richmond, at Numbers) *9pm 1st Sat only*

Numbers [★MW,D,S,V,WC] 3811 Park Blvd (at University) **619/294-7583** *patio, bear night 1st Sat*

Rich's [★M,D,V,S,YC] 1051 University Ave (at Vermont) **619/295-2195** *open Wed-Sun, theme nights, L.L. Bear [B,L] 3rd Sat*

■CAFES

Babycakes [BW] 3766 5th Ave (at Robinson) **619/296-4173** *9am-11pm, till midnight Fri-Sat, patio*

The Big Kitchen [WC] 3003 Grape St (at 30th) **619/234-5789** *8am-2pm*

Claire de Lune 2906 University Ave **619/688-9845** *6am-10pm, till midnight Fri-Sat*

Espresso Roma UCSD Price Center #76 (at Voight), La Jolla **858/450-2141** *7am-10pm, 8am-4pm wknds*

Extraordinary Desserts 2929 5th Ave **619/294-2132** *also store in Little Italy: 1430 Union, 619/249-7001, the name says it all*

Gelato Vero [WI] 3753 India St **619/295-9269** *7am-midnight, great desserts (yes, the gelato is truly delicious) & coffee*

Twiqqs 4590 Park Blvd (at Madison Ave, University Heights) **619/296-0616** *7am-11pm*

■Restaurants

Adams Avenue Grill [BW,WC,GO] 2201 Adams Ave (at Mississippi) **619/298-8440** *brkfst, lunch & dinner, bistro*

Arrivederci 3845 4th Ave **619/299-6282** *lunch & dinner*

Bai Yook Thai 1260 University Ave **619/296-2700** *lunch & dinner, dinner only Sun*

Baja Betty's [★MW,WC] 1421 University Ave (at Normal St) **619/269-8510** *11am-midnight, till 1am Fri-Sat, Mexican, patio*

Bamboo Lounge 1475 University Ave (at Herbert St) **619/291-8221** *4pm-midnight, till 1am wknds, sushi*

Bangkok Thai Bistro 540 University Ave **619/269-9209** *11am-10pm, till 11pm Fri-Sat*

Brian's American Eatery [B,BW] 1451 Washington St **619/296-8268** *6:30am-10pm, 24hrs Fri-Sat*

Cafe 222 222 Island Ave **619/236-9902** *7am-2pm, great brkfst*

Celadon 3671 5th Ave (at Pennsylvania) **619/297-8424** *lunch & dinner, upscale Thai*

California • USA

Cody's La Jolla [E,R] 8030 Girard Ave (at Coast Blvd S), La Jolla **858/459-0040** *brkfst & lunch daily, contemporary California cuisine, live music*

The Cottage 7702 Fay (at Klein), La Jolla **858/454-8409** *7:30am-3pm, dinner June-Sept*

Crazee Burger [BW] 4201 30th St (at Howard) **619/282-6044** *11am-9pm, till 11pm Fri, till 10pm Sat*

Crest Cafe [WC] 425 Robinson (btwn 4th & 5th) **619/295-2510** *7am-midnight*

Hash House A Go Go 3628 5th Ave **619/298-4646** *brkfst, lunch & dinner, clsd Mon, great brkfst*

Hillcrest Brewing Company [MW] 1458 University Ave **619/491-0400** *first gay brewery in California*

Inn at the Park [★M] 525 Spruce St (btwn 5th & 6th) **619/296-0057** *dinner nightly, also bar [P]*

Jimmy Carter's Mexican Cafe 3172 5th Ave (at Spruce) **619/295-2070** *7am-9pm*

Kous Kous 3940 4th Ave, Ste 110 (beneath Martinis on Fourth) **619/295-5560** *5pm-11pm, Moroccan*

Lips [DS] 3036 El Cajon Blvd **619/295-7900** *5pm-close, Sun gospel brunch, clsd Mon, "the ultimate in drag dining," Bitchy Bingo Wed, celeb impersonation Th, DJ wknds*

Luna Grill 350 University **619/296-5862** *11am-10pm, Near East & Mediterranean, plenty veggie/ vegan*

Martinis Above Fourth [C,P,GO] 3940 4th Ave, Ste 200 (btwn Washington & University) **619/400-4500** *open 5pm, from 4pm Fri-Sat, clsd Sun*

The Mission 3795 Mission Blvd (at San Jose), Mission Beach **858/488-9060** *7am-3pm*

Ono Sushi 1236 University Ave (at Richmond) **619/298-0616** *lunch wknds, dinner nightly*

The Prado 1549 El Prado (in Balboa Park) **619/557-9441** *lunch & dinner, Latin/ Italian fusion*

The Range 1220 University Ave **619/269-1222** *lunch & dinner, brkfst wknds*

Roberto's 3202 Mission Blvd **858/488-1610** *open 24hrs, the best rolled tacos & guacamole, multiple locations*

Rudford's [★] 2900 El Cajon Blvd (at Kansas St) **619/282-8423** *24hrs, homestyle cooking*

Saigon on Fifth 3900 5th Ave, Ste 120 **619/220-8828** *11am-3am, Vietnamese*

South Park Abbey [E] 1946 Fern St (at Grape St) **619/696-0096** *3pm-1:30am, from 9am Sat-Sun, till midnight Sun-Mon, clsd Tue*

Terra 3900 block of Vermont St (at 10th Ave) **619/293-7088** *lunch & dinner, clsd for dinner*

Urban Mo's [★MW,D,E,WC] 308 University Ave (at 3rd) **619/491-0400** *9am-2am, 10am-midnight Sun, 3 full bars (Club Mo's), patio*

Veg N Out 3442 30th St (North Park) **619/546-8411** *11am-9pm, from noon Sun, vegetarian/ vegan*

Waffle Spot 1333 Hotel Circle S (at King's Inn) **619/297-2231** *7am-2pm*

West Coast Tavern 2895 University Ave **619/295-1688** *lunch & dinner, upscale, also lounge*

■ ENTERTAINMENT & RECREATION

Diversionary Theatre 4545 Park Blvd #101 (at Madison) **619/220-0097** (box office #), **619/220-6830** *LGBT theater*

Ocean Beach I-8 West to Sunset Cliffs Blvd *very dog-friendly*

Torrey Pines Beach State Park ("Blacks Beach") *popular nude beach*

■ BOOKSTORES

Traveler's Depot 1655 Garnet Ave (btwn Jewell & Ingraham) **858/483-1421** *10am-6pm, 11am-5pm wknds, guides, maps & more*

■RETAIL SHOPS

Auntie Helen's [WC] 4028 30th St (at Lincoln) **619/584-8438** *10am-6pm, 11am-5pm Sun-Mon, thrift shop benefits PWAs*

Babette Schwartz [GO] 421 University Ave (at 5th Ave) **619/220-7048** *11am-9pm, till 5pm Sun, campy novelties & gifts*

Flesh Skin Grafix 1155 Palm Ave, Imperial Beach **619/424-8983** *tattoos & piercing*

House Boi [GO] 1435 University Ave **619/298-5200** *noon-8pm, 11am-7pm Sun, clsd Mon, clothing, house furnishings*

Mankind 3425 5th Ave (at Upas St) **619/497-1970** *11am-10pm, noon-6pm Sun*

Obelisk Shoppe [★WC] 1037 University Ave (btw 10th & Vermont) **619/297-4171** *10am-9pm, till 10pm wknds, LGBT*

■PUBLICATIONS

Blade California 562/314-7674

The Bottomline 3314 4th Ave **619/291-6690** *bi-weekly, news, entertainment & listings, covers San Diego & Palm Springs*

San Diego LGBT Weekly 1850 5th Ave (at Fir) **619/450-4288**

San Diego PIX 1010 University Ave **877/727-5446**

■GYMS & HEALTH CLUBS

Urbanbody Gym 3148 University Ave (at Iowa St, North Park) **619/795-9712**

■MEN'S CLUBS

Club San Diego [★PC] 3955 4th Ave (btwn Washington & University) **619/295-0850** *24hrs*

■MEN'S SERVICES

►**MegaMates** 619/308-0800 *Call to hook up with HOT local men. FREE to listen & respond to ads. Use FREE code DAMRON. MegaMates.com.*

■EROTICA

Adult Emporium [GO] 3576 Main St (at San Diego) **619/239-1878** *24hrs*

Barnett Ave Adult Superstore 3610 Barnett Ave (near intersection of Barnett & Jessop Ln) **619/224-0187** *24hrs*

The Crypt 3847 Park Blvd (at University) **619/692-9499**

Gemini Adult Books [WC] 5265 University Ave (at 52nd) **619/287-1402**

Pleasures & Treasures Adult/ Leather Shop [GO] 2525 University Ave (at Arnold) **619/822-4280** *11am-11pm, till 6pm Sun*

Romantix Adult Superstore 1407 University Ave (at Richmond) **619/299-7186**

■CRUISY AREAS

Please Note: All cruisy areas for San Diego have been removed because the SDPD aggressively polices these areas.

SAN FRANCISCO

San Francisco is divided into 7 geographical areas:
SF—Overview
SF—Castro & Noe Valley
SF—South of Market
SF—Polk Street Area
SF—Downtown & North Beach
SF—Mission District
SF—Haight, Fillmore, Hayes Valley

SF—Overview

■INFO LINES & SERVICES

AA Gay/ Lesbian 1821 Sacramento St **415/674-1821** *check www.aasf.org for meeting times*

The Center for Sex & Culture 1349 Mission St (btwn 10th & 11th St) **415/902-2071** *very queer-friendly classes, workshops, gatherings, events, readings & more*

Crystal Meth Anonymous 415/835-4747

GLBT Hotline of San Francisco **415/355-0999** *5pm-9pm Mon-Fri, peer-counseling, info*

hope
healing
remembrance

Photo: Mike Shriver

Honor a Life Touched by AIDS by Engraving a Name in the Circle of Friends

NATIONAL · AIDS · MEMORIAL GROVE

In 1996, Congress and the President of the United States designated the AIDS Memorial Grove as a national memorial to commemorate all lives touched by AIDS. Located in San Francisco's Golden Gate Park, the National AIDS Memorial Grove is a place of natural beauty and serenity, and home to the Circle of Friends.

The Circle of Friends, engraved in a flagstone terrace near the eastern entrance to the Grove, is surrounded by redwood trees and flowering dogwoods. It is a special place – a place of remembrance. Like the Vietnam Veterans Memorial, the Circle of Friends offers a testament to the individual lives touched by AIDS, making permanent a personal message of love and loss.

By engraving a name in the Circle of Friends, your own, that of someone you honor, love, or miss, you tell the world that this global tragedy must never be forgotten, and that everyone lost to AIDS will be remembered always.

Names are inscribed in November annually, prior to our World AIDS Day national observance on December 1st.

For more information, please call 415-765-0497, or visit www.aidsmemorial.org.

BEATBOX

IT'S WHERE WE
DANCE

314 11TH ST AT FOLSOM ST
SAN FRANCISCO, CA
BEATBOXSF.COM

California • USA

LYRIC (Lavender Youth Recreation/ Information Center) 127 Collingwood (btwn 18th & 19th) 415/703-6150 *peer-run support line for LGBT youth under 24*

Magnet [★] 4122 18th St 415/581-1600 *center for gay men's health*

The San Francisco LGBT Community Center 1800 Market St (at Octavia) 415/865-5555 *noon-10pm, from 9am Sat, clsd Sun, cybercenter, cafe, classes & more*

■NIGHTCLUBS

Frisco Disco Events *gay dance events in San Francisco, www.thediscosf.com*

Gus Presents [★] *guspresents.com*

Trannyshack [★M,D,TG,E,GO] *occasional events, check trannyshack.com for info*

■RESTAURANTS

Beach Chalet Brewery & Restaurant [E] 1000 Great Hwy (at Fulton St) 415/386-8439

■ENTERTAINMENT & RECREATION

Baker Beach Lincoln Blvd at Bowley, in the Presidio *popular nude beach*

Black Sand Beach first exit past Golden Gate Bridge (Alexander) (go left under fwy, right on Outlook Rd, look for dirt parking lot), Golden Gate Nat'l Rec Area *popular nude beach, look for trail*

Castro Theatre 429 Castro (at Market) 415/621-6120 *art house cinema, many LGBT & cult classics, live organ evenings*

Cruisin' the Castro Tours tour meets at the rainbow flag at Harvey Milk Plaza (corner of Castro & Market) 415/255-1821 *"a TOP city tour & walking w/ pride since 1989! Diverse, fun, informative & NO hills!"*

Femina Potens 415/864-1558 *nonprofit art & performance promoting women & transfolk in the arts*

►Frameline [★] 415/703-8650 *LGBT media arts foundation that sponsors annual SF Int'l LGBT Film Festival in June*

Golden Gate Bridge Beach/ Marshall Beach, aka "Nasty Boy Beach" [M,N,AYOR] Lincoln Blvd at Langdon Ct, in the Presidio *can get very crowded!*

The Intersection for the Arts [GF] 925 Mission St #109 415/626-2787 *San Francisco's oldest alternative arts space (since 1965!) w/ plays, art exhibitions, live jazz, literary series, performance art & much more*

Local Tastes of the City Tours [GO] 415/665-0480, 888/358-8687 *explore history & culture of local neighborhoods as "we eat our way through San Francisco"*

The Marsh 1062 Valencia (at 22nd St) 415/826-5750, 415/282-3055 *queer-positive theater*

National AIDS Memorial Grove [WC] Golden Gate Park (on corner of Middle Drive East & Bowling Green Dr) 415/765-0497, 888/294-7683 *guided tours available 9am-noon every 3rd Sat*

New Conservatory Theatre Center 25 Van Ness Ave, Lower Lobby (at Market) 415/861-8972 *LGBT themed dramas, comedies & musicals, full bar*

QComedy Gay Comedy Showcase [★MW,$] 415/533-9133 *see www.qcomedy.com for location*

San Francisco Pride 1800 Market St, PMB #Q31 94102 415/864-3733

Steve Silver's Beach Blanket Babylon [★] 678 Beach Blanket Babylon Ave (formerly Green St) (btwn Powell & Columbus, in Club Fugazi) 415/421-4222 *the USA's longest running musical revue & wigs that must be seen to be believed; also restaurant & full bar*

Thanks Babs, the Day Tripper [GO] 702/370-6961

Theatre Rhinoceros 1360 Mission St #200 800/838-3006, 415/552-4100 *LGBT theater*

Victorian Home Walks [GO] 415/252-9485 *custom-tailored walking tours w/ San Francisco resident*

FOLSOM
STREET FAIR ®

The San Francisco Original

folsomstreetfair.com

California • *USA*

Yerba Buena Center for the Arts
[GF] 701 Mission St (at 3rd St)
415/978-2787 (box office) *annual season includes wide variety of contemporary dance, theater & music, also film theater & gallery*

■PUBLICATIONS

BAR (Bay Area Reporter)
415/861-5019 *the weekly LGBT newspaper*

Bay Times **415/503-1386** *bi-weekly, good Bay Area resource listings*

➤**Gloss Magazine** **415/552-5070**
CA arts/ entertainment magazine, bi-weekly

■MEN'S CLUBS

SF Jacks **415/267-6999** *2nd & 4th Mon, doors open 7:30pm-8:30pm only, mandatory clothes check, call hotline for location*

■MEN'S SERVICES

➤**MegaMates** **415/430-1199** *Call to hook up with HOT local men. FREE to listen & respond to ads. Use FREE code DAMRON. MegaMates.com.*

SF—Castro & Noe Valley

■ACCOMMODATIONS

24 Henry & Village House
[M,NS,WI,GO] 24 Henry St (btwn Sanchez & Noe) **415/864-5686, 800/900-5686** *B&B, some shared baths*

Andrew Whelan House [GS,NS,WI,GO]
415/621-7736 *Victorian home & garden, shared baths*

Beck's Motor Lodge [GF,WC] 2222 Market St (at Sanchez) **415/621-8212** *in the heart of the Castro (ie, cruisy)*

Castro Suites [GS,NS,WI,GO] 927 14th St (at Noe) **415/437-1783** *furnished apts, kitchen*

Edwardian San Francisco [GF,NS] 1668 Market St (btwn Franklin & Gough) **415/864-1271, 888/864-8070** *some shared baths, hot tub, jacuzzi*

Inn on Castro [MW,NS,WI,GO] 321 Castro St (btwn 16th & 17th) **415/861-0321** *full brkfst*

The Parker Guest House
[★M,NS,WI,GO] 520 Church St (at 17th) **415/621-3222, 888/520-7275** *guesthouse complex w/ gardens, steam spa*

The Willows Inn [MW,NS,WI,GO] 710 14th St (at Church) **415/431-4770, 800/431-0277** *"amenities, comfort, great location"*

■BARS

440 Castro [★M,NH,B,L] 440 Castro St **415/621-8732** *noon-2am, very cruisy*

Beaux [M,D] 2344 Market St (at Castro) **415/863-4027** *2pm-2am*

Blackbird [GS,NH,GO] 2124 Market St **415/503-0630** *3pm-2am*

Boy Bar [M,D] 2369 Market St (at Castro, at the Cafe) *Fri only*

The Cafe [MW,D,YC] 2369 Market St (at Castro) **415/861-3846** *5pm-2am, from 3pm Sat-Sun*

The Edge [M,NH,L] 4149 18th St **415/863-4027** *noon-2am, classic cruise bar*

Harvey's [★MW,NH,E,DS,WC] 500 Castro St **415/431-4278** *11am-11pm, 9am-2am wknds, also restaurant*

Hi Tops [MW,F] 2247 Market St **415/551-2500** *noon-2am, from 10am Sun*

Last Call Bar [M,NH] 3988 18th St **415/861-1310** *noon-2am*

The Lookout [★M,F] 3600 16th St (at Market) **415/431-0306** *3:30pm-2am, from 12:30pm wknds*

Martuni's [GS,NH,P] 4 Valencia St (at Market) **415/241-0205** *4pm-2am, lounge, great martinis*

Midnight Sun [★M,V] 4067 18th St (at Castro) **415/861-4186** *2pm-2am, from 1pm Sat-Sun*

The Mint [MW,K] 1942 Market St (at Buchanan) **415/626-4726** *noon-2am, popular karaoke bar nights, also sushi restaurant*

The Mix [M,NH] 4086 18th St **415/431-8616** *3pm-2am, from 8am wknds, heated patio*

Moby Dick [M,NH,V] 4049 18th St (at Hartford) *2pm-2am, from noon wknds*

California • *USA*

Pan Dulce [MW,D,MR-L] 2369 Market St (at the Cafe) **415/861-3846** *9pm-2am Th only, "The Castro's Biggest Latino Party!"*

Pilsner Inn [★M,NH,YC] 225 Church St (at Market) **415/621-7058** *10am-2am, great patio*

Q Bar [★M,NH,D,WC] 456 Castro St **415/864-2877** *4pm-2am, from 2pm wknds, sidewalk patio*

SF Badlands [★M,NH,D,V,WC] 4121 18th St (at Castro) **415/626-9320** *2pm-2am, Sun beer bust*

Swirl [\] 572 Castro St (at 19th) **415/864-2262** *1pm-8pm, till 9pm Fri-Sat, wine bar & wine store, tastings & events*

Twin Peaks Tavern [M,OC] 401 Castro St (at Market & 17th) **415/864-9470** *noon-2am, from 8am Th-Sun*

■CAFES

Cafe Flore [★MW,WI] 2298 Market St (at Noe) **415/621-8579** *7am-2am, full bar, great patio to see & be seen, come early for a seat*

Duboce Park Cafe [F] 2 Sanchez St (at Duboce) **415/621-1108** *7am-8pm, outdoor seating*

Orbit Room Cafe 1900 Market St (at Laguna) **415/252-9525** *4pm-2am, till midnight Sun, also bar*

Samovar Tea Lounge 498 Sanchez St (at 18th St) **415/626-4700** *10am-10pm*

■RESTAURANTS

Anchor Oyster Bar [MW,BW] 579 Castro St (at 19th) **415/431-3990** *11:30am-10pm, from 4pm Sun*

Catch [E] 2362 Market St **415/431-5000** *lunch & dinner [R], wknd brunch, seafood*

Chow [★] 215 Church St (at Market) **415/552-2469** *8am-11pm, till midnight wknds, patio*

Cove Cafe [★WC] 434 Castro St **415/626-0462** *8am-9pm, till 10pm Fri-Sat*

Eric's Chinese Restaurant [★] 1500 Church St (at 27th St) **415/282-0919** *11am-9pm*

Eureka Restaurant & Lounge 4063 18th St (at Hartford) **415/431-6000** *dinner nightly, lounge upstairs*

Firewood Cafe 4248 18th St (at Diamond St) **415/252-0999** *11am-11pm, rotisserie chicken, pastas, oven-fired pizzas, salads*

Hot Cookie 407 Castro St **415/621-2350** *11am-1am, hot cookies!*

It's Tops 1801 Market St (at Octavia) **415/431-6395** *8am-3pm daily, 8pm-3am Wed-Sat, vintage diner*

Kasa Indian Eatery 4001 18th St (at Noe) **415/621-6940** *11am-10pm, till 11pm Fri-Sat, plenty veggie*

La Mediterranée [BW] 288 Noe (at Market) **415/431-7210** *11am-10pm, till 11pm Sat-Sun*

Mama Ji's 4415 18th St **415/626-4416** *9:30am-9:30pm, great Dim sum in the Castro*

Orphan Andy's [GO] 3991 17th St **415/864-9795** *24hrs, diner*

Pesce [WC] 2223 Market St **415/928-8025** *simply prepared fare served Venetian Cichéti style*

Poesia Osteria Italiana [★] 4072 18th St (at Collingwood) **415/252-9325** *dinner nighly, Italian, great food & full bar*

The Sausage Factory [MW,BW] 517 Castro St **415/626-1250** *11:30am-midnight, pizza & pasta*

Sparky's 242 Church St (at Market) **415/626-8666** *24hrs, diner, popular after-hours*

Takara Sushi [MW] 4243 18th St (at Diamond) **415/626-7864** *lunch & dinner, clsd Tue, cont'l/ Japanese*

Thailand Restaurant 438-A Castro St **415/863-6868** *11am-10pm, plenty veggie*

Woodhouse Fish Co 2073 Market St (at 14th) **415/437-2722** *noon-9:30pm, New England clam shack-style seafood*

Zuni Cafe [★] 1658 Market St (at Franklin) **415/552-2522** *lunch & dinner, clsd Mon, upscale cont'l/ Mediterranean, full bar*

Tan Line Optional

California • *USA*

■ENTERTAINMENT & RECREATION

Castro Country Club [MW] 4058 18th St (at Hartford) 415/552-6102 *alcohol- & drug-free space, cafe*

GLBT History Museum 4127 18th St (at Castro) 415/621-1107 *11am-7pm, noon-5pm Sun, clsd Tue*

➤Great Tan 329 Noe St 415/701-1080 *7am-9:30pm, till 6:30pm Sat-Sun, also at 2286 Union St*

Pink Triangle Park near Market & Castro *"in remembrance of LGBT victims of the Nazi regime"*

■BOOKSTORES

Aardvark Books 227 Church St 415/552-6733 *10:30am-10:30pm, mostly used, good LGBT section*

Books, Inc [WC] 2275 Market St 415/864-6777 *10am-10pm, LGBT section, readings*

■RETAIL SHOPS

HRC Action Center & Store 575 Castro St 415/431-2200 *10am-9pm, till 10pm wknds, Human Rights Campaign merchandise & info*

Kenneth Wingard 2319 Market St (btwn Castro & Noe) 415/431-6900

Rolo [★] 2351 Market St 415/431-4545 *11am-8pm, till 7pm Sun, designer labels*

Under One Roof [WC] 541 Castro 415/503-2300 *11am-7pm, till 2pm Mon, noon-6pm Sun, 100% donated to AIDS relief*

■GYMS & HEALTH CLUBS

SF Fitness Castro 2301 Market St 415/348-6377 *day passes available*

■MEN'S CLUBS

Eros [PC] 2051 Market St (btwn Church & Dolores) 415/864-3767 *noon-midnight, till 3am Fri-Sat, safer-sex club, theme nights, massage available, day passes*

■EROTICA

Auto-Erotica 4077-A 18th St, 2nd flr 415/861-5787 *"purveyor of vintage porn & fine dildos"*

Chaps 4057 18th St (btwn Castro & Hartford) 415/863-1699 *10am-11pm, till midnight Fri-Sat*

Rock Hard 518 Castro St (at 18th St) 415/437-2430 *9:30am-11pm, till midnight Fri-Sat, toys, DVDs, lube, leather, cockrings & more*

■CRUISY AREAS

Collingwood Park [AYOR] (btwn 18th & 19th Sts) *Castro merry-go-round, after bars close*

SF—South of Market

■ACCOMMODATIONS

Holiday Inn Civic Center [GF,SW,WI,WC] 50 8th St (at Market) 415/626-6103, 877/252-1169

The Mosser Hotel [GS,NS] 54 4th St (btwn Market & Mission) 415/986-4400, 800/227-3804 *1913 landmark, also restaurant & full bar*

The Westin San Francisco Market Street [GF,NS] 50 3rd St 415/974-6400, 888/627-8561 *sauna*

■BARS

Club OMG [GS,D] 43 6th St 415/896-64s3 *6pm-2am, gay bollywood events*

The Eagle Tavern [★M,L,E] 398 12th St (at Harrison) 415/626-0880 *noon-2am, great beer bust Sun, patio*

Hole in the Wall Saloon [★M,NH,L] 1369 Folsom (btwn 9th & 10th) 415/431-4695 *noon-2am, "a nasty little biker bar"*

Lone Star Saloon [★M,B,L] 1354 Harrison St (btwn 9th & 10th) 415/863-9999 *noon-2am, from 9am wknds, patio, bear bar, beer bust wknds*

Powerhouse [M,NH,L] 1347 Folsom St (at Dore Alley) 415/552-8689 *4pm-2am, theme nights, popular wknds w/ DJ, patio, cruisy*

■NIGHTCLUBS

Asia SF [★GS,D,MR-A,S,$] 201 9th St (at Howard) 415/255-2742 *10pm-close Wed-Sat, theme nights, go-go boys, also Cal-Asian restaurant w/ en-drag dinner service*

➤**BeatBox** [GS,D] 314 11th St 415/500-2675 *theme nights*

Bootie SF [★GF,D,E,$] 375 11th St (at Harrison, at DNA Lounge) **415/626-1409 (DNA info line)** *9pm-3am Sat,, mashups, bootlegs, bastard pop*

Cat Club [GS,D] 1190 Folsom St (at 8th) **415/703-8965** *hosts many one-night clubs & events*

The Crib SF [MW,D,V,18+,$] 715 Harrison St (at 3rd) *9:30pm-2am Th only*

Endup [GS,D,MR] 401 6th St (at Harrison) **415/646-0999 (info line), 415/357-0827** *theme nights, popular Sun mornings*

Fever [M,D] 401 6th St (at Harrison, at Endup) *11pm-11am Fri only*

Go BANG! [MW,D] 399 9th St (at The Stud) *1st Sat only, underground 70s-80s disco*

GusPresents.com *The host w/ the most—Gus is always throwing one hell of a party for the boys!*

Honey Soundsystem [M,D,B] 1535 Folsom St (at Holy Cow) *Sun only, local DJ collective*

Mezzanine [GS,D,MR,TG,E,WC,$] 444 Jessie (at Mint) **415/625-8880** *9pm-close, live music, big name DJs, call for events*

The Stud [★MW,D,YC] 399 9th St (at Harrison) **415/863-6623** *5pm-2am, theme nights*

■RESTAURANTS

Ame [R] 689 Mission St (at 3rd St, in St Regis Hotel) **415/284-4040** *lunch & dinner, full bar*

Ananda Fuara 1298 Market St (at 9th) **415/621-1994** *8am-8pm, till 3pm Wed, clsd Sun, vegetarian*

Anchor & Hope 83 Minna St (at 2nd St) **415/501-9100** *lunch Mon-Fri, dinner nightly, seafood*

Butter 354 11th St (btwn Folsom & Harrison) **415/863-5964** *6pm-2am, clsd Mon, "white trash bistro," full bar, theme nights*

Don Ramon's Mexican Restaurant 225 11th St (btwn Howard & Folsom) **415/864-2700** *lunch Tue-Fri, dinner nightly, clsd Mon, some veggie, full bar*

Dottie's True Blue Cafe [GO] 28 6th St **415/885-2767** *7:30am-3pm, clsd Tue-Wed, great brkfst*

Fringale [WC] 570 4th St (btwn Bryant & Brannan) **415/543-0573** *lunch Tue-Fri & dinner nightly, French bistro*

Rocco's Cafe [★] 1131 Folsom St (at 7th) **415/554-0522** *brkfst & lunch daily, dinner Wed-Sat only*

The Slanted Door [★R] 1 Ferry Building #3 **415/861-8032** *lunch & dinner, Vietnamese, full bar*

Supperclub [E] 657 Harrison St (btwn 2nd & 3rd) **415/348-0900** *6:30pm-close, live performance art & acrobatics, also full bar & nightclub*

Ted's 1530 Howard St (at 11th) **415/552-0309** *6am-6pm, 8am-5pm wknds, excellent deli sandwiches*

Tu Lan 8 6th St (at Market) **415/626-0927** *lunch & dinner, clsd Sun, Vietnamese, dicey neighborhood but delicious (& cheap) food*

■RETAIL SHOPS

Dandelion [GO] 55 Potrero Ave (at Alameda St) **415/436-9500, 888/548-1968** *10am-7pm, till 6pm Fri-Sat, noon-5pm Sun*

Mr S Leather & Fetters USA San Francisco 385 8th St (at Harrison) **415/863-7764, 800/746-7677** *11am-7pm, erotic goods, custom leather & latex*

Stompers 323 10th St (at Folsom) **415/255-6422, 888/BOOTMAN** *11am-6pm, noon-4pm Sun, clsd Mon, boots, cigars & gloves*

■GYMS & HEALTH CLUBS

SF Fitness [★] 1001 Brannan St (at 9th) **415/348-6377** *day passes available*

■MEN'S CLUBS

Blow Buddies [★MO,LV,PC,GO] 933 Harrison (btwn 5th & 6th) **415/777-4323** *open late Wed-Sun, clsd Mon-Tue*

California • *USA*

Playspace [MO] 962 Folsom St *open Th-Sun, the ideal hook-up location*

■EROTICA

Folsom Gulch 947 Folsom (btwn 5th & 6th) 415/495-6402 *10am-2am, 24hrs Fri-Sat, hot arcade action, serving the gay community for over 25 years!*

Good Vibrations [★W,WC] 899 Mission St (at 5th St) 415/513-1635, 800/289-8423 *10am-9pm, till 10pm Fri-Sat, clean, well-lighted sex toy store*

Pop Sex 960 960 Folsom St (btwn 5th & 6th) 415/543-2124 *10am-2am, 24hrs wknds, the best in adult entertainment*

■CRUISY AREAS

Folsom St [AYOR] btwn 5th & 6th *late*

SF—Polk Street Area

■ACCOMMODATIONS

Inn On Broadway [GF,WI,WC] 2201 Van Ness Ave (at Broadway) 415/776-7900, 800/727-6239 *motel close to Fisherman's Wharf*

The Monarch Hotel [GF] 1015 Geary St (at Polk) 415/673-5232, 800/777-3210 *Edwardian boutique-style hotel*

Nob Hill Motor Inn [GF,NS,WI,WC] 1630 Pacific Ave (at Van Ness Ave) 415/775-8160, 800/343-6900 *hotel*

The Phoenix Hotel [★GF,SW,WI] 601 Eddy St (at Larkin) 415/776-1380, 800/248-9466 *1950s-style motor lodge, fave of celebrity rockers*

Radisson Hotel Fisherman's Wharf [GF,SW,WI,WC] 250 Beach St (at Hyde) 415/392-6700

San Francisco City Center Hostel [GF,NS,WI] 685 Ellis St (at Larkin) 415/474-5721 *hostel, shared & private rooms available, free brkfst, kids ok*

■BARS

The Cinch [M,NH,WI,WC] 1723 Polk St (at Clay) 415/776-4162 *9am-2am, patio, lots of pool tables & no attitude, [D] Th-Sat, [DS] Fri*

Edinburgh Castle [GF,NH,E] 950 Geary St (at Polk) 415/885-4074 *5pm-2am, Scottish pub w/ single malts & authentic fish & chips*

Gangway [M,NH] 841 Larkin St (btwn Geary & O'Farrell) 415/776-6828 *8am-2am*

Lush Lounge [GS,NH,WC] 1092 Post (at Polk) 415/771-2022 *3pm-2am, from noon wknds*

■NIGHTCLUBS

Divas [M,NH,D,TG,DS] 1081 Post St (at Larkin) 415/474-3482 *7am-2am, TS/TVs & their admirers*

■CAFES

La Boulange de Polk 2310 Polk St (at Green St) 415/345-1107 *7am-7pm, French bakery & cafe, outdoor seating, Parisian down to the attitude*

■RESTAURANTS

Grubstake II [MW,BW] 1525 Pine St (at Polk) 415/673-8268 *5pm-4am, diner/ Portuguese*

Rex Cafe 2323 Polk St 415/441-2244 *dinner from 5:30pm, brunch 10am-3pm wknds, American, full bar*

Street 2141 Polk St (btwn Broadway & Vallejo) 415/775-1055 *dinner, clsd Mon, incredible hamburgers*

■BOOKSTORES

Books Inc Opera Plaza [★] 601 Van Ness Ave (at Turk) 415/776-1111 *8:30am-9pm, general, LGBT section, readings*

■EROTICA

Frenchy's 1020 Geary St (at Polk) 415/776-5940 *24hrs*

Glass Kandi 569 Geary St (at Taylor) 415/931-2256 *4pm-9pm, noon-9pm Sat, till 7pm Sun, glass dildos*

Good Vibrations [★W] 1620 Polk St (btwn Sacramento & Clay) 415/345-0400

■CRUISY AREAS

Polk St [AYOR] btwn Geary & California Sts *hustlers*

SF—Downtown & North Beach

■ ACCOMMODATIONS

Adante Hotel [GS,NS,WC] 610 Geary St (at Jones) 415/673-9221, 888/423-0083 *in Union Square/ Theater District, kids ok*

Andrews Hotel [GF,NS,WI] 624 Post St (btwn Taylor & Jones) 415/563-6877, 800/926-3739 *Victorian hotel, also Italian restaurant*

Argonaut Hotel [GF,NS,WC] 495 Jefferson St (at Hyde) 415/563-0800, 800/790-1415 *boutique hotel in Fisherman's Wharf*

Dakota Hotel/ Hostel [GF,WI] 606 Post St (at Taylor) 415/931-7475 *near Union Square*

Executive Hotel Vintage Court [GF,NS,WI,WC] 650 Bush St (at Powell) 415/392-4666, 888/388-3932 *also world-famous 5-star Masa's restaurant, French*

Galleria Park Hotel [GS,WI,NS,WC] 191 Sutter St (at Kearny) 415/781-3060, 800/792-9639 *boutique hotel*

Grand Hyatt San Francisco [GF,WI] 345 Stockton St (at Sutter) 415/398-1234 *restaurant & lounge, gym*

Halcyon Hotel [GF,NS,WI] 649 Jones St (at Post) 415/929-8033, 800/627-2396

Handlery Union Square Hotel [GF,SW,WI,WC] 351 Geary St 415/781-7800, 800/995-4874 *steps from Union Square*

Harbor Court Hotel [GF,SW,WI,WC] 165 Steuart St (btwn Howard & Mission) 415/882-1300, 866/792-6283 *in the heart of the Financial District, gym*

Hilton San Francisco Financial District [GS] 750 Kearny St (at Clay) 415/433-6600, 800/424-8292

Hotel Abri [GF,WI] 127 Ellis St (at Powell) 415/392-8800, 866/778-6169 *boutique hotel*

Hotel Adagio [GF,WC] 550 Geary St (at Shannon) 415/775-5000, 800/228-8830

Hotel Bijou [GS,NS,WI,WC] 111 Mason St (at Eddy) 415/771-1200, 800/771-1022

The Hotel California [GF,NS] 580 Geary St (at Jones) 415/441-2700, 800/227-4223 *also popular Millennium gourmet vegetarian restaurant & bar*

Hotel Carlton [GF] 1075 Sutter (at Larkin) 415/673-0242, 800/922-7586 *also Saha restaurant, Arabic-fusion*

Hotel Diva [GF,NS,WI] 440 Geary (at Mason) 415/885-0200, 800/553-1900 *hip hotel, gym*

Hotel Fusion [GS,NS,WI,WC] 140 Ellis St (at Powell St) 415/568-2525, 866/753-4244

Hotel Griffon [GS,WI,WC] 155 Steuart St (at Mission) 415/495-2100, 800/321-2201 *also restaurant, bistro/ cont'l*

Hotel Mark Twain [GF,WI,WC] 345 Taylor St (at Ellis) 415/673-2332, 877/854-4106 *also Fish & Farm restaurant*

Hotel Metropolis [GF,WI,NS] 25 Mason St (at Eddy) 415/775-4600, 877/628-4412 *near Union Square shopping*

Hotel Monaco [GF] 501 Geary St (at Taylor) 415/292-0100, 866/622-5284 *pets ok, also Grand Cafe restaurant, French*

Hotel Nikko San Francisco [GF,SW,NS,WC] 222 Mason St (at Ellis) 415/394-1111, 866/645-5673 *health club & spa, also ANZU restaurant*

Hotel Palomar [GS,WI] 12 4th St (at Market) 415/348-1111, 866/373-4941 *boutique hotel*

The Hotel Rex [GF,WC] 562 Sutter St (at Powell) 415/433-4434, 800/433-4434 *full bar*

Hotel Triton [GF,WI,WC] 342 Grant Ave (at Bush) 415/394-0500, 800/800-1299 *designer theme rooms*

Hotel Union Square [GF,WI] 114 Powell St (at Ellis) 415/397-3000, 800/553-1900 *1930s art deco lobby*

California • *USA*

Hotel Vitale [GF,NS,WI,WC] 8 Mission St (at Steuart) 415/278-3700, 888/890-8688 *4-star, full-service waterfront luxury hotel, rooftop spa, restaurant & bar*

Hotel Zetta [GS,WI] 55 5th St 415/543-8555

Hyatt Regency San Francisco [GF,NS,WI] 5 Embarcadero Center (at California) 415/788-1234, 800/233-1234 *luxury waterfront hotel*

The Inn at Union Square [GF,NS,WI] 440 Post St (at Powell) 415/397-3510, 800/288-4346 *complimentary breakfast and wine and cheese daily*

JW Marriott Hotel San Francisco [GF,NS,WI,WC] 500 Post St (at Mason) 415/771-8600, 888/236-2427

Kensington Park Hotel [GF,NS,WI] 450 Post St 415/788-6400 *on Union Square, also Farallon Restaurant*

King George Hotel [GS,F,WI,WC] 334 Mason St (at Geary) 415/781-5050

Larkspur Hotel [GF,WI,NS] 524 Sutter St (at Powell) 415/421-2865, 866/823-4669 *B&B-inn on Union Square, afternoon tea, wine hour*

Luz Hotel [GS] 725 Geary St (at Leavenworth) 415/928-1917 *clothing-optional jacuzzi*

Nob Hill Hotel [GS,NS,WC] 835 Hyde St (btwn Bush & Sutter) 415/885-2987, 877/662-4455 *European-style hotel, jacuzzi*

Petite Auberge [GF,NS] 863 Bush St (at Taylor) 415/928-6000, 800/365-3004

Prescott Hotel [GF,NS,WI] 545 Post St (btwn Taylor & Mason) 415/563-0303, 866/271-3632 *small luxury hotel*

Serrano Hotel [GF,WI,WC] 405 Taylor St (at O'Farrell) 415/885-2500, 866/289-6561 *in Theater District*

Sir Francis Drake Hotel [GF,WI] 450 Powell St (at Sutter) 415/392-7755, 800/795-7129 *1928 landmark, also restaurant & Starlight Room*

The Stratford Hotel [GS,WI,WC] 242 Powell St (at Geary) 415/397-7080, 866/688-0038 *near Union Square*

Tuscan Inn [GF,WC] 425 N Point St (at Mason) 415/561-1100, 888/648-4626

Union Square Plaza Hotel [GF] 432 Geary St (at Mason) 415/776-7585, 800/841-3135 *1 block from Union Square*

Vertigo Hotel [GS,NS,WI,WC] 940 Sutter St (at Leavenworth) 415/885-6800, 888/444-4605 *boutique hotel*

Villa Florence Hotel [GF,WI] 225 Powell St (at Geary) 415/397-7700, 866/823-4669 *Union Square boutique hotel, also Kuleto's restaurant, Italian*

■BARS

Aunt Charlie's Lounge [M,NH,DS] 133 Turk St (at Taylor) 415/441-2922 *10am-midnight, till 2am Fri- Sat*

Bourbon & Branch [GS,R] 501 Jones St (at O'Farrell) 415/931-7292 *in Prohibition-era speakeasy, drinks are worth the price*

■NIGHTCLUBS

Hero [★M,D,S] 420 Mason (at Geary, at Ruby Skye) *occasional Sun T-dance, check local listings for dates*

■CAFES

Caffe Trieste [★] 601 Vallejo St 415/392-6739 *get a taste of the real North Beach (past & present)*

Sugar Cafe [F,WI] 679 Sutter St (at Taylor) 415/441-5678 *10am-2am, from 8am wknds, cafe by day, cocktails by night*

■RESTAURANTS

Ar Roi 643 Post St (at Jones) 415/771-5146 *lunch & dinner, clsd Sun, Thai*

The Buena Vista 2765 Hyde St (at Beach) 415/474-5044 *9am-2am, from 8am wknds, the restaurant that introduced Irish coffee to America*

Cafe Claude [E,BW] 7 Claude Ln (near Bush & Kearny) 415/392-3515 *11:30am-10:30pm, from 5:30pm Sun, as close to Paris as you can get in SF*

Canteen 415/928-8870 *dinner nightly, brkfst wknds*

Le Colonial 20 Cosmo Pl (btwn Taylor & Jones) **415/931-3600** *dinner nightly, wknd brunch, Vietnamese, full bar*

Golden Era [★] 572 O'Farrell St **415/673-3136** *11am-9pm, clsd Tue, vegetarian/ vegan*

Mario's Bohemian Cigar Store Cafe [BW,WI] 566 Columbus Ave (at Union) **415/362-0536** *10am-close, great foccaia sandwiches*

Millennium 580 Geary St (at Jones) **415/345-3900** *dinner only, Euro-Mediterranean, upscale vegetarian*

■ENTERTAINMENT & RECREATION

Rrazz Room [★GS,C,WC] 222 Mason (at Nikko Hotel) **415/394-1189, 800/380-3095** *cabaret w/ world-class performers*

Sunday's A Drag@The Starlight Room [MW,E,$] 450 Mason St (at Sutter) **415/395-8595** *Sun brunch, noon & 2:30pm drag shows*

■BOOKSTORES

Book Passage 1 Ferry Bldg #42 **415/835-1020** *10am-8pm, from 8am Sat, 10am-7pm Sun-Mon, independent*

City Lights Bookstore 261 Columbus Ave (at Pacific) **415/362-8193** *10am-midnight, historic beatnik bookstore, many progressive titles, LGBT section, whole floor dedicated to poetry*

■SEX CLUBS

Power Exchange [GS] 220 Jones St **415/487-9944**

■EROTICA

Nob Hill Adult Theatre & Video Arcade [MO,$] 729 Bush St (at Powell) **415/397-6758** *11:30am-1:30am*

Video Secrets 389 Bay St (at Mason) **415/391-9349**

SF—Mission District

includes Bernal Heights

■ACCOMMODATIONS

Elements [★GS,F,WI] 2515 Mission St (at 21st St) **415/647-4100, 866/327-8407** *hostel w/ private or shared rooms*

The Inn San Francisco [GF,NS,WI] 943 S Van Ness Ave (btwn 20th & 21st) **415/641-0188, 800/359-0913** *Victorian mansion, hot tub*

Noe's Nest B&B [GF,NS] 1257 Guerrero St (btwn 24th & 25th Sts) **415/821-0751** *kitchens, fireplace*

■BARS

El Rio [★GS,NH,MR,E] 3158 Mission St (at Cesar Chavez) **415/282-3325** *5pm-close Mon-Th, from 3pm wknds, patio*

Esta Noche [M,D,MR-L,TG,S] 3079 16th St (at Mission) **415/861-5757** *1pm-2am, salsa & disco in a classic Tijuana dive*

Lexington Club [★W,NH,GO] 3464 19th St (btwn Mission & Valencia) **415/863-2052** *5pm-2am, from 3pm Fri-Sun*

Lone Palm [GS] 3394 22nd St (at Guerrero) **415/648-0109** *4pm-2am, a bar for grown ups (we know you're out there)*

Nihon [GS,D,F] 1779 Folsom St (at 14th St) **415/552-4400** *6pm-close, clsd Sun, whiskey lounge, also Japanese restaurant*

Phone Booth [MW,NH] 1398 S Van Ness Ave (at 25th) **415/648-4683** *1pm-2am*

Pop's Bar [GS,NH,WC] 2800 24th St (btwn York & Bryant) **415/401-7677** *4pm-2am, photobooth*

Truck Bar [M,NH,F,GO] 1900 Folsom St (at 15th) **415/252-0306** *4pm-2am, clsd Mon (winter)*

Wild Side West [GS,WC] 424 Cortland, Bernal Heights (at Wool) **415/647-3099** *1pm-2am, patio, magic garden*

Zeitgeist [★GS,F] 199 Valencia St (at Duboce) **415/255-7505** *9am-2am, divey biker bar & beer garden*

■NIGHTCLUBS

Hard French [MW,D,MR,F,$] 3158 Mission (at El Rio) *3pm-8pm 1st Sat only, soul dance party*

The Make-Out Room [GS,D,E] 3225 22nd St (at Mission) • **415/647-2888** *6pm-2am*

California • *USA*

Mighty [GF,D] 119 Utah St (at 15th St) **415/762-0151**

Stay Gold [MW,D] 161 Erie St (at Mission, at Public Works) *10:30pm last Wed only*

Sundance Saloon [★MW,D,CW,GO,$] 550 Barneveld Ave (at space550, 2 blocks off Bayshore Blvd at Industrial) **415/820-1403** *5pm-10:30pm Sun (lessons at 5:30pm) & 6:30pm-10:30pm Th (lessons at 7pm)*

■CAFES

Dolores Park Cafe [★F,E] 501 Dolores St (at 18th St) **415/621-2936** *7am-8pm, outdoor seating overlooking Dolores Park, live music Fri*

Farleys [E] 1315 18th St (at Texas St, Potrero Hill) **415/648-1545** *6:30am-9:30pm, from 7:30am wknds*

The Revolution Cafe [E] 3248 22nd St (btwn Mission & Bartlett) **415/642-0474** *9am-1am*

Tartine Bakery [★] 600 Guerrero St (at 18th St) **415/487-2600** *8am-7pm, from 9am Sun, French bakery w/ a line out the door*

■RESTAURANTS

Aslam's Rasoi 1037 Valencia St (at 21st) **415/695-0599** *5pm-11pm, Indian & Pakistani*

Boogaloos [★] 3296 22nd St (at Valencia) **415/824-4088** *8am-3pm, worth the wait*

Delfina [★R] 3621 18th St (at Dolores) **415/552-4055** *5:30pm-10pm, excellent Tuscan cuisine, full bar, patio (summers)*

El Farolito [★] 2779 Mission St (at 24th) **415/824-7877** *10am-3am, delicious, cheap burritos & more*

Farina 3560 18th St (at Guerrero) **415/565-0360** *dinner nightly, Sun brunch, Italian*

Just For You [★MW] 732 22nd St (at 3rd St) **415/647-3033** *7:30am-3pm, Southern brkfst*

Luna Park 694 Valencia St (at 18th) **415/553-8584** *lunch & dinner, wknd brunch*

Maverick 3316 17th St (btwn Mission & Valencia) **415/863-3061** *dinner nightly, also wknd brunch, upscale American, great wine selection*

Medjool [★WC] 2522 Mission St (at 21st St) **415/550-9055** *5pm-10pm, till 11pm Fri-Sat, clsd Sun, tapas, also cafe, lounge & rooftop bar*

Moki's Sushi & Pacific Grill 615 Cortland Ave (at Moultrie) **415/970-9336** *dinner nightly*

Pauline's Pizza Pie [★MW,BW] 260 Valencia St (btwn 14th & Duboce) **415/552-2050** *5pm-10pm, clsd Sun-Mon, gourmet pizza*

Picaro [BW,WC] 3120 16th St (at Valencia) **415/431-4089** *5pm-10pm, from 9:30am wknds, Spanish tapas bar*

Pork Store Cafe [★BW] 3122 16th St (at Valencia) **415/626-5523** *8am-4pm daily & 7pm-3am Fri-Sat, American/ diner food, great breakfasts; also 1451 Haight St, 415/864-6981*

Range [★] 842 Valencia St (btwn 19th & 20th Sts) **415/282-8283** *dinner nightly, California contemporary, full bar*

Slow Club [WC] 2501 Mariposa (at Hampshire) **415/241-9390** *lunch Mon-Fri, dinner Mon-Sat, wknd brunch, full bar*

■ENTERTAINMENT & RECREATION

Dolores "Beach" Church & 19th St (at the top corner of Dolores Park) *popular "beach" in Dolores Park, crowded on sunny days*

■BOOKSTORES

Dog Eared Books 900 Valencia St (at 20th) **415/282-1901** *10am-10pm, till 8pm Sun, new & used, good LGBT section*

Modern Times Bookstore [WC] 2919 24th St (at Alabama) **415/282-9246**

■RETAIL SHOPS

Black & Blue Tattoo [★TG] 381 Guerrero St (at 16th St) **415/626-0770** *noon-7pm, queer-, gender-fluid-, trans- & POC-friendly*

Body Manipulations 3234 16th St (btwn Guerrero & Dolores) **415/621-0408** *noon-7pm, from 2pm Mon-Th, piercing (walk-in basis), jewelry*

■EROTICA

Good Vibrations [★W,WC] 603 Valencia St (at 17th St) 415/522-5460, 800/289-8423 *11am-7pm, till 8pm Th, till 9pm Fri-Sat, clean, well-lighted sex toy store*

Mission St News 2086 Mission St (at 17th) 415/626-0309 *24hrs*

SF—Haight, Fillmore, Hayes Valley

■ACCOMMODATIONS

The Chateau Tivoli B&B [GF,NS,WI] 1057 Steiner St (at Golden Gate) 415/776-5462, 800/228-1647 *historic SF B&B*

Hayes Valley Inn [GS,NS,WI] 417 Gough St (at Hayes) 415/431-9131, 800/930-7999 *European-style pension, shared baths*

Hotel Del Sol [★GS,NS,SW,WI,WC] 3100 Webster St (at Greenwich) 415/921-5520, 877/433-5765

Hotel Drisco [GF,NS] 2901 Pacific Ave (at Broderick) 415/346-2880, 800/634-7277

Hotel Kabuki [GF,WC] 1625 Post St (at Laguna) 415/922-3200, 800/533-4567 *in Japantown*

Hotel Majestic [GF,NS,WI,WC] 1500 Sutter St (at Gough) 415/441-1100, 800/869-8966 *one of SF's earliest grand hotels, also restaurant, full bar*

Hotel Tomo [GF,NS,WI] 1800 Sutter St (at Buchanan) 415/921-4000, 888/822-8666 *in Japantown, restaurant & bar*

Inn at the Opera [GF,NS,WI,WC] 333 Fulton St (at Franklin) 415/863-8400, 866/729-7182

Jackson Court [GF,NS,WI] 2198 Jackson St (at Buchanan) 415/929-7670

The Laurel Inn [GF,NS] 444 Presidio Ave (at Sacramento) 415/567-8467, 800/552-8735

Metro Hotel [GF,WI] 319 Divisadero St (at Haight) 415/861-5364 *European-style pension*

Queen Anne Hotel [GF,NS,WI,GO] 1590 Sutter St (at Octavia) 415/441-2828, 800/227-3970

San Francisco Fisherman's Wharf Hostel [GS,F,WI,NS,WC] Fort Mason, Bldg 240 (at Franklin) 415/771-7277 *hostel, shared baths*

Shannon-Kavanaugh Guest House [GF,NS,GO] 722 Steiner St (at Hayes) 415/563-2727 *1-bdrm garden apt in house on SF's famous "Postcard Row"*

Stanyan Park Hotel [GF,NS,WC] 750 Stanyan St (at Waller) 415/751-1000 *historic Victorian*

■BARS

Rickshaw Stop [★GF,F,E] 155 Fell St (btwn Van Ness & Franklin) 415/861-2011 *Wed-Sat only, hipster bar, nightclub (live bands) & restaurant*

Trax [M,NH] 1437 Haight St (at Masonic) 415/864-4213 *noon-2am*

■NIGHTCLUBS

Cockblock [MW,D,MR] 155 Fell St (at Rickshaw Shop) *10pm-2am 2nd Sat*

Cockfight [M,D,A] 424 Haight St (at Webster, at Underground SF) 415/864-7386 *9pm 1st Sat only*

Underground SF [GS,D,A] 424 Haight St (at Webster) 415/864-7386 *5:30pm-2am, clsd Mon, theme nights, call for events, more gay Sat*

■CAFES

Blue Bottle Coffee Company [★] 315 Linden St (at Gough St) 415/252-7535 *7am-5pm, from 8am wknds, organic coffee & treats from kiosk in front of artists' workshop—wonderful hidden treat*

■RESTAURANTS

Absinthe Brasserie & Bar 398 Hayes St (at Gough) 415/551-1590 *lunch & dinner, bar till 2am Fri-Sat, clsd Mon*

Alamo Square Seafood Grill 803 Fillmore (at Grove) 415/440-2828 *dinner only*

Burma Superstar [★] 309 Clement St 415/387-2147 *lunch & dinner, Burmese food that will rock your world*

Cheese Steak Shop 1716 Divisadero St (btwn Bush & Sutter) 415/346-3712 *9am-10pm, from 11am Sun, from 10am Mon, best cheese steak outside Philly, also veggie versions*

Eliza's [★] 2877 California (at Broderick) 415/621-4819 *lunch Mon-Wed, dinner nightly, excellent Chinese food*

Ella's 500 Presidio Ave (at California) 415/441-5669 *brkfst & lunch Mon-Fri, popular wknd brunch*

Garibaldi's [WC,GO] 347 Presidio Ave (at Sacramento) 415/563-8841 *lunch weekdays, dinner nightly, Mediterranean, full bar*

Greens [★] Fort Mason, Bldg A (near Van Ness & Bay) 415/771-6222 *lunch Tue-Sat, dinner Mon-Sat, Sun brunch, gourmet vegetarian, spectacular view of the Golden Gate Bridge*

Little Star Pizza [★BW] 846 Divisadero St (btwn Fulton & McAllister Sts) 415/441-1118 *5pm-10pm, till 11pm Fri-Sat, clsd Mon, Chicago-style deep dish pizza*

Memphis Minnie's BBQ [★] 576 Haight St 415/864-7675 *11am-10pm, till 9pm Sun, clsd Mon*

Nopa 560 Divisadero St (at Hayes) 415/864-8643 *dinner 6pm-1am, bar from 5pm, urban rustic*

Park Chow [★] 1238 9th Ave (btwn Irving & Lincoln) 415/665-9912 *11am-10pm, brunch from 10am wknds, eclectic & affordable*

Patxi's Chicago Pizza 511 Hayes St (at Octavia St) 415/558-9991 *11am-10pm, clsd Mon, Chicago-style deep dish pizza, also thin crust*

Pluto's Fresh Food for a Hungry Universe 627 Irving St (btwn 7th & 8th Aves) 415/753-8867 *11am-10pm, design your own sandwiches*

Suppenküche [BW,GO] 601 Hayes (at Laguna) 415/252-9289 *dinner, Sun brunch, German cuisine served at communal tables*

Thep-Phanom [★BW] 400 Waller St (at Fillmore) 415/431-2526 *5:30pm-10:30pm, excellent Thai food, worth the wait!*

■**BOOKSTORES**

Bibliohead Bookstore [GO] 334 Gough St (at Hayes) 415/621-6772 *eclectic used books, queer section*

The Booksmith 1644 Haight St 415/863-8688 *cool independent, big-name author readings*

■**RETAIL SHOPS**

Cold Steel America 1783 Haight St 415/621-7233 *noon-8pm, piercing & tattoo studio*

Flight 001 525 Hayes St (btwn Octavia & Laguna) 415/487-1001, 877/354-4481 *11am-7pm, till 6pm Sun, way cool travel gear*

Timbuk 2 Store 506 Hayes St 415/252-9860 *11am-7pm, noon-6pm Sun, messenger-style bags & backpacks*

■**GYMS & HEALTH CLUBS**

Kabuki Springs & Spa 1750 Geary Blvd (at Fillmore) 415/922-6000 *10am-9:45pm, traditional Japanese bath w/ extensive menu of spa sevices*

■**CRUISY AREAS**

Buena Vista Park [AYOR] Haight St (btwn Baker & Central) *evenings in northern & highest part*

Land's End [AYOR] NW tip of SF *inquire locally*

San Jose

includes Campbell & Los Gatos; see also Cupertino, Santa Clara & Sunnyvale

■**INFO LINES & SERVICES**

AA Gay/ Lesbian 274 E Hamilton Ave, Ste D, Campbell 408/374-8511 *24hr helpline, check www.aasanjose.org for meetings*

Billy DeFrank LGBT Community Center [WC] 938 The Alameda 408/293-3040 *3pm-9pm, from 10am Wed, clsd Sat-Mon*

■**ACCOMMODATIONS**

Hotel De Anza [GF,F,E,WC,NS] 233 W Santa Clara St 408/286-1000, 800/843-3700 *art deco gem*

Moorpark Hotel [GF,SW,WC] 4241 Moorpark Ave 408/864-0300, 877/740-6622 *also bar & restaurant*

■BARS

Brix [MW,NH,D,MR,TG,K,V,WC] 349 S 1st St (at San Salvadore) 408/947-1975 *6pm-2am, from 4pm Sun*

Mac's Club [M,NH] 39 Post St (btwn 1st & Market) 408/288-8221 *noon-2am, patio*

Renegades [M,NH,B,L] 501 W Taylor St (at Coleman Ave) 408/275-9902 *2pm-2am, patio*

■NIGHTCLUBS

Splash [M,D,K,DS,V,GO] 65 Post St (at 1st) 408/292-2222 *4pm-2am ,from 3pm Sun*

■RESTAURANTS

Eulipia Restaurant & Bar 374 S 1st St (at San Carlos) 408/280-6161 *dinner only, clsd Mon*

Pasta Pomodoro 1205 The Alameda (at Race) 408/292-9929 *Italian*

Vin Santo 1346 Lincoln Ave 408/920-2508 *dinner nightly, clsd Mon, Northern Italian, wine bar*

■ENTERTAINMENT & RECREATION

Tech Museum of Innovation 201 S Market St (at Park Ave) 408/294-8324 *10am-5pm, IMAX Dome Theater, a must-see for digital junkies*

■MEN'S CLUBS

Watergarden [★WI,18+,PC] 1010 The Alameda 408/275-1215 *24hrs, great outdoor patio & jacuzzi, Latino Th*

■MEN'S SERVICES

➤**MegaMates** 408/514-1111 *Call to hook up with HOT local men. FREE to listen & respond to ads. Use FREE code DAMRON. MegaMates.com.*

■EROTICA

Leather Masters 969 Park Ave (at Race St) 408/293-7660 *noon-8pm, clsd Sun-Mon, fetish clothes, toys, etc*

Party Time 1456 W San Carlos St 408/998-0925 *arcade*

San Luis Obispo

■INFO LINES & SERVICES

GALA/ Gay & Lesbian Alliance of the Central Coast 1060 Palm St (at Santa Rosa St) 805/541-4252 *8am-noon & 1pm-5pm , clsd wknds*

■ACCOMMODATIONS

The Madonna Inn [GF,F,SW] 100 Madonna Rd 805/543-3000, 800/543-9666 *one-of-a-kind theme rooms*

The Palomar Inn [GS,NS,WI] 1601 Shell Beach Rd, Shell Beach 888/384-4004 *motel*

Sycamore Mineral Springs Resort [GF] 1215 Avila Beach Dr 805/595-7302, 800/234-5831 *hot mineral spring spa, integrative retreat center, also restaurant*

■BARS

Fuel Dock [GF] 900 Main St, Morro Bay 805/772-8478

Gaslight Lounge [GF] 2143 Broad St 805/541-4262 *dive bar*

Legends [GF] 899 Main St, Morro Bay 805/772-2525

The Library [GF,D,WC] 723 Higuera St 805/542-0199

■CAFES

Linnaea's Cafe [E,WI] 1110 Garden St (near Marsh) 805/541-5888 *6:30am-11pm*

Outspoken Cafe [GO] 1422 Monterey St (at California) 805/788-0885 *7am-5pm, clsd wknds, cafe & juice bar*

West End Espresso & Tea [GO] 670 Higuera St #A (at Nipomo) 805/543-4902, 805/544-3581 *6:30am-7pm, till 9pm Th, till 8pm Fri-Sat, outdoor seating*

■RESTAURANTS

Big Sky Cafe 1121 Broad St (btwn Higuera & Marsh Sts) 805/545-5401 *7am-10pm, 8am-9pm Sun-Th, plenty veggie/ vegan*

High Street Deli 350 High St 805/541-4738 *7am-7pm, 8am-3pm Sun*

California • *USA*

Novo 726 Higuera St **805/543-3986** *lunch & dinner*

Vieni Vai 690 Higuera St **805/544-5282** *lunch & dinner, Sun brunch, Italian*

■ ENTERTAINMENT & RECREATION

Pirate's Cove Beach [GS,N,AYOR] 404 Front St, Avila Beach

■ BOOKSTORES

Coalesce Bookstore 845 Main St, Morro Bay **805/772-2880** *10am-5:30pm, 11am-4pm Sun*

Volumes of Pleasure [WC,GO] 1016 Los Osos Valley Rd, Los Osos **805/528-5565** *10am-6pm, clsd Sun-Mon*

■ PUBLICATIONS

GALA News & Reviews **805/541-4252** *news & events for Central California coast*

■ CRUISY AREAS

Embarcadero Boat Ramp [AYOR] Tidelands Park

Morro Bay Rock [AYOR] Coleman Dr

San Rafael
see Marin County

San Ramon
see East Bay

Santa Ana
see Orange County

Santa Barbara
see also Ventura

■ INFO LINES & SERVICES

Pacific Pride Foundation 126 E Haley St #A-11 **805/963-3636** *9am-5pm Mon-Fri*

■ ACCOMMODATIONS

Canary Hotel [GF] 31 W Carrillo **805/884-0300, 866/999-5401**

Inn of the Spanish Garden [GF,SW,NS,WC] 915 Garden St (at Carrillo) **805/564-4700, 866/564-4700** *luxury hotel*

Old Yacht Club Inn [GF,NS,WI] 431 Corona Del Mar Dr **805/962-1277, 800/676-1676** *only B&B on beach*

The Orchid Inn at Santa Barbara [GS,NS,WI,WC,GO] 420 W Montecito St **805/965-2333, 800/427-2156** *1900s Victorian*

White Jasmine Inn [GS,NS,WI] 1327 Bath St (at Sola) **805/966-0589** *cottages, full brkfst, fireplaces*

■ BARS

Reds Wine Bar [GS,F,E,WI] 211 Helena Ave **805/966-5906** *2pm-10pm, till 2am Th-Sat, clsd Mon*

■ NIGHTCLUBS

Wildcat Lounge [★GS,D] 15 W Ortega St **805/962-7970** *more gay Sun*

■ CAFES

Our Daily Bread 831 Santa Barbara St **805/966-3894** *6am-5:30pm, 7am-4pm Sat, clsd Sun, bakery/ cafe*

■ RESTAURANTS

Joe's Cafe 536 State St **805/966-4638** *7:30am-11pm*

The Natural Cafe 508 State St **805/962-9494** *11am-9pm*

Opal Restaurant & Bar 1325 State St (at Sola St) **805/966-9676** *lunch (Mon-Sat) & dinner nightly, full bar*

Sojourner Cafe [BW,WC] 134 E Canon Perdido (at Santa Barbara) **805/965-7922** *11am-10pm, till 11pm Th-Sat*

■ ENTERTAINMENT & RECREATION

Santa Barbara Mission 2201 Laguna St **805/682-4713** *the "queen of the missions"; take a self-guided tour btwn 9am-4:30pm*

■ BOOKSTORES

Chaucer's Books [★] 3321 State St (at Las Positas Rd, Loreto Plaza) **805/682-6787** *9am-9pm, till 6pm Sun*

■ EROTICA

For Adults Only 223 Anacapa St **805/963-9922** *24hrs*

The Riviera Adult Superstore 4135 State St (at Hwy 154 intersection) 805/967-8282 *10am-midnight, pride items, community resources*

Santa Clara

■ ACCOMMODATIONS

Avatar Hotel [GS,WI,NS,WC] 4200 Great America Pkwy 408/235-8900, 800/586-5691

Biltmore Hotel & Suites [GF,SW,NS,WI] 2151 Laurelwood Rd (at Montague Expwy) 408/988-8411, 800/255-9925

■ NIGHTCLUBS

A Tinker's Damn (TD's) [M,D,DS] 46 N Saratoga Ave (at Stevens Creek) 408/243-4595 *3pm-2am, from 1pm wknds*

■ EROTICA

Hot Stuff 56 Saratoga Ave 408/241-9971 *arcade*

L'Amour Shoppe 2329 El Camino Real 408/296-7076 *24hrs, arcade*

Santa Cruz

■ INFO LINES & SERVICES

AA Gay/ Lesbian 5732 Soquel Dr, Soquel 831/475-5782 (AA#) *call or visit www.aasantacruz.org for meetings*

The Diversity Center [WI] 1117 Soquel Ave (at Cayuga) 831/425-5422 *open daily, call for events*

■ ACCOMMODATIONS

Chaminade Resort & Spa [GF,SW,NS,WC] 1 Chaminade Ln (at Soquel Ave) 831/475-5600, 800/283-6569

Dream Inn [GS,F,SW,WI] 175 W Cliff Dr 831/426-4330, 866/774-7735

■ BARS

Mad House [GS,NH,D,DS,GO] 529 Seabright Ave (at Murray St) 831/425-2900 *4pm-2am, clsd Mon, more gay Th*

■ NIGHTCLUBS

Blue Lagoon [GF,D,A,E,TG,V,WC] 923 Pacific Ave 831/423-7117 *3:30pm-2am, theme nights, live bands*

■ RESTAURANTS

Betty Burgers 505 Seabright Ave (at Murray) 831/423-8190 *10am-10pm, retro burger joint, outdoor seating*

Cafe Limelight [TG,WC,GO] 1016 Cedar St (at Locust St) 831/425-7873 *lunch & dinner, clsd Mon, European*

Cilantros Mexican Restaurant 1934 Main St (in Town Center strip mall), Watsonville 831/761-2161 *lunch & dinner*

Crêpe Place [E,WC] 1134 Soquel Ave (at Seabright, across from Rio Theater) 831/429-6994 *11am-midnight, from 9am Sat-Sun, full bar, garden patio*

Saturn Cafe [GO] 145 Laurel St (at Pacific) 831/429-8505 *10am-3am, vegetarian diner*

Silver Spur 2650 Soquel Dr 831/475-2725 *6am-3pm, clsd Sun*

■ ENTERTAINMENT & RECREATION

Bonny Doon Beach [GS,N,AYOR] Hwy 1 at Bonny Doon Rd (at milepost 27.6, N of Santa Cruz) *park in paved parking lot; nude side of beach to the north*

■ BOOKSTORES

Bookshop Santa Cruz [WC] 1520 Pacific Ave 831/423-0900 *9am-10pm*

■ GYMS & HEALTH CLUBS

Kiva Retreat House Spa 702 Water St (at Ocean) 831/429-1142 *noon-11pm, till midnight Fri-Sat, check for women-only & men-only hours*

■ MEN'S SERVICES

➤**MegaMates** 831/515-1020 *Call to hook up with HOT local men. FREE to listen & respond to ads. Use FREE code DAMRON. MegaMates.com.*

■ EROTICA

Frenchy's Cruzin Books & Video 3960 Portola Dr (at 41st Ave) 831/475-9221 *arcade*

■ CRUISY AREAS

Laguna Creek Beach [AYOR] 7 miles N of town

Santa Rosa

see Sonoma County

California • *USA*

Saratoga

■RETAIL SHOPS

Vine Life 14572-A Big Basin Way **408/872-1500** *11am-5pm, wine, cards & gifts*

Sausalito

see Marin County

Sebastopol

see also Russian River & Sonoma County

Sonoma County

see also Russian River

■INFO LINES & SERVICES

AA Meetings in Sonoma County **707/544-1300** (AA#), **800/224-1300** *call or visit www.sonomacountyaa.org for meetings*

➤**Sonoma County Tourism Bureau** **707/522-5800, 800/576-6662** *see ad in front color section*

■ACCOMMODATIONS

An Inn 2 Remember [GF,NS,WI] 171 W Spain St (at First St W), Sonoma **707/938-2909** *located in Wine Country, whirlpool baths & fireplaces, free use of bikes*

Beltane Ranch [GF] 11775 Sonoma Hwy (Hwy 12), Glen Ellen **707/996-6501** *1892 New Orleans-style ranch house*

Best Western Dry Creek Inn [GS,SW,WI] 198 Dry Creek Rd, Healdsburg **707/433-0300, 800/222-5784**

Camellia Inn [GF,SW,NS,WI] 211 North St (at Fitch), Healdsburg **707/433-8182, 800/727-8182** *Italianate Victorian, full brkfst*

The Gaige House [GF,SW,WI] 13540 Arnold Dr, Glen Ellen **707/935-0237, 800/935-0237** *in the Wine Country*

Grape Leaf Inn [GF,WI] 539 Johnson St, Healdsburg **707/433-8140, 866/433-8140** *Queen Anne Victorian, full brkfst*

Hyatt Vineyard Creek Hotel [GF,SW,WI,WC] 170 Railroad St (at Third St), Santa Rosa **707/284-1234** *resort, seafood restaurant*

Madrona Manor [GF,F,SW,NS,WC] 1001 Westside Rd, Healdsburg **707/433-4231, 800/258-4003** *also restaurant*

Magliulo's Rose Garden Inn [GF,WI,WC] 681 Broadway (at Andrieux), Sonoma **707/996-1031**

Sonoma Chalet [GF] 18935 5th St W, Sonoma **707/938-3129, 800/938-3129**

Sonoma's Best Guest Cottages [GF,WI] 1190 E Napa St (at 8th St E), Sonoma **707/933-0340, 800/291-8962**

■CAFES

A' Roma Roasters [MW,E,WC,GO] 95 5th St (Railroad Square), Santa Rosa **707/576-7765** *6am-close, from 7am Sat-Sun*

Coffee Catz [E,WI] 6761 Sebastopol Ave #300 (in Gravenstein Station), Sebastopol **707/829-6600** *7am-6pm, till 10pm Wed (open mic), till 10pm Fri-Sat (live bands), garden*

Screamin' Mimi's 6902 Sebastopol Ave (intersection of Hwy 12 & 116), Sebastopol **707/823-5902** *espresso drinks & homemade ice cream*

Sonoma's Best 1190 E Napa St (at 8th St E), Sonoma **707/996-7600** *7am-6pm, 8am-5pm Sun, local products—cheese, wine, olive oils & more—all under one roof*

■RESTAURANTS

Estate 400 W Spain St, Sonoma **707/933-3663** *lunch & dinner, Sun brunch, clsd Mon, Italian*

Fig Cafe & Wine Bar 13690 Arnold Dr, Glen Ellen **707/938-2130** *dinner nightly, Sun brunch*

Mom's Apple Pie 4550 Gravenstein Hwy N, Sebastopol **707/823-8330** *pie worth stopping for on your way to & from Russian River!*

Singletree Inn [GO] 165 Healdsburg Ave, Healdsburg **707/433-8263** *7am-3pm, good brkfsts, famous BBQ sandwiches, some veggie, local wines, outdoor seating*

Slice of Life 6970 McKinley St, Sebastopol **707/829-6627** *11am-9pm, from 9am Sat-Sun, clsd Mon, vegan & vegetarian*

Syrah Bistro 205 5th St (at Davis), Santa Rosa **707/568-4002** *dinner nightly, California/ French*

■ENTERTAINMENT & RECREATION

Out In The Vineyard [GO] **707/495-9732** *tours of the wine country*

River's Edge Kayak & Canoe Company [GO] **707/433-7247** *river excursions*

■RETAIL SHOPS

Grower's Collective Tasting Room **707/996-1364** *noon-5:30pm, clsd Tue-Th, open wknds only in winter*

■MEN'S SERVICES

▶**MegaMates** **707/583-1112** *Call to hook up with HOT local men. FREE to listen & respond to ads. Use FREE code DAMRON. MegaMates.com.*

■EROTICA

Secrets Santa Rosa 3301 Santa Rosa Ave (at Todd), Santa Rosa **707/542-8248**

Springville

■ACCOMMODATIONS

Great Energy [MW,SW,NS] PO Box 473, 93265 **559/539-2382** *retreat in foothills of Sierra Nevada mtns*

Stockton

see also Modesto

■NIGHTCLUBS

Paradise Club [MW,D,F,E,YC] 10100 N Lower Sacramento Rd (near Grider) **209/477-4724** *6pm-2am, from 3pm Sun*

■EROTICA

Suzie's Adult Superstores 3126 E Hammer Ln **209/952-6900** *24hrs, arcade*

■CRUISY AREAS

Oak Park [AYOR] Alpine Ave

Sunnyvale

see also San Jose

■ACCOMMODATIONS

Wild Palms Hotel [GF,SW,WI,WC] 910 E Fremont Ave (at Wolfe Ave) **408/738-0500, 800/538-1600** *hot tub*

■MEN'S SERVICES

▶**MegaMates** **408/331-7400** *Call to hook up with HOT local men. FREE to listen & respond to ads. Use FREE code DAMRON. MegaMates.com.*

Temecula

■NIGHTCLUBS

Aloha J's [MW,D,F] 27497 Ynez Rd **951/506-9889** *gay/ straight, more gay Wed*

Club Velocity [MW,D,F] 27725 Jefferson Ave Ste 101 (at Johnny G's) **951/506-0399** *9pm Sun only; also Wed at Aloha J's*

Tiburon

see Marin County

Twentynine Palms

see Joshua Tree Nat'l Park

Ukiah

■BARS

Perkins St Lounge [GF,D,E,K] 228 E Perkins St **707/462-0327** *3pm-2am*

Upland

■NIGHTCLUBS

Oasis [M,D,F,DS,WC] 1386 E Foothill Blvd #H (at Grove) **909/920-9590** *6pm-2am Wed-Sat, from 8pm Sun,*

■EROTICA

Sensations Love Boutique 1656 W Foothill Blvd (at Mountain) **909/985-1654**

California • *USA*

The Toy Box 1999 W Arrow Rte (at Central) **909/920-1135** *24hrs*

Vacaville

■INFO LINES & SERVICES
Solano Pride Center 1125 Missouri St #203-D, Fairfield **707/398-3463** *call for meeting times*

■EROTICA
Secrets Adult Super Store 564 Parker Rd (at Union Ave), Fairfield **707/437-9297** *arcade*

■CRUISY AREAS
Lee Bell Park [AYOR] Travis Blvd (at Union Ave), Fairfield

Vallejo
includes Benicia

■BARS
Town House Cocktail Lounge [GS,NH,GO] 401-A Georgia St (at Marin) **707/553-9109** *1pm-midnight, from 10am Sat-Sun*

■BOOKSTORES
Bookshop Benicia [WC] 856 Southampton Rd, Benicia **707/747-5155** *10am-7pm, till 6pm wknds*

Van Nuys

■MEN'S SERVICES
➤**MegaMates** 818/465-0500 *Call to hook up with HOT local men. FREE to listen & respond to ads. Use FREE code DAMRON. MegaMates.com.*

Ventura
see also Santa Barbara

■INFO LINES & SERVICES
AA Gay/ Lesbian 805/389-1444 (AA#), 800/990-7750

■BARS
Paddy McDermott's [MW,D,F,E,K] 2 W Main St (at Ventura) **805/652-1071** *2pm-2am, beer busts*

■EROTICA
Three Star Books 359 E Main St **805/653-9068** *24hrs*

■CRUISY AREAS
Surfers Point [AYOR] N of the Ventura Pier (btwn fairgrounds & Ocean) *go N along beach to Hobo's Jungle*

Victorville

■BARS
Ricky's [GS,D,F,K,DS,WC] 13728 Hesperia Rd #12 **760/951-5400** *6pm-2am, clsd Mon*

■EROTICA
Oasis Adult Dept Store 14949 Palmdale Rd **760/241-0788** *arcade*

■CRUISY AREAS
Deep Creek Hot Springs [AYOR] Apple Valley *from I-15, take Bear Valley Cutoff & turn right onto Central Rd; go left onto Ocotillo Rd for 2 miles & turn right onto Bowen Ranch Rd (unmarked dirt road)*

Grady Trammel Park [AYOR] 3/4 mile N of West Side 15 bar (on Stoddard Wells Rd) *watch out for rangers (!)*

Walnut Creek
see East Bay

■MEN'S SERVICES
➤**MegaMates** 925/300-9999 *Call to hook up with HOT local men. FREE to listen & respond to ads. Use FREE code DAMRON. MegaMates.com.*

Yosemite Nat'l Park

■ACCOMMODATIONS
The Ahwahnee Hotel [GF,F,SW,NS] Yosemite Valley Floor **866/875-8456** **(reservations)** *incredibly dramatic & expensive grand fortress*

Highland House B&B [GF,WI] 3125 Wild Dove Ln (at Jerseydale Rd), Mariposa **209/966-3737**

The Homestead [GF,NS,WI] 41110 Rd 600, Ahwahnee **559/683-0495, 800/483-0495** *cottages & 2-bdrm house*

June Lake Villager [GF,WI] 2640 Hwy 158 (2.5 miles W of Hwy 395), June Lake **760/648-7712, 800/655-6545**

Narrow Gauge Inn [GF,SW,NS] 48571 Hwy 41, Fish Camp **559/683-7720, 888/644-9050**

Queen's Inn by the River
[GS,NS,WI,WC,GO] 41139 Hwy 41,
Oakhurst 559/683-4354 *garden w/
river view, lesbian-owned*

Tenaya Lodge at Yosemite [GF,F,SW]
1122 Hwy 41, Fish Camp
559/683-6555, 888/514-2167

Yosemite View Lodge [GF,SW,WC]
11136 Hwy 140, El Portal
209/379-2681, 888/742-4371 *3
pools, 2 restaurants & lounge*

Yosemite's Apple Blossom Inn B&B
[GF,NS,WC] 559/642-2001,
888/687-4281

■**CRUISY AREAS**
Rest Stop [AYOR] at turn to Glacier
Point on road to valley

COLORADO

Aspen

■**ACCOMMODATIONS**
Aspen Mountain Lodge [GF,SW,NS]
311 W Main St 970/925-7650,
800/362-7736

Hotel Aspen [GF,SW,NS,WI] 110 W Main
St 970/925-3441, 800/527-7369
hot tub, après-ski wine & cheese

Hotel Lenado [GF] 200 S Aspen St
970/925-6246, 800/321-3457

St Moritz Lodge [GF,SW,NS,WI,GO] 334
W Hyman Ave 970/925-3220,
800/817-2069

■**RESTAURANTS**
Jimmy's 205 S Mill St (at Hopkins)
970/925-6020 *5:30pm-11pm, Sun
brunch, also bar from 4:30pm, patio*

Syzygy [E,WC] 308 E Hopkins Ave
970/925-3700 *seasonal, 6pm-10pm,
bar till 2am*

■**BOOKSTORES**
Explore Booksellers & Bistro
[F,WI,WC] 221 E Main St (at Aspen)
970/925-5336, 800/562-7323
10am-10pm, also vegetarian restaurant

Beaver Creek

■**ACCOMMODATIONS**
Beaver Creek Lodge [GF,SW,NS,WI,WC]
26 Avondale Ln (at Village Rd)
970/845-9800, 800/525-7280 *also
restaurant, mtn chic, steam room, gym*

Boulder

■**INFO LINES & SERVICES**
Out Boulder 2132 14th St (at Pine)
303/499-5777 *LGBT resource center*

■**ACCOMMODATIONS**
The Briar Rose B&B [GF,NS,WI] 2151
Arapahoe Ave (at 22nd St)
303/442-3007, 888/786-8440 *full
organic brkfst*

■**CAFES**
Walnut Cafe [★WC] 3073 Walnut St
(at 30th) 303/447-2315 *7am-3:30pm,
patio*

■**ENTERTAINMENT &
RECREATION**
Boulder Area Bicycle Adventures
[GO] 303/918-7062 *bike tours of
Boulder & annual LGBT ride in June*

■**RETAIL SHOPS**
Enchanted Ink [GO] 1200 Pearl St #35
(at Broadway) 303/440-6611 *tattoos,
piercing, henna*

■**CRUISY AREAS**
Dream Canyon [SW,N] Lost Angel Rd
(off Sugarloaf Mtn Rd) *inquire locally
for detailed directions*

Colorado Springs
(includes Manitou Springs)

■**INFO LINES & SERVICES**
Colorado Springs Pride Center [WI]
719/471-4429 *noon-5pm*

■**ACCOMMODATIONS**
Blue Skies Inn B&B [GS,NS,WI,WC] 402
Manitou Ave (at Mayfair), Manitou
Springs 719/685-3899,
800/398-7949

Blue Skies Inn B&B [GS,NS,WI,WC] 402
Manitou Ave (at Mayfair), Manitou
Springs 719/685-3899,
800/398-7949

Colorado • USA

Old Town Guesthouse [GF,NS,WI,WC] 115 S 26th St **719/632-9194, 888/375-4210** *full brkfst, hot tub*

Pikes Peak Paradise [GF,NS,WI,GO] 236 Pinecrest Rd, Woodland Park **719/687-6656, 800/728-8282** *full brkfst, hot tub, mansion w/ view of Pikes Peak*

Two Sisters Inn—A B&B [★GF,NS] 10 Otoe Pl (at Manitou Ave), Manitou Springs **719/685-9684**

■BARS

Club Q [★M,NH,D,F,E,K,S,18+,WC,GO] 3430 N Academy Blvd (at N Carefree) **719/501-1429** *6pm-2am, till 4am Sat, clsd Mon*

Underground [M,NH,D,F,K,GO] 110 N Nevada Ave (at Kiowa St) **719/578-7771** *4pm-2am, from 2pm Sun*

■CAFES

Spice of Life an Ingredients Emporium [WI] 727 Manitou Ave, Manitou Springs **719/685-5284** *7am-6pm*

■RESTAURANTS

Dale Street Bistro Cafe 115 E Dale (at Nevada) **719/578-9898** *lunch & dinner, brunch wknds*

■MEN'S CLUBS

Buddies [MO,MR,V,18+,N,PC,GO] 3430 N Academy Blvd (N Carefree) **719/591-7660** *3pm-4am, clsd Mon-Tue, beer bust Sun*

■MEN'S SERVICES

➤**MegaMates 719/520-9797** *Call to hook up with HOT local men. FREE to listen & respond to ads. Use FREE code DAMRON. MegaMates.com.*

■EROTICA

First Amendment Adult Bookstore 220 E Fillmore St (at Nevada) **719/630-7676**

XXX-Treme Mature Fantasy Store 620 Peterson Rd (Platte -Hwy 24) **719/638-0200**

■CRUISY AREAS

Palmer Park [AYOR] *many undercover cops*

Denver

■INFO LINES & SERVICES

Gay/ Lesbian AA 303/322-4440

The GLBT Center of Colorado (The Center) [WC] 1301 E Colfax **303/733-7743** *10am-8pm Mon-Fri, from noon Sat, extensive resources & support groups*

■ACCOMMODATIONS

The Brown Palace [GF,WI] 321 17th St (at N Broadway) **303/297-3111, 800/321-2599** *sun in every room, also restaurant & spa*

Capitol Hill Mansion B&B [GF,NS,WI] 1207 Pennsylvania St (at 12th) **303/839-5221, 800/839-9329** *full brkfst, hot tub*

Castle Marne B&B [GF,WI] 1572 Race St (at 16th Ave) **303/331-0621, 800/926-2763** *hot tubs on private balconies*

The Curtis-a DoubleTree by Hilton [GF,SW,WI] 1405 Curtis St **303/571-0300, 800/525-6651** *hip hotel, restaurant*

Hotel Monaco [GF,NS,WI] 1717 Champa St (at 17th) **303/296-1717, 800/990-1303** *gym, spa, also Italian restaurant*

Hotel Teatro [GF,NS,WI] 1100 14th St **303/228-1100, 888/727-1200** *luxury boutique hotel, 2 restaurants*

The Oxford Hotel [GF,F,WI] 1600 17th St **303/628-5400, 800/228-5838** *health club & spa, also restaurant & art deco lounge*

■BARS

Aqua Lounge [MW,E,V,WI] 1417 Krameria (btwn 14th & Colfax) **720/287-0584** *4pm-2am, piano bar*

Barker Lounge [M,NH] 475 Santa Fe Dr (at 5th St) **303/778-0545** *noon-2am, also large patio w/ bar, dogs welcome*

The Beauty Bar [GS,D,E] **720/542-8024** *5pm-2am , from 7pm Sat, clsd Sun-Mon*

Black Crown Piano Lounge [M,F,E] 1446 S Broadway **720/353-4701** *4pm-midnight, till 2am Fri-Sat, from 11am Sat-Sun*

Boyztown [M,NH,S,WI] 117 Broadway (btwn 1st & 2nd Aves) 303/722-7373 *3pm-2am, from noon wknds, male dancers Tue-Sun*

Broadways [M,NH,DS,WI] 1027 Broadway (at 11th Ave) 303/623-0700 *2pm-2am, from noon Sat-Sun, cool mix of folk*

Charlie's [★M,D,CW,K,DS,WC] 900 E Colfax Ave (at Emerson) 303/839-8890 *11am-2am, country bar & house music room*

The Compound/Basix [★M,NH,D] 145 Broadway (at 2nd Ave) 303/722-7977 *7am-2am, [D] Fri-Sat*

Dazzle [GF,F,E] 930 Lincoln St (btwn 9th & 10th Aves) 303/839-5100 *from 4pm Sun-Th, from 11am Fri, also Sun brunch , jazz club & restaurant*

Denver Eagle [M,NH,B,L,WC,GO] 3600 Blake St (at 36th) 303/291-0250 *4pm-2am, from 2pm Sun, clsd Mon*

The Denver Wrangler [M,B,WC] 1700 Logan St (at 17th Ave) 303/837-1075 *11am-2am, levi/ bear bar, popular Sun beer bust*

Eden [W,F,E] 3090 Downing St (at 31st Ave) 303/832-5482 *4pm-2am, from 11am Sun (brunch till 4pm)*

El Chapultepec [★GF,F,E,$] 1962 Market St (at 20th) 303/295-9126 *9am-2am, live jazz & blues, 1-drink minimum per set*

El Potrero [GS,DS,MR-L,E,F] 4501 E Virginia Ave, Glendale 303/388-8889 *Mexican restaurant from 3pm, Latino gay bar late, clsd Mon-Tue*

li'l Devil's [M,NH] 255 S Broadway 303/733-1156 *3pm-2am, from noon wknds*

R&R Denver [MW,NH] 4958 E Colfax Ave (at Elm St) 303/320-9337 *3pm-2am, from 1pm Fri, from 11am wknds*

X Bar [MW,D,F] 629 E Colfax Ave 303/832-2687 *3pm-2am, from noon Sun*

■**NIGHTCLUBS**

Beta Nightclub [GS,D,$] 1909 Blake St (btwn 19th & 20th) 303/383-1909 *more gay Th*

Climax Sunday at Club Vinyl [MW,D] 1082 Broadway 303/832-8628 *4pm-2am Sun, great rooftop patio*

Coco Breeze Lounge & Cafe [M,D,K,CW,18+] 539 W 43rd Ave (at Fox) 303/480-4244 *4pm-4am, till 2am Mon-Tue*

La Rumba [GF,D,E,$] 99 W 9th Ave (at Broadway) 303/572-8006 *salsa dancing & lessons Th & Sat, more gay Fri for Lipgloss (Brit-pop & indie music)*

Lannie's Clocktower Cabaret [GF,F,E,C] 16th St Mall at Arapahoe (in historic D&F Tower) 303/293-0075 *upscale cabaret w/ variety of acts weekly, including drag & burlesque*

Lipstick [MW,D] 989 Sheridan Blvd 303/482-1003 *9pm-2am Th-Sat*

Tracks [GS,D,DS,MR] 3500 Walnut St (at 36th) 303/863-7326 *9pm-2am, clsd Sun-Wed, 2 rooms, theme nights*

■**CAFES**

City, O City 206 E 13th Ave (at Sherman) 303/831-6443 *7am-2am, from 8am wknds, vegetarian/ vegan, also bar*

Common Grounds [WI] 1550 17th St 303/296-9248 *6:30am-10pm, till 9pm Sun*

Jelly Cafe 600 E 13th Ave (at Pearl) 303/831-6301 *7am-3pm, a whole lotta Jelly filled fun*

The Market at Larimer Square 1445 Larimer Sq (btwn 14th & 15th) 303/534-5140 *6am-11pm, till midnight Fri-Sat, till 10pm Sun*

Paris on the Platte [E,WI] 1553 Platte St (at 15th) 303/455-2451 *7am-2am, soups, salads, sandwiches, live music*

■**RESTAURANTS**

Annie's Cafe & Bar [★] 3100 E Colfax (at St Paul) 303/355-8197 *7am-10pm, from 8am Sat, diner*

The Avenue Grill 630 E 17th Ave (at Washington) 303/861-2820 *11am-11pm, till midnight Fri-Sat, till 10pm Sun*

Banzai Sushi 6665 Leetsdale Dr (E of Colorado Blvd) 303/329-3366 *lunch Mon-Fri, dinner nightly*

Barricuda's 1076 Ogden St (at E 11th) 303/860-8353 *10am-2am, also dive bar*

Colorado • *USA*

Beatrice & Woodsley [R] 38 S Broadway **303/777-3505** *one of America's top restaurants*

Benny's Restaurante y Tequila Bar 301 E 7th Ave (at Grant St) **303/894-0788** *lunch & dinner, patio*

The Corner Office Restaurant & Martini Bar 1405 Curtis St (at Curtis Hotel) **303/825-6500** *6am-midnight, till 2am Fri-Sat, groovy Sun disco brunch*

Devil's Food 1020 S Gaylord St (at E Tennessee) **303/733-7448** *7am-10pm, till 4pm Sun-Mon, yummy desserts*

Duo 2413 W 32nd Ave (at Zuni) **303/477-4141** *dinner nightly, wknd brunch, hip, organic, creative American, full bar*

Euclid Hall Bar & Kitchen 1317 14th St **303/595-4255** *11:30am-1am-, till 2am Fri-Sat, American tavern focuses on high quality and innovative pub food*

Fruition 1313 E 6th Ave **303/831-1962** *5pm-10pm, till 8pm Sun, contemporary French*

Hamburger Mary's/ Club M [★GS,D,K,DS] 700 E 17th Ave (at Washington St, across from JR's bar) **303/832-1333** *11am-2am, from 10am Sun*

Il Vicino 550 Broadway **303/861-0801** *11am-10pm, pizza*

Las Margaritas Uptown [★GO] 1035 E 17th Ave (at Downing) **303/830-2199** *11am-1am, Mexican, also bar*

Racine's 650 Sherman St (at 6th Ave) **303/595-0418** *brkfst, lunch, dinner, late night & Sun brunch, full bar*

Steuben's 523 E 17th Ave **303/830-1001** *11am-11pm, American comfort food served up hip, patio, full bar*

Sunny Gardens 6460 E Yale Avenue **303/691-8830** *Chinese, plenty veggie/ vegan*

Thai Pot Cafe 1550 S Colorado Blvd (at E Florida) **303/639-6200** *lunch & dinner*

Tom's Home Cookin' [WC,GO] **303/388-8035** *11am-3pm, clsd Sat-Sun, Southern comfort food*

Vesta Dipping Grill 1822 Blake St (near 18th St) **303/296-1970** *5pm-10pm Sun-Th, till 11pm Fri-Sat, upscale*

WaterCourse Foods 837 E 17th Ave (at Clarkson) **303/832-7313** *7am-9pm, till 10pm Fri-Sat, vegetarian/ vegan*

Wazee Supper Club [WC] 1600 15th St (at Wazee) **303/623-9518, 303/825-3199 (pizza delivery)** *11am-2am, noon-midnight Sun, classic comfort food, full bar*

▪ENTERTAINMENT & RECREATION

Rocky Mountain Rainbeaus **303/863-7739** *all-inclusive, all-levels, high-energy square dance club*

▪BOOKSTORES

Tattered Cover Book Store [WC] 2526 Colfax Ave (at Elizabeth St) **303/322-7727, 800/833-9327** *9am-9pm, 10am-6pm Sun, independent, cafe; also 1628 16th St, 303/ 436-1070*

▪RETAIL SHOPS

CJ's Leather 135 Broadway **303/715-1157** *11am-5pm, clsd Sun-Mon*

▪PUBLICATIONS

Out Front Colorado **303/778-7900** *statewide bi-weekly LGBT newspaper, since 1976*

▪GYMS & HEALTH CLUBS

Pura Vida Fitness & Spa 2955 E 1st Ave #200 **303/321-7872**

▪MEN'S CLUBS

Denver Swim Club [★MO,V,YC,SW,PC] 6923 E Colfax Ave (at Olive) **303/322-4023**

Midtowne Spa—Denver [PC] 2935 Zuni St (at 29th) **303/458-8902** *24hrs*

▪MEN'S SERVICES

►MegaMates **303/433-6789** *Call to hook up with HOT local men. FREE to listen & respond to ads. Use FREE code DAMRON. MegaMates.com.*

▪EROTICA

Circus Cinema 5580 N Federal Blvd **303/455-3144** *24hrs*

Crypt Adult Entertainment 139 Broadway (btwn 1st & 2nd) 303/778-6584 *10am-2am, all-male theaters & arcades*

The Crypt on Broadway 8 Broadway (at Ellsworth) 303/733-3112 *11am-11pm, leather, clubwear & more*

Dove Theater 3480 W Colfax (at King St) 303/893-0037 *8:30am-12:30am, 24hrs wknds*

Pleasure Entertainment Center 127 S Broadway (at Bayaud) 303/722-5852 *open 23hrs; also 3250 W Alameda, 303/934-2373 & 3490 W Colfax, 303/825-6505*

Romantix Adult Superstore 633 E Colfax Ave (at Washington) 303/831-8319

■CRUISY AREAS
Cheesman Park [AYOR] *near Pavilion beware of undercover cops!*

Durango

■ACCOMMODATIONS
Leland House B&B [GF,NS,WI,WC] 721 E 2nd Ave 970/385-1920

Mesa Verde Far View Lodge [GF,NS,WI] 1 Navajo Hill, Mesa Verde National Park 602/331-5210, 800/449-2288 *inside nat'l park at 8250' elevation*

Rochester Hotel [★GF,NS,WC] 721 E 2nd Ave 800/664-1920 *Western-style house, full brkfst*

■RESTAURANTS
Palace Restaurant [WC,GO] 505 Main Ave (at 5th St) 970/247-2018 *11am-10pm, clsd Sun in winter, full bar, patio*

Estes Park

■ACCOMMODATIONS
Stanley Hotel [GF,SW,WI] 333 Wonderview Ave 800/976-1377, 970/577-4000 *the inspiration for Stephen King's The Shining*

Fort Collins

■ACCOMMODATIONS
Archer's Poudre River Resort [GF,GO] 33021 Poudre Canyon Hwy, Bellvue 970/881-2139, 888/822-0588

■BARS
Choice City Shots [MW,NH,D,K,S,WC,GO] 124 LaPorte Ave (at College) 970/221-4333 *6:30pm-midnight, till 1:30am Th-Sat*

Grand Junction

■RESTAURANTS
Leon's Taqueria 505 30th Rd 970/242-1388 *11am-9pm*

■EROTICA
24 Road Video Exchange 639 24 Rd (at Mesa Mall) 970/243-4112 *10am-11pm*

Junction News 754 North Ave (at 7th St) 970/242-9702 *24hrs, till midnight Sun Mon*

■CRUISY AREAS
Hawthorne Park [AYOR]

Walker Wildlife Area [AYOR] Hwy 6/50 W, past Mesa Mall (near the CO River) *in the woods*

Hotchkiss

■ACCOMMODATIONS
Leroux Creek Inn & Vineyards [GF] 12388 3100 Rd 970/872-4746

■RESTAURANTS
North Fork Valley Restaurant & Thirsty Parrot Pub [E] 140 W Bridge St 970/872-4215 *11am-8pm, American/ Mexican*

Pueblo

■BARS
Pirate's Cove [MW,NH,WC] 105 Central Plaza (off 1st & Union) 719/543-2683 *4pm-2am, call for Sun hrs, clsd Mon*

■CRUISY AREAS
City Park Pueblo Blvd & Thatcher *N side near gazebo*

Stratton

■ACCOMMODATIONS
Claremont Inn & Winery [GS,F,WI,GO] 800 Claremont St (off exit 419, I-70) 719/348-5125, 888/291-8910 *2 hours from Denver, full brkfst*

Connecticut • *USA*

Vail

■RESTAURANTS

Larkspur Restaurant & Market [WC] 458 Vail Valley Dr (in the Golden Peak Lodge) **970/754-8050** *lunch & dinner, fine dining, also bar, patio, ski-in/ out*

Sweet Basil [WC] 193 E Gore Creek Dr **970/476-0125** *lunch & dinner, bar*

CONNECTICUT

Bethel

■CAFES

Molten Java [E,GO] 213 Greenwood Ave **203/739-0313** *6am-9pm, till 10pm Fri-Sat, 8am-8pm Sat-Sun*

■RESTAURANTS

Bethel Pizza House 206 Greenwood Ave **203/748-1427** *11am-11pm, till midnight Fri-Sat*

Bridgeport

■RESTAURANTS

Bloodroot Restaurant & Bookstore 85 Ferris St (at Harbor Ave) **203/576-9168** *lunch Tue & Th-Sat, dinner Tue-Sat, brunch only Sun, clsd Mon, vegetarian*

■MEN'S SERVICES

➤**MegaMates 203/612-9962** *Call to hook up with HOT local men. FREE to listen & respond to ads. Use FREE code DAMRON. MegaMates.com.*

■EROTICA

Boston Book & Video 2053 Boston Ave **203/335-9705** *open till 2am*

Romantix Adult Superstore 410 North Ave **203/332-7129**

Bristol

■EROTICA

Amazing Superstore 167 Farmington Ave **860/582-9000**

■CRUISY AREAS

Rockwell Park [AYOR] Rte 72

Colebrook

■ACCOMMODATIONS

Rock Hall Luxe Lodging [GS,SW,NS,WI] 19 Rock Hall Rd **860/379-2230**

Danbury

■ACCOMMODATIONS

Maron Hotel & Suites [GF,WI,WC] 42 Lake Ave Extension (off I-84) **203/791-2200, 866/811-2582** *kids/ pets ok*

■BARS

Triangles Cafe [★MW,D,K,DS,V,GO] 66 Sugar Hollow Rd, Rte 7 **203/798-6996** *5pm-1am, till 2am Fri-Sat, patio*

■RESTAURANTS

Sesame Seed 68 W Wooster St **203/743-9850** *lunch & dinner, clsd Sun, Mediterranean/ Italian*

Thang Long [BYOB] 56 Padanaram Rd (near North Street Shopping Center) **203/743-6049** *lunch & dinner, Vietnamese*

Enfield

■EROTICA

Bookends 44 Enfield St/ Rte 5 **860/745-3988**

Groton

■EROTICA

Amazing 591 Rte 12 #8 **860/448-0787**

Hartford

■INFO LINES & SERVICES

Hartford Gay & Lesbian Health Collective 1841 Broad St (at New Britain Ave) **860/278-4163** *9am-5pm, till 9pm Th, clsd wknds*

True Colors 30 Arbor St (at Capital Ave) **860/232-0050, 888/565-5551** *support & mentoring for LGBT youth*

■ACCOMMODATIONS

Butternut Farm [GS,NS,WI] 1654 Main St, Glastonbury **860/633-7197** *full brkfst*

Inn at Kent Falls [GS,SW,NS,WI,WC,GO] 107 Kent Cornwall Rd, Kent **860/927-3197** *1 hr from Hartford*

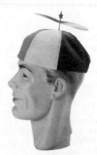

Connecticut • *USA*

The Mansion Inn [GF] 139 Hartford Rd (at Main St), Manchester 860/646-0453

■**BARS**

Chez Est [★MW,D,F,K,DS] 458 Wethersfield Ave (at Main St) 860/525-3243 *3pm-1am, till 2am Fri-Sat*

Polo [MW,D,E,K,DS,S] 678 Maple Ave (btwn Preston & Mapleton) 860/278-3333 *9pm-1am, till 2am Fri-Sat, clsd Sun-Wed*

■**CAFES**

Tisane Tea & Coffee Bar [F,K,WI] 537 Farmington Ave (at Kenyon) 860/523-5417 *8am-1am, till 2am Sat, also bar, men's night Tue*

■**RESTAURANTS**

Arugula [R,WC] 953 Farmington Ave, West Hartford 860/561-4888 *lunch & dinner, clsd Mon, Mediterranean*

Firebox 539 Broad St 860/246-1222 *11:30am-10:30pm, 4:30pm-8:30pm Sun, contemporary American, also farmers market Th (April-Oct)*

Peppercorns Grill 357 Main St 860/547-1714 *lunch Mon-Fri, dinner nightly, clsd Sun, Northern Italian*

Pond House Cafe [BYOB,WC] 1555 Asylum Ave, W Hartford 860/231-8823 *lunch & dinner Tue-Sat, wknd brunch, patio*

Trumbull Kitchen 150 Trumbull St (at Pearl St) 860/493-7417 *lunch Mon-Sat dinner nightly, global cuisine/ tapas*

■**ENTERTAINMENT & RECREATION**

Real Art Ways [WI] 56 Arbor St 860/232-1006 *contemporary art, cinema, performance, also lounge*

■**RETAIL SHOPS**

➤**MetroStore** 493 Farmington Ave (at Sisson Ave) 860/231-8845 *8:30am-8pm, till 5:30pm Tue, Wed & Sat, clsd Sun, magazines, travel guides, leather, DVD rentals & more*

■**PUBLICATIONS**

➤**Metroline** 860/233-8334 *regional newspaper & entertainment guide, covers CT, RI & MA*

■**MEN'S SERVICES**

➤**MegaMates** 860/242-3600 *Call to hook up with HOT local men. FREE to listen & respond to ads. Use FREE code DAMRON. MegaMates.com.*

■**EROTICA**

Erotic Zone [AYOR] 35 W Service Rd (at Hwy 91 N) 860/549-1896 *8am-6pm*

Very Intimate Pleasures 100 Brainard Rd (exit 27, off I-91) 860/246-1875

■**CRUISY AREAS**

Bushnell Park [AYOR] S of Asylum Ave (downtown exit off I-84)

Meriden

■**CRUISY AREAS**

Hubbard Park [AYOR]

Middletown

■**ENTERTAINMENT & RECREATION**

Wednesday Night Supper Club [M,B,F,GO] 825 Saybrook Rd (at Tommy's Restaurant) 860/346-8686 *6:30pm-close Wed only*

Mystic

■**ACCOMMODATIONS**

House of 1833 B&B Resort [GF,SW,NS,WI,GO] 72 N Stonington Rd 860/536-6325, 800/367-1833

The Mare's Inn B&B [GF,NS,WC,GO] 333 Colonel Ledyard Hwy, Ledyard 860/572-7556

Mermaid Inn of Mystic [GS,WI,NS,GO] 2 Broadway 860/536-6223, 877/692-2632

The Old Mystic Inn [GF,NS,WI,GO] 52 Main St (at Rte 27), Old Mystic 860/572-9422

New Britain

■**CRUISY AREAS**

Martha Hart Park [AYOR] off Corbin Ave

New Haven

■**INFO LINES & SERVICES**

New Haven Pride Center [WC] 14 Gilbert St, West Haven 203/387-2252

■ACCOMMODATIONS

Linden Point House [GF,WI] 30 Linden Point Rd, Stony Creek **203/481-0472**

Omni New Haven Hotel at Yale [GF,WI,WC] 155 Temple St (at Chapel) **203/772-6664, 800/843-6664**

■BARS

168 York St Cafe [MW,F,GO] 168 York St **203/789-1915** *3pm-1am, till 2am Fri-Sat, also restaurant, dinner Mon-Sat, Sun brunch, patio*

The Bar [GS,D,E,F,WC] 254 Crown St (at College) **203/495-8924** *11:30am-1am, from 5pm Mon-Tu, more gay Tue*

Partners [MW,D,L,K,DS] 365 Crown St (at Park St) **203/776-1014** *5pm-1am, till 2am Fri-Sat, from 8pm Mon-Tue & Sat-Sun*

■NIGHTCLUBS

Gotham Citi Cafe [★GS,D,DS,18+,WC] 169 East St **203/498-2484** *9pm-4am, clsd Sun-Wed, more gay Sat*

■CAFES

Atticus Bookstore/ Cafe 1082 Chapel St (at York St) **203/776-4040** *7am-9pm*

■RESTAURANTS

116 Crown 116 Crown St **203/777-3116** *upscale tapas, great mixed drinks*

Beachhead [E] 3 Cosey Beach Ave, East Haven **203/469-5450** *4pm-close, from 1pm Sun, seafood, Italian, patio*

Bentara 76 Orange St **203/562-2511** *lunch Mon-Sat, dinner nightly, Malaysian, plenty veggie*

Claire's Corner Copia [WI,WC] 1000 Chapel St (at College St) **203/562-3888** *8am-9pm, till 10pm Fri-Sat, vegetarian*

Mezcal 14 Mechanic St (at Lawrence) **203/782-4828** *lunch Tue-Sun, dinner nightly, authentic Mexican*

Miya Sushi 58 Howe St (at Chapel St) **203/777-9760** *lunch & dinner, clsd Sun-Mon*

Soul de Cuba 238 Crown St **203/498-2822** *lunch & dinner, full bar*

■EROTICA

Fairmount Theatre 33 Main St Annex **203/467-3832**

Very Intimate Pleasures 170 Boston Post Rd, Orange **203/799-7040**

■CRUISY AREAS

East Rock State Park [AYOR] lower parking lot *days*

New London

■BARS

Frank's Place [M,D,F,E,K,WI,WC] 9 Tilley St (at Bank) **860/442-2782** *4pm-1am, till 2am Fri-Sun, patio*

O'Neill's Brass Rail [M,K,DS,WI] 52 Bank St **860/443-6203** *noon-1am, till 2am Fri-Sat*

Norwalk

■INFO LINES & SERVICES

Triangle Community Center 16 River St (at Elm St) **203/853-0600** *call for info*

■CRUISY AREAS

Merritt Pkwy Park & Ride [AYOR] Rte 15, exit 38 (Rte 123, New Canaan Ave) *main lot, turn right*

Ridgefield

■RESTAURANTS

Caputo's East Ridge Cafe 5 Grove St **203/894-1940** *11:30am-10pm, also mellow, upscale bar*

■CRUISY AREAS

Riverside on Rte 7 [AYOR] opposite Ridgefield Motor Inn

Stamford

■CRUISY AREAS

Cove Island Park [AYOR] intersection of Cove Rd & Weed Ave

Waterbury

■EROTICA

Video Book of Waterbury 90 S Main St **203/573-1066**

■CRUISY AREAS

Lakewood Park/ Twin Lakes Annex [AYOR] Farmwood Rd *days*

Delaware • *USA*

Westport

ENTERTAINMENT & RECREATION

Sherwood Island State Park Beach
left to gay area

Willimantic

EROTICA

Dan's Adult World 1110 Main St
860/456-3780

DELAWARE

New Castle

EROTICA

Bob's Discount Books 174 S DuPont
Hwy (near 13/40 split) 302/328-4812
clsd Sun, arcade

Rehoboth Beach

INFO LINES & SERVICES

Camp Rehoboth Community Center
37 Baltimore Ave 302/227-5620
*9am-5:30pm Mon-Fri, 10am-4pm
wknds, community center, HIV testing &
counseling, also magazine*

Gay & Lesbian AA 302/856-6452
noon Th

Narcotics Anonymous 37 Baltimore
Ave (at Camp Rehoboth center)
302/227-5620 *5:30pm Sun*

ACCOMMODATIONS

At Melissa's B&B [GS,NS,WI] 36
Delaware Ave (btwn 1st & 2nd)
302/227-7504, 800/396-8090

Bellmoor Inn [GF,SW,WI] 6 Christian St
(at Delaware) 866/227-5800,
800/425-2355 *upscale inn & spa*

Bewitched & BEDazzled B&B
[GS,NS,WI,WC,GO] 67 Lake Ave (at
Rehoboth Ave) 302/226-3900,
866/732-9482

Breakers Hotel & Suites [GF,SW,WC]
105 2nd St (at Olive) 302/227-6688,
800/441-8009

Cabana Gardens B&B [GS,SW,NS,GO]
20 Lake Ave (at 3rd St) 302/227-5429

Canalside Inn [GS,SW,NS,WI,WC,GO]
Canal at 6th 302/226-2006,
866/412-2625

The Homestead at Rehoboth B&B
[GF,NS,WI,WC,GO] 35060 Warrington Rd
(at Old Landing Rd) 302/226-7625

Lazy L at Willow Creek [GS,SW,WI,GO]
16061 Willow Creek Rd (at Hwy 1),
Lewes 302/644-7220

The Lighthouse Inn B&B
[GS,NS,WI,GO] 20 Delaware Ave (at 1st
St) 302/226-0407

The Ram's Head [MO,SW,N,GO] 35006
Warrington Rd (at John J Williams Hwy)
302/226-9171

Rehoboth Guest House
[MW,NS,WI,GO] 40 Maryland Ave (btwn
1st & 2nd Sts) 302/227-4117,
800/564-0493

The Royal Rose Inn [GS,GO] 41
Baltimore Ave (at 1st St)
302/226-2535

Shore Inn at Rehoboth [MO,WI,N,GO]
37239 Rehoboth Ave (across from
Double L Bar) 302/227-8487

Silver Lake Guest House
[MW,NS,WI,GO] 20388 Silver Lake Dr (at
Robinson Dr) 302/226-2115,
800/842-2115 *near Poodle Beach*

Summer Place Hotel [GS] 30 Olive Ave
(at 1st) 302/226-0766,
800/815-3925

BARS

The Blue Moon [★MW,E,DS,K] 35
Baltimore Ave (btwn 1st & 2nd)
302/227-6515 *6pm-2am, clsd Jan,
also restaurant*

Dogfish Head Brewings & Eats
[GF,F,E] 320 Rehoboth Ave (at 4th)
302/226-2739

Double L Bar [M,D,L,B,D,E] 622
Rehoboth Ave (at Church)
302/227-0818 *4pm-2am, patio*

Finbar Pub & Grill [GF,F,E] 316-318
Rehoboth Ave (at 4th) 302/227-1873
*from 3pm, from noon Fri-Sun, popular
happy hour*

Frogg Pond [GF,NH,F,E,K] 3 S 1st St
(near Rehoboth Ave) 302/227-2234
11am-1am

Rigby's Bar & Grill [GS,F,E,K] 404 Rehoboth Ave (at State St) 302/227-6080 *3pm-1am, from 10am Sun*

■ CAFES

The Coffee Mill [WI,GO] 127B Rehoboth Ave 302/227-7530 *7am-11pm, till 5pm (off-season)*

Lori's Cafe [GO] 39 Baltimore Ave (at 1st) 302/226-3066 *seasonal, call for hours, courtyard*

■ RESTAURANTS

Aqua Grill [E] 57 Baltimore Ave 302/226-9001 *seasonal, deck, full bar*

Back Porch Cafe 59 Rehoboth Ave 302/227-3674 *lunch & dinner, Sun brunch, seasonal*

Big Sissies Bar & Grill 37385 Rehoboth Ave 302/226-7600 *3pm-1am*

Buttery [R] 102 2nd St, Lewes 302/645-7755 *lunch, dinner, Sun brunch*

Cafe Sole 44 Baltimore Ave 302/227-7107 *lunch daily, dinner Wed-Sun, patio, also full bar*

Cloud 9 [D,WC] 234 Rehoboth Ave (at 2nd) 302/226-1999 *4pm-2am, Sun brunch from 11am, also bar*

The Cultured Pearl 301 Rehoboth Ave (2nd flr) 302/227-8493 *dinner only, pan-Asian/ sushi, cocktail lounge*

Dos Locos [★] 208 Rehoboth Ave (across from Fire Company) 302/227-3353 *11:30am-10pm, till 11pm Fri-Sat, Mexican*

Eden [★WC] 23 Baltimore Ave 302/227-3330 *dinner Tue-Sat, seasonal, wine list & martini bar*

Espuma 28 Wilmington Ave 302/227-4199 *5pm-10pm, clsd Mon, full bar*

Fins 243 Rehoboth Ave 302/226-3467 *dinner nightly, lunch Sat-Sun, fish house & raw bar*

Go Fish! 24 Rehoboth Ave 302/226-1044 *11:30am-9:30pm (in-season), authentic British fish & chips*

Hobos Restaurant & Bar 56 Baltimore Ave 302/226-2226 *from 11am (in-season)*

Iguana Grill 52 Baltimore Ave 302/727-5273 *lunch & dinner (summers), Southwestern, full bar, patio*

JD's Filling Station 329 Savannah Rd, Lewes 302/644-8400 *7:30am-9pm*

Jerry's Seafood 108 2nd St, Lewes 302/645-6611 *lunch & dinner daily, "home of the crab bomb"*

Mariachi [WC] 302/227-0115 *11am-9pm, till 11pm Fri-Sat, Mexican-Latin American*

Planet X Cafe 35 Wilmington Ave 302/226-1928 *seasonal, lunch, dinner, Sun brunch*

Purple Parrot Grill [K,DS,WC] 134 Rehoboth Ave 302/226-1139 *lunch & dinner daily, brunch Sun, karaoke & drag shows wknds*

Seafood Shack [K] 42 1/2 Baltimore Ave (at 1st St) 302/227-5881 *patio seating, live music wknds*

■ ENTERTAINMENT & RECREATION

Cape Henlopen State Park Beach 42 Cape Henlopen Dr, Lewes 302/645-8983 *8am-sunset*

Poodle Beach S of boardwalk at Queen St *popular gay beach*

■ BOOKSTORES

Proud Bookstore 149 Rehoboth Ave (at Village of the Sea Shops) 302/227-6969

■ RETAIL SHOPS

Leather Central 36983 Rehoboth Ave 302/227-0700 *leather uniforms, toys, accessories*

■ PUBLICATIONS

Letters from Camp Rehoboth 302/227-5620 *newsmagazine w/ events & entertainment listings*

■ GYMS & HEALTH CLUBS

Midway Fitness 34823 Derrickson Dr 302/645-0407

Wilmington

■NIGHTCLUBS

Crimson Moon Tavern [M,D,DS,V]
1909 W 6th St (at Union St)
302/654-9099 *6pm-2am, from 7pm Sat, clsd Sun-Tue*

■RESTAURANTS

Eclipse 1020 Union St 302/658-1588
lunch Mon-Fri, dinner nightly, upscale

The Green Room [E] 11th & Market St
(at Hotel Dupont) 302/594-3154
brkfst, lunch & dinner, Sun brunch, bar

Mrs Robino's [WC] 520 N Union St (at
Pennsylvania) 302/652-9223 *11am-9pm, till 10pm Fri-Sat, family-style Italian, full bar*

■MEN'S SERVICES

➤**MegaMates** 302/397-0111 *Call to hook up with HOT local men. FREE to listen & respond to ads. Use FREE code DAMRON. MegaMates.com.*

Washington

■INFO LINES & SERVICES

➤**Kasper's Livery Service** [GO] 201
Eye St SW 202/554-2471,
800/455-2471 *limousine service serving DC, MD & VA*

Triangle Club 202/659-8641 *various 12-Step groups, call for times*

■ACCOMMODATIONS

Beacon Hotel & Corporate Quarters
[GF,F,WC] 1615 Rhode Island Ave NW (at
17th) 202/296-2100, 800/821-4367

➤**The Bed & Breakfast at the
William Lewis House** [★M,GO] 1309 R
St NW (at 13th) 202/462-7574,
800/465-7574 *turn-of-the-century, hot tub, full brkfst wknds*

District of Columbia • *USA*

The Carlyle Suites Hotel [GS,F,WI,WC] 1731 New Hampshire Ave NW (btwn R & S Sts) 202/234-3200, 800/964-5377 *art deco, gay Sun brunch*

Donovan House [GS,WI] 1155 14th St NW (at Massachusetts Ave NW) 202/737-1200 *stylish hotel, rooftop bar*

Embassy Suites Hotel at the Chevy Chase Pavilion [GF,SW,WC] 4300 Military Rd NW (at Wisconsin) 202/362-9300

Grand Hyatt Washington [GF,SW,NS,WI,WC] 1000 H St NW 202/582-1234

Hamilton Crowne Plaza Hotel [GF,NS,WC] 14th & K St, NW 202/682-0111, 800/263-9802

Hotel George [GF,WI] 15 E St NW 202/347-4200, 800/546-7866

Hotel Helix [GF,WC,NS,WI] 1430 Rhode Island Ave NW 202/462-9001, 800/706-1202 *full-service boutique hotel, also Helix Lounge*

Hotel Monaco Washington DC [GF,WC,WI] 700 F St NW (at 7th) 202/628-7177, 800/649-1202 *boutique hotel*

Hotel Palomar [GF,F,SW,WI,WC] 2121 P St NW (at 21st St) 202/448-1800, 866/866-3070 *in Dupont Circle*

Hotel Rouge [GF,WI,WC] 1315 16th St NW (at Rhode Island) 202/232-8000, 800/738-1202 *also restaurant & bar*

Kalorama Guest House [GS,NS,WI] 2700 Cathedral Ave NW (off Connecticut Ave) 202/328-0860, 800/974-9101

Madison Hotel [GF,WI] 1177 15th St NW (at M St NW) 202/862-1600, 800/424-8577 *luxury hotel, also restaurant & spa*

Morrison-Clark Historic Hotel & Restaurant [GF,WI] 1015 L St NW (at Massachusetts Ave NW) 202/898-1200, 800/322-7898 *hotel in 2 Victorian town houses w/ very popular restaurant*

The River Inn [GF,WI,WC] 924 25th St NW (at K St) 202/337-7600, 888/874-0100 *also Dish + Drinks restaurant*

Savoy Suites Hotel [GF,WI,WC] 2505 Wisconsin Ave NW (near Georgetown) 202/337-9700, 800/944-5377 *also restaurant*

Topaz Hotel [GF,WI,WC] 1733 N St NW (at Massachusetts Ave NW) 202/393-3000, 800/775-1202 *also restaurant & bar*

■ BARS

Back Door Pub [M,MR-AF,S,WC] 1104 8th St SE, 2nd flr (at L St) 202/546-5979 *5pm-2am, till 3am Fri-Sat*

The Black Cat [GS,D,E,WC] 1811 14th St NW (at the Black Cat) 202/667-4490 *many queer events, live music, dance parties, also cafe*

DC Bear Crue [M,D,B,K] *Fri nights and Sun beer bust, check dcbearcrue.com for details*

DC Eagle [★M,L,WC] 639 New York Ave NW (btwn 6th & 7th) 202/347-6025 *4pm-2am, till 3am Fri-Sat, 2pm-2am Sun*

DIK Bar/ Windows [M,D,K,OC] 1637 17th St NW (at R St NW, upstairs) 202/328-0100 *4pm-2am, aka Dupont Italian Kitchen*

The Fireplace [M,NH,MR,V,WC] 2161 P St NW (at 22nd St) 202/293-1293 *1pm-2am, till 3am Fri-Sat*

Green Lantern [M,NH,D,B,K,V,WC] 1335 Green Court NW (in alley L St, btwn 13th & 14th) 202/347-4533 *4pm-2am, till 3am wknds*

JR's [★M,NH,F,V,YC] 1519 17th St NW (at Church) 202/328-0090 *2pm-2am, till 3am Fri, 1pm-3am Sat, 1pm-2am Sun*

Larry's Lounge [MW,NH,F,WC,GO] 1840 18th St NW (at T St) 202/483-1483 *4pm-1am, till 2am Fri-Sat, patio*

Mova [M] 2204 14 St NW 202/797-9730 *5pm-3am*

Mr Henry's Capitol Hill [GF,M,MR,E,NS,WC] 601 Pennsylvania Ave SE (at 6th St) 202/546-8412 *11:30am-11:30pm, also restaurant*

Washington • District of Columbia

Nellie's Sports Bar [M,NH] 900 U St NW (at 9th) **202/332-6355** *5pm-midnight, 3pm-2am Fri, from 11am wknds*

Number Nine [MW,NH] 1435 P St NW (at 15th St NW) **202/986-0999** *5pm-close*

POV Roof Terrace Bar [GF,F] 515 15th Street NW (at Alexander Hamilton Pl) **202/661-2400** *11am-2am, pricey cocktails; superior views of the White House & Lincoln Memorial*

Wisdom [GS,F] 1432 Pennsylvania Ave SE **202/543-2323** *5pm-2am, till 3am Fri-Sat*

■ NIGHTCLUBS

Bachelors Mill [★M,D,MR-AF,K,S,WC] 1104 8th St SE (downstairs at Back Door Pub) **202/546-5979** *11pm-3am Th-Sat only*

Blowoff [★M,A,D,$] 815 V St NW (at 9th, at 9:30 Club) *10:30pm-3am monthly, varying dates*

Chief Ike's Mambo Room [GF,D,E,WC] 1725 Columbia Rd NW (at Ontario Rd) **202/332-2211** *4pm-2am, till 3am Fri, 6pm-3am Sat*

Cobalt/ 30 Degrees Lounge [★M,D,E,DS] 1639 R St NW (at 17th) **202/232-4416** *5pm-2am, till 3am Fri-Sat*

Delta Elite [MW,D,MR-AF] 3734 10th St NE (at Perry St NE, in Brookland) **202/529-0626** *midnight-4am Fri-Sat only, ladies night Fri, men's night Sat till 5am*

Mixtape [MW,D] *2nd Sat only, alternative queer dance party, check mixtapedc.com for info*

She Rex [W,D,E,WC] 1725 Columbia Rd NW (at Ontario Rd, at Chief Ike's) **202/332-2211**

Town Danceboutique [★M,D,B,DS,18+] 2009 8th St NW (at U St NW) **202/234-8696** *9pm-4am Fri-Sat, 18+ Fri*

Ziegfield's/ Secrets [M,D,DS,S] 1824 Half St SW **202/863-0670** *9pm-close Wed-Sun, [DS] downstairs, strippers upstairs*

■ CAFES

Cosi [★WI] 1647 20th St NW **202/332-6364** *7am-11pm, till midnight Fri-Sat, 8am-10pm Sun, full bar from 4pm, make your own s'mores*

Hello Cupcake 1361 Connecticut Avenue NW **202/861-2253** *10am-7pm, till 9pm Fri-Sat, 11am-6pm Sun, cupcakes!*

Jolt 'n' Bolt [★] 1918 18th St NW (at Florida) **202/232-0077** *7am- 8:30pm, patio*

Soho Tea & Coffee [F,WI,WC] 2150 P St NW (at 21st St) **202/463-7646** *7am-1am, till 2am wknds, patio*

■ RESTAURANTS

18th & U Duplex Diner [GS] 2004 18th St NW (at Ave U) **202/265-7828** *6pm-11pm, till 12:30am Tue-Wed, till 1:30am Fri-Sat, American comfort food, full bar*

2 Amys Pizza [WC] 3715 Macomb St NW **202/885-5700** *lunch & dinner Tue-Sun, dinner only Mon*

Acadiana [R] 901 New York Ave NW **202/408-8848** *lunch Mon-Fri, dinner nightly, brunch Sun, Cajun, great bourbon selection*

Annie's Paramount Steak House [★WC] 1609 17th St NW (at Corcoran) **202/232-0395** *10am-11:30pm, till 1am Th & Sun, 24hrs Fri-Sat, full bar*

Banana Cafe & Piano Bar [E,P,GO] 500 8th St SE (at E St) **202/543-5906** *11am-10:30pm, till 11pm Fri-Sat, Puerto Rican/ Cuban, famous margaritas*

Bar Pilar 1833 14th St NW (at Swann St) **202/265-1751** *dinner nightly, Sun brunch, new American*

Beacon Bar & Grill [★] 1615 Rhode Island Ave NW (at 17th, at Beacon Hotel) **202/872-1126** *brkfst, lunch & dinner, popular Sun brunch, patio*

Busboys & Poets [★] 2021 14th St NW (at V St) **202/387-7638** *8am-midnight, till 2am Fri-Sat, 10am-midnight Sun, also bookstore, live jazz & poetry*

Cafe Japoné [★MR-A,K] 2032 P St NW (at 21st) **202/223-1573** *6pm-1:30am, till 2:30am Fri-Sat, Japanese, full bar, live jazz*

Cafe La Ruche 1039 31st St 202/965-2684 *dinner, Sun brunch, French, patio*

Cafe Saint Ex/ Gate 54 1847 14th St NW 202/265-7839 *lunch, dinner, Sun brunch, modern American, also Gate 54 club downstairs, popular Th [GF,D]*

Dupont Italian Kitchen & Bar [WC] 1637 17th St NW (at R St) 202/328-3222, 202/328-0100 *11am-11pm, bar 4pm-2am*

Firefly 1310 New Hampshire Ave NW 202/861-1310 *lunch & dinner, wknd brunch, plenty veggie*

Floriana [GO] 1602 17th St NW (at Q St NW) 202/667-5937 *dinner nightly, Italian, full bar, patio*

Food For Thought [WC] 1811 14th St NW (at the Black Cat) 202/667-4490 *8pm-1am, 7pm-2am Fri-Sat, mostly vegan/ veggie, indie/ punk music shows, readings*

Guapo's [WC] 4515 Wisconsin Ave NW (at Albemarle) 202/686-3588 *lunch & dinner, Mexican, full bar*

Jaleo [E,WC] 480 7th St NW (at E St) 202/628-7949 *lunch & dinner, tapas, full bar, Sevillanas dancers Wed*

Java Green Eco Cafe 1020 19th St NW 202/775-8899 *8am-8pm, 10am-6pm Sat, clsd Sun, organic cafe, plenty veggie/ vegan*

Level One 1639 R St NW (at 17th) 202/745-0025 *dinner nightly, wknd brunch*

Logan Tavern [GO] 1423 P St NW 202/332-3710 *lunch & dinner, wknd brunch, American comfort food, also bar*

Occidental Grill 1475 Pennsylvania Ave NW (btwn 14th & 15th) 202/783-1475 *lunch Mon-Sat, dinner nightly, clsd Sun, upscale, political player hangout*

Perry's 1811 Columbia Rd NW (at 18th) 202/234-6218 *5:30pm-11:30pm, popular drag Sun brunch, contemporary American & sushi, full bar*

Pizza Paradiso 2003 P Street NW 202/223-1245 *11am-11pm, till midnight wknds,Gluten-Free Crust*

Posto 1515 14th St NW 202/332-8613 *dinner nightly, terrific Italian*

Rasika [WC] 633 D St NW 202/637-1222 *lunch Mon-Fri, dinner Mon-Sat, clsd Sun, Indian*

Rice 1608 14th St NW (at 'Q') 202/234-2400 *lunch & dinner, Thai*

Rocklands 2418 Wisconsin Ave NW (at Calvert) 202/333-2558 *11am-10pm, till 9pm Sun, BBQ & take-out*

Sala Thai 1301 U St NW (at 13th) 202/462-1333 *lunch & dinner*

Smoke & Barrell [E] 2471 18th St NW 202/319-9353 *beer, bbq & bourbon*

Soul Vegetarian Exodus 2606 Georgia Ave NW 202/328-7685 *11am-9pm, till 3pm Sun (brunch), all-vegan menu, no frills*

Thaitanic 1326 14th St NW (at Rhode Island Ave) 202/588-1795 *lunch & dinner, Thai, plenty veggie*

Zaytinia 701 9th Street NW (at G St) 202/638-0800 *lunch & dinner, Greek/ Mediterranean*

■ENTERTAINMENT & RECREATION

Anecdotal History Tours [GF] 301/294-9514 *guided tours, by appt only*

Bike & Roll Washington DC [GF] 1100 Pennsylvania Ave NW (off 12th St, at Old Post Office Pavilion) 202/842-2453

Capital Bikeshare 877/430-2453 *look for the red bikes at parking stations around the city; join for 24hrs or longer*

Hillwood Museum & Gardens [R] 4155 Linnean Ave NW (at Tilden St NW) 202/686-5807 *10am-5pm Tue-Sat, Fabergé, porcelain, furniture & more*

Phillips Collection 1600 21st St NW (at Q St) 202/387-2151 *clsd Mon, America's first museum of modern art, near Dupont Circle*

■BOOKSTORES

G Books [GO] 1520 U St NW, BSMT (btwn 15th St & U St) 202/986-9697 *4pm-10pm, used gay books, mags, movies, pride items*

Kramerbooks & Afterwords Cafe & Grill [E,F,WC] 1517 Connecticut Ave NW (at Q St) **202/387-1400** *7:30am-1am, 24hrs wknds, also cafe & bar*

■RETAIL SHOPS

HRC Action Center & Store 1640 Connecticut Avenue NW **202/232-8621** *10am-9pm, till 10pm wknds, Human Rights Campaign merchandise & info*

Leather Rack 1723 Connecticut Ave NW (btwn R & S Sts) **202/797-7401**

Pulp 1803 14th St NW **202/462-7857** *11am-7pm, till 5pm Sun, cards, gifts, music*

Universal Gear 1529 14th St NW (btwn P & Q) **202/319-0136** *11am-10pm, till midnight Fri-Sat, casual, club, athletic & designer clothing*

■PUBLICATIONS

Metro Weekly 202/638-6830 *LGBT newsmagazine, extensive club listings*

Washington Blade 202/747-2077 *LGBT newspaper*

■GYMS & HEALTH CLUBS

Washington Sports Club 1835 Connecticut Ave NW (at Columbia & Florida) **202/332-0100**

■MEN'S CLUBS

Crew Club 1321 14th St NW (at Rhode Island) **202/319-1333** *24hrs*

Glorious Health Club [MO] 2120 West Virginia Ave NE **202/269-0226**

■MEN'S SERVICES

➤**MegaMates 202/822-1666** *Call to hook up with HOT local men. FREE to listen & respond to ads. Use FREE code DAMRON. MegaMates.com.*

■EROTICA

Pleasure Place [WC] 1063 Wisconsin Ave NW, Georgetown (btwn M & K Sts) **800/386-2386**

■CRUISY AREAS

Rock Creek Park [AYOR] Beach Dr N of Military Rd *area behind Francis swimming pool*

FLORIDA

Statewide

■PUBLICATIONS

➤**Ambush Mag 504/522-8047** *LGBT newspaper for the Gulf South (TX through FL)*

HOTSPOTS! Magazine 954/928-1862 *"South Florida's largest gay publication"*

Bonifay

■CRUISY AREAS

Wayside Park Hwy 79 *parking lot & woods 6 miles N of Bonifay at Holmes Creek bridge*

Boynton Beach

see also West Palm Beach

Bradenton

see also Sarasota

■MEN'S SERVICES

➤**MegaMates 941/527-0527** *Call to hook up with HOT local men. FREE to listen & respond to ads. Use FREE code DAMRON. MegaMates.com.*

Cape Coral

see Fort Myers

Clearwater

see also Dunedin, New Port Richey, Port Richey & St Petersburg

■ACCOMMODATIONS

Holiday Inn Select [GF,F,SW,WI,WC] 3535 Ulmerton Rd (Rte 688 W) **727/577-9100, 888/465-4329**

■BARS

Pro Shop Pub [★M,NH,B,GO] 840 Cleveland St (at Prospect) **727/447-4259** *1pm-2am*

■RETAIL SHOPS

Skinz 2027 Gulf to Bay Blvd (aka State Rd 60, at Hercules Rd) **727/441-8789** *10am-6pm, clsd Sun*

■MEN'S SERVICES

➤MegaMates 727/230-0030 *Call to hook up with HOT local men. FREE to listen & respond to ads. Use FREE code DAMRON. MegaMates.com.*

Cocoa

■BARS

The Ultra Lounge [M,NH] 407 Brevard Ave, Cocoa Village 321/690-0096 *6pm-2am, from 4pm wknds*

Cross City

■ACCOMMODATIONS

Southern Comfort Campground [M,SW,NS,WI,WC,GO] 50 SE 74th Ave (at Hwy 19) 352/498-0490, 352/210-6953

Daytona Beach

■ACCOMMODATIONS

The August Seven Inn [GF,NS,WI,GO] 1209 S Peninsula Dr (at Silver Beach) 386/248-8420 *1 block from ocean*

Mayan Inn [GF,SW,WI,WC] 103 S Ocean Ave 386/252-2378, 800/329-8622

The Villa B&B [GF,SW,N,NS,WI,GO] 801 N Peninsula Dr 386/248-2020

■BARS

Streamline Lounge [GF,D,E,WI] 140 S Atlantic Ave (at Streamline Hotel) 386/258-6937 *11am-3am, penthouse lounge*

■CAFES

Java Joint & Eatery 2201-E N Oceanshore Blvd, Flagler Beach 386/439-1013 *7am-4pm*

■RESTAURANTS

Anna's Trattoria [BW] 304 Seabreeze Blvd 386/239-9624 *5pm-10pm, clsd Sun-Mon, Italian*

The Clubhouse 600 Wilder Blvd (at Daytona Beach Golf & Country Club) 386/257-0727 *6am-7:30pm*

Frappes North [E,WC] 123 W Granada Blvd (at S Yonge St), Ormond Beach 386/615-4888 *lunch Tue-Fri, dinner nightly, clsd Sun*

Sapporo 501 Seabreeze Ave 386/257-4477

■PUBLICATIONS

Watermark 407/481-2243 *bi-weekly LGBT newspaper for Central FL*

■EROTICA

The Banned Bookstore 701 N Ridgewood Ave 386/248-0072

X-Mart Boutique 2591 W International Speedway Blvd 386/252-8707 *24hrs*

Dunedin

see also St Petersburg

■NIGHTCLUBS

Blur Nighclub [M,D,K,DS] 325 Main St 727/736-0206 *8pm-2am, clsd Sun-Mon*

■CRUISY AREAS

Honeymoon Island State Recreation Area [AYOR] end of Causeway Blvd *nude sunbathing & beach*

Fort Lauderdale

■INFO LINES & SERVICES

Greater Fort Lauderdale Convention & Visitors Bureau 100 E Broward Blvd, Ste 200 800/227-8669 (code 187), 954/765-4466

Lambda South Inc [WC] 1306 E Las Olas Blvd *meeting space for LGBT in recovery*

The Pride Center at Equality Park [WC] 2040 N Dixie Hwy, Wilton Manors 954/463-9005 *10am-10pm, noon-5pm wknds, outreach*

■ACCOMMODATIONS

15 FTL Guesthouse [M,SW,N,WI,WC,GO] 908 NE 15th Ave (at Sunrise) 954/523-7829, 888/234-5494 *Key West-style guest-house*

Alcazar Resort [MO,SW,N,NS,WI,GO] 555 N Birch Rd (at Terramar) 954/567-2525, 888/830-9931 *at the beach*

Bungalow Six Guesthouse [M,SW,WI,GO] 2726 NE 6th Ln (at 27th St), Wilton Manors 954/561-5454, 877/210-6317

Florida • *USA*

The Cabanas [★M,SW,NS,WI,GO] 2209 NE 26th St **954/564-7764, 866/564-7764** *riverfront, kayaks available, clothing-optional jacuzzi, spa*

Cheston House [MO,SW,N,NS,WI,GO] 520 N Birch Rd (at Viramar) **954/566-7950, 866/566-7950**

►**Coconut Cove Guesthouse** [MO,SW,N,NS,WI,GO] 3012 Granada St (at Birch St & A1A) **954/523-3226, 888/414-3226** *courtyard gardens*

Coral Reef Guesthouse [MO,SW,N,NS,WI,WC,GO] 2609 NE 13th Ct (off Sunrise Blvd) **954/568-0292, 888/365-6948** *very secluded*

Ed Lugo Resort [★GF,SW,WI,GO] 2404 NE 8th Ave (Wilton Manors) **954/275-8299**

Elysium Resort [MO,SW,N,NS,WI,GO] 552 N Birch Rd (at Terramar) **954/564-9601, 800/533-4744** *sundeck, near beach*

The Flamingo—Inn Amongst the Flowers [MO,SW,NS,WI,GO] 2727 Terramar St (near Birch) **954/561-4658, 888/286-8218**

The Grand Resort & Spa [MO,SW,N,NS,WI,WC,GO] 539 N Birch Rd (at Windamar) **954/630-3000, 800/818-1211** *sundeck, spa, gym, clothing-optional courtyard, gay-owned & operated since 1999*

Hotel Lush Royale [MO,SW,NS,WI] 2901 Terramar St (at Orton) **954/564-6442**

►**Inn Leather Guesthouse** [★MO,L,SW,N,WI,GO] 610 SE 19th St (at SW 1st Ave) **954/467-1444, 877/532-7729** *sling in each room & dungeon*

Island Sands Inn [GS,SW,WI,GO] 2409 NE 7th Ave **954/990-6499**

Liberty Apartment & Garden Suites [MO,SW,WI,WC,GO] 1501 SW 2nd Ave (at Sheridan), Dania Beach **954/927-0090, 877/927-0090**

Florida • *USA*

Manor Inn [MO,SW,N,NS,WI,GO] 2408 NE 6th Ave (at NE 24th St), Wilton Manors **954/565-8223, 866/682-7456**

Mary's Resort [M,SW,NS,WI,GO] 1115 Tequesta St (at 11th Ave) **954/523-3500, 866/805-6570**

Palm Plaza Resort [MO,L,SW,N,WI,WC,GO] 2801 Riomar St (at Birch) **954/260-6568**

Pineapple Point Guest House [★MO,SW,N,NS,WI,WC,GO] 315 NE 16th Terr (at NE 3rd Ct) **954/527-0094, 888/844-7295** *luxury guesthouse, gym*

The Royal Palms Resort & Spa [★M,F,SW,NS,WI,GO] 717 Breakers Ave **954/564-6444, 800/237-7256**

The Schubert Resort [★MO,SW,NS,WI,WC,GO] 855 NE 20th Ave **954/763-7434, 866/763-7435**

Sea Grape House Inn [M,SW,N,NS,WI,GO] 1109 NE 16th Pl (at Dixie Hwy) **954/525-6586, 800/377-8802**

Villa Venice Men's Resort [MO,SW,NS,WI,GO] 2900 Terramar St (at Orton) **954/563-6819, 800/445-7036** *2 blocks to beach*

Windamar Beach Resort [M,SW,N,WI,GO] 543 Breakers Ave (near Bayshore) **954/561-0039, 866/554-6816** *just steps from the gay beach*

▶The Worthington Guest House [MO,SW,NS,WI,GO] 543 N Birch Rd (at Terramar) **954/563-6819, 800/445-7036** *resort, clothing-optional hot tub*

■BARS

Andy's Lounge [GS,NH,CW] 12450 W State Rd 84, Davie **954/472-7081** *3pm-8am, Sun gay night*

Bill's [M,NH,DS,K,WC] 2209 Wilton Dr (off NE 23rd St) **954/567-5978** *2pm-2am, till 3am Fri-Sat, from noon Sat-Sun*

Boardwalk [★M,NH,S,18+] 1721 N Andrews Ave **954/463-6969** *3pm-2am, till 3am Fri-Sat, strippers from 5pm*

Cubby Hole [M,NH,B,F,WI] 823 N Federal Hwy (at 8th St) **954/728-9001** *11am-2am, till 3am Fri-Sat*

The Drive [M,F] 2390 Wilton Dr **954/561-9000** *11am-2am, till 3am Fri-Sat*

Georgie's Alibi [MW,F,V,NS,WI,WC] 2266 Wilton Dr (at NE 4th Ave) **954/565-2526** *11am-2am*

Infinity Lounge [M] 2184 Wilton Dr **754/223-3619** *3pm-2am*

Jackhammer in Exile [★M,D,B,L,WC] 2232 Wilton Dr (at Boom, in Wilton Manors) **954/630-3556** *Sun only T-dance*

Johnny's/ Club 11 [M,NH,F,S,WC] 1116 W Broward Blvd (at 11th Ave) **954/522-5931** *2pm-2am, from noon Sun, male dancers nightly*

The Manor Complex [MW,D,F,E,C] 2345 Wilton Dr, Wilton Manors **954/626-0082** *11am-11pm, also Epic nightclub, also restaurant & cafe*

Mona's [M,NH,K] 502 E Sunrise Blvd (at 5th Ave) **954/525-6662** *noon-2am, till 3am wknds*

Monkey Business [M,NH,C,DS] 2740 N Andrews Ave **954/514-7819** *9am-2am, till 3am wknds*

Naked Grape [GF] 2163 Wilton Dr (at NE 20th St), Wilton Manors **954/563-5631** *4pm-midnight, 2pm-1am Fri-Sat, clsd Sun-Mon, wine bar*

Noche Latina Saturday [M,D,E,MR] 2345 Wilton Dr (at Manor Complex), Wilton Manors **954/626-0082** *11pm Sat*

PJ's Corner Pocket [M,NH,MR-A,V] 924 N Flagler Dr **954/533-0257** *4pm-2am, from 7pm Sat, clsd Wed*

Ramrod [★M,B,L] 1508 NE 4th Ave (at 16th St) **954/763-8219** *3pm-2am, till 3am wknds, cruisy, patio, also LeatherWerks leather store*

Rumors [M,NH,F,WC] 2426 Wilton Dr, Wilton Manors **954/565-8853** *11am-2am, till 3am Fri-Sat*

Scandals [M,D,CW,B,E,F,K,OC,WC] 3073 NE 6th Ave, Wilton Manors **954/567-2432** *noon-2am, patio*

Shannon & Anthony's Corner Pub [GS,NH,GO] 1915 N Andrews Ave **954/564-7335** *11am-2am*

Sidelines Sports Bar [★MW,NH] 2031 Wilton Dr, Wilton Manors **954/563-8001** *3pm-2am, from noon wknds*

Smarty Pants [★M,NH,F,E,K,DS,WC] 2400 Oakland Park Blvd **954/561-1724** *9am-2am, till 3am Sat, noon-2am Sun*

The Stable Bar [M,NH,DS] 205 E Oakland Park Blvd (at Andrews) **954/565-4506** *2pm-2am, noon-3am Fri-Sat*

■NIGHTCLUBS

Boom [M,D,E,K,DS,V,GO] 2232 Wilton Dr, Wilton Manors **954/630-3556** *3pm-2am, till 3am wknds, T-dance Sun*

The Castle Lounge #2 [M,DS] 840 E Oakland Park Blvd, Wilton Manors **954/868-6346**

Dudes Bar [MO,E,P,S,V] 3270 NE 33rd St **954/568-7777** *2pm-2am, till 3am Fri-Sat*

Living Room [M,D] 300 SW 1st Ave (at Brickell) **888/992-7555** *gay Fri only*

Torpedo [M,D,S] 2829 W Broward Blvd (at 28th Ave) **954/587-2500** *10pm-dawn*

■CAFES

Cafe Emunah [F] 3558 N Ocean Blvd **954/561-6411** *11am-10pm, clsd Fri, sunset-1am Sat*

Java Boys [★WI] 2230 Wilton Dr, Wilton Manors **954/564-8828** *7am-11pm*

Jimmies Chocolates & Cafe 148 N Federal Hwy, Dania Beach **954/921-0688** *bistro w/ fresh fare & wine*

Storks [WC] 2505 NE 15th Ave (at NE 26th St, Wilton Manors) **954/567-3220** *6:30am-midnight, bear night Th*

■RESTAURANTS

La Bonne Crêpe 815 E Las Olas Blvd **954/761-1515** *7am-9:30pm, till 11:30pm Fri-Sat, patio*

Canyon 1818 E Sunrise Blvd **954/765-1950** *Southwestern, full bar*

Courtyard Cafe [GO] 2211 Wilton Dr **954/563-2499** *7am-11pm, 24hrs Th-Sat*

Flip Flops 3051 NE 32nd Ave **954/567-1672** *11am-9pm, till 10pm Fri-Sat, casual waterfront dining*

The Floridian [WC] 1410 E Las Olas Blvd **954/463-4041** *24hr diner*

Fuego Latino Cuban [BW] 1417 E Commercial Blvd **954/351-7754** *11am-10pm, till 11pm Fri-Sat, from noon Sun*

Galanga 2389 Wilton Dr, Wilton Manors **954/202-0000** *dinner nightly, lunch weekdays, Thai, also sushi*

Hi-Life Cafe [R] 3000 N Federal Hwy (at Oakland Park Blvd, in the Plaza 3000) **954/563-1395** *dinner, clsd Mon*

Humpy's 2244 Wilton Dr, Wilton Manors **954/566-2722** *11am-10pm, till 2am Th-Sat, pizza & panini*

J Marks Restaurant [GO] 1245 N Federal Hwy **954/390-0770** *11am-10pm, till 11pm Fri-Sat, full bar*

Kitchenetta [WC] 2850 N Federal Hwy **954/567-3333** *dinner nightly, clsd Mon*

La Bamba [WC] 4245 N Federal Hwy **954/568-5662** *more gay Mon night*

Lester's Diner [★WC] 250 State Rd 84 **954/525-5641** *24hrs, more gay late nights*

Lips [K,DS] 1421 E Oakland Park Blvd (at Dixie Hwy) **954/567-0987** *6pm-close, from noon Sun, clsd Mon, "the ultimate in drag dining"*

Mason Jar Cafe [GO] 2980 N Federal Hwy **954/568-4100** *11:30am-3pm Mon-Fri, dinner nightly, upscale comfort food*

Mojo [E] 4140 N Federal Hwy **954/568-4443** *open 4pm, clsd Sun, full bar*

Le Patio [GO] 2401 NE 11th Ave **954/530-4641**

PL8 Kitchen 210 SW 2nd St **954/524-1818** *lunch & dinner, till 2am wknds, small plates*

Rosie's Bar & Grill [★] 2449 Wilton Dr, Wilton Manors **954/563-0123** *11am-11pm*

SAIA [WI] 999 N Fort Lauderdale Beach Blvd **954/302-5252** *authentic Asian cuisine*

Sublime 1431 N Federal Hwy
954/539-9000 *5:30pm-10pm, clsd
Mon, vegan/ vegetarian*

Tequila Sunrise Mexican Grill [E]
4711 N Dixie Hwy **954/938-4473**
*11:30am-10pm, till 11pm Th-Sat, 1pm-
10pm Sun*

Tropics Cabaret & Restaurant
[GO,WC] 2000 Wilton Dr (at 20th)
954/537-6000 *lunch & dinner, Sun
brunch, till 3am Sat, piano bar*

■BOOKSTORES

Pride Factory 850 NE 13th St
954/463-6600 *10am-9pm, 11am-
7pm Sun*

■RETAIL SHOPS

GayMartUSA 2240 Wilton Dr (at NE
6th Ave) **954/630-0360** *10am-
midnight*

LeatherWerks [L,18+,GO] 1226 NE 4th
Ave (at 13th St) **954/761-1236**
*11am-8pm, noon-6pm Sun, leatherwear
& gear, adult toys; also inside the
Ramrod (8pm-close)*

Out of the Closet 2097 Wilton Dr,
Wilton Manors **954/358-5580** *10am-
7pm, till 6pm Sun*

The Poverello Center 2056 N Dixie
Hwy **954/561-3663** *thrift store to
support PWAs*

To The Moon [GO] 2205 Wilton Dr (at
6th Ave), Wilton Manors
954/564-2987 *10am-11pm, pride
gifts, cards & candy candy candy!*

■PUBLICATIONS

Genre Latino/ Latin Boys Magazine
*get the dirt on Latin nights & clubs in
Southern FL*

What's Happening Magazine
407/690-0809 *statewide LGBT entertainment & lifestyle magazine*

■GYMS & HEALTH CLUBS

Island City Health & Fitness 2270
Wilton Dr, Wilton Manors
954/318-3900 *5am-11pm, 8am-8pm
wknds*

■MEN'S CLUBS

Club Fort Lauderdale [★SW,18+,PC]
110 NW 5th Ave (at Broward)
954/525-3344 *24hrs*

Clubhouse II [V,PC] 2650 E Oakland
Park Blvd **954/566-6750** *24hrs, gym,
[L] Tue*

Slammer [MO,BYOB,PC] 321 W Sunrise
Blvd **954/524-2625** *8pm-close*

■MEN'S SERVICES

➤**MegaMates 954/761-7070** *Call to
hook up with HOT local men. FREE to
listen & respond to ads. Use FREE code
DAMRON. MegaMates.com.*

■EROTICA

Fetish Factory 855 E Oakland Park
Blvd **954/563-5777** *11am-9pm,
noon-6pm Sun*

Rock Hard 2301 Wilton Dr, Wilton
Manors **954/318-7625**

Secrets of Romance 10145 NW 46th
St, Sunrise **954/748-5855** *10am-2pm,
clsd Sun, cross dressing store*

Tropixxx Video 1514 NE 4th Ave (at
NE16th St), Wilton Manors
888/464-5988

■CRUISY AREAS

Beach at Sebastian St [AYOR]

Fort Lauderdale Beach [AYOR] opposite 18th St NE (btwn Oakland Park &
Sunrise Blvds) *dune area cruisy all night
& gay beach during the day*

Holiday Park [AYOR] Sunrise Blvd (on
right side at Federal Hwy) *exit I-95 at
Sunrise Blvd & head E toward beach,
open 5am-midnight*

Pompano Beach [AYOR] 16th St & A1A
(N of Atlantic)

Fort Myers

■INFO LINES & SERVICES

Gay AA Lambda Drummers [WC]
3049 McGregor Blvd (at St John the
Apostle MCC) **239/275-5111** (AA#)
8pm Tue & Sat in social hall

■BARS

Boston Ale N Tale [GF,F] 3441 Colonial
Blvd (in Sunsports Plaza)
239/274-8253 *4pm-closing*

The Office Pub [M,NH,B] 3704
Cleveland Ave (at Grove)
239/936-3212 *noon-2am, theme
nights*

Tubby's City Hangout [M,K,S,GO] 4810 Vincennes St, Cape Coral, FL **239/541-3540** *2pm-2am*

■NIGHTCLUBS

The Bottom Line (TBL) [MW,D,K,DS,V,WC] 3090 Evans Ave (at Hanson) **239/337-7292** *2pm-2am*

■RESTAURANTS

McGregor Grill [GO] 15675 McGregor Blvd, Ste 24 **239/437-3499** *11:30am-2am, from 4pm Sun, pub fare, some outdoor dining*

The Oasis [BW,WC] 2260 Dr Martin Luther King Blvd **239/334-1566** *breakfast, lunch & dinner*

■MEN'S SERVICES

➤**MegaMates 239/337-3100** *Call to hook up with HOT local men. FREE to listen & respond to ads. Use FREE code DAMRON. MegaMates.com.*

■CRUISY AREAS

Bowditch Point Recreational Park [AYOR] 50 Estero Blvd (at end of street), Fort Myers Beach

Bunche Beach [AYOR] John Morris Pkwy *S end of beach*

Horton Park [AYOR] Everest Pkwy (go E on Del Prado to end), Cape Coral *open sunrise to sunset*

Fort Pierce

■EROTICA

The Lion's Den Adult Superstore 7100 Okeechobee Rd (exit 129 off I-95) **772/466-6323**

Gainesville

■INFO LINES & SERVICES

Free to Be AA 3131 NW 13th St (The Pride Center) **352/372-8091 (AA#)** *7:30pm Sun, LGBT AA group*

Pride Community Center 3131 NW 13th St #62 **352/377-8915** *3pm-7pm, noon-4pm Sat, clsd Sun*

■BARS

Spikes [MW,NH,WC] 4130 NW 6th St **352/376-3772** *5pm-2am, till 11pm Sun*

The University Club [★MW,D,K,DS,S,YC,WC] 18 E University Ave (enter rear) **352/378-6814** *5pm-2am, from 9pm Sat, till 11pm Sun, 3 levels, patio*

■ENTERTAINMENT & RECREATION

Ponte Vedra LGBT Beach *Go N from Gainesville on Waldo Rd to N 301, then E on I-10. I-10 becomes 95. Go S on 95, then take a left. Go E onto Butler Blvd, which ends at A1A. Turn right onto A1A & then drive 5 to 7 minutes looking for Guana Boat Landing parking lot on the right.*

■BOOKSTORES

Wild Iris Books [TG,E,WC] 802 W University Ave (at 8th St) **352/375-7477** *1pm-9pm, till 5pm Sat, clsd Sun-Mon*

■CRUISY AREAS

Bolen's Bluff Dock [AYOR] US 441 S (past Praynes Prairie, on the right) *days*

Hollywood

■ACCOMMODATIONS

Rooftop Resort [GS,SW,N,WI] 1215 N Ocean Dr **954/925-0301** *the premier nudist swinger resort hotel in S Florida*

■NIGHTCLUBS

The Castle Lounge [M,DS] 1322 N Dixie Hwy **954/840-9683**

Trixie's II [M,TG,DS] 1322 N Dixie Hwy **954/793-5394** *7pm-2am*

■MEN'S SERVICES

➤**MegaMates 954/342-0342** *Call to hook up with HOT local men. FREE to listen & respond to ads. Use FREE code DAMRON. MegaMates.com.*

■EROTICA

Hollywood Spice 600 N State Rd 7 (btwn Hollywood Blvd & Johnson St) **954/983-4687** *arcade*

Pleasure Emporium 1321 S 30th Ave **954/927-8181**

Sensations Video 106 S State Rd 7 **954/894-7701** *arcade*

■CRUISY AREAS

Holland Park [AYOR] Johnson St (at Intracoastal)

Florida • *USA*

Inverness

■ACCOMMODATIONS

Camp David [MO,SW,N] 2000 S Bishop Point Rd 352/344-3445 *camping/ RV retreat, membership req'd*

Islamorada

■ACCOMMODATIONS

Casa Morada [GF,SW] 136 Madeira Rd 305/664-0044, 888/881-3030 *luxury all-suite hotel w/ private island*

Lookout Lodge Resort [GF,NS,WI] 87770 Overseas Hwy (at Plantation Blvd) 305/852-9915, 800/870-1772 *waterfront resort*

Jacksonville

■INFO LINES & SERVICES

Free to Be LGBT AA 634 Lomax St 904/399-8535 (AA#) *6:30pm Mon*

■ACCOMMODATIONS

Comfort Inn Oceanfront [GF,F,SW,WI,WC] 1515 N 1st St, Jacksonville Beach 904/241-2311, 800/654-8776

Hilton Garden Inn Jacksonville JTB/ Deerwood Park [GF,SW,WI,WC] 9745 Gate Pkwy (at Southside Blvd) 904/997-6600, 877/782-9444

Spring Hill Suites Jacksonville [GF,SW,NS,WI] 4385 Southside Blvd (at J Turner Butler Blvd) 904/997-6650, 888/287-9400

■BARS

616 Bar [MW,NH,B,K] 616 Park St (at I-95) 904/358-6969 *4pm-2am, patio*

AJ's Bar & Grill [W,D,F,E,DS,WC] 10244 Atlantic Blvd (in Regency Walk Shopping Ctr) 904/805-9060 *4pm-2am, from 1pm Sun, men very welcome*

Bo's Coral Reef [MW,NH,D,DS] 201 5th Ave N (at 2nd St), Jacksonville Beach 904/246-9874 *2pm-2am*

In Cahoots [M,D,A,MR,E,K,DS,V,WC] 711 Edison Ave (btwn Riverside & Park) 904/353-6316 *8pm-2am, from 4pm Sun, clsd Mon-Tue*

The Metro [★MW,D,DS,P,S,V,18+,WC] 859 Willow Branch Ave 904/388-8719 *2pm-2am, till 4am Fri-Sat*

The New Boot Rack Saloon [M,CW,K,BW,WI,WC] 4751 Lenox Ave (at Cassat Ave) 904/384-7090 *3pm-2am*

Park Place Lounge [MW,NH,D,WC] 931 King St (at Post) 904/389-6616 *noon-2am*

■RESTAURANTS

Al's Pizza 1620 Margaret St, Ste 201 904/388-8384 *in Riverside/ Little 5 Points area*

Biscotti's [★] 3556 Saint Johns Ave (Talbot Ave) 904/387-2060 *10:30am-10pm, till midnight Fri-Sat, from 8am Sat-Sun*

Bistro Aix 1440 San Marco Blvd 904/398-1949 *11am-10pm, till 11pm Fri, 5pm-11pm Sat, 5pm-9pm Sun*

European Street Cafe [★BW,WC,GO] 2753 Park St (at King) 904/384-9999 *10am-10pm, deli, patio*

Mossfire Grill 1537 Margaret St 904/355-4434 *lunch & dinner, full bar*

■RETAIL SHOPS

Metro Gift Shop 859 Willow Branch Ave (inside The Metro) 904/388-8719 *2pm-2am Fri-Sat only*

Rainbows & Stars 1046 Park St (in historic 5 Points) 904/356-7702 *10am-7pm Wed-Fri, noon-7pm Sat, noon-5pm Sun, clsd Mon-Tue*

■MEN'S CLUBS

Club Jacksonville [★SW,PC,WI] 1939 Hendricks Ave (at Atlantic Blvd) 904/398-7451 *24hrs*

■MEN'S SERVICES

➤MegaMates 904/721-9999 *Call to hook up with HOT local men. FREE to listen & respond to ads. Use FREE code DAMRON. MegaMates.com.*

■CRUISY AREAS

Willowbranch Park [AYOR] Park St (btwn Willow Branch Ave & Cherry St) *take Roosevelt Blvd to McDuff Ave & head toward river*

Key Biscayne

■CRUISY AREAS

Bear Cut Park [AYOR] in Crandon Beach Park *head W on beach; beware cops (even undercover)!*

Key West

■ INFO LINES & SERVICES

Gay & Lesbian Community Center
[WI] 513 Truman Ave **305/292-3223**
many meetings & groups

Keep It Simple (Gay/ Lesbian AA)
305/296-8654 (AA #) *8pm Mon-Sat,
5:30pm Sun*

➤**Key West Business Guild**
305/294-4603, 800/535-7797
see ad in front color section

■ ACCOMMODATIONS

Alexander Palms Court [GF,SW,WC,GO]
715 South St (at Vernon)
305/296-6413, 800/858-1943

Alexander's Guest House
[★MW,SW,N,WI,WC,GO] 1118 Fleming St
(at Frances) **305/294-9919,
800/654-9919**

Ambrosia House Tropical Lodging
[GF,SW,WI,WC] 615 & 618-622 Fleming
St (at Simonton) **305/296-9838**

Andrews Inn [GF,SW,NS,WI] Zero
Whalton Ln (at Duval) **305/294-7730,
888/263-7393**

The Artist House [GS,NS,WI] 534 Eaton
St (at Duval) **305/296-3977,
800/582-7882**

Avalon B&B [GF,SW,WI] 1317 Duval St
(at United) **305/294-8233,
800/848-1317**

Curry House [GS,SW,NS,WI] 806
Fleming St (at William) **305/294-6777,
800/633-7439**

Cypress House & Guest Studios
[GF,SW,NS,WI,WC] 601 Caroline (at
Simonton) **305/294-6969,
800/525-2488**

Equator Guest House
[MO,SW,N,NS,WI,WC,GO] 818 Fleming St
(at William) **305/294-7775,
800/278-4552**

The Grand Guesthouse [MW,WI,NS,GO]
1116 Grinnell St **305/294-0590,
888/947-2630**

Heartbreak Hotel [GS,GO] 716 Duval
St (near Petronia) **305/296-5558**

Heron House Court [GF,SW,NS,WI,WC]
412 Frances St (at Eaton)
800/932-9119

Island House [MO,F,SW,N,NS,WI,GO]
1129 Fleming St (at White)
305/294-6284, 800/890-6284 *cafe
& bar, very cruisy*

Key West Harbor Inn B&B
[GS,SW,NS,WI] 219 Elizabeth St (at
Greene) **305/296-2978,
800/608-6569**

Knowles House B&B [GS,SW,N,NS,GO]
1004 Eaton St (at Grinnell)
305/296-8132, 800/352-4414

La Te Da [★MW,S,21+,SW,WI,WC,GO]
1125 Duval St (at Catherine)
305/296-6706, 877/528-3320

Marquesa Hotel [★GF,SW,NS,WI,WC]
600 Fleming St (at Simonton)
305/292-1919, 800/869-4631 *also
Cafe Marquesa 6pm-10:30pm, full bar*

**The Mermaid & the Alligator—A
Key West B&B** [GS,SW,NS,WI,GO] 729
Truman Ave (at Windsor Ln)
305/294-1894, 800/773-1894

The New Orleans House Guesthouse
[M,SW,N,WI,GO] 724 Duval St, upstairs
(at Petronia) **305/293-9800,
888/293-9893** *sundeck, hot tub,
garden bar, play areas*

Pearl's Key West
[★GS,SW,NS,WI,WC,GO] 525 United St
(at Duval) **305/292-1450,
800/749-6696** *all-welcome historic
inn offering guesthouse ambiance*

Pilot House Guest House
[GS,SW,N,NS,WI,WC] 414 Simonton St (at
Eaton) **305/293-6600,
800/648-3780**

Seascape Inn [GF,SW,NS,WI] 420 Olivia
St (at Duval) **305/296-7776,
800/765-6438**

**Simonton Court Historic Inn &
Cottages** [GF,SW,NS,WI] 320 Simonton
St (at Caroline) **305/294-6386,
800/944-2687**

Tropical Inn [GF,SW,WI] 812 Duval St
(near Petronia) **305/294-9977,
888/611-6510** *hot tub, sundeck*

■ BARS

The 801 Bourbon Bar
[★MW,NH,D,K,C,DS,P,S] 801 Duval St (at
Petronia) **305/294-4737** *10am-4am,
from noon Sun, also Saloon One [M,L]*

Bobby's Monkey Bar [M,NH,E,K,WI,WC] 900 Simonton St (at Olivia) 305/294-2655 *noon-4am*

Bourbon Street Pub [★M,S,V,SW,WC] 724 Duval St (at Petronia) 305/293-9800 *11am-4am, from noon Sun, popular daytime bar*

Garden of Eden [GS,D,E,N] 224 Duval St 305/296-4565 *10am-4am, from noon Sun*

Hog's Breath Saloon [GF,F,E] 400 Front St 305/296-4222

La Te Da [★MW,F,C,P,WC,GO] 1125 Duval St (at Catherine) 305/296-6706

Virgilio's [GS,D,F,E] 524 Duval St (at Fleming in La Trattoria) 305/296-8118 *7pm-4am, martini bar, garden*

■NIGHTCLUBS

Aqua [★MW,D,E,K,DS,V,WC,GO] 711 Duval St 305/294-0555 *3pm-2am*

Bottle Cap Lounge [GS,D] 305/296-2807 *noon-4am*

■CAFES

Croissants de France [BW] 816 Duval St 305/294-2624 *bakery 7:30am-6pm, restaurant open till 10pm, patio*

■RESTAURANTS

Antonia's Restaurant [★] 615 Duval St (at Southard) 305/294-6565 *lunch & dinner, Italian, full bar*

Azur 425 Grinnell St 305/292-2987 *Mediterranean*

Blue Heaven [E] 729 Thomas St 305/296-8666 *great brkfst, also lunch & dinner*

Bo's Fish Wagon [★] 801 Caroline (at William) 305/294-9272 *lunch & dinner, "seafood & eat it"*

Cafe Sole 1029 Southard St (at Frances) 305/294-0230 *dinner nightly, Sun brunch, romantic, candlelit backyard*

Camille's 1202 Simonton (at Catherine) 305/296-4811 *brkfst, lunch & dinner, bistro, hearty brkfst*

El Meson de Pepe [E] 410 Wall St (in Mallory Sq) 305/295-2620 *Cuban*

The Flaming Buoy Filet Co [WC] 1100 Packer St (at Virginia) 305/295-7970 *lunch & dinner*

Grand Cafe Key West 314 Duval St 305/292-4740 *lunch & dinner*

Half Shell Raw Bar 231 Margaret St 305/294-7496 *11am-10pm, waterfront*

Hurricane Hole 305/294-8025, 305/294-0200 *10am-10pm, dockside bar*

Jack Flats [WC] 509 Duval St 305/294-7955 *11am-2am*

Kelly's Caribbean Bar Grill & Brewery 301 Whitehead St (at Caroline) 305/293-8484 *lunch & dinner, owned by actress Kelly McGillis*

La Trattoria Venezia 524 Duval St (at Fleming) 305/296-1075 *5pm-10:30pm*

Lobos Mixed Grill [BW] 5 Key Lime Sq (south of Southard St) 305/296-5303 *11am-6pm*

Louie's Backyard [★] 700 Waddell Ave (at Vernon) 305/294-1061 *11:30am-1am, deck*

Mangia Mangia [BW] 900 Southard St (at Margaret St) 305/294-2469 *dinner only, fresh pasta, patio*

Mangoes [WC] 700 Duval St (at Angela) 305/292-4606 *lunch & dinner, bar till 1am, "Floribbean" cuisine, full bar*

Michaels 532 Margaret St 305/295-1300 *dinner only, steakhouse*

New York Pasta Garden 1075 Duval St (Duval Square) 305/292-1991 *11am-10pm*

Nine One Five 915 Duval St 305/296-0669 *dinner only, tapas, full bar*

Sarabeth's 530 Simonton St 305/293-8181 *8am-9pm, American*

Seven Fish [★] 632 Olivia St (at Elizabeth) 305/296-2777 *6pm-10pm, clsd Tue*

Square One [WC] 1075 Duval St (at Truman) 305/296-4300 *4pm-11pm*

■ENTERTAINMENT & RECREATION

BluQ Sailing [M,GO] 200 Margaret St 305/923-7245 *all-gay sails*

Fort Zachary Taylor Beach *more gay to the right*

Gay & Lesbian Trolley Tour
305/294-4603

SkinnyDipperCruises.com Garrison
Bight Marina (Palm Ave)
305/240-0517 *clothing-optional
chartered cruises*

Venus Charters [★GO] Garrison Bight
Marina 305/304-1181

■BOOKSTORES

Key West Island Books 513 Fleming
St (at Duval) 305/294-2904 *10am-
9pm, till 6pm Sun*

■RETAIL SHOPS

Fausto's Food Palace 522 Fleming St
(at Duval) 305/296-5663 *8am-8pm,
till 7pm Sun, cruisy grocery store*

In Touch Gay Pride Store 706 ∧
Duval St (at Angela) 305/294-1995
9am-9pm, gay gifts

■GYMS & HEALTH CLUBS

Key West Island Gym [GO] 1119 White
St 305/295-8222

■MEN'S SERVICES

➤**MegaMates** 305/390-0390 *Call to
hook up with HOT local men. FREE to
listen & respond to ads. Use FREE code
DAMRON. MegaMates.com.*

■EROTICA

Fairvilla Megastore 520 Front St
305/292-0448

Leather Master 418 Appelrouth Ln
305/292-5051 *11am-10pm, noon-
8pm Sun*

Truman Adult Books & Video 922
Truman Ave 305/295-0120 *arcade*

■CRUISY AREAS

Higgs Beach [AYOR] on White St

Little Hamaca Park [AYOR] on
Government Rd *from downtown, go E
on Flagler Rd, turn right on Government,
follow past airport to park at end of road*

Lake Worth

see also West Palm Beach

■INFO LINES & SERVICES

Compass LGBT Community Center
[WC] 201 N Dixie Hwy 561/533-9699
*9am-9pm, till 7pm Fri, 3pm-7pm Sat,
clsd Sun*

■BARS

The Bar [MW,NH,D,K,GO] 2211 N Dixie
Hwy 561/370-3954 *2pm-2am, noon-
midnight Sun*

The Mad Hatter Bar & Grill
[M,NH,V,OC,GO] 1532 N Dixie Hwy (16th
Ave) 561/547-8860 *1pm-2am, noon-
midnight Sun*

■NIGHTCLUBS

Mara [M,D] 1132 N Dixie Hwy
561/827-6468 *7pm-2am Wed, 10pm-
2am Th-Fri, till 5am Sat, from 6pm Sun*

■CAFES

Mother Earth Coffee & Gifts [E,GO]
561/460-8647 *8am-7pm, till 10pm
Fri-Sat*

■RESTAURANTS

The Cottage [WC] 522 Lucerne Ave
561/586-0080 *dinner only, also bar*

Lakeland

■MEN'S SERVICES

➤**MegaMates** 863/248-0100 *Call to
hook up with HOT local men. FREE to
listen & respond to ads. Use FREE code
DAMRON. MegaMates.com.*

■CRUISY AREAS

Lake Morton [AYOR] *beware cops
(including undercover)!*

Largo

■BARS

Quench Lounge [M,D,K,S] 13284 66th
St N 727/754-5900 *2pm-2am*

■EROTICA

Buddies of Largo 13801 66th St
727/539-7979

Madison

■ACCOMMODATIONS

The Mystic Lake Manor
[MO,R,SW,N,WI,WC,GO] 850/973-8435
full brkfst, hot tub

Marathon

■ACCOMMODATIONS

Tropical Cottages [GF,V,NS] 243 61st St
Gulf 305/743-6048

Florida • *USA*

■ENTERTAINMENT &
RECREATION

Bahia Honda State Park & Beach 12
miles S of Marathon

Melbourne

■ACCOMMODATIONS

Crane Creek Inn B&B [GS,SW,NS,WI]
907 E Melbourne Ave 321/768-6416

■BARS

Cold Keg [MW,D,C,DS,18+,WC] 4060 W
New Haven Ave (1/2 mile E of I-95)
321/724-1510 *4pm-2am, clsd Sun*

■EROTICA

Hot Flixx 3369 Sarno Rd (Bldg A)
321/752-8805

MIAMI

Miami is divided into 3 geographi-
cal areas:
Miami—Overview
Miami—Greater Miami
Miami—Miami Beach/ South Beach

Miami—Overview

■INFO LINES & SERVICES

➤**Greater Miami CVB**
305/539-3000, 800/933-8448
*plan your Miami vacation! see ad in
front color section*

Switchboard of Miami
305/358-1640 *24hrs, gay-friendly
info & referrals for Dade County*

■ENTERTAINMENT &
RECREATION

Sailboat Charters of Miami [MW]
3400 Pan American Dr (at S Bayshore
Dr) 305/772-4221 *private sailing
charters aboard all-teakwood 46-foot
clipper to Bahamas & the Keys*

■PUBLICATIONS

Genre Latino/ Latin Boys Magazine
*get the dirt on Latin nights & clubs in
Southern FL*

What's Happening Magazine
407/690-0809 *statewide LGBT entertainment & lifestyle magazine*

Miami—Greater Miami

■BARS

The Dugout [M] 3215 NE 2nd Ave (at
NE 32nd St) 305/438-1117 *4pm-3am,
from 6pm Sat-Sun*

Eros Lounge [M,NH,K,DS] 8201 Biscayne
Blvd 305/754-3444 *4pm-3am, till
midnight Sun-Mon*

Jamboree [M,NH,DS] 7005 Biscayne
Blvd (at NE 70th) 305/759-0066
7pm-2am, dive bar, patio

■NIGHTCLUBS

Club Boi [M,D,MR,18+] 1060 NE 79th St
305/836-8995 *11pm-close Tue & Fri-
Sat*

Club Sugar [MW,D,MR-L,DS] 2301 SW
32nd Ave (at Coral Wy) 305/443-7657
*10:30pm-5am Th-Sat, 8pm-3am Sun,
clsd Mon-Wed*

Discotekka [M,D,18+] 950 NE 2nd Ave
(at Metropolis Nightclub)
305/371-3773 *after hours Sat only*

Johnny's Miami [M,D,S] 62 NE 14th St
305/640-8749 *5pm-5am, stripper bar*

Kaffe Krystal [GF,D,MR-L] 10855 SW
72nd St (at SW 107th Ave)
305/274-1112 *clsd Mon-Tue*

Space Miami [GF,D] 34 NE 11th St (at
NE 1st Ave) 305/375-0001 *popular
club w/ int'l visiting DJs*

■CAFES

Gourmet Station 7601 Biscayne Blvd
(at NE 71st St) 305/762-7229 *8am-
9pm, till 8pm Fri, clsd Sat-Sun*

■RESTAURANTS

Area 31 [WC] 270 Biscayne Blvd Way
(at the Epic Hotel) 305/424-5234
brkfst, lunch & dinner, amazing view

Cafeina 297 NW 23rd St (W of Miami
Ave) 305/438-0792 *5pm-3am Th-Fri,
from 9pm Sat, clsd Sun-Wed, tapas, also
gallery, bands, events*

Habibi's Grill 93 SE 2nd St (at NE 1st
Ave) 786/425-2699 *11am-8pm, clsd
Sun, Lebanese/ Mediterranean*

Jimmy's East Side Diner [WC] 7201
Biscayne Blvd 305/754-3692 *7am-
4pm*

Joey's 2506 NW 2nd Ave 305/438-0488 *lunch & dinner, clsd Sun, Italian, patio*

The Magnum Lounge & Restaurant [★NH,E,P,R] 709 NE 79th St 305/757-3368 *6pm-midnight, bar open 5pm-2am, clsd Mon*

Michy's 6927 Biscayne Blvd (at NE 69th) 305/759-2001 *dinner only, "luxurious comfort food"*

Ortanique on the Mile 278 Miracle Mile (at Salzedo), Coral Gables 305/446-7710 *Caribbean, full bar*

Ristorante Fratelli Milano [WC] 213 SE 1st St (at 2nd Ave) 305/373-2300 *11am-10pm*

Royal Bavarian Schnitzel Haus 1085 NE 79th St 305/754-0002 *5pm-11pm, German fare*

Soyka 5556 NE 4th Ct 305/759-3117 *lunch & dinner, wknd brunch, full bar*

UVA 69 6900 Biscayne Blvd (at NE 69th St) 305/754-9022 *11am-11pm, full bar, patio*

Wynwood Kitchen & Bar 2550 NW 2nd Ave 305/722-8959 *5:30pm-midnight, Latin, great art*

■ENTERTAINMENT & RECREATION

Awarehouse Miami 550 NW 29th St 305/576-4004 *artsy venue w/ live music, art shows & more*

Roam Rides 888/760-7626 *Vespa scooter rental, delivered to your hotel; also guided tours of Wynwood neighborhood art murals*

■BOOKSTORES

Lambda Passages Bookstore 7545 Biscayne Blvd (at NE 76th) 305/754-6900 *11am-9pm, noon-6pm Sun, LGBT/ feminist*

■RETAIL SHOPS

Creative Male 222 NE 25th St #116 305/573-3080 *noon-8pm, till 6pm Sun*

■MEN'S CLUBS

Club Aqua Miami [MO,SW,PC] 2991 Coral Wy (at S Red Rd) 305/448-2214 *24hrs*

■EROTICA

Miami Playground 2657 NW 36th St 305/638-4957 *24hrs*

■CRUISY AREAS

Matheson Hammock Beach [AYOR] on Old Cutler Rd (S of Kendall Dr) *also Indian Hammocks Park on 117 Ave in Kendall*

Miami—Miami Beach/ South Beach

■ACCOMMODATIONS

The Angler's [GS,SW,WI] 660 Washington Ave 305/534-9600, 866/729-8800 *restaurant & lounge*

Beachcomber Hotel [GF,NS,WI] 1340 Collins Ave (at 13th St) 305/531-3755, 888/305-4683

Blue Moon Hotel [GF,SW,WI] 944 Collins Ave 305/673-2262

The Cardozo Hotel [GF,F,WI,WC] 1300 Ocean Dr 305/535-6500, 800/782-6500

The Century [GF,F,NS,WI,WC] 140 Ocean Dr 305/674-8855, 877/659-8855

Chesterfield Hotel, Suites & Day Spa [GS] 855 Collins Ave 305/531-5831, 877/762-3477

Circa 39 Hotel [GF,SW,NS,WI,WC] 3900 Collins Ave (at 39th St) 305/538-4900, 877/824-7223

The Colony Hotel [GF,F,WI,WC] 736 Ocean Dr (at 7th St) 305/673-0088

Delano Hotel [GF,F,SW,WC] 1685 Collins Ave 305/672-2000, 800/697-1791

The European Guesthouse [MW,SWWI,GO] 721 Michigan Ave (btwn 7th & 8th) 305/673-6665

The Hotel [GF,F,SW,NS,WI,WC] 801 Collins Ave 305/531-2222, 877/843-4683

Hotel Ocean [GS,F,WI,WC] 1230-38 Ocean Dr 305/672-2579

Island House South Beach [GS,GO] 1428 Collins Ave 305/864-2422, 800/382-2422

Florida • *USA*

The King & Grove Tides [GS,F,SW,WI] 1220 Ocean Dr (at 12th St) **305/604-5070, 305/503-3268** *private beach area, also La Marea restaurant*

Lords of South Beach [M,F,SW,NS,WC] 1120 Collins Ave **305/674-7800, 877/448-4754**

The National Hotel [GS,F,SW,WI,WC] 1677 Collins Ave **305/532-2311, 800/327-8370** *luxury hotel on the beach*

Penguin Hotel [MW,F,WI,WC] 1418 Ocean Dr **305/534-9334**

The Raleigh, Miami Beach [GF,SW,WI,WC] 1775 Collins Ave (at Ocean Front) **305/534-6300, 800/848-1775**

South Seas [GF,F,SW,WI] 1751 Collins Ave **305/538-1411, 800/345-2678**

The Winterhaven [GS,WI,WC] 1400 Ocean Dr **305/531-5571**

■BARS

Buck15 Lounge [GS,E] 437 Lincoln Ln **305/538-3815** *10pm-5am, clsd Sun-Mon, more gay Th*

Creme Lounge [MW,NH,D] 725 Lincoln Ln N (upstairs from Score) **305/535-1163** *open Tue & Th-Sat*

Palace Bar & Grill [MW,F,DS,GO] 1200 Ocean Dr (at 12th St) **305/531-7234** *10am-1am, till 2am Fri-Sat*

■NIGHTCLUBS

Mova Lounge [MW] 1625 Michigan Ave (at Lincoln Rd) **305/534-8181** *3pm-3am*

Score [★MW,D,K,DS,V] 1437 Washington Ave **305/535-1111** *lounge opens 3pm, dance club 10pm-5am Tue & Th-Sat*

Twist [★M,D,K,DS,S,V,WC] 1057 Washington Ave (at 11th) **305/538-9478** *1pm-5am*

■CAFES

News Cafe 800 Ocean Dr (at 8th St) **305/538-6397** *24hrs, bookstore & bar*

■RESTAURANTS

11th Street Diner 1065 Washington (at 11th) **305/534-6373** *24hrs, full bar*

B&B: Burger & Beer Joint 1766 Bay Rd (at 18th St) **305/672-3287** *lunch & dinner*

Balans 1022 Lincoln Rd (btwn Michigan & Lennox) **305/534-9191** *8am-midnight*

Big Pink 157 Collins (at 2nd St) **305/532-4700** *8am-midnight, open late wknds*

David's Cafe II 1654 Meridian Ave **305/672-8707** *24hrs, Cuban*

Juice & Java [WC] 1346 Washington Ave (at 14th St) **305/531-6675** *9am-9pm, 10am-6pm Sun,, healthy fast food*

Larios on the Beach [WC] 820 Ocean Dr (at 8th) **305/532-9577** *11:30am-midnight, Cuban*

Nexxt Cafe 700 Lincoln Rd (at Euclid Ave) **305/532-6643** *11:30am-11pm*

Spiga 1228 Collins Ave (at 12th St) **305/534-0079**

Sushi Rock Cafe [★] 1351 Collins Ave (at 14th) **305/532-2133** *noon-midnight*

Tiramesu 721 Lincoln Rd **305/532-4538** *lunch & dinner, Italian*

■ENTERTAINMENT & RECREATION

Fritz's Skate & Bike 1620 Washington Ave **305/532-1954**

The Gay Beach/ 12th St Beach 12th St & Ocean *where the boys are*

Lincoln Rd Lincoln Rd (btwn Bay Rd & Collins Aves) *pedestrian mall*

South Beach Bike Tours [GO] **305/673-2002**

■RETAIL SHOPS

Pink Palm 723 Lincoln Rd (at Meridian Ave) **305/397-8097** *10am-11pm*

■GYMS & HEALTH CLUBS

Crunch 1259 Washington Ave **305/674-8222**

David Barton Gym 2323 Collins Ave **305/534-1660**

■MEN'S SERVICES

➤**MegaMates** **305/250-9909** *Call to hook up with HOT local men. FREE to listen & respond to ads. Use FREE code DAMRON. MegaMates.com.*

■EROTICA

Pleasure Boutique 1019 5th St
305/673-3311

Sensations Video 1317 Washington
Ave 305/534-2330 *24hrs*

X Spot 19800 S Dixie Hwy
305/255-2190 *24hrs*

■CRUISY AREAS

Haulover Beach Park [AYOR] North
Miami Beach *popular nude beach, N of
station #27; beware of cops (even
undercover)!*

Mt Dora

■ACCOMMODATIONS

Adora Inn [GS,NS,WI,GO]
352/735-3110 *full brkfst*

Naples

see also Fort Myers

■BARS

Bambusa Bar & Grill [GF,NH,F,V,GO]
600 Goodlette Rd N (at 5th Ave N)
239/649-5657 *4pm-midnight*

■CAFES

Sunburst Cafe [WC] 2340 Pine Ridge
Rd (at Airport Pulling Rd)
239/263-3123 *7am-3pm*

■RESTAURANTS

Caffe dell'Amore [BW,R,WC,GO] 1400
Gulf Shore Blvd N (at Banyan Blvd)
239/261-1389 *dinner only, clsd Sun-
Mon in summer, Italian*

The Real Macaw 3275 Bayshore Dr
239/732-1188 *occasionally have gay
events*

New Port Richey

■BARS

Chill Chamber [MW,D,E,WC] 3501
Universal Plaza (at Moog Rd & US 19)
727/844-3474 *2pm-2am*

Ocala

■BARS

Copa/ Tropix [M,D,DS,F] 2330 S Pine
Ave 352/351-5721 *2pm-2am*

The Pub [M,NH] 14 NW 5th St
352/857-7256 *8pm-2am*

Orlando

■INFO LINES & SERVICES

**GLBT Community Center of Central
Florida** 946 N Mills Ave
407/228-8272 *9am-9pm, noon-5pm
Sat-Sun*

■ACCOMMODATIONS

Eo Inn & Spa [GS,F,NS,WI] 227 N Eola
Dr (at Robinson) 407/481-8485,
888/481-8488 *boutique hotel, rooftop
terrace, hot tub, cafe on-site*

Four Points by Sheraton Studio City
[GF,SW,WI,WC] 5905 International Dr (at
Kirkman) 407/351-2100,
866/716-8105 *bar & restaurant*

Grand Bohemian Hotel Orlando
[GF,SW,NS,WI,WC] 325 S Orange Ave
407/313-9000, 888/213-9110

Hyatt Residency Grand Cypress
[GF,SW,WI,WC] 1 Grand Cypress Blvd
407/239-1234

The Parliament House Resort
[★MW,D,MR,F,S,YC,SW,WC,GO] 410 N
Orange Blossom Tr 407/425-7571
also 6 bars (open at 8pm)

Rick's B&B [M,N,SW,WI,GO] PO Box
22318, 32830 407/396-7751,
407/414-7751 (cell) *full brkfst, patio,
near Walt Disney World*

Wyndham Orlando Resort [GF,SW,WC]
8001 International Dr 407/351-2420

■BARS

Bar Codes [M,NH,B,L,BW] 4453
Edgewater Dr (at Thistledown Rd)
407/412-6917 *noon-2am, patio*

Bear's Den [M,B] 410 N Orange
Blossom Tr (at Parliament House)
407/425-7571 *6pm-2am, from noon
wknds, also restaurant*

Copper Rocket [GF,BW,WC] 106 Lake
Ave (at 17-92), Maitland
407/645-0069 *4pm-2am, also restaurant*

Hank's [M,NH,BW,WC] 5026 Edgewater
Dr (at Lee Rd) 407/291-2399 *noon-
2am, patio*

The New Phoenix [MW,NH,D,E,K,DS]
7124 Aloma Ave (at Forsythe), Winter
Park 407/678-9070 *6pm-2am, from
4pm Th-Sat*

Florida • USA

The Peacock Room [GF,NH,E] 1321 N Mills Ave (at Montana) 407/228-0048 4:30pm-2am, from 8pm wknds, art shows, live music

Savoy [M,S] 1913 N Orange Ave (at Berkshire) 407/898-6766 5pm-2am, male dancers nightly

Stonewall Bar [M,D,F,K,S,WC,GO] 741 W Church St (at Glenn Ln) 407/373-0888 5pm-2am

NIGHTCLUBS

Parliament House Resort [★MW,D,MR,F,S,V,18+,SW,WC,GO] 410 N Orange Blossom Tr 407/425-7571 10:30am-3am, 6 bars

Pulse Orlando [M,D,DS,18+] 1912 S Orange Ave (at Kaley St) 407/649-3888 9pm-2am, clsd Sun

Revolution [MW,D,MR,DS,S,V,18+,WC] 375 S Bumby Ave (at South St) 407/228-9900 4pm-close, from 10pm Sun, go-go dancers, patio

CAFES

Pom Pom's 67 N Bumby Ave 407/894-0865 11am-5am, 24hrs Fri-Sat, tea & sandwiches

White Wolf Cafe & Antique Shop [E,BW,WC] 1829 N Orange Ave (at Princeton) 407/895-9911 7am-9pm, till 10pm Fri-Sat, 8am-3pm Sun

RESTAURANTS

Dandelion Communitea Cafe [BW] 618 N Thornton Ave (at Colonial) 407/362-1864 11am-10pm, till 3pm Mon, till 5pm Sun, vegetarian/ vegan

Dexter's Thornton Park [E] 808 E Washington St 407/648-2777 lunch & dinner, also Winter Park & Lake Mary locations

Ethos Vegan Kitchen [WI,WC] 601-B New York Ave (at Fairbanks) 407/228-3898 11am-10pm, 10am-3pm Sun

Funky Monkey Wine Company [DS] 407/427-1447 5pm-11pm, sushi

Garden Cafe [WC] 810 W Colonial Dr (at Westmoreland) 407/999-9799 11am-10pm, clsd Mon, vegetarian Chinese

Hamburger Mary's Orlando [E,K,V,WC,GO] 110 W Church St (at Garland) 321/319-0600 11am-midnight, till 1am Th-Sat, full bar

Houston's [WC] 215 South Orlando Ave, Winter Park 407/740-4005 lunch & dinner

Hue 629 E Central Blvd (at N Summerlin Ave) 407/849-1800 lunch & dinner, full bar

Loving Hut [WC] 2101 E Colonial Dr (at Palm Dr) 407/894-5673 11am-9pm, from 3pm Sun, clsd Tue, vegetarian/ vegan

The Rainbow Cafe [MW] at Parliament House 407/425-7571 7am-11pm

BOOKSTORES

Mojo 930 N Mills Ave (at E Marks St) 407/896-0204 1pm-8pm, 3pm-6pm Sun, LGBT

RETAIL SHOPS

A Comic Shop 114 South Semoran Blvd, Winter Park 407/332-9636 11am-7pm, till 9pm Wed, till midnight Fri-Sat

Fairvilla's Sexy Things 7631 International Blvd 407/826-1627 gifts, adult toys

PUBLICATIONS

Hotspots 954/928-1862 weekly entertainment guide

Watermark PO Box 533655 32853 407/481-2243 bi-weekly LGBT newspaper for Central FL

What's Happening Magazine 407/690-0809 statewide LGBT entertainment & lifestyle magazine

MEN'S CLUBS

Club Orlando [SW,PC] 450 E Compton St (at Delaney Ave) 407/425-5005 24hrs

MEN'S SERVICES

►**MegaMates** 407/657-4500 Call to hook up with HOT local men. FREE to listen & respond to ads. Use FREE code DAMRON. MegaMates.com.

EROTICA

Fairvilla Megastore 1740 N Orange Blossom Tr 407/425-6005 9am-2am

Midnight News at Parliament House 407/425-7571 *6pm-2am*

■CRUISY AREAS

Mead Botanical Gardens [AYOR] Denning Rd & Garden St, Winter Park *take I-4 to Fairbanks exit & go E to Denning Rd, turn right & go 1 mile, on left*

Split Oak Park [AYOR] Narcoossee Rd *Take Narcoossee Rd, 5 miles S of 417, to Clapp Sims Duda Rd & turn left. Go for 1.5 miles to park*

Turkey Lake Rest Area [AYOR] *take FL Turnpike N from I-4 to milepost 263 btwn exits 259 & 265*

Palm Beach

■ACCOMMODATIONS

The Chesterfield Hotel [GF,SW] 363 Coconut Row 561/659-5800

■RESTAURANTS

Ta-boo [WC] 221 Worth Ave 561/835-3500 *11:30am-10pm, till 11pm Fri-Sat, cont'l*

■EROTICA

Adult Video Warehouse 501 Northlake Blvd, North Palm Beach 561/863-9997

Panama City

■ACCOMMODATIONS

Casa de Playa [MW,SW,NS,GO] 20304 Front Beach Rd, Panama City Beach 850/236-8436, 850/381-1351 *guesthouse, steps from Gulf of Mexico*

Wisteria Inn [GS,SW,NS] 20404 Front Beach Rd, Panama City Beach 850/234-0557 *tropical inn, hot tub*

■BARS

La Royale Lounge & Liquor Store [MW,NH,WC] 100 Harrison (at Beach Dr) 850/763-1755 *3pm-3am, till 4am Fri-Sat, from 7pm Sun, courtyard*

Splash Bar [M,NH,DS,S,V,18+,YC,WC,GO] 6520 Thomas Dr, Panama City Beach 850/236-3450 *6pm-2am, till 4am Th-Sat, also pride shop*

■NIGHTCLUBS

Fiesta Room [MW,D,DS,WC] 110 Harrison Ave (at Beach Dr) 850/763-1755 *3pm-3am*

■CRUISY AREAS

Tyndall Bridge [AYOR] on Tyndall Pkwy (toward Air Force base) *parking lot*

Pensacola

■INFO LINES & SERVICES

GLBT AA Group 716 9th Ave (at Jackson) 850/433-4191 (AA#) *6pm Sun*

■BARS

The Cabaret [MW,E,K,WC] 101 S Jefferson St 850/607-2020 *3pm-2:30am*

The Round-Up [★M,NH,B,L,V,WC] 560 E Heinberg St 850/433-8482 *2pm-3am, patio*

■NIGHTCLUBS

Emerald City [★MW,D,DS,S,18+,WC] 406 E Wright St (at Alcaniz) 850/433-9491 *3pm-3am, clsd Tue, patio*

■CAFES

End of the Line Cafe [★E,WI,WC] 610 E Wright St 850/429-0336 *10am-10pm, 11am-5pm Sun, clsd Mon, vegetarian; also live music & art*

■CRUISY AREAS

The Bluffs [AYOR] Scenic Dr *beware of cops!*

Pompano Beach

■NIGHTCLUBS

Club Cinema [GS,D] 3251 N Federal Hwy 786/597-4088

Swinging Richard's [M,F,S,$] 1350 SW 2nd St 954/357-2532 *5pm-2am, clsd Mon, gay strip club, nude dancers*

■RESTAURANTS

J Marks Restaurant [E,WC,GO] 1490 NE 23rd St (at Federal Hwy/ US1) 954/782-7000 *11am-10pm, till 11pm Fri-Sat, full bar*

Sarasota

■INFO LINES & SERVICES

Gay AA 7225 N Lockwood Ridge Rd (in Pierce Hall, Church of the Trinity MCC) **941/355-0847 (church #)** *7pm Sun & 7pm Th*

■ACCOMMODATIONS

The Cypress [GF,NS,WI] 621 Gulfstream Ave S **941/955-4683**

Turtle Beach Resort [GF,SW,WI,WC] 9049 Midnight Pass Rd **941/349-4554**

■NIGHTCLUBS

Throb [M,D,DS,GO] 2201 Industrial Blvd **941/358-6969** *3pm-2am, till 9pm Mon,Th & Sun*

■RESTAURANTS

Caragiulos 69 S Palm Ave **941/951-0866** *lunch & dinner, Italian-American*

■PUBLICATIONS

What's Happening Magazine **407/690-0809** *statewide LGBT entertainment & lifestyle magazine*

■MEN'S SERVICES

➤MegaMates 941/870-0800 *Call to hook up with HOT local men. FREE to listen & respond to ads. Use FREE code DAMRON. MegaMates.com.*

■CRUISY AREAS

Gravel Pit Lake [AYOR] Honore Ave (N of 17th St at Cooper Creek Park) *road has no sign, turn right after passing power lines*

South Beach

see Miami Beach/ South Beach

St Augustine

see also Jacksonville

■ACCOMMODATIONS

Alexander Homestead [GF,NS,WI] 14 Sevilla St **904/826-4147, 888/292-4147**

Casa Monica [GF,SW,NS,WC] 95 Cordova St **904/827-1888, 888/213-8903**

The Inn at Camachee Harbor [GF,F,WI] 201 Yacht Club Dr (at May St) **904/825-0003, 800/688-5379**

Our House B&B [GS,WI,GO] 7 Cincinnati Ave **904/347-6260**

■RESTAURANTS

Collage [★R] 60 Hypolita St **904/829-0055** *dinner nightly, "artful global dining"*

■CRUISY AREAS

Riverdale Park [AYOR] CR 13 (at SR 207) *take Hwy 207 to CR 305, follow through Racey Point & then Riverdale, days*

Vilano Beach Walkway [AYOR] *go N on A1A 2 miles, 2nd crosswalk over A1A, beachside*

St Petersburg

see also Tampa

■ACCOMMODATIONS

Bay Palms Waterfront Resort [GF,SW,NS,WI,GO] 4237 Gulf Blvd, St Petersburg Beach **727/360-7642, 800/257-8998**

Dicken's House B&B [GS,WI,GO] 335 8th Ave NE **727/822-8622, 800/381-2022**

Flamingo Resort [M,E,SW,F,WI,WC] 4601 34th St South **727/321-5000**

GayStPete House [M,SW,N,NS,WI,WC,GO] 4505 5th Ave N (at 45th) **727/365-0544**

La Veranda B&B [GS] 111 5th Ave N **727/224-1057** *1 block from the beach*

The Pier Hotel [GS,NS,WI] 253 2nd Ave N (at 2nd St) **727/822-7500, 800/735-6607**

Postcard Inn on the Beach [GF,F,SW,WI] 6300 Gulf Blvd **727/367-2711, 800/237-8918**

Villa Da Costa [MO,N,GO] 7555 46th Ave N **727/546-1477** *motel*

■BARS

Gran Central Garage [M,K] 2729 Cental Ave **727/258-4850**

Haymarket Pub [M,NH,WC] 8308 4th St N (at 83rd) **727/577-9621** *5pm-3am*

Lucky Star Lounge [M] 2760 Central Ave (28th St) *2pm-2am*

Oar House [MW,NH,F,K] 4807 22nd Ave S **727/327-1691** *9am-2am, from 11am Sun*

Sporters Bar [M,NH,B,CW,L,WC,GO] 187 Dr Martin Luther King St N **727/821-1920** *2pm-2am*

■NIGHTCLUBS

Georgie's Alibi [MW,NH,D,F,DS,S,V,WI,WC,GO] 3100 3rd Ave N (at 31st St N) **727/321-2112** *11am-3am, patio*

■RESTAURANTS

Central Avenue Oyster Bar 249 Central Ave **727/897-9728** *11am-midnight*

Sea Porch Cafe 3400 Gulf Blvd (at Don Cesar Beach Resort) **727/360-1884** *beach views*

Skyway Jack's 2795 34th St S **727/867-1907** *5am-3pm, Southern cooking (diner-style)*

■ENTERTAINMENT & RECREATION

Bedrocks Beach/ Sunset Beach W Gulf Blvd (at S end of Treasure Island, Sunset Beach) *popular park*

Dali Museum 1 Dali Blvd **727/823-3767, 800/442-3254**

Fort DeSoto Park Pinellas Bayway S

■MEN'S SERVICES

►**MegaMates 727/490-0800** *Call to hook up with HOT local men. FREE to listen & respond to ads. Use FREE code DAMRON. MegaMates.com.*

■EROTICA

XTC Adult Supercenter 4800 34th St S **727/865-6977** *arcade*

■CRUISY AREAS

Fort DeSoto Park [AYOR] Pinellas Bayway S *days, beautiful beach, after leave North Beach parking lot & cross rainbow bridge*

North Shore Park [AYOR]

Tallahassee

■INFO LINES & SERVICES

The Family Tree 5126C Woodlane Cir **850/222-8555** *LGBT community ctr*

■ACCOMMODATIONS

Hampton Inn Quincy [GF,SW,WI,WC] 165 Spooner Rd (Pat Thomas Pkwy), Quincy **850/627-7555**

■MEN'S SERVICES

►**MegaMates 850/385-9900** *Call to hook up with HOT local men. FREE to listen & respond to ads. Use FREE code DAMRON. MegaMates.com.*

■EROTICA

Rick's Toy Box 618 W Tennessee St **850/577-9000**

X-Mart Adult Supercenter [AYOR] 5021 W Tennessee (US 90) (Capital Circle W) **850/575-2169** *24hrs, arcade*

Tampa

see also St Petersburg

■ACCOMMODATIONS

Don Vicente de Ybor Inn [GS] 1915 Republica de Cuba **813/241-4545, 866/206-4545** *historic boutique hotel*

Gram's Place Hostel [GS,N,NS,WI] 3109 N Ola Ave **813/221-0596**

Hampton Inn & Suites [GS,SW,WI,WC] 1301 East 7th Ave **813/247-6700**

Hyatt Regency [GS,F,SW,WI,WC] 211 N Tampa St **813/225-1234**

Sawmill Camping Resort [M,D,E,K,SW,N,GO] 21710 US Hwy 98, Dade City **352/583-0664** *RV hookups, cabins, tent spots*

■BARS

2606 [★M,L,S,WC,GO] 2606 N Armenia Ave (at St Conrad) **813/875-6993** *3pm-3am, also leather shop from 9pm*

Baxter's [M,NH,K,S,WC] 1519 S Dale Mabry (at W Neptune) **813/258-8830** *noon-3am*

Body Shop Bar [M,NH,K,S,GO] 14905 N Nebraska **813/971-3576** *3pm-3am*

Bradley's on 7th [M,D,DS] 1510 E 7th Ave, Ybor City **831/241-2723** *4pm-3am*

Chelsea Lounge [★MW,NH,D,K,DS] 1502 N Florida Ave (at Hwy 275) **813/228-0139** *3pm-3am*

Florida • *USA*

City Side [MW,D,NH,K,WI] 3703 Henderson Blvd (at Dale Mabry) 813/350-0600 *11am-3am, patio*

Hamburger Mary's [MW,F,K,DS,WC] 1600 E 7th Ave (at N 16th St) 813/241-6279 *11am-11pm, till 3am wknds*

Reservoir Bar [GS,NH,WC] 1518 E 7th Ave 813/248-1442 *7pm-3am*

▇NIGHTCLUBS

The Castle [GS,D] 2004 N 16th St 813/247-7547 *10:30pm-3am, clsd Tue-Wed, theme nights*

Crowbar [GS,D,E,K] 1812 N 17th St 813/241-8600 *10pm-3am*

G Bar [★MW,D,DS,V,18+,GO] 1401 E 7th Ave 813/247-1016 *4pm-3am, clsd Sun-Mon*

Liquid [M,D,DS] 1502 E 7th Ave 813/248-6104 *4pm-3am, from 7pm Sat, clsd Mon*

Steam Fridays [★M,D,DS,18+] 1507 E 7th Ave (at the Honey Pot) 813/247-4663 *10pm Fri only, 3 flrs*

Valentines Nightclub [★M,D,K,DS,S] 7522 N Armenia Ave (btwn Sligh & Waters) 813/936-1999 *3pm-3am*

Ybor City Social Club/ Eagle Club [M,D,B,L] 1909 N 15th St (btwn 8th & 9th), Ybor City *10pm-3am, Eagle downstairs*

▇CAFES

Joffrey's Coffee [F,WI] 1600 E 8th Ave 813/247-4600 *7am-10pm, till midnight wknds*

Sacred Grounds Cafe [MW,E,WI] 4819 E Busch Blvd (at Hyaleah Rd) 813/983-0837 *6pm-midnight, till 2am Fri-Sat, open mic Mon*

Tre Amici [BW] 1907 19th St N 813/247-6964 *8am-5pm, till 11pm Th, clsd Sun, cafe & wine bar*

▇RESTAURANTS

Bernini 1702 E 7th Ave 813/248-0099 *lunch Mon-Fri, dinner nightly, Italian*

Centro Cantina 1600 E 8th Ave 813/241-8588 *Tex Mex, great balcony*

Columbia 2117 E 7th Ave 813/248-4961 *11am-close, from noon Sun, Cuban & Spanish*

Crabby Bill's 401 Gulf Blvd, Indian Rocks Beach 727/595-4825 *inexpensive seafood joint*

Gaspar's Grotto [E,K,WI] 1805 E 7th Ave 813/248-5900 *11am-3am, patio*

JJ's Cafe & Bar 1601 E 7th Ave (at N 16th St) 813/247-4125 *11am-10pm, till 2:30am wknds*

The Laughing Cat [WC] 1820 N 15th St 813/241-2998 *Italian*

The Metro Restaurant & Lounge [DS] 511 N Franklin St 813/225-1111 *4:30pm-11pm, till 1am Fri-Sat, clsd Mon, drag shows wknds*

The Queen's Head 2501 Central Ave, St Petersburg 727/498-8584 *4:30pm-2am, from noon wknds, clsd Mon, full bar*

▇ENTERTAINMENT & RECREATION

Picnic Island Picnic Island Blvd (across from the military base, on E side) *gay beach at end of park*

▇RETAIL SHOPS

King Corona Cigars 1523 E 7th Ave 888/248-3812 *local, handmade cigars.also cafe & bar*

The MC Film Festival 1901 N 15th St (at 8th Ave) 813/247-6233 *LGBT pride gift store*

Urban Body 715 S Howard Ave #1301 813/251-5522 *11am-7pm, noon-5pm Sun*

▇PUBLICATIONS

Watermark 813/655-9890, 877/926-8118 *bi-weekly LGBT newspaper for Central FL*

What's Happening Magazine 407/690-0809 *statewide LGBT entertainment & lifestyle magazine*

▇MEN'S CLUBS

Rainbow Cabaret [AYOR,WI] 4421 N Hubert Ave (behind Playhouse Theatre) 813/877-7585 *24hrs*

Tampa Men's Club 4061 W Crest Ave (at Hillsborough & Lois) 813/876-6367 *24hrs*

Wilton Manors • Florida

Ybor Resort & Spa [MO,WI,PC] 1512 E 8th Ave **813/242-0900** *full accommodations*

■**MEN'S SERVICES**
➤**MegaMates** 813/251-4744 *Call to hook up with HOT local men. FREE to listen & respond to ads. Use FREE code DAMRON. MegaMates.com.*

■**EROTICA**
Buddies Video 4322 W Crest Ave (at Hillsborough) **813/876-8083**

Planet X 9921 Adamo Dr **813/740-8484** *24hrs*

Playhouse Theatre [AYOR] 4421 N Hubert Ave (at Alva) **813/873-9235**

Tres Equis [★] 6220 Adamo Dr (behind Goldrush topless bar) **813/740-8664**

■**CRUISY AREAS**
Al Lopez Park [AYOR] N Himes Ave (1 blk S of Hillsborough), West Tampa *take I-275 N toward Ocala, take Hillsborough exit, then go W on Hillsborough Ave for 2 1/2 miles, turn left on Himes Ave*

Picnic Island [AYOR] Picnic Island Blvd (across from the military base, on E side) *gay beach at end of park, past the last parking lot & beyond the mangroves*

Venus

■**ACCOMMODATIONS**
Camp Mars [M,SW,N,GO] 326 Goff Rd **863/699-6277** *campground w/ cabins, tents, RV hookups, 2 hours from Fort Lauderdale & Miami*

West Palm Beach

■**ACCOMMODATIONS**
Grandview Gardens B&B [GF,SW,NS,WI,WC,GO] 1608 Lake Ave (at Palm) **561/833-9023**

Hotel Biba [GF] 320 Belvedere Rd **561/832-0094** *mid-century chic motor lodge*

Scandia Lodge [GS,SW,NS] 625 S Federal Hwy (at 6th Ave), Lake Worth **561/586-3155**

■**BARS**
Fort Dix [★M,D,NH,WC] 6205 Georgia Ave (at Colonial) **561/533-5355** *noon-3am, till 4am Fri-Sat, patio*

HG Rooster's [★M,NH,F,K,DS,S,WC] 823 Belvedere Rd (btwn Parker & Lake) **561/832-9119** *3pm-3am, till 4am Fri-Sat*

■**NIGHTCLUBS**
Monarchy [GF,D] 221 Clematis St **561/835-6661** *10pm-3am, till 4am Fri-Sat, clsd Sun, Tue & Th*

Respectable Street [GF,D,A,E,18+] 518 Clematis St **561/832-9999** *9pm-3am, till 4am Fri-Sat, clsd Sun-Tue, retro & new wave nights*

■**RESTAURANTS**
Rhythm Cafe [BW] 3800-A S Dixie Hwy **561/833-3406** *6pm-10pm, clsd Sun-Mon*

Thai Bay 1900 Okeechobee Blvd (in Palm Beach Market Pl) **561/640-0131** *lunch & dinner, clsd Sun*

■**ENTERTAINMENT & RECREATION**
MacArthur Beach Singer Island, N Palm Beach

■**BOOKSTORES**
Changing Times Bookstore 911 Village Blvd #806 (at Palm Beach Lakes) **561/640-0496** *10am-7pm, till 5pm Sat-Sun*

■**RETAIL SHOPS**
Eurotique 814 Northlake Blvd, North Palm Beach **561/684-2302** *10am-8pm, till 6pm Sat, noon-5pm Sun*

■**MEN'S SERVICES**
➤**MegaMates** 561/909-1100 *Call to hook up with HOT local men. FREE to listen & respond to ads. Use FREE code DAMRON. MegaMates.com.*

■**EROTICA**
Redlight Adult Video Outlet 3900 Byron Dr **561/629-7331**

■**CRUISY AREAS**
Jupiter Beach [AYOR] Jupiter *going S on A1A, it's the 3rd catwalk past Jupiter Key on the left*

Wilton Manors
see Fort Lauderdale

USA

GEORGIA

Athens

■ACCOMMODATIONS

Ashford Manor B&B [GF,SW,NS,WI,GO] 5 Harden Hill Rd (at Main St), Watkinsville **706/769-2633**

■BARS

The Globe [GF,F] 199 N Lumpkin St (at Clayton) **706/353-4721** *11am-2am, till midnight Sun, 40 single-malt scotches*

■NIGHTCLUBS

Forty Watt Club [GF,E,WC] 285 W Washington St (at Pulaski) **706/549-7871** *call for events, live music venue*

■CAFES

Jittery Joe's Coffee [WI,WC] 297 E Broad St (at Jackson) **706/613-7449** *7am-11pm, from 8am wknds*

■RESTAURANTS

The Grit [WC] 199 Prince Ave **706/543-6592** *11am-10pm, great wknd brunch 10am-3pm*

■CRUISY AREAS

Ben Burton Park [AYOR] Mitchell Bridge Rd (just before Oconee River Bridge)

Kangaroo Truck Stop [AYOR] Hwy 29 N

Atlanta

■INFO LINES & SERVICES

Galano Club 585 Dutch Valley Rd (at Monroe) **404/881-9188** *meetings throughout the day, LGBT recovery club*

■ACCOMMODATIONS

The Georgian Terrace Hotel [GF,SW,WI,WC] 659 Peachtree St NE (at Ponce de Leon) **404/897-1991, 800/651-2316** *hosted Gone w/ the Wind world-premier reception in 1939*

Glenn Hotel [GS,WI] 110 Marietta St NW (at Spring) **404/521-2250, 888/717-8851** *boutique hotel, also restaurant & rooftop lounge*

Hello B&B [MW,NS,WI,GO] 1865 Windemere Dr **404/892-8111** *hot tub*

Hotel Indigo [WI] 683 Peachtree St NE (at 3rd) **404/874-9200, 800/863-7818** *cozy, stylish no-frills hotel, workout room, also restaurant*

In the Woods Campground & Resort [M,N,SW,GO] 142 Casey Ct (at Hwy 327 & Hwy 51), Canon **706/246-0152** *campground w/ 36+ campsites & 20+ RV hookups*

Stonehurst Place Bed & Breakfast [GS,NS,WI,GO] 923 Piedmont Ave NE (at 8th St) **404/881-0722, 877/285-2246**

W Atlanta Midtown [GS,WI,SW] 188 14th St NE (at Juniper St NE) **404/892-6000** *stylish hotel, convenient location*

■BARS

Amsterdam [★M,D,F,V] 502 Amsterdam Ave NE **404/892-2227** *11:30am-close, video & sports bar*

Atlanta Eagle [★M,D,B,L,GO] 306 Ponce de Leon Ave NE (at Argonne) **404/873-2453** *7pm-3am, from 5pm Sat, clsd Sun, also leather store*

BJ Roosters [M,NH,WC,GO] 2345 Cheshire Bridge Rd NE (at La Vista) **404/634-5895** *2:30pm-3am, till midnight Sun, go-go boys*

Blake's on the Park [★MW,NH,F,K,S,V] 227 10th St (at Piedmont) **404/892-5786** *3pm-3am, from 1pm Fri-Sun, till midnight Sun*

Bulldogs [★M,NH,D,L,MR-AF] 893 Peachtree St NE (btwn 7th & 8th) **404/872-3025** *4pm-4am Sun-Fri, till 3am Sat, clsd Sun*

Burkhart's Pub [MW,NH,F,K,S,WC] 1492-F Piedmont Ave NE (at Monroe, in Ansley Square) **404/872-4403** *4pm-3am, from 2pm wknds, till midnight Sun, patio*

The Cockpit [M,NH,F] 465 Boulevard SE (off I-20) **404/343-2450** *5pm-close*

The Daiquiri Factory [MW] 889 W Peachtree St (at 7th) **404/881-8188** *11am-2:30am, the name says it all*

Eddie's Attic [GS,E] 515-B N McDonough St (at Trinity Place), Decatur **404/377-4976** *5pm-close Mon-Th, till 2am Fri-Sat, open 1 hr before showtime Sun, live music, comedy, also restaurant, rooftop deck*

Felix's on the Square [M,F,K,WC] 1510-G Piedmont Ave NE (Ansley Square) **404/249-7899** *2pm-2:30am, from noon Sat, 12:30pm-midnight Sun*

Friends on Ponce [MW,NH,V,WC] 736 Ponce de Leon NE (at Ponce de Leon Pl) **404/817-3820** *2pm-3am, from noon Sat, till midnight Sun, rooftop patio*

Halo Lounge [GS,F] 817 W Peachtree St (6th St, btwn W Peachtree & Peachtree) **404/962-7333** *9pm-3am, from 6pm Sat, clsd Sun*

The Hideaway [M,NH,OC,WC] 1544 Piedmont Ave NE #124 (at Monroe, in Ansley Mall) **404/874-8247** *2pm-2am Mon-Th, till 3am Fri-Sat, 12:30pm-midnight Sun*

Le Buzz [MW,NH,D,F,K,DS,S,WC] 585 Franklin Rd A-10 (at S Marietta Pkwy, in Longhorn Plaza), Marietta **770/424-1337** *5pm-3am, clsd Sun, DJ Fri, patio*

Mary's [MW,NH,D,K,V,WC] 1287B Glenwood Ave (at Flat Shoals) **404/624-4411** *5pm-3am, clsd Sun-Mon*

Mixx [M,NH,D,K,P,B,F] 1492-B Piedmont Ave NE (at Monroe, in Ansley Square) **404/228-4372** *4pm-2am, till 3am Fri-Sat, clsd Sun*

Model T [M,NH,F,K,DS,OC,WC] 699 Ponce de Leon NE #11 (at Barnett) **404/872-2209** *9am-3am, till midnight Sun, cruisy*

Opus I [M,NH,WC] 1086 Alco St NE (at Cheshire Bridge) **404/634-6478** *11am-3am, 12:30pm-midnight Sun*

Oscar's Video Bar [M,S] 1510-C Piedmont Ave NE (in Ansley Mall) **404/815-8841** *2pm-2:30am, clsd Sun*

Tripps [M,NH,F] 1931 Piedmont Circle (at Cheshire Bridge) **404/724-0067** *2pm-3am, 12:30pm-midnight Sun*

Woofs on Piedmont [★M,NH,F,GO] 2425 Piedmont Rd NE (at Lindbergh) **404/869-9422** *noon-2am, sports bar*

NIGHTCLUBS

Bliss [MO,D] 2284 Cheshire Bridge Rd **404/320-1924** *7pm-3am Wed-Sat, nude dancers*

The Heretic [★M,D,L,F,S,WC] 2069 Cheshire Bridge Rd (at Piedmont) **404/325-3061** *9am-3am, clsd Sun, till 11pm Mon-Tue, patio, theme nights, also Heretic Leathers store*

Swinging Richard's [M,S,$] 1400 Northside Dr NW (btwn I-75 & Northside Dr) **404/352-0532** *6:30pm-close, clsd Sun-Mon, gay strip club, nude dancers*

Traxx [M,D,MR-AF,$] **866/602-5553** *dance parties & events around Atlanta*

Wild Mustang/ Jungle [★MW,D,DS,$] 2115 Faulkner Rd NE (off Cheshire Bridge Rd NE) **404/844-8800** *10pm-3am, clsd Sun, also 11pm Mon for Stars of the Century [DS]*

XS Ultra Lounge [M,D,MR-AF] 708 Spring St (at 3rd) **678/705-5537, 866/602-5553**

CAFES

Apache Cafe [MR,F,E] 64 3rd St NW **404/876-5436** *food served, poetry readings, events, gallery*

Aurora Coffee 468 Moreland Ave **404/523-6856** *6:30am-9pm, from 7am wknds*

Intermezzo [WI] 1845 Peachtree Rd NE **404/355-0411** *noon-11pm, full bar, great desserts,*

RESTAURANTS

Amuse 560 Dutch Valley Rd **404/888-1890** *dinner only, wknd brunch, clsd Mon, full bar, int'l bistro*

Apres Diem 931 Monroe Dr #C-103 **404/872-3333** *11:30am-midnight, till 2am Fri-Sat, from 11am wknds, brunch Sat-Sun, French bistro, live jazz Wed, full bar*

Aria 490 E Paces Ferry **404/233-7673** *dinner only, clsd Sun*

Aurum [GS] 915 Peachtree St (at 8th St) **404/815-9426** *9pm-2am, till 3am wknds, lounge*

Bacchanalia/ Star Provisions/ Quinones 1198 Howell Mill Rd NW **404/365-0410** *dinner only, clsd Sun, upscale*

Buckhead Diner 3073 Piedmont Rd NE **404/262-3336** *lunch Mon-Sun, dinner nightly, Sun brunch, upscale diner fare*

Cafe Sunflower 2140 Peachtree Rd NW (at Bennett St NW) **404/352-8859** *lunch & dinner, clsd Sun, vegetarian*

The Colonnade 1879 Cheshire Bridge Rd NE **404/874-5642** *dinner nightly, lunch wknds, traditional Southern*

Cowtippers [TG,WC] 1600 Piedmont Ave NE (at Monroe) **404/874-3751** *11am-11pm, till midnight Fri-Sat, steak house*

Ecco [R,WC] 40 7th St NE **404/347-9555** *5:30pm-10pm, till 11pm Fri-Sat, till 10pm Sun, Italian*

Einstein's [★WC] 1077 Juniper St (at 12th) **404/876-7925** *11am-11pm, till midnight Fri-Sat, from 9am Sun, wknd brunch, full bar, patio*

The Flying Biscuit Cafe [★BW,WC] 1655 McLendon Ave (at Clifton) **404/687-8888** *7am-10pm, healthy brkfst all day; multiple locations*

Fresh To Order 860 Peachtree St NE (at 7th St NE) **404/593-2333** *11am-10pm, patio brunch Sun from 10am, healthy fast food, patio*

Frogs 931 Monroe Dr NE **404/607-9967** *11am-10pm, till 11pm wknds, Mexican*

Gilbert's Cafe & Bar 219 10th St NE (at Piedmont Ave) **404/872-8012** *dinner Tue-Sun, wknd brunch, food till 2am, bar till 3am, till midnight Sun*

Hobnob [WC] 1551 Piedmont Ave NE (at Monroe) **404/968-2288** *11am-11pm, till 3pm Sun*

Joe's On Juniper 1049 Juniper St **404/875-6634** *11am-2am, till midnight Sun, American*

Las Margaritas [E,WC] 1842 Chesire Bridge Rd **404/873-4464** *lunch & dinner, Latin fusion*

The Lobby at Twelve [R] 361 17th St **404/961-7370** *brkfst, lunch & dinner, upscale American*

Majestic Diner [★AYOR,WC] 1031 Ponce de Leon Ave (at Highland) **404/875-0276** *24hrs, diner right from the '50s, cantankerous waitresses included*

Mi Barrio Restaurante Mexicano [WC] 571 Memorial Dr SE **404/223-9279** *lunch Tue-Sat, dinner nightly, clsd Sun*

Murphy's [★WC] 997 Virginia Ave NE (at N Highland Ave) **404/872-0904** *11am-10pm, till midnight Fri-Sat, from 8am wknds*

No Más! Cantina [GO] 180 Walker St **404/574-5678** *lunch & dinner daily, wknd brunch, Mexican, also huge furniture & gift store*

Pastries A Go Go [WC] 235 Ponce De Leon Place (at Commerce), Decatur **404/373-3423** *7:30am-4pm, clsd Tue, delicious baked goods*

R Thomas Deluxe Grill [BW,WC] 1812 Peachtree Rd NW (btwn 26th & 27th) **404/872-2942, 404/881-0246** *24hrs, healthy Californian/ juice bar, popular late night*

Ria's Bluebird Cafe [★BW,TG,WC] 421 Memorial Dr (at Cherokee) **404/521-3737** *8am-3pm, gourmet brunch in quaint old diner in Grant Park*

Roxx Tavern & Diner [WC] 1824 Cheshire Bridge Rd NE (at Manchester) **404/892-4541** *lunch & dinner, Sun brunch, patio*

Sawicki's 250 W Ponce De Leon Ave, Decatur **404/377-0992** *11am-7pm, till 8pm Fri-Sat, noon-5pm Sun, deli, great sandwiches*

The Shed at Glenwood 475 Bill Kennedy Way **404/835-4363** *dinner nightly, Sun brunch, also bar*

Swan Coach House 3130 Slaton Dr NW **404/261-0636** *11am-2:30pm, clsd Sun, also gift shop & art gallery*

Table 1280 1280 Peachtree St NE (at Woodruff Arts Center) **404/897-1280** *lunch & dinner, wknd brunch, clsd Mon, also lounge, upscale American & tapas*

TWO urban licks [E,R] 820 Ralph McGill Blvd **404/522-4622** *dinner nightly, brunch Sun, great grill, full bar, live blues*

The Vortex [18+] 438 Moreland Ave NE (at Euclid) **404/688-1828** *11am-midnight, till 3am wknds, biker ambiance, great burgers*

Watershed [WC] 1820 Peachtree St **404/809-3561** *11am-10pm, Sun brunch, wine bar, also gift shop, owned by Emily Saliers of the Indigo Girls*

■ ENTERTAINMENT & RECREATION

AIDS Memorial Quilt/ NAMES Project 14th St **404/688-5500** *visit The Quilt at the foundation offices*

Ansley Park Playhouse 1545 Peachtree St **404/941-7453** *some LGBT-themed productions*

Joining Hearts, Inc Piedmont Park Pool **678/318-1446** *great dance/ pool party in July, 100% of every dollar raised is donated*

Little 5 Points, Moreland & Euclid Ave S of Ponce de Leon Ave *hip & funky area w/ too many restaurants & shops to list*

Martin Luther King, Jr Center for Non-Violent Social Change 449 Auburn Ave NE **404/526-8900** *includes King's birth home, the church where he preached in the '60s & his gravesite*

Piedmont Park [AYOR] NE of Piedmont at 10th *hilltop sunbathing*

■ BOOKSTORES

Brushstrokes/ Capulets [GO] 1510 Piedmont Ave NE (near Monroe) **404/876-6567** *10am-10pm, till 11pm Fri-Sat, LGBT variety store*

■ RETAIL SHOPS

The Boy Next Door 1447 Piedmont Ave NE (btwn 14th & Monroe) **404/873-2664** *10am-8pm, noon-6pm Sun, clothing*

The Junkman's Daughter [WC] 464 Moreland Ave NE (at Euclid) **404/577-3188** *11am-7pm, till 8pm Fri, till 9pm Sat, from noon Sun, hip stuff*

■ PUBLICATIONS

David Atlanta **404/418-8901** *gay entertainment magazine w/ extensive nightlife calendar, maps & directory*

Fenuxe **404/835-2016** *the voice of Atlanta's Gay Community*

Georgia Voice **404/815-6941** *bi-weekly LGBT publication*

■ GYMS & HEALTH CLUBS

Gravity Fitness 2201 Faulkner Rd (off Cheshire Bridge Rd) **404/486-0506** *day passes available*

Urban Body Fitness 500 Amsterdam Ave **404/885-1499**

■ MEN'S CLUBS

The Den [MO,MR-AF,PC] 2135 Liddell Dr (at Cheshire Bridge) **404/292-7746**

Flex [SW,WI] 76 4th St NW (at Spring St) **404/815-0456** *24hrs*

Manifest4u 2103 Faulkner Rd NE (off Cheshire Bridge Rd) **404/549-2815** *10pm-3am Th, till 6am Fri-Sat, from 9pm Sun, theme nights, also yoga classes*

■ MEN'S SERVICES

➤**MegaMates** **404/244-7000** *Call to hook up with HOT local men. FREE to listen & respond to ads. Use FREE code DAMRON. MegaMates.com.*

■ EROTICA

Inserection 1739 Cheshire Bridge Rd **404/262-9113**

Southern Nights Videos 2205 Cheshire Br Rd (at Woodland Ave NE) **404/728-0701** *24hrs*

Starship 2275 Cheshire Bridge Rd **404/320-9101, 800/215-1053** *24hrs, many locations in Atlanta*

■ CRUISY AREAS

Piedmont Park [AYOR] 10th St (at Monroe)

Georgia • *USA*

Augusta

■ACCOMMODATIONS

▶**Parliament Resort**
[MO,L,V,18+,BYOB,SW,N,WI,PC,GO] 1250 Gordon Hwy **706/722–1155** *24hrs, motel complex w/ hot tub, video lounge, maze, novice dungeon*

■BARS

The Filling Station [M] 1258 Gordon Hwy **706/828–7400** *8pm-close Th-Sat only*

■NIGHTCLUBS

Club Argos [NH,D,TG,K,DS,V,GO] 1923 Walton Way (at Heckle) **706/481–8829** *9pm-2am, clsd Sun-Tue*

Cartersville

■EROTICA

The Lion's Den Adult Superstore 33 Kent Dr (exit 296, off I-75) **770/607–5113** *24hrs*

Dewy Rose

■ACCOMMODATIONS

The River's Edge [M,F,E,SW,N,NS,WC] 2311 Pulliam Mill Rd **706/213–8081** *cabins, camping, RV*

Lake Lanier

■ENTERTAINMENT & RECREATION

Gay Cove btwn Athens Park Rd & Frank Boyd Rd (Channel Marker 21) *a rainbow rendezvous for the pleasure-boating crowd—look for the rainbow flag*

Macon

■CRUISY AREAS

Central City Park [AYOR] Walnut St (at 7th)

Rest Area [AYOR] I-475 bypass (off I-75, after Mercer University Dr)

Savannah

■ INFO LINES & SERVICES

First City Network 307 E Harris St
912/236-2489 *info & events line,
social group, newsletter*

■ ACCOMMODATIONS

The Azalea Inn & Gardens
[GF,SW,NS,WI] 217 E Huntingdon St (at
Abercorn St) 912/236-6080,
800/582-3823 *19th-c Italianate,
vintage gardens, full Southern brkfst*

Catherine Ward House Inn [GS,WI,NS]
118 E Waldburg St (at Abercorn)
912/234-8564, 800/327-4270 *full
brkfst*

The Galloway House [GS] 107 E 35th
St 912/658-4419 *furnished apts,
cont'l brkfst*

Kehoe House [GF,WI] 123 Habersham
St 912/232-1020, 800/820-1020
full brkfst

Mansion on Forsyth Park
[GF,SW,NS,WI,WC] 700 Drayton St
912/238-5158, 888/213-3671

Statesboro Inn [GF,WI] 106 S Main,
Statesboro 912/489-8628,
800/846-9466 *full brkfst*

Thunderbird Inn [GF,NS,WI,GO] 611 W
Oglethorpe Ave (at MLK Blvd)
912/232-2661, 866/324-2661

■ BARS

Chuck's Bar [GS,NH,YC] 305 W River St
912/232-1005 *hrs vary, clsd Sun*

■ NIGHTCLUBS

Club One [MW,D,F,K,C,DS,S,V] 1
Jefferson St (at Bay) 912/232-0200
*5pm-3am, till 2am Sun, "home of the
Lady Chablis"*

■ CAFES

Cafe Gelatohhh 202 W St Julian St
912/234-2344 *artisanal gelato; also
coffee, sandwiches*

The Sentient Bean 13 E Park Ave (at
Bull St) 912/232-4447 *7am-10pm,
food served, vegetarian/vegan, shows at
night*

Wright Square Cafe [★GO] 21 W York
St 912/238-1150 *7:30am-5pm, from
9am Sat, clsd Sun, patio*

■ RESTAURANTS

The 5 Spot [★] 4430 Habersham St
912/777-3021
7am-10pm, till 11pm Fri-Sat

B Matthews [WC] 325 E Bay St
912/233-1319 *8am-9pm, till 10pm
Fri-Sat, till 3pm Sun, casual bistro*

Bar Food [WC,GO] 4523 Habersham St
912/355-5956 *4pm-1am, clsd Sun*

Casbah 20 E Broughton St
912/234-6168 *dinner nightly,
Moroccan, also entertainment*

Churchill's Pub 13 W Bay St
912/232-8501 *5pm-1am*

Clary's Cafe 404 Abercorn (at Jones)
912/233-0402 *7am-4pm, from 8am
Sat-Sun, country cookin*

The Distillery [WC] 416 W Liberty St
912/236-1772 *11am-1am, till 3am
Fri-Sat, noon-9pm Sun*

Fannie's on the Beach [D,E] 1613
Strand Ave (at Silver Ave), Tybee Island
912/786-6109 *noon-11pm, till 2am
wknds*

Firefly Cafe [WC] 321 Habersham St
912/234-1971

Green Truck Neighborhood Pub
[BW,WC,GO] 2430 Habersham St
912/234-5885 *11am-11pm, clsd Sun-
Mon*

Local 11 Ten 1110 Bull St
912/790-9000 *dinner nightly, upscale
dining in a restored 1950s bank; also
Perch rooftop bar*

Mellow Mushroom [WC] 11 W Liberty
St 912/495-0705 *11am-10pm, pizza &
beer*

Olde Pink House/ Planters Tavern [E]
23 Abercorn St 912/232-4286
*upscale Southern dining upstairs, cozy
bar downstairs, live jazz*

Rocks on the Roof 102 W Bay St (on
the roof of The Bohemian Hotel)
912/721-3900 *7am-10pm, till 11pm
wknds, fantastic views*

Soho South Cafe 12 W Liberty St
912/233-1633 *11am-4pm daily,
eclectic*

Hawaii • *USA*

■ENTERTAINMENT &
RECREATION

Savannah Walks, Inc [GF]
912/238-9255, 888/728-9255
walking tours of downtown Savannah

■MEN'S SERVICES

➤MegaMates 912/344-9494 *Call to
hook up with HOT local men. FREE to
listen & respond to ads. Use FREE code
DAMRON. MegaMates.com.*

Unadilla

■EROTICA

Lion's Den 790 Pine St (Exit 121, off I-
75) 478/627-2782 *24hrs*

Valdosta

■CRUISY AREAS

Langdale Park [AYOR] N Valdosta Rd
days

Washington

■RESTAURANTS

Talk of the Town [GO] 10 West Public
Sq 706/678-7661 *11am-2pm, clsd
Sun*

HAWAII

Please note that cities are grouped
by islands:
Hawaii (Big Island)
Kauai
Maui
Molokai
Oahu (includes Honolulu)

HAWAII (BIG ISLAND)

■MEN'S SERVICES

➤MegaMates 808/930-3300 *Call to
hook up with HOT local men. FREE to
listen & respond to ads. Use FREE code
DAMRON. MegaMates.com.*

Captain Cook

■ACCOMMODATIONS

Aloha Guest House
[GS,N,NS,WI,WC,GO] 84-4780
Mamalahoa Hwy 808/328-8955,
800/897-3188

Areca Palms Estate B&B [GF,NS]
808/323-2276, 800/545-4390

Horizon Guest House
[GS,SW,NS,WI,WC,GO] 808/938-7822

Ka'awa Loa Plantation [GS,NS,WI,GO]
82-5990 Napoopoo Rd 96704
808/323-2686 *plantation-style B&B
on 5-acre start-up coffee farm*

Kealakekua Bay B&B [GS,NS]
808/328-8150, 800/328-8150

South Kona Hideaway [GS,WI,GO] 83-
5399 Middle Keei Rd (at Mamalahoa
Hwy)

Hilo

■RESTAURANTS

Cafe Pesto [E] 308 Kamehameha Ave
808/969-6640 *pizzas, salads, pastas*

■ENTERTAINMENT &
RECREATION

Best of Hilo Adventures Tours [GO]
1477 Kalanianaole Ave 808/987-3905

Richardson Beach at end of
Kalanianaole Ave (Keaukaha)

■CRUISY AREAS

Reeds "Gay" Bay Tearooms [AYOR]
Banyan Dr *1st beach S of the hotels*

Honaunau-Kona

■ACCOMMODATIONS

**Dragonfly Ranch Healing Arts
Center** [GS,NS,WI] 1 1/2 miles down
City of Refuge Rd 808/328-2159 *eco-
spa; luxuriously rustic upscale treehouse*

Kailua-Kona

■INFO LINES & SERVICES

Gay AA 808/329-1212

■ACCOMMODATIONS

1st Class B&B Kona Hawaii
[GF,NS,WI] 77-6504 Kilohana St
808/329-8778, 888/769-1110

**KonaLani Hawaiian Inn & Coffee
Plantation** [MW,NS,WI,GO] 76-5917H
Mamalahoa Hwy 808/324-0793

Royal Kona Resort
[GF,F,E,SW,NS,WI,WC] 75-5852 Ali'i Dr
808/329-3111, 800/222-5642

■Bars

The Mask-querade
[★MW,NH,D,B,E,K,GO] 75-5660 Kopiko
St 808/329-8558 *noon-2am*

My Bar [GF,K] 74-5606 Luhia St (btwn
Kaiwi & Eho St) 808/331-8789 *11am-
2am, from 10am wknds*

■Restaurants

Agnes' Portuguese Bake Shop 46
Hoolai St 808/262-5367 *6am-6pm,
till 2pm Sun, clsd Mon*

Buzz's Original Steak House [WC] 413
Kawailoa Rd 808/261-4661 *across
from beach, great Mai Tais*

Huggo's [E,K] 75-5828 Kahakai Rd (on
Kailua Bay) 808/329-1493 *dinner
only, also bar, patio*

Moke's Bread & Breakfast 27 Ho'olai
St 808/261-5565 *6:30am-3pm, clsd
Tue, great brkfst*

■Bookstores

Kona Stories 78-6831 Ali'i Dr #142
(in the Keauhou Shopping Ctr)
808/324-0350 *bookstore that hosts
PFLAG meetings & other LGBT groups*

■Retail Shops

The Wright Gallery [GO] 73-5590
Kauhola St 808/333-6572 *10am-
5pm, clsd Mon*

■Cruisy Areas

67 Beach Old Puako Rd *take Rte 19 N
to Puako Beach Rd, take 1st right onto
Old Puako Rd, look for telephone pole
#67, then go north for about 0.5 miles.
You drive to the shore on an unpaved
lane & walk to the water*

Honokohau Beach [AYOR] 5 miles S of
airport, Kailua-Kona *far N end of beach*

Kahaluu Beach Park [AYOR]

Old Airport Park *the beach area just
north of the end of the parking area,
which is the old airport runway*

Pahoa

■Accommodations

Absolute Paradise B&B
[MO,SW,N,NS,WI,GO] 808/965-1828,
888/285-1540 *B&B, outdoor hot tub,
some shared baths*

Coconut Cottage B&B [GS,GO]
808/965-0973, 866/204-7444

**Isle of You Naturally Farm &
Retreat** [M,NS,GO] 808/965-1639
cabin & yurts on naturist farm retreat

Kalani [GS,F,SW,N,NS,WI,WC,GO]
808/965-7828, 800/800-6886

Pamalu–Hawaiian Country House
[GS,SW,NS,WI,GO] 808/965-0830
secluded country retreat

Rainbow Retreat Center
[GS,SW,NS,WI,WC,GO] 808/965-9011

■Entertainment &
  Recreation

Kehena Beach off Hwy 137 (trailhead
at 19-mile marker phone booth) *lava
rock trail to clothing-optional black-
sand beach*

■Cruisy Areas

Steam Vents [AYOR] 3 miles S of Pahoa
on Keaau-Pahoa Rd *early evenings*

Volcano Village

■Accommodations

**The Artist Cottage at Volcano
Garden Arts** [GF,WI] 19-3834 Old
Volcano Rd (at Wright Rd)
808/985-8979

The Chalet Kilauea Collection
[GF,NS,WI] 19-4178 Wright Rd (at
Laukapu) 808/967-7786,
800/937-7786

Hale Ohia Cottages [GS,NS,WI,GO]
808/967-7986, 800/455-3803

■Cafes

Ono Cafe 19-3834 Old Volcano Rd (at
Wright St, at Volcano Garden Arts)
808/985-8979 *11am-3pm*

Kauai

■Men's Services

▶**MegaMates** 808/240-3300 *Call to
hook up with HOT local men. FREE to
listen & respond to ads. Use FREE code
DAMRON. MegaMates.com.*

Anahola

■ACCOMMODATIONS

Mahina Kai Ocean Villa
[GS,SW,N,NS,GO] 4933 Aliomanu Rd
808/822-9451, 800/337-1134

Hanalei

■NIGHTCLUBS

Tahiti Nui [GF,D,F,E,K,WC] 5-5134 Kuhio
Hwy (near Hanalei Center)
808/826-6277 *11am-2am, 4pm-11pm
Sun, also restaurant*

Kapaa

■ACCOMMODATIONS

17 Palms Kauai [GS,NS,WI,WC,GO]
808/822-5659, 888/725-6799 *2
secluded cottages 200 steps from beach*

Anuenue Plantation B&B
[M,NS,WI,GO] 808/823-8335,
888/371-7716

Fern Grotto Inn [GS,WI,NS] 4561
Kuamoo Rd (at Kuhio Hwy)
808/821-9836, 808/822-4845

Plantation Hale Suites [GF,SW,WI,WC]
525 Aleka Loop 808/822-4941, 800
/775-4253 *mention DAMRON for a
10% discount off our best available rate*

■RESTAURANTS

Eggbert's [WC] 4-484 Kuhio Hwy (in
Coconut Plantation Marketplace)
808/822-3787 *7am-1pm, light fare
until 6pm Mon-Sat*

Mema [BYOB,WC] 4-369 Kuhio Hwy (in
shopping center) 808/823-0899
*lunch Mon-Fri, dinner nightly, Thai &
Chinese*

■CRUISY AREAS

Coconut Marketplace 484 Kuhio Hwy
(NW corner)

Donkey Beach [AYOR] off Hwy 56, N of
Kapaa (btwn 11 & 12-mile markers)
*walk along cane field, down through
ironwood trees & then to the right on the
dirt road to the beach*

Kilauea

■CRUISY AREAS

Secret Beach [AYOR] *inquire locally*

Lihue

■ACCOMMODATIONS

Kauai Beach Resort [GF,SW,NS,WI]
4331 Kauai Beach Dr 808/245-1955,
866/971-2782 *also restaurant/ bar*

■ENTERTAINMENT &
RECREATION

Lydgate State Park Beach off Hwy 56
btwn Lihue & Kapaa (S of Wailua River)
*gay beach btwn the condos & the golf
course*

Puunene

■RESTAURANTS

Roy's Poipu Bar & Grill 2360 Kiahuna
Plantation Dr (in Poipu Shopping Ctr)
808/742-5000 *5:30pm-10pm*

Wailua

■RESTAURANTS

Caffe Coco [E,BYOB,WC] 4-369 Kuhio
Hwy 808/822-7990 *lunch Tue-Fri,
dinner nightly, clsd Mon*

Waimea

■ACCOMMODATIONS

Aston Waimea Plantation Cottages
[GF,SW,WI] 808/338-1625,
877/997-6667

MAUI

■INFO LINES & SERVICES

Both Sides Now *LGBT community
resources & events*

■MEN'S SERVICES

➤**MegaMates** 808/270-3300 *Call to
hook up with HOT local men. FREE to
listen & respond to ads. Use FREE code
DAMRON. MegaMates.com.*

Hana

■ACCOMMODATIONS

Hana Accommodations [GS,NS,GO]
808/248-7868, 800/228-4262
studios & tropical cottages, hot tub

Get a Room!

Receive 10% OFF
when you book online!

Use promo code DAMRON

808.879.1261
MauiSunseeker.com

BOOK ONLINE 24/7

MAUI
SUNSEEKER

LGBT
RESORT

Kaanapali

■ACCOMMODATIONS

The Royal Lahaina Resort
[GF,F,SW,WC] 2780 Kekaa Dr
808/661-3611, 800/222-5642

Kihei

■ACCOMMODATIONS

Eva Villa [GF,SW,WI,WC] 815 Kumulani
Dr 808/874-6407, 800/884-1845
near Wailea beaches

➤**Maui Sunseeker LGBT Resort**
[★MW,SW,N,NS,WI,GO] 551 S Kihei Rd
(at Wailana Place) 808/879-1261,
800/532-6284 *beachfront island
hideaway*

■BARS

Diamond's Ice Bar & Grill [GF,F,E]
1279 S Kihei Rd 808/874-9299
11am-2am, from 7am Sun

■NIGHTCLUBS

Ambrosia Martini Lounge [GS,D,E,WC]
1913 S Kihei Rd #H (in Kihei Kalama
Village) 808/891-1011 *6pm-2am*

■CAFES

Cafe at La Plage [WI,WC] 2395 S Kihei
Rd (at Kam Beach I) 808/875-7668
7am-5pm, till 3pm Sun

■RESTAURANTS

Jawz Tacos [WC] 1279 S Kihei Rd
808/874-8226 *11am-9pm*

Stella Blues Cafe [E,WC] 1279 S Kihei
Rd (in Azeka II Shopping Center)
808/874-3779 *7:30am-11pm*

■ENTERTAINMENT &
  RECREATION

Maui Massage for Men [GO]
808/280-7175

■EROTICA

The Love Shack 1913 S Kihei Rd (in
Kalama Vlg) 808/875-0303

■CRUISY AREAS

Kalama Park [AYOR]

Kula

■ACCOMMODATIONS

The Upcountry B&B [GF,NS,WI,WC]
4925 Lower Kula Rd (at Copp St)
808/878-8083

Lahaina

■RESTAURANTS

Betty's Beach Cafe [★] 505 Front St
808/662-0300 *8am-10pm, more gay
at bar till midnight*

Lahaina Coolers [WC] 180 Dickenson
St 808/661-7082 *8am-1am, patio*

■RETAIL SHOPS

Skin Deep Tattoo 626 Front St (across
from the Banyan Tree) 808/661-8531
10am-10pm, till 8pm Sun-Mon

■CRUISY AREAS

Front St [AYOR] along Beach Walk

Makawao

■ACCOMMODATIONS

Aloha Cottage [GS,WI,GO]
808/573-8555, 888/328-3330
*designed for comfort, style, charm &
seclusion, outdoor soaking tub*

Hale Ho'okipa Inn B&B [GF,NS,WI,WC]
32 Pakani Pl 808/572-6698,
877/572-6698 *gracious old Hawaiian
plantation home*

■RESTAURANTS

Casanova Restaurant & Deli [D,E]
1188 Makawao Ave 808/572-0220
*lunch & dinner, Italian, full bar till 2am,
live music*

Makena

■ENTERTAINMENT &
  RECREATION

Little Beach at Makena [MW] *Pilani
Hwy S to Wailea, right at Wailea Ike Dr,
left on Wailea Alanui Dr to public beach,
then take trail up hill at right end of
beach*

Wailea

■ACCOMMODATIONS

Ho'olei at Grand Wailea
[GF,SW,WI,WC] 146 Ho'olei Cir (at
Wailea Alanui Dr) 877/346-6534

Wailuku

■INFO LINES & SERVICES

AA Gay/ Lesbian 70 Central Ave #1 808/244-9673 *7:30am Sun*

■ACCOMMODATIONS

Maalaea Kai Condo [GF] 70 Hauoli St (Maalaea Village) 562/212-3312

MOLOKAI

Kaunakakai

■RESTAURANTS

Kanemitsu Bakery & Coffee Shop 79 Ala Malama St 808/553-5855 *5:30am-5pm, clsd Tue, great sweet bread*

OAHU

■PUBLICATIONS

Odyssey Magazine Hawaii 808/955-5959 *everything you need to know about gay Hawaii*

Aiea

■EROTICA

Video Warehouse 98-019 Kamehameha Hwy (at Hekaha St) 808/487-1750 *24hrs, booths*

Honolulu

■INFO LINES & SERVICES

Gay/ Lesbian AA 310 Pa`okalani Ave, Room 203A 808/946-1438 *7pm & 8pm Sat*

■ACCOMMODATIONS

Aqua Palms Waikiki [GF,SW,NS,WI,WC] 1850 Ala Moana Blvd (at Kalia & Ena) 808/947-7256, 866/406-2782

Aston Waikiki Circle Hotel [GF,NS,WI] 2464 Kalakaua Ave (at Uluniu St, Waikiki) 808/923-1571, 877/997-6667

Hotel Renew [GF,NS,WI] 129 Paoakalani Ave (at Lemon Rd, Waikiki) 808/687-7700, 888/485-7639

Waikiki Grand Hotel [M,NS,SW] 134 Kapahulu Ave 808/923-1814, 808/923-1511 *rentals above Hula's Bar, near gay beach*

■BARS

Bacchus Waikiki [MW,NH,] 408 Lewers St 808/926-4167 *noon-2am*

In Between [M,NH,K] 2155 Lau'ula St (off Lewers, across from Planet Hollywood, Waikiki) 808/926-7060 *noon-2am*

Lo Jax [MW,NH,F,V,WI] 2256 Kuhio Ave, 2nd flr (at Seaside, Waikiki) 808/922-1422 *noon-2am*

Tapa's Restaurant & Lanai Bar [GS,E,F,K,GO] 407 Seaside, 2nd flr (at Kuhio Ave) 808/921-2288 *9am-2am, lanai bar, also restaurant for dinner & Sun brunch*

Wang Chung's [MW,K,WC] 2410 Koa Ave (at Kaiulani) 808/921-9176 *5pm-2am*

■NIGHTCLUBS

Bar 7 [GS,D,MR-A,S,YC,WC] 1344 Kona St (at Piikoi Rd) 808/955-2640 *9pm-4am, [DS] Sat*

Fusion Waikiki [M,D,TG,K,DS,S,V] 2260 Kuhio Ave, 2nd flr (at Seaside) 808/924-2422 *10pm-4am, from 8pm Fri-Sat*

➤Hula's Bar & Lei Stand [★,M,D,TG,F,S,V,YC,WI] 134 Kapahulu Ave (2nd flr of Waikiki Grand Hotel) 808/923-0669 *10am-2am, near gay beach, go-go boys Th-Sun, weekly catamaran cruise*

■CAFES

Leonard's Bakery 933 Kapahulu Ave 808/737-5591 *5:30am-9pm, till 10pm Fri-Sat, irresistible malasadas & doughnuts*

Mocha Java Cafe [WI,WC] 1200 Ala Moana Blvd (in Ward Center) 808/591-9023 *8am-9pm, till 6pm Sun, outdoor seating*

Tapa's II [WI,GO] 1888 Kalakaua Ave, C106 (in Waikiki Landmark Building) 808/979-2299 *9am-2am, clsd wknds, full bar, patio*

■RESTAURANTS

Alan Wong's 1857 S King St (at Pumehana St) 808/949-2526 *dinner only, upscale*

Arancino di Mare 2552 Kalakaua Ave (in Waikiki Beach Marriott) **808/931-6273** *brkfst, lunch & dinner, Italian*

Cafe Che Pasta [MW,D,E] 1001 Bishop St, Ste 108 (enter off Alakea St) **808/524-0004** *lunch & dinner, clsd Sun, full bar*

Cafe Sistina [WC] 1314 S King St **808/596-0061** *lunch Mon-Fri, dinner nightly, northern Italian, full bar*

Cha Cha Cha 342 Seaside Ave **808/923-7797** *lunch & dinner, Mexican, happy hour, full bar*

Cheeseburger in Paradise 2500 Kalakaua Blvd **808/923-3731** *7am-11pm, full bar*

Eggs 'n' Things 2464 Kalakaua Ave **808/923-3447** *6am-2pm, 5pm-10pm; also at 2464 Kalakaua Ave, 808/926-3447*

House Without A Key 2199 Kalia Rd (at Lewers St, at Halekulani Hotel) **808/923-2311** *7am-9pm, stunning sunset views, Hawaiian music nightly*

Hula Grill [E] 2335 Kalakaua Ave (in Outrigger Hotel) **808/923-4852**

Indigo [E,WC] 1121 Nu'uanu Ave **808/521-2900** *lunch Tue-Fri, dinner Tue-Sat, Eurasian*

Keo's in Waikiki [R,WC] 2028 Kuhio Ave **808/951-9355** *5pm-10pm, Thai*

La Cucaracha 2446 Koa Ave **808/924-3366** *noon-11pm, Mexican, full bar*

Liliha Bakery [WC] 515 N Kuakini St (at Liliha St) **808/531-1651** *open 24hrs, till 8m Sun, clsd Mon, diner fare & baked goods*

Lulu's [E] 2586 Kalakaua Ave **808/926-5222** *7am-2am, full bar*

Rock Island Cafe 131 Kaiulani Ave (off Kalakaua, in King's Village Waikiki) **808/923-8033** *old-fashioned soda fountain*

Singha Thai [E] 1910 Ala Moana Blvd **808/941-2898** *4pm-10pm*

Tiki's Grill & Bar [E] 2570 Kalakaua Ave (in ResortQuest Hotel) **808/923-8454**

■ENTERTAINMENT & RECREATION

Diamond Head Beach [GS] *take road from lighthouse to beach; some nude sunbathing*

Hawaii Gay Tours [GO] 1947 Alaeloa St **218/234-2310**

Honolulu Gay/ Lesbian Cultural Foundation 1670 Makaloa St #204 **808/675-8428** *last wknd of May Honolulu Rainbow Film Festival*

Queen's Surf Beach Kapiolani Park (off Kalakaua) *popular gay beach at far end of Kuhio Beach*

Rainbow Sailing Charters [MW,GO] **808/347-0235** *day & overnight sailing adventures*

■RETAIL SHOPS

Over Easy Down Under 2299 Kuhio Ave (at Aqua Waikiki Wave Hotel) **808/926-4994** *10am-8pm, 11am-4pm Sun, men's swimwear*

■PUBLICATIONS

Expression Magazine 808/393-7994 *monthly glossy LGBT magazine*

Odyssey Magazine Hawaii **808/955-5959** *everything you need to know about gay Hawaii*

■MEN'S CLUBS

Max's Gym [V,18+,PC] 438 Hobron Ln, 4th flr (at Ala Moana Blvd, in Eaton Square) **808/951-8232** *noon-4am, 24hrs wknds*

■MEN'S SERVICES

▶**MegaMates** 808/599-6999 *Call to hook up with HOT local men. FREE to listen & respond to ads. Use FREE code DAMRON. MegaMates.com.*

■EROTICA

Suzie's Secrets 1370 Kapiolani Blvd **808/949-4383** *24hrs*

Velvet Video 2155 Lau'ula St, 2nd flr (above In Between, Waikiki) **808/924-0868** *24hrs, booths, toys*

■CRUISY AREAS

Ala Moana Beach Park [AYOR] *near Waikiki Yacht Club*

Alan Davis Beach Rte 27 *turn past Sandy Beach but before Makapuu Point Lighthouse*

Diamond Head Road [AYOR] *on trails across the street from the lighthouse*

Windward Coast

■ACCOMMODATIONS

Ali'i Bluffs Windward B&B [GS,SW,NS,WI,GO] 46–251 Ikiiki St, Kane'ohe 808/235-1124, 800/235-1151

IDAHO

Statewide

■PUBLICATIONS

Diversity Newsmagazine 208/336-3870 *statewide LGBT newspaper, monthly*

Boise

■INFO LINES & SERVICES

The Community Center 305 E 37th St, Garden City 208/336-3870 *volunteer staff*

■ACCOMMODATIONS

Bed & Buns [MO,N,NS,WI,GO] 208/866-2759, 208/362-1802 *B&B, hot tub*

Hotel 43 [GS,F,WI] 981 Grove St 800/243-4622

The Modern Hotel & Bar [GF,WI] 1314 W Grove St 208/424-8244, 866/780-6012

■BARS

The Lucky Dog [M,NH,B,L,WI] 2223 W Fairview Ave (at 23rd) 208/333-0074 *2pm-2am, from noon wknds, patio*

Neurolux [GF,D,E] 111 N 11th St (at W Idaho) 208/343-0886 *1pm-2am, live music*

■NIGHTCLUBS

The Balcony Club [★MW,D,K,WC,GO] 150 N 8th St #226 (at Idaho) 208/336-1313 *4pm-2am, theme nights*

■CAFES

Flying M Coffeehouse [WI] 500 W Idaho St (at 5th St) 208/345-4320 *6:30am-11pm, from 7:30am wknds, till 6pm Sun*

River City Coffee 5517 W State St 208/853-9161 *6am-5pm, till 4pm Sun*

Tully's [WI] 794 Broad St 208/472-1308 *7am-8pm, till 6pm Sat, 8am-5pm Sun*

■RESTAURANTS

Lucky 13 Pizza 3662 S Eckert Rd 208/344-6967 *11am-9pm, till 10pm wknds*

■ENTERTAINMENT & RECREATION

The Flicks [F,E,BW,WC] 646 Fulton St 208/342-4222 *opens 4pm, from noon Fri-Sun, 4 movie theaters, patio*

■RETAIL SHOPS

The Record Exchange [E] 1105 W Idaho St (at 11th) 208/344-8010 *9am-9pm, till 7pm Sun, also cafe*

■MEN'S SERVICES

➤**MegaMates** 208/343-8500 *Call to hook up with HOT local men. FREE to listen & respond to ads. Use FREE code DAMRON. MegaMates.com.*

■EROTICA

The O!Zone 1615 Broadway Ave (at Howe) 208/395-1977

Pleasure Boutique 5022 Fairview Ave (at Orchard) 208/433-1161

Vixen Video [GO] 5777 W Overland Rd 208/672-1844

■CRUISY AREAS

Ann Morrison Park [AYOR] *near baseball fields*

Coeur d'Alene

see also Spokane, Washington

■ACCOMMODATIONS

The Clark House on Hayden Lake [GF,NS,WI,GO] 5250 E Hayden Lake Rd, Hayden Lake 208/772-3470, 800/765-4593

Lava Hot Springs

see also Pocatello

■ACCOMMODATIONS

Aura Soma Lava [GS,SW] 196 E Main St **208/776-5800, 800/757-1233** *also retail store*

Moscow

■INFO LINES & SERVICES

Inland Oasis LGBTA Center 1320 S Mountain View Rd **208/596-4449** *HIV testing, youth group & more*

■BOOKSTORES

Bookpeople 521 S Main (btwn 5th & 6th) **208/882-2669** *9:30am-6:30pm, till 8pm Fri-Sat*

Nampa

■CAFES

Flying M Coffee Garage [E] 1314 2nd St S **208/467-5533** *7am-11pm, till 6pm wknds*

Pocatello

■NIGHTCLUBS

Club Charleys [MW,D,E,DS,K,WC] 331 E Center St **208/232-9606** *5pm-2am, clsd Sun*

■CAFES

Main St Coffee & News 234 N Main St (btwn Lander & Clark) **208/234-9834** *6:30am-4pm, from 8am Sat, from 9am Sun*

■EROTICA

Main Street Video 657 N Main St **208/235-9457**

Pegasus Book Store 246 W Center St **208/232-6493**

■CRUISY AREAS

Ross Park [AYOR] *upper level*

Powell

■CRUISY AREAS

Jerry Johnson Hot Springs [AYOR] US 12 *days*

Twin Falls

■CAFES

Annie's Lavender & Coffee Cafe [F,WC] 591 Addison Ave W (at 8th St) **208/736-2003** *6am-5pm, seasonal wknd hrs*

■RESTAURANTS

Pizza Planet 720 Main St (at 8th St), Buhl **208/543-8560** *11am-8pm, till 9pm Fri-Sat*

■CRUISY AREAS

City Park [AYOR] Shoshone & 4th Ave E

Rock Creek Park [AYOR] W on Hwy 30 *days*

ILLINOIS

Alton

see also St Louis, Missouri

■NIGHTCLUBS

Bubby & Sissy's [MW,D,DS,K,F,WC] 602 Belle St (at 6th) **618/465-4773** *3pm-2am, till 3am Fri-Sat, clsd Mon*

■CRUISY AREAS

Rock Springs Park [AYOR] College Ave (at Rock Springs Dr)

Arlington Heights

see Chicago

Bloomington

■CAFES

Coffee Hound [WI] 407 N Main St **309/827-7575** *6:30am-6pm, 8am-5pm Sun*

Kelly's Bakery & Cafe [WC] 113 N Center St **309/820-1200** *7am-6pm, till 2pm Sat, clsd Sun*

Blue Island

see also Chicago

■NIGHTCLUBS

Club Krave [MW,NH,TG,F,K,C,DS,S,WI,WC] 13126 S Western Ave (at Grove) **708/597-8379** *8pm-2am, till 3am Fri-Sat, from 6pm Mon*

Illinois • *USA*

Bradley

■RESTAURANTS
La Villetta 801 W Broadway St 815/939-4960 *11am-9pm, till 8pm Sun, Italian*

■EROTICA
Slightly Sinful 101 N Kinzie Ave (at Broadway) 815/937-5744

Calumet City

■CRUISY AREAS
Clayhole Woods, Shabonna Woods & Sandridge Forest Preserves [AYOR]

Carbondale

■INFO LINES & SERVICES
AA Lesbian/ Gay 618/549-4633

■NIGHTCLUBS
Two 13 [GF,NH,D,E,DS] 213 E Main St 618/549-4270 *8pm-2am*

■CRUISY AREAS
Crab Orchard Lake [AYOR] Cambria Neck Ln *exit off Rte 13 onto Cambria Rd, drive 1 mile N, on right side of Cambria Rd is side road called Cambria Neck Ln, turn right onto it*

Centreville

see also St Louis, Missouri

■NIGHTCLUBS
Boxers 'n' Briefs [M,D,F,DS,18+,WC,$] 55 Four Corners Ln (next to PT's Show Club) 618/332-6141 *7pm-4am, till 6am Fri-Sat, till 3am Sun, clsd Mon, nude dancers*

Champaign/ Urbana

■ACCOMMODATIONS
Sylvia's Irish Inn [GF,E,NS,WI] 312 W Green St, Urbana 217/384-4800

■BARS
Emerald City Lounge [MW,F,E,WC,GO] 118 N First St (at University Ave), Champaign 217/398-8661 *5pm-2am Th-Sat, from 10am Sun*

Mike 'N Molly's [GF,E,U] 105 N Market St (at University), Champaign 217/355-1236 *4pm-2am, live music, beer garden*

■NIGHTCLUBS
Chester Street [MW,D,DS,GO] 63 Chester St (at Water St), Champaign 217/356-5607 *5pm-2am*

■CAFES
Aroma Cafe 118 N Neil St, Champaign 217/356-3200 *7am-10pm, from 8am wknds*

Cafe Kopi [WI] 109 N Walnut (at University), Champaign 217/359-4266 *7am-midnight, espresso bar with sandwiches*

Espresso Royale 602 E Daniel St (at 6th St), Champaign 217/328-1112 *7am-midnight*

Pekara Bakery & Bistro 116 N Neil St, Champaign 217/359-4500 *7am-8pm, from 8am Sun*

■RESTAURANTS
Boltini Lounge 211 N Neil St, Champaign 217/378-8001 *4pm-2am, from 6pm Sat, clsd Sun, also full bar*

The Courier Cafe 111 N Race St, Urbana 217/328-1811 *7am-11pm*

Dos Reales [WC] 1407 N Prospect Ave, Champaign 217/351-6879 *11am-10pm, Mexican*

Farren's Pub & Eatery [WC] 308 N Randolph St, Champaign 217/359-6977 *11am-9pm, till 10pm Fri, from noon wknds, full bar*

Fiesta Cafe [GO] 216 S 1st St (at E Clark), Champaign 217/352-5902 *11am-11pm, bar till 1am, Mexican*

The Great Impasta [E,WC] 156C Lincoln Sq, Urbana 217/359-7377 *11am-9pm, till 10pm Fri, 5pm-10pm Sat*

Radio Maria 119 N Walnut St, Champaign 217/398-7729 *4pm-2am, wknd brunch, eclectic Mexican cuisine*

Silvercreek [E] 402 N Race St, Urbana 217/328-3402 *lunch & dinner, brunch Sun*

■RETAIL SHOPS
Dandelion 9 Taylor St, Champaign 217/355-9333 *11am-6pm, noon-5pm Sun, vintage clothing*

■GYMS & HEALTH CLUBS
Refinery [GF] 2302 W John St, Champaign 217/355-4444

■EROTICA

Fantasy's 3604 N Cunningham Ave (Cunningham exit off I-74 E), Urbana 217/328-1199 *24hrs, video booths*

Illini Video Arcade 33 E Springfield Ave (S Neil exit, off I-74), Champaign 217/359-8529 *24hrs*

■CRUISY AREAS

Crystal Lake Park [AYOR] at Park & University Sts, Urbana

CHICAGO

Chicago is divided into 5 geographical areas:
Chicago—Overview
Chicago—North Side
Chicago—Boystown/ Lakeview
Chicago—Near North
Chicago—South Side

Chicago—Overview

includes some listings for Greater Chicagoland; please check individual cities like Oak Park as well

■INFO LINES & SERVICES

AA/ New Town Alano Club [WC] 909 W Belmont Ave, 2nd flr (btwn Clark & Sheffield) 773/529-0321 *5pm-11pm, from 8:30am wknds*

The Center on Halsted 3656 N Halsted St (at Waveland) 773/472-6469, 773/472-1277 **(TTY)** *8am-10pm, LGBT center, organic grocery store, cafe, theater, gym, technology center*

■ENTERTAINMENT & RECREATION

Chicago Neighborhood Tours [GF] 77 E Randolph St (at Michigan Ave, at Chicago Cultural Center) 312/742-1190 *the best way to make the Windy City your kind of town*

Heartland Cafe 7000 N Glenwood Ave (in Rogers Park) 773/465-8005 *cafe w/ full bar, theater, lots of live music*

John Hancock Observatory 875 N Michigan Ave (in John Hancock Center) 312/751-3681, 888/875-8439 *9am-11pm, also check out the "Signature Lounge at the 96th"*

Leather Archives & Museum 6418 N Greenview Ave 773/761-9200 *11am-7pm Th-Fri, till 5pm Sat-Sun, membership required (purchase at door)*

Second City [GF,E] 1616 N Wells St (at North) 312/337-3992, 312/337-3992 *legendary comedy club, call for reservations*

■PUBLICATIONS

boi magazine 773/975-0264 *slick glossy w/ bar listings, articles, photos & circuit dish*

Nightspots 773/871-7610 *weekly LGBT nightlife magazine*

PINK & PINK PAGES 773/765-4712 *LGBT business directory & lifestyle magazine*

Windy City Times 773/871-7610 *weekly LGBT newspaper & calendar guide*

■MEN'S SERVICES

▶**MegaMates** 312/377-6533 *Call to hook up with HOT local men. FREE to listen & respond to ads. Use FREE code DAMRON. MegaMates.com.*

■CRUISY AREAS

Humboldt Park [AYOR] North Ave & Sacramento *near pavilion & bushes*

Marquette Park [AYOR] 7100 S Kedzie Avenue (at 71st Street W) *use S entrance*

Chicago—North Side

■ACCOMMODATIONS

House 5863 B&B [GS,NS,WI,GO] 5863 N Glenwood (at Admore) 773/682-5217

■BARS

The Anvil [M,MW,V] 1137 W Granville (E of Broadway) 773/973-0006 *9am-2am*

Big Chicks [MW,NH,D,F,V,WI,WC] 5024 N Sheridan (btwn Foster & Argyle) 773/728-5511 *4pm-2am, from 3pm wknds, patio, Sun BBQ*

The Call [MW,D,CW,DS,V,WC] 1547 W Bryn Mawr (at Clark) 773/334-2525 *4pm-2am*

Crew [MW,F,V] 4804 N Broadway St (at Lawrence) **773/784-2739** *11:30am-midnight, 11am-2am Fri-Sat, sports bar & grill, patio*

The Glenwood [MW,NH,WC] 6962 N Glenwood Ave (at Morse) **773/764-7363** *3pm-2am, from noon Sun, sports bar*

Green Mill [★GS,E] 4802 N Broadway Ave (at Lawrence) **773/878-5552** *noon-4am, noted jazz venue, hosts the Uptown Poetry Slam*

In Fine Spirits [GS,F] 5420 N Clark St (at Rascher Ave) **773/334-9463** *4pm-midnight, 3pm-2am Fri-Sat, wine bar, patio, also wine store*

Jackhammer [★M,NH,D,K,L,S,V] 6406 N Clark St (at Devon) **773/743-5772** *5pm-4am, till 5am Sat, from 2pm Sun, patio*

Marty's [GF,F] 1511 W Balmoral Ave (at Clark) **773/321-7481** *5pm-2am, upscale wine & martini bar*

Parlour on Clark [★MW,D,C,DS] 6341 N Clark St **773/564-9274** *7pm-2am, from noon Sun, clsd Mon-Tue*

Scot's [M,NH] 1829 W Montrose Ave (at Damen) **773/528-3253** *3pm-2am, 1pm-3am Sat, from 11am Sun*

Sidecar [GS] 6920 N Glenwood Ave (at Morse) **773/764-2826** *5pm-close, martini lounge*

The Sofo Tap [M,NH,V,WC] 4923 N Clark St (at W Argyle) **773/784-7636** *5pm-2am, from 3pm Fri, from noon wknds, backyard beer garden*

Spyner's Pub [W,NH,K] 4623 N Western Ave (at W Eastwood) **773/784-8719**

T's [W,NH,F,K,WC] 5025 N Clark St (at Winnemac) **773/784-6000** *5pm-2am, 11am-3am, till 2am Sun*

T's Bar & Restaurant [GS,NH,F] 5025 N Clark St **773/784-6000** *5pm-2am from 11am wknds, nice patio & good burgers*

Touché [★M,L] 6412 N Clark St (at Devon) **773/465-7400** *5pm-4am, 3pm-5am Sat, noon-4am Sun*

◼NIGHTCLUBS

Atmosphere [MW,D,DS,C,S,WI,GO] 5355 N Clark St (at W Balmoral Ave) **773/784-1100** *6pm-2am, till 3am Sat, from 3pm Sat-Sun, clsd Mon*

◼CAFES

Charmer's Cafe [MW,WI,WC] 1500 W Jarvis (at Greenview) **773/743-2233** *6am-6pm, from 7am wknds*

Coffee Chicago [F,WI,WC] 5256 N Broadway St (btwn Berwyn & Foster) **773/784-1305** *7am-9pm, from 8am wknds*

KOPI: A Traveler's Cafe [E,F,WC] 5317 N Clark St **773/989-5674** *8am-11pm*

Metropolis Coffee [★WI] 1039 W Granville Ave (at Kenmore) **773/764-0400**

◼RESTAURANTS

A Taste of Heaven [GO] 5401 N Clark St **773/989-0151** *brunch, dinner and delicious. savory and sweet items*

Andie's [WC] 5253 N Clark (btwn Berwyn & Farragut) **773/784-8616** *11am-11pm, eastern Mediterranean, full bar*

Anteprima [WC] 5316 N Clark St (at Summerdale) **773/506-9990** *dinner nightly, Italian*

Deluxe Diner [K] 6349 N Clark St (at Devon) **773/743-8244** *24hr diner*

Fat Cat [WC] 4840 N Broadway (at Lawrence Ave) **773/506-3100** *4pm-2am, from 11am wknds, full bar*

Fireside [WI,WC] 5739 N Ravenswood (at Rosehill) **773/561-7433** *11am-4am, Cajun & pizza, patio, full bar*

Hamburger Mary's/ Rec Room/ Attic [MW,E,K,DS,WC] 5400 N Clark St (at Balmoral) **773/784-6969** *11:30am-midnight, till 2am Wed-Sun, from 10:30am wknds, also full bar*

Hot Woks Cool Sushi 30 S Michigan Ave (at Madison) **312/345-1234** *11am-9pm, sushi/ Thai*

Jin Ju [WC] 5203 N Clark St (at Summersdale) **773/334-6377** *dinner only, clsd Mon, Korean, also bar*

Pauline's [WC] 1754 W Balmoral (at Ravenswood) **773/561-8573** *7am-3pm, hearty brkfsts*

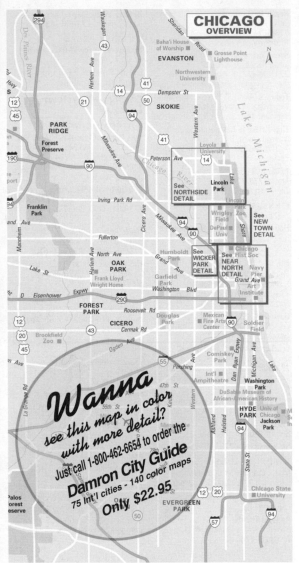

CHICAGO OVERVIEW

EVANSTON

Baha'i House of Worship

Grosse Point Lighthouse

Northwestern University

SKOKIE

Dempster St

PARK RIDGE

Forest Preserve

Loyola University

Peterson Ave

See NORTHSIDE DETAIL

Lincoln Park

Franklin Park

Irving Park Rd

Wrigley Field

DePaul Univ

Park

See NEW TOWN DETAIL

Fullerton

OAK PARK

North Ave

Humboldt Park

Grand Ave

See WICKER PARK DETAIL

See NEAR NORTH DETAIL

Chicago Hist Soc

Navy Pier

Frank Lloyd Wright Home

Garfield Park

Washington Blvd

Grand Ave

Art Institute

FOREST PARK

Eisenhower Expwy

Roosevelt Rd

Douglas Park

CICERO

Cermak Rd

Mexican Fine Arts Center

Soldier Field

Brookfield Zoo

Ogden Ave

Comiskey Park

Pershing

Int'l Amphitheatre

Washington Park

47th St

DuSable Museum of African-American History

HYDE PARK

Univ of Chicago

Jackson Park

EVERGREEN PARK

Chicago State University

Illinois • USA

Reza's Restaurant [WC] 5255 N Clark
(btwn Berwyn & Farragut)
773/561-1898 *lunch & dinner
Mediterranean/ Persian, full bar*

Svea Restaurant [WC] 5236 N Clark
(btwn Berwyn & Farragut)
773/275-7738 *7am-2pm, till 3pm
wknds, Swedish/ American comfort food*

Tedino's [★WC] 5335 N Sheridan Rd (at
Broadway) 773/275-8100 *11am-
midnight, from 3pm Mon, pizza, full bar*

Thai Pastry & Restaurant [WC] 4925
N Broadway St, Unit E (at Argyle)
773/784-5399 *11am-10pm, till 11pm
Fri-Sat*

Tweet [WI] 5020 N Sheridan Rd (at
Argyle) 773/728-5576 *9am-3pm, clsd
Tue, brkfst & brunch, cash only*

■ENTERTAINMENT & RECREATION

Hollywood /Osterman Beach [★] at
Hollywood & Sheridan Sts *"the" gay
beach*

■RETAIL SHOPS

Enjoy, An Urban General Store 4727
N Lincoln Ave (Lincoln Square)
773/334-8626 *10am-7pm, till 6pm
Sun, pride items*

Gaymart 3457 N Halsted St (at
Cornelius) 773/929-4272 *11am-8pm,
till 6pm Sun*

Leather 6410 [GO] 6410 N Clark St (at
Devon, btwn Jackhammer & Touché)
773/508-0900 *noon-midnight, till
4am Th, till 5am Fri, till 6am Sat, from
4pm Sun-Mon*

■GYMS & HEALTH CLUBS

Cheetah Gym 5248 N Clark St (at
Foster) 773/728-7777,
866/961-6840

Sir Spa [GS,GO] 773/271-7000

■MEN'S CLUBS

Man's Country [PC,S] 5015 N Clark St
(at Argyle) 773/878-2069 *24hrs, nude
strippers Fri-Sat*

■EROTICA

Admiral Theater 3940 W Lawrence
Ave (at Pulaski) 773/478-8111,
773/478-8263

Banana Video 4923 N Clark St (at
Argyle, 2nd flr) 773/561-8322 *arcade*

■CRUISY AREAS

Hollywood Beach [AYOR] along lake (at
5700 N)

Lincoln Park [AYOR] E of Lake Shore Dr
(btwn Foster & Montrose)

Chicago—Boystown/ Lakeview

■ACCOMMODATIONS

**Best Western Plus Hawthorne
Terrace** [GF,WI,WC] 3434 N Broadway St
(at Hawthorne Pl) 773/244-3434,
888/860-3400 *in heart of Chicago's
gay community, gym*

City Suites Hotel [GF,WI] 933 W
Belmont Ave (btwn Clark & Sheffield)
773/404-3400, 800/248-9108
European style

Majestic Hotel [GF,NS,WI] 528 W
Brompton Ave (at Addison)
773/404-3499, 800/727-5108

The Willows [GS,NS,WI] 555 W Surf St
(at Broadway) 773/528-8400,
800/787-3108

■BARS

3160 [MW,NH,E,P,C,WC] 3160 N Clark St
(at Belmont) 773/327-5969 *3pm-
2am, noon-3am Sat, 11am-2am Sun*

Beat Kitchen [GF,F,E] 2100 W Belmont
(btwn Hoyne & Damen)
773/281-4444 *4pm-2am, from
11:30am Sat-Sun, till 3am Sat, live
bands, also grill*

Blues [★GF,E] 2519 N Halsted St (at Lill
Ave) 773/528-1012 *8pm-2am, till
3am Sat, classic Chicago blues spot*

Bobby Love's [MW,NH,K,WC] 3729 N
Halsted St (at Waveland)
773/525-1200 *3pm-2am, from noon
wknds, till 3am Sat*

Buck's Saloon [M,NH] 3439 N Halsted
St (btwn Cornelia & Newport)
773/525-1125 *noon-2am, till 3am
Sat, from 11am Sun, great beer garden*

Cell Block [M,B,L,WC] 3702 N Halsted St
(at Waveland) 773/665-8064 *2pm-
3am, back bar wknds from 10pm*

Charlie's Chicago [M,D,CW,K] 3726 N Broadway St (btwn Waveland & Grace) **773/871-8887** *3pm-4am, till 5am Sat, club music after 1am*

The Closet [★MW,NH,K,V] 3325 N Broadway St (at Buckingham) **773/477-8533** *4pm-4am, noon-5am Sat, till 4am Sun*

D.S. Tequila Company [GS,F] 3352 N Halsted St (at Roscoe) **773/697-9127** *5pm-2am, noon-3am wknds*

Elixir [M] 3452 N Halsted St (at Cornelia) **773/975-9244** *6pm-close, swank cocktails*

Little Jim's [★M,NH] 3501 N Halsted St (at Cornelia) **773/871-6116** *noon-4am, till 5am Sat*

The Lucky Horseshoe Lounge [M,NH,S] 3169 N Halsted St (at Briar) **773/404-3169** *3pm-2am, 1pm-3am Sat*

Manhandler Saloon [★M,NH,V] 1948 N Halsted St (at Armitage) **773/871-3339** *noon-4am, till 5am Sat, patio*

Minibar [★MW,F,WC] 3341 N Halsted St (at Roscoe) **773/871-6227** *5pm-2am, from 11am wknds*

The North End [M,NH,WC] 3733 N Halsted St (at Grace) **773/477-7999** *2pm-2am, from 11am wknds, sports bar*

Roscoe's [★MW,NH,D,F,K,DS,S,V] 3354-56 N Halsted St (at W Roscoe) **773/281-3355** *4pm-2am, from 3pm Fri, from 2pm Sat, patio*

Scarlet [M,E,C,P] 3320 N Halsted St (at Aldine) **773/348-1053** *6pm-2am, from 2pm wknds, piano bar*

Sidetrack [★MW,NH,V,WC] 3349 N Halsted St (at Roscoe) **773/477-9189** *3pm-2am, till 3am Sat*

■NIGHTCLUBS

Berlin [★MW,D,TG,S,V,WC] 954 W Belmont (at Sheffield) **773/348-4975** *5pm-4am, from 8pm Sun-Mon*

Circuit/Rehab [M,D,MR,S] 3641 N Halsted St (at Addison) **773/325-2233** *9pm-4am, till 5am Sat, clsd Mon-Wed, Latin nights Th & Sun (T-dance)*

Hydrate [★GS,D,E,DS,S] 3458 N Halsted St (at Cornelia) **773/975-9244** *8pm-4am, till 5am Sat, opens earlier in summer*

Planet Earth [GS,D] 3534 W Belmont (at Late Bar) **773/267-5283** *10pm-5am Sat, New Wave*

Smart Bar [★GF,D,A,E] 3730 N Clark St (downstairs at the Metro) **773/549-0203** *10pm-4am, till 5am Sat, clsd Mon-Tue, theme nights*

Spin [MW,D,K,DS,S,V,YC] 800 W Belmont (enter on Halsted) **773/327-7711** *4pm-2am, till 3am Sat, from 2pm wknds*

Stardust Thursdays [W,D,F] 954 W Belmont (at Berlin) **773/348-4975**

Urbano [M,D,MR-AF,MR-L] 3641 N Halsted St (at Addison) **773/325-2233**

■CAFES

Caribou Coffee [WI] 3300 N Broadway St (at Aldine) **773/477-3695** *from 5:30am, from 6:30am Sat, till midnight Fri-Sat*

The Coffee & Tea Exchange 3311 N Broadway St (at Roscoe) **773/528-2241** *8am-8pm, 10am-6pm Sun*

■RESTAURANTS

Angelina Ristorante [WC] 3561 N Broadway St (at Addison) **773/935-5933** *5:30pm-11pm, wknd brunch, Italian, full bar*

Ann Sather's [★] 909 W Belmont Ave (at Sheffield) **773/348-2378** *7am-3pm, till 4pm Sat-Sun, Swedish diner & Boystown fixture*

Cesar's [WI] 2924 N Broadway (at Oakdale) **773/296-9097** *"home of the killer margaritas"*

Chicago Diner [BW] 3411 N Halsted St (at Roscoe) **773/935-6696** *11am-10pm, from 10am wknds, till 11pm Fri-Sat, hip & vegan*

Halsted's Bar & Grill [★MW,GO] 3441 N Halsted St (btwn Newport & Cornelia) **773/348-9696** *dinner nightly, brunch wknds, neighborhood sports bar*

Home Bistro [★BYOB,WC] 3404 N Halsted St (at Roscoe, btwn Addison & Belmont) **773/661-0299** *dinner only, clsd Mon*

Horizon Cafe [WC] 3805 N Broadway St (corner w/ Halsted & Grace) 773/883-1565 *7am-9pm, till 10pm Fri-Sat, brkfst anytime*

Joy's Noodles & Rice [WC] 3257 N Broadway St (at Melrose) 773/327-8330 *11am-10pm, till 11pm Fri-Sat, Thai, patio*

Kanok [BYOB,WC] 3422 N Broadway St (at W Hawthorne Pl) 773/529-2525 *4pm-10:30pm, sushi/ Asian*

Kit Kat Lounge & Supper Club [C,DS,GO] 3700 N Halsted St (at W Waveland Ave) 773/525-1111 *5:30pm-1am, brunch Sun (seasonal)*

Kitsch'n On Roscoe 2005 W Roscoe (at Damen) 773/248-7372 *8:30am-3pm, dinner served in summer, full bar*

Las Mananitas [★WC] 3523 N Halsted St (at Cornelia) 773/528-2109 *11am-11pm, till midnight Fri-Sat, strong margaritas*

Melrose Restaurant 3233 N Broadway St 773/327-2060 *24hrs, great food*

Mon Ami Gabi 2300 N Lincoln Park W (at Belden) 773/348-8886 *dinner only, French bistro*

Nookie's Tree [★BYOB,WC] 3334 N Halsted St (at Roscoe) 773/248-9888 *7am-midnight, 24hrs wknds*

Orange 2413 N Clark St 773/549-7833 *8am-3pm, popular brunch spot*

Panino's Pizzeria [WC] 3702 N Broadway (at Waveland) 773/472-6200 *11:30am-11pm, till 10pm Sun, full bar*

Pick Me Up Cafe 3408 N Clark St (at Roscoe) 773/248-6613 *11am-3am, 24hrs Fri-Sat, brkfst all day*

Pie Hole Pizza 3477 N Broadway 773/525-8888 *5pm-3am, noon-5am wknds*

Pingpong [WC] 3322 N Broadway St 773/281-7575 *5pm-midnight, noon-10pm Sun, Asian fusion, patio*

The Raw Bar & Grill [E,WC] 3720 N Clark St (at Waveland) 773/348-7291, 773/348-7961 *11am-2am, till 3am Sat, seafood*

Stella's Diner 3042 N Broadway St 773/472-9040 *7am-10pm*

Sushisamba Rio [WC] 504 N Wells St (at W Illinois) 312/595-2300 *lunch & dinner, popular brunch, glitzy lounge atmosphere*

Tapas Gitana [MW] 3445 N Halsted St (btwn Newport & Cornelia) 773/296-6046 *5pm-11pm, clsd Mon, full bar, patio*

Taverna 750 [WC] 750 W Cornelia Ave (at Halsted) 773/904-7466 *5:30-late, Sun brunch, upscale Italian, full bar*

Yoshi's Cafe [★WC] 3257 N Halsted St (at Melrose) 773/248-6160 *dinner Tue-Sun, also Sun brunch, Asian-inspired French*

■ BOOKSTORES

Unabridged Books [★] 3251 N Broadway St (at Aldine) 773/883-9119 *10am-9pm, till 7pm wknds, LGBT section*

■ RETAIL SHOPS

Brown Elephant 3651 N Halsted St 773/549-5943 *11am-6pm, all purchases benefit Howard Brown general health center; also in Andersonville and Oak Park*

Uncle Fun 1338 W Belmont (at Racine) 773/477-8223 *heaven for kitsch lovers*

■ MEN'S CLUBS

Steamworks Men's Gym/ Sauna [WI] 3246 N Halsted St (N of Belmont) 773/929-6080 *24hrs*

■ EROTICA

Batteries Not Included 3420 N Halsted St (at Newport) 773/935-9900 *11am-midnight, till 1am Fri, 10am-2am Sat*

Cupid's Treasures 3519 N Halsted St (at Cornelia) 773/348-3884 *11am-midnight*

The Pleasure Chest 3436 N Lincoln Ave (btwn Roscoe & Addison) 773/525-7152, 800/525-7152 *clsd Sun*

The Ram Bookstore 3511 N Halsted St (at Addison) 773/525-9528

■ CRUISY AREAS

Belmont Rocks [AYOR]

Chicago—Near North

■ACCOMMODATIONS

ACME Hotel Company Chicago
[GF,WI,WC] 15 E Ohio St (at State St)
312/894-0900

Allegro Chicago [GF,F,E,WI,WC] 171 W
Randolph St (at LaSalle)
312/236-0123, 866/672-6143

Dana Hotel & Spa [GF,F,NS,WC] 660 N
State St (at Erie) 312/202-6000,
888/301-7946

Flemish House of Chicago
[GS,NS,WI,GO] 68 E Cedar St (btwn Rush
& Lake Shore Dr) 312/664-9981 *B&B,
studios & apts*

Gold Coast Guest House B&B
[GF,NS,WI] 113 W Elm St (btwn Clark &
LaSalle) 312/337-0361

The Hotel Burnham [GF,NS,WI] One W
Washington St (at State)
312/782-1111, 866/690-1986

Hotel Indigo Chicago Gold Coast
[GF,WI,WC] 1244 N Dearborn Pkwy
(btwn Goethe & Division)
312/787-4980, 866/521-6950

Hotel Monaco [GF,WI,NS] 225 N
Wabash (at S Water & Wacker Pl)
312/960-8500, 800/397-7661

Millennium Knickerbocker Hotel
[GF,F,WC] 163 E Walton Pl (Michigan
Ave) 312/751-8100, 800/621-8140

Old Town Chicago Guest House 1442 N North Park Ave (near
Wells & North) 312/440-9268

Palmer House Hilton [GF,SW] 17 E
Monroe St (at State St) 312/726-7500

W Chicago—City Center
[GF,NS,WI,WC] 172 W Adams St (at
LaSalle) 312/332-1200,
877/WHOTELS (reservations only) *in
the Loop, also restaurant & bar*

W Chicago—Lakeshore
[GF,SW,NS,WI,WC] 644 N Lake Shore Dr
(at Ontario) 312/943-9200,
877/WHOTELS (reservations only)

■BARS

Club Foot [GF,NH,D] 1824 W Augusta
Blvd (at Honore, in Wicker Park)
773/489-0379 *8pm-2am, till 3am Sat,
kitschy*

Davenport's [GS,C,P] 1383 N Milwaukee
(in Wicker Park) 773/278-1830 *7pm-
midnight, till 2am Fri-Sat, till 11pm Sun,
clsd Tue*

Downtown [★M,E,C,P,V] 440 N State (at
Illinois) 312/464-1400 *3pm-2am, till
3am Sat*

Second Story Bar [M,NH] 157 E Ohio
St (at Michigan Ave) 312/923-9536
1pm-2am, 2pm-3am Sat

Wang's [GS] 3317 N Broadway St
773/296-6800 *4pm-11pm, till 2am
Fri-Sat, noon-10pm Sun, more gay men
late night*

■NIGHTCLUBS

Baton Show Lounge [MW,DS,WC] 436
N Clark St (btwn Illinois & Hubbard)
312/644-5269 *showtimes at 8:30pm,
10:30pm, 12:30am, clsd Mon-Tue, reservations advised, since 1969!*

Chances Dances [MW,D] 2011 W North
Ave (at Damen, at Subterranean)
10pm-2am 3rd Mon; also 2nd Tue at
Danny's, 1959 W Dickens Ave

Sound Bar/ Y Bar [GS,D] 226 W
Ontario (btwn Franklin & Wells)
312/787-4480 *10pm-4am, till 5am
Sat, clsd Sun-Wed*

Underground Wonder Bar [GF,E,MR,P]
710 N Clark St (at Huron)
312/266-7761 *5pm-close*

■CAFES

Earwax Cafe & Film [F,WC] 1561 N
Milwaukee Ave (in Wicker Park)
773/772-4019 *11am-5pm, till 8pm
wknds, food served, some vegan*

■RESTAURANTS

Blackbird 619 W Randolph St (at Des
Plaines) 312/715-0708 *lunch Mon-Fri,
dinner nightly, clsd Sun*

Catch 35 35 W Wacker Dr (at
Dearborn) 312/346-3500,
312/346-3535 *lunch Mon-Fri, dinner
nightly, steak & seafood*

Fireplace Inn 1448 N Wells St (at
North Ave) 312/664-5264,
312/664-5264 *lunch & dinner, BBQ,
full bar open late*

Girl and the Goat [GO] 809 W Randolph St **312/492-6262** *4:30pm-11pm, clsd Mon-Wed*

Hot Chocolate [WC] 1747 N Damen Ave (in Wicker Park) **773/489-1747** *lunch, dinner & dessert, wknd brunch, clsd Mon*

Ina's 1235 W Randolph St (at Racine) **312/226-8227** *brkfst & lunch, full bar*

Kiki's Bistro [WC] 900 N Franklin St (at Locust) **312/335-5454** *lunch Mon-Fri, dinner nightly, clsd Sun, French, full bar*

Lou Mitchell's 565 W Jackson Blvd (at Jefferson) **312/939-3111** *great brkfst*

Manny's [WC] 1141 S Jefferson St (at Roosevelt) **312/939-2855** *6am-8pm, clsd Sun, killer corned beef*

Moonshine 1824 W Division St (at Honore, in Wicker Park) **773/862-8686** *dinner nightly, lunch Wed-Fri, wknd brunch, American, also bar*

Nacional 27 325 W Huron (at N Orleans) **312/664-2727** *dinner nightly, clsd Sun, Nuevo Latino, also lounge open late*

Park Grill 11 N Michigan Ave (in Millennium Park) **312/521-7275** *11am-10pm*

Parthenon Restaurant [WC] 314 S Halsted St (near W Jackson) **312/726-2407** *11am-midnight, full bar, "best gyros in Chicago"*

Shaw's Crab House [E,WC] 21 E Hubbard St (at State St) **312/527-2722** *lunch & dinner, full bar*

Topolobampo/ Frontera Grill 445 N Clark St (btwn Illinois & Hubbard) **312/661-1434** *lunch & dinner, Sat brunch (Frontera only), clsd Sun-Mon*

Vermilion [★WC] 10 W Hubbard St (at State) **312/527-4060** *lunch Mon-Fri, dinner nightly, Latin-Indian fusion, full bar, patio*

■**BOOKSTORES**

After-Words New & Used Books [WI] 23 E Illinois St (btwn State & Wabash) **312/464-1110** *10:30am-10pm, till 11pm Fri-Sat, noon-7pm Sun*

Quimby's Bookstore [WC] 1854 W North Ave (at Wolcott, in Wicker Park) **773/342-0910** *noon-9pm, 11am-10pm Sat, noon-6pm Sun*

■**RETAIL SHOPS**

Flight 001 1133 N State St (at Elm) **312/944-1001** *11am-6pm, till 7pm Sat, way cool travel gear*

■**GYMS & HEALTH CLUBS**

Cheetah Gym 1934 W North Ave (at Damen, in Wicker Park) **773/394-5900**

■**EROTICA**

Bijou Theatre 1349 N Wells St (at North Ave) **312/943-5397** *24hrs*

Frenchy's 872 N State St (at Delaware) **312/337-9190** *24hrs*

Lover's Playground 109 W Hubbard (at Clark) **312/828-0953** *24hrs*

Lover's Warehouse [WC] 1246 W Randolph (at Elizabeth) **312/226-5222** *24hrs*

Wells Books 178 N Wells (at Lake) **312/263-9266**

Chicago—South Side

■**BARS**

Club Escape [MW,D,DS,MR-AF,F] 1530 E 75th St (at Stoney Island Ave) **773/667-6454** *4pm-2am, till 3am Sat*

Inn Exile [M,D,V,WI,WC] 5758 W 65th St (at Menard, near Midway Airport; 1 mile W of Midway hotel center at 65th & Cicero) **773/582-3510** *8pm-2am, till 3am Sat*

Jeffery Pub [★MW,D,MR-AF,DS,WC] 7041 S Jeffery Blvd (at 71st) **773/363-8555** *noon-4am, till 5am Sat, clsd Mon*

■**NIGHTCLUBS**

Escapades [M,D,V] 6301 S Harlem Ave (at 63rd) **773/229-0886** *9pm-4am, till 5am Sat*

■**BOOKSTORES**

57th St Books 1301 E 57th St, Hyde Park (at Kimbark St) **773/684-1300** *10am-8pm*

Powell's Bookstore [★WC] 1218 S Halsted St (at W Roosevelt) **312/243-9070** *9am-9pm, 10am-6pm Sun, also 1501 E 57th St, 773/ 955-7780*

De Kalb

■NIGHTCLUBS

Otto's [GF,E] 118 E Lincoln Hwy
815/758-2715 *6:30pm-close, live music venue*

■EROTICA

Paperback Grotto 157 E Lincoln Hwy (at 2nd) **815/758-8061**

Decatur

■BARS

The Flashback Lounge [MW,NH,D] 2239 E Wood St (at 22nd) **217/422-3530** *9am-2am*

■RESTAURANTS

Robbie's Grill 122 N Merchant St **217/423-0448** *11am-10pm, till 3am Sat, clsd Sun, full bar*

■EROTICA

Romantix Adult Superstore 2015 N 22nd St **217/362-0105** *booths*

■CRUISY AREAS

Fairview Park [AYOR] *in the back*

Elk Grove Village

see also Chicago

■CRUISY AREAS

Busse Woods Forest Preserve [AYOR]

Elkhart

■CAFES

Bluestem Bake Shop 107 Governor Oglesby St **217/947-2222** *9am-4pm, clsd Mon, Wed & Sat*

Forest Park

■NIGHTCLUBS

Hideaway [M,D,K,DS,V] 7301 W Roosevelt Rd (at Marengo) **708/771-4459** *3pm-2am, till 3am Fri-Sat, male dancers*

Forest View

■BARS

Forest View Lounge [W,F,E] 4519 S Harlem Ave **208/484-9778** *11am-midnight, till 2am wknds, clsd Sun*

Galesburg

■MEN'S CLUBS

Hole in the Wall [MO,B,L,MR,F,V,18+,N,PC,WC,GO] 1438 Knox Hwy 9 (off I-74 at Exit 51) **309/289-2375** *10am-11pm, 24hrs Th-Sun, clsd Mon-Tue, steam room*

■EROTICA

Romantix Adult Superstore 595 N Henderson St (at Losey) **309/342-7019**

Hoffman Estates

■CRUISY AREAS

Beverly Lake Forest Preserve [AYOR] Rte 72 (btwn 25 & 59)

Ina

■CRUISY AREAS

Rend Lake [AYOR] off I-57 (S of Mt Vernon, N of Carbondale) *near boat ramp, beware of cops*

Joliet

■INFO LINES & SERVICES

Community Alliance & Action Network [WI] 68 N Chicago St #401 (at Jefferson) **815/726-7906** *by appointment, LGBT community center*

■NIGHTCLUBS

Maneuvers & Co [MW,D,TG,DS] 118 E Jefferson (at Chicago) **815/727-7069** *8pm-2am, till 3am Fri-Sat, patio, frequent events*

■CRUISY AREAS

Hammill Woods [AYOR] Rte 59 (2 miles N of Hwy 52) *beware of cops*

Kankakee

■CRUISY AREAS

Kankakee River State Park [AYOR] Rte 102 *across from main entrance, Dan Uze Area*

Illinois • USA

LaGrange

CRUISY AREAS
Possum Hollow Woods [AYOR] 31st St (W of LaGrange Rd)

Leroy

CRUISY AREAS
Moraine View State Park [AYOR] *around Dawson Lake & Timber Point*

Monticello

RESTAURANTS
The Brown Bag 212 W Washington St 217/762-9221 *9am-7pm, till 8pm Tue & Fri, till 4pm Sat, clsd Sun*

Morris

EROTICA
Forty-Seven Video 50 Gore Rd (N of exit 112, off I-80) 815/942-8309 *24hrs*

Normal

CAFES
Coffeehouse & Deli [E,WI] 114 E Beaufort St 309/452-6774 *7am-10pm, vegetarian/ vegan*

O'Fallon

RESTAURANTS
Paulo's at the Mansion [WC,GO] 1680 Mansion Wy (at Lakepointe Center Dr) 618/624-0629 *5pm-9pm Tue-Th, till 10pm Fri-Sat, steakhouse*

Oak Park

see also Berwyn & Chicago

Oakwood

EROTICA
Oasis Books & Video 504 N Oakwood St (off I-74) 217/354-4820 *24hrs, arcade*

Ottawa

EROTICA
Brown Bag Video 3042 N State Rte 71 (at I-80, exit 93) 815/313-4125 *24hrs*

CRUISY AREAS
Matthiessen State Park [AYOR] 1 mile E of I-39 (at Exit 54) *river area*

Peoria

ACCOMMODATIONS
Hotel Pere Marquette [GF,WI] 501 Main St 309/637-6500, 800/447-1676 *buffet brkfst*

BARS
Buddies On Adams [MW,NH,K,WI] 807 SW Adams St (at Oak St) 309/676-7438 *6pm-1am, till 4am Fri-Sat, clsd Mon*

CAFES
One World [WI,WC] 1245 W Main St (at University) 309/672-1522 *7am-11pm, from 8am wknds*

RESTAURANTS
Two 25 225 NE Adams St (at Mark Twain Hotel) 309/282-7777 *lunch Mon-Fri, dinner nightly, clsd Sun*

EROTICA
The Green Door 2610 W Farmington Rd (near Sterling Ave) 309/674-4337

Swingers World 335 SW Adams (at Harrison) 309/676-9275

Quincy

NIGHTCLUBS
Irene's Cabaret [★MW,D,B,L,MR,TG,E,K,DS,WC,GO] 124 N 5th St (at Washington Park, enter rear) 217/222-6292 *9pm-2:30am, from 7pm Fri-Sat, till 3:30am Sat, clsd Sun-Tue*

EROTICA
Chelsea Entertainment 4804 Gardner Expwy 217/224-7000

CRUISY AREAS
Parker Heights Park [AYOR] *parking lot by archery range*

Rockford

NIGHTCLUBS
The Office Niteclub [★MW,D,E,K,DS,S,V] 513 E State St (btwn 2nd & 3rd) 815/965-0344 *noon-2am*

■RESTAURANTS

Lucerne's Fondue & Spirits [R,WC]
845 N Church St (at Whitman)
815/968-2665 *5pm-11pm, clsd Mon*

Maria's 828 Cunningham St (at Corbin)
815/968-6781 *4:30pm-9pm, clsd Sun-Mon, full bar*

Schiller Park

■CRUISY AREAS

Schiller Woods [AYOR] Irving Park Rd
(btwn N Cumberland Ave & River Rd)

Springfield

■INFO LINES & SERVICES

The Phoenix Center 109 E Lawrence Ave **217/528-5253** *8:30am-4:30pm, clsd wknds*

■ACCOMMODATIONS

The State House Inn [GF,WI,WC] 101 E Adams St (at First St) **217/528-5100**

■BARS

The Station House [MW,NH,D,WC]
304-306 E Washington (btwn 3rd & 4th Sts) **217/525-0438** *5pm-1am, till 3am Th-Sat*

■RETAIL SHOPS

New Age Tattoos & Body Piercings
2915 S MacArthur Blvd **217/546-5006**
11am-8pm, till 6pm Sun

■MEN'S SERVICES

►**MegaMates** 217/801-9220 *Call to hook up with HOT local men. FREE to listen & respond to ads. Use FREE code DAMRON. MegaMates.com.*

■CRUISY AREAS

Douglas Park [AYOR] MacArthur & Mason

Riverside Park [AYOR] Peoria Rd N, past river

Waukegan

■CRUISY AREAS

Green Belt Forest Preserve Hwy 120 E, right on Green Bay Rd

INDIANA

Anderson

■EROTICA

After Dark 2012 Mounds Rd
765/649-7597 *10am-11pm, till midnight Fri-Sat, noon-10pm Sun*

Bloomington

■BARS

Uncle Elizabeth's [MW,NH,D,K,DS] 1614 W 3rd St **812/331-0060** *4pm-3am, 7pm-midnight Sun, patio*

■CAFES

Rachael's Cafe [E] 300 E 3rd St
812/330-1882 *8am-9pm, till 7pm Sun*

Soma Coffee House [WI] 322 E Kirkwood Ave (below Laughing Planet) **812/331-2770** *7am-11pm, from 8am Sun*

■RESTAURANTS

Laughing Planet Cafe 322 E Kirkwood Ave (enter on Grant) **812/323-2233** *11am-9pm, outdoor seating*

Village Deli 409 E Kirkwood
812/336-2303 *7am-9pm, 8am-9pm wknds*

■ENTERTAINMENT & RECREATION

BloomingOut WFHB 91.3 & 98.1 & 100.7 & 106.3FM **812/325-7870** & **323-1200** *6pm Th, "your midwest queer connection"*

■RETAIL SHOPS

Athena Gallery [WC] 116 N Walnut **812/339-0734** *10:30am-7pm, till 8:30pm Fri, noon-5pm Sun, clothing, drums, incense, gifts, etc*

■EROTICA

College Adult Bookstore 1013 N College Ave (at 14th) **812/332-5160** *24hrs*

■CRUISY AREAS

Cascades Park [AYOR] *beware of cops late evenings!*

Indiana • *USA*

Columbus

■CRUISY AREAS
Nobblitt Park [AYOR] 17th St (1 1/2 blocks W of Washington) *walk to train bridge*

Elkhart

see also **South Bend**

Evansville

■NIGHTCLUBS
Someplace Else [MW,D,K,DS] 930 Main St (at Sycamore) **812/424-3202** *4pm-3am*

■EROTICA
Bookmart of Evansville 519 N Main (by Lucky Lady) **812/423-2011** *24hrs*

Exotica 4605 Washington Ave **812/401-7399**

Fulton Ave Adult Books 201 S Fulton Ave (at 2nd) **812/421-0222**

■CRUISY AREAS
Mesker Park [AYOR] *police patrols are heavy*

Fort Wayne

■INFO LINES & SERVICES
Gay/ Lesbian AA 501 W Berry St (at Plymouth church) **260/423-9424** *2nd Tue at 6:30pm, 1pm every Sun*

■NIGHTCLUBS
After Dark [M,D,K,DS,S,WC,GO] 1601 S Harrison St (at Grand St) **260/456-6235** *noon-3am, 6pm-12:30am Sun*

Babylon [M,D,K] 112 E Masterson Ave **260/247-5092** *8pm-3am Fri-Sat only*

■CAFES
Firefly [E,WI] 3523 N Anthony Blvd **260/373-0505** *6:30am-8pm, from 8am wknds*

■RESTAURANTS
The Loving Cafe [WC] 7605 Coldwater Rd **260/489-8686** *10am-8pm, clsd Sun, vegetarian/ vegan*

■RETAIL SHOPS
Boudoir Noir 512 W Superior St **260/420-0557** *10am-midnight, noon-8pm Sun, gifts, toys, leather*

■CRUISY AREAS
Swinney Park [AYOR] *be alert—major crackdown on cruising in Fort Wayne*

Gary

see also **Chicago, Illinois**

■EROTICA
Romantix Adult Superstore 8801 W Melton Rd/ US 20 (at Ripley Rd) **219/938-2194** *24hrs*

Trucker's World [AYOR] 5480 W 25th Ave (off I-80/ 94, at Burr St) **219/844-3123**

Goshen

see also **South Bend**

■CAFES
The Electric Brew [E] 136 S Main St **574/533-5990** *6am-10pm, noon-7pm Sun*

Hammond

■ACCOMMODATIONS
Sibley Courtyard Inn [MO,NS,WI,PC,GO] 629 Sibley Blvd (at Calumet Ave) **219/933-9604** *gay men's guesthouse w/ bathhouse facilities: steam room, sauna, hot tub, private courtyard*

■BARS
Dick's R U Crazee? [M,NH,K,DS] 1221 E 150th St **219/852-0222** *8pm-3am, from 7pm wknds*

Hebron

■EROTICA
The Lion's Den Adult Superstore 18010 Colorado St (exit 240, off I-65) **219/696-1276** *24hrs*

Indiana Dunes

■ACCOMMODATIONS
The Gray Goose Inn B&B [GS,WI] 350 Indian Boundary Rd (at I-95), Chesterton **219/926-5781**, **800/521-5127** *full brkfst*

Indianapolis

■INFO LINES & SERVICES

AA Gay/ Lesbian 317/632-7864
*various LGBT meeting, check web
(www.indyaa.org) for meeting times &
locations*

■ACCOMMODATIONS

The Alexander [GF] 333 S Delaware St
855/200-3002 *boutique-style art
hotel*

The Fort Harrison State Park Inn
[GF,NS,WC] 5830 N Post Rd
317/638-6000 *luxury inn in historic
Fort Harrison in NE Indianapolis*

Stone Soup Inn [GS,WI] 1304 N
Central Ave (at 13th St)
317/639-9555, 866/639-9550 *in
the heart of the historic Old Northside*

Sycamore Knoll B&B [GS,NS,WI,GO]
10777 Riverwood Ave, Noblesville
317/776-0570 *1886 estate near the
White River, full brkfst, lesbian-owned*

The Villa [GS,WI] 1456 N Delaware St
(at 15th) **317/916-8500** ,
866/626-8500 *spa and restaurant*

Wyndham Indianapolis West
[GF,SW] 2544 Executive Dr (off Airport
Expy) **317/248-2481, 800/444-2326**
WJ in lobby, restaurant & lounge

■BARS

501 Eagle [★M,D,B,L] 501 N College (at
Michigan St) **317/632-2100** *5:30pm-
3am, from 7:30pm Sat, 4pm-12:30am
Sun*

Downtown Olly's [M,NH,K,V,WC] 822 N
Illinois St (at St Clair) **317/636-5597**
*open 24hrs, sports & video bar, brkfst,
lunch, dinner*

The Metro Nightclub & Restaurant
[★MW,F,K,P,WC] 707 Massachusetts Ave
(at College) **317/639-6022** *3pm-3am,
noon-midnight Sun, patio, also restaurant, giftshop*

Noah Grant's Grill House & Raw Bar
[GF,NH,F] 65 S 1st St (at W Oak St),
Zionsville **317/732-2233** *4pm-close,
clsd Mon, wine bar & bistro, full serving
lunch & dinner, Sun brunch, patio*

Varsity Lounge [M,NH,F,K,WI] 1517 N
Pennsylvania Ave (S of 16th)
317/635-9998 *10am-3am, till
midnight Sun*

Zonie's Closet [GS,K,DS] 1446 E
Washington St (at Arsenal)
317/266-0535 *8am-3am, noon-
midnight Sun*

■NIGHTCLUBS

Greg's [★M,D,DS,CW,V,WC] 231 E 16th
St (at Alabama) **317/638-8138** *4pm-
3am, patio*

Talbott Street [★GS,D,DS,GO] 2145 N
Talbott St (at 22nd St) **317/931-1343**
9pm-2am Fri-Sat

The Ten [★MW,D,DS,S,WC] 1218 N
Pennsylvania St (at 12th, enter rear)
317/638-5802 *6pm-3am, till 1am
Wed, till midnight Sun, clsd Mon-Tue*

■CAFES

Bjava 5510 Lafayette Rd (at 56th St)
317/280-1236 *6am-5pm, 7am-3pm
Sat, clsd Sun*

Cornerstone Coffeehouse [F,WI] 651 E
54th St (at N College Ave, Broad Ripple)
317/726-1360 *6am-10pm, from 7am
Sat, till 9pm Sun, also full bar*

Earth House Collective [WI] 237 N
East St **317/636-4060** *11am-9pm,
clsd Sun, coffeehouse, also art, music &
classes*

Henry's on East Street [★F,WI,GO] 627
N East St **317/951-0335** *7am-7pm,
till 9pm Fri, from 8am wknds*

Hubbard & Cravens [F,WI] 4930 N
Pennsylvania St (in Broad Ripple)
317/251-5161 *6am-7pm, 7am-3pm
Sun*

Monon Coffee Company 920 E
Westfield Blvd (at Guilford)
317/255-0510 *6:30am-8pm, till 10pm
Fri, from 7am Sat, 8am-8pm Sun*

■RESTAURANTS

14 West 14 W Maryland St
317/636-1414 *lunch & dinner,
seafood & steaks, patio*

Adobo Grill [WC] 110 E Washington
317/822-9990 *lunch Fri-Sun, dinner
nightly, Mexican, full bar*

Aesop's Tables [BW,WC] 600 E Massachusetts Ave **317/631-0055** *lunch & dinner, clsd Sun, authentic Mediterranean*

BARcelona 201 N Delaware St **317/638-8272** *11am-11pm, also full bar, tapas*

Bazbeaux Pizza 329 Massachusetts Ave **317/636-7662** *lunch & dinner*

Cafe Zuppa 320 N Meridian St (at New York St) **317/634-9877** *7am-2:30pm, Sun brunch buffet*

Creation Cafe & Euphoria 337 W 11th St (in Buggs' Temple) **317/955-2389** *8am-9pm, clsd Sun, outdoor seating*

English Ivy's [WI,WC] 944 S Alabama (at 10th) **317/822-5070** *11am-3am from 10am wknds, also full bar*

India Garden [WC] 830 Broad Ripple Ave (btwn Carrollton & Guilford) **317/253-6060** *lunch & dinner, Indian; also 207 N Delaware St, 317/634-6060*

King David Dogs 15 N Pennsylvania St *great hot dogs*

La Piedad 6524 Cornell Ave **317/475-0988** *lunch & dinner, Mexican*

Mama Carolla's [★WC] 1031 E 54th St (at Winthrop) **317/259-9412** *dinner only, clsd Sun-Mon, traditional Italian*

Naked Tchopstix [★BW] 6253 N College Ave (in Broad Ripple) **317/252-5555** *lunch & dinner, Korean, Japanese, Chinese cuisine, also sushi bar*

Oakley's Bistro [★WC] 1464 W 86th St (at Ditch Rd) **317/824-1231** *lunch & dinner, clsd Sun-Mon, gourmet cont'l, reservations suggested*

Pancho's Taqueria [★WC] 7023 Michigan Rd (at Westlane) **317/202-9015** *11am-9pm, authentic Mexican*

Sawasdee [WC] 1222 W 86th St (at Ditch Rd) **317/844-9451** *lunch Mon-Sat, dinner nightly, Thai, some veggie*

Three Sisters Cafe 6360 N Guilford Ave (at Main St) **317/257-5556** *8am-9pm, till 3pm Sun, plenty veggie & vegan, popular Sun brunch*

Usual Suspects 6319 Guilford Ave (at Broad Ripple) **317/251-3138** *5pm-10pm, till 11pm Fri-Sat, till 9pm Sun, clsd Mon, eclectic, full bar, patio*

Yats [★WC] 659 Massachusetts Ave (at Walnut) **317/686-6380** *11am-9pm, till 10pm Fri-Sat, till 7pm Sun, Cajun; also also 5363 N College Ave & 8352 E 96th St*

■ ENTERTAINMENT & RECREATION

Indy Indie Artist Colony 26 E 14th St **317/295-9302** *noon-5pm Th-Sat, largest artist community in the city with 72 artist live/work spaces*

Theatre on the Square 627 Massachusetts Ave (at East) **317/685-8687**

■ BOOKSTORES

Big Hat Books 6510 Cornell Ave **317/202-0203** *10am-6pm, noon-5pm Sun, general independent*

Bookmamas 9 S Johnson Ave (at E Washington St, in Irvington) **317/375-3715** *open Wed-Sat, call for hours, used bookstore*

■ RETAIL SHOPS

All My Relations 7218 Rockville Rd **317/227-3925** *noon-6pm, till 7pm Wed-Th, 10am-6pm Sat, New Age/meta-physical store, also classes*

Metamorphosis [18+] 828 Broad Ripple Ave (at Carrollton) **317/466-1666** *1pm-9pm, till 5pm Sun, tattoo & piercing parlor*

■ PUBLICATIONS

Nuvo 317/254-2400 *Indy's alternative weekly*

►The Word 317/632-8840 *LGBT newspaper*

■ MEN'S CLUBS

Club Indianapolis [18+,SW,PC] 620 N Capitol Ave (at North & Walnut) **317/635-5796** *24hrs, steam, sauna, gym, outdoor patio*

The Works [WI,PC,GO] 4120 N Keystone Ave (at 38th) **317/547-9210** *24hrs*

■ MEN'S SERVICES
➤ MegaMates 317/322-9000 *Call to hook up with HOT local men. FREE to listen & respond to ads. Use FREE code DAMRON. MegaMates.com.*

■ EROTICA
Annex Bookstore 6767 E 38th St (at Massachusetts) 317/549-3522 *9am-3am*

■ CRUISY AREAS
Damron does not list here as there are 9 cops to every 1 cruiser [AYOR]

Kokomo

■ BARS
Bar Blue [★MW,D,F,K,DS,S] 1400 W Markland Ave (at Park) 765/456-1400 *open Sat only, patio*

■ CRUISY AREAS
Highland Park [AYOR] near "Old Ben"

Lafayette

■ INFO LINES & SERVICES
Pride Lafayette, Inc 640 Main St #218 765/423-7579 *community center 6pm-8pm, 5pm-9pm wknds, support/social activities*

■ EROTICA
Fantasy East 2315 Concord Rd (at Teal) 765/474-2417 *10am-1am*

Logansport

■ CRUISY AREAS
Spencer Park [AYOR] near tennis courts & trails along Eel River

Madison

■ CRUISY AREAS
Clifty St Park [AYOR] btwn poplar & oak groves

Vaughn Dr [AYOR] along river

Indiana • *USA*

Marion

■EROTICA

After Dark 1311 W Johnson St
765/662-3688 *10am-11pm, till
midnight Fri-Sat, noon-10pm Sun*

Michigan City

■ACCOMMODATIONS

Duneland Beach Inn & Restaurant
[GF] 3311 Pottawattomie Trail (at
Duneland Beach Dr) 219/874-7729,
800/423-7729 *also restaurant/ bar,
private beach, 60 miles from Chicago*

Tryon Farm Guest House [GF,NS,WI]
1400 Tryon Rd (at Hwy 212)
219/879-3618 *full brkfst, hot tub*

Mishawaka

see also South Bend

■ACCOMMODATIONS

The Beiger Mansion [GF,SW,NS,WI,GO]
317 Lincolnway E 574/255-6300,
800/437-0131 *B&B in 4-level neo-
classical limestone mansion*

Morgantown

■ACCOMMODATIONS

Camp Buckwood [MO,SW,GO] 8670
Spearsville Rd 812/597-2450 *lodge
w/ tents & RV sites, cabins, play areas*

Muncie

■CRUISY AREAS

McCulloch Park [AYOR] on Broadway
(past the Muncie Mall)

New Albany

see Louisville, KY

Richmond

■EROTICA

Exotic Fantasies 12 S 11th St
765/935-5827

South Bend

■ACCOMMODATIONS

Innisfree B&B [GF,NS] 702 W Colfax
574/283-0740 *1892 Queen Anne
minutes from Notre Dame, full brkfst*

■BARS

Jeannie's Tavern [GF,NH,TG,GO] 621 S
Bendix (at Ford St) 574/288-2962
2pm-2am

Vickies Inc [GS,NH,TG,F,GO] 112 W
Monroe St (at S Michigan St)
574/232-4090 *2pm-2am, football
party every Sat in season*

■ENTERTAINMENT &
    RECREATION

GLBT Resource Center of Michiana
574/254-1411 *5pm-8pm Mon &
11am-2pm Sat*

■EROTICA

Romantix Adult Superstore 2715 S
Main St (at Eckman St) 574/291-1899

■CRUISY AREAS

Rum Village Park [AYOR] W Ewing Ave

Terre Haute

■NIGHTCLUBS

Zim Marss Nightclub [MW,D,TG,DS,S]
1500 Locust St (at 15th St)
812/232-3026 *8pm-3am, 7pm-
12:30am Sun, clsd Mon-Tue*

■CRUISY AREAS

Deming Park [AYOR]

Fairbanks Park [AYOR] S 1st Ave

Valparaiso

■ACCOMMODATIONS

Inn at Aberdeen [GF,NS,WI,WC] 3158 S
State Rd 2 219/465-3753,
866/761-3753 *1880s Queen Anne, full
brkfst*

Vevay

■CAFES

Java Bean Cafe & Confectionery
[GO] 117 W Main St 812/427-2888
7am-7pm, clsd Sun

Vincennes

■CRUISY AREAS

**George Rodgers Clark Memorial
Park** [AYOR]

Iowa

Statewide

PUBLICATIONS
The ACCESSline 712/560-1807 *the Heartland's LGBT newspaper*

Ames

RESTAURANTS
Lucullan's Italian Grill 400 Main St (at Burnett) 515/232-8484 *dinner Tue-Sun, Italian, full bar*

EROTICA
Romantix Adult Superstore 117 Kellogg St (at Lincoln Wy) 515/232-7717 *9am-4am*

Boone

CRUISY AREAS
Roadside Park [AYOR] 1 mile W on US-30

Burlington

ACCOMMODATIONS
Arrowhead Motel, Inc [GF,WI,WC,GO] 2520 Mt Pleasant St 319/752-6353

BARS
Steve's Place [GS,F,WC,GO] 852 Washington St (at Central Ave) 319/754-5868 *9am-2am, clsd Sun, full menu*

EROTICA
Risque IV 421 Dry Creek Ave, West Burlington 319/753-5455 *8am-midnight, 24hrs Th-Sat*

CRUISY AREAS
Hunt Woods [AYOR] 1 mile S of town *days*

Cedar Falls
see also Waterloo

Cedar Rapids

BARS
The Piano Lounge [GS,E] 208 2nd Ave SE 319/363-0606 *4pm-2am, clsd Sun*

NIGHTCLUBS
Club Basix [MW,D,L,TG,DS,GO] 3916 1st Ave NE (btwn 39th & 40th) 319/363-3194 *5pm-2am, from noon wknds*

CAFES
Blue Strawberry [NS] 118 2nd St SE 319/247-2583 *7am-8pm, 8am-5pm Sun*

ENTERTAINMENT & RECREATION
CSPS Arts Center 1103 3rd St SE 319/364-1580 *many LGBT events*

EROTICA
Adult Shop 630 66th Ave SW (at 6th St) 319/362-4939 *24hrs*

Adult Shop North 5539 Crane Ln NE 319/294-5360 *24hrs*

Clinton

EROTICA
ABC Books 135 5th Ave S 563/242-7687

Council Bluffs
see also Omaha, Nebraska

RESTAURANTS
Dixie Quick's [R] 157 W Broadway 712/256-4140 *lunch & dinner, brunch from 9am wkds, clsd Mon, Southern*

EROTICA
Romantix Adult Superstore 3216 1st Ave (at Broadway) 712/328-2673 *24hrs*

Romantix Adult Superstore 50662 189th St 712/366-1764 *24hrs*

Davenport

ACCOMMODATIONS
Hotel Blackhawk [GF] 200 East 3rd St 563/322 5000, 888/525-4455

BARS
Mary's on 2nd [MW,NH,D,E,V,WC] 832 W 2nd St (btwn Warren & Brown) 563/884-8014 *4pm-2am, patio*

NIGHTCLUBS
Connections [MW,D,DS,K] 822 W 2nd St (at Brown) 563/322-1121 *5pm-2am*

Iowa • USA

■EROTICA

TR Video 3727 Hickory Grove Rd (at Fairmont & Hickory Grove) 563/386-7914

Venus News 902 W 3rd St (at Warren) 563/322-7576

■CRUISY AREAS

Credit Island Park [AYOR] W River Dr (W end) *daytime*

Davenport Levee [AYOR] under the Centennial Bridge *dusk*

Le Clair Park [AYOR] on riverfront from Main to Ripley *late*

Des Moines

■INFO LINES & SERVICES

The Center/ Equality Iowa 515/243-0313

■ACCOMMODATIONS

Hotel Fort Des Moines [GF,SW,NS,WI,WC] 1000 Walnut St (at 10th St) 515/243-1161, 800/532-1466

The Renaissance Savery Hotel [GF,F,SW,WI,WC] 401 Locust St (at 4th) 515/244-2151, 800/514

■BARS

The Blazing Saddle [★M,D,L,DS,S,WI,WC] 416 E 5th St (btwn Grand & Locust) 515/246-1299 *2pm-2am, from noon wknds*

Buddy's Corral [GF,K] 418 E 5th St (btwn Grand & Locust) 515/244-7140 *noon-2am, from 10am Sat*

■NIGHTCLUBS

The Garden [MW,D,K,S,V,YC,WC] 112 SE 4th St 515/243-3965 *8pm-2am, 5pm-midnight Sun, clsd Mon-Tue, patio*

Le Boi Bar [MW,D,DS] 508 Indianola Ave (at 7th) 515/284-1074 *8pm-2am, 3pm-midnight Sun, clsd Mon-Tue*

■CAFES

Drake Diner [F,WC] 1111 25th St (btwn University & Cottage Grove) 515/277-1111 *7am-11pm, try the cake shake, patio, also full bar*

Java Joe's [E,NS,WI,WC] 214 4th St (at Court Ave) 515/288-5282 *7am-11pm, till midnight Th-Sat, till 10pm Sun*

Ritual Cafe [E] 1301 E Locust St 515/288-4872 *7am-7pm, till 11pm Fri-Sat, clsd Sun*

Zanzibar's Coffee Adventure [WC] 2723 Ingersoll Ave (at 28th St) 515/244-7694 *6:30am-8pm, till 9pm Fri-Sat, 8am-6pm Sun*

■RESTAURANTS

Cafe di Scala [E,WC] 644 18th St (at Woodland) 515/244-1353 *dinner Th-Sat only*

■ENTERTAINMENT & RECREATION

First Friday Breakfast Club, Inc [MO,R] 1501 Woodland (at 15th) 515/288-2500, 515/284-0880 *7am-8:15am 1st Fri, gay & bisexual men, cont'l brkfst, guest speakers, call to reserve*

■RETAIL SHOPS

Liberty Gifts 333 E Grand Ave, Ste 105 (entrance on E 4th St) 515/508-0825 *10am-8pm, 11am-7pm Sun pride store*

■MEN'S SERVICES

➤**MegaMates** 515/267-0900 *Call to hook up with HOT local men. FREE to listen & respond to ads. Use FREE code DAMRON. MegaMates.com.*

■EROTICA

Gallery Book Store 1000 Cherry St (at 10th) 515/244-2916

Minx Love Boutique 1510 NE Broadway 515/266-2744 *also Minx Show Palace*

Romantix Adult Superstore 2020 E Euclid Ave (at Delaware) 515/266-7992 *24hrs*

■CRUISY AREAS

West River Dr [AYOR] N of downtown, by the river (off 2nd Ave N)

Dubuque

■CAFES

Cafe Manna Java [WI,GO] 700 Locust St (Roshek Building) 563/588-3105 *7am-9pm, 8am-2am Sun, full bar*

■CRUISY AREAS

Julien Dubuque Monument Park [AYOR]

Fort Dodge

■EROTICA
Romantix Adult Superstore 15 N 5th St (on the square) 515/955-9756

Iowa City

■INFO LINES & SERVICES
AA Gay/ Lesbian 500 N Clinton (at church) 319/338-9111 (AA#) *5pm Sun*

■BARS
Deadwood Tavern [★GF,NH,WC] 6 S Dubuque St 319/351-9417 *11am-2am, mostly straight, college crowd*

Studio 13 [MW,D,DS,S,19+,GO] 13 S Linn St (in the alley btwn Linn & Dubuque Sts) 319/338-7185 *7pm-2am, clsd Mon*

■RESTAURANTS
The Mill [E] 120 E Burlington St 319/351-9529 *lunch & dinner, wknd brunch, live music*

■BOOKSTORES
Prairie Lights Bookstore [WC] 15 S Dubuque St (at Washington) 319/337-2681, 800/295-2665 *9am-9pm, till 6pm Sun, also cafe & wine bar*

■RETAIL SHOPS
New Pioneer Co-op & Bakehouse [GF,WC] 22 S Van Buren (at Washington) 319/338-9441 *7am-11pm, health food store & deli; also Coralville location at 1101 2nd St*

■EROTICA
Romantix Adult Superstore 315 Kirkwood Ave (at Gilbert) 319/351-9444 *8am-4am*

Marshalltown

■EROTICA
Adult Odyssey 907 Iowa Ave E 641/752-6550 *10am-11pm. till 3am Fri-Sat*

Newton

■EROTICA
The Lion's Den Adult Superstore 7717 Hwy F 48 West (Exit 159, off I-80) 641/792-9301 *24hrs*

Ottumwa

■EROTICA
Cinema X 317 E Main St (downtown exit, off Rte 34) 641/683-1481 *clsd Mon*

■CRUISY AREAS
Greater Ottumwa Park [AYOR]

Sioux City

■NIGHTCLUBS
Jones Street Station [GS,D,MR,TG,K,DS,V,WC,GO] 412 Jones St (at 5th St) 712/258-6338 *8pm-2am, clsd Sun-Mon*

■EROTICA
Romantix Adult Superstore 511 Pearl St 712/277-8566 *8am-4am, noon-2am Sun*

Waterloo

■ACCOMMODATIONS
Stella's Guesthouse & Gardens [MW,N,NS,GO] 324 Summit Ave (at Chicago) 319/232-2122 *B&B in 107-year-old home, full brkfst, hot tub, shared baths*

■NIGHTCLUBS
Kings & Queens Knight Club [GF,D,TG,DS,V,YC,WC] 304 W 4th St (at Jefferson) 319/232-3001 *6:30pm-2am, clsd Sun-Mon*

■EROTICA
Adult Cinema 16 315 E 4th St (at Mulberry) 319/234-7459 *9am-2am, till midnight Sun*

Romantix Adult Superstore 1507 La Porte Rd (at Lock) 319/234-9340 *24hrs*

KANSAS

Statewide

■PUBLICATIONS

The Liberty Press 316/652-7737
Kansas statewide LGBT newspaper

Abilene

■EROTICA

The Lion's Den Adult Superstore
2349 Fair Rd (exit 272 off I-70)
785/263-9898

Great Bend

■CRUISY AREAS

Fort Zarah Rest Area [AYOR] on Santa
Fe Trail (on Hwy 56) *2 miles E of Great
Bend*

Hutchinson

■CRUISY AREAS

Carey Park [AYOR] Main St (at the very
S end)

Junction City

■NIGHTCLUBS

Xcalibur Club [MW,D,E,DS,18+,GO] 384
Grant Ave **785/762-2050** *6pm-2am,
clsd Mon-Tue*

■EROTICA

After Dark Video 785/762-4747
9am-2am, cruisy

Kansas City

see also Kansas City, Missouri

■MEN'S SERVICES

➤**MegaMates** 913/904-9974 *Call to
hook up with HOT local men. FREE to
listen & respond to ads. Use FREE code
DAMRON. MegaMates.com.*

■CRUISY AREAS

Pierson Park [AYOR] Wyandotte County
(off Nieman Rd) *Mon-Fri*

Lawrence

■NIGHTCLUBS

Granada [GS,D,E,NS,WC] 1020
Massachusetts (at 11th)
785/842-1390 *hours vary, live bands*

Jazzhaus [GF,E,K,WI] 926-1/2
Massachusetts St **785/749-3320,
785/749-1387** *8pm-2am*

Wilde's Chateau [GS,D] 2412 Iowa St
785/856-1514 *9pm-2am Wed, Fri-Sat
only*

■CAFES

Henry's [★WI] 11 E 8th St (btwn
Massachusetts St & New Hampshire St)
785/331-3511 *7am-2am, cafe downstairs, bar from 5pm upstairs*

Java Break [GO] 17 E 7th St (at New
Hampshire) **785/749-5282** *24hrs,
sandwiches, desserts*

■RESTAURANTS

Teller's Restaurant & Bar [WC] 746
Massachusetts St (at 8th)
785/843-4111 *11am-10pm, till 11pm
Fri-Sat, from 10am Sun, Italian*

■BOOKSTORES

The Dusty Bookshelf [GO] 708
Massachusetts St **785/749-4643**
*10am-8pm, till 10pm Fri-Sat, noon-6pm
Sun, LGBT section*

■CRUISY AREAS

Memorial Drive [AYOR] E of Jayhawk
Blvd

Riverfront Park [AYOR] Hwy 24/40 (at
N 2nd St)

Manhattan

■BOOKSTORES

The Dusty Bookshelf [GO] 700 N
Manhattan Ave **785/539-2839** *10am-
8pm, till 6pm Sat, noon-5pm Sun*

■CRUISY AREAS

Tuttle Creek Park [AYOR]

Olathe

■CRUISY AREAS

Cedar Lake [AYOR] on Lone Elm Rd

Overland Park

■ACCOMMODATIONS

Hawthorn Suites [GF,SW,NS,WI,WC]
11400 College Blvd **913/826-6167**

Salina

■CRUISY AREAS

Thomas Park [AYOR] 1/2 mile S of I-70 (at 9th St exit)

Topeka

■INFO LINES & SERVICES

Freedom Group AA 3916 SW 17th St (at Gage, at St David's church) **785/272-9483** *8pm Fri*

■BARS

Skivies [M,NH,D,DS,CW,B,L,GO] 921 S Kansas Ave (near 10th St) **785/234-0482** *3pm-2am*

■CRUISY AREAS

Gage Park [AYOR] *beware of cops!*

Shunga Park [AYOR] 29th St & Fairlawn Rd

Wichita

■INFO LINES & SERVICES

One Day at a Time Gay AA 156 S Kansas Ave (at MCC, enter on English) **316/684-3661** *8pm Tue & Th*

■ACCOMMODATIONS

Hawthorn Suites [GF,WI,WC] 2405 N Ridge Rd **316/729-5700** *brkfst buffet*

■BARS

J's Lounge [MW,E,K,C,WC] 513 E Central Ave (at N Emporia St) **316/262-1363** *4pm-2am, cabaret, patio, "an upscale dive"*

Rain Cafe & Lounge [MW,D,F,K,GO] 518 E Douglas Ave **316/261-9000** *11am-2am*

The Store [W,NH] 3210 E Osie **316/683-9781** *2pm-2am, men welcome*

■NIGHTCLUBS

Fantasy Complex [MW,D,CW,K,DS,S,18+,WC] 3201 S Hillside (at 31st) **316/682-5494** *8pm-2am Th-Sun, also South Forty [CW]*

■CAFES

Riverside Perk [E,WI,WC] 1144 N Bitting Ave (at 11th) **316/264-6464** *7am-10pm, till midnight Fri-Sat, from 10am Sun; also Lava Lounge juice bar next door*

The Vagabond [WI] 614 W Douglas Ave **316/303-1110** *7am-2am, also art gallery & bar, theme nights*

■RESTAURANTS

Moe's Sub Shop 2815 S Hydraulic St (at Wassall) **316/524-5511** *11am-8pm, clsd Sun*

Oh Yeah! China Bistro [WC] 3101 N Rock Rd **316/425-7700** *lunch & dinner*

Old Mill Tasty Shop 604 E Douglas Ave (at St Francis) **316/264-6500** *11am-3pm, from 8am Sat, clsd Sun, old-fashioned soda fountain*

Rain Cafe & Lounge [★D] 518 E Douglas (btwn St Francis & Emporia) **316/261-9000** *11am-2am, from 1pm Sun, full menu till 9pm, full bar, DJ on wknds*

River City Brewing Company 150 N Mosley St **316/263-2739** *11am-10pm, till 2am wknds, also live music*

Riverside Cafe 739 W 13th St (at Bitting) **316/262-6703** *6am-8pm, till 2pm Sun*

■ENTERTAINMENT & RECREATION

Cabaret Oldtown Theatre 412 1/2 E Douglas Ave (at Topeka) **316/265-4400** *edgy, kitschy productions*

Mosley Street Melodrama [F,$] 234 N Mosley St (btwn 1st & 2nd St) **316/263-0222** *melodrama, homestyle buffet & full bar!*

Wichita Arts 334 N Mead **316/462-2787** *promotes visual & performing arts; ArtScene publication has extensive cultural calendar*

■PUBLICATIONS

The Liberty Press 316/652-7737 *statewide LGBT newspaper*

■MEN'S SERVICES

►**MegaMates** 316/267-8500 *Call to hook up with HOT local men. FREE to listen & respond to ads. Use FREE code DAMRON. MegaMates.com.*

■EROTICA

Adult Superstore 5858 S Broadway **316/522-9040** *24hrs*

Kansas • USA

After Dark 7805 W Kellogg (at Tyler exit) **316/721-3160**

Circle Cinema/ Video 2570 S Seneca St (at Crawford St) **316/264-2245** *24hrs*

Fetish Lingerie 2150 S Broadway St (btwn E Clark & E Kinkaid Sts) **316/264-7800** *11:30-7pm, clsd Sun-Mon*

Patricia's 6143 W Kellogg (at Dugan) **316/942-1244** *9am-1am, from noon-10pm Sun*

Xcitement Video 3909 W Pawnee St **316/942-0200** *24hrs*

■CRUISY AREAS

Chisholm Trail Park [AYOR] Oliver & 29th St *days*

KENTUCKY

Ashland

■CRUISY AREAS

Central Park [AYOR] *beware of cops on bikes!*

Campbellsville

■CRUISY AREAS

Green River Dam [AYOR] Hwy 55 (below dam)

Covington

see also Cincinnati, Ohio

■BARS

701 Bar & Lounge [GF,NH,D,F,E,K] 701 Bakewell St (at 7th St) **859/431-7011** *3pm-1am, from 1pm Sun*

Bar Monet [MW,D,F,S] 837 Willard St **859/491-2403** *4pm-1am*

Rosie's Tavern [GS,NH,GO] 643 Bakewell St (at 7th St) **859/291-9707** *3pm-2:30am*

Yadda Club [MW,NH,MR,F,E,K,WC] 404 Pike St (at Main St) **859/491-5600** *8pm-2:30am Wed-Sun, patio*

■CAFES

Pike Street Lounge [K] 266 Pike St **859/916-5430** *8am-1am, from 11am wknds, coffee & cocktails, local art*

■CRUISY AREAS

Devou Park [AYOR] Covington exit, off Rte 75

Jamestown

■CRUISY AREAS

Kendall Recreation Area [AYOR] below Wolf Creek Dam (10 miles S on Hwy 127) *also pull-off areas & overlook above dam*

Lexington

■INFO LINES & SERVICES

Gay/ Lesbian AA 530 E High St (at Woodland Church) **859/225-1212** **(AA#)** *8pm Wed, also 7:30pm Fri at 205 E Short St*

GLSO Pride Center of the Bluegrass 389 Waller Ave #100 **859/253-3233** *10am-3pm Mon-Fri*

■ACCOMMODATIONS

The Bear & Boar B&B Resort [MO,SW,WI,GO] Wood Creek Lake **606/862-6557** *also camping, theme parties*

Hyatt Regency Lexington [GF,F,SW,WC] 401 W High St **859/253-1234**

Ramada Limited [GF,SW,NS,WI,WC] 2261 Elkhorn Rd (off I-75) **859/294-7375, 800/272-6232**

■BARS

The Bar Complex [★MW,D,DS,S,WI,WC] 224 E Main St (at Esplanade) **859/255-1551** *4pm-midnight, till 2am wknds*

Crossings [M,NH,K,L,S,WC] 117 N Limestone St **859/233-7266** *4pm-2am*

Soundbar [GS,D,K] 208 S Limestone **859/523-6338** *4:30pm-close*

■CAFES

Third Street Stuff [F] 257 N Limestone **859/255-5301** *6:30am-11pm, from 8am Sun, also funky boutique*

■RESTAURANTS

Alfalfa Restaurant [E] 141 E Main St **859/253-0014** *lunch & dinner, brunch wknds, healthy multi-ethnic, folk music wknds*

Natasha's Bistro & Bar [E] 112 Esplanade (at Main St) 859/259-2754 *lunch & dinner, clsd Sun, eclectic dining, plenty veggie, also live theater & music*

■BOOKSTORES

Joseph-Beth [WI,WC] 161 Lexington Green Circle (at Nicholasville Rd) 859/273-2911, 800/248-6849 *9am-10pm, till 11pm Fri-Sat, 11am-9pm Sun, also cafe*

Sqecial Media 371 S Limestone St (btwn Pine & Winslow) 859/255-4316 *10am-8pm, noon-6pm Sun, also pride items*

■PUBLICATIONS

LinQ 859/253-3233 *local news & calendar*

■EROTICA

Hook Novelty 940 Winchester Rd 859/252-2093

Romantix Adult Superstore 933 Winchester Rd (at Liberty Rd) 859/252-0357 *24hrs*

■CRUISY AREAS

Jacobson Park [AYOR] Richmond Rd (3 miles W of Lexington) *take 3 rights inside park to sunbathing area*

Woodland Park [AYOR] E High St

Louisville

■INFO LINES & SERVICES

Gay AA 1722 Bardstown Rd (Bardstown Rd Pres Ch) 502/587-6225 *6:30pm Wed, 7pm Fri; also 4:30pm Sun & 6pm Mon at MCC 1432 Highland Ave*

■ACCOMMODATIONS

21c Museum Hotel Louisville [★GF] 700 W Main St 502/217-6300, 877/217-6400 *boutique hotel w/ museum*

The Brown Hotel [GF,WI,NS] 335 W Broadway (at 4th) 502/583-1234, 888/387-0498 *also restaurant & bar*

Columbine B&B [GF,NS,WI,GO] 1707 S 3rd St (near Lee St) 502/635-5000, 800/635-5010 *1896 Greek Revivial mansion, full brkfst*

Galt House Hotel & Suites [GF] 140 N 4th St (at W Main) 502/589-5200, 800/843-4258 *waterfront hotel*

Inn at the Park [GF,NS,WI] 1332 S 4th St (at Park Ave) 502/638-0045 *restored mansion, full brkfst*

■BARS

The Levee [GS,NH,D,K,WI] 1005 W Market, Jeffersonville, IN 4pm-3am

Magnolia Bar [GF,NH] 1398 S 2nd St (at Magnolia) 502/637-9052 *2pm-4am*

Teddy Bears Bar & Grill [M,NH,WC] 1148 Garvin Pl (at St Catherine) 502/589-2619 *11am-4am, from 1pm Sun*

Tryangles [M,K,S,WC] 209 S Preston St (at Market) 502/583-6395 *4pm-4am, from 1pm Sun*

■NIGHTCLUBS

Boots [★M,L] 120 S Floyd St (in Connections Complex) 502/585-5752 *open 9pm Fri-Sate, dress code, fireplace, patio*

The Connection Complex [★MW,D,C,P,V,WC] 120 S Floyd St (at Market) 502/585-5752 *8pm-4am, till 2am Mon-Tue, 5 bars*

Lisa'a Oak Street Lounge [GS,E,K] 1004 E Oak St 502/637-9315 *9pm-1am, 7pm-3am Fri-Sat*

■RESTAURANTS

The Bodega at Felice [WI,GO] 829 E Market St 502/569-4100 *7am-7pm, till 11pm Fri, 9am-4pm Sat, clsd Sun, gourmet market & deli, coffee bar*

Cafe Mimosa 1543 Bardstown Rd (at Stevens Ave) 502/458-2233 *lunch & dinner, Vietnamese, Chinese & sushi*

El Mundo [★WC] 2345 Frankfort Ave 502/899-9930 *11:30am-10pm, full bar till 2am Th-Sat, clsd Sun-Mon, Mexican*

Havana Rumba 4115 Oechsli Ave (off State Hwy 1447) 502/897-1959 *lunch & dinner, Cuban*

Jack Fry's [WC] 1007 Bardstown Rd 502/452-9244 *lunch & dinner, steak/ Southern, live jazz*

Mayan Cafe 813 E Market St 502/566-0651 *lunch Mon-Fri, dinner nightly, clsd Sun, Mayan/ Mexican*

Kentucky • USA

Porcini 2730 Frankfort Ave (at Bayly) **502/894-8686** *dinner nightly, clsd Sun, Italian*

Proof on Main 702 W Main St (at 7th, at 21c Hotel) **502/217-6360** *brkfst & lunch Mon-Fri, dinner nightly, upscale, American w/ Tuscan influence*

Ramsi's Cafe on the World [WC] 1293 Bardstown Rd **502/451-0700** *11am-1am, till 2am Fri-Sat, Sun brunch, eclectic menu*

Third Avenue Cafe [WC] 1164 S 3rd St (at W Oak) **502/585-2233** *11am-9pm, till 10pm Fri-Sat, clsd Sun, vegan/ vegetarian, patio*

Vietnam Kitchen [WC] 5339 Mitscher Ave **502/363-5154** *clsd Wed, plenty veggie*

Zen Garden [WC] 2240 Frankfort Ave **502/895-9114** *lunch & dinner, clsd Sun, Asian, vegetarian*

■ENTERTAINMENT & RECREATION

Pandora Productions PO Box 4185 40204 **502/216-5502** *LGBT-themed productions*

Rudyard Kipling [E] 422 W Oak St (btwn 4th & Garvin) **502/636-1311** *live music & theater, also restaurant, open wknds*

■BOOKSTORES

Carmichael's 1295 Bardstown Rd (at Longest Ave) **502/456-6950** *8am-10pm, till 11pm Fri-Sat,*

■PUBLICATIONS

The Community Letter *LGBT newspaper*

■MEN'S SERVICES

➤**MegaMates** **502/561-6666** *Call to hook up with HOT local men. FREE to listen & respond to ads. Use FREE code DAMRON. MegaMates.com.*

■EROTICA

Arcade Adult Bookstore 2822 7th St (at Arcade) **502/637-8388**

Blue Movies 140 W Jefferson St (at 2nd) **502/585-4627** *9am-1am*

Louisville Manor 4600 Dixie Hwy (at San Jose Ave) **502/449-1443** *24hrs*

Metro Station 4948 Poplar Level Rd **502/968-2353**

Showboat Adult Bookstore 3524 S 7th St (at Berry Blvd) **502/361-0007** *hustlers*

Theatair X 4505 Hwy 31 E (1/2 mile N of I-65), Clarksville, IN **812/282-6976** *24hrs*

Madisonville

■CRUISY AREAS

Grapevine Lake [AYOR]

Madisonville City Park [AYOR] Park Ave (off Pennyrile Pkwy) *go W thru 3 traffic lights, go left & drive 1 mile*

Midway

■CAFES

Tavern 815 [WI] 131 E Main St (inside Le Marché boutique mall) **859/846-4688** *11am-3pm, till 4pm Sat*

Morehead

■CRUISY AREAS

Cave Run State Park [AYOR]

Daniel Boone Campground [AYOR]

Newport

see also Cincinnati, Ohio

■BARS

The Crazy Fox Saloon [GS,NH,E] 901 Washington Ave (at 9th) **859/261-2143** *3pm-2:30am, patio*

■CRUISY AREAS

James Taylor Park [AYOR] on Newport Levee

Paducah

■EROTICA

Romantix Adult Superstore 243 Brown (at Irvin Cobb Dr) **270/442-5584**

Somerset

■CRUISY AREAS

Alpine Rest Area [AYOR] S Hwy 27 Daniel Boone Nat'l Forest

Upton

■EROTICA
The Lion's Den Adult Superstore
2833 Weldon Loop (exit 76 off I-65)
270/369-8171

Whitesburg

■CRUISY AREAS
Carr Creek Dam [AYOR] Hazard

LOUISIANA

Statewide

■PUBLICATIONS
➤**Ambush Mag** 504/522-8049
oldest LGBT newspaper for the Gulf South (Texas through Florida)

Alexandria

■EROTICA
Alexandria Adult Emporium 3117 Masonic Dr (across from Bringhurst Park) 318/561-0306 *24hrs*

Capri Video #3 1820 N MacArthur Dr (off Hwy 1) 318/767-1669 *arcade*

■CRUISY AREAS
Bringhurst Park [AYOR] 3016 Masonic Dr

Baton Rouge

■INFO LINES & SERVICES
Freedom of Choice/ Gay AA 7747 Tom Dr (at MCC) 225/930-0026 (AA#) *8pm Th & Sat*

■BARS
George's Place [★MW,NH,K,S,V,WC] 860 St Louis 225/387-9798 *3pm-2am, from 5pm Sat, clsd Sun, [S] Fri*

Hound Dogs [MW,NH,WC] 668 Main St (at 7th) 225/344-0807 *2pm-2am, from 4pm Mon-Tue, from noon Sun*

■NIGHTCLUBS
Splash [★MW,D,DS,18+,WC] 2183 Highland Rd 225/242-9491 *9pm-2am, clsd Sun-Wed*

■RESTAURANTS
Drusilla Seafood 3482 Drusilla Ln (at Jefferson Hwy) 225/923-0896, 800/364-8844 *11am-10pm*

Mestizo 2323 Acadian Thruway (just off I-10) 225/387-2699 *lunch & dinner, Louisiana-Mexican fusion*

Ralph & Kacoo's [WC] 6110 Bluebonnet Blvd (off I-10 & Perkins) 225/766-2113 *11am-9:30pm, till 10:30pm Fri-Sat, Cajun, full bar*

■PUBLICATIONS
➤**Ambush Mag** 504/522-8049
LGBT newspaper for the Gulf South (TX through FL)

■EROTICA
Grand Cinema Station 10732 Florida Blvd 225/272-2010

■CRUISY AREAS
Capitol Lakes Park [AYOR] New Orleans *also adjacent area*

Manchac Park [AYOR] Hwy 73 (N of Bayou Manchac)

Breaux Bridge

■ACCOMMODATIONS
Maison des Amis [GF,WI] 111 Washington St (at Bridge St) 337/507-3399

Egan

■EROTICA
The Lion's Den Adult Superstore 191 Bocage Rd (exit 72 off I-10) 337/783-5000 *24hrs*

Lafayette

■INFO LINES & SERVICES
AA Gay/ Lesbian 115 Leonie St 337/991-0830 (AA#) *call for times & locations*

■NIGHTCLUBS
Bolt [MW,D,K] 116 E Vermilion St 337/524-1380 *8pm-2am, 6pm-midnight Sun, clsd Mon-Tue*

■CRUISY AREAS
Acadiana Park, Beaver Park & Moore Park [AYOR]

Lake Charles

■ACCOMMODATIONS
Aunt Ruby's B&B [GS,WI] 504 Pujo St (at Hodges) 337/430-0603 *full brkfst*

Louisiana • USA

■NIGHTCLUBS

Crystal's [MW,D,CW,F,DS,WC,GO] 112 E Broad (at Ryan) 337/433-5457 *9pm-2am, till 4am Fri*

■RESTAURANTS

Pujo St Cafe [GO] 901 Ryan St (at Pujo) 337/439-2054 *11am-9pm, till 10pm Fri-Sat, clsd Sun, full bar*

■CRUISY AREAS

Pindarosa Park [AYOR] Sampson St, Westlake

Prien Lake Park & Tuten Park [AYOR]

Metairie

see New Orleans

Monroe

■BARS

The Corner Bar [MW,NH,MR,E,K,DS,18+,GO] 512 N 3rd St (at Pinc) 318/329-0046 *8pm-2am, 3pm-midnight Sun, clsd Mon & Wed, seasonal hrs*

■NIGHTCLUBS

Club Pink [M,NH,D,K,18+,WC,GO] 1914 Roselawn Ave 318/654-7030 *7pm-2am*

■CRUISY AREAS

Forsythe Park [AYOR] Forsythe Ave (at Riverside Dr)

Natchitoches

■ACCOMMODATIONS

Chez des Amis B&B [GS,NS,WI,GO] 910 Washington St (btwn Texas & Pavie) 318/352-2647 *full brkfst*

Judge Porter House B&B [GS,WI,GO] 321 Second St 318/527-1555, 800/441-8343

New Iberia

■EROTICA

Leisure Time Entertainment 7600 Hwy 90 W 337/364-1883 *24hrs, arcade*

New Orleans

■INFO LINES & SERVICES

AA Lambda Center 1024 Elysian Fields Ave 504/838-3399 **(general AA office #)** *daily meetings, call for schedule*

LGBT Community Center of New Orleans [WC] 504/945-1103 *noon-8pm, noon-6pm Fri-Sat, call first*

■ACCOMMODATIONS

1896 O'Malley House B&B [GS,NS,WI,GO] 120 S Pierce St (at Canal St) 504/488-5896, 866/226-1896

5 Continents B&B [GS,WI,GO] 1731 Esplanade Ave (at Claiborne) 504/324-8594, 800/997-4652 *full brkfst*

Aaron Ingram Haus [GS,WI,GO] 1012 Elysian Fields Ave (btwn N Rampart & St Claude) 504/949-3110 *guesthouse, apts, courtyard*

Andrew Jackson Hotel [GF,WI,NS] 919 Royal St (btwn St Philip & Dumaine) 504/561-5881, 800/654-0224 *historic inn*

Antebellum Guest House [GS,N,NS,WI,GO] 1333 Esplanade Ave (at Marais St) 504/943-1900 *full brkfst*

Ashton's B&B [GF,NS,WI] 2023 Esplanade Ave (at Galvez) 504/942-7048, 800/725-4131

Auld Sweet Olive B&B [★GS,NS,WI] 2460 N Rampart St (at Spain) 504/947-4332, 877/470-5323

B&W Courtyards B&B [GF,NS,WI,GO] 2425 Chartres St (btwn Mandeville & Spain) 504/324-3396, 800/585-5731

Biscuit Palace Guest House [GF,WI,WC] 730 Dumaine (btwn Royal & Bourbon) 504/525-9949 *1820s Creole mansion in the French Quarter*

Bon Maison Guest House [GS,NS,GO] 835 Bourbon St (btwn Lafitte's & Bourbon Pub) 504/561-8498

Bourbon Orleans Hotel [GF,F,SW,WI,NS] 717 Orleans (at Bourbon St) 504/523-2222, 866/513-9744

►**Bourgoyne Guest House** [★MW] 839 Bourbon St (at Dumaine St) 504/524–3621, 504/525–3983 *1830s Creole mansion furnished w/ antiques, courtyard*

The Burgundy B&B [GS,NS,WI,GO] 2513 Burgundy St (at St Roch) 504/261–9477 *1890s "double shotgun" in Faubourg Marigny, near French Quarter, hot tub [N]*

Canal Street Inn [GS,NS,WI] 3620 Canal St (at Telemachus) 504/483–3033

Chez Palmiers B&B [GS,SW,NS,WI,GO] 1744 N Rampart St (at St Anthony) 504/208–7044, 877/233–9449

The Chimes B&B [GF,NS,WI] 1146 Constantinople St (in Garden District) 504/899–2621, 504/453–2183

The Cornstalk Hotel [GF,WI] 915 Royal St 504/523–1515, 800/759–6112

Crescent City Guest House [GS,N,NS,WI,GO] 612 Marigny St (at Chartres) 504/944–8722, 877/281–2680 *near French Quarter, hot tub*

Elysian Guest House [GF,NS,WI,GO] 1008 Elysian Fields Ave (at Rampart St) 504/324–4311

The Frenchmen Hotel [GS,SW,NS,WI,WC] 417 Frenchmen St (where Esplanade, Decatur & Frenchmen intersect) 504/948–2166, 800/831–1781

The Green House Inn [MW,SW,NS,WI,GO] 1212 Magazine St (at Erato) 504/525–1333, 800/966–1303 *gym, hot tub*

Harrah's Casino [GF,F,WC] 228 Poydras St 504/533–6000, 800/847–5299

Historic Rentals [GS,WI,NS,GO] 800/537–5408 *1- & 2-bdrm apts in French Quarter*

Louisiana • *USA*

Hotel Monteleone [GF,WI,SW] 214 Royal St (at Iberville) 504/523-3341, 800/535-9595

Kerlerec House [GS,NS,WI,GO] 928 Kerlerec St (at Dauphine St) 504/944-8544 *1 block from the French Quarter, gardens*

La Dauphine, Residence des Artistes [GS,NS,WI,GO] 2316 Dauphine St (btwn Elysian Fields & Marigny) 504/948-2217 *B&B, no unregistered overnight guests*

La Maison Marigny B&B on Bourbon [GS,NS,WI,GO] 1421 Bourbon St (at Esplanade) 504/948-3638, 800/570-2014 *on the quiet end of Bourbon St*

Lafitte Guest House [GS,NS,WI] 1003 Bourbon St (at St Philip) 504/581-2678, 800/331-7971 *elegant French manor house*

Lamothe House Hotel [GS,SW,NS,WI,GO] 621 Esplanade Ave (btwn Royal & Chartres) 504/947-1161, 800/367-5858

Maison Dupuy Hotel [GF,SW,WI] 1001 Toulouse St 504/586-8000, 800/535-9177

The Olivier House [GF,SW,WI,WC] 828 Toulouse (at Bourbon) 504/525-8456, 866/525-9748

Pierre Coulon Guest House [GS,NS,WI,GO] 504/943-6692, 877/943-6692 *quiet apt*

Royal Street Courtyard [GS,WI,GO] 2438 Royal St (at Spain) 504/943-6818, 888/846-4004 *historic 1850s guesthouse, hot tub*

W New Orleans—French Quarter [GF,SW,WI,WC] 316 Chartres St 504/581-1200, 877/WHOTELS (reservations only) *also Bacco restaurant*

■ BARS

700 Club [MW,V,F,WC] 700 Burgundy (at St Peter) 504/561-1095 *noon-4am, kitchen clsd Mon-Tue*

Big Daddy's [MW,NH,WC] 2513 Royal St (at Franklin) 504/948-6288 *24hrs*

Bourbon Pub & Parade [★MW,D,DS,S,V,18+,YC,WI] 801 Bourbon St (at St Ann) 504/529-2107 *24hrs, theme nights, Sun T-dance*

Cafe Lafitte in Exile/ The Balcony Bar [★M,D,S,V] 901 Bourbon St (at Dumaine) 504/522-8397 *24hrs*

The Corner Pocket [★M,NH,DS,S] 940 St Louis (at Burgundy) 504/568-9829 *noon-2am, 24hrs Fri-Sat, male dancers nightly*

Country Club [★GS,F,V,K,S,SW,N,WI] 634 Louisa St (at Royal) 504/945-0742 *11am-1am, not your father's country club!*

Cutter's [MW,NH,E,WI,WC] 706 Franklin Ave (at Royal) 504/948-4200 *3pm-3am, from 11am wknds*

The Double Play [M,NH,TG] 439 Dauphine (at St Louis) 504/523-4517 *24hrs*

The Four Seasons [M,NH,E,DS,GO] 3229 N Causeway Blvd (at 18th), Metairie 504/832-0659 *3pm-close, also the Out Back Bar summers, patio*

The Friendly Bar [★M,NH,WC] 2301 Chartres St (at Marigny) 504/943-8929 *11am-close*

Good Friends Bar [M,NH,K,WC] 740 Dauphine (at St Ann) 504/566-7191 *also Queens Head Pub upstairs Fri-Sun, popular piano sing-along 4pm-8pm*

JohnPaul [M,D,E,DS] 940 Elysian Fields Ave (at N Rampart) 504/948-1888 *3pm-2am, from noon wknds*

Le Roundup [M,NH,TG] 819 St Louis St (at Dauphine) 504/561-8340 *24hrs, very MTF-friendly crowd*

Michael's in the Park [MW,NH,DS,WC] 834 N Rampart (at Dumaine) 504/267-3615 *noon-2am, 24hrs Fri-Sun, patio*

Napoleon's Itch [★MW,E] 734 Bourbon (at St Ann) 504/237-4144 *noon-2am, till 4am Fri-Sat, wine & martini bar*

Orlando's Society Page Lounge [M,NH,TG] 542 N Rampart (at Toulouse) 6pm-2am, from 3pm wknds

Phoenix [★M,NH,B,L,F,GO] 941 Elysian Fields Ave (at N Rampart) 504/945-9264 *24hrs, cruise room, beer busts, also The Eagle [D] 9pm-5am*

Rawhide 2010 [M,NH,D,A,B,L,V] 740 Burgundy St (at St Ann) **504/525-8106** *1pm-5am*

Rubyfruit Jungle/ 1135 [GS,D,TG,V,18+] 1135 Decatur St (at Governor Nicholls) **504/571-1863** *goth theme nights & electronica*

Spotted Cat [GF,E,D,WC] 623 Frenchmen St **206/337-3273** *4pm-2am, excellent live jazz in the Faubourg Marigny*

Tubby's Golden Lantern [M,NH,DS,S] 1239 Royal St (at Barracks) **504/529-2860** *8am-2am*

■ **NIGHTCLUBS**

All Ways Lounge & Theater [M,NH,D,CW,E,WI] 2240 St Claude Ave (at Marigny) **504/218-5778** *open 6pm, clsd Mon,*

Club Fusions [M,D,MR-AF] 2004 AP Tureaud Ave (at N Galvez St) **504/301-5121** *10pm-4am Sat & Mon only, hip hop club*

Oz [★M,D,E,DS,S,V,YC,WC] 800 Bourbon St (at St Ann) **504/593-9491, 850/433-7499** *24hrs*

■ **CAFES**

Cafe Rose Nicaud [WI] 632 Frenchmen St (btwn Royal & Chartres) **504/949-3300** *7am-7pm*

CC's Coffee House [WI] 941 Royal St **504/581-6996** *7am-9pm*

Croissants d'Or [WC] 617 Ursulines St **504/524-4663** *6am-3pm, clsd Tue, delicious pastries*

The Orange Couch [F,E,WI,WC] 2339 Royal St **504/267-7327** *7am-10pm, ultra mod cafe*

Royal Blend Coffee & Tea House 621 Royal St **504/523-2716** *6am-8pm, till midnight wknds, on a quiet, hidden courtyard, also salads & sandwiches*

Z'otz [E] 8210 Oak St **504/861-2224** *7am-1am, coffee shop & art space*

■ **RESTAURANTS**

13 Monaghan's [WC] 517 Frenchmen St **504/942-1345** *11am-4am, brkfst, lunch & dinner all the time, full bar*

Acme Oyster House 724 Iberville St (at Royal) **504/522-5973** *11am-10pm, till 11pm wknds, long line moves quickly, worth the wait!*

Angeli on Decatur [WI,WC] 1141 Decatur St (at Gov Nicholls) **504/566-0077** *11am-2am, till 4am Fri-Sat, pizza*

Brennan's [R] 417 Royal St (at Conti) **504/525-9711** *brkfst, lunch & dinner, upscale*

Cafe Amelie 912 Royal St (in Princess of Monaco Courtyard) **504/412-8965** *lunch & dinner, Sun brunch, clsd Mon-Tue, Creole*

Cafe Negril [E,D,WC] 606 Frenchman St (at Chartres St) **504/944-4744** *dinner, clsd Sun-Mon, Caribbean*

Casamento's [WC] 4330 Magazine St (at Napoleon Ave) **504/895-9761** *lunch, dinner Th-Sat, clsd Sun-Mon (also clsd June-Aug), best oyster loaf in city*

Clover Grill [★] 900 Bourbon St (at Dumaine) **504/598-1010** *24hrs, diner fare*

Commander's Palace [★R,WC] 1403 Washington Ave (at Coliseum St, in Garden District) **504/899-8221** *lunch Mon-Fri, dinner nightly, jazz brunch wknds, upscale Creole, dress code*

Coquette [WC] 2800 Magazine St (at Washington Ave) **504/265-0421** *lunch Wed-Sat, dinner Mon-Sat*

The Court of Two Sisters 613 Royal St **504/522-7261** *daily jazz brunch buffet 9am-3pm, dinner nightly, Creole*

Dante's Kitchen [WC] 736 Dante St (at River Rd) **504/861-3121** *dinner nightly, wknd brunch, clsd Tue, Cajun*

EAT New Orleans 900 Dumaine St (at Dauphine) **504/522-7222** *lunch & dinner, Sun brunch, clsd Mon, Cajun/Creole, some veggie, cute waiters*

Elizabeth's 601 Gallier St **504/944-9272** *7am-10pm, from 8am wknds, clsd Mon, Cajun*

Feelings Cafe [P,WC] 2600 Chartres St (at Franklin Ave) **504/945-2222** *dinner Th-Sun, also Sun brunch, Creole, also piano bar*

Fiorella's Cafe 45 French Market Pl (at Gov Nicholls & Ursulines) **504/553-2155** *noon-midnight, till 2am Fri-Sat, awesome Fried Chicken*

Gott Gourmet Cafe 3100 Magazine St (at 8th St) **504/373-6579** *11am-9pm, 8am-5pm wknds*

Gumbo Shop 630 St Peter St (at Chartres) **504/525-1486** *award-winning gumbo*

Herbsaint 701 St Charles Ave **504/524-4114** *lunch & dinner, bistro menu afternoons, clsd Sun, French/ Southern*

La Peniche 1940 Dauphine St (at Touro St) **504/943-1460** *24hrs, clsd Tue-Wed, Southern comfort foods, popular for brkfst*

Marigny Brasserie 640 Frenchmen St **504/945-4472** *lunch Mon-Fri, dinner nightly, wknd brunch, French*

Meauxbar Bistro 942 N Rampart St (at St Philip) **504/569-9979** *6pm-10pm, clsd Sun-Mon*

Mike's On The Avenue [WC] 628 St Charles Ave (in the Lafayette Hotel) **504/523-7600** *lunch & dinner, great views of St Charles Ave*

Mona Lisa [BW,GO,WC] 1212 Royal St (at Barracks) **504/522-6746** *11am-10pm, from 5pm Mon-Th, Italian*

Mona's 504 Frenchmen St **504/949-4115** *11am-10pm, till 11pm Fri-Sat, noon-9pm Sun, cheap Middle Eastern eats*

Moon Wok 800 Dauphine St **504/523-6910** *11am-9pm, till 10pm Fri-Sat, Chinese*

Napoleon House [WC] 500 Chartres St **504/524-9752** *lunch daily, dinner only Mon, clsd Sun, po' boys & muffulettas*

Olivier's [WC] 204 Decatur St **504/525-7734** *5pm-10pm, Creole*

Orleans Grapevine [WC] 718-720 Orleans Ave **504/523-1930** *4pm-10:30pm, till 11:30pm Fri-Sat, wine bar & bistro*

Phillips [WC,GO] 733 Cherokee St (at Maple) **504/865-1155** *4pm-2am, upscale*

Praline Connection [E] 542 Frenchmen St (at Chartres) **504/943-3934** *11am-10pm, soul food*

Restaurant August [WC] 301 Tchoupitoulas St (at Gravier St) **504/299-9777** *lunch Mon-Fri, dinner nightly, upscale French/ Mediterranean*

Sammy's Seafood 627 Bourbon St (across from Pat O' Brien's) **504/525-8442** *11am-11pm, Cajun/ Creole*

Stanley 547 St Ann St (at Chartres) **504/587-0093** *7am-10pm, upscale diner fare*

Stella [WC] 1032 Chartres St (at Ursulines Ave) **504/587-0091** *dinner nightly, upscale global fusion cuisine*

The Upperline Restaurant [WC] 1413 Upperline St **504/891-9822** *dinner Wed-Sun, Creole, fine dining, full bar*

■ENTERTAINMENT & RECREATION

Cafe du Monde [WC] 800 Decatur St (at St Ann, corner of Jackson Square) **504/525-4544, 800/772-2927** *till you've had a beignet—fried dough, powdered w/ sugar, that melts in your mouth—you haven't been to New Orleans & this is "the" place to have them 24hrs a day*

Haunted History Tour **504/861-2727, 888/644-6787** *guided 2-1/2-hour tours of New Orleans' most famous haunts, including Anne Rice's former home*

Mardi Gras World 1380 Port of New Orleans Pl **504/361-7821** *tour this year-round Mardi Gras float workshop*

Pat O'Brien's [GF,F,WC] 718 St Peter St (btwn Bourbon & Royal) **504/525-4823, 800/597-4823** *more than just a bar—come for the Hurricane, stay for the kitsch*

Preservation Hall [NS,$] 726 St Peter St (btwn Bourbon & Royal) **504/522-2841, 888/946-5299** *8pm-midnight, set begins at 8:30pm, come & hear the music that started jazz: New Orleans-style jazz!*

Louisiana • *USA*

St Charles Streetcar St Charles St (at Canal St) 504/248-3900 *it's not named Desire, but you should still ride it, Blanche, if you want to see the Garden District*

■BOOKSTORES

FAB -Faubourg Marigny Art & Books 600 Frenchmen St (at Chartres) 504/947-3700 *1pm-11pm, LGBT books & art*

Garden District Book Shop 2727 Prytania St (at Washington) 504/895-2266 *10am-6pm, till 4pm Sun*

Kitchen Witch Cook Books [GF] 631 Toulouse St (at Royal St) 504/528-8382 *10am-7pm, clsd Tue, cookbooks from rare to campy*

■RETAIL SHOPS

Angela King Gallery [GO] 241 Royal St 504/524-8211

Bourbon Pride 909 Bourbon St (at Dumaine) 504/566-1570 *10am-8pm, till 11pm wknds, LGBT cards, gifts*

Hit Parade 741 Bourbon St 504/524-7700 *3pm-11pm, 11am-2am Fri-Sat, 11am-midnight Sun, gift and clothing store*

NOLA Tattoo 1820 Hampson St (Uptown, at Riverbend) 504/524-6147 *tattoos & piercing*

Rab-Dab 918 Royal St (at Dumaine) 504/525-6662 *noon-6pm, men's clothing/ clubwear & gifts*

Second Skin Leather 521 St Philip St (btwn Decatur & Chartres) 504/561-8167 *noon-8pm, till 10pm wknds*

■PUBLICATIONS

➤**Ambush Mag** 504/522-8049 *LGBT newspaper for the Gulf South (TX through FL)*

■MEN'S CLUBS

The Club New Orleans [18+,PC,V,WI] 515 Toulouse St (at Decatur) 504/581-2402 *24hrs*

■MEN'S SERVICES

➤**MegaMates** 504/733-3939 *Call to hook up with HOT local men. FREE to listen & respond to ads. Use FREE code DAMRON. MegaMates.com.*

■EROTICA

Airline Adult Books 1404 26th St (off Bainbridge), Kenner 504/468-2931 *super-arcade w/ 30 rooms*

Mr Binky's 107 Chartres St (off Canal St) 504/302-2095 *24hrs*

Paradise Adult Video [WC] 41 W 24th St (at Crestview), Kenner 504/461-0000 *arcade*

Shreveport

■ACCOMMODATIONS

Twenty-Four Thirty-Nine Fairfield [GF,WI] 2439 Fairfield Ave 318/424-2424, 877/251-2439 *1905 Victorian*

■BARS

Korner Lounge II [M,NH,K] 800 Louisiana Ave (near Cotton) 318/222-9796 *3pm-2am*

■NIGHTCLUBS

Central Station [★MW,D,CW,DS,TG,WC] 1025 Marshall St (btwn Fairfield & Creswell) 318/222-2216 *5pm-close, till 4am Fri-Sat*

■EROTICA

Capri Video 2010 Nelson St 318/221-5427 *10am-midnight, includes 2 theaters*

Fun Shop Too 9434 Mansfield Rd 318/688-2482 *clsd Sun, adult, novelty & gag gifts & toys*

Slidell

■BARS

Anything Geauxs [M,D,DS,TG.E,K] 1540 W Lindberg Dr (at Gause Blvd) 504/722-2101 *6pm-2am, clsd Mon-Wed*

Billy's [MW,NH,K,DS,WI] 2600 Hwy 190 W 985/847-1921 *6pm-1am*

MAINE

Albion

■ACCOMMODATIONS

Twin Ponds Lodge [MO,SW,N,WI] 96 York Town Rd (at Libby Hill Rd) 207/437-2200

Aroostook County

■ACCOMMODATIONS

Magic Pond Wildlife Sanctuary & Guest House [MW,NS,GO] Blaine 215/287-4174

Augusta

■ACCOMMODATIONS

Annabessacook Farm [★GS,SW,NS,WI,GO] 192 Annabessacook Rd, Winthrop 207/377-3276 *restored 1810 farmhouse, full brkfst*

Maple Hill Farm Inn [GS,NS,WI,WC,GO] Hallowell 207/622-2708, 800/622-2708 *historic Victorian farmhouse, full brkfst*

■RESTAURANTS

Slates [E] 167 Water St (Franklin), Hallowell 207/622-9575, 207/622-4104 *lunch Tue-Fri, dinner Mon-Sat, brunch wknds, also bakery*

Bangor

■BOOKSTORES

Pro Libris Bookshop 10 3rd St (at Union) 207/942-3019 *10am-6pm, clsd Sun-Mon, new & used*

■CRUISY AREAS

Valley Avenue Park [AYOR] along river bank

Bar Harbor

■ACCOMMODATIONS

Aysgarth Station [GF,NS,WI] 20 Roberts Ave (at Cottage St) 207/288-9655 *10-minute drive from Acadia, cats on premises*

The Colonial Inn [GF,SW,WI] 321 High St (at US1), Ellsworth 207/667-5548, 888/667-5548

Manor House Inn [GF,NS,WI] 106 West St (near Bridge St) 207/288-3759, 800/437-0088 *open April-Oct, 1887 Victorian mansion, full brkfst, some rooms w/ whirlpools*

■RESTAURANTS

Mama DiMatteo's [GO] 34 Kennebec Pl (at Firefly Ln) 207/288-3666 *4:30pm-10pm, full bar*

■ENTERTAINMENT & RECREATION

ImprovAcadia 15 Cottage St (2nd flr) 207/288-2503 *live improvised theater*

■CRUISY AREAS

Lake Wood [AYOR] off Crooked Rd (1 mile from Hulls Cove) *follow trail to the "Ledges"*

Thompson Island [AYOR] Mt Desert Island *beware of cops!*

Bath

■ACCOMMODATIONS

The Galen C Moses House [GS,NS,WI,GO] 1009 Washington St 207/442-8771, 888/442-8771 *full brkfst*

The Inn at Bath [GS,NS,WC] 969 Washington St (at North St) 207/443-4294, 800/423-0964 *1810 Greek Revival B&B, full brkfst*

Boothbay Harbor

■ACCOMMODATIONS

Hodgdon Island Inn [GS,SW,NS,WI] PO Box 603, Boothbay 04571 207/633-7474, 800/314-5160 *1810 sea captain's home, full brkfst*

Sur La Mer Inn [GF,NS,GO] 18 Eames Rd, PO Box 663, 04538 207/633-7400, 207/380-6400 *seasonal luxury oceanfront B&B, May-Oct*

Brunswick

■BOOKSTORES

Gulf of Maine Books 134 Maine St (at Pleasant) 207/729-5083 *9:30am-5:30pm, clsd Sun*

Maine • *USA*

Bucksport

■ACCOMMODATIONS

Williams Pond Lodge B&B [GS,WI,GO]
207/460-6064

Corea

■ACCOMMODATIONS

**The Black Duck Inn on Corea
Harbor** [GS,NS,WI,GO] 207/963-2689
*full brkfst, restored farmhouse on
harbor, also cottages*

Deer Isle

■RESTAURANTS

Fisherman's Friend 5 Atlantic Ave,
Stonington 207/367-2442 *seasonal,
11am-9pm, till 10pm Fri-Sat*

Dexter

■ACCOMMODATIONS

Brewster Inn [GF,NS,WI,WC] 37 Zion's
Hill Rd (at Dexter St) 207/924-3130
historic mansion, full brkfst

Farmington

■BOOKSTORES

Devany, Doak & Garrett Booksellers
193 Broadway (at High St)
207/778-3454 *10am-5pm, till 5:30pm
Th, till 6:30pm Fri, 9am-5pm Sat, noon-
3pm Sun, LGBT section*

Freeport

■ACCOMMODATIONS

The Royalsborough Inn [GF,NS,WI]
1290 Royalsborough Rd, Durham
207/353-6372, 800/765-1772 *full
brkfst, spa services, massage, also alpaca
farm*

■RESTAURANTS

Harraseeket Lunch & Lobster Co 36
Main St (at Harraseeket Rd), S Freeport
207/865-4888, 207/865-3535 *open
May-Oct*

Hancock

■RESTAURANTS

Le Domaine Restaurant & Inn
207/422-3395, 800/554-8498 *open
June-Oct, 6pm-9pm, Sun brunch, clsd
Mon*

Kennebec Valley

■ACCOMMODATIONS

The Sterling Inn [GF,WI,GO] 1041 US
Route 201, Caratunk 207/672-3333
mention Damron for special rates

Kennebunkport

■ACCOMMODATIONS

Hidden Pond Maine [GF] 354 Goose
Rocks Rd 207/967-9050,
888/967-9050

White Barn Inn & Spa [GF,SW,F,NS,WI]
37 Beach Ave 207/967-2321 *also
restaurant*

■RESTAURANTS

Bartley's Dockside [WI] 4 Western Ave
207/967-6244, 207/233-6037 *lunch
& dinner, full bar*

Nunan's Lobster Hut 9 Mills Rd
207/967-4362 *seasonal*

Kittery

see also Portsmouth, New
Hampshire

■EROTICA

Amazing 92 Rte 236 N (1 mile from
traffic circle), Eliot 207/439-6285

Lewiston

■EROTICA

Paris Adult Book Store 297 Lisbon St
(at Chestnut) 207/783-6677,
800/581-6901

Naples

■ACCOMMODATIONS

Lambs Mill Inn [GS,NS,WI,GO] Lambs
Mill Rd (1/2 mile off Rte 302)
207/693-6253 *1860s farmhouse, full
brkfst, lesbian-owned*

Newcastle

■ACCOMMODATIONS

The Tipsy Butler B&B [GF,NS,WI] 11
High St 207/563-3394 *on the
Damariscotta River*

Ogunquit

■ACCOMMODATIONS

2 Village Square Inn Ogunquit [M,SW,NS,WI,GO] 14 Village Square Ln (at Main St) 207/646-5779 open May-Oct, Victorian w/ ocean views, hot tub

Abalonia Inn [GS,SW,WI,GO] 268 Main St (at Shore Rd) 207/646-7001 pets ok

Beaver Dam Campground [GF,SW] 551 School St, Rte 9, Berwick 207/698-2267 campground on 20-acre spring-fed pond

Belm House Vacation Units [MW,WI,GO] 207/641-2637 rental units w/ kitchens

Black Boar Inn [MW,NS,GO] 277 Main St (at Ogunquit Rd) 207/646-2112 weekly rentals only

Leisure Inn [GF,NS,WI] 73 School St (at Main St) 207/646-2737 seasonal

Meadowmere Resort [GF,SW,NS,WI,WC] 74 S Main St (at Rte 1) 207/646-9661, 800/633-8718 health club & spa

Moon Over Maine B&B [MW,NS,WI,GO] Berwick Rd 207/646-6666 hot tub

Ogunquit Beach Inn [MW,WI,GO] 67 School St 207/646-1112 5 minutes walk to beach

The Ogunquit Inn [MW,NS,WI,GO] 17 Glen Ave 207/646-3633, 866/999-3633 clsd Nov-March, Victorian B&B

OgunquitCottages.com [MW,NS,GO] 25 Mill St, N Reading, MA 01864 207/646-3840, 978/664-5813 weekly rentals, seasonal (June-Sept), near bars & beach

Rockmere Lodge B&B [GS,NS,GO] 150 Stearns Rd 207/646-2985, 800/646-2985 Maine shingle cottage, near beach

Yellow Monkey Guest Houses & Motel [GS,WC,GO] 280 Main St 207/646-9056 seasonal, jacuzzi, ocean view, gym

■BARS

Front Porch Cafe [GS,F,P] 9 Shore Rd (at Beach St) 207/646-4005 seasonal, lunch & dinner

Vine Cafe [F] 478 Main St 207/646-0288, 877/646-0288 seasonal, 4pm-close, also restaurant, good wine selection

■NIGHTCLUBS

Maine Street [★MW,D,F,K,C,GO] 195 Main St/ US Rte 1 207/646-5101 5pm-1am, T-dance from 3pm wknds, seasonal

■CAFES

Bread & Roses 246 Main St 207/646-4227 7am-7pm, seasonal

Fancy That Cafe Main St (at Beach St & Rte 1) 207/646-4118 April-Oct, 6:30am-11pm

■RESTAURANTS

Amore Breakfast 309 Shore Rd 207/646-6661, 866/641-6661 brkfst only, seasonal

Angelina's Ristorante 655 Main St 207/646-0445 dinner, Italian

Arrows [★R] 41 Berwick Rd (2 miles W of Rte 1), Cape Neddick 207/361-1100 open April-Dec, 6pm-9pm Th-Sun, eclectic

Beachfire Bar & Grill 658 Main St 207/646-8998 dinner nightly, wknd brunch, outdoor fire pit

Bessie's 8 Shore Rd (Rte 1) 207/646-0888 brkfst, lunch & dinner, also bar

Clay Hill Farm [P] 220 Clay Hill Rd (off Logging Rd), Cape Neddick (York) 207/361-2272 dinner only, seafood, also piano bar

Five-O [★] 50 Shore Rd 207/646-5001 5pm-midnight, martini bar & restaurant, full bar

Jonathan's [E,WC] 92 Bourne Ln 207/646-4777 dinner nightly, steak/ seafood, full bar

La Pizzeria [BW,GO] 239 Main St 207/646-1143 open April-Dec, lunch & dinner

Maine • USA

Wild Blueberry Cafe & Bistro [E] 82 Shore Rd 207/646-0990 *brkfst, lunch & dinner, jazz brunch 10am-1pm Sun*

■ENTERTAINMENT & RECREATION

Ogunquit Playhouse 10 Main St 207/646-5511 (box office), 207/646-2402 *summer theater, some LGBT-themed productions*

■CRUISY AREAS

Ogunquit Beach [AYOR] off Rte 1 *200 yds N of beach entrance*

Portland

■ACCOMMODATIONS

The Chadwick B&B [GS,WI,GO] 140 Chadwick St 207/774--5141, 800/774-2137

The Inn at St John [GS,NS,WI,GO] 939 Congress St 207/773-6481, 800/636-9127

The Inn by the Sea [GF,SW,NS,WC] 40 Bowery Beach Rd, Cape Elizabeth 207/799-3134, 800/888-4287

The Percy Inn [GF,WI,NS] 15 Pine St (at Longfellow Square) 207/871-7638, 888/417-3729

The Pomegranate Inn [GF,NS,WI] 49 Neal St (at Carroll St) 207/772-1006, 800/356-0408

Sea View Inn [GS,SW,NS,WI,WC] 65 W Grand Ave (at Atlantic Ave), Old Orchard Beach 207/934-4180, 800/541-8439 *motel*

West End Inn [GF,NS,WI] 146 Pine St (at Neal St) 207/772-1377, 800/338-1377

Wild Iris Inn [GF,NS,WI] 273 State St (at Grant St) 207/775-0224, 800/600-1557

■BARS

Blackstones [M,NH,WC] 6 Pine St (off Longfellow Square) 207/775-2885 *4pm-1am, from 3pm wknds, [L] 3rd Sat, theme nights*

The Wine Bar [GS,F] 38 Wharf St 207/772-6976 *5pm-close*

■NIGHTCLUBS

Styxx [★MW,D,E,DS,GO] 3 Spring St (at Center St) 207/828-0822 *7pm-1am, from 4pm Th-Sat*

■CAFES

Coffee by Design 43 Washington Ave (at Oxford St) 207/879-2233 *8am-5pm, clsd wknds*

■RESTAURANTS

Becky's [WC] 390 Commercial St (at High St) 207/773-7070 *4am-10pm, great brkfst & chowdah*

Grace 15 Chestnut St 207/828-4422 *fine dining in renovated old church*

Katahdin 27 Forest Ave 207/774-1740 *5pm-11pm, clsd Sun-Mon, American menu, bar*

Portland & Rochester Public House 118 Preble St 207/773-2000 *3pm-1am, bistro & pub in the Bayside neighborhood*

Street & Co [★BW,WC] 33 Wharf St (btwn Dana & Union) 207/775-0887 *5:30pm-9:30pm, till 10pm Fri-Sat, seafood*

Walter's Cafe [WC] 2 Portland Sq (at Union) 207/871-9258 *lunch & dinner, dinner nightly, seafood/ pasta*

■BOOKSTORES

Longfellow Books 1 Monument Way 207/772-4045 *9am-7pm, till 6pm Sat, 9:30am-5pm Sun, LGBT section*

■RETAIL SHOPS

The Corner General Store 154 Middle St (at Market) 207/253-5280 *8am-1am, great wine selection*

Emerald City [GO] 564 Congress St 207/774-8800 *10am-6pm, First Friday Art Walk; gifts, pride items & more*

■MEN'S SERVICES

➤**MegaMates** 207/828-0000 *Call to hook up with HOT local men. FREE to listen & respond to ads. Use FREE code DAMRON. MegaMates.com.*

■EROTICA

Condom Sense 424 Fore St (at Union) 207/871-0356, 877/871-0356 *10am-8pm, till 9pm Th, till 10pm Fri-Sat, till 6pm Sun*

Video Expo 666 Congress St (at State) 207/774-1377

■ CRUISY AREAS

Cutter Street [AYOR] *at the foot of the street on the Eastern Promenade*

Rockland

■ ACCOMMODATIONS

Captain Lindsey House Inn [GF,NS,WI,WC] 5 Lindsey St 207/596-7950, 800/523-2145

The Old Granite Inn [GF,NS,WI] 546 Main St 207/594-9036, 800/386-9036 *1880s stone guesthouse, full brkfst*

Rockport

■ RESTAURANTS

Chez Michel 2530 Atlantic Hwy (at Rte 1), Lincolnville 207/789-5600 *dinner Wed-Sun, full bar, some veggie*

Lobster Pound [WC] Rte 1, Lincolnville Beach 207/789-5550 *11:30am-8pm May-Oct, full bar, patio*

Tenants Harbor

■ ACCOMMODATIONS

Eastwind Inn [GF,F] 207/372-6366, 800/241-8439 *clsd Dec-April, full brkfst, rooms & apts*

Waterville

■ EROTICA

Treasure Chest II [★GO] 5 Sanger Ave (at Main) 207/873-7411

Video 54 [★GO] 18 Water St (at Sherwin St) 207/873-4201

Western Mtns

■ ACCOMMODATIONS

Mountain Village Farm B&B [GF,NS,WI] 164 Main St, Kingfield 04947 207/265-2030 *rural & sophisticated B&B, full brkfst*

York Harbor

■ RESTAURANTS

York Harbor Inn 480 York St 207/363-5119, 800/343-3869 *lunch Mon-Sat, dinner nightly, Sun brunch, also the Cellar Pub, also lodging*

MARYLAND

Annapolis

■ INFO LINES & SERVICES

AA Gay/ Lesbian 199 Duke of Gloucester St (at St Anne's Parish) 410/268-5441 *8pm Tue*

■ ACCOMMODATIONS

Two-O-One B&B [GS,NS,WI,GO] 201 Prince George St (at Maryland Ave) 410/268-8053 *full brkfst*

■ RESTAURANTS

Cafe Sado 205 Tackle Cir (at Castle Marina Rd), Chester 410/604-1688 *lunch & dinner, sushi/ Asian fusion*

Baltimore

■ INFO LINES & SERVICES

AA Gay/ Lesbian 410/663-1922 *6:30pm Sat, call for other mtg times*

Gay, Lesbian, Bisexual & Transgender Community Center of Baltimore 241 W Chase St (at Read) 410/837-5445

■ ACCOMMODATIONS

Abacrombie Fine Food & Accommodations [GS,NS] 58 W Biddle St (at Cathedral) 410/244-7227, 888/922-3437

Hotel Monaco Baltimore [GS,WI,WC] 2 N Charles St 443/692-6170, 888/752-2636

Pier 5 Hotel [GS,F,WI,WC] 711 Eastern Ave (at President) 410/539-2000, 866/583-4162

Scarborough Fair B&B [GF,GO] 801 S Charles St 410/837-0010, 877/954-2747

■ BARS

Club Bunns [MW,D,MR-AF,S] 608 W Lexington St (at Greene St) 410/234-2866 *5pm-2am, 7pm-1am Sun*

The Drinkery [M,NH,K] 205 W Read St (at Park) 410/225-3100 *11am-2am*

The Gallery Bar & Studio Restaurant [MW,WC] 1735 Maryland Ave (at Lafayette) 410/539-6965 *6pm-1am, dinner Mon-Fri*

Maryland • *USA*

Grand Central [★MW,D,F,K,DS,V,18+] 1001 N Charles St (at Eager) 410/752-7133 *4pm-close, 3 bars*

Hippo [★MW,D,TG,E,K,DS,P,V,WC] 1 W Eager St (at Charles) 410/547-0069 *4pm-2am, 3 bars*

Jay's on Read [M,P] 225 W Read St 410/225-0188 *4pm-1am*

Leon's [MW,NH,B,F,WI,WC] 870 Park Ave (at Chase) 410/539-4993, 410/539-4850 *4pm-2am, also Singer's restaurant*

Mixers [MW,NH,D,E,K] 6037 Belair Rd (at Glenarm Ave) 410/483-6011 *5pm-2am*

The Quest [M,NH] 3607 Fleet St (at Conkling) 410/563-2617 *4pm-2am*

The Rowan Tree [GS,K] 1633 S Charles St (at E Heath) 410/468-0550 *noon-2am, "where diversity is our name"*

Ziascoz [GS,NH,K,MR-AF] 1313 E Pratt St (at Eden) 410/276-5790 *7pm-2am*

■NIGHTCLUBS

Club 1722 [GS,D,MR,18+,PC] 1722 N Charles St (at Lafayette) 410/547-8423 *afterhours club, Fri-Sat only, 2am-close, BYOB*

Club Orpheus [GS,D] 1003 E Pratt St 410/276-5599

The Paradox [★GS,D,MR,F,E,V,WC] 1310 Russell St (at Ostend) 410/837-9110 *11pm-5am, midnight-6am Sat, more 3rd gay Sat*

■CAFES

Station North Arts Cafe 1816 N Charles St 410/625-6440 *8am-3pm, from 10am Sat, clsd Sun, also art gallery, events*

■RESTAURANTS

Aldos [★WC] 306 S High St 410/727-0700 *dinner nightly, Italian*

Alonso's [NS,WC] 415 W Cold Spring Ln (at Keswick Rd) 410/235-3433 *4pm-10:30pm, from 11:30am Fri-Sat, full bar*

Cafe Hon [WC] 1002 W 36th St (at Roland) 410/243-1230 *11am-10pm, from 9am-close wknds*

The Dizz 300 W 30th St 443/869-5864 *10am-2am, full bar*

Golden West Cafe 1105 W 36th St 410/889-8891 *brkfst, lunch & dinner, New Mexican, also bar, live bands*

Jerry D's Seafood 7804 Harford Rd, Parkville 410/668-1299

Mari Luna 1225 Cathedral St 410/637-8013 *modern Mexican, also lounge*

Mount Vernon Stable & Saloon 909 N Charles St (btwn Eager & Read) 410/685-7427 *11:30am-midnight, till 1am Fri-Sat, Sun brunch, also bar*

Trinidad Gourmet 418 E 31st St 410/243-0072 *7am-8:30pm, clsd Sun, Caribbean, delicious & inexpensive*

Viccino 1317 N Charles St 410/347-0349 *11am-11pm, till 9pm Sun, New American, full bar*

Woodberry Kichen [WC] 2010 Clipper Park Rd #126 410/464-8000 *dinner nightly, wknd brunch, organic & sustainable, full bar*

XS Baltimore 1307 N Charles St 410/468-0002 *7am-midnight, till 2am Fri-Sat, sushi restaurant, cafe & lounge*

■PUBLICATIONS

Baltimore OUTloud 410/244-6780

Gay Life 410/837-7748 *LGBT newspaper*

■MEN'S SERVICES

►**MegaMates** 410/468-4000 *Call to hook up with HOT local men. FREE to listen & respond to ads. Use FREE code DAMRON. MegaMates.com.*

■EROTICA

Big Top Video & News 429 E Baltimore 410/547-2495

Chained Desires 136 W Read St 410/528-8441 *11am-8pm, till 9pm Fri-Sat, clsd Mon*

Greenmount Books 3222 Greenmount Ave (at 33rd St) 410/467-0403

Sugar [TG,GO] 927 W 36th St (at Roland) 410/467-2632

■CRUISY AREAS

Druid Hill Park [MR-AF,YC,AYOR] W side of town (near Park Cir)

Lake Montebello Park [AYOR] Lake Montebello Terr (at Harford Rd) *in the woods*

Wyman Dell Park [AYOR] Charles St (btwn 29th & 33rd) *hustlers on the sidewalk, cruising on the Wyman Park Dr side*

Beltsville

see Washington, District of Columbia

College Park

see Washington, District of Columbia

Cumberland

■RESTAURANTS
Acropolis 45 E Main St, Frostburg 301/689-8277 *4pm-10pm, clsd Sun-Mon, full bar*

Edgewood

■EROTICA
Bush River Books & Video 3909 Pulaski Hwy (Rte 40), Abingdon 410/676-9051

Frederick

■CRUISY AREAS
Gambrill State Park [AYOR] W of Frederick (off I-70) *go to the summit, turn left*

Greenbelt

see also Washington, District of Columbia

■CRUISY AREAS
Greenbelt Park [AYOR]

Hagerstown

■NIGHTCLUBS
The Lodge [M,D,DS,MR,K,TG,GO] 21614 National Pike, Boonsboro 301/591-4434 *9pm-2am, till midnight Sun, clsd Mon-Th*

Laurel

see also Washington, District of Columbia

■BARS
PW's Sports Bar & Grill [MW,NH,F,DS,K,WI,GO] 9855 N Washington Blvd (at Whiskey Bottom Rd) 301/498-4840, 301/498-4841 *5am-2am, sports bar*

■EROTICA
Route 1 News Agency 106 Washington Blvd (at Main) 410/880-4253

Potomac

see Washington, District of Columbia

Princess Anne

■ACCOMMODATIONS
The Alexander House Booklovers B&B [GF,NS] 30535 Linden Ave (at corner of Beckford) 410/651-5195 *literary-themed B&B, full brkfst*

Rock Hall

■ACCOMMODATIONS
Tallulah's on Main [GS,NS,WC,GO] 5750 Main St (at Sharp St) 410/639-2596 *small suite hotel*

Rockville

see also Washington, District of Columbia

■CRUISY AREAS
Lake Needwood [AYOR] N of Rte 28 (off Avery Rd)

Salisbury

■EROTICA
Salisbury News Agency 616 S Salisbury Blvd (near Vine) 410/543-4469

Silver Spring

see Washington, District of Columbia

Snow Hill

■ACCOMMODATIONS
River House Inn [GF,SW,WI,GO] 201 E Market St (at Green St) 410/632-2722

MASSACHUSETTS

Amherst

see also Northampton

■BOOKSTORES

Amherst Books 8 Main St
413/256-1547, 800/503-5865
*6:30am-9pm, till 5pm Sun, independent,
LGBT section*

Food For Thought [WC] 106 N
Pleasant St (at Main) 413/253-5432
10am-6pm, progressive bookstore

Attleboro

■EROTICA

State Line Video 1124 Washington St
(off I-95, Broadway exit), South
Attleboro 508/761-4900 *arcade*

Barre

■ACCOMMODATIONS

Jenkins Inn & Restaurant
[GF,F,NS,WI,GO] 978/355-6444,
800/378-7373 *also restaurant & full
bar*

Berkshires

■ACCOMMODATIONS

The B&B at Howden Farm [GS,NS,GO]
303 Rannapo Rd, Sheffield
413/229-8481 *on 250-acre working
farm, full brkfst*

Broken Hill Manor [GF,NS,WI,GO] 771
West Rd (at Rte 23), Sheffield
413/528-6159, 877/535-6159 *B&B,
full brkfst*

Gateways Inn [GF,NS,WI] 51 Walker St
(at Church St), Lenox 413/637-2532,
888/492-9466 *also bar & restaurant*

Guest House at Field Farm
[GF,TG,NS,SW,WI] 554 Sloan Rd,
Williamstown 413/458-3135

Mount Greylock Inn [GS,GO] 6 East St,
Adams 413/743-2665 *views of Mt
Greylock*

River Bend Farm B&B [GF,NS] 643
Simonds Rd, Williamstown
413/458-3121

The Rookwood Inn [GS,NS,WI] 11 Old
Stockbridge Rd (at Walker St/ Rte 183),
Lenox 413/637-9750, 800/223-9750
Victorian inn near Tanglewood & skiing

The Thaddeus Clapp House [GF,NS] 74
Wendell Ave, Pittsfield 413/499-6840,
888/499-6840

Topia Inn [GS,NS,WI,WC,GO] 10 Pleasant
St (at Rte 8), Adams 413/743-9600,
888/868-6742

Windflower Inn [GF,SW,NS,WI] 684 S
Egremont Rd, Great Barrington
413/528-2720, 800/992-1993
country inn in the Berkshires, full brkfst

■RESTAURANTS

Allium Restaurant + Bar 42 Railroad
St (at Main), Great Barrington
413/528-2118 *5pm-9pm, till 10pm
Fri-Sat, bar open late*

Cafe Lucia 80 Church St (at Tucker),
Lenox 413/637-2640 *dinner only, clsd
Mon, seasonal*

Church Street Cafe 65 Church St (at
Franklin), Lenox 413/637-2745 *lunch
& dinner, seasonal, American bistro*

Mezze Bistro + Bar 777 Cold Spring
Rd, Williamstown 413/458-0123
5pm-9pm, till 10pm Fri-Sat, seasonal hrs

■ENTERTAINMENT &
    RECREATION

Tanglewood [E] 197 Rte 183, Lenox
888/266-1200 *summer home of the
Boston Symphony/ Pops*

Williamstown Theatre Festival just E
of Rte 2 & Rte 7 junction, Williamstown
413/597-3400, 413/458-3200 *call
for season calendar*

■EROTICA

Amazing.net Video Store 1021 South
St/ Rte 20, Pittsfield 413/496-8055

■CRUISY AREAS

Onota Lake [AYOR] parking lot near
woods, Pittsfield

Boston

◼ INFO LINES & SERVICES

Fenway Health 1340 Boylston St (at Jersey St) **617/267-0900, 888/242-0900** *medical & HIV services, LGBT health resources*

Gay AA 12 Channel St #604 **617/426-9444 (AA#)**

GLBT Helpline 617/267-9001, **888/340-4528** *6pm-11pm*

◼ ACCOMMODATIONS

463 Beacon St Guest House [GS,NS,WI,GO] 463 Beacon St **617/536-1302**

Beacon Hill Hotel & Bistro [GS,F,WI] 25 Charles St (at Chestnut St) **617/723-7575**

Chandler Inn [GF,NS,WI] 26 Chandler St (at Berkeley) **617/482-3450, 800/842-3450** *European-style hotel*

The Charles Hotel [GF] 1 Bennett St (at Eliot), Cambridge **617/864-1200, 800/882-1818**

The Charles Street Inn [GS,NS,WC,GO] 94 Charles St (at Mount Vernon, Beacon Hill) **617/314-8900, 877/772-8900**

Clarendon Square Inn [GS,NS,WI,GO] 198 W Brookline St (btwn Tremont & Columbus) **617/536-2229**

Encore B&B [GF,NS,GO] 116 W Newton St (at Tremont) **617/247-3425** *19th-c town house in Boston's South End*

Fifteen Beacon Hotel [GF,F,WI] 15 Beacon St (at Somerset) **617/670-1500, 877/982-3226**

Holiday Inn Express & Suites Boston Garden [GF,WI,NS,WC] 280 Friend St (at Causeway) **617/720-5544**

Hotel 140 [GS,NS,WC] 140 Clarendon St (at Stuart St) **617/585-5600, 800/714-0140**

Hotel Onyx [GF,WI,NS] 155 Portland St (at Causeway) **617/557-9955, 866/660-6699**

Massachusetts • *USA*

The Liberty Hotel [GF,NS,WI,WC] 215 Charles St (at Cambridge St) 617/224-4000, 866/507-5245 *in the former Charles St Jail*

Nine Zero Hotel [GF,WI,NS,WC] 90 Tremont St (at Bosworth) 617/772-5800, 866/646-3937 *luxury hotel, full brkfst, jacuzzi*

➤**Oasis Guest House** [★GS,NS,WI,WC,GO] 22 Edgerly Rd (at Westland) 617/267-2262, 800/230-0105 *in Back Bay*

Whitman House Inn [GS,NS,WI,GO] 17 Worcester St (at Norfolk St), Cambridge 617/945-5350, 617/913-6189

■BARS

The Alley [★M,NH,D,B,K,WC,GO] 14 Pi Alley (at 275 Washington St) 617/263-1449 *10pm-2am, from noon wknds*

Bella Luna Restaurant & Milky Way Lounge [GS,F,E,K] 284 Amory St, Jamaica Plain 617/524-3740 *6pm-1am, live music, also restaurant*

Boston Eagle [M,NH,WC] 520 Tremont St (near Berkeley) 617/542-4494 *3pm-2am, from noon Sun*

Boston Ramrod [★M,D,B,L,WC] 1254 Boylston St (at Ipswich, 1 block from Fenway Park) 617/266-2986 *noon-2am*

➤**Club Cafe Restaurant, Nightclub & Cabaret** [★MW,D,F,E,K,P,V,WC] 209 Columbus Ave (at Berkeley St) 617/536-0966 *11am-2am, incredible Sunday brunch buffet along with lunch other days*

Encore Lounge [GS,E,WC] 275 Tremont St (at Stuart St, in hotel) 617/728-2162 *5pm-2am, lounge & cabaret*

Fritz [★MW,NH,WC] 26 Chandler St (in the Chandler Inn) 617/482-4428 *noon-2am, brunch Sat-Sun, sports bar*

Jacque's [★M,TG,C,DS,$] 79 Broadway (at Stuart) 617/426-8902 *11am-midnight, from noon Sun*

Paradise [M,D,S,K,V] 180 Massachusetts Ave, Cambridge 617/868-3000 *9pm-1am, 7pm-2am Th-Sat*

Ryles [GS,F,E] 212 Hampshire St (at Cambridge St, in Inman Square), Cambridge 617/876-9330 *great wknd jazz brunch*

Sister Sorel/ Tremont 647 [MW,NH,WC] 647 Tremont (at W Brookline) 617/266-4600 *dinner only, wknd brunch*

■NIGHTCLUBS

dbar [GS,D,WC] 1236 Dorchester Ave (at Hancock St), Dorchester 617/265-4490 *5pm-midnight, till 2am wknds, also restaurant, dinner nightly*

Epic Saturday [M,D] 15 Lansdowne St (House of Blues) 888/693-2583 *10:30pm Sat only*

The Estate [GS,D,19+,$] 1 Boylston Pl (at The Alley) 617/351-7000 *gay Th only for Glam Life*

Foxy [M,D] 474 Massachusetts Ave (at Zuzu), Cambridge 617/864-3278 *1st & 3rd Sun only, foxy boys*

The Glam Life [MW,D,$] 1 Boylston Pl (at The Estate) 617/819-4297 *Th only, hip-hop*

Hot Mess Sundays [M,D,$] 275 Tremont St (at Underbar) 617/819-4297 *Sun only*

Machine [★M,D,V,S,YC,WC] 1254 Boylston St (at Park, below Boston Ramrod) 617/536-1950 *10pm-2am*

The Middle East & ZuZu [GF,A,F,E,YC,$] 472 Massachusetts Ave (in Central Square), Cambridge 617/864-3278 *11am-1am, till 2am wknds, live music*

➤**Napoleon Cabaret** [★E,F,P,OC,WC] 209 Columbus Ave (at Club Cafe) 617/536-0966 *nightly piano & vocals*

Rise [GS,D,PC] 306 Stuart St (btwn Berkeley & Arlington) 617/423-7473 *1am-6am 2nd Sat of the month only*

■CAFES

1369 Cafe 757 Massachusetts Ave (in Central Square), Cambridge 617/576-4600 *7am-11pm*

Berkeley Perk [F,WC,GO] 69 Berkeley St (at Chandler) 617/426-7375 *6:30am-5pm, from 7:30am Sat, clsd Sun*

NINETEENEIGHTYTHREE

XXX

THIRTY

TWENTYTHIRTEEN

It all started in 1983.
Thirty years of dining, drinks, dancing,
entertainment, cabaret, singing, comedy, drag,
videos, fashion, music, sports, dates, birthdays,
anniversaries, weddings, fundraisers, flirting,
love lost and love found.

Thirty years of pride!

Club Café

DINE DRINK DANCE

209 Columbus Avenue in Boston
617 536 0966 clubcafe.com

Diesel Cafe [WC,GO] 257 Elm St (in Davis Square), Somerville **617/629-8717** *6am-11pm, from 7am wknds*

Fiore's Bakery [GO] 55 South St (at Bardwell), Jamaica Plain **617/524-9200** *7am-7pm, from 8am wknds, some vegan*

Francesca's [WC] 564 Tremont St (at Clarendon) **617/482-9026** *8am-11pm*

South End Buttery [WC] 314 Shawmut Ave (at Union Park St) **617/482-1015** *cupcakes! also brkfst, lunch & dinner, full bar*

▪RESTAURANTS

BarLola [E] 160 Commonwealth Ave (at Dartmouth) **617/266-1122** *4pm-midnight*

Boston Pita Pit [WC] 479 Harvard St (at Commonwealth), Brookline **617/738-7482** *10am-midnight, till 2am wknds*

Casa Romero 30 Gloucester St (at Commonwealth) **617/536-4341** *dinner, Mexican, also bar*

Charlie's Sandwich Shoppe [WC] 429 Columbus Ave (at Pembroke St) **617/536-7669** *great brkfst, clsd Sun*

City Girl Cafe [BW,GO] 204 Hampshire St (at Inman), Cambridge **617/864-2809** *noon-10pm, from 10am Sat-Sun, clsd Mon, Italian, great sandwiches*

►Club Cafe [★E,P,V,WC] 209 Columbus Ave (adjacent to Club Cafe) **617/536-0966** *dinner & Sun brunch, also 3 bars*

Ecco 107 Porter St **617/561-1112** *4pm-midnight, from noon Sun, Sun gay event night 8pm*

Johnny D's Restaurant & Music Club [E,WC] 17 Holland St (in Davis Square), Somerville **617/776-2004** *dinner nightly, lunch Th-Sun*

My Thai Cafe 3 Beach St, 2nd flr (at Washington) **617/451-2395** *11am-10pm, till 11pm Fri-Sat, Asian, vegetarian/ vegan*

Rabia's [WC] 73 Salem St (at Cross St) **617/227-6637** *11am-10:30pm, fine Italian*

Ristorante Lucia [WC] 415 Hanover St (at Harris) **617/367-2353** *great North End pasta*

Stella [WI,WC] 1525 Washington St (at W Brookline) **617/247-7747** *dinner & Sun brunch, full bar till 2am, also cafe 7am-3pm*

Sweet Cheeks Q [GO] 1381 Boylston St **617/266-1300** *11:30am-11pm, American south north of the Mason Dixon*

Trattoria Pulcinella 147 Huron Ave (at Concord), Cambridge **617/491-6336** *5pm-10pm, fine Italian*

Veggie Planet 47 Palmer St (at Club Passim), Cambridge **617/661-1513** *11:30am-10:30pm*

▪ENTERTAINMENT & RECREATION

Freedom Trail **617/357-8300** *start at the Visitor Information Center in Boston Common (at Tremont & West Sts), the most famous cow pasture & oldest public park in the US, then follow the red line to some of Boston's most famous sites*

New Repertory Theatre 321 Arsenal St, Watertown **617/923-8487 (box office), 617/923-7060**

Urban AdvenTours 103 Atlantic Ave (at Richmond St) **617/670-0637, 800/979-3370** *guided bike tours & bike rentals*

▪BOOKSTORES

Calamus Bookstore [★] 92-B South St **617/338-1931, 888/800-7300** *9am-7pm, noon-6pm, complete GLBT bookstore*

Trident Booksellers & Cafe [F,BW,WI,WC] 338 Newbury St (off Mass Ave) **617/267-8688** *8am-midnight*

▪PUBLICATIONS

Bay Windows **617/464-7280** *LGBT newspaper*

The Rainbow Times **413/282-8881, 617/444-9618** *bi-weekly LGBT news magazine for MA, northern CT & southern VT*

■MEN'S SERVICES

➤**MegaMates** 617/423-6666 *Call to hook up with HOT local men. FREE to listen & respond to ads. Use FREE code DAMRON. MegaMates.com.*

■EROTICA

Amazing Express 57 Stuart St 617/338-1252

Good Vibrations [★WC] 308 Harvard St, Brookline 617/264-4400 *10am-9pm, till 10pm Th-Sat*

Hubba Hubba 534 Massachusetts Ave (at Brookline, in Central Square), Cambridge 617/492-9082 *fetish & drag gear*

■CRUISY AREAS

Carson Beach [AYOR] William J Day Blvd

Charles River Esplanade [AYOR] across foot bridge at end of Dartmouth St, near lagoon *go to the right*

The Fens (FenwayVictory Gardens) [AYOR] near the Ramrod bar

Brookline

see Boston

Cambridge

see Boston

Cape Cod

see also Provincetown listings

■INFO LINES & SERVICES

Gay/ Lesbian AA 508/775-7060 *call for info*

■ACCOMMODATIONS

The Colonial House Inn & Restaurant [GF,SW,WI,GO] 277 Main St, Rte 6A (at Strawberry Ln), Yarmouthport 508/362-4348, 800/999-3416 *dinner & light brkfst included, jacuzzi, also restaurant & lounge*

Lamb & Lion Inn [GF,NS,SW,WI] 2504 Main St (Rte 6A), Barnstable 508/362-6823, 800/909-6923

White Swan B&B [GF,NS,WI] 146 Manomet Point Rd, Plymouth 508/224-3759 *in 200-year-old farmhouse, open year-round, at mouth of Cape Cod*

Woods Hole Passage [GF,NS,WI] 186 Woods Hole Rd, Falmouth 508/548-9575, 800/790-8976 *full brkfst, near beaches*

■CRUISY AREAS

Boardwalk [AYOR] Jarvis St (off 6-A, exit 1), Sandwich *nights*

Crow's Pasture [AYOR] N on 6-A to South St, past cemetery, Dennis *in dunes*

Kalmus Park Beach [AYOR] end of Ocean St, Hyannis *behind parking lot*

Ryder Woods Conservation Area [AYOR] Rte 130 to Cotuit Rd (toward Mashpee for 3.5 miles), Sandwich *trails along the lake*

Skaket Beach [AYOR] Dennis *off to the right*

Chelsea

see Boston

Greenfield

■ACCOMMODATIONS

Brandt House [GF,NS,WI] 29 Highland Ave 413/774-3329, 800/235-3329 *16-rm estate on hill, full brkfst, formal garden*

■RESTAURANTS

Hope & Olive 44 Hope St 413/774-3150 *lunch & dinner, clsd Mon*

■BOOKSTORES

World Eye Bookshop 156 Main St (at Miles St) 413/772-2186 *9:30am-6:30pm, 9am-5pm Sat, 11am-4pm Sun, LGBT section*

Haverhill

■CAFES

Wicked Big Cafe [WI,WC,GO] 19 Essex St (at Wingate) 978/556-5656 *7am-4pm, 8am-1pm Sat, clsd Sun*

Ipswich

■CRUISY AREAS

Crane's Beach [AYOR] 1/2 mile to the right

Lenox

see Berkshires

Massachusetts • *USA*

Lowell

■EROTICA
Tower News 101 Gorham St
978/452-8693

Lynn

■BARS
The Cirque [MW,NH,D,L,K,DS,V,GO] 47
Central Ave **781/586-0551** *11am-
1am, DJ wknds*

Fran's Place [MW,D,WC] 776
Washington St (at Sagamore)
781/598-5618 *3pm-1am, also sports
bar*

Martha's Vineyard

■ACCOMMODATIONS
Arbor Inn [GF,NS] 222 Upper Main St,
Edgartown **508/627-8137,
888/748-4383** *some shared baths*

Martha's Vineyard Surfside Motel
[GF,NS,WI,WC] 7 Oak Bluffs Ave, Oak
Bluffs **508/693-2500, 800/537-3007**

The Shiverick Inn [GS,NS,WI,GO] 5
Pease's Pt Wy, Edgartown (at Pent Ln)
508/627-3797, 800/723-4292

■RESTAURANTS
The Black Dog Tavern [WC] Beach St
Extension #21 (at Water St)
508/693-9223 *brkfst, lunch & dinner,
seasonal*

Le Grenier [BW] 96 Main St (at
Drummer Ln), Vineyard Haven
508/693-4906 *dinner, French*

■BOOKSTORES
Bunch of Grapes 44 Main St (at
Center St), Vineyard Haven
508/693-2291, 800/693-0221 *9am-
6pm, 11am-5pm Sun, some LGBT titles*

Medford

■EROTICA
Amazing.net Video Store 423 Mystic
Ave/ Rte 38 781/391-7438

New Bedford

■BARS
Le Place [★MW,D,K] 20 Kenyon St (at
Belleville Ave) **508/990-1248** *2pm-
2am*

■EROTICA
Amazing.net Video Store 10
Sconticut Neck Rd/Rte 6, Fairhaven
508/991-8191

Newton
see Boston

North Adams
see Berkshires

Northampton
see also Amherst

■ACCOMMODATIONS
Clarion Hotel & Conference Center
[GF,SW,NS,WI,WC] 1 Atwood Dr
413/586-1211, 800/582-2929 *also
restaurants & bar*

Corner Porches [GS,NS] 82 Baptist
Corner Rd (at Main), Ashfield
413/628-4592 *30 minutes from
Northampton*

The Hotel Northampton
[GF,NS,WI,WC] 36 King St (near Bridge
St) **413/584-3100, 800/547-3529**
cafe & historic tavern

■NIGHTCLUBS
Diva's [★MW,D,E,K,DS,S,YC] 492 Pleasant
St (at Conz St) **413/586-8161** *9pm-
2am, clsd Sun-Mon, theme nights, [18+]
Tue-Fri*

Pearl Street [GS,D,E,YC] 10 Pearl St (at
Main) **413/586-8686** *7pm-1am, live
music*

■CAFES
Haymarket Cafe [★F,WC] 185 Main St
413/586-9969 *7am-10pm, till 11pm
Fri-Sat, also restaurant*

■RESTAURANTS
Bela [WC,GO] 68 Masonic St
413/586-8011 *noon-8:30pm, clsd
Sun-Mon, vegetarian*

Blue Heron Restaurant [GO] 112 N
Main St, Sunderland **413/665-2102**

Bueno Y Sano 134 Main St (at Center
St) **413/586-7311** *11am-10pm, till
9pm Sun, Mexican*

The Old Creamery Co-op [GO] 445
Berkshire Tr, Cummington
413/634-5560 *7am-7:30pm*

Paul & Elizabeth's [BW,WC] 150 Main St (in Thorne's Marketplace) **413/584-4832** *lunch & dinner, Sun brunch, seafood*

■ENTERTAINMENT & RECREATION

The Iron Horse 20 Center St (at Main) **413/586-8686** *5:30pm-close, live music, all ages*

■RETAIL SHOPS

Oh My A Sensuality Shop 122 Main St (at Center) **413/584-9669** *noon-7pm, till 8pm Fri-Sat, noon-5pm Sun*

Pride & Joy [WC,GO] 150 Main St (at Old South St, at Thornes Marketplace) **413/727-3758** *open 7 days, LGBT books & gifts*

■CRUISY AREAS

Northampton Meadows [AYOR] next to the Connecticut River (dirt roads) *not far from I-91 rest areas*

Pulaski Park [AYOR] Main St *summer nights*

Provincetown

see also Cape Cod listings

■INFO LINES & SERVICES

Provincetown Business Guild **508/487-2313**

■ACCOMMODATIONS

A Secret Garden Inn [MW,NS] 300-A Commercial St **508/487-9027**

Admiral's Landing [MW,NS,WI] 158 Bradford St (btwn Conwell & Pearl) **508/487-9665, 800/934-0925**

Aerie House & Beach Club [MW,WI,GO] 184 Bradford St (at Miller Hill) **508/487-1197, 800/487-1197**

Ampersand Guesthouse [M,NS,WI,GO] 6 Cottage St (at Commercial) **508/487-0959, 800/574-9645**

Anchor Inn Beach House [GS,NS,WC] 175 Commercial St (at Winthrop) **508/487-0432, 800/858-2657** *private beach*

Bayberry Accommodations [MW,NS,WI,GO] 16 Winthrop St (at Commercial) **508/487-4605, 800/422-4605**

Beaconlight Guest House [M,NS,WI,GO] 12 Winthrop St (at Bradford) **508/487-9603, 800/696-9603**

Benchmark Inn [MW,SW,NS,WI,WC,GO] 6-8 Dyer St **508/487-7440, 888/487-7440**

The Black Pearl Inn [MW,NS,WI,GO] 11 Pearl St (at Bradford) **508/487-0302, 800/761-1016** *"friends of Bill welcome"*

Boatslip Resort [★M,SW,GO] 161 Commercial St **508/487-1669, 877/786-9662** *seasonal, also several bars & popular T-dance*

The Bradford Carver House [MW,NS,WI,GO] 70 Bradford St **508/487-0728, 800/826-9083** *restored mid-19th-c home, centrally located*

Brass Key Guesthouse [★M,SW,NS,WI,WC,GO] 67 Bradford St (at Carver) **508/487-9005, 800/842-9858**

Captain's House B&B [M,B,NS,WI,GO] 350-A Commercial St (at Center) **508/487-9353, 800/457-8885**

Carl's Guest House [MO,N,NS,WI,GO] 68 Bradford St (at Court St) **508/487-1650** *sundeck*

Carpe Diem Guesthouse & Spa [MW,NS,WI,GO] 12 Johnson St **508/487-4242, 800/487-0132**

The Carriage House Guesthouse [GS,GO] 7 Central St (at Commercial) **508/487-8855, 800/309-0248**

Chicago House [MW,NS,WI,GO] 6 Winslow St (at Bradford) **508/487-0537, 800/733-7869** *rooms & apts*

Christopher's by the Bay [MW,NS,WI,GO] 8 Johnson St (at Commercial) **508/487-9263** *some shared baths, patio*

Crown & Anchor [MW,SW,NS,WI,GO] 247 Commercial St **508/487-1430** *also cabaret & poolside bars*

Crowne Pointe Historic Inn & Shui Spa [MW,SW,NS,WI,WC,GO] 82 Bradford St **508/487-6767, 877/276-9631** *also restaurant*

Massachusetts • *USA*

Designer's Dock [GS,WI,GO] 349 Commercial St **508/776-5746, 800/724-9888** *weekly condos in town & on beach, seasonal*

Enzo [GS,WI] 186 Commercial St (at Court) **508/487-7555, 888/873-5001** *Italian restaurant & piano bar on premises*

Fairbanks Inn [★MW,NS,WI,GO] 90 Bradford St **508/487-0386, 800/324-7265** *parking*

Gabriel's at The Ashbrooke Inn [★MW,NS,WI,GO] 102 Bradford St **508/487-3232** *full brkfst, hot tub*

The Gallery Inn [MW] 3 Johnson St (at Commercial) **508/487-3010, 800/676-3010**

Gifford House Inn [MW,WI,GO] 11 Carver St **508/487-0688, 800/434-0130** *seasonal, also several bars & restaurant*

Grand View Inn [MW,NS,GO] 4 Conant St (at Commercial) **508/487-9193**

Heritage House [MW,WI,GO] 7 Center St **508/487-3692** *shared baths, lesbian-owned*

The Inn at Cook Street [GF,NS,GO] 7 Cook St (at Bradford) **508/487-3894, 888/266-5655**

Inn at the Moors [GF,SW,WI,GO] 59 Provincelands Rd **508/487-1342, 800/842-6379** *motel, across from Nat'l Seashore Province Lands, seasonal*

John Randall House [MW,NS,WI,GO] 140 Bradford St (at Center) **508/487-3533, 800/573-6700**

Land's End Inn [GS,NS,WI] 22 Commercial St **508/487-0706, 800/276-7088**

Lotus Guest House [MW,WI,GO] 296 Commercial St (at Standish) **508/487-4644, 888/508-4644** *seasonal, decks, garden*

Moffett House [MW,GO] 296-A Commercial St (at Ryder) **508/487-6615, 800/990-8865**

Prince Albert Guest House [M,NS,WI,GO] 164-166 Commercial St (at Central) **508/487-1850**

Ravenwood Guest House [MW,NS,WC,GO] 462 Commercial St (at Cook) **508/487-3203** *private beach*

The Red Inn [GF,NS,WC,GO] 15 Commercial St (at Point) **508/487-7334, 866/473-3466**

Revere Guesthouse [MW,NS,GO] 14 Court St (btwn Commercial & Bradford) **508/487-2292, 800/487-2292**

Romeo's Holiday [MW,N,WI,GO] 97 Bradford St (btwn Gosnold & Masonic) **508/487-6636, 877/697-6636** *hot tub*

Rose & Crown Guest House [GS,GO] 158 Commercial St (at Central) **508/487-3332**

Sage Inn & Lounge [GS,WI,WC] 336 Commercial St **508/487-6424**

Salt House Inn [MW,NS,WI,GO] 6 Conwell St (at Railroad) **508/487-1911** *sundeck*

Sandcastle Resort and Club [GS,SW,WI] 929 Commercial St **508/487-9300**

Seasons, An Inn for All [MW,NS,WI,GO] 160 Bradford St (at Pearl) **508/487-2283, 800/563-0113** *Victorian B&B, full brkfst*

Snug Cottage [GS,NS,WI,GO] 178 Bradford St **508/487-1616, 800/432-2334**

Somerset House [MW,NS,WI,GO] 378 Commercial St (at Pearl) **508/487-0383, 800/575-1850**

Sunset Inn [MW,N,NS,WI,GO] 142 Bradford St (at Center) **508/487-9810, 800/965-1801** *seasonal, some shared baths*

Surfside Hotel & Suites [GS,SW,NS,WI] 543 Commercial St (at Kendall Ln) **508/487-1726, 800/421-1726** *seasonal, waterfront hotel w/ lots of amenities, private beach*

The Tucker Inn [MW,NS,WI,GO] 12 Center St (at Bradford) **508/487-0381, 800/477-1867**

Victoria House [MW,WI,NS,GO] 5 Standish St **508/487-4455, 877/867-8696**

The Waterford [GS,WI] 386 Commercial St (at Pearl) 508/487-6400, 800/487-0784 *deck w/ full bar, also restaurant*

Watermark Inn [GS,NS,WI] 603 Commercial St 508/487-0165

Watership Inn [M,WI,GO] 7 Winthrop St (at Commercial St) 508/487-0094, 800/330-9413

West End Inn [GF,WI,NS,GO] 44 Commercial St 508/487-9555, 800/559-1220 *seasonal*

White Porch Inn [M,WI] 7 Johnson St 508/364-2549, 866/922-0333

White Wind Inn [MW,WI,GO] 174 Commercial St (at Winthrop) 508/487-1526, 888/449-9463

■BARS

The Boatslip Resort [★MW,D,F,YC] 161 Commercial St 508/487-1669, 877/786-9662 *seasonal, popular T-dance 4pm daily, special events, outdoor/ waterfront grill*

Governor Bradford [GF,F,E,K,DS] 312 Commercial St (at Standish) 508/487-2781 *11am-1am, from noon Sun, also restaurant in summer*

PiedBar [★MW,D,F,E,P,S,WC] 193-A Commercial St (at Court St) 508/487-1527 *seasonal May-Oct, noon-1am, mostly men 6:30pm-9:30pm at After Tea T-Dance*

Porchside Lounge [M,NH,P] 11 Carver St (in the Gifford House) 508/487-0688 *5pm-1am, Lobby Bar from 10pm, also restaurant*

Shipwreck Lounge [MW] 10 Carver St (at Bradford) 508/487-1472 *upscale lounge, outdoor seating w/ fire pit*

Vault [MO,B,L] 247 Commercial St (downstairs in the Crown & Anchor) 508/487-1430 *9pm-1am Th-Sun only*

Wave Video Bar [MW,NH,K] 247 Commercial St (in the Crown & Anchor) 508/487-1430 *6pm-1am, from noon in season, T-dance Sun*

■NIGHTCLUBS

Atlantic House (The "A-House") [★M,D] 6 Masonic Pl 508/487-3169 *10pm-1am, 3 bars, weekly theme parties, also The Little Bar [M,NH] & the Macho Bar [M,L]*

Club Purgatory [MW,D,L] 9-11 Carver St (at Bradford St, in the Gifford House) 508/487-8442 *opens 7pm, from 9pm Sun (in season)*

Paramount [★MW,D,E,C,DS,$] in the Crown & Anchor 508/487-1430 *10pm-1am wknds, seasonal*

■CAFES

Post Office Cafe Cabaret [E] 303 Commercial St (upstairs) 508/487-3892 *8am-11pm, seasonal hours*

■RESTAURANTS

Bayside Betsy's [WC] 177 Commercial St 508/487-6566 *brkfst, lunch & dinner, bar till 10pm, on waterfront*

Big Daddy's Burritos 205 Commercial St 508/487-4432 *11am-10pm (May-Oct)*

Bubala's by the Bay [★] 183-185 Commercial 508/487-0773 *lunch & dinner, bar till 1am, patio*

Ciro & Sal's [R] 4 Kiley Ct (btwn Bangs St & Lovett's Ct) 508/487-6444 *dinner from 5:30pm, Northern Italian*

Fanizzi's [★WC] 539 Commercial St (at Kendall Lane) 508/487-1964

Front Street Restaurant [BW] 230 Commercial St 508/487-9715 *seasonal, bistro 6pm-10:30pm, bar till 1am*

Lobster Pot [WC] harborside (at 321 Commercial St) 508/487-0842 *11:30am-10pm (April-Nov)*

The Mews Restaurant & Cafe [★E,WC] 429 Commercial St (at Bangs St) 508/487-1500 *dinner, seasonal Sun brunch, waterfront dining*

Napi's Restaurant [WC] 7 Freeman St 508/487-1145, 800/571-6274 *dinner (lunch Oct-April), int'l/ seafood*

Massachusetts • USA

The Red Inn [GF,NS,WC,GO] 15 Commercial St (at Point) **508/487-7334, 866/473-3466** *dinner nightly, brunch Th-Sun, clsd Jan-April, reservations a must, full bar*

Relish 93 Commercial St **508/487-8077** *yummy baked goods, pick up a sandwich on the way to the beach!*

Spiritus Pizza [★] 190 Commercial St **508/487-2808** *noon-2am, great espresso shakes & late-night hangout for a slice*

■ENTERTAINMENT & RECREATION

Art House Theatre & Cafe 214 Commercial St **508/487-9222**

Art's Dune Tours [GO] 4 Standish St **508/487-1950, 800/894-1951** *day trips, sunset tours & charters through historic sand dunes & Nat'l Seashore Park*

Dolphin Fleet Whale Watch [GF,WC] 305 Commercial St **508/240-3636, 800/826-9300** *3-hr day & evening cruises*

Herring Cove Beach

Ptown Bikes [GO] 42 Bradford **508/487-8735** *9am-6pm, rentals*

Spaghetti Strip *nude beach, 1.5 miles S of Race Point Beach*

■RETAIL SHOPS

HRC Action Center & Store 209-211 Commercial St **508/487-7736, 888/932-7472** *Human Rights Campaign merchandise & info*

■PUBLICATIONS

Provincetown Banner 167 Commercial St **508/487-7400** *newspaper*

Provincetown Magazine **508/487-1000** *seasonal, Provincetown's oldest weekly magazine*

■GYMS & HEALTH CLUBS

Mussel Beach Health Club 35 Bradford St (btwn Montello & Conant) **508/487-0001** *6am-9pm, till 8pm in winter*

Provincetown Gym 82 Shank Painter Rd (at Winthrop) **508/487-2776**

■EROTICA

Full Kit Gear Shop 192 Commercial St **508/413-9676** *leather, latex, fetish-wear*

■CRUISY AREAS

Dick Dock [AYOR] behind Boatslip Beach Club *late*

Herring Cove Beach [AYOR]

Quincy

see also Boston

■NIGHTCLUBS

My House [MW,D,F,K] 609 Washington St (at Cleverly Ct) **617/302-4285** *6pm-1am, clsd Mon*

Randolph

■BARS

Randolph Country Club/ RCC [★MW,D,F,K,C,S,V,SW,WC] 44 Mazzeo Dr **781/961-2414** *2pm-2am, from 10am summer, 2 dance clubs, cabaret, poolside grill, volleyball*

Raynham

■EROTICA

Video Xtra 508/821-7800

Somerville

see Boston

Springfield

■BARS

Pure [M,NH,F,WC] 234 Chestnut St (E of Main) **413/205-1483** *noon-2am*

■NIGHTCLUBS

The X Room [M,D,S] 395 Dwight St **413/732-4562** *7pm-2am, from 2pmTh-Sun, nude dancers*

■MEN'S SERVICES

➤**MegaMates** **413/271-3700** *Call to hook up with HOT local men. FREE to listen & respond to ads. Use FREE code DAMRON. MegaMates.com.*

Stoneham

■CRUISY AREAS

Sheep's Fold Conservation Area [AYOR] Rte I-93 exit 33 (off Rte 28) *top of the hills*

Taunton

■BARS

Bobby's Place [MW,D,F,K,DS] 62 Weir St (at Route 44, 138 & 140, at Taunton Green) **508/824-9997** *5pm-1am, till 2am Fri-Sat, from 2pm Sun*

Weymouth

■EROTICA

Amazing.net Video Store 138 Bridge St (Rte 3A), North Weymouth **781/335-0446**

Williamstown

see Berkshires

Worcester

■BARS

MB Lounge [MW,NH,WI,WC,GO] 40 Grafton St (at Franklin) **508/799-4521** *5pm-2am, from 3pm wknds*

Mixers Cocktail Lounge [MW,D] 105 Water St **508/756-2227** *6pm-2am, clsd Mon*

■NIGHTCLUBS

Club Remix [M,D,K] 105 Water St (at Harrison) **508/756-2227** *9pm-2am, from 8pm Wed, clsd Mon-Tue*

■RETAIL SHOPS

Glamour Boutique 850 Southbridge St, Auburn **508/721-7800** *large-size dresses, wigs, etc*

■PUBLICATIONS

Central Mass Pride Magazine *centralmasspridemag.com*

MICHIGAN

Statewide

■PUBLICATIONS

Out Post 313/702-0272 *bi-weekly nightlife guide for SE Michigan*

Albion

■EROTICA

The Lion's Den 2101 N Concord Rd (exit 127, off I-94) **517/531-5051** *24hrs*

Ann Arbor

■INFO LINES & SERVICES

The Jim Toy Community Center 319 Braun Ct **734/995-9867** *LGBT resource center, HIV testing 5pm-7pm Sun*

Lesbian/ Gay AA 734/482-5700

■BARS

\'aut\ Bar [★MW,NH,F,WC] 315 Braun Ct (at Catherine) **734/994-3677** *4pm-2am, from 11am Sat, 10 am Sun, patio*

■NIGHTCLUBS

The Necto [GS,D,V,18+,YC] 516 E Liberty (at Maynard) **734/994-5436** *9pm-2am, theme nights, gay night Fri*

■CAFES

Cafe Verde [★F] 214 N Fourth Ave (at Catherine St) **734/994-9174** *7am-9:30pm, 9am-8pm Sun, fair trade & organic coffee & tea*

■RESTAURANTS

Dominick's [BW,WC] 812 Monroe St (at Tappan Ave) **734/662-5414** *10am-10pm, clsd Sun, Italian, full bar*

The Earle [BW,WC] 121 W Washington (at Ashley) **734/994-0211** *5:30pm-9pm, till 11pm Fri-Sat, 5pm-8pm Sun*

Mani Osteria & Bar 341B E Liberty **734/769-6700** *11:30am-10pm, from 4pm wknds, clsd Mon, great pizza*

Seva 314 E Liberty (at 5th Ave) **734/662-1111** *11am-9pm, from 10am wknds, vegetarian, also cafe & wine bar*

Zingerman's Delicatessen [GO] 422 Detroit St (at Kingsley) **734/663-3354, 888/636-8162** *7am-10pm, also ship food worldwide*

■ENTERTAINMENT & RECREATION

The Ark [GF,E] 316 S Main St (btwn William & Liberty) **734/761-1818, 734/761-1800** *concert house*

■BOOKSTORES

Common Language [WC] 317 Braun Ct (at 4th) **734/663-0036** *11am-10pm, till midnight Fri-Sat, till 7pm Sun, LGBT*

Michigan • *USA*

Crazy Wisdom Books & Tea Room
114 S Main St (btwn Huron &
Washington) 734/665-2757 *11am-
9pm, till 11pm Fri-Sat, 11am-8pm Sun*

Battle Creek

■NIGHTCLUBS

Partners [MW,D,K,S,V,WC] 910 North
Ave (at Morgan) 269/964-7276 *7pm-
2am, clsd Mon*

■EROTICA

Romantix Adult Superstore 690 W
Michigan Ave (at Grand)
269/964-3070

Bay City

■BARS

Malickey's Pub [GS,DS] 501 S Madison
989/414-6667 *11:30am-1:30am*

Bellaire

■ACCOMMODATIONS

Applesauce Inn B&B [GF,WI,NS] 7296
S M-88 231/533-6448 *B&B in 100-
year-old farmhouse*

Bellaire B&B [GS,WI,GO] 212 Park St (at
Antrim) 231/533-6077,
800/545-0780 *stately 1879 home, full
brkfst*

Big Rapids

■EROTICA

Fantasies Unlimited 13480 Northland
Dr (at Arthur Rd) 231/792-8052

Cheboygan

■EROTICA

Fantasies Unlimited 1116 E State St
231/627-4665

Copemish

■ACCOMMODATIONS

Jeralan's Farm B&B [GF,NS] 18361
Viaduct Rd (at Simpson Rd)
231/378-2926, 866/250-8444 *1872
farmhouse on 80 acres of woods &
ponds*

Detroit

■INFO LINES & SERVICES

Affirmations Community Center 290
W 9 Mile Rd (at Planavon), Ferndale
800/398-4297 *9am-9pm, clsd Sun,
helpline line 4pm-9pm*

Helpline 800/398-4297 *4pm-9pm
Tue-Sat, support & resources line*

■ACCOMMODATIONS

The Atheneum Suite Hotel [GF,WI,WC]
1000 Brush Ave (at Lafayette)
313/962-2323, 800/772-2323

**Detroit Marriott at the Renaissance
Center** [GF,WC] 400 Renaissance Center
Dr 313/568-8000, 800/228-9290

Honor & Folly [GS,WI] 2138 Michigan
Ave (above Slows BBQ) *design-focused
B&B with cooking classes, bike rentals
and goods made by local designers &
artisans*

Milner Hotel [GF] 1538 Centre St (at
Grand River Ave) 313/963-3950,
877/645-6377

■BARS

Adam's Apple [M,NH,K,GO] 18931 W
Warren Ave (at Artesian)
313/240-8482 *3pm-2am, from noon
wknds*

Centaur Bar [GS,F] 2233 Park Ave (at
W Montcalm St) 313/963-4040 *4pm-
2am*

Club Gold Coast [★M,D,DS,S,WI,WC]
2971 E 7 Mile Rd (at Conant)
313/366-6135 *7pm-2am, male
dancers nightly*

Gigi's [M,D,TG,K,DS,S,GO] 16920 W
Warren (at Clayburn, enter rear)
313/584-6525 *noon-2am, from 2pm
wknds*

Hayloft Saloon [M,NH,B,L,OC,WI,WC]
8070 Greenfield Rd (S of Joy Rd)
313/581-8913 *3pm-2am*

Male Box Bar [M,NH,D,K,DS,18+,GO]
23365 Hoover Rd (N of 9 Mile), Warren
313/893-7696 *2pm-2am*

Menjo's [★M,D,K,V,YC] 928 W
McNichols Rd (at Hamilton)
313/863-3934 *1pm-2am, popular
happy hour*

Pronto [★MW,F,V] 608 S Washington (at 6th St), Royal Oak **248/544-7900** *11am-2am, patio*

R&R Saloon [M,NH,D,L,F,WI] 7330 Michigan Ave (at Central) **313/849-2751** *2pm-2am, till 5am Wed & wknds, may be relocating*

Soho [MW,K] 205 W 9 Mile (at Woodward), Ferndale **248/542-7646** *4pm-close, from 6pm wknds*

The Woodward Video Bar & Grill [★M,D,MR,F,K,V] 6426 Woodward Ave (at Milwaukee, rear entrance) **313/872-0166** *2pm-2am*

The Works Detroit [GS,D,V] 1846 Michigan Ave (at Rosa Parks) **313/961-1742** *10pm-3am Th, till 5am Fri-Sat, mostly gay Sat*

▪ NIGHTCLUBS

Birdcage [MW,DS] 6640 E 8 Mile Rd (at Sherwood) **313/891-1020** *4pm-2am Fri-Sun*

Escape [MW,NH,F,DS,GO] 19404 Sherwood (at 7 Mile) **313/892-1765** *10pm-5am*

Hellbound **248/541-3979** *this party is held at various nightclubs and venues in the Detroit area every 2 to 3 months, check www.noirleather.com*

Leland City Club [GF,D,A,18+] 400 Bagley St (at Leland Hotel) **313/962-2300** *10pm-4:30am Fri-Sat, goth/ alternative crowd*

Luna [GF,D,A] 1815 N Main St (at 12 Mile), Royal Oak **248/589-3344** *from 9pm, clsd Sun-Tue, theme nights*

Stiletto's [MW,D,DS,E,K] 1641 Middlebelt Rd (btwn Michigan Ave & Cherry Hill Rd), Inkster **734/729-8980** *8pm-2am Th-Sun*

Temple [GS,D,MR-AF,TG,WC] 2906 Cass Ave (btwn Charlotte & Temple) **313/832-2822** *1pm-2am, popular wknds*

▪ CAFES

Avalon International Breads [GO] 422 W Willis (at Cass) **313/832-0008** *6am-6pm, clsd Sun-Mon*

Coffee Beanery Cafe [WI] 28557 S Woodward Ave (S of 12 Mile), Berkley **248/336-9930** *7am-11pm*

Five 15 [E,WI,GO] 515 S Washington St, Royal Oak **248/515-2551** *11am-5pm, till 5pm Sun, clsd Mon, Drag Bingo Fri-Sat, performances, art shows*

▪ RESTAURANTS

Amici's 3249 12 Mile Rd (at Gardner Ave), Berkley **248/544-4100** *gourmet pizza & martinis*

Atlas Global Bistro 3111 Woodward Ave (at Charlotte) **313/831-2241** *lunch & dinner, Sun brunch, American/ int'l, upscale*

Cacao Tree Cafe 204 W 4th St, Royal Oak **248/336-9043** *9am-9pm, gourmet raw food/ vegan*

Cass Cafe [WI] 4620 Cass Ave (at Forest) **313/831-1400** *11am-2am, 5pm-1am Sun, full bar*

Coach Insignia 200 Renaissance Ctr, 71st Fl **313/567-2622** *dinner, clsd Sun, steakhouse*

Como's [WC] 22812 Woodward (at 9 Mile), Ferndale **248/548-5005** *11am-2am, till 4am Fri-Sat, Italian, full bar, patio*

Elwood Bar & Grill 300 Adams (at Brush, by Comerica Park) **313/962-2337** *11am-8pm, till 2pm Mon, clsd Sun (unless there's a Tiger's game); Art Deco diner*

Inn Season 500 E 4th St (at Knowles), Royal Oak **248/547-7916** *lunch & dinner, Sun brunch, clsd Mon, organic vegetarian/ vegan*

La Dolce Vita [MW,WC] 17546 Woodward Ave (at McNichols) **313/865-0331** *lunch & dinner, Sun brunch, clsd Mon, Italian, patio*

Mercury Burger & Bar 2163 Michigan Ave **313/964-5000** *11am-11pm*

One-Eyed Betty's [GO] 175 W Troy, Ferndale **248/808-6633** *4pm-2am, from 9am wknds*

Red Star 13944 Michigan Ave, Dearborn **313/581-1451** *Chinese, plenty veggie/ vegan*

Roast 1128 Washington Ave (at State St) **313/961-2500** *dinner nightly, steakhouse*

Seva 66 E Forest **313/974-6661** *11am-9pm, till 11pm Fri-Sat, vegetarian*

Michigan • *USA*

Sweet Lorraine's Cafe & Bar [★WC] 29101 Greenfield Rd (at 12 Mile), Southfield **248/559-5985** *11am-10pm, till 11pm Fri-Sat, till 9:30pm Sun*

Traffic Jam & Snug [WC] 511 W Canfield St (at SE corner of 2nd Ave) **313/831-9470** *11am-10:30pm, till midnight Fri-Sat, till 9pm Sun, also full bar, bakery, dairy & brewery*

Vivio's [WC] 2460 Market St (at Napoleon St) **313/393-1711** *lunch & dinner, clsd Sun, full bar*

Wolfgang Puck Grille 1777 3rd St (at the MGM Grand Hotel) **313/465-1648** *5pm-10pm, 9am-2pm Sat-Sun, clsd Mon-Tue*

■ENTERTAINMENT & RECREATION

Charles H Wright Museum of African American History 315 E Warren Ave (at Cass) **313/494-5800**

Motown Historical Museum 2648 W Grand Blvd **313/875-2264**

■BOOKSTORES

Just 4 Us [GO] 211 W 9 Mile Rd (at Woodward), Ferndale **248/547-5878** *11am-8pm, till 10pm Th-Fri, till 5pm Sun, also cafe*

■RETAIL SHOPS

Royal Oak Tattoo 820 S Washington Ave (at Lincoln), Royal Oak **248/398-0052** *tattoo & piercing studio*

■PUBLICATIONS

Between the Lines 734/293-7200 *statewide LGBT weekly*

Metra Magazine PO Box 71844, Madison Heights 48071 **248/543-3500** *covers IN, IL, MI, OH, PA, WI & Ontario, Canada*

■MEN'S CLUBS

Body Zone Health Club [MO,V,18+,PC,GO] 1617 E McNichols (at I-75) **313/366-9663** *24hrs*

TNT Health Club [MO,V,18+,PC,GO,$] 13333 W 8 Mile Rd (at Schaefer, enter rear) **313/341-7250** *11am-8pm*

■MEN'S SERVICES

➤**MegaMates** 313/962-5000 *Call to hook up with HOT local men. FREE to listen & respond to ads. Use FREE code DAMRON. MegaMates.com.*

■EROTICA

Blue Moon Video 7041 W 8 Mile Rd (2 blocks W of Livernois) **313/340-1730** *11am-1am, till 10pm Sun*

Escape Adult Bookstore 18728 W Warren Ave (8 blocks W of Southfield) **313/336-6558** *10am-midnight, from noon Sun*

Noir Leather [WC] 124 W 4th St (at S Center St), Royal Oak **248/541-3979** *11am-9pm, till 10pm Fri-Sat, noon-7pm Sun*

Uptown Book Store 16541 Woodward Ave (at 6 Mile Rd), Highland Park **313/869-9477**

Douglas

see Saugatuck

Escanaba

■EROTICA

Sensual Arts Adult Bookstore [GO] 615 N Lincoln Rd (at 6th Ave N) **906/786-9020**

Flint

■BARS

MI [★MW,D,MR,WI] 2406 N Franklin Ave (at Belle Ave) **810/234-9481** *5pm-2am*

Pachyderm Pub [MW,NH,D,MR,TG,K,F,WI,GO] G-1408 E Hemphill Rd (btwn I-475 & Saginaw St), Burton **810/744-4960** *3pm-2am, from 5pm wknds, patio*

■NIGHTCLUBS

Club Triangle [★MW,D,S,18+] 2101 S Dort (at Lippincott) **810/767-7550** *9pm-close Wed-Sun*

■CAFES

The Good Beans Cafe [E,WI,WC,GO] 328 N Grand Traverse (at 1st Ave) **810/237-4663** *7:30am-4pm, till 9pm Th-Fri, open some wknds*

Marquette • Michigan

■MEN'S SERVICES
➤MegaMates 810/597-0597 *Call to hook up with HOT local men. FREE to listen & respond to ads. Use FREE code DAMRON. MegaMates.com.*

Frankfort

■ACCOMMODATIONS
Wayfarer Lodgings [GF,NS,WI] 1912 S Scenic Hwy (M-22) 231/352-9264, 800/735-8564

Grand Rapids

■INFO LINES & SERVICES
Lesbian/ Gay Network of W Michigan 343 Atlas Ave SE (behind Spirit Dreams in Eastown) 616/458-3511 *11am-5:30pm, clsd wknds*

■ACCOMMODATIONS
Radisson Riverfront Hotel [GF,NS,SW,WI,WC] 270 Ann St NW (at Turner Ave) 616/363-9001, 800/395-7046

■BARS
Apartment Lounge [M,NH,WC] 33 Sheldon NE (at Library) 616/451-0815 *1pm-2am, from noon wknds*

Diversions [★MW,D,K,V,18+,WC] 10 Fountain St NW (at Division) 616/451-3800 *8pm-2am*

Pub 43 [MW,NH,F] 43 S Division St (at Weston) 616/458-2205 *3pm-2am*

■NIGHTCLUBS
Rumors Nightclub [MW,D,DS,K,S,V,WC,GO] 69 S Division Ave (at Oakes St) 616/454-8720 *4pm-2am*

■RESTAURANTS
Brandywine 1345 Lake Dr SE (in East Town) 616/774-8641 *7am-8pm, from 7:30am Sat, 8am-2:30pm Sun*

Cherie Inn [WC] 969 Cherry St SE (at Lake Dr) 616/458-0588 *7am-3pm, from8am wknds, clsd Mon*

Gaia Cafe 209 Diamond Ave SE (at Cherry St) 616/454-6233 *8am-8pm, till 3pm wknds, clsd Mon, vegetarian*

■MEN'S CLUBS
Diplomat Health Club [PC] 2324 Division Ave (at Whithey) 616/452-3754 *24hrs*

Grayling

■EROTICA
Fantasies Unlimited 6131 M-72 West 989/348-4665

Kalamazoo

■INFO LINES & SERVICES
Kalamazoo Gay/ Lesbian Resource Center 629 Pioneer St 269/349-4234 *9am,-5pm, clsd wknds*

Lansing

■BARS
Esquire [MW,NH,K] 1250 Turner St (at Clinton) 517/487-5338 *3pm-2am*

■NIGHTCLUBS
Spiral [M,D,S,DS,18+,WC] 1247 Center St (at Clinton) 517/371-3221 *8pm-2am, clsd Mon-Tue, theme nights*

■BOOKSTORES
Everybody Reads 2019 E Michigan Ave 517/346-9900 *11am-7pm, 10am-4pm Sun, cool general bookstore, also coffeehouse*

■MEN'S SERVICES
➤MegaMates 517/318-0333 *Call to hook up with HOT local men. FREE to listen & respond to ads. Use FREE code DAMRON. MegaMates.com.*

■EROTICA
Fantasies Unlimited 3208 S MLK Blvd (at Southland Ave) 517/393-1159

Marquette

■ACCOMMODATIONS
The Landmark Inn [GF,NS,WI] 230 N Front St (at Ridge St) 906/228-2580, 888/752-6362 *historic boutique hotel overlooking Lake Superior, restaurant & bar*

■CRUISY AREAS
Presque Isle Point [AYOR]

Michigan • *USA*

Mount Pleasant

■CRUISY AREAS
Mission Creek Park [AYOR] Harris St *summers*

Petoskey

■ACCOMMODATIONS
Coach House Inn [GF,WI,NS,GO] 1011 N US 31 (at Mitchell) **231/347-8281, 877/347-8088** *basic amenities*

Pontiac

■BARS
Liberty Bar [MW,D,F] 85 N Saginaw **248/758-0771** *11:30am-2am, from 2pm wknds*

■EROTICA
Fantasies Unlimited 974 Joslyn Ave **248/338-2442**

■CRUISY AREAS
Hawthorne Park [AYOR] N Telegraph Rd (at Dixie Hwy)

Port Huron

■NIGHTCLUBS
Seekers [MW,D,DS] 3301 24th St (btwn Oak & Little) **810/985-9349** *7pm-2am*

■CRUISY AREAS
Pine Grove Park [AYOR]

Saginaw

■NIGHTCLUBS
The Mixx Nightclub [MW,D,F,K,V,18+,WC] 115 N Hamilton St (at Court St) **989/498-4022** *5pm-close Th-Sun*

Saugatuck

■ACCOMMODATIONS
Beechwood Manor Inn & Cottage [GS,NS,WI,GO] 736 Pleasant St (at Allegan) **269/857-1587, 877/857-1587**

Bella Vita Spa & Suites [GF,WI] 119 Butler St **269/857-8482** *also day spa*

The Belvedere Inn & Restaurant [GF,NS,WI,GO] 3656 63rd St **269/857-5777, 877/858-5777** *full brkfrst*

Bird Center Resort [GF,WI] 584-586 Lake St **269/857-1750** *cottages across from Sautatuck Harbo*

The Bunkhouse B&B at Campit [MW,SW,NS,WI,GO] **269/543-4335, 877/226-7481**

Campit Outdoor Resort [MW,SW,WI,GO] 6635 118th Ave, Fennville **269/543-4335, 877/226-7481** *seasonal, campsites & RV hookups, membership required*

Douglas House B&B [GS,NS,GO] 41 Spring St (at Wall St), Douglas **269/857-1119** *near gay beach*

The Dunes Resort [MW,D,TG,F,E,DS,SW,WC,GO] 333 Blue Star Hwy, Douglas **269/857-1401**

Hidden Garden Cottages & Suites [GF,NS,WI] 247 Butler St **269/857-8109, 888/857-8109**

Hillby Thatch Cottages [GS,NS] 1438-1440 71st St, Glenn **847/864-3553**

The Hunter's Lodge [GS,NS,WI,GO] 2790 68th St (at US 31), Fennville **269/857-5402** *seasonal, vintage rustic log cabin*

J Paules Fenn Inn [GF,NS] 2254 S 58th St, Fennville **269/561-2836, 877/561-2836** *full brkfst*

The Kingsley House B&B [GF,NS,WI,GO] 626 West Main St, Fennville **269/561-6425, 866/561-6425** *full brkfst*

Kirby House [GS,SW,NS,WI,GO] 294 Center St (at Blue Star Hwy) **269/857-2904, 800/521-6473** *full brkfst,*

Maple Ridge Cottages [GS,NS,GO] 713-719 Maple **269/857-5211 (Pines #)** *quaint cottages, hot tubs*

The Newnham SunCatcher Inn [GF,SW,NS,WI] 131 Griffith (at Mason) **269/857-4249, 800/587-4249**

The Park House Inn B&B [GF,NS,WI] 888 Holland St **269/857-4535, 866/321-4535** *B&B in one of Saugatuck's oldest residences*

The Pines Motor Lodge & Cottages [GS,NS,WI,GO] 56 Blue Star Hwy (at Center St), Douglas **269/857-5211** *boutique retro motel, also retro gift gallery*

St Ignace • Michigan

The Spruce Cutter's Cottage [GS,GO] 6670 126th Ave (at Blue Star Hwy & M-89), Fennville **269/543-4285, 800/493-5888**

■**BARS**

Dunes Disco [MW,D,TG,E,C,DS,GO] 333 Blue Star Hwy (at the Dunes Resort) **269/857-1401** *9am-2am*

■**CAFES**

Uncommon Grounds [WI] 127 Hoffman (at Water) **269/857-3333** *6:30am-10pm, coffee & juice bar*

■**RESTAURANTS**

Back Alley Pizza Joint 22 Main St (at Center), Douglas **269/857-7277** *11am-10pm, till 11pm Fri-Sat*

Chequers 220 Culver St **269/857-1868** *11:30am-9pm, seasonal, great fish & chips*

Everyday People Cafe [E,WC] 11 Center St (at Main), Douglas **269/857-4240** *call for hours*

Kalico Kitchen [WC] 312 Ferry St, Douglas **269/857-2678** *7am-9pm winter, till 10pm summer*

Marro's Italian [D] 147 Water St (at Mason St) **269/857-4248** *dinner only, clsd Mon-Tue, nightclub till 2am Fri-Sat*

Monroe's Cafe-Grille 302 Culver St (at Griffith) **269/857-1242** *8am-9pm, clsd Nov-March*

Phil's Bar & Grille 215 Butler St (at Mason) **269/857-1555** *11:30am-10pm, till 11pm Fri-Sat, patio*

Pumpernickel's [WI] 202 Butler St (at Mason) **269/857-1196** *8am-4pm*

Restaurant Toulouse [R,E,WC] 248 Culver **269/857-1561** *dinner nightly, lunch wknds (seasonal), full bar*

Scooters 322 Culver St (at Griffith) **269/857-1041** *noon-9pm, till 10pm wknds, clsd Tue, great pizza*

The White House Bistro [E] 149 Griffith (at Mason) **269/857-3240** *4pm-10pm, 9am-midnight Sat, 9am-9pm Sun, live music*

Wicks Park [E,WC] 449 Water St **269/857-2888** *dinner nightly, live music wknds*

Wild Dog Grill 24 W Center St (at Spring), Douglas **269/857-2519** *dinner nightly, from noon wknds, clsd Mon-Tue*

■**ENTERTAINMENT & RECREATION**

Earl's Farm Market [GO] 1630 Blue Star Hwy, Fennville **269/227-2074** *8am-9pm May-Oct only, pick your own berries!*

Oval Beach consult local map for driving directions, Douglas *popular beach on Lake Michigan*

Tulip Time Festival Holland **800/822-2770**

■**RETAIL SHOPS**

Amaru Leather 322 Griffith St (at Hoffman St) **269/857-3745** *"original & custom creations in leather by two resident designers"*

Groovy! Groovy! Retro Gift Gallery [GO] 56 Blue Star Hwy (at Center St), Douglas **269/857-5211** *seasonal hours, antiques, funky gifts & goods*

Hoopdee Scootee 133 Mason (at Butler) **269/857-4141** *seasonal, clothing, gifts*

Saugatuck Drug Store 201 Butler St (at Mason) **269/857-2300** *seasonal, old-fashioned corner drug store, including actual soda fountain!*

■**GYMS & HEALTH CLUBS**

Pump House Gym 6492 Blue Star Hwy (at 135th) **269/857-7867** *day passes*

■**CRUISY AREAS**

Oval Beach [AYOR] *walk north*

South Haven

■**ACCOMMODATIONS**

Yelton Manor B&B [GS,NS,WI,WC] 140 North Shore Dr (at Dyckman) **269/637-5220** *full brkfst*

St Ignace

■**ACCOMMODATIONS**

Budget Host Inn & Suites [GF,SW,WI,WC] 700 N State St **906/643-9666, 800/872-7057**

Traverse City

ACCOMMODATIONS

Neahtawanta Inn [GF,SW,NS,WI,WC]
1308 Neahtawanta Rd (at Peninsula Dr)
231/223-7315, 800/220-1415
sauna

NIGHTCLUBS

Side Traxx [MW,D,V,GO] 520 Franklin St
(at E 8th) **231/935-1666** *5pm-2am,
cruise bar*

BOOKSTORES

The Bookie Joint 124 S Union St
(btwn State & Front) **231/946-8862**
*noon-6pm, clsd Sun, pride gifts, used
books*

CRUISY AREAS

Westend Beach Hwy 31 (N of Munson
Hospital)

Union Pier

ACCOMMODATIONS

Blue Fish Guest House & Cottage
[GS,NS,GO] 10234 Community Hall Rd
269/469-0468 x112 *cottages &
guesthouses*

Fire Fly Resort [GS,NS,GO] 15657
Lakeshore Rd **269/469-0245** *1- &
2-bdrm units*

Ypsilanti

see also Ann Arbor

MINNESOTA

Bemidji

CRUISY AREAS

Diamond Point Park [AYOR] *summers*

The Indian Trail [AYOR] below Lake
Blvd (btwn 10th & 12th St)

Duluth

see also Superior, Wisconsin

ACCOMMODATIONS

The Olcott House B&B Inn
[GF,NS,WI,GO] 2316 E 1st St (at 23rd
Ave) **218/728-1339, 800/715-1339**

BARS

Duluth Flame [MW,D,E,K,DS] 28 N 1st
Ave W **218/727-2344** *3pm-2:30am*

CAFES

Jitters [WI] 102 W Superior St
218/720-6015 *7am-7pm, 9am-1pm
Sun*

RESTAURANTS

At Sara's Table Chester Creek Cafe
[E,WI,WC] 1902 E 8th St (at 19th)
218/724-6811 *7am-8pm*

MEN'S CLUBS

Duluth Family Sauna 18 N 1st Ave E
218/726-1388 *noon-10:30pm*

EROTICA

Wabasha Books 114 E 1st St
218/723-1980

Lanesboro

ACCOMMODATIONS

Stone Mill Hotel & Suites
[GS,NS,WI,WC,GO] 100 E Beacon St (at
Parkway Ave) **507/467-8663,
866/897-8663**

Mankato

CAFES

The Coffee Hag [E,WC] 329 N
Riverfront Dr **507/387-5533** *7am-
10pm, till 11pm Fri-Sat*

EROTICA

Pure Pleasure 2102 N Riverfront Dr
507/388-6871 *24hrs*

Minneapolis/ St Paul

INFO LINES & SERVICES

AA Intergroup 952/922-0880

OutFront Minnesota 310 E 38th St
#204, Minneapolis **612/822-0127,
800/800-0350** *info line w/ 24hr pre-
recorded visitor info*

Quatrefoil Library 1619 Dayton Ave
#105, St Paul **651/641-0969** *7pm-
9pm, 10am-5pm Sat, 1pm-5pm Sun,
LGBT resource center*

ACCOMMODATIONS

The Depot Renaissance Minneapolis
[GF,F] 225 3rd Ave S, Minneapolis
612/375-1700, 866/211-4611

Graves 601 Hotel [GF,NS,WI] 601 1st
Ave N (at 6th St N), Minneapolis
612/677-1100, 866/523-1100

Hotel 340 [GF,SW,WI] 340 Cedar St 651/280-4120

Le Meridien Chambers [GF,WI,WC] 901 Hennepin Ave, Minneapolis **612/767-6900, 800/543-4300** *art-filled hotel; also restaurant & bar*

Namaste Cafe 2512 Hennepin Ave S, Minneapolis **612/827-2496** *11am-10pm, full bar, great Indian & Napali food*

Water Street Inn [GF,WI,WC] 101 S Water St, Stillwater **651/439-6000** *also restaurant & pub*

■BARS

19 Bar [M,NH,WC] 19 W 15th St (at Nicollet Ave), Minneapolis **612/871-5553** *3pm-2am, from 1pm wknds*

Bev's Wine Bar [GF,F,WC] 250 3rd Ave N #100 (at Washington Ave), Minneapolis **612/337-0102** *4:30pm-1am, patio*

Brass Rail [★M,K,P,S,V,WC] 422 Hennepin Ave (at 4th) Minneapolis **612/332-7245** *noon-2am*

Bryant Lake Bowl [GF,F,E,WC] 810 W Lake St (near Bryant), Minneapolis **612/825-3737** *8am-2am, bar, theater & bowling alley*

Camp Bar [★M,D,F,K,S,V,WC] 490 N Robert St (at 9th St), St Paul **651/292-1844** *4pm-2am, bear party 4th Fri*

Eagle Bolt Bar [M,B,L,F] 515 Washington Ave S (btwn Portland & 5th Ave), Minneapolis **612/338-4214** *4pm-2am, from 10am Sat-Sun, beer bust Sun, also Bolt underground dance bar*

Jetset [MW,D,K] 115 N First St (at 1st Ave N), Minneapolis **612/339-3933** *5pm-close, from 6pm Sat, clsd Sun-Mon*

Lush Food Bar [MW,D,C,DS,F] 990 Central Ave (at Spring St), Minneapolis *8am-2am, clsd Mon, brunch served everyday till 2pm*

Lush Food Bar [MW,D,F] 990 Central Avenue NE, Minneapolis **612/612-0000** *8am-2am, clsd Mon*

The Town House [★MW,D,E,F,K,C,DS,P,GO] 1415 University Ave W (at Elbert), St Paul **651/646-7087** *2pm-2am, from noon wknds*

■NIGHTCLUBS

The Boys Present [M,D] Minneapolis *seasonal monthly party,check* www.theboyspresent.com

Gay 90s [★MW,D,MR,F,E,K,DS,18+,WC] 408 Hennepin Ave (at 4th St S), Minneapolis **612/333-7755** *8am-2am (dinner Wed-Sun), also Men's Room [MO,L]*

Ground Zero [★GS,D,S,WC] 15 NE 4th St (at Hennepin), Minneapolis **612/378-5115** *10pm-2am Th-Sat only, more gay Sat for Bondage-A-Go-Go*

Kitty Cat Klub [GF,F,E] 315 14th Ave SE (at SE University Ave) **612/331-9800** *lounge w/ eclectic decor, live bands*

The Saloon [★M,D,F,S,YC,WC,GO] 830 Hennepin Ave (at 9th), Minneapolis **612/332-0835** *noon-2am, from 11am Sun*

■CAFES

Anodyne at 43rd [F,E,WC] 4301 Nicollet Ave S (at 43rd), Minneapolis **612/824-4300** *7am-10pm, till 8pm Fri-Sun*

Black Dog Coffee & Wine Bar [BW,F] 308 Prince St (at Broadway), St Paul **651/228-9274** *7am-10pm, till 11pm Fri-Sat, 8am-8pm Sun*

Blue Moon [WI,GO] 3822 E Lake St, Minneapolis **612/721-9230** *7am-10pm, from 8am wknds*

Cahoots [WI,WC] 1562 Selby Ave (at Snelling), St Paul **651/644-6778** *6:30am-10:30pm, from 7am wknds*

Cuppa Java [BW,WI] 400 Penn Ave S, Minneapolis **612/374-4806** *7am-10pm, deliver 9am-3pm*

Moose & Sadie's [WI,WC] 212 3rd Ave N (at 2nd St), Minneapolis **612/371-0464** *7am-8pm, 9am-2pm wknds*

Quixotic Coffee [WI] 769 Cleveland, St Paul **651/699-5448** *7am-9pm, till 6pm Sun*

Uncommon Grounds 2809 Hennepin Ave (at W 28th St), Minneapolis **612/872-4811** *noon-midnight, till 1am Fri-Sat, patio*

Minnesota • USA

The Urban Bean [WI,WC] 3255 Bryant Ave S (at 33rd), Minneapolis 612/824–6611 *6:30am-11pm*

Wilde Roast Cafe [BW,WC,GO] 65 Main St SE (at Hennepin Ave), Minneapolis 612/331–4544 *7am-10pm*

■ RESTAURANTS

Al's Breakfast [★] 413 14th Ave SE (at 4th), Minneapolis 612/331–9991 *6am-1pm, from 9am Sun, great hash*

Barbette 1600 W Lake St (at Irving), Minneapolis 612/827–5710 *8am-1am, till 2am Fri-Sat*

Birchwood Cafe [WI,WC] 3311 E 25th St, Minneapolis 612/722–4474 *7am-9pm, from 8am Sat, 9am-8pm Sun, veggie/ vegan*

Brasa Premium Rotisserie [BW,WC] 600 E Hennepin, Minneapolis 612/379–3030

French Meadow [BW] 2610 Lyndale Ave S, Minneapolis 612/870–7855 *6:30am-9pm, till 10pm Fri-Sat organic & local, plenty veggie/ vegan*

Hard Times Cafe [WI] 1821 Riverside Ave, Minneapolis 612/341–9261 *6am-4am, vegan/ vegetarian, punk rock ambiance*

Hell's Kitchen 80 9th St S, Minneapolis 612/332–4700 *7:30am-10pm, till 2am Fri-Sat, great brkfst & free music wknds 11am-2pm*

Loring Kitchen & Bar [GO] 1359 Willow St, Minneapolis 612/843–0400 *11am-11pm, till 1am Fri-Sat, from 9am Sat-Sun*

Lucia's Restaurant & Wine Bar [WC] 1432 W 31st St, Minneapolis 612/25–1572 *lunch & dinner, clsd Mon*

Monte Carlo [WC] 219 3rd Ave N, Minneapolis 612/333–5900 *lunch & dinner, bar till 1am*

Murray's 26 S 6th St (at Hennepin), Minneapolis 612/339–0909 *lunch Mon-Fri, dinner nightly*

Nye's Polonaise [E,P] 112 E Hennepin 612/379–2021 *4pm-2am, from 11am Fri-Sa*

Psycho Suzi's Motor Lounge [E,WC] 2519 Marshall St NE, Minneapolis 612/788–9069 *11am-2am, pu-pu's & pizza*

Punch Neapolitan Pizza [WC] 704 Cleveland Ave S, St Paul 651/696–1066 *11am-9:30pm; also at 210 E Hennepin Ave*

Red Stag Supperclub [E,WC] 509 1st Ave NE (at 5th St), Minneapolis 612/767–7766 *11am-2am, from 9am Sat-Sun*

Restaurant Alma 528 University Ave SE, Minneapolis 612/379–4909 *dinner nightly, organic New American*

Seward Cafe [WC] 2129 E Franklin Ave, Minneapolis 612/332–1011 *7am-3pm, 8am-4pm wknds, vegetarian/ vegan*

Toast Wine Bar & Cafe 415 N 1st St (in the Heritage Landing Bldg) 612/333–4305 *5pm-11pm, till midnight Fri-Sat*

Trattoria da Vinci [E,WC] 400 Sibley St, St Paul 651/222–4050 *11am-9pm, 5pm-10pm Sat, clsd Sun-Mon*

■ ENTERTAINMENT & RECREATION

Calhoun 32nd Beach 3300 E Calhoun Pkwy (33rd & Calhoun Blvd), Minneapolis 612/230–6400

Twin Lake Beach [N] in Wirth Park (33rd & Calhoun Blvd), Minneapolis *aka Hidden Lake, hard to find, inquire locally*

■ RETAIL SHOPS

The Rainbow Road [WC] 109 W Grant St (at LaSalle), Minneapolis 612/872–8448 *10am-10pm, LGBT*

■ PUBLICATIONS

Lavender Magazine 612/436-4660, 877/515–9969 *LGBT newsmagazine for IA, MN, ND, SD, WI*

Scene 612/886-3151 *LGBTQA Twin Cities publication*

■ MEN'S SERVICES

▶**MegaMates** 952/938–8700 *Call to hook up with HOT local men. FREE to listen & respond to ads. Use FREE code DAMRON. MegaMates.com.*

■ EROTICA

Cockpit 2321 Hennepin Ave S *11am-8pm, till 6pm Sat, noon-5pm Sun*

Fantasy Gifts 1437 University Ave, St Paul 651/256–7484 *noon-8pm, clsd Sun-Tue*

Lickety Split 251 3rd Ave S, Minneapolis 612/333-0599

SexWorld 241 2nd Ave N (at Washington), Minneapolis 612/672-0556 *24hrs*

The Smitten Kitten [TG,GO] 3010 Lyndale Ave S, Minneapolis 612/721-6088, 888/751-0523

■**CRUISY AREAS**

"Bare Ass" Beach [AYOR] E bank of the Mississippi (btwn the Franklin Ave & I-94 bridges), Minneapolis *especially summer afternoons*

Loring Park [AYOR] 15th St (near 35 W & I-94 exchange), Minneapolis

Moorhead

see also Fargo, North Dakota

■**INFO LINES & SERVICES**

Pride Collective & Community Ctr 810 4th Ave S #220 218/287-8034 *6pm-7:30pm Tue & 1pm-3pm Sat*

■**CAFES**

Atomic Coffee [E,GO] 16 4th St S (at Main) 218/299-6161 *6:30am-9pm, from 8am Sun, also gallery*

Owatonna

■**EROTICA**

The Lion's Den Adult Superstore 1178 W Frontage Rd (exit 42B, off I-35) 507/214-3900 *24hrs*

MISSISSIPPI

Biloxi

■**BARS**

Club Veaux [M,D,F] 834 Howard Ave 228/207-3271

Just Us Lounge [MW,NH,D,E,K,DS,S] 906 Division St (at Cailavet) 228/374-1007 *24hrs*

■**CRUISY AREAS**

Hiller Park [AYOR] off Pass Rd

Gulfport

■**BARS**

Knuckle Heads [GF,NH,D,K] 1105 Broad Ave (at Railroad) 228/864-0463

The Other Bar [MW,D,DS,WC] 2218 25th Ave 228/284-1674 *4pm-close*

Jackson

■**INFO LINES & SERVICES**

Lambda AA 4866 N State St (at Unitarian Church) 601/856-5337 *6:30pm Mon*

■**BARS**

Bottoms Up [MW,D] 3911 Northview Dr 601/981-2188 *9pm Fri-Sat only*

Jack's Construction Site (JC's) [MW,NH,BYOB,WI] 425 N Mart Plaza 601/362-3108 *5pm-2am, from 7pm Th-Sat, clsd Mon*

■**CRUISY AREAS**

Battlefield Park [AYOR] Terry Rd (at Hwy 80) *afternoons*

Natchez

■**ACCOMMODATIONS**

Historic Oak Hill Inn B&B [NS,WI,GO] 409 S Rankin St (at Orleans St) 601/446-2500, 601/446-8641 *antebellum mansion near the Mississippi*

Mark Twain Guesthouse [GF] 25 Silver St 601/446-8023 *above Under the Hill Saloon*

■**BARS**

Under the Hill Saloon [GF,NH,E,WI] 25 Silver St 601/446-8023 *10am-close*

Oxford

■**CRUISY AREAS**

Pat Lamar Park [AYOR]

Tupelo

■**CRUISY AREAS**

Chickasaw Village & Old Town Site Scenic Overlooks [AYOR] Natchez Trace Pkwy *closes at sunset*

Confederate Grave Site [AYOR] Hwy 78-Natchez Trace Pkwy interchange (5 miles N)

Vicksburg

■**CRUISY AREAS**

Rest Stop I-20 E (2nd rest stop)

MISSOURI

Ava

■ACCOMMODATIONS

Cactus Canyon Campground
[MO,N,GO] 16 miles E of Ava on Hwy 14
(N 1 mile on County 223)
417/683-9199

Boonville

■MEN'S CLUBS

Megaplex Health Club & Spa [MO,V]
11674 Old Hwy 40 (off I-70 exit 98)
660/882-0008

■EROTICA

Passions Video 17701 Old Five Dr (off
I-70 exit 103) **660/882-9426**

Branson

see also Springfield & Eureka
Springs, Arkansas

■ACCOMMODATIONS

Branson Stagecoach RV Park
[GF,SW,WI] 5751 State Hwy 165
417/335-8185, 800/446-7110 *pull-
thru & back-in RV sites, cabins*

■CRUISY AREAS

Table Rock Lake Dam [AYOR] Fish
Hatchery area

Bridgeton

■EROTICA

Spanky's Video 3419 N Lindbergh Blvd
(at Morrow Dr) **314/209-7779**

Cape Girardeau

■ACCOMMODATIONS

Rose Bed Inn [GS,F,NS,WI,WC,GO] 611 S
Sprigg St **573/332-7673,
866/767-3233** *full brkfst, hot tub,
gourmet dining*

■NIGHTCLUBS

Independence Place [MW,D,TG,DS] 5 S
Henderson St (at Independence, at
Holiday Happenings) **573/334-2939**
*8:30pm-1:30am, from 7pm Fri-Sat, clsd
Sun*

■CRUISY AREAS
Capaha Park [AYOR]

Clinton

■CRUISY AREAS

Sparrowfoot Park [AYOR] 4 miles S off
Hwy 13 Lithuania *swimming & boat
launch area at Truman Lake*

Columbia

■BARS

The Arch & Column Pub
[M,NH,K,WC,GO] 1301 Business Loop 70
E (at College) **573/441-8088** *5:30pm-
1:30am, clsd Sun*

SoCo Club [MW,D,F,K,DS,V,WC] 119 S
7th St **573/499-9483** *3:30pm-
1:30am, till midnight Sun, clsd Mon*

■CAFES

Ernie's Cafe 1005 E Walnut St (at
10th) **573/874-7804** *6:30am-3pm*

Uprise Baker/ RagTag Cinema [F,BW]
10 Hitt St (Broadway) **573/443-4359,
573/441-8504** *5pm-close, from 2pm
wknds, independent & alternative
cinema, also theater, music & dance*

■RESTAURANTS

Main Squeeze [WI,WC] 28 S 9th St (at
Cherry St) **573/817-5616** *10am-8pm,
till 5pm Sun, local organic ingredients,
vegetarian*

■BOOKSTORES

The Peace Nook 804 C East Broadway
(btwn 8th & 9th) **573/875-0539**
*10am-9pm, noon-6pm Sun, LGBT
section, books, pride products*

■EROTICA

Bocomo Bay [★] 1122-A Wilkes Blvd
573/443-0873 *smoke shop too*

**Olde Un Theatre/ Midwest Adult
Book Store** 101 E Walnut St (at 1st)
573/442-6622 *7am-midnight*

Venus [GO] 1010 Old Hwy 63 N
573/442-4319 *24hrs Tue-Sat, till 1pm
Sun, from 9am-1am Mon*

■CRUISY AREAS

Cosmopolitan Park [AYOR] W side of
town (off Business Loop 70)

Hannibal

■ACCOMMODATIONS

Garden House B&B [GF,WI,NS,GO] 301 N 5th St (at Bird) 573/221-7800, 866/423-7800

Rockcliffe Mansion [GF,NS,WI,GO] 1000 Bird St (at 10th St) 573/221-4140, 877/423-4140

■RESTAURANTS

LaBinnah Bistro [BW,GO] 207 N 5th St (at Center) 573/221-7800 *dinner only, in a Victorian home*

Joplin

■INFO LINES & SERVICES

Gay Lesbian Family & Corporate Center 417/434-1149

Kansas City

see also Kansas City & Overland Park, Kansas

■INFO LINES & SERVICES

Lesbian & Gay Community Center of Greater Kansas City 4008 Oak St #10 816/931-4420 *call for events*

Live & Let Live AA 3901 Main St #211 (at 39th) 816/531-9668 *6pm daily, noon Sun*

■ACCOMMODATIONS

Hotel Phillips [GF,WI] 816/221-7000, 800/433-1426 *art deco landmark in downtown KC*

Ken's Place [MW,SW,WI,GO] 18 W 38th St (at Baltimore) 816/753-0533 *some shared baths, near gay bars*

Q Hotel & Spa [★GF,WI,WC] 560 Westport Rd (at Mill St) 816/931-0001, 800/942-4233

The Raphael [GF,F,WI] 325 Ward Pkwy (at Wornall Rd) 816/756-3800, 800/821-5343

Su Casa B&B [GF,SW,NS,WI] 9004 E 92nd St (off James A Reed Rd) 816/965-5647, 816/916-3444 (cell) *Southwest-style home*

■BARS

Buddies [M,NH] 3715 Main St (at 37th) 816/561-2600 *6am-3am, clsd Sun*

Hamburger Mary's KC [MW,K,F,E] 101 Southwest Blvd (at Baltimore Ave) 816/842-1919 *11am-1:30am, juicy burgers w/ a side of camp*

Missie B's/ Bootleggers [MW,NH,D,L,TG,K,DS,S] 805 W 39th St (at SW Trafficway) 816/561-0625 *noon-3am*

Sidekicks [MW,D,CW,DS,WC] 3707 Main St (at 37th) 816/931-1430 *2pm-3am, from 4pm Sun, clsd Mon*

Sidestreet Bar [M,NH,GO] 413 E 33rd St (at Gillham Rd) 816/531-1775 *10am-1:30am, clsd Sun*

Social [MW,D,F,K,WC,GO] 1118 McGee 816/472-4900 *3pm-3am, from 5pm Sat, clsd Sun-Mon*

The View [M,NH,GO] 204 Orchard St (at Tenny Ave), KS 913/281-0833 *4pm-2am, from noon Sun, clsd Mon*

■CAFES

Broadway Cafe [F,NS] 4106 Broadway (at Westport) 816/531-2432 *7am-9pm; also 412 Washington*

■RESTAURANTS

Beer Kitchen [E] 435 Westport Rd (at Pennsylvania) 816/389-4180 *11am-3am, from 10am wknds, gastro pub, live music*

Bistro 303 [★WC,GO] 303 Westport Rd 816/753-2303 *open 3pm, from 11am Sat-Sun, patio*

Blue Bird Bistro [WC] 1700 Summit St (at W 17th St) 816/221-7559 *7am-10pm, 10am-2pm Sun, organic fare*

Cafe Trio/ Starlet Lounge [P,GO] 4558 Main St 816/756-3227 *5pm-11pm, clsd Sun, live jazz*

Chubby's [WC] 3756 Broadway St (at 38th) 816/931-2482 *open 24hrs, popular late nights, diner fare*

Classic Cup Cafe [WC] 301 W 47th St (at Central) 816/753-1840 *brkfst, lunch, dinner, Sun brunch*

Grand Street Cafe [NS,WC] 4740 Grand St (at 47th St) 816/561-8000 *lunch & dinner, Sun brunch, patio seating*

Le Fou Frog 400 E 5th St (at Oak St) 816/474-6060 *dinner only, French bistro*

McCoy's Public House 4057 Pennsylvania Ave **816/960-0866** *11am-3am, till midnight Sun, huge patio*

The Mixx [WC] 4855 Main St (at W 48th) **816/756-2300** *lunch & dinner, fast & healthy, huge selection of salads*

Tannin Wine Bar **816/842-2660** *11:30am-1:30am, from 4pm wknds, wine & cheese flights, patio seating*

YJ's Snack Bar [WC] 128 W 18th St (at W Baltimore Ave) **816/472-5533** *8am-10pm, 24hrs Th-Sat*

■ENTERTAINMENT & RECREATION

First Fridays Art Walk Crossroads District (Baltimore & 20th) **816/994-9325** *5pm-10pm 1st Fri, art gallery walk, also live music & vendors*

Nelson-Atkins Museum 4525 Oak St **816/751-1278** *American Indian galleries*

■MEN'S SERVICES

➤**MegaMates** 816/326-9926 *Call to hook up with HOT local men. FREE to listen & respond to ads. Use FREE code DAMRON. MegaMates.com.*

■EROTICA

Erotic City 8401 E Truman Rd (off I-435, at Alice Ave) **816/252-3370**

Hollywood at Home 9063 Metcalf Ave (at 91st), Overland Park, KS **913/649-9666** *10am-11pm*

Video Mania [GO] 208 Westport Rd **816/561-6397**

Moberly

■CRUISY AREAS
Rothwell Park [AYOR]

Osage Beach

■ACCOMMODATIONS
Utopian Inn [MW,NS,GO] 1962 Alcorn Hollow Rd, Roach **573/347-3605** *3 bdrm rental on a lake*

Overland

■EROTICA
Patricia's 10210 Page Ave (E of Ashby) **314/423-8422**

Springfield

■INFO LINES & SERVICES
AA Gay/ Lesbian [NS] 518 E Commercial St **417/823-7125 (AA #)** *6pm Sat*

Gay & Lesbian Community Center of the Ozarks [WC] 518 E Commercial St **417/869-3978** *many groups, newsletter*

■BARS
Martha's Vineyard [MW,NH,D,DS,18+,WC,$] 219 W Olive St (at S Patton) **417/864-4572** *5pm-1:30am, from 2pm Sun, clsd Mon patio*

Mud Lounge [GF,F] 321 E Walnut **417/865-6964** *4pm-1:30am, clsd Sun*

■CAFES
Mudhouse [F] 323 South Ave **417/832-1720** *7am-midnight, 9am-8pm Sun*

■EROTICA
Patricia's 1918 S Glenstone (at E Cherokee) **417/881-8444**

■CRUISY AREAS
Lake Springfield Park [AYOR] *NW side, north of power plant, days*

Phelps Grove Park [AYOR]

St Joseph

■CRUISY AREAS
Riverfront Park [AYOR] *downtown*

St Louis

■ACCOMMODATIONS
➤**A St Louis Guesthouse** [M,N,NS,WI,GO] 1032 Allen Ave (at Menard) **314/773-1016** *in historic Soulard district, hot tub, cash discount*

Brewers House B&B [MW,NS,WI,GO] 1829 Lami St (at Lemp) **314/771-1542, 888/767-4665** *1860s home, jacuzzi*

The Cheshire [GS,SW,WI] 6300 Clayton Rd **314/647-7300**

Dwell 912 B&B [GF,NS,WI,GO] 912 Hickory St (at S 9th St) **314/599-3100**

Grand Center Inn [GS,WI,NS,GO] 3716 Grandel Sq (at N Grand Blvd) **314/533-0771**

■Bars

Absolutli Goosed Martini Bar, Etc
[MW,NH,WC,GO] 3196 S Grand (at Wyoming) 314/771-9300 *4pm-midnight, till 1am Fri-Sat, clsd Sun, also desserts, appetizers, patio*

Bad Dog Bar & Grill [M,NH,B,L,F,GO]
3960 Chouteau Ave (at S Vandeventer Ave) 314/652-0011 *4pm-1:30am, 2pm-midnight Sun*

Cicero's [GS,E,F] 6691 Delmar Blvd (at Kingsland Ave), University City 314/862-0009 *11am-12:30am, till 11pm Sun, Italian restaurant*

Clementine's [★M,NH,L,F,WC] 2001 Menard St (at Allen) 314/664-7869 *10am-midnight, from 11am Sun, patio*

Club Escapades [MW,D,DS,F,K,S,WI] 133 W Main St (at 2nd), Belleville, IL 618/222-9597 *6pm-2am, clsd Sun-Mon*

Erney's 32 Degree [M,D] 4200 Manchester Ave (at Boyle) 314/652-7195 *8pm-3am, clsd Mon*

Grey Fox Pub [MW,NH,TG,DS,S] 3503 S Spring (at Potomac) 314/772-2150 *2pm-1:30am, noon-midnight Sun, patio*

Hummel's Pub [MW,NH,F,K,GO] 7101 S Broadway (at Blow St) 314/353-5080 *11am-1am, from 2pm Mon*

JJ's Clubhouse & Bar [M,NH,B,L,WC] 3858 Market St (at Vandeventer) 314/535-4100 *3pm-3am*

Just John [MW,NH,D,K,V] 4112 Manchester Ave 314/371-1333 *3pm-3am, from noon-1am Sun*

Keypers Piano Bar [MW,NH,P,F] 2280 S Jefferson (at Shenandoah) 314/664-6496 *1pm-1:30am, 2pm-midnight Sun, patio*

Korners Bar [MW,D,DS] 7109 S Broadway (at Blow St) 314/352-3088 *4pm-1:30am, clsd Sun-Mon*

Meyer's Grove [MW,DS] 4510 Manchester Ave 314/932-7003 *4pm-1:30pm, clsd Sun*

Missouri • *USA*

Premium Lounge [GS,F] 4199 Manchester Rd (at Boyle) 314/652-8585 *opens 4pm, clsd Sun*

Rehab Lounge [GS,NH,F] 4052 Chouteau Ave (at Boyle) 314/652-3700 *11am-1:30am, also restaurant*

Rosie's Place [GS,NH] 4573 Laclede Ave 314/361-6423 *11am-1:30am*

Soulard Bastille [M,NH] 1027 Russell Blvd (at Menard) 314/664-4408 *11am-1:30am*

Sub Zero Vodka Bar [GS,F] 308 N Euclid Ave 314/367-1200 *11:30am-1:30am, sushi and burgers*

■NIGHTCLUBS

Atomic Cowboy [GS,F,E,WI] 4140 Manchester Ave (btwn Kentucky & Talmadge) 314/775-0775 *11am-3am, from 5pm Sat-Sun, also Fresh-Mex Mayan grill*

Attitudes [MW,D,DS,K] 4100 Manchester Ave (at S Sarah) 314/534-0044 *7pm-3am, clsd Mon*

Bubby & Sissy's [MW,D,E,F,K,DS,V,WC] 602 Belle St (at 6th St), Alton, IL 618/465-4773 *3pm-2am, till 3am Fri-Sat*

Magnolia's [MW,D,MR-AF] 5 S Vandeventer Ave (at Laclede) 314/652-6500 *hip hop/ R&B club*

■CAFES

Coffee Cartel [★F,WI,WC] 2 Maryland Plaza (at Euclid) 314/454-0000 *24hrs*

MoKaBe's [★E,WC] 3606 Arsenal (at S Grand) 314/865-2009 *8am-midnight, from 9am Sun*

Soulard Coffee Garden Cafe [F,WI,WC] 910 Geyer Ave (btwn 9th & 10th) 314/241-1464 *6:30am-4pm, from 8am wknds*

■RESTAURANTS

Billie's Diner [WC] 1802 S Broadway 314/621-0848 *5am-2:30pm, midnight-1:30pm wknds*

Cafe Osage 4605 Olive St 314/454-6868 *7am-2pm, till 5pm Th-Sat, from 9am Sun*

City Diner [★WC] 3139 S Grand Blvd 314/772-6100 *7am-11pm, 24hrs Fri-Sat, till 10pm Sun*

Dressel's [E,WC] 419 N Euclid (at McPherson) 314/361-1060 *11am-1am, till midnight Sun, great Welsh pub food, full bar*

Eleven Eleven Mississippi 1111 Mississippi 314/241-9999 *lunch Mon-Fri, dinner nightly, clsd Sun, wine country bistro*

Hamburger Mary's [E,K] 3037 Olive St 314/533-6279 *11am-midnight, till 1am Th-Sat*

Joanie's Pizza 2101 Menard St 314/865-1994 *11am-11pm, till midnight wknds*

Majestic Cafe [WC] 4900 Laclede Ave (at Euclid) 314/361-2011 *6am-10pm, bar till 1:30am, Greek-American diner fare*

Mango 1101 Lucas Ave 314/621-9993 *11am-10pm, bar till 1:30am Fri-Sat, 4pm-9pm Sun, Latin American/ Peruvian*

Meskerem 3210 S Grand Blvd 314/772-4442 *lunch & dinner, Ethiopian, plenty veggie*

Mojo Tapas 3117 S Grand Blvd (at Arsenal St) 314/865-0500 *4pm-11pm, full bar till 1:30am*

Molly's in Soulard [E,K] 816 Geyer Ave 314/241-6200 *11am-9pm, full bar till 1:30am, old-world New Orleans charm, huge patio*

Pappy's Smokehouse 3106 Olive St 314/535-4340 *11am-8pm, till 4pm Sun, excellent BBQ*

Rue 13 [D,C] 1311 Washington 314/588-7070 *5pm-3am, clsd Sun-Mon, sushi, full bar*

Ted Drewes Frozen Custard [★WC] 6726 Chippewa (at Jameson) 314/481-2652, 314/481-2124 *11am-10pm, seasonal, a St Louis landmark; also 4224 S Grand Blvd, 314/352-7376*

Three Monkey's 153 Morgan Ford Rd 314/772-9800 *11am-1:30am*

Tony's [R,WC] 410 Market St (at Broadway) 314/231-7007 *dinner only, clsd Sun-Mon, Italian fine dining*

Van Goghz [WI,WC] 3200 Shenandoah (at Compton) **314/865-3345** *11am-11pm, till 1:30am Fri-Sat, 9:30am-3pm Sun, also martini bar*

Vin de Set [WC] 2017 Chouteau Ave (at S 21st St) **314/241-8989** *lunch & dinner, dinner only wknds, clsd Mon, rooftop bar & bistro*

The Wild Flower Restaurant & Bar [WC] 4590 Laclede Ave (at Euclid) **314/367-9888** *lunch & dinner, bar till 1:30am, clsd Tue, Sun brunch*

■**BOOKSTORES**

Left Bank Books [★] 399 N Euclid Ave (at McPherson) **314/367-6731** *10am-10pm, 11am-6pm Sun, feminist & LGBT titles; also at 321 N 10th St*

Not Just A Bookstore [WI] 4507 Manchester Ave **314/531-5900** *10am-6pm, also herbal loose teas and all natural soaps and oils*

■**RETAIL SHOPS**

CheapTRX [WC] 3211 S Grand Blvd (at Wyoming St) **314/664-4011** *alternative shopping, body piercing, tattoos*

■**PUBLICATIONS**

Vital Voice **314/256-1196** *bi-weekly news & features publication*

■**MEN'S CLUBS**

Club St Louis [PC,SW,18+] 2625 Samuel Shepard Dr (at Jefferson) **314/533-3666** *24hrs*

■**MEN'S SERVICES**

➤**MegaMates** **314/209-0300** *Call to hook up with HOT local men. FREE to listen & respond to ads. Use FREE code DAMRON. MegaMates.com.*

■**EROTICA**

Patricia's 3552 Gravois Ave (at Grand) **314/664-4040**

■**CRUISY AREAS**

Creve Coeur Park [AYOR] Dorset Rd W (off Hwy 2-70)

Steele

■**EROTICA**

The Lion's Den Adult Superstore 36 E Outer Rd (exit 8, off I-55) **573/695-7294**

MONTANA

Billings

■**BARS**

The Loft [MW,D,E,K,WC] 1123 1st Ave N (at 12th) **406/259-9074** *10am-2am*

■**EROTICA**

Big Sky Books 1203 1st Ave N (at 12th St) **406/259-0051**

The Victorian [P] 2019 Minnesota Ave (at 21st) **406/245-4293** *noon-midnight, clsd Sun-Mon, also HIV & Hep B/C testing*

Bozeman

■**ACCOMMODATIONS**

Lehrkind Mansion Inn [GS,NS,WI,GO] 719 N Wallace Ave **406/585-6932**

■**CAFES**

The Leaf & Bean [E,WC] 35 W Main St **406/587-1580** *6am-9pm, till 10pm Fri-Sat; also 1500 N 19th Ave*

The Nova Cafe 312 E Main St (at Rouse Ave) **406/587-3973** *7am-2pm*

■**EROTICA**

Erotique 12 N Willson Ave (at Main) **406/586-7825**

Butte

■**RESTAURANTS**

Four Seasons 3030 Elm St **406/723-3888** *11am-9:30pm, from noon wknds*

Matt's Place 2339 Placer St (btwn Montana & Rowe) **406/782-8049** *11:30am-7pm, clsd Sun-Mon, classic soda-fountain diner*

Pork Chop John's 2400 Harrison Ave **406/782-1783** *10:30am-10:30pm,clsd Sun; also 8 W Mercury, 406/782-0812*

Uptown Cafe [WC] 47 E Broadway **406/723-4735** *lunch weekdays & dinner nightly, bistro, full bar*

Kalispell

■**INFO LINES & SERVICES**

Flathead Valley Alliance **406/758-6707** *LGBT referral service*

Montana • *USA*

Missoula

■INFO LINES & SERVICES

KISMIF Gay/ Lesbian AA 405 University Ave (at church) **406/543-0011** *7pm Mon*

Western Montana Gay/ Lesbian Community Center 127 N Higgins Ave #202 **406/543-2224** *LGBT resource ctr*

■BARS

The Oxford [★GF] 337 N Higgins Ave (at Pine) **406/549-0117** *8am-2am, 24hr cafe & casino*

■CAFES

The Catalyst 111 N Higgins **406/542-1337** *7am-3pm*

■RESTAURANTS

Montana Club [WC] 2620 Brooks **406/543-3200** *6am-10pm, till 11pm Fri-Sat, casino open till 2am*

■BOOKSTORES

Fact & Fiction [WC] 220 N Higgins **406/721-2881** *9am-6pm, 10am-5pm Sat, noon-4pm Sun*

■RETAIL SHOPS

Jeannette Rankin Peace Center 519 S Higgins Ave **406/543-3955** *10am-6pm, noon-4pm Sun, fair trade gift store; also peace resource center*

■PUBLICATIONS

Out Words 127 N Higgins Ave #202 **406/543-2224** *MT's LGBT publication*

■CRUISY AREAS

McCormick Park [AYOR] W side of Orange St Bridge

Swan Valley

■ACCOMMODATIONS

Holland Lake Lodge [GF,WI,WC,GO] 1947 Holland Lake Rd (at Hwy 83) **406/754-2282, 877/925-6343** *resort w/ lakefront cabins, restaurant & bar*

NEBRASKA

Columbus

■CRUISY AREAS

Pawnee Park [AYOR]

Lincoln

■INFO LINES & SERVICES

Rainbow Group Gay/ Lesbian AA 2325 S 24 St (at Sewell, at St Matthew's) **402/438-5214** *7:30pm Mon & Fri*

■BARS

Panic [MW,E,WI,WC,GO] 200 S 18th St (at N St) **402/435-8764** *4pm-1am, from 1pm wknds, patio*

■NIGHTCLUBS

The Q [MW,D,E,DS,S] 226 S 9th St (btwn M & N Sts) **402/475-2269** *8pm-1am, clsd Mon*

■CRUISY AREAS

15th St [AYOR] from A St to State Capitol

Pioneers & Van Dorn Parks [AYOR]

Norfolk

■CRUISY AREAS

Tahazooka Park [AYOR]

Omaha

■INFO LINES & SERVICES

AA Gay/ Lesbian 851 N 74th St (at Presbyterian Church) **402/556-1880** *8:15pm Fri*

Rainbow Outreach Center 1719 Leavenworth St **402/341-0330** *call for hrs*

■ACCOMMODATIONS

Castle Unicorn [GS,NS,WI,GO] 57034 Deacon Rd (at Hwy 34 & I-29), Pacific Jct, IA **712/527-5930** *medieval-style B&B*

The Cornerstone Mansion Inn [GF,NS,WI] 140 N 39th St (at Dodge) **402/558-7600, 888/883-7745**

■BARS

The Omaha Mining Company [M,D,S,18+,WC] 1715 Leavenworth St (btwn 17th & 18th) **402/449-8703** *2pm-1am, till 4am Fri-Sat, very cruisy*

■NIGHTCLUBS

Flixx Lounge [M,D,C,DS] 1019 S 10th St **402/408-1020** *5pm-1am*

The Max [★M,D,DS,S,V,WC,$] 1417 Jackson St (at 15th St) 402/346-4110 *4pm-1am, till 2am Th-Sat, patio*

■RESTAURANTS

The Boiler Room [WC] 1110 Jones St 402/916-9274 *dinner only, clsd Sun, full bar*

California Tacos & More [BW,WC] 3235 California St 402/342-0212 *11am-9pm, clsd Sun*

The Flatiron Cafe [WC] 1722 St Marys Ave 402/345-7477 *dinner only, clsd Sun, full bar*

M's Pub [WC] 422 S 11th St 402/342-2550 *11am-1am, from 5pm Sun, full bar*

McFoster's Natural Kind Cafe [WC] 302 N 38th St 402/345-7477 *lunch & dinner, vegetarian, full bar*

■MEN'S SERVICES

►**MegaMates** 402/341-4000 *Call to hook up with HOT local men. FREE to listen & respond to ads. Use FREE code DAMRON. MegaMates.com.*

■CRUISY AREAS

Glen Cunningham Lake [AYOR] along W side

Scottsbluff

■CRUISY AREAS

Riverside Zoo Park [AYOR]

NEVADA

Carson City

■ACCOMMODATIONS

West Walker Motel [GF,WI] 106833 Hwy 395, Walker, CA 530/495-2263 *in Toiyabe Nat'l Forest near West Walker River*

■MEN'S SERVICES

►**MegaMates** 775/888-9995 *Call to hook up with HOT local men. FREE to listen & respond to ads. Use FREE code DAMRON. MegaMates.com.*

Elko

■CRUISY AREAS

Elko City Park [AYOR]

Lake Tahoe

see also Lake Tahoe, California

Las Vegas

■INFO LINES & SERVICES

Alcoholics Together 900 E Karen, 2nd flr #A-202 (at Sahara, in Commercial Center) 702/598-1888 *12:15pm & 8pm daily, call for other mtgs*

The Gay/ Lesbian Community Center of Southern Nevada 953 E Sahara Ave #B-31 702/733-9800 *11am-7pm, clsd wknds*

■ACCOMMODATIONS

►**Blue Moon Resort** [MO,SW,N, WI,NS,WC,GO] 2651 Westwood Dr 702/784-4500, 866/798-9194 *private resort, sundeck, steam room & jacuzzi grotto*

El Cortez Cabana [GF] 651 E Ogden Ave (at 7th St) 702/385-5200, 800/634-6703 *recently renovated*

Lucky You B&B [M,SW,N,GO] 702/384-1129 *hot tub, sauna, shared baths*

Paris, Las Vegas Resort & Casino [GF] 3655 Las Vegas Blvd S 702/946-7000, 800/630-7933

Vdara Hotel & Spa [GF,SW,NS] 2600 W Harmon Ave 702/590-2767, 866/745-7767

■BARS

Badlands Saloon [M,NH,D,CW,WC,GO] 953 E Sahara #22 (in Commercial Center) 702/792-9262 *24hrs*

Charlie's Las Vegas [★M,D,DS,CW,WC] 5012 S Arville St (at Tropicana) 702/876-1844 *24hrs, dance lessons 7pm-9pm Mon, Th-Sat*

Club Metro [M,D] 1000 E Sahara Ave 702/629-2368 *4pm-5am*

Escape Lounge [MW,NH,V,WC] 4213 W Sahara Ave 702/364-1167 *24hrs*

Flex [MW,D,DS,S,WC] 4347 W Charleston (at Arville) 702/385-3539, 702/878-3355 *24hrs*

Freezone [MW,NH,D,TG,F,K,DS,S,YC,GO] 610 E Naples 702/794-2300 *24hrs, also restaurant*

Nevada • *USA*

Border Grill 3950 Las Vegas Blvd S (at the Mandalay Bay Resort & Casino) 702/632-7403 *11:30am-close, Mexican, full bar, patio*

Chicago Joe's 820 S 4th St (at Gass Ave) 702/382-5637 *11am-10pm, from 5pm Sat, clsd Sun-Mon, old-school Italian, in downtown arts district*

Cupcakery 7175 W Lake Mead 702/835-0060

The Egg & I [★WC] 4533 W Sahara Ave (near Arville) 702/364-9686 *6am-3pm*

Firefly [WC] 3900 Paradise Rd #A 702/369-3971 *11am-2am, tapas, also bar*

Go Raw 2381 E Windmill Ln 702/450-9007 *8am-8pm, till 5pm Sun, organic vegan, also juice bar; also at 2910 Lake East Dr, 702/254-5382*

Grand Lux Cafe 3355 Las Vegas Blvd S (at the Venetian) 702/414-3888 *open 24hrs, generous portions*

Lindo Michoacan [★] 2655 E Desert Inn Rd (near Eastern) 702/735-6828 *11am-11pm, till midnight wknds, Mexican*

Lotus of Siam [★WC] 953 E Sahara Ave #A-5 (in Commercial Center) 702/735-3033 *lunch Mon-Fri, dinner nightly, Thai*

Mon Ami Gabi [WC] 3655 Las Vegas Blvd S (at Paris Las Vegas) 702/944-4224 *7am-11pm, outdoor seating*

Paymon's Mediterranean Cafe & Lounge [WC] 4147 S Maryland Pkwy (at E Flamingo Rd) 702/731-6030 *11am-1am, plenty veggie, also at 8380 W Sahara Ave, 702/731-6030*

Society Cafe Encore 3121 Las Vegas Blvd S (at Encore) 702/248-3463 *7am-11pm, till 1am wknds, upscale*

■ ENTERTAINMENT & RECREATION

Cupid's Wedding Chapel [GS] 827 Las Vegas Blvd S (1 block N of Charleston) 702/598-4444, 800/543-2933 *commitment ceremonies*

Erotic Heritage Museum 3275 Industrial Rd 702/369-6442 *6pm-10pm Wed-Th, 3pm-midnight Fri, from noon wknds, clsd Mon-Tue*

Frank Marino's Divas Las Vegas [DS] 3535 Las Vegas Blvd S (at the Imperial Palace) 702/794-3261, 888/777-7664 *show at 7:30pm, Frank Marino & friends impersonate the divas, from Joan Rivers to Tina Turner*

Onyx Theatre 953 E Sahara Ave # 16A (at Maryland Pkwy) 702/732-7225 *alternative films & performances*

Thanks Babs, the Day Tripper [GO] 702/370-6961

Viva Las Vegas Wedding Chapel [GO] 1205 Las Vegas Blvd 800/574-4450

■BOOKSTORES

Get Booked 4640 S Paradise Rd #15 (at Naples) 702/737-7780 *10am-midnight, till 2am Fri-Sat, LGBT*

■RETAIL SHOPS

Glamour Boutique II 714 E Sahara Ave #104 (at S 6th St) 702/697-1800, 866/692-1800 *clsd Sun, large-size dresses, wigs, etc*

The Rack [WC] 953 E Sahara Ave, Ste 101, Bldg 16 (in Commercial Center) 702/732-7225 *leather, fetish*

■PUBLICATIONS

Las Vegas Night Beat 702/369-8441

QVegas 702/650-0636 *monthly LGBT news & entertainment magazine*

■GYMS & HEALTH CLUBS

The Las Vegas Athletic Club [GF] 2655 S Maryland Pkwy 702/734-5822 *day passes*

■MEN'S CLUBS

Entourage Vegas [MO,SW] 953 E Sahara Ave #A19 (near Paradise & Maryland, at Commercial Center entrance) 702/650-9191 *24hrs*

Hawks Gym [MO,PC,AYOR,GO,$] 953 E Sahara (at SE corner of Commercial Center) 702/731-4295 *24hrs wknds*

Power Exchange [TG,18+,$] 3610 S Highland Dr 702/255-4739 *play space open to hetero, gay, bi, trans, men & women; cover charge for men*

■MEN'S SERVICES

➤**MegaMates** 702/932-7373 *Call to hook up with HOT local men. FREE to listen & respond to ads. Use FREE code DAMRON. MegaMates.com.*

■EROTICA

Adult World/ Mini Theaters [V] 3781 Meade Ave (at Valley View) 702/579-9735 *24hrs*

Bare Essentials Fantasy Fashions [GO] 4029 W Sahara Ave (near Valley View Blvd) 702/247-4711 *exotic/ intimate apparel, toys*

Desert Adult Books 4350 N Las Vegas Blvd (at Craig Rd) 702/643-7982 *24hrs*

Fantasy World Arcade/ Theaters 6760 Boulder Hwy (btwn Sunset & Russell) 702/433-6311 *24hrs*

Industrial Road Adult Books 3427 Industrial Rd (at Spring Mtn) 702/734-7667 *24hrs*

Rancho Adult Entertainment Center 4820 N Rancho Dr (at Lone Mtn) 702/645-6104 *24hrs*

Tropicana Adult Superstore 3850 W Tropicana (at Valley View) 702/798-0144 *24hrs, cruisy theaters*

Wild J's 2923 S Industrial Rd (behind Circus Circus) 702/892-0699 *24hrs*

■CRUISY AREAS

Jaycee Park [AYOR] Eastern & St Louis (N of Sahara)

Sunset Park [AYOR]

Laughlin

see Bullhead City, Arizona

Reno

■ACCOMMODATIONS

Silver Legacy Resort & Casino [GF,F,SW] 407 N Virginia St 775/325-7401, 800/687-8733

■BARS

Cadillac Lounge [MW,NH] 1114 E 4th St (at Sutro) 775/324-7827 *noon-2am*

Carl's Pub [M,NH,D,L] 3310 S Virginia St (at Moana) 775/829-8886 *2pm-2am, till midnight Sun, patio, theme nights*

Chapel Tavern [GS,E] 1099 S Virginia St (at Vassar) **775/324-2244** *2pm-4am, from 10am wknds*

Five Star Saloon [GS,NH,D,TG,WI,WC] 132 West St (at 1st) **775/329-2878** *24hrs*

The Patio [MW,NH,E,K] 600 W 5th St (btwn Washington & Ralston) **775/323-6565** *11am-2am*

■**NIGHTCLUBS**

Tronix [★GS,D,MR-L, DS] 340 Kietzke Ln (btwn Glendale & Mill) **775/786-2121** *2pm-close, clsd Sun-Tue*

■**RESTAURANTS**

4th Street Bistro 3065 W 4th St **775/323-3200** *dinner nightly, clsd Sun-Mon, upscale, extensive wine list*

Brasserie Saint James 901 S Center St **775/348-8888** *11am-11pm, till 1am Fri-Sat, full bar & great roof deck*

The Daily Bagel 495 Morill Ave # 102 **775/786-1611** *6:30am-2pm, till 3pm Wed-Fri, 8am-2pm, Sat, clsd Sun*

Old Granite Street Eatery 243 S Sierra St **775/622-3222** *11am-11pm, from 10am wknds, full bar*

Pneumatic Diner 501 W 1st St (in Truckee River Apts, 2nd flr) **775/786-8888 x106** *11am-10pm, from 8am Sun, vegetarian*

■**ENTERTAINMENT & RECREATION**

Brüka Theatre 99 N Virginia St **775/323-3221** *alternative theater & performance space*

■**BOOKSTORES**

Sundance Books 1155 W 4th St #106 (at Keystone) **775/786-1188** *9am-9pm, 9am-5pm wknds, independent*

■**PUBLICATIONS**

Reno Gay Page 775/453-4058 *monthly, bar & resource listings, community events, arts & entertainment*

■**MEN'S CLUBS**

Steve's [PC] 1030 W 2nd St (at Keystone) **775/323-8770** *24hrs, spa*

■**MEN'S SERVICES**

➤**MegaMates 775/334-6666** *Call to hook up with HOT local men. FREE to listen & respond to ads. Use FREE code DAMRON. MegaMates.com.*

■**EROTICA**

Suzie's 195 Kietzke Ln (at E 2nd St) **775/786-8557** *24hrs*

■**CRUISY AREAS**

Crissie Caughlin Park [AYOR] W end of the park *days*

Winnemuca

■**BARS**

Cheers [GF,NH] 320 S Bridge St **775/623-2660** *9am-close*

■**CRUISY AREAS**

Button Point [AYOR] I-80, exit 187 (3 miles E of Winnemuca)

NEW HAMPSHIRE

Concord

■**CRUISY AREAS**

Rollings Park [AYOR] S end of town

Franklin

■**ACCOMMODATIONS**

Gile House Inn [M,SW,WI,GO] 40 Giile Rd **603/491-8584**

Keene

■**ACCOMMODATIONS**

The Lane Hotel [GS,F,NS,WI,WC] 30 Main St **603/357-7070, 888/300-5056**

Manchester

■**ACCOMMODATIONS**

Radisson Hotel Manchester [GF,F,SW,WI,WC] 700 Elm St **603/625-1000, 800/395-7046**

■**BARS**

The Breezeway [MW,NH,D,C,DS,GO] 14 Pearl St **603/621-9111** *4pm-1am, theme nights*

Club 313 [★MW,D,F,E,K,DS,NS,WI,WC] 93 S Maple St (at S Willow) **603/628-6813** *7pm-1am, clsd Sun-Mon & Wed*

Doogie's Bar & Grill [M,NH,F,D,WC,GO] 37 Manchester St **603/232-0732** *4pm-1am, patio*

Element Lounge [MW,D,F,K,DS] 1055 Elm St **603/627-2922** *3pm-1:30am, clsd Mon*

Nashua

■ACCOMMODATIONS

Radisson Hotel [GF,SW,WI,WC] 11 Tara Blvd **603/888-9970**

Newfound Lake

■ACCOMMODATIONS

The Inn on Newfound Lake [GS,SW,NS,WI,GO] 1030 Mayhew Tpke Rte 3-A, Bridgewater **603/744-9111, 800/745-7990** *private beach on cleanest lake in NH, also restaurant, full bar*

Portsmouth

■ACCOMMODATIONS

Ale House Inn [GF,WI,GO] 121 Bow St (at Market St) **603/431-7760**

■CAFES

Breaking New Grounds [WI] 14 Market Square **603/436-9555** *6:30am-11pm*

■RESTAURANTS

The Mombo [WC] 66 Marcy St (at State St) **603/433-2340** *dinner only, clsd Sun-Mon*

■EROTICA

Moonlight Reader 940 Rte 1 Bypass N **603/436-9622**

White Mtns

■ACCOMMODATIONS

Beal House [GF,WI] 2 W Main St, Littleton **603/444-2661** *also restaurant*

The Horse & Hound Inn [GF,F,NS,WI,GO] 205 Wells Rd, Franconia **603/823-5501, 800/450-5501** *also restaurant*

The Inn at Bowman [GS,SW,NS,WC,GO] 1174 Rte 2 (Presidential Hwy), Randolph **603/466-5006**

Inn at Crystal Lake [GS,NS,WI,GO] 2356 Eaton Rd (at Rte 16), Eaton **603/447-2120, 800/343-7336**

The Notchland Inn [GS,F,NS,GO] 2 Morey Rd, Hart's Location **603/374-6131, 800/866-6131**

Riverbend Inn B&B [GS,NS,WI,GO] 273 Chocorua Mtn Hwy (at Rte 113), Chocorua **603/323-7440, 800/628-6944** *full brkfst*

Wildcat Inn & Tavern [GF,E,NS] Rte 16A, Jackson Village **603/383-4245, 855/532-7727**

Wyatt House Country Inn [GS,WI,GO] 3046 White Mountain Hwy, N Conway **603/356-7977 , 800/527-7978**

■RESTAURANTS

Polly's Pancake Parlor 672 Rte Sugar Hill Rd (exit 38 off 93 N), Sugar Hill **603/823-5575** *7am-2pm, till 3pm wknds, clsd winters*

The Red Parka Steakhouse & Pub Rte 302, Glen **603/383-4344** *open from 3pm, also bar*

■ENTERTAINMENT & RECREATION

Reel North Fly Fishing [GO] **603/858-4103** *casting lessons, half & full day river trips*

■CRUISY AREAS

Scenic Rest Area [AYOR] on left of Rte 16 N, Chocorua

NEW JERSEY

Statewide

■PUBLICATIONS

Out in Jersey 743 Hamilton Ave, Trenton 08629 **609/213-9310** *bimonthly glossy magazine for all of New Jersey's LGBT community*

Asbury Park

■ACCOMMODATIONS

Empress Hotel [GF,SW,WI] 101 Asbury Ave **732/774-0100** *also Empress Lobby Lounge on wknds*

■**BARS**

Georgie's [MW,NH,F,K,DS] 812 5th Ave (at Main) 732/988-1220 *2pm-2am*

■**NIGHTCLUBS**

Paradise [MW,D,E,P,SW] 101 Asbury Ave (at Ocean Ave) 732/988-6663 *4pm-2am, from 2pm Sat, from noon Sun, 2 dance flrs, also piano bar & tiki/ pool bar in summer*

■**RESTAURANTS**

Bistro Olé [★BYOB, GO] 230 Main St 732/897-0048 *dinner nightly, clsd Mon-Tue, Spanish-Portuguese*

Moonstruck [E] 517 Lake Ave (at Grand) 732/988-0123 *dinner only, clsd Mon-Tue, also bar, live music wknds*

Atlantic City

■**ACCOMMODATIONS**

The Carisbrooke Inn [GF,NS,WI] 105 S Little Rock Ave, Ventnor 609/822-6392 *on a beach block*

Ocean House [MO,V,N,GO] 127 S Ocean Ave 609/345-8203

Tropicana Casino & Resort [GF,SW] 2831 Boardwalk (at Brighton) 609/340-4000, 800/345-8767

■**BARS**

Rainbow Room [MW,NH] 55 S Bellevue Ave 609/317-4593 *6pm-2am*

■**NIGHTCLUBS**

Pro Bar [MW,D,DS] 1133 Boardwalk (at Resorts Casino) 800/334-6378 *8pm-3am, clsd Mon-Wed*

■**RESTAURANTS**

Dock's Oyster House [WC] 2405 Atlantic Ave 609/345-0092 *5pm-10pm, till 11pm Fri-Sat*

White House Sub Shop 2301 Arctic Ave (at Mississippi) 609/345-1564 *10am-8pm, till 9pm Fri-Sat*

Belmar

■**CRUISY AREAS**

Belmar Beach [AYOR] *under fishing pier*

Boonton

■**NIGHTCLUBS**

Switch [MW,D,CW,F,S] 202 Myrtle Ave (off Washington) 973/263-4000 *3pm-2am*

Camden

■**ENTERTAINMENT & RECREATION**

The Walt Whitman House 30 Mickle Blvd (btwn S 3rd & S 4th Sts) 856/964-5383 *the last home of America's great & controversial poet*

Cape May

■**ACCOMMODATIONS**

Congress Hall [GF,SW,WI] 251 Beach Ave 609/884-8421, 888/944-1816

Cottage Beside the Point [NS,GO] 609/204-0549, 609/898-0658 *studio*

Highland House [GF,NS] 131 N Broadway (at York) 609/898-1198

The Virginia Hotel [GF,WI] 25 Jackson St (btwn Beach Dr & Carpenter's Ln) 609/884-5700, 800/732-4236 *also The Ebbitt Room restaurant*

■**BARS**

The King Edward Room [M] 301 Howard St (at The Chalfonte Hotel) 609/884-8409 *3pm-1am summer only*

■**CAFES**

Higher Grounds [E,WI] 479B W Perry St 609/884-1131 *8:30am-4:30pm, clsd Sun*

■**CRUISY AREAS**

Cape May Promenade [AYOR] Beach Ave (btwn Broadway & 2nd)

Higbee Beach [AYOR]

Cherry Hill

■**CRUISY AREAS**

Cooper River Park [AYOR] Cuthbert Blvd S (off Rte 70)

Cliffwood

■**CRUISY AREAS**

Cliffwood Beach [AYOR]

Hammonton

■NIGHTCLUBS

Club In Or Out [MW,D,DS,TG,E,K] 19 N Egg Harbor Rd (at Orchard Ave) **609/561-2525** *6pm-3am Fri-Sat, 5pm-1am Sun*

Highland Park

■INFO LINES & SERVICES

Pride Center of New Jersey 85 Raritan Ave (at S 1st Ave) **732/846-2232** *info line & meeting space for various groups*

Hoboken

■NIGHTCLUBS

Maxwell's [★GF,A,F] 1039 Washington St **201/653-1703** *live music venue*

Jamesburg

■RESTAURANTS

Fiddleheads [BYOB,GO] 27 E Railroad Ave **732/521-0878** *lunch & dinner, Sun brunch, clsd Mon-Tue, upscale bistro*

Jersey City

■INFO LINES & SERVICES

Hudson Pride Connections 32 Jones St **201/963-4779** *"serving the LGBT communities & all people living w/ HIV, since 1993"*

■ACCOMMODATIONS

Hyatt Regency Jersey City [GF,SW,NS,WC] 2 Exchange Pl (on the Hudson) **201/645-4712, 201/469-1234** *luxury waterfront hotel, short ride to NYC*

■BARS

Lamp Post [GS,F] 382 2nd St **201/222-1331** *11:30am-2am, till 3am Fri-Sat, live bands*

LITM [GS] 140 Newark Ave (at Grove) **201/536-5557** *5pm-1am, till 2am Fri-Sat, 11am-midnight Sun, also restaurant & gallery*

■RESTAURANTS

Baja 117 Montgomery St **201/915-0062** *lunch & dinner, Mexican, DJ wknds*

Linden

■BARS

Duval Bar & Lounge [MW,D,F,K] 9 Cedar Ave **908/290-3535** *6pm-2am, till 3am Th-Sat, clsd Sun-Mon*

Lodi

■RESTAURANTS

Penang Malaysian & Thai Cuisine [WC,GO] 334 N Main St (at Garibaldi Ave) **973/779-1128** *11am-11pm, full bar*

Morristown

■INFO LINES & SERVICES

GAAMC (Gay Activist Alliance in Morris County) 21 Normandy Hts Rd (at Columbia Rd, Unitarian Fellowship) **973/285-1595** *info line 7:30pm-9pm*

New Brunswick

■BARS

The Den [M,D,MR,DS,V,WC] 700 Hamilton St (at Douglas), Somerset **732/545-7354** *8pm-2am Wed-Sat only*

■RESTAURANTS

The Frog & the Peach [WC] 29 Dennis St (at Hiram Square) **732/846-3216** *lunch Mon-Fri, dinner nightly, full bar, upscale*

Sofie's Bistro 700 Hamilton St (at Douglas), Somerset **732/545-7778** *dinner only, clsd Mon, patio*

Stage Left [★WC,GO] 5 Livingston Ave (at George) **732/828-4444** *full bar, expensive*

Newark

■NIGHTCLUBS

Rainbow Tuesday [M,D,DS] 70 Jabez St (at XL Lounge) **973/207-4261** *Tue only*

■MEN'S SERVICES

▶**MegaMates** **973/679-2020** *Call to hook up with HOT local men. FREE to listen & respond to ads. Use FREE code DAMRON. MegaMates.com.*

New Jersey • *USA*

■EROTICA
Little Theatre 562 Broad St
973/623-5177

Ocean City

■CRUISY AREAS
58th St Pavilion [AYOR] *late*

Princeton

■CRUISY AREAS
Herrontown Woods Park [AYOR] off
Snowden Ln, btwn mailbox 586 & 603
(no sign, entrance looks like private
driveway) *beware of cops!*

River Edge

■NIGHTCLUBS
Feathers [★M,D,K,S,V,YC,WC] 77
Kinderkamack Rd (at Grand)
201/342-6410 *9pm-2am, till 3am Sat,
clsd Mon-Tue*

■CRUISY AREAS
Park & Ride [AYOR] off Rte 4 (across
the street from Feathers nightclub)

Sandy Hook

■ENTERTAINMENT &
RECREATION
Gunnison Nude Beach Beach G parking lot (near Gunnison Park, S end) *at
the beach go right (all the way) to the
gay section, cruisy area year-round*

Sayreville

■NIGHTCLUBS
iKon Lounge [M,D] 1979 Hwy 35 South
732/727-6410 *9pm-2am, gay Tue &
Fri only*

Toms River

■CRUISY AREAS
Winding River [AYOR] Rte 37 (near
Garden State Pkwy)

NEW MEXICO

Alamogordo

■ACCOMMODATIONS
Best Western Desert Aire Motor Inn
[GF,SW,WI,WC] 1021 S White Sands Blvd
505/437-2110, 800/637-5956

■CRUISY AREAS
Alameda Park [AYOR] off White Sands
Blvd *nights*

Foothills Park [AYOR] 1st St E (past
Scenic Dr) *days*

Albuquerque

includes Bernalillo, Corrales,
Placitas & Rio Rancho

■INFO LINES & SERVICES
AA Gay/ Lesbian [NS,WC]
505/266-1900 (AA#)

Common Bond Info Line
505/891-3647 *24hrs, covers LGBT
community*

■ACCOMMODATIONS
Adobe Nido [GF,NS,WI] 1124 Major Ave
NW (at 12th St & Candilaria NW)
505/344-1310, 866/435-6436 *B&B,
also aviary*

Bottger Mansion of Old Town
[GF,TG,WI] 110 San Felipe (at Central
Ave) 505/243-3639, 800/758-3639
B&B

**Brittania & W E Mauger Estate
B&B** [GF,NS,WI] 701 Roma Ave NW (at
7th) 505/242-8755, 800/719-9189

Casa Manzano B&B [GS,GO] 103
Forest Rd 321 (at State Rte 55), Tajique
505/384-9767

Casas de Suenos [GS] 310 Rio Grande
Blvd SW (btwn York & Alhambra)
505/247-4560, 800/665-7002

La Casita B&B [GF,NS,WI] 317 16th St
NW (at Lomas Blvd) 505/242-0173
adobe guesthouse

Golden Guesthouses [MW,NS,GO] 2645
Decker NW (at Glenwood)
505/344-9205, 888/513-GOLD

The Nativo Lodge [GF] 6000 Pan
American Fwy NE 505/798-4300,
888/628-4861

Sheraton Albuquerque Airport Hotel [GF,F,SW] 2910 Yale Blvd SE (at Gibson) **505/843-7000, 800/325-3535**

■BARS

Albuquerque Social Club [★MW,D,PC] 4021 Central Ave NE (at Morningside, enter rear) **505/262-1088** 3pm-2am, noon-midnight Sun

Sidewinders Ranch [M,D,CW,B,K,WC] 8900 Central SE (at Wyoming) **505/554-2078** 4pm-2am, till midnight Sun, clsd Mon

■NIGHTCLUBS

Effex [MW,D] 420 Central SW (at 5th) **505/842-8870** 9pm-2am Th-Sat

■CAFES

Java Joe's 906 Park Ave SW **505/765-1514** 6:30am-3:30pm, coffee & pastries, monthly art shows

■RESTAURANTS

Artichoke Cafe [WC] 424 Central Ave SE (at Arno St) **505/243-0200** lunch Mon-Fri, dinner nightly, seafood

Cafe Cubano at Laru Ni Hati [GO] 3413 Central Ave NE (btwn Tulane & Amherst) **505/255-1575** 10am-9pm, till 8pm Sat, noon-5pm Sun, clsd Mon, cigars & cheap Cuban food, also unisex hair salon

Copper Lounge [WC] 1504 Central Ave SE (at Maple) **505/242-7490** 11am-2am, clsd Sun, pizza, burgers, full bar

Desert Fish 4214 Central Ave SE **505/266-5544** dinner nightly, wknd brunch, clsd Mon, seafood

El Patio [★YC,BW,WC] 142 Harvard St SE (at Central) **505/268-4245** 11am-9pm, plenty veggie

El Pinto 10500 4th St NW (at Roy Ave) **505/898-1771** lunch & dinner, Sun brunch, Mexican

Flying Star Cafe [WI,WC] 3416 Central Ave SE (2 blocks W of Carlisle) **505/255-6633** 6am-11pm, till midnight Fri-Sat

Frontier 2400 Central Ave SE (at Cornell) **505/266-0550** 5am-1am, good breakfast burritos

The Original Garcia's Kitchen [WC] 1113 4th St NW (at Mountain) **505/247-9149** 7am-9pm, awesome little down home place

The Range Cafe 2200 Menaul NE (at University Blvd) **505/888-1660** 7:30am-9pm, Southwestern

Romano's Macaroni Grill [WC] 2100 Louisiana NE (at Winrock Mall) **505/881-3400** 11am-10pm, Italian

Sadie's Cocinita [★WC] 6230 4th St NW (near Osuna) **505/345-5339** 11am-10pm, 10am-9pm Sun, New Mexican

Zinc Wine Bar & Bistro [E,R] 3009 Central Ave NE (at Dartmouth) **505/254-9462** lunch & dinner, brunch wknds, also Blues Cellar till 1am Mon-Sat, live music

■ENTERTAINMENT & RECREATION

Bio Park Botanic Garden 2601 Central Ave NW (at New York Ave) **505/768-2000** an oasis in the desert: native & exotic plants, butterflies

■BOOKSTORES

Page One 11018 Montgomery NE (at Juan Tabo Blvd) **505/294-2026, 800/521-4122** 9am-9pm, till 6pm Sun, "New Mexico's Largest Independent Bookstore"

■MEN'S SERVICES

►**MegaMates** 505/268-1111 Call to hook up with HOT local men. FREE to listen & respond to ads. Use FREE code DAMRON. MegaMates.com.

■EROTICA

Castle Megastore 5110 Central Ave SE (at San Mateo) **505/262-2266**

Self Serve [GO] 3904-B Central Ave SE (at Morningside) **505/265-5815** noon-7pm, till 8pm Fri, till 6pm Sun

Video Maxxx 810 Comanche NE (at I-25) **505/341-4000** leather, novelties, books, etc

Viewpoint [★] 6406 Central Ave SE (at San Pedro) **505/268-6373** 24hrs

New Mexico • *USA*

Chimayo

■ACCOMMODATIONS

Casa Escondida B&B [GF,NS,WI] 505/351-4805, 800/643-7201 *full brkfst, hot tub*

Clovis

■CRUISY AREAS

Main St [AYOR] btwn 2nd & 7th

Farmington

■ACCOMMODATIONS

Quality Inn [GF,WI,WC] 1901 E Broadway 505/325-3700, 877/424-6423

Hobbs

■EROTICA

Oasis Video & Bookstore 515 Hwy 132 (at Hwy 83), Lovington 575/392-2310

Stateline Video 6100 W Carlsbad Hwy 62 (across from airport) 575/393-3616

Las Cruces

■ACCOMMODATIONS

Hotel Encanto de Las Cruces [GF] 705 S Telshor Blvd 575/522-4300, 866/383-0443

■RETAIL SHOPS

Spirit Winds Gifts & Cafe [E,F,WI,WC] 2260 S Locust St (at Thomas Dr) 575/521-0222 *7:30am-7pm, 8am-6pm Sun, patio*

■CRUISY AREAS

Burn Lake [AYOR] btwn W Amador & Westgate

Madrid

■BARS

Mineshaft Tavern [GF,F,E] 2846 State Hwy 14 505/473-0743 *11:30am-close, also restaurant*

■CAFES

Java Junction [WI] 2855 State Hwy 14 505/438-2772 *7am-4pm, till 5pm wknds, also giftshop & B&B*

Ramah

■ACCOMMODATIONS

El Morro RV Park, Cabins & Cafe [GS,NS,WI,GO] 4018 Hwy 53 505/783-4612 *in Zuni Mtns, full brkfst, lesbian-owned*

Ruidoso

■ENTERTAINMENT & RECREATION

Mountain Annie's Center for the Arts [E,NS,WC] 2710 Sudderth Dr (at Grindstone Canyon Rd) 575/257-7982

■CRUISY AREAS

Cedar Creek [AYOR] off Mechem Dr

Santa Fe

■INFO LINES & SERVICES

AA Gay/ Lesbian 1601 S St Francis Dr 505/982-8932 *6pm Mon; also 6pm Tue at Friendship Club, 1915 Rosina St*

■ACCOMMODATIONS

Bishop's Lodge Resort & Spa [GF,SW,NS,WC] 1297 Bishops Lodge Rd 505/983-6377, 800/419-0492 *on 450 acres*

El Farolito B&B [GS,NS,WI,GO] 514 Galisteo St (at Paseo de Peralta) 505/988-1631, 888/634-8782 *adobe compound w/ casitas*

Four Kachinas Inn [GS,NS,WI,WC,GO] 512 Webber St 505/982-2550, 800/397-2564 *courtyard, near the Plaza*

Hacienda Nicholas [GS,NS,WI,WC] 320 E Marcy St 505/986-1431, 888/284-3170 *full brkfst*

Inn at Vanessie [GF,NS,WI,WC] 427 W Water St 505/984-1193, 800/646-6752 *historic adobe inn, also restaurant & live music club*

The Inn of the Five Graces [GF] 150 E DeVargas St 505/992-0957, 866/992-0957

➤**Inn of the Turquoise Bear B&B** [MW,NS,WI,GO] 342 E Buena Vista St (at Old Santa Fe Tr) 505/983-0798, 800/396-4104 *Out & About Editors' Choice Award 1999-03 & Santa Fe Heritage Preservation Award 1999, New Mexico Preservation Award 2000*

Inn on the Alameda [GF,WI,WC] 303 E Alameda (at Canyon Rd) 505/984-2121, 888/984-2121 *afternoon wine reception, hot tubs*

Las Palomas [GF,NS,WI,WC] 460 W San Francisco St 505/982-5560, 877/982-5560 *luxury hotel 3 blocks from historic Plaza*

The Madeleine Inn [GS,NS,WI] 106 Faithway St 505/982-3465, 888/877-7622 *Queen Anne Victorian, full brkfst, hot tub, also spa*

Rosewood Inn of the Anasazi [GF,WI,NS,WC] 113 Washington Ave 505/988-3030, 888/767-3966 *luxury hotel 1/2 block from historic Plaza, also restaurant*

The Triangle Inn—Santa Fe [MW,WI,WC,GO] 14 Arroyo Cuyamungue (12 miles N of Santa Fe) 505/455-3375, 877/733-7689 *adobe casitas, nonsmoking available, hot tub, lesbian-owned*

■**BARS**

The Matador [GF,NH] 116 W San Francisco St (at Galisteo) 505/984-5050 *friendly neighborhood dive bar*

Starlight Lounge [MW,E,DS] 500 Rodeo Rd 505/428-7777 *5pm-midnight Wed-Sun*

■**RESTAURANTS**

Anasazi Restaurant [WC] 113 Washington Ave (at Inn of the Anasazi) 505/988-3030 *brkfst, lunch, dinner & wknd brunch*

Cafe Pasqual's [★BW,WC] 121 Don Gaspar Ave (at Water St) 505/983-9340, 800/722-7672 *brkfst, lunch, dinner & Sun brunch, Southwestern*

New York • USA

■Bars

Cathode Ray [M,NH,V,WC] 26 Allen St (at N Pearl) **716/884-3615** *1pm-4am*

Fugazi [GS,V] 503 Franklin St (near Allen St) **716/881-3588** *5pm-2am, cocktail lounge*

K Gallagher's [GF,NH,MR,F,WC] 73 Allen St **716/886-6676** *lunch & dinner, till 3pm Sun*

Q [MW,NH] 44 Allen St **716/332-2223** *3pm-4am, from noon wknds*

The Underground [M,NH,D,K] 274 Delaware Ave (at Johnson) **716/853-0092** *noon-4am*

■Nightclubs

Club Marcella [MW,D,DS,WC,18+] 622 Main St **716/847-6850** *10pm-4am, clsd Mon-Wed*

■Cafes

Cafe 59 [WI,GO] 59 Allen St (at Franklin) **716/883-1880** *7am-4pm, 10am-4pm Sat, clsd Sun*

■Restaurants

Allen Street Hardware Cafe [E] 245 Allen St (at College) **716/882-8843** *from 5pm daily, full bar, live music, art*

Anchor Bar 1047 Main St **716/886-8920, 716/884-4083** *11am-10pm, till midnight Fri-Sat, home of the original Buffalo Chicken Wing*

Atmosphere 62 62 Allen St (at Franklin) **716/881-0062** *from 4pm Wed-Sat, full bar*

Mothers 33 Virginia Pl (at Virginia St) **716/882-2989** *4pm-11pm, till 2am Sat*

Rue Franklin 341 Franklin St (at W Tupper) **716/852-4416** *5:30pm-10pm, clsd Sun-Mon, upscale, contemporary French*

Tempo 581 Delaware Ave (at Allen St) **716/885-1594** *dinner only, clsd Sun, upscale Italian/ American*

Towne Restaurant 186 Allen St **716/884-5128** *7am-5am, clsd Sun, Greek*

■Entertainment & Recreation

Babeville 341 Delaware Ave (at W Tupper) **716/852-3835** *Ani Di Franco's rehabbed church performance space, also Hallwalls Arts Center*

Buffalo United Artists 119 Chippewa (btwn Delaware & Elmwood) **716/886-9239** *gay-themed theater company*

■Bookstores

Talking Leaves 3158 Main St (btwn Winspear & Hertel Aves) **716/837-8554** *10am-6pm, till 8pm Wed-Th, clsd Sun; also 951 Elmwood Ave*

■Publications

Outcome Buffalo 495 Linwood Ave **716/228-8828** *monthly*

■Men's Services

➤**MegaMates 716/852-4800** *Call to hook up with HOT local men. FREE to listen & respond to ads. Use FREE code DAMRON. MegaMates.com.*

■Erotica

Elmwood Books Adult Mart 3102 Delaware Ave (at Sheridan), Kenmore **716/874-1045** *24hrs*

Video Liquidators 1770 Elmwood Ave **716/874-7223** *24hrs*

■Cruisy Areas

South Park Lake [AYOR] 15 minutes from downtown *best btwn 5pm & midnight*

Canton

■Restaurants

Spicy Iguana 21 Miner St **315/714-2155** *4pm-9pm, till 2am Fri-Sat, clsd Sun-Mon, Mexican*

Capital District

includes Albany, Cohoes, Salem, Schenectady & Troy

■Info Lines & Services

Capital District Lesbian/ Gay Community Center 332 Hudson Ave, Albany **518/462-6138** *social & human service programs; also Rainbow Cafe 6pm-9pm, clsd Sat*

Gay AA 332 Hudson Ave (at L/G Community Center), Albany **518/462-6138** *7pm Sun, men only 7:30pm Mon*

■**ACCOMMODATIONS**

The Morgan State House [GF,NS,WI] 393 State St, Albany **518/427-6063, 888/427-6063** *1800s town house*

■**BARS**

Clinton Street Pub [MW,NH,D,E,K] 159 Clinton St, Schenectady **518/377-8555** *11am-close, from 8am Sat, from noon Sun*

Oh Bar [MW,NH,MR,K,V,WC] 304 Lark St (at Madison), Albany **518/463-9004** *2pm-4am*

Rocks [MW,NH,K,GO] 77 Central Ave (at Elk), Albany **518/472-3588** *2pm-4am*

Waterworks Pub [M,NH,D,F,E,K,18+,WC] 76 Central Ave (btwn Lexington & Northern), Albany **518/465-9079** *1pm-4am, garden bar, DJ wknds*

■**NIGHTCLUBS**

Fuze Box [GS,D,E,GO] 12 Central Ave, Albany **518/703-8937** *8pm-4am Th-Sat, swing dancing*

■**RESTAURANTS**

Bomber's Burrito Bar [GO] 258 Lark St, Albany **518/463-9636** *11am-2am, till 3am wknds, plenty veggie*

Bomber's Burrito Bar [GO] 447 State St, Schenectady **518/374-3548** *11am-2am, till 3am wknds, plenty veggie*

Debbie's Kitchen 456 Madison Ave (btwn Lark St & Washington Park), Albany **518/463-3829** *10am-7pm, 11am-6pm Sat, clsd Sun*

El Loco Mexican Cafe 465 Madison Ave (btwn Lark & Willett), Albany **518/436-1855** *lunch Wed-Sat, dinner nightly, clsd Mon, full bar*

Midtown Tap & Tea Room [WC,GO] 289 New Scotland Ave, Albany **518/435-0202** *11am-10pm, from 4pm Sat, clsd Mon*

Yono's [E,WC] 25 Chapel St (at Sheridan), Albany **518/436-7747** *5:30pm-10pm, clsd Sun-Mon*

■**RETAIL SHOPS**

Romeo's Gifts 299 Lark St (at Madison), Albany **518/434-4014** *noon-9pm, till 5pm Sun*

■**MEN'S CLUBS**

River Street Club [MO,V,N,NS,PC,WC,GO] 540 River St (at corner of River & Hoosick St), Troy **518/272-0340** *7am-11pm, from noon wknds*

■**MEN'S SERVICES**

➤**MegaMates** Albany **518/207-0707** *Call to hook up with HOT local men. FREE to listen & respond to ads. Use FREE code DAMRON. MegaMates.com.*

■**CRUISY AREAS**

Empire State Plaza [AYOR] Albany

Catskill Mtns

■**ACCOMMODATIONS**

Bradstan Country Hotel [GF,C,P] 1561 Rte 17-B, White Lake **845/583-4114** *also piano bar & cabaret from 9pm-1am Fri-Sat*

Clark House [GS,NS] 3292 Rte 23A, Palenville **518/678-5649** *Victorian guesthouse, full brkfst, hot tub*

Country Suite [GF,NS,GO] Rte 23, Windham **518/734-4079** *B&B, Victorian-style farmhouse, full brkfst, antique shop*

Cuomo's Cove [GF,NS] 33 Cumo's Cove Rd (at South St), Windham **518/734-5903, 800/734-5903**

ECCE B&B [GS,NS,WI,GO] 19 Silverfish Rd, Barryville **845/557-8562, 888/557-8562** *above Upper Delaware River, full brkfst*

Fairlawn Inn [GF,WI,GO] 7872 Main St, Hunter **518/263-5025**

Kate's Lazy Meadow Motel [GF,NS,WI] 5191 Rte 28, Mt Tremper **845/688-7200** *love shack owned by Kate Pierson of the B-52s*

The Roxbury, Contemporary Catskill Lodging [GS,NS,WI,WC,GO] 2258 County Hwy 41 (at Bridge St), Roxbury **607/326-7200** *hip country motel, kids ok*

Village Green [GO] **845/679-0313**

New York • *USA*

■BARS

Public Restaurant & Lounge [GF]
2318 City Hwy 41 (Bridge St), Roxbury
607/326-4026 *5pm-9pm, till midnight Fri-Sat, clsd Mon-Tue*

■RESTAURANTS

Catskill Rose 5355 Rte 212, Mt
Tremper **845/688-7100** *5pm-close Th-Sun, full bar, patio, also lodging*

■BOOKSTORES

Golden Notebook [WC] 29 Tinker St,
Woodstock **845/679-8000** *11am-6pm, till 7pm Fri-Sat*

■EROTICA

Exotic Gifts & Videos Old Rte 52 (at Rte 52), Liberty **845/292-1140**

Cherry Creek

■ACCOMMODATIONS

The Cherry Creek Inn [GF] 1022 West
Rd (CR68) (at Center Rd)
716/296-5105 *B&B, full brkfst*

Cooperstown

■ACCOMMODATIONS

Cobblescote on the Lake [GF,WI,F,GO]
6515 State Hwy 80 **607/437-1146**
spectacular views at refurbished waterfront resort

Corning

■ACCOMMODATIONS

Black Sheep Inn [GS,WI] 8329 Pleasant
Valley Rd (Rte 54), Hammondsport
607/569-3767, 877/274-6286

Hillcrest Manor B&B [GF,NS,WI,GO]
227 Cedar St (at Fourth St)
607/936-4548, 607/654-9136 *1890
mansion*

Rufus Tanner House B&B
[GS,NS,WI,WC] 60 Sagetown Rd, Pine
City **607/732-0213, 800/360-9259**
full brkfst, hot tub

Croton-on-Hudson

■ACCOMMODATIONS

Alexander Hamilton House
[GS,SW,NS,WI] 49 Van Wyck St
914/271-6737 *full brkfst, 1889
Victorian*

Elmira

■BARS

Chill [MW,NH,D,F,K,DS,GO] 200 W 5th
607/738-9343 *6pm-1am, clsd Sun-Tue*

■EROTICA

Deluxe Books 123 Lake St
607/734-9656

Findley Lake

■ACCOMMODATIONS

Blue Heron Inn [GF,NS] 10412 Main St
(at Shadyside Rd) **716/769-7852** *B&B,
full brkfst*

Fire Island

see also Long Island

■INFO LINES & SERVICES

AA 631/654-1150 *call for meeting
times*

■ACCOMMODATIONS

►**Belvedere Guest House for Men**
[MO,SW,WC,GO] 631/597-6448
*Venetian-style palace, hot tub, jacuzzi,
gym*

Dune Point Guesthouse [GF,NS,WC]
631/597-6261, 631/560-2200 (cell)
hot tub

Grove Hotel [M,SW,N,WC,GO] Dock
Walk, Cherry Grove **631/597-6600**
nonsmoking room available, also 4 bars

Hotel Ciel [M,F,SW,WC] Harbor Walk
631/597-6500 *also restaurant*

The Madison Fire Island Pines
[M,SW,NS,WI,GO] 22 Atlantic Walk
631/597-6061 *near beach, roof deck,
hot tub*

Pines Bluff Overlook [M]
631/597-3064

■BARS

Blue Whale [★MW,D,F,WC] Harbor
Walk, The Pines **631/597-6500**
seasonal, popular Low Tea dance

Cherry's On the Bay [★MW,D,F,E,DS,P]
158 Bayview Walk, Cherry Grove
631/597-7859 *seasonal, noon-4am,
patio, also restaurant*

Belvedere

GUEST HOUSE FOR MEN
FIRE ISLAND'S FINEST

www.belvederefireisland.com
(631) 597-6448

BOOK NOW!
online
or call

Pines Bistro & Martini Bar [M,D,E,P] 36 Fire Island Blvd, The Pines **631/597-6862** *seasonal, opens 6pm*

Sip • n • Twirl [M,D,E] 36 Fire Island Blvd, The Pines **631/597-3599** *seasonal, noon-4am*

■NIGHTCLUBS

Ice Palace [MW,D,DS,WC] Bayview Walk, Cherry Grove **631/597-6600** *hours vary*

■CAFES

Canteen [★M,F,WC] Harbor Walk, The Pines **631/597-6500** *coffee, smoothies, cocktails & food*

■RESTAURANTS

Cherry Grove Pizza Dock Walk (under the GroveHotel), Cherry Grove **631/597-6766** *seasonal, 11am-10pm*

Marina Meat Market Harbor Walk, The Pines **631/597-6588** *great sandwiches*

Pines Pizza 36 Fire Island Blvd, The Pines **631/597-3597** *seasonal, 11am-11pm*

Sand Castle 140 Lewis Walk, Cherry Grove **631/597-4174** *seasonal, lunch & dinner, also bar*

■ENTERTAINMENT & RECREATION

Cherry Grove Beach [MW] *nude beach; head left for gay section*

Invasion of the Pines The Pines dock (July 4th wknd) *come & enjoy the annual fun as boatloads of drag queens from Cherry Grove arrive to terrorize the posh Pines*

The Pines Beach [M] *nude beach*

■GYMS & HEALTH CLUBS

Deck Pool & Gym Harbor Walk, The Pines *7am-6pm, day passes available*

■CRUISY AREAS

Meat Rack [AYOR] trail btwn Cherry Grove & W end of Pines *where the boys of Fire Island really work out*

Geneva

■ACCOMMODATIONS

Belhurst [GF,F] 4069 Rte 14 S (near Snell Rd) **315/781-0201** *fireplaces, also restaurant*

Glens Falls

■ACCOMMODATIONS

Glens Falls Inn [GF,WI] 25 Sherman Ave **646/743-9365** *Victorian B&B, full brkfst*

Hamptons

see Long Island—Suffolk/ Hamptons

Hudson Valley

Hudson Valley includes Catskill, High Falls, Highland, Hudson, Hyde Park, Kinderhook, Kingston, New Paltz, Poughkeepsie, Rhinebeck & Saugerties

■ACCOMMODATIONS

Barclay Heights B&B [GF,NS] 158 Burt St (at Trinity Place), Saugerties **845/246-3788** *full brkfst*

The Country Squire B&B [GS,NS,WI,GO] 251 Allen St (at 3rd), Hudson **518/822-9229**

Harmony House B& B [GS,WI,GO] 1659 Route 212, Saugertie **845/679-1277**

Van Schaack House [GF,NS,GO] 20 Broad St (at Albany Rd), Kinderhook **518/758-6118** *B&B, full brkfst*

■RESTAURANTS

Armadillo Bar & Grill 97 Abeel St, Kingston **845/339-1550** *lunch wknds, dinner nightly, clsd Mon*

Northern Spy Cafe [WC] Rte 213, High Falls **845/687-7298** *dinner only, clsd Mon*

Rock & Rye 215 Hugenot St (behind conference center), New Paltz **845/255-7888** *5pm-close, Sun brunch 11am-3pm, clsd Mon-Tue*

Terrapin 6426 Montgomery St, Rhinebeck **845/876-3330** *lunch & dinner, bistro, also bar, patio*

The Would Restaurant [GO] 120 North Rd (off Rte 9 W), Highland **845/691-9883** *dinner nightly, clsd Sun, full bar, patio*

■**ENTERTAINMENT & RECREATION**

Dia:Beacon Riggio Galleries 3 Beekman St (at Rte 9D), Beacon **845/440-0100** *modern art museum*

■**EROTICA**

Hamilton Book & Video 216 N Hamilton St (at Parker), Poughkeepsie 845/473-1776

Ulster Video & Gifts 584 Ulster Ave, Kingston 845/331-6023

Ithaca

■**INFO LINES & SERVICES**

AA Gay/ Lesbian 607/273-1541

■**ACCOMMODATIONS**

Juniper Hill B&B [GF,NS,WI,GO] 16 Elm St (at Main St), Trumansburg **607/387-3044, 888/809-1367** *full brkfst*

Noble House Farm [GF,NS,WC,GO] 215 Connecticut Hill Rd, Newfield **607/277-4798** *near gorges & wine tours*

William Henry Miller Inn [GF,WI] 303 N Aurora St (at E Buffalo St) 607/256-4553, 877/256-4553

■**BARS**

Felicia's Atomic Lounge [GF,F,E,P,GO] 508 W State St (Meadow St) **607/273-2219** *4pm-1am, clsd Mon*

Oasis [★MW,D,MR,E,WC] 1230 Danby Rd/ Rte 96-B (at Comfort) **607/273-1505** *4pm-1am, clsd Mon, also restaurant*

■**CAFES**

Sarah's Patisserie [GO] 200 Pleasant Grove Rd (at Hanshaw Rd) **607/257-4257** *10am-6pm, clsd Sun-Mon*

■**ENTERTAINMENT & RECREATION**

Out Loud Chorus 607/280-0374

■**CRUISY AREAS**

Stewart Park [AYOR]

Jamestown

■**ACCOMMODATIONS**

Fairmount Motel [GF,WI,GO] 138 W Fairmount (Rte 394) **716/763-9550** *near Lake Chautauqua*

■**BARS**

Sneakers [MW,WC] 100 Harrison (at Institute) **716/484-8816** *2pm-2am, clsd Mon*

■**ENTERTAINMENT & RECREATION**

The Lucille Ball/ Desi Arnaz Center 2 W 3rd St (at Main) **716/484-0800, 877/582-9326** *for those who love Lucy*

Little Falls

■**CAFES**

Piccolo Cafe 365 Canal Pl **315/823-9856** *lunch Tue-Fri, dinner Wed-Sun, clsd Mon*

LONG ISLAND

Long Island is divided into 2 geographical areas:
Long Island—Nassau
Long Island—Suffolk/ Hamptons
see also Fire Island

Long Island—Nassau

■**INFO LINES & SERVICES**

Long Island GLBT Center 400 Garden City Plaza #110, Garden City **516/323-0011** *Long Island GLBT services network*

■**BARS**

Blanche [M,NH,K,E,S] 47 Boundary Ave, South Farmingdale **516/694-6906** *5pm-4am, from 3pm Sun*

■**RESTAURANTS**

RS Jones 153 Merrick Ave (off Sunrise), Merrick **516/378-7177** *dinner, clsd Mon, Tex-Mex*

■**ENTERTAINMENT & RECREATION**

Jones Beach walk E from Field #6, Wantagh

New York • *USA*

Pride for Youth Coffeehouse [MW]
2050 Bellmore Ave, Bellmore
516/679-9000 *7:30pm-11:30pm Fri,
ages 13-20, live music*

Long Island—Suffolk/ Hamptons

▇INFO LINES & SERVICES

The Center at Bay Shore 34 Park Ave,
Bay Shore 631/665-2300 *drop-in
lounge w/ cybercenter, events*

The Hamptons GLBT Center 44
Union St, Sag Harbor 831/899-4950
Long Island GLBT services network

▇ACCOMMODATIONS

The Atlantic [GF,SW,WC] 1655 Country
Rd 39, Southampton 631/283-6100

East Hampton Village B&B [GS,NS,WI]
172 Newtown Ln (at McGuirk St), East
Hampton 631/324-1858 *lovely turn-
of-the-century home*

Mill House Inn [GF,NS,WI,WC] 31 N
Main St (at Newtown Lane), East
Hampton 631/324-9766 *full brkfst,
kids/ dogs ok*

Stirling House B&B [GF,NS,WI,GO] 104
Bay Ave, Greenport 631/477-0654,
800/551-0654 *full brkfst, jacuzzi*

Sunset Beach [GF,F] 35 Shore Rd,
Shelter Island 631/749-2001 *seasonal*

▇BARS

The Long Island Eagle [M,NH,L] 94 N
Clinton St (at Union Blvd), Bay Shore
631/968-2750 *5pm-4am, from 9pm
Sun*

Nuts & Bolts [M,NH,D] 1083 Main St,
Holbrook 631/737-6887 *8pm-close,
from 4pm Sun*

▇NIGHTCLUBS

Bunkhouse [M,D,K,S,WC,GO,$] 620
Waverly Ave, Patchouge *theme nights*

Wall Street Saturdays [MW,D] 575
Nesconset Hwy/ Rte 347, Hauppauge
516/909-4779 *Sat only*

▇RESTAURANTS

Babette's 66 Newtown Ln, East
Hampton 631/329-5377 *seasonal,
brkfst, lunch & dinner, healthy*

▇EROTICA

Sugar Bush 290A Knickerbocker Ave
(btwn Sunrise & Vets Hwy), Bohemia
631/567-9779

▇CRUISY AREAS

Fowler Beach [AYOR] Southampton *go
right*

Smith Point Park [AYOR] Fire Island
Nat'l Seashore (at end of William Floyd
Pkwy), Shirley

Middletown

▇ACCOMMODATIONS

Best Western Inn at Hunt's Landing
[GF,SW,WI] 120 Rtes 6 & 209,
Matamoras, PA 570/491-2400,
800/528-1234 *restaurant & bar*

Montgomery

▇ACCOMMODATIONS

The Borland House B&B [GF,WI] 130
Clinton St 845/457-1513

NEW YORK CITY

New York City is divided into 9
geographical areas:
NYC—Overview
NYC—Soho, Greenwich & Chelsea
NYC—Downtown
NYC—Midtown
NYC—Uptown
NYC—Brooklyn
NYC—Queens
NYC—Bronx
NYC—Staten Island

NYC—Overview

▇INFO LINES & SERVICES

AA Gay/ Lesbian Intergroup at
Lesbian/ Gay Community Center
212/647-1680

LGBT Community Center [WC] 208 W
13th (at 7th Ave) 212/620-7310 *tons
of groups & resources, museum*

▇ENTERTAINMENT & RECREATION

**Before Stonewall: A Lesbian & Gay
History Tour** meet: Washington Square
Arch (at Big Onion Walking Tours)
212/439-1090

New York • *USA*

■PUBLICATIONS

Gay City News 646/229-1890 *LGBT newspaper, weekly*

Get Out Magazine 646/761-3325 *content from the hottest gay and gay-friendly spots in New York*

MetroSource 212/691-5127 *LGBT lifestyle & resource directory*

Next Magazine *entertainment & nightlife paper*

►**Odyssey Magazine** 323/874-8788 *dish on NYC's club scene*

■MEN'S SERVICES

►**MegaMates** 212/971-7272 *Call to hook up with HOT local men. FREE to listen & respond to ads. Use FREE code DAMRON. MegaMates.com.*

NYC—Soho, Greenwich & Chelsea

■INFO LINES & SERVICES

Audre Lorde Project [TG] 147 W 24th St 212/463-0342 *1pm-7pm Tue-Th only, LGBT center for people of color, events, resources, HIV services*

■ACCOMMODATIONS

Ace Hotel [GF] 20 W 29th St (at Broadway) 212/679-2222 *hip hotel near Flatiron District*

Chelsea Mews Guest House [MO,NS,GO] 344 W 15th St (btwn 8th & 9th Aves) 212/255-9174 *some shared baths*

►**Chelsea Pines Inn** [MW,WI,GO] 317 W 14th St (btwn 8th & 9th Aves) 212/929-1023, 888/546-2700 *"Chelsea Pines is the premier LGBT choice in the heart of the community," featured in the NY Times*

The Chelsea Savoy Hotel [GS,WI,WC] 204 W 23rd St (at 7th Ave) 212/929-9353, 866/929-9353

Chelsea Star Hotel [GS,WI] 300 W 30th St (at 8th Ave) **212/ 244-7827, 877/ 827-6969**

➤**Colonial House Inn** [MW,N,NS,GO] 318 W 22nd St (btwn 8th & 9th Aves) **212/243-9669, 800/689-3779** *1850 brownstone in Chelsea, rooftop patio*

Crosby Street Hotel [GF,WI] 79 Crosby St (at Spring) **212/226-6400** *chic boutique hotel in Soho*

Eventi [GF] 851 6th Ave (at 30th St) **212/564-4567, 866/996-8396**

➤**The GEM Hotel Chelsea** [GF,WI,WC] 300 W 22nd St (at 8th Ave) **212/675-1911**

➤**The GEM Hotel SoHo** [GF,WI,WC] 135 E Houston St (btwn 1st & 2nd Aves) **212/358-8844**

Gershwin Hotel [GF,WI] 7 E 27th St (at 5th Ave) **212/545-8000** *artsy hotel w/ model's floor dorms & rooms*

Hotel 17 [GF] 225 E 17th St **212/475-2845** *"East Village chic" budget hotel, shared baths*

Incentra Village House [GS,NS,WI] 32 8th Ave (at W 12th St) **212/206-0007** *in 2 red-brick buildings built in 1841*

➤**The Jade Hotel** [GF] 52 W 13th St (at 6th Ave) **212/375-1300**

The Jane [GS,WI] 113 Jane St (at Hudson River Pk) **212/924-6700** *inspired by luxury train cabins, some shared baths*

Soho Grand Hotel [GF,WI,WC] 310 W Broadway (at Canal St) **212/965-3000, 800/965-3000** *big, glossy, over-the-top hotel*

The Standard Hotel [GF,SW,WI] 848 Washington St (at W 13th) **212/645-4646, 877/550-4646** *ultra-modern, luxe hotel straddling the High Line*

Tribeca Grand [GS,WI] 2 Ave of the Americas **212/519-6600**

Washington Square Hotel [GF,F,WI] 103 Waverly Pl (at MacDougal St) **212/777-9515, 800/222-0418** *on historic Washington Square Park*

➤**Wyndham Garden Hotel Chelsea**
[GF,WI,WC] 37 W 24th St
212/243-0800

■**BARS**

Arrow Bar [GS,D] 85 Ave A (btwn 5th &
6th) 212/673-1775 *4pm-close, theme
nights*

Barracuda [★M,S] 275 W 22nd St (at
8th Ave) 212/645-8613 *4pm-4am,
live DJs*

Beauty Bar [GS,D,E] 231 E 14th St (at
3rd Ave) 212/539-1389 *5pm-4am,
from 7pm wknds*

The Boiler Room [M,NH,WI] 86 E 4th
St (at 2nd Ave) 212/254-7536 *4pm-
4am*

Boots & Saddle [M,NH,B,L,MR,S,18+,YC]
76 Christopher St (at 7th Ave S)
212/633-1986 *noon-4am, go-go
dancers*

Boxers NYC [M,NH,F,V,WC] 37 W 20th
St (at 6th Ave) 212/255-5082 *4pm-
2am, from 1pm wknds*

Cake Shop [GF] 152 Ludlow St (btwn
Stanton & Rivington) 212/253-0036
*9am-2am, till 4am wknds, cafe/ bakery
by day, punk bands at night*

The Cock [M,K,S,$] 29 2nd Ave (1 blk
above Houston) 212/473-9406 *4pm-
4am, a "sleazy rock 'n' roll bar," live DJs*

Cubbyhole [MW,NH] 281 W 12th St (at
4th St) 212/243-9041

The Dalloway [GO] 525 Broome St (at
7th Ave) 212/966-9620

Duplex [GF,C,P,$] 61 Christopher St (at
7th Ave) 212/255-5438 *4pm-4am,
piano bar from 9pm*

The Eagle [★M,L] 554 W 28th St (btwn
10th & 11th) 646/473-1866 *10pm-
4am*

Eastern Bloc [★MW,D,S,WC] 505 E 6th
St (at Ave A) 212/777-2555 *7pm-
4am, trendy lounge*

G Lounge [★M,GO] 225 W 19th St (at
7th Ave) 212/929-1085 *4pm-4am,
lounge, live DJs*

Joe's Legendary Famous Club

Busiest Corner in the Village

THE MONSTER ®

80 Grove St. • NY NY • (212) 924-3558

Gym Sports Bar [M,NH] 167 8th Ave (btwn 18th & 19th) 212/337-2439 *4pm-close, from 1pm wknds*

The Hangar [M,DS,S] 115 Christopher St (at Bleecker) 212/627-2044 *3pm-4am*

Julius' [M,NH,F] 159 W 10th St 212/243-1928 *11am-2am, till 4am wknds, good burgers*

Marie's Crisis [MW,P] 59 Grove St (at 7th Ave) *4pm-4am, piano bar from 9:30pm*

►**The Monster** [★M,D,C,P,WC] 80 Grove St (at W 4th St, Sheridan Square) 212/924-3558 *4pm-4am, from 2pm wknds, piano bar, T-dance style*

Nowhere [MW,NH,TG] 322 E 14th St (btwn 1st & 2nd) 212/477-4744 *3pm-4am*

Phoenix [MW,NH] 447 E 13th St (at Ave A) 212/477-9979 *4pm-4am, patio*

Pieces [M,NH,D,K,C] 8 Christopher St (btwn 6th & 7th) 212/929-9291 *2pm-4am*

Play-Boy [M,D,YC] 447 E. 13th St (at Phoenix) *Sat only*

Rockbar [M,NH,E,WC] 185 Christopher St (at Weehawken St) 212/242-9113 *noon-close*

The Rusty Knot [GS,NH,F,WC] 425 West St (at 11th St) 212/645-5668 *noon-close*

Secret Lounge [M,MR-A,S] 525 W 29th St (at 10th Ave) 212/268-5580 *10pm-4am, clsd Sun-Wed*

Stonewall Inn [M,NH,D,DS,B,E] 53 Christopher St (at 7th Ave) 212/488-2705 *2pm-4am*

Ty's [M,NH,L,B,GO] 114 Christopher St (btwn Bleecker & Hudson) 212/741-9641 *3pm-4am*

■NIGHTCLUBS

Alegria [★M,D] *8 parties a year, during holiday wknds & Black Party in March*

Bar 13 [GS,D,YC] 35 E 13th St (btwn Broadway & 5th Ave) 212/979-6677 *check local listings for gay events*

Big Apple Ranch [MW,D,CW,BW,$] 39 W 19th St, 5th flr (btwn 5th & 6th, at Dance Manhattan) 8pm-1am Sat only, two-step lessons

Boys Night Out [M,D,YC] 369 W 46th St (at the Ritz) *Th only*

Eleven Eleven [M,D] 244 E Houston St (at Essex, at Open House) *11pm Fri, dancing, drag & debauchery*

Happy Ending [GS,D,E] 302 Broome St (at Forsyth) 212/334-9676 *7pm-4am, from 10pm Tues, clsd Sun-Mon, theme nights*

Hot Rabbit [W,D] 80 Grove St (at W 4th, at the Monster) *10pm Fri only*

Les Garcons [M,D] 32 Mulberry St (at Bayard, at Le Baron) *11pm Wed only, exclusive, fashion-forward crowd*

Penthaus Fridays [M,D,YC] 760 8th Ave (btwn 46th & 47th, at the Copa) *11pm Fri, rooftop dancing & cocktails*

Pyramid [GS,D] 101 Ave A (at 7th St) 212/228-4888 *theme nights*

Saint-At-Large [★M,D] 212/674-8541 *producers of the Black Party in March*

Sea Tea [M,D,MR,F,P,S,GO,$] *leaves from Pier 40 (West Side Hwy at Houston St)* 212/675-2971 *6pm-10pm Sun (June-Sept)*

Sweet Fox [MW,D] 92 2nd Ave (at Lit Lounge) *10pm Th only*

Westgay [M,D,YC] 75 Clarkson St, at Westway (btwn Washington & West) *Tue only, freaky dance party*

XES Lounge [★M,D,K,C,V,GO] 157 W 24th St (at 7th Ave) 212/604-0212 *4pm-4am, smoking patio*

■CAFES

Brown Cup Cafe 334 8th Ave (at 27th St) 212/675-7765 *7am-8pm, 8am-6pm Sat, clsd Sun*

■RESTAURANTS

7A [★] 109 Ave A (at 7th St) 212/475-9001 *24hrs, great fake meat & tasty mimosas!*

Agave 140 Seventh Ave (btwn 10th St & Charles) 212/989-2100 *noon-close, Southwestern, popular brunch*

Angelica Kitchen 300 E 12th St (at 1st Ave) 212/228-2909 *11:30am-10:30pm, vegetarian/ vegan*

Awash 338 E 6th (btwn 1st & 2nd Aves) 212/982-9589 *11am-11pm, Ethiopian*

Benny's Burritos 113 Greenwich (at Jane) **212/633-9210** *11am-11pm, till midnight Fri-Sat, cheap and huge*

Big Gay Ice Cream Shop 125 E 7th St (at 1st Ave) **212/533-9333** *1pm-midnight; also Big Gay Ice Cream Truck from May-Oct*

Blue Ribbon [WC] 97 Sullivan St (at Spring St) **212/274-0404** *4pm-4am, cont'l/ American, chef hangout*

Bone Lick Park [WC] 75 Greenwich Ave (at 7th Ave) **212/647-9600** *BBQ, full bar*

Budhu Lounge 531 Hudson St (at Charles St) **917/262-0836** *5:30pm-2am, till 4am Fri-Sat, 11am-midnight Sun*

Cola's [★] 148 8th Ave (at 17th St) **212/633-8020** *lunch & dinner, Italian*

Cowgirl Hall of Fame 519 Hudson St (at W 10th) **212/633-1133** *lunch, dinner, wknd brunch*

Crispo 240 W14th St (at 7th) **212/229-1818** *dinner only, great caramelized cauliflower & carbonara*

The Dish 201 8th Ave (btwn 20th & 21st) **212/352-9800, 212/352-3003** *brkfst, lunch & dinner, also bar*

East of Eighth 254 W 23rd St (at 8th) **212/352-0075** *lunch & dinner, bar open late*

Elmo 156 7th Ave (at 20th St) **212/337-8000** *lunch & dinner, lounge*

Les Enfants Terribles 37 Canal St (at Ludlow) **212/777-7518** *8am-4am, African/Moroccan, Brazilian, French, full bar & DJ*

Gobo 401 Ave of the Americas (at W 8th) **212/255-3242** *11:30am-11pm, vegetarian/ vegan*

Intermezzo 202 8th Ave (at 21st St) **212/929-3433** *noon-midnight, Italian, great wknd brunch*

LaVagna 545 E 5th (btwn Aves A & B) **212/979-1005** *dinner only, affordable Italian*

The Meatball Shop [★] 200 9th St **212/257-4363** *6pm-midnight, till 1am Fri-Sat, also on 84 Stanton, 64 Greenwich & 170 Bedford*

The Noho Star 330 Lafayette St (at Bleecker) **212/925-0070** *8am-midnight, from 10:30am wknds, eclectic European & Chinese*

Omai 158 9th Ave (at 19th St) **212/633-0550** *dinner nightly, Vietnamese*

Philip Marie 569 Hudson St (at 11th St) **212/242-6200** *noon-11pm, clsd Mon*

Red Bamboo 140 W 4th St (at MacDougal) **212/260-1212** *noon-midnight, vegetarian/ vegan*

Sacred Chow [WC] 227 Sullivan St (btwn W 3rd St & Bleecker) **212/337-0863** *11am-10pm, till 11pm Fri-Sat, gourmet vegan*

Sigiri 91 1st Ave (btwn 5th & 6th Sts) **212/614-9333** *lunch & dinner, Sri Lankan*

Trattoria Pesce Pasta 262 Bleecker St (at 6th Ave) **212/645-2993** *noon-midnight*

Veselka 144 2nd Ave (at 9th St) **212/228-9682** *24hrs, Ukrainian, great pierogi*

■ ENTERTAINMENT & RECREATION

Chelsea Classics 260 W 23rd St (btwn 7th & 8th, at Clearview Cinema) **212/691-5519** *Th night only, drag diva Hedda Lettuce hosts camp movies*

Dixon Place 161 Chrystie St (at Delancey) **212/219-0736** *many gay-themed productions; also HOT Festival of queer performance in July*

High Line Gansevoort & W 30th St (btwn 9th & 11th Ave) **212/500-6035** *elevated train track converted to beautiful urban park*

La Mama 74 E 4th St **212/475-7710** *experimental theater*

Leslie/ Lohman Gay Art Foundation & Gallery 26 Wooster St (btwn Grand & Canal) **212/431-2609** *noon-6pm, clsd Sun-Mon*

PS 122 150 1st Ave (at E 9th St) **212/477-5829, 212/352-3101 (tickets)** *it's rough, it's raw, it's real New York performance art*

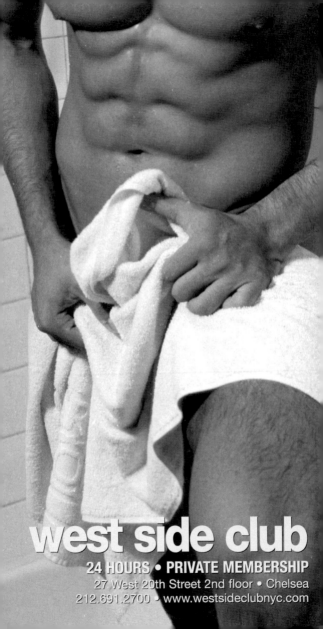

west side club

New York • USA

The Will Clark Show 8 Christopher St (at 6th Ave, at Pieces) *8pm Wed, Porno Bingo, cheap drinks, cheap men!*

■ BOOKSTORES

The Bureau of General Services—Queer Division 27 Orchard St (nr Canal St) 646/457-0859 *11am-7pm, noon-6pm Sun, clsd Mon, queer bookstore and event space hosted by Strange Loop Gallery*

■ RETAIL SHOPS

Flight 001 96 Greenwich Ave (btwn Jane & 12th) 212/989-0001, 877/354-4481 *11am-8pm, noon-6pm Sun, way cool travel gear*

Nasty Pig 265 West 19th St (at 8th Ave) 212/691-6067 *noon-8pm, 1pm-6am Sun*

Rainbows & Triangles 192 8th Ave (at 19th St) 212/627-2166 *11am-10pm, noon-9pm Sun, LGBT cards, books, gifts & more*

■ MEN'S CLUBS

Hard Drive [MO,BYOB] 250 W 26th St (btwn 7th & 8th, at Paddles) 212/366-9339 *8pm Wed only, dungeon party*

►**West Side Club** [★M,PC] 27 W 20th St, 2nd flr (at 6th Ave) 212/691-2700 *24hrs*

■ EROTICA

Blue Door Video 87 1st Ave (at 6th St) 212/995-2248 *24hrs, gay movie theater*

Leather Man 111 Christopher St (at Bleecker) 212/243-5339

Pleasure Chest 156 7th Ave S (at Charles) 212/242-2158

Purple Passion [GO] 211 W 20th St (at 7th Ave) 212/807-0486 *fetishwear*

Unicorn 277-C W 22nd St (btwn 7th & 8th Ave) 212/924-2921

NYC—Downtown

■ ACCOMMODATIONS

Gild Hall Wall Street [GS,WC] 15 Gold St (at Platt) 212/232-7700, 212/232-7800 (reservations) *high-tech boutique hotel, also restaurant & lounge*

Millenium Hilton [SW,WC] 55 Church St 212/693-2001, 877/692-4458

■ RESTAURANTS

La Flaca [WC] 384 Grand St 646/692-9259 *noon-4am, Mexican, full bar*

NYC—Midtown

■ ACCOMMODATIONS

Chambers Hotel [GF] 15 W 56th St (at 5th Ave) 212/974-5656, 866/204-5656 *upscale boutique hotel; fabulous art collection*

Comfort Inn - Midtown West [GF,WI,WC] 442 W 36th St (btwn 9th & 10th) 212/714-6699

Distrikt Hotel [GF,WI] 342 W 40th St (at 9th Ave) 646/831-6780 , 888/444-5610 *upscale boutique hotel*

►**The GEM Hotel Midtown West** [GF,WI,WC] 449 W 36th St (at 10th Ave) 212/967-7206

Hotel 57 [GF,NS,WI,WC] 130 E 57th St (at Lexington) 212/753-8841, 800/497-6028

The Hotel Metro [GF,WI,WC] 45 W 35th St (at 5th Ave) 212/947-2500, 800/356-3870

Hudson Hotel [GF,WI,WC] 356 W 58th St (at 9th) 512/554-6000, 800/697-1791 *magical hotel w/ trendy bars*

Ink48 [GF,WI] 653 11th Ave (at 48th St) 212/757-0088, 877/843-8869 *luxe hotel in former printing house*

The MAve [GF,WI] 61 Madison Ave (at 27th St) 212/532-7373

The Out NYC [MW] 510 W 42nd S 212/947-2999, 855/568-8692 *NYC's first straight-friendly urban resort; restaurant & club on site*

The Pod Hotel [NS,WI,WC] 230 E 51st Street (near 2nd Ave) 212/355-0300, 800/742-5945 *compact rooms, rooftop lounge*

Room Mate Grace [GF,SW,NS,WI,WC] 125 W 45th St (near Sixth Ave) 212/354-2323

The Strand [GF,WI] 33 W 37th St 212/448-1024

➤**Travel Inn** [GF,SW,WC] 515 W 42nd St (at 10th Ave) **212/695-7171, 800/869-4630** *fitness center*

The Tuscany [GS,WI,WC] 120 E 39th St (at Park Ave) **212/686-1600, 877/WHOTELS (reservations only)** *also Parisian-style cafe-bar*

■ BARS

9th Avenue Saloon [M,NH,K] 656 9th Ave (at 46th St) **212/307-1503** *noon-4am*

Adonis [M,S,$] 221 E 58th St (at Evolve) **845/536-3323** *7pm-1am Wed, M4M Weekly Strip Show*

Atlas Social Club 753 9th Ave (btw 59th & 51) **212/262-8527** *4pm-4am, decorated like an old school boxing gym*

Bar Centrale [GS] 324 W 46th St (at 8th Ave) **212/581-3130** *5pm-close, celebs a-plenty*

Bar Tini Ultra Lounge [M] 642 10th Ave (at 45th) **917/388-2897** *4pm-4am, theme nights*

Barrage [M] 401 W 47th St (at 9th Ave) **212/586-9390** *5pm-2am*

Don't Tell Mama [★GF,C,P,YC,$] 343 W 46th St (at 9th Ave) **212/757-0788** *4pm-4am, cover + 2-drink minimum for [C]*

Evolve [M,E,DS,S,V,GO] 221 E 58th St (at 2nd Ave) **212/355-3395** *4pm-4am, theme nights*

Fairytail Lounge [M,NH] 500 W 48th St **646/684-3897** *5pm-2am, tiny, trippy lounge*

Flaming Saddle's Saloon [MW,D,CW] 793 9th Ave **212/713-0481** *4pm-2am, from 2pm Sat-Sun*

Hardware [M] 697 10th Ave (at 48th) **212/924-9885** *4pm-2am*

HK Hell's Kitchen [MW] 523 9th Ave (at 39th St) **212/913-9092** *swank lounge, theme nights, also restaurant*

Industry [M] 355 W 52nd St (at 9th Ave) **646/476-2747** *4pm-4am*

New York • *USA*

Posh Bar & Lounge [M,NH] 405 W 51st St (at 9th Ave) **212/957-2222** *4pm-4am, popular happy hour, DJ nightly*

The Ritz [M,D,DS] 369 W 46th St (btwn 8th & 9th Aves) **212/333-2554** *4pm-4am, great place for a drink pre- or post-theater*

Therapy [MW,F,E,C] 348 W 52nd St (at 9th) **212/397-1700** *5pm-4am*

Townhouse Bar [M,E,C,P] 236 E 58th St (btwn 2nd Ave & 3rd Ave) **212/754-4649** *4pm-3am, till 4am Fri-Sat, upscale, dress code*

Vlada [M] 331 W 51st St (btwn 8th & 9th) **212/974-8030** *4pm-4am, slick gay lounge*

■NIGHTCLUBS

Escuelita [M,D,MR-L,TG,DS,S,18+,$] 301 W 39th St (at 8th Ave) **212/631-0588** *10pm-5am , clsd Mon & Wed*

The XL [M,D,E,C,DS] 512 W 42nd S **917/239-2999** *4pm-4am*

■RESTAURANTS

44 1/2 [WC,GO] 626 10th Ave (btwn 44 & 45) **212/399-4450** *5:30pm-close, brunch wknds*

44 & X Hell's Kitchen [WC,GO] 622 10th Ave (at 44th St) **212/977-1170** *lunch & dinner*

A Voce [R] 41 Madison Ave (at 26th) **212/545-8555** *lunch Mon-Fri, dinner nightly, Italian*

Arriba Arriba [★] 762 9th Ave (at 51st) **212/489-0810** *noon-midnight, till 1am wknds, Mexican, great margaritas*

Bamboo 52 344 W 52nd St (btwn 8th & 9th Aves) **212/315-2777** *noon-4am, from 4pm Sun, sushi, also sake bar, garden*

Bann 350 W 50th St (btwn 8th & 9th Aves) **212/582-4446** *lunch Mon-Fri, dinner nightly, Korean*

Lips [DS] 227 E 56th St (at 3rd Ave) **212/675-7710** *6pm-midnight, till 1:30am Fri-Sat, gospel brunch Sun, clsd Mon, full bar, "the ultimate in drag dining"*

Lucky Cheng's [★K,DS] 240 W 52nd St (btw B'way & 8th) **212/995-5500** *5:30pm-midnight, Asian/fusion, full bar, drag shows*

Market Cafe [GO] 496 9th Ave (at 38th St) **212/967-3892** *lunch & dinner, wknd brunch*

Vynl 754 9th Ave (at 51st St) **212/974-2003** *11am-11pm, also bar; also at 102 8th Ave*

■ENTERTAINMENT & RECREATION

Ars Nova 511 W 54th St (at 10th Ave) **212/489-9800** *many gay-themed productions*

Empire State Building 350 5th Ave (btwn 33rd & 34th) *spectacular views of the city; visit day or night*

Naked Boys Singing [WC] 340 W 50th St (btwn 8th & 9th) **212/302-4848** *Off-Broadway smash hit*

Sex & the City Hotspots Tour [R] 5th Ave, in front of the Pulitzer Fountain (at 58th St) **212/209-3370** *3 hours, reservations a must!*

■MEN'S CLUBS

➤**East Side Club** [★PC] 227 E 56th St, 6th flr (btwn 2nd & 3rd) **212/753-2222, 212/888-1884** *24hrs*

NYC—Uptown

■ACCOMMODATIONS

710 Guest Suites [GF] 710 St Nicholas Ave (at 145th) **212/491-5622** *modern, chic apt suites*

BB Lodges [GS,NS,WI,GO] 1598 Lexington Ave (btwn 101st & 102nd) **917/345-7914** *private rooms w/ private kitchens*

Harlem Renaissance House [GS,NS,WI,GO] **212/226-1590**

Hotel Newton [GS,NS,WC] 2528 Broadway (btwn 94th & 95th) **212/678-6500, 800/643-5553** *nearest hotel to Columbia University*

Mount Morris House B&B [GS,WI,GO] 12 Mount Morris Park W (at 121st St) **917/478-6214**

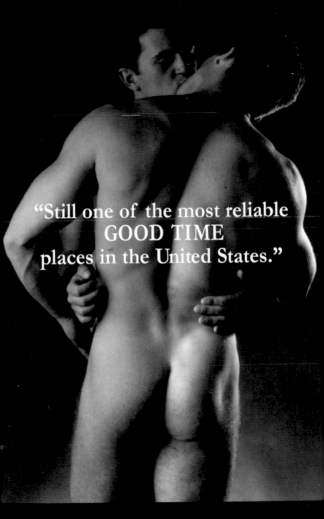

"Still one of the most reliable
GOOD TIME
places in the United States."

east side club

New York • USA

■BARS

Brandy's Piano Bar [MW,P] 235 E 84th St (at 2nd Ave) **212/650-1944** *4pm-4am, piano from 9:30pm*

Candle Bar [M,NH] 309 Amsterdam Ave (at 74th) **212/799-0062** *4pm-4am, from 3pm wknds*

Cava Wine Bar [GF] 185 W 80th St (at Amsterdam) **212/724-2282** *5:30pm-2am, from 3:30pm Sun, also tapas*

Suite [M,NH,K,DS] 992 Amsterdam (at 109th St) **212/222-4600** *5pm-4am*

Tool Box [M,NH,V] 1742 2nd Ave (at 91st St) **212/348-1288** *8pm-4am, cruisy*

■RESTAURANTS

Billie's Black [E,K,GO] 271 W 119th St (at St Nicholas Ave) **212/280-2248** *noon-midnight, till 4am Fri-Sat, soul food, also full bar, live music Th-Fri*

Joanne Trattoria 70 W 68th St (btw Columbus & Central Park W), New York **212/721-0068**

■EROTICA

Les Hommes 217-B W 80th St, 2nd flr (btwn Broadway & Amsterdam) **212/580-2445** *10am-2am, till 3am Fri Sat*

■CRUISY AREAS

The Rambles [AYOR] in Central Park

NYC—Brooklyn

■INFO LINES & SERVICES

Audre Lorde Project [TG] 85 S Oxford St **718/596-0342** *1pm-7pm Tue-Th only, LGBT center for people of color*

■ACCOMMODATIONS

Hotel Le Bleu [GF,WI] 370 4th Ave **718/625-1500, 866/427-6073**

Hotel Le Jolie [GF] 235 Meeker Ave **718/625-2100, 866/526-4097**

The Loralei B&B [GS,NS,WI,GO] 667 Argyle Rd (at Foster Ave) **646/228-4656** *1904 Victorian*

■BARS

The Abbey [GS,NH] 536 Driggs Ave (btwn N 7th & 8th), Williamsburg **718/599-4400** *3pm-4am*

Alligator Lounge [GS,F,K] 600 Metropolitan Ave (at Lorimer) **718/599-4440** *3pm-4am, from 1pm wknds, free pizza from 6pm*

Bar 4 [GS,NH,E] 444 7th Ave (at 15th St, in Park Slope) **718/832-9800** *6pm-4am, DJ Fri-Sat*

Branded Saloon [GS,NH,E,K,GO] 603 Vanderbilt Ave (at Bergen) **718/484-8704**

Excelsior [MW] 390 5th Ave (btwn 6th & 7th) **718/832-1599** *6pm-4am, from 2pm wknds, patio*

Ginger's Bar [MW,NH,E] 363 5th Ave (btwn 5th & 6th Sts, in Park Slope) **718/788-0924** *5pm-4am, from 2pm wknds, patio*

Metropolitan [MW,NH,D,WI] 559 Lorimer St (at Metropolitan Ave), Williamsburg **718/599-4444** *3pm-4am, comfy bar w/ fireplaces & patio*

Sugarland [MW,D,E,K] 221 N 9th St (at Driggs Ave) **718/599-4044** *9pm-4am*

This N That [MW,NH] 108 N 6th St (at Berry), Williamsburg **718/599-5959** *4pm-4am*

■NIGHTCLUBS

Club Langston [M,D,MR-AF] 1073 Atlantic Ave (btwn Franklin & Classon) **718/622-5183** *11pm-4am Th-Sun*

Glasslands Gallery [GS,D] 289 Kent Ave, Williamsburg (btwn S 1st & S 2nd) **718/599-1450** *performance, art & dance space*

Public Assembly [GF] 70 N 6th St **718/384-4586**

■CAFES

Outpost [MW,YC,BW,GO] 1014 Fulton St (at Downing) **718/636-1260** *7:30am-midnight, 9am-11pm wknds, also lounge, art gallery*

■RESTAURANTS

Alma 187 Columbia St (at Degraw) **718/643-5400** *dinner nightly, wknd brunch, upscale Mexican, outdoor rooftop seating w/ view of Manhattan, also B61 Bar downstairs*

Beast 638 Bergen St (at Vanderbilt Ave) **718/399-6855** *dinner nightly, wknd brunch, also bar from 5pm*

Bogota Latin Bistro [E,GO] 141 5th Ave (at St John's Pl) 718/230-3805 dinner nightly, wknd brunch, clsd Tue

ChipShop [★] 383 5th Ave (at 6th St) 718/244-7746 noon-10pm, till 11pm Th-Sat, from 11am wknds, home of the famous fried Twinkie!

home made [GO] 293 Van Brunt St (btwn Pioneer & King) 347/223-4135

Johnny Mack's [E] 1114 8th Ave (btwn 11th & 12th) 718/832-7961 4pm-2am, from noon wknds

Krescendo 364 Atlantic Ave famed chef Elizabeth Falkner makes pizza

Nita Nita 146 Wythe Ave (at N 8th) 718/388-5328 4pm-2am, brunch wknds, also full bar, tapas

Santa Fe Grill [WC] 62 7th Ave (at Lincoln) 718/636-0279 5pm-close, from noon wknds, also bar

Superfine [E,GO] 126 Front St (at Pearl St) 718/243-9005 11:30am-3am, 2pm-11pm Sat, 11am-10pm Sun, clsd Mon, also bar

Tandem 236 Troutman St (btwn Wilson & Knickerbocker, in Bushwick) 718/386-2369 6pm-4am, also full bar, occasional gay parties

■ENTERTAINMENT & RECREATION

Galapagos Art Space 16 Main St (at Water St) 718/222-8500 performance & art space; occasional gay parties

Ova the Rainbow [MW,TG,E] 59 Montrose Ave (at The Spectrum) monthly queer dance party

The Spectrum [MW,TG,E] 59 Montrose Ave queer performance space

■EROTICA

Babeland 462 Bergen St (at 5th Ave) 718/638-3820 noon-9pm, till 7pm Sun

NYC—Queens

■BARS

Albatross [GS,NH,GO] 36-19 24th Ave (at 37th), Astoria 718/204-9045 6pm-4am, more gay wknds

Bungalo Astoria [GS,F] 32-03 Broadway (at 32nd St) 718/204-7010 5pm-4am, from 3pm Fri-Sat, dress code

Elixir Lounge [M,D,K,DS] 43-03 Broadway, Astoria 347/642-5804

Friend's Tavern [M,NH,MR-L] 78-11 Roosevelt Ave, Jackson Hts 718/397-7256 4pm-4am, DJ Wed-Sun

Hell Gate Social [GS,D] 12-21 Astoria Blvd (at 14th St) 718/204-8313 7pm-4am

Hombres Lounge [M,NH,K] 85-25 37th Ave #206, Jackson Heights 718/930-0886 5pm-4pm

True Colors [M,NH,D,MR-L] 79-15 Roosevelt Ave (btwn 79th & 80th Sts, Jackson Hts) 718/672-7505 4pm-4am

■NIGHTCLUBS

Divine [M,D,DS,MR-L] 102-01 44th Ave, Corona 718/424-0900

Evolution [MW,D,MR-L,DS] 76-19 Roosevelt Ave (at 77th St), Jackson Hts 718/457-3939 4pm-4am

Lucho's Place [M,NH,D,TG,C,DS,18+,YC] 38-19 69th St, Woodside 718/424-9181 10pm-4am Wed-Sun

■RESTAURANTS

Monika's Cafe Bar 3290 36th St, Astoria 718/204-5273 10am-2am, till 4am Fri-Sat, Th gay night

■MEN'S CLUBS

Northern Men's Sauna [PC] 3365 Farrington St, Flushing 718/445-9775 11am-10pm, run-down

NYC—Bronx

■BARS

Le Boy [M,D,MR-L] 104 Dyckman St (at Nagle) 646/692-4630 6pm-4am Wed-Sun

No Parking [M,D,K,MR-L] 4168 Broadway (at 177th St) 212/923-8700 6pm-3am, go-go boys

■NIGHTCLUBS

Boyz Nightz/ Escandalo [M,D] 3534 Broadway (at 145th St, at El Morocco) 646/479-2361 Sun only, gay Latin night

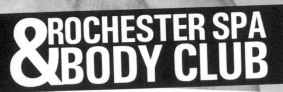

&ROCHESTER SPA
&BODY CLUB

NEW YORK STATE'S LEGENDARY SPA
NO MEMBERSHIP FEES EVER

ROOMS • LOCKERS • SUITES • FANTASY ROOMS
SNACKS & REFRESHMENTS • TANNING • SUNDECK
TOYS & NOVELTIES • VIDEO ROOMS • TV LOUNGE
FITNESS CENTER • FREE PARKING

109 LIBERTY POLE WAY, ROCHESTER NY 14604
WWW.ROCHESTERSPA.COM • 585 454 1074

Nyack

■ NIGHTCLUBS

Barz [MW,D,A,K] 327 Rte 9 W
845/353-4444 *8pm-4am, from 3pm Sun, clsd Sun-Mon*

Orange County

■ EROTICA

Exotic Gifts & Videos 658 Rte 211 E (exit 120, off Rte 17), Middletown **845/692-6664**

Rochester

■ INFO LINES & SERVICES

AA Gay/ Lesbian 17 Fitzhugh St (St Lukes & Simon Church) **585/232-6720** (AA#) *8pm Sun*

Gay Alliance of the Genesee Valley (GAGV) 875 E Main St, 5th flr **585/244-8640** *events, education, SAGE & youth services*

■ ACCOMMODATIONS

Silver Waters Bed & Breakfast [GS,GO] 8420 Bay St (at Lummis), Sodus Point **315/483-8098**

■ BARS

140 Alex Bar & Grill [MW,D,E,K,DS,V,GO] 140 Alexander St (at Broadway) **585/256-1000** *4pm-2am, from 2pm Sun, also restaurant*

Avenue Pub [★M,NH,D] 522 Monroe Ave (at Goodman) **585/244-4960** *4pm-2am, patio*

The Bachelor Forum [M,B,L] 670 University Ave (at Atlantic) **585/271-6930** *2pm-2am*

■ NIGHTCLUBS

Tilt Nightclub [GS,D,DS] 444 Central Ave **585/232-8440** *10pm-2:30am Th-Sat*

Vertex [GS,D] 169 N Chestnut St **585/232-5498** *10pm-2am Wed-Sat, goth club*

■ CAFES

Little Theatre Cafe [★E,BW,WC] 240 East Ave **585/258-0400** *5pm-10pm, till 11pm Fri-Sat, till 8pm Sun*

■ RETAIL SHOPS

Equal Grounds 750 South Ave (at Caroline) **585/256-2362** *7am-midnight, from 10am wknds, LGBT gifts & books, also coffeehouse*

Outlandish [GO] 274 N Goodman St (in the Village Gate) **585/760-8383** *11am-9pm, noon-5pm Sun*

■ PUBLICATIONS

Empty Closet **585/244-8640** *LGBT newspaper, resource listings*

■ MEN'S CLUBS

➤**Rochester Spa & Body Club** [PC] 109 Liberty Pole Way **585/454-1074** *24hrs*

■ MEN'S SERVICES

➤**McgaMates** **585/563-2820** *Call to hook up with HOT local men. FREE to listen & respond to ads. Use FREE code DAMRON. MegaMates.com.*

Saratoga Springs

■ ACCOMMODATIONS

The Inn at Round Lake [GF,SW,NS,WI,GO] 14 Covel Ave (at Burlington), Round Lake **518/899-4914** *Victorian B&B*

The Mansion [GF,NS,WC,GO] 801 Rte 29, Rock City Falls **518/885-1607, 888/996-9977** *1860 Victorian mansion, full brkfst*

■ BARS

Desperate Annie's [GF,NH] 12 Caroline St (off Broadway) **518/587-2455** *4pm-close*

■ RESTAURANTS

Esperanto [★YC] 6 1/2 Caroline St (off Broadway) **518/587-4236** *11am-close, doughboys!*

Little India [BW] 60 Court St **518/583-4151** *lunch & dinner*

Sharon Springs

■ ACCOMMODATIONS

American Hotel [GS,F,NS,WI,WC,GO] 192 Main St **518/284-2105** *1847 Nat'l Register hotel, also restaurant & bar*

Edgefield [GS,NS,GO] 153 Washington St **518/284-3339** *well-appointed English Country house*

The TurnAround Spa Lodge [MW,F,NS,GO] 105 Washington St **518/284-9708** *small hotel & health spa, full brkfst, hot tub*

Syracuse

■INFO LINES & SERVICES
AA Gay/ Lesbian 315/463-5011 (AA#) *call for meeting schedule*

■BARS
Rain Lounge [M,NH,MR,TG,E,K,GO] 103 N Geddes St **315/218-5951** *4pm-2:30am*

Wolf's Den [MW,NH,K] 617-619 Wolf St **315/560-5637** *4pm-2am, till midnight Sun-Tue, from noon Sun for brunch*

■NIGHTCLUBS
Trexx [M,D,DS,S,V,18+WC] 319 N Clinton St (exit 18, off Rte 81) **315/474-6408** *8pm-2am, till 4am Fri-Sat, clsd Sun-Wed, go-go dancers*

■RESTAURANTS
Cafe Mira [WC,GO] 14 Main St, Adams **315/232-4470** *open 5pm Wed-Sat only*

■EROTICA
Boulevard Books 2576 Erie Blvd E (at Seeley) **315/446-1595** *24hrs*

Salt City Book & Video 2807 Brewerton Rd **315/454-0629** *24hrs*

■CRUISY AREAS
Thornden Park [AYOR] *pink triangle rock*

Utica

■NIGHTCLUBS
That Place [M,D,YC,WC] 216 Bleecker St (at Genesee) *9pm-2am Th & Sat*

■RESTAURANTS
The Hadley [E,WC,GO] 2008 Genesee St (at Arnold Ave) **315/507-4264** *5pm-10pm, clsd Sun, also bar*

Westchester

■BARS
B Lounge [MW,D,K] 4 Broadway, Valhalla **914/437-5093** *5pm-1am, till 4am Wed-Fri, 8pm-4am Sat, 6pm-1am Sun*

White Plains

■INFO LINES & SERVICES
The LOFT 252 Bryant Ave **914/948-2932, 914/948-4922** (helpline) *LGBT community center, call for hours, also newsletter*

NORTH CAROLINA

Asheville

■INFO LINES & SERVICES
Lambda AA 9 Swan St (at Cathedral of All Souls Episcopal Church) **828/254-8539** (AA#), **800/524-0465** *7pm Mon & Wed, 8pm Fri*

■ACCOMMODATIONS
1889 WhiteGate Inn & Cottage [GS,NS,WI,GO] 173 E Chestnut St **828/253-2553, 800/485-3045**

The 1900 Inn on Montford [GF,NS,WI] 296 Montford Ave **828/254-9569, 800/254-9569**

Biltmore Village Inn [GF,NS,WI,GO] 119 Dodge St (at Irwin) **828/274-8707, 866/274-8779**

Cedar Crest Inn [GS,GO] 674 Biltmore Ave **828/252-1389 , 877/251-1389**

Mountain Laurel B&B [MW,NS,WI,GO] 139 Lee Dotson Rd, Fairview **828/628-9903, 828/712-6289** (cell)

North Lodge on Oakland B&B [GS,WI,GO] 84 Oakland Rd (at Victoria Rd) **828/252-6433, 800/252-3602**

The Tree House [W,TG,NS,GO] 190 Tessie Ln, Black Mountain **828/669-3889**

■BARS
O Henry's/ The Underground [M,NH,D,B,L,DS,WC] 237 Haywood St **828/254-1891** *4pm-2am; Underground from 10pm Fri-Sat only*

Smokey's After Dark [M,NH] 18 Broadway 828/253-2155 *4pm-2am*

Tressa's [GS,D,E] 28 Broadway 828/254-7072 *4pm-2:30am, from 6pm Sat, clsd Sun, jazz/ cigar bar*

■NIGHTCLUBS

Club Hairspray [MW,NH,D,E,K,C,DS] 38 N French Broad Ave (at Patton Ave) 828/258-2027 *8pm-2am, patio*

Scandals [MW,D,DS,V,18+,PC,WC] 11 Grove St (at Patton) 828/252-2838 *10pm-3am Th-Sun*

■CAFES

Edna's of Asheville [BW,WI,PC,WC,GO] 870 Merrimon Ave 828/255-3881 *6am-10pm*

Laurey's [★WC,GO] 67 Biltmore Ave 828/252-1500 *9am-6pm, till 4pm Sat, clsd Sun*

■RESTAURANTS

Avenue M 791 Merrimon Ave 828/350-8181 *5pm-late, 10am-2:30pm daily, clsd Mon, full bar*

Barley's Taproom & Pizzeria [E] 42 Biltmore 828/255-0504 *11:30am-2am, till midnight Sun*

Charlotte Street Grill & Pub [WI,GO] 157 Charlotte St 828/252-2948 *noon-2am*

Early Girl Eatery 8 Wall St 828/259-9292 *brkfst & lunch daily, dinner Tue-Sun, wknd brunch*

Firestorm Cafe & Books [E,WI] 48 Commerce St 828/255-8115 *10am-11pm, clsd Sun, vegetarian*

Laughing Seed Cafe [BW,WC] 40 Wall St (at Haywood) 828/252-3445 *11:30am-9pm, till 10pm Fri-Sat, Sun brunch from 10am, clsd Tue, vegetarian/ vegan, patio*

Table 48 College St 828/254-8980 *11am-2:30pm & 5:30pm-11pm, Sun brunch, clsd Tue*

Tupelo Honey Cafe 12 College St 828/255-4404 *9am-10pm*

■ENTERTAINMENT & RECREATION

LaZoom Tours [BYOB] 90 Biltmore Ave 828/225-6932 *city-wide comedy tours of Asheville, afternoons & evenings*

■BOOKSTORES

Malaprop's Bookstore/ Cafe [E] 55 Haywood St (at Walnut) 828/254-6734, 800/441-9829 *9am-9pm, till 7pm Sun*

■EROTICA

BedTyme Stories 2334 Hendersonville Rd, Arden 828/684-8250

■CRUISY AREAS

The Blue Ridge Parkway [AYOR] Sleepy Gap & Chestnut Cove overlooks (at mile marker 397 & 398)

Blowing Rock

■ACCOMMODATIONS

Blowing Rock Victorian Inn [GF,NS,WI,GO] 242 Ransom St (at US 321) 828/295-0034

Brevard

■ACCOMMODATIONS

Ash Grove Mountain Cabins & Camping [GS,NS,WI,GO] 749 E Fork Rd 828/885-7216 *camping & cabins*

Charlotte

■INFO LINES & SERVICES

Acceptance Group Gay/ Lesbian AA 2830 Dorcester Pl (at St. Paul United Methodist Church) 704/377-0244, 877/233-6853 *8pm Fri*

The Lesbian/ Gay Community Center 2508 N Davidson St 704/333-0144 *5pm-8pm Tue-Th, 10am-1pm Fri-Sat, clsd Sun-Mon*

■ACCOMMODATIONS

VanLandingham Estate [GF,NS,WI,GO] 2010 The Plaza (at Belvedere) 704/334-8909, 888/524-2020

■BARS

The Bar At 316 [★MW,NH,V,PC] 316 Rensselaer Ave (at South Blvd) 704/910-1478 *5pm-2am, from 3pm Sun*

Hartigan's Irish Pub [★GS,NH,D,F,E,K,WI,GO] 601 S Cedar St (at W Hill St) 704/347-1841 *11am-10pm, till 2am wknds, clsd Sun*

Petra's Piano Bar [GS,E,K,WI] 1917 Commonwealth Ave (at Thomas) **704/332-6608** *5pm-2am, clsd Mon*

Sidelines Sports Bar & Billiards [GF,NH,F,WI,PC,WC,GO] **704/525-2608** *4pm-2am, from noon wknds*

The Woodshed [M,NH,B,L,PC,WC] 4000 Queen City Dr (at Little Rock) **704/394-1712** *5pm-2am, from 3pm Sun, also patio bar*

■NIGHTCLUBS

Cathode Azure Club [M,D,DS] 1820 South Blvd (near East Blvd) **704/823-6066** *7pm-2am, from noon Sun*

Chasers [M,D,S,V,PC,WC] 3217 The Plaza (at 36th) **704/339-0500** *6pm-2am*

Marigny Dance Club [★GS,D,S] 1440 S Tryon St #110 **704/910-4444** *10pm-2am, clsd Sun-Wed*

The Nickel Bar [MW,D,MR-AF] **704/916-9389** *9pm-2am, from 5pm Sun, clsd Mon-Wed*

Scorpio's [★MW,D,MR,DS,V,18+,PC,WC] 2301 Freedom Dr (at Berryhill Rd) **704/373-9124** *9pm-3am Wed & Fri-Sun*

UpStage [GS,E] 3306 N Davidson St (at E 36th St) **704/430-4821** *performing arts and creative events*

■CAFES

Amelie's French Bakery 2424 N Davidson St **704/376-1781** *open 24hrs*

Smelly Cat Coffee 514 E 36th St **704/374-9656** *7am-10pm, till 1am Fri-Sat*

■RESTAURANTS

300 East [WC] 300 East Blvd (at Cleveland) **704/332-6507** *11am-10pm, Sun brunch, full bar*

Alexander Michael's 401 W 9th St (at Pine) **704/332-6789** *lunch & dinner, clsd Sun, full bar*

Cosmos Cafe 300 N College (at 6th) **704/372-3553** *11am-2am, clsd Sun, also martini lounge*

Dish 1220 Thomas Ave (at Central) **704/344-0343** *11am-10pm, till 11pm Fri-Sat, clsd Sun, patio*

Lupie's Cafe [★] 2718 Monroe Rd (near 5th St) **704/374-1232** *11am-10pm, from noon Sat, clsd Sun*

Penguin Drive-In 1921 Commonwealth Ave (at Thomas) **704/375-1925** *11am-1am, till 2am wknds, full bar*

■ENTERTAINMENT & RECREATION

One Voice Chorus [GO] PO Box 9241 28299

■BOOKSTORES

Paper Skyscraper [WC] 330 East Blvd (at Euclid Ave) **704/333-7130** *10am-7pm, till 6pm Sat, noon-5pm Sun, books & funky gifts*

White Rabbit Books 920 Central Ave (at E 10th) **704/377-4067** *10am-9pm, noon-6pm Sun, LGBT, also magazines, T-shirts, DVDs, novelties*

■PUBLICATIONS

Q Notes **704/531-9988** *bi-weekly LGBT newspaper for the Carolinas*

■MEN'S SERVICES

➤**MegaMates** **704/556-0006** *Call to hook up with HOT local men. FREE to listen & respond to ads. Use FREE code DAMRON. MegaMates.com.*

■EROTICA

Carolina Video Source 8829 E Harris Blvd (at Albemarle Rd) **704/566-9993**

Hwy 74 Video & News 3514 Barry Dr (at Wilkinson Blvd) **704/399-7907**

■CRUISY AREAS

Freedom Park [AYOR]

Fayetteville

■NIGHTCLUBS

Alias [MW,D,MR,TG,E,S,V,18+,PC,GO] 984 Old McPherson Church Rd (at Raeford Rd) **910/484-7994** *9pm-2:30am Fri-Sat only*

■EROTICA

Cupid's Boutique 137 N Reilly Rd (at Morganton) **910/860-7716**

Fort Video & News 4431 Bragg Blvd (near 401 overpass) **910/868-9905** *24hrs*

Priscilla McCall's 3800 Sycamore Dairy Rd (at Bragg Blvd) 910/860-1776

Greensboro

■INFO LINES & SERVICES

Live & Let Live AA 617 N Elm St (at Presbyterian Church) 336/854-4278 (AA#) 8pm Tue; also Free Spirit, 8pm Sat, 2105 W Market St (at Episcopal Church)

■ACCOMMODATIONS

Biltmore Greensboro Hotel [GS,NS,WI,GO] 111 W Washington St (at Elm St) 336/272-3474, 800/332-0303

O Henry Hotel [GF,SW,WC] 624 Green Valley Rd (at Benjamin Pkwy) 336/854-2000, 800/965-8259 bar/ restaurant popular w/ local gay community

■BARS

The Q [MW,NH,D,18+,WI] 708 W Market St 336/272-2587 4pm-close, from 9pm Sat, from 7pm Sun, patio

■NIGHTCLUBS

Chemistry [M,D,K,DS] 2901 Spring Garden St 336/617-8571 8pm-2:30am, from 5pm Fri & Sun

Warehouse 29 [M,D,DS,S,V,18+,PC] 1011 Arnold St 336/333-9333 9:30pm-2:30am Th-Sun, T-dance Sun (summers), also patio bar

■MEN'S SERVICES

►**MegaMates** 336/617-2032 Call to hook up with HOT local men. FREE to listen & respond to ads. Use FREE code DAMRON. MegaMates.com.

■EROTICA

New Vision Video & News [PC,$] 507 Mobile St (off Randleman Rd) 336/274-6443

Greenville

■CRUISY AREAS

Green Springs Park [AYOR] 5th St (behind Pizza Hut)

Havelock

■NIGHTCLUBS

Club Above & Beyond [MW,D,DS,PC] 114 Crocker Rd 252/266-0114 open 8pm, from 10pm Sat, clsd Wed

Hickory

■NIGHTCLUBS

Club Cabaret [MW,D,S,WI,PC,WC] 101 N Center St (at 1st Ave) 828/322-8103 8pm-2am, from 9pm Fri-Sat, clsd Mon-Wed

■CAFES

Taste Full Beans [GO] 29 2nd St NW 828/325-0108 7am-5:30pm, till 2:30pm Sat, clsd Sun, art exhibits

Jacksonville

■EROTICA

Priscilla McCall's 113-A Western Blvd 910/355-0765

Little Switzerland

■ACCOMMODATIONS

La Petite Chalet [GS,GO] 38 Orchard Ln (at Hwy 226A) 888/828-1654

Madison

■ACCOMMODATIONS

Hunter House B&B [GS,SW,NS,WI,GO] 216 W Hunter St 336/445-4730 patio, gardens, pets on premises

Mooresville

■RESTAURANTS

Pomodoro's Italian American Cafe [BW,WC,GO] 168 Norman Station Blvd 704/663-6686 11am-10pm, till 11pm Fri-Sat

Raleigh/Durham/Chapel Hill

■INFO LINES & SERVICES

Common Solutions Gay/ Lesbian AA Crownwell Bldg, East Campus (at Duke University), Durham 919/286-9499 (AA#) 6:30pm Mon

LGBT Center of Raleigh 411 Hillsborough St, Raleigh 919/832-4484

North Carolina • *USA*

■ACCOMMODATIONS

Heartfriends Inn B&B [GS,WI,WC,GO] 4389 Siler City/Snow Camp Rd (at Ed Clapp Rd), Siler City 919/663-1707, 877/679-0980

The King's Daughters Inn [GF] 204 N Buchanan Blvd, Durham 919/354-7000, 877/534-8534

■BARS

Flex [★M,B,E,K,DS,PC] 2 S West St (at Hillsborough), Raleigh 919/832-8855 *5pm-close, from 2pm Sun*

Hibernian Restaurant & Pub [GF,F,E] 311 Glenwood Ave (at W Lane St), Raleigh 919/833-2258 *11am-2am*

■NIGHTCLUBS

313 [M,D,MR,P,DS,18+,WI,PC,WC] 313 W Hargett St (at Harrington), Raleigh 919/755-9599 *8pm-close*

The Bar [MW,D,E,K,PC,GO] 711 Rigsbee Ave, Durham 919/956-2929 *4pm-2am*

Icon Nightclub [MW,D,DS,K,MR-AF,18+,PC,WC] 320 E Durham Rd, Cary 919/460-4343 *8pm-2am Tue & 9pm-3:30am Fri-Sat*

Legends/ View [MW,D,DS,S,YC,PC,WC] 330 W Hargett St (at S Harrington St), Raleigh 919/831-8888 *5pm-2:30am*

The Pinhook [GS,E] 117 W Main St, Durham 991/667-1100 *5pm-2am, 6pm-midnight Sun, patio*

Stir [M,D] 157 E Rosemary (at The Thrill), Chapel Hill 919/929-0024 *9pm Sun only*

The T [MW] 423 W Franklin St (at the Lantern), Chapel Hill 919/969-8846 *10pm Tue only, chic, eclectic crowd*

■CAFES

Bean Traders 105-249 W NC Hwy 54, Durham 919/484-2499 *6am-8pm, from 8am wknds*

Cafe Helios [F,BW] 413 Glenwood Ave (at North St), Raleigh 919/838-5177 *7am-10pm, 8am-6pm Sun*

Caffe Driade [E,BW] 1215 E Franklin St #A (at Elizabeth St), Chapel Hill 919/942-2333 *7am-11pm*

Third Place [F] 1811 Glenwood Ave (at W Whitaker Mill Rd), Raleigh 919/834-6566 *6am-7pm*

■RESTAURANTS

Blu Seafood & Bar 2002 Hillsborough Rd (at 9th St), Durham 919/286-9777 *lunch & dinner, clsd Sun*

The Borough [WI] 317 W Morgan St, Raleigh 919/832-8433 *4pm-2am, also bar*

Crooks Corner [WC] 610 Franklin St (at Merritt Mill Rd), Chapel Hill 919/929-7643 *dinner nightly, Sun brunch, clsd Mon, Southern cooking, full bar*

Dain's Place [WI] 754 9th St (at Markham), Durham *11am-2am, from 5pm Mon, 9am Sat, great burgers & pub food, also bar*

Elmo's Diner 776 9th St (in the Carr Mill Mall), Durham 919/416-3823 *6:30am-10pm*

Five Star 511 W Hargett St (at West St), Raleigh 919/833-3311 *5:30pm-2am, Asian-fusion*

Humble Pie 317 S Harrington St (at Martin), Raleigh 919/829-9222 *5pm-11pm, bar open late, brunch only Sun, small plates*

Irregardless Cafe [E] 901 W Morgan St (at Hillsborough), Raleigh 919/833-8898 *lunch Tue-Fri, dinner Tue-Sat, Sun brunch, clsd Mon*

Lantern 423 W Franklin St, Chapel Hill 919/969-8846 *dinner nightly, clsd Sun, Asian, also cocktail lounge till 2am*

The Mad Hatter's Bakeshop & Cafe [WI] 1802 W Main St (at Broad), Durham 919/286-1987 *7am-9pm, 8am-3pm Sun*

The Pit 328 W Davie St (at S Dawson), Raleigh 919/890-4500 *11am-10pm, till 11pm wknds, upscale BBQ*

Rue Cler 401 E Chapel Hill St (at Mangum St), Durham 919/682-8844 *lunch & dinner, wknd brunch, French*

Solas 919/755-0755 *dinner, Sun brunch, upscale dining, dress code, also rooftop lounge & nightclub*

Spotted Dog 111 E Main St (at N Greensboro St), Carrboro **919/933-1117** *11:30am-midnight, clsd Mon, plenty veggie*

Sunrise Biscuit Kitchen 1305 E Franklin St, Chapel Hill **919/933-1324** *great brkfst, drive-thru only*

Vivace 4209 Lassiter Mill Rd #115 (at Pamlico Dr), Raleigh **919/787-7747** *lunch & dinner, Sun brunch, Italian, patio seating, full bar*

■BOOKSTORES

Internationalist Books & Community Center 405 W Franklin St (at Kenan St), Chapel Hill **919/942-1740** *11am-8pm, noon-6pm Sun, progressive/ alternative, cooperatively run*

Quail Ridge Books 3522 Wade Ave (at Ridgewood Center), Raleigh **919/828-1588, 800/672-6789** *9am-9pm, LGBT section*

The Regulator Bookshop 720 9th St (btwn Hillsborough & Perry), Durham **919/286-2700** *10am-9pm, noon-6pm Sun*

■MEN'S SERVICES

►**MegaMates 919/829-7300** *Call to hook up with HOT local men. FREE to listen & respond to ads. Use FREE code DAMRON. MegaMates.com.*

■EROTICA

Capitol Blvd News 2236 Capitol Blvd, Raleigh **919/831-1400**

Castle Video & News 1210 Capitol Blvd, Raleigh **919/836-9189** *24hrs*

Cherry Pie [18+] 1819 Fordham Blvd, Chapel Hill **919/928-0499** *10am-midnight*

Eagles/ Videos for the Mature 9016 Glenwood Ave, Raleigh **919/787-0016** *24hrs*

Frisky Business Boutique 1720 New Raleigh Hwy, Durham **919/957-4441**

Our Place 327 W Hargett (at Harrington), Raleigh **919/833-8968**

Rocky Mount

■NIGHTCLUBS

Liquid Nightclub [M,D,A,S,MR-AF,AYOR] 313 Falls Rd **252/266-6464** *8pm-3am Sat only*

Washington

■CAFES

Back Water Jack's Tiki Bar [WC] 1052 E Main St (at Havens St) **252/975-1090** *lunch & dinner, clsd Mon, also bar*

Wilmington

■ACCOMMODATIONS

Best Western Coastline Inn [GS,NS,WC,WI,GO] 503 Nutt St **910/763-2800**

Rosehill Inn B&B [GF,NS,WI] 114 S 3rd St (at Dock St) **910/815-0250, 800/815-0250**

The Taylor House Inn [GS,NS] 14 N 7th St **910/763-7581, 800/382-9982**

■BARS

Costello's [M,E,P,V,PC,WC,GO] 211 Princess St (btwn 2nd & 3rd) **910/470-9666** *7pm-2am, from 5pm Fri*

Tool Box [M,NH,D,K,WI,GO] 2325 Burnett Blvd **910/343-6988** *7pm-1am, till 2am Th-Sat*

■NIGHTCLUBS

Ibiza [M,D,K,DS,S,YC,PC,WC,GO] 118 Market St (rear) **910/251-1301** *8pm-3am Wed-Sun only*

■RESTAURANTS

Caffe Phoenix [GO] 9 S Front St **910/343-1395** *11:30am-10pm, Sun brunch, Mediterranean, some veggie*

■ENTERTAINMENT & RECREATION

Cinematique 310 Chestnut St (at Thalian Hall) **910/343-1640** *classic, foreign & notable films*

Winston-Salem

■MEN'S SERVICES

►**MegaMates 336/201-5553** *Call to hook up with HOT local men. FREE to listen & respond to ads. Use FREE code DAMRON. MegaMates.com.*

■EROTICA

New Vision Video & News 1045 N Cherry St (at N Huff) **336/725-8034** *also* 3061 Kennersville Rd, 336/788-0020

NORTH DAKOTA

Fargo

■INFO LINES & SERVICES

Pride Collective & Community Center 116 12th St S (at Main Ave), Moorhead, MN **218/287-8034** *6pm-7:30pm Tue, referrals, support/ social groups, check www.pridecollective.com for events*

■ACCOMMODATIONS

The Hotel Donaldson [GS,F,WI] 101 Broadway **701/478-1000** , **888/478-8768**

■CAFES

Atomic Coffee [F,WI] **701/478-6160** *7am-11pm, 8pm-10pm Sun*

■RESTAURANTS

Fargo's Fryn' Pan [★WC] 300 Main St (at 4th) **701/293-9952** *24hrs*

Mom's Kitchen 1322 Main St **701/235-4460** *6am-10pm, full bar*

■RETAIL SHOPS

Zandbroz Variety 420 N Broadway **701/239-4729** *9am-8pm, noon-5pm Sun, books & gifts*

■EROTICA

Romantix Adult Superstore 417 N Pacific Ave **701/235-2640** *9am-3am*

■CRUISY AREAS

Island Park [AYOR] *near pool*

Grand Forks

■EROTICA

Romantix Adult Superstore 102 S 3rd St (at Kittson) **701/772-9021**

Mandan

■EROTICA

Risque's II 2113 Memorial Hwy **701/663-9013**

Minot

■EROTICA

Risque's 1514 S Broadway **701/838-2837**

■CRUISY AREAS

Rest Area [AYOR] Hwy 2 (10 miles E of town)

OHIO

Statewide

■PUBLICATIONS

Gay People's Chronicle **216/916-9338** *Ohio's largest bi-weekly LGBT newspaper w/ extensive listings*

Outlook 614/268-8525 *statewide LGBT newsweekly*

Akron

■INFO LINES & SERVICES

AA Intergroup 330/253-8181 (AA#)

Akron Pride Center 895 N Main St **330/252-1559** *call for meeting schedule*

■BARS

Adams Street Bar [★M,D,F,P,S,WI] 77 N Adams St (at Upson) **330/434-9794** *4pm-2am, from 9pm Sun, [P] Wed*

Cocktails [M,D,DS,V] 1009 S Main St (at Crosier) **330/376-2625** *11am-2:30am, Daddy's [L] upstairs wknds*

The Office Bistro & Lounge [GF,NH,MR,P,WI,WC] 778 N Main St (at Cuyahoga Falls Ave) **330/376-9550** *11am-2:30am, bistro & lounge, bi-sexual friendly*

Tear-Ez [MW,NH,DS,WI,WC] 360 S Main St (near Exchange St) **330/376-0011** *11am-2:30am, from noon Sun*

■NIGHTCLUBS

Interbelt [MW,D,DS,S,V] 70 N Howard St (near Perkins & Main) **330/253-5700** *9pm-2:30am, patio*

Square [M,D,E,K,WC,GO] 820 W Market St (near Portage Path) **330/374-9661** *5pm-2:30am, from 8pm Sat, from 7pm Sun*

■CAFES

Angel Falls Coffee Company
[WC,WI,GO] 792 W Market St (btwn S Highland & Grand) 330/376-5282
7am-10pm, patio

■RESTAURANTS

Aladdin's Eatery 782 W Market St (at Grand) 330/535-0110 *11am-10pm, Middle Eastern*

Bricco [GO] 1 W Exchange St (at S Main St) 330/475-1600 *11am-midnight, till 1am Fri-Sat, 4pm-9pm Sun, Italian, also bar*

Bruegger's Bagels 1821 Merriman Rd 330/867-8394 *6am-4pm*

■MEN'S CLUBS

Akron Steam & Sauna [PC] 41 S Case Ave (near River Rd) 330/252-2791 *noon-midnight, 24hrs wknds*

■MEN'S SERVICES

►**MegaMates** 330/315-3000 *Call to hook up with HOT local men. FREE to listen & respond to ads. Use FREE code DAMRON. MegaMates.com.*

Brunswick

see also Akron & Cleveland

■RESTAURANTS

Pizza Marcello 67-A Pearl Rd (near Boston Rd) 330/225-1211 *3pm-close, from noon wknds, Italian*

Canton

■NIGHTCLUBS

Crew [MW,D,K,C] 304 Cherry Ave NE (at 3rd) 330/452-2739 *6pm-2:30am, from 9pm Sat-Sun*

Cincinnati

■INFO LINES & SERVICES

AA Gay/ Lesbian 328 W McMillan St (enter at 445 Herman St), Corryville 513/351-0422 (AA#) *8pm Wed, call for locations of wknd meetings*

Gay/ Lesbian Community Center of Greater Cincinnati 4119 Hamilton Ave (near Blue Rock) 513/591-0200 *6pm-9pm, noon-4pm Sat, clsd Sun*

■ACCOMMODATIONS

Cincinnatian Hotel [GF,NS,WI,WC] 601 Vine St (at 6th St) 513/381-3000, 800/942-9000 *restaurant & lounge*

Crowne Plaza [GF,SW,WI,WC] 5901 Pfeiffer Rd (at I-71) 513/793-4500, 800/468-3597

First Farm Inn [GF,NS,WI,WC] 2510 Stevens Rd, Petersburg, KY 859/586-0199 *20 minutes from Cincinnati*

Millennium Hotel Cincinnati [GF,SW,WI,WC] 150 W 5th St 513/352-2100, 800/876-2100 *outdoor rooftop pool & sundeck*

Weller Haus B&B [GF,NS,WI] 319 Poplar St, Bellevue, KY 859/391-8315, 800/431-4287

■BARS

Below Zero Lounge [GS,D,F,E,K,WI] 1120 Walnut St (at E Central Pkwy) 513/421-9376 *4pm-2:30am, clsd Mon-Tue*

Junkers Tavern [GF,NH,K,E] 4158 Langland St (at Chase) 513/541-5470 *9am-1am, live bands*

The Main Event [GS,NH] 835 Main St (at 9th) 513/421-1294 *6am-2:30am, from 11am Sun*

Milton's [GF,NH] 301 Milton St (at Sycamore) 513/784-9938 *4pm-2:30am*

On Broadway [M,NH,CW,B,L,K,DS,V,GO] 817 Broadway (at 9th) 513/421-2555 *4pm-2:30am*

The Serpent [M,L] 4042 Hamilton Ave (at Blue Rock) 513/681-6969 *9pm-2:30am,clsd Mon*

Shooters [M,D,CW,K,S] 927 Race St (at Court) 513/381-9900 *4pm-2:30am, [K] Wed*

Simon Says [★M,NH,P,WC] 428 Walnut St (at 5th) 513/381-7577 *11am-2:30am, from 1pm Sun*

■NIGHTCLUBS

Adonis [MW,D,TG,DS] 4601 Kellogg Ave (at Stites Rd) 513/871-1542 *9pm-3am Sat only*

The Cabaret [M,DS] 1122 Walnut St (at E Central Pkwy) 513/284-2050 *10pm-2am Th-Sun*

Ohio • USA

The Dock [★MW,D,DS,MR-AF,19+,WC]
603 W Pete Rose Wy (near Central)
513/241-5623 *10pm-3am, till 4am
Fri-Sat, clsd Mon-Wed*

■CAFES

College Hill Coffee Co [E,WI,WC] 6128
Hamilton Ave (at North Bend Rd)
513/542-2739 *6:30am-6:30pm, till
10pm Fri, 8:30am-10pm Sat, till 4pm
Sun, clsd Mon*

Zen & Now [WI] 4453 Bridgetown Rd
513/598-8999 *7am-7pm, till 10pm
Fri-Sat, clsd Sun*

■RESTAURANTS

Boca [WC] 3200 Madison Rd (at Brazee
St), Oakley 513/542-2022 *dinner Tue-
Sat, clsd Sun-Mon, full bar*

Honey [WC] 4034 Hamilton Ave (at
Blue Rock) 513/541-4300 *dinner &
Sun brunch, clsd Mon, casual fine dining*

The Loving Hut 6227 Montgomery Rd
(at Woodmont) 513/731-2233 *11am-
7pm, clsd Sun-Mon, vegetarian/ vegan*

Melt Eclectic Deli 4165 Hamilton Ave
(at Lingo St) 513/681-6358 *11am-
9pm, 10am-3pm Sun*

Myra's Dionysus 121 Calhoun St (at
Dennis St) 513/961-1578 *11am-
10pm, till 11pm Fri-Sat, from 5pm Sun,
diverse menu, plenty veggie*

Tucker's [WC] 1637 Vine St (at Green)
513/721-7123 *great brkfst hole in
wall, vegan too*

■ENTERTAINMENT & RECREATION

Ensemble Theatre of Cincinnati 1127
Vine St (at 12th) 513/421-3555

Know Theatre 1120 Jackson St (at
Central Pkwy) 513/300-5669
contemporary multicultural theater

■RETAIL SHOPS

Park & Vine 1202 Main St
513/721-7275 *eco-friendly
merchandise*

Pink Pyramid 907 Race St (btwn 9th &
Court) 513/621-7465 *noon-9pm, till
11pm Fri-Sat, 1pm-7pm Sun, pride items,
also leather*

■PUBLICATIONS

CNKY Scene 513/309-9729 *LGBT
publication*

Gay People's Chronicle
440/986-0051

■MEN'S SERVICES

➤**MegaMates** 513/821-4500 *Call to
hook up with HOT local men. FREE to
listen & respond to ads. Use FREE code
DAMRON. MegaMates.com.*

Cleveland

■INFO LINES & SERVICES

AA Gay/ Lesbian 6600 Detroit Ave (at
LGBT Center) 216/241-7387,
800/835-1935

LGBT Community Center [WC] 6600
Detroit Ave 216/651-5428 *1pm-8pm,
clsd wknds*

■ACCOMMODATIONS

Clifford House [GS,NS,WI,GO] 1810 W
28th St (at Jay) 216/589-0121 *near
downtown*

Radisson Hotel Cleveland–Gateway
[GF,WI,WC] 651 Huron Rd (at Prospect)
216/377-9000, 800/967-9033

Stone Gables B&B [GS,WI,WC,GO]
3806 Franklin Blvd (at W 38th)
216/961-4654, 877/215-4326 *full
brkfst, sauna*

■BARS

ABC The Tavern [GF,NH,F] 1872 W
25th St 216/861-3857 *4pm-2:30am,
from noon wknds, dive bar w/ great food*

Bounce [★MW,F,V,GO] 2814 Detroit Ave
(at W 28th) 216/357-2997 *5pm-
2:30am*

Cocktails Cleveland [★M,D,L,B,K,S,V,WI]
9208 Detroit Ave (at W 93rd St)
216/961-3115 *4pm-2:30am, patio*

The Hawk [MW,NH,WC] 11217 Detroit
Ave (at 112th St) *noon-2:30am, from
1pm Sun*

Leather Stallion Saloon [★M,NH,B,L,F]
2205 St Clair Ave (near E 21st St)
216/589-8588 *4pm-2am, DJ Sun,*

Now That's Class [GF,NH,E,WC] 11213
Detroit Ave (at 112th St) 216/221
-8576 *4pm-close, punk & metal bands;
food served, plenty veggie/ vegan*

Twist [★MW,NH,D,P] 11633 Clifton (at 117th St) **216/221-2333** *11:30am-2:30am, from noon Sun*

■NIGHTCLUBS

Mean Bull 1313 E 26th St (at St Clair) **216/812-3304** *11:30pm-2:30am Fri-Sat only*

■CAFES

Grumpy's Cafe 2621 W 14th St **216/241-5025** *7am-9pm, till 3pm Sun-Mon*

Gypsy Beans & Baking Co [★WI,WC] 6425 Detroit Ave (at W 65th St, next to Cleveland Public Theatre) **216/939-9009** *7am-9pm, till 11pm Fri-Sat, fresh-baked gourmet pastries, soups, sandwiches*

Lucky's Cafe [WI,WC] 777 Starkweather Ave (at Professor Ave) **216/622-7773** *7am-5pm, 8am-3pm wknds, popular wknd brunch, cafe & bakery, outdoor seating*

Phoenix Coffee [★E,WI,WC] 2287 Lee Rd (at Essex), Cleveland Heights **216/932-8227** *6am-10pm, till 11pm Fri, from 7am Sat, 7am-7pm Sun, great sandwiches, patio*

■RESTAURANTS

Ali Baba [★BYOB] 12021 Lorain Ave (at W 120th St) **216/251-2040** *5pm-10pm Th-Sat, the best Middle Eastern food you'll have outside the Middle East, plenty veggie*

Bar Cento [BW,WC] 1948 W 25th St (at Lorain Ave) **216/274-1010** *4:30pm-2am, from noon Sat, great pizza*

Battiste & Dupree Cajun Grill & Bar [WC] 1992 Warrensville Ctr Rd (at Wyncote) **216/381-3341** *lunch & dinner, clsd Sun-Mon*

Cafe Tandoor [WC] 2096 S Taylor Rd (at Cedar), Cleveland Heights **216/371-8500** *lunch & dinner, 3pm-9pm Sun, Indian*

The Coffee Pot 12415 Madison Ave (at Robin), Lakewood **216/226-6443** *6am-4pm, till 3pm Sat, till 2pm Sun, clsd Mon, diner*

Crop Bistro 2537 Lorain Ave (at 25th) **216/696-2767** *lunch Tue-Fri, dinner nightly, clsd Mon, innovative American*

Diner on Clifton [M] 11637 Clifton Blvd (at W 117th St) **216/521-5003** *7am-11pm*

Flying Fig 2523 Market Ave (at W 25th St) **216/241-4243** *lunch & dinner, wknd brunch*

The Greenhouse Tavern 2038 E 4th St **216/241-5025** *11am-11pm, till 1am Fri-Sat*

Hecks [★WC] 2927 Bridge Ave (at W 30th) **216/861-5464, 800/677-8592** *lunch & dinner, brunch Sun, gourmet burgers*

Hodge's 668 Euclid Ave **216/771-4000** *11am-10pm, from 4pm wknds, global comfort food*

The Inn on Coventry [WC] 2785 Euclid Heights Blvd (at Coventry), Cleveland Heights **216/371-1811** *7am-8:30pm, from 8:30am-3pm wknds, homestyle, popular Bloody Marys*

Johnny Mango World Cafe & Bar 3120 Bridge Ave (btwn Fulton & W 32nd, in Ohio City) **216/575-1919** *11am-10pm, till 11pm Fri-Sat, healthy world food & juice bar, also full bar till 1am*

Latitude 41N [WI,WC,GO] 5712 Detroit Ave (at W 58th St, Detroit Shoreway) **216/961-0000** *8am-9pm, till 10pm Fri, till 3pm Sun, restaurant & cafe*

Lolita 900 Literary Rd (at Professor Ave, in Tremont) **216/771-5652** *5pm-11pm, till 1am Fri-Sat, 4pm-9pm Sun, clsd Mon, upscale cont'l, full bar*

Luchita's [★] 3456 W 117th St (at Governor) **216/252-1169** *lunch & dinner, clsd Mon, Mexican, full bar*

Luxe [E,WC] 6605 Detroit Ave (at W 65th St) **216/920-0600** *5pm-midnight, lounge till 2am, gourmet comfort food, also lounge*

Momocho [WC] 1835 Fulton Rd (at Woodbine Ave) **216/694-2122** *5pm-close, from 4pm Sun, modern Mexican, also bar*

My Friend's Deli & Restaurant [WI,BW] 11616 Detroit Ave (at W 117th) **216/221-2575** *24hrs*

Pearl of the Orient [WC] 19300 Detroit Rd (in Beachcliff Market Sq), Rocky River **440/333-9902** *lunch & dinner, pan-Asian, some veggie, also restaurant on East Side*

Tommy's [WI,WC] **216/321-7757** *9am-9pm, till 10pm Fri, 7:30am-10pm Sat, plenty veggie, great milkshakes*

■ENTERTAINMENT & RECREATION

Rock & Roll Hall of Fame 1100 Rock & Roll Blvd (at E 9th & Lake Erie) **216/781-ROCK** *even if you don't like rock, stop by & check out IM Pei's architectural gift to Cleveland*

■BOOKSTORES

Loganberry Books 13015 Larchmere Blvd, Shaker Heights **216/795-9800** *10am-6pm, till 8pm Th, clsd Sun, used & rare books*

Mac's Backs 1820 Coventry Rd (next to Tommy's), Cleveland Heights **216/321-2665** *10am-9pm, till 10pm Fri-Sat, 11am-8pm Sun, great new & used, 3 floors, reading series, some LGBT titles*

■RETAIL SHOPS

The Dean Rufus House of Fun 1422 W 29th St (at Detroit) **216/348-1386** *1pm-midnight, till 2:30am Fri-Sat, clsd Mon, clothing, DVDs*

Torso [GO] 11520 Clifton Blvd (at Warren), Lakewood **216/862-3987** *11am-9pm, till 5pm Sun, clsd Mon, clothing*

■PUBLICATIONS

Gay People's Chronicle **216/916-9338** *Ohio's largest bi-weekly LGBT newspaper w/ extensive listings*

■MEN'S CLUBS

Flex [★MR,SW,V,PC] 2600 Hamilton Ave **216/812-3304** *24hrs*

■MEN'S SERVICES

►**MegaMates** **216/912-6000** *Call to hook up with HOT local men. FREE to listen & respond to ads. Use FREE code DAMRON. MegaMates.com.*

■EROTICA

Adult Mart 16700 Brookpark Rd (at W 150th) **216/267-9019**

Adult Mart 19121 Neff Rd **216/738-0133**

Bank News 4025 Clark Ave (at W 41st St) **216/281-8777** *general magazine store w/ section for adult videos, magazines, toys*

Inz & Outz 11424 Lorain Ave (at W 115th St) **216/251-3330** *11am-10pm, noon-5pm Sun, "one stop GLBT shop"*

Rocky's Entertainment & Emporium 13330 Brookpark Rd (at W 130th) **216/267-4659**

Columbus

■INFO LINES & SERVICES

AA Gay/ Lesbian **614/253-8501, 800/870-3795** (in OH)

Stonewall Columbus Community Center/ Hotline [WC] 1160 N High St (at E 4th Ave) **614/299-7764** *9am-5pm, clsd wknds*

■ACCOMMODATIONS

The Blackwell [GF,F,WI] 2110 Tuttle Park Pl (at Lane Ave) **614/247-4000, 866/247-4000** *on OSU campus*

Harrison House B&B [GF,NS,WI] 313 W 5th Ave (at Neil Ave) **614/421-2202, 800/827-4203**

The Lofts [GF,WI] 55 E Nationwide Blvd (at High St) **614/461-2663, 800/735-6387**

The Westin Columbus [GF] 310 S High St (at Main) **614/223-3800, 800/937-8461**

■BARS

Arch City Tavern [★MW,NH,D,F,K,E] 862 N High (at 1st Ave) **614/421-9697** *6pm-2am, clsd Mon, karaoke, live bands*

AWOL [M,NH,K,WC] 49 Parsons Ave (at Oak) **614/621-8779** *2pm-2:30am, from noon wknds*

The Bow Wow [M,NH] 1602 S 4th St **614/444-5520** *strippers*

Cavan Irish Pub [GF,E,K] 1409 S High St (at Jenkins) **614/725-5502** *2pm-2:30am, from noon wknds*

Columbus • Ohio

Club 20 [M,NH,K] 20 E Duncan (at N Pearl) 614/261-9111 *noon-2:30am, from 1pm Sun, patio*

Club Diversity [MW,E,P,WI] 863 S High St (at Whittier) 614/224-4050 *4pm-midnight, till 2:30am Fri, noon-2:30am Sat*

Exile [★M,NH,L,S,WC] 893 N 4th St (at 2nd Ave) 614/299-0069 *4pm-2:30am*

Inn Rehab [M,D,F,K,DS] 627 Greenlawn Ave (at Harmon) 614/754-7326 *11am-2:30am*

Level Dining Lounge [GS,F,D,K,WC] 614/754-7111 *11am-2:30am*

Slammers [W,D,F,E,WI,WC] 202 E Long St (at N 5th St) 614/221-8880 *11am-12:30am, till 2:30am Fri-Sat, from 4pm wknds, clsd Mon-Tue*

The South Bend Tavern [MW,NH,DS,WC] 126 E Moler St (at 4th St) 614/444-3386 *noon-2:30am*

Tremont [M,NH,OC] 708 S High St (at Frankfort) 614/445-9365 *1pm-2:30am*

Union Cafe [★MW,F,V,WI,WC] 782 N High St (at Hubbard) 614/421-2233 *11am-2:30am*

NIGHTCLUBS

Axis [★M,D,C,DS,S,18+,WC,GO] 775 N High St (at Hubbard) 614/291-4008 *10pm-2:30am Fri-Sat only, also Pump lounge*

Wall Street [★MW,D,CW,DS,P,YC,WC] 144 N Wall St (at Spring St) 614/464-2800 *9pm-2:30am, from 10pm Wed, 8pm-midnight Th, clsd Mon-Tue*

CAFES

Cup O Joe Cafe [F,WI,WC] 627 S 3rd St (at Sycamore) 614/221-1563 *6am-10pm, till 11pm Fri-Sat, from 7am wknds, till 10pm Sun*

RESTAURANTS

Alana's Food & Wine 2333 N High St (at Patterson) 614/294-6783 *from 5pm, clsd Sun-Tue*

Banana Leaf [WC] 816 Bethel Rd (at Olentangy River Rd) 614/459-4101 *11:30am-9:30pm, vegetarian/ vegan Indian*

Betty's [E] 680 N High St 614/228-6191 *11am-2am, plenty veggie, also bar*

Blue Nile 2361 N High St (at W Patterson) 614/421-2323 *lunch & dinner, clsd Mon, Ethiopian*

Cap City Diner 1299 Olentangy River Rd (at W 5th) 614/291-3663 *11am-10pm, till 11pm Fri-Sat, till 9pm Sun*

L'Antibes [WC,GO] 772 N High St #106 (at Warren) 614/291-1666 *dinner from 5pm, clsd Sun-Mon*

Lemongrass [★R] 641 N High (at Russell) 614/224-1414 *lunch & dinner, clsd Sun-Mon, Asian*

Northstar Cafe [★] 951 N High St (at W 2nd Ave) 614/298-9999 *9am-10pm, plenty veggie*

Surly Girl Saloon [E] 1126 N High St (at W 4th Ave) 614/294-4900 *11am-2am, plenty veggie, also bar*

Till 247 King Ave 614/298-9986 *lunch & dinner, wknd brunch, patio*

Tip Top Kitchen & Cocktails 73 E Gay St (at 3rd St) 614/221-8300 *11am-2am*

Whole World Bakery & Restaurant [WC] 3269 N High St (at W Como Ave) 614/268-5751 *11am-8pm, Sun brunch, clsd Mon, vegetarian/ vegan*

BOOKSTORES

The Book Loft of German Village 631 S 3rd St (at Sycamore) 614/464-1774 *10am-11pm, till midnight Fri-Sat, LGBT section*

RETAIL SHOPS

Hausfrau Haven 769 S 3rd St (at Columbus) 614/443-3680 *10am-7pm, noon-5pm Sun, cards, wine & gifts*

Piercology [GO,WC] 190 W 2nd Ave (at Hunter Ave) 614/297-4743 *noon-8pm*

Schmidt's Fudge Haus 220 E Kossuth St (in Historic German Village) 614/444-2222 *noon-close, old fashioned fudge & candy, gifts*

Ohio • *USA*

Torso [GO] 772 N High St (at Warren) 614/421-7663 *11am-10pm, till 5pm Sun-Mon, clothing*

■PUBLICATIONS

Gay People's Chronicle 440/986-0051

Outlook Weekly 614/268-8525 *statewide LGBT weekly*

■MEN'S CLUBS

The Club Columbus [SW] 795 W 5th Ave (at Olentangy River Rd) 614/291-0049 *gym, steam, sauna*

■MEN'S SERVICES

▶**MegaMates** 614/888-7777 *Call to hook up with HOT local men. FREE to listen & respond to ads. Use FREE code DAMRON. MegaMates.com.*

■EROTICA

The Garden 1174 N High St (btwn 4th & 5th Ave) 614/294-2869 *11am-3am, noon-midnight Sun*

The Lion's Den Adult Superstore 4315 Kimberly Pkwy (off Hamilton Rd) 614/861-6770 *6am-midnight*

Dayton

■INFO LINES & SERVICES

AA Gay/ Lesbian 20 W 1st St (off Main, at Christ Episcopal Church) 937/222-2211 *8pm Sat*

Greater Dayton Lesbian/ Gay Center 117 E 3rd St 937/274-1776

■ACCOMMODATIONS

Dayton Marriott [GF] 1414 S Patterson Blvd 937/223-1000, 800/450-8625

■BARS

MJ's Cafe [M,D,F,K,S] 119 E 3rd St (at S Jefferson) 937/223-3259 *3pm-2:30am, deck*

Stage Door [M,L,WC] 44 N Jefferson St (at 2nd) 937/223-7418 *3pm-2:30am*

■NIGHTCLUBS

Masque [★M,D,DS,S,18+] 34 N Jefferson St (btwn 2nd & 3rd) 937/228-2582 *8pm-2:30am, till 5am wknds*

■CAFES

Expressions Coffee House 937/308-8345 *7am-9pm, 9am-2pm Sat, clsd Sun, live music*

■RESTAURANTS

Cold Beer & Cheeseburgers [WC] 33 S Jefferson St (at 4th St) 937/222-2337 *11am-close, clsd Sun, grill, full bar*

The Spaghetti Warehouse 36 W 5th St (at Ludlow) 937/461-3913 *11am-10pm, till 11pm wknds, more gay Tue w/ Friends of the Italian Opera*

■BOOKSTORES

Books & Co 4453 Walnut St (in Greene Shopping Ctr) 937/429-2169 *9am-11pm, till 8pm Sun*

■PUBLICATIONS

Gay Dayton 937/623-1590 *monthly LGBT publication*

■MEN'S SERVICES

▶**MegaMates** 937/395-9001 *Call to hook up with HOT local men. FREE to listen & respond to ads. Use FREE code DAMRON. MegaMates.com.*

■EROTICA

Adult Total X [V] 6388 N Dixie Dr (at Needmore Ave) 937/454-9999

Findlay

■EROTICA

Findlay Adult Books & Video 623 Trenton Ave (at I-75, exit 159) 419/422-1301

Kent

■BARS

The Zephyr Pub [GF,E] 106 W Main St (at Water St) 330/678-4848 *3pm-close*

Lima

■NIGHTCLUBS

Somewhere in Time [MW,D,DS,S] 804 W North St (at Baxter) 419/227-7288 *5pm-2:30am, from 8pm wknds*

Logan

■ACCOMMODATIONS

Glenlaurel—A Scottish Country Inn [GS,NS,WC] 14940 Mt Olive Rd (off State Rte I-80), Rockbridge 740/385-4070, 800/809-7378 *full brkfst, hot tub*

Inn & Spa at Cedar Falls [GS,NS,WI,WC] 21190 State Rte 374
740/385-7489, 800/653-2557

Lazy Lane Cabins [GF,NS]
740/385-3475, 877/225-6572
secluded cabins sleep 2-8, hot tubs, fireplaces

Lorain

■BARS

Tim's Place [MW,NH,D,DS,WC] 2223
Broadway (btwn 22nd & 23rd)
440/218-2223 *8pm-2:30am, clsd Mon, patio*

Monroe

■BARS

Old Street Saloon [MW,NH,D,K,DS] 13
Old St (at Elm St) **513/539-9183**
8pm-2am Th-Sat, till 1am Wed, clsd Sun-Tue

Niles

■EROTICA

Niles Books 5970 Youngstown Warren
Rd (off Rte 46) **330/544-3755**

Oberlin

■ACCOMMODATIONS

Hallauer House B&B [GF,SW,WI] 14945
Hallauer Rd **440/774-3400,
877/774-3406** *eco-friendly historic
inn 3 miles S of Oberlin*

■RESTAURANTS

The Feve [★NS] 30 S Main St (at
College St) **440/774-1978** *11am-
midnight, popular weekend brunch,
plenty veggie, full bar from 5pm*

Weia Teia [WC] 9 S Main St (at College
St) **440/774-8880** *lunch & dinner,
Thai/ Asian fusion, upscale, some veggie*

■BOOKSTORES

MindFair Books 13 W College St
(shares storefront w/ Ben Franklin)
440/774-6463 *10am-6pm, till 8pm
Fri, noon-5pm Sun*

Oxford

■CRUISY AREAS

Hueston Woods State Park [AYOR]
mornings & at dusk

Perrysville

■ACCOMMODATIONS

Circle JJ Ranch [M,21+] 1104
Amsterdam Rd SE, Scio **330/627-3101**
*open April-Oct, special events, theme
wknds*

Quaker City

■EROTICA

The Lion's Den Adult Superstore
65799 Batesville Rd (exit 193, off I-70)
740/758-5210 *24hrs*

Sandusky

■NIGHTCLUBS

Crowbar [MW,NH,D,K,GO] 206 W Market
St (at Jackson St) **419/624-0109**
6pm-2:30am, clsd Tue

■RESTAURANTS

Mona Pizza Gourmet [MR,TG,GO] 135
Columbus Ave (at Market St)
419/626-8166 *11am-10pm, till 3am
wknds*

■CRUISY AREAS

Boeckling Boat Dock [AYOR]

Springfield

■NIGHTCLUBS

Diesel [GF,D,E,K] 1912-14 Edwards Ave
(at N Belmont Ave) **937/324-0383**
8:30pm-2:30am, clsd Mon-Tue, patio

■CRUISY AREAS

Clarence J Brown Reservoir Beach
[AYOR]

Steubenville

■EROTICA

Past Time Adult Bookstore & Arcade
118 N 6th St **740/282-1907**

Toledo

■INFO LINES & SERVICES

AA Gay/ Lesbian 3535 Executive Pkwy
(at Unity) **419/380-9862** *8pm Wed*

■ACCOMMODATIONS

Mansion View Inn [GF,NS,WI] 2035
Collingwood Blvd (at Irving)
419/244-5676 *1887 Victorian near
downtown*

Ohio • USA

BARS

Blush [M,DS] 119 N Erie St
419/255-4010 *9pm-2:30am Fri-Sat only*

Outskirts [W,D,K,18+] 5038 Lewis Ave
419/476-1577 *5pm-2:30am, till midnight Sun & Wed, clsd Mon, Tue & Th*

R House [M,D] 5534 Secor Rd (btwn Laskey & Alexis) 419/474-2929 *4pm-2:30am, patio*

Rip Cord [M,NH,K,S,DS,F] 115 N Erie St (btwn Jefferson & Monroe)
419/243-3412 *9am-2:30am, Sun brunch*

NIGHTCLUBS

Bretz [MW,D,K,DS,S,18+,WC] 2012 Adams St 419/243-1900 *9pm-2:30am, till 4:30am Fri-Sat, clsd Mon-Tue, patio*

MEN'S CLUBS

Diplomat Health Club [PC] 1313 N Summit St (along Maumee River) 419/255-3700 *24hrs*

MEN'S SERVICES

►**MegaMates** 419/873-3000 *Call to hook up with HOT local men. FREE to listen & respond to ads. Use FREE code DAMRON. MegaMates.com.*

Warren

NIGHTCLUBS

Club 441 [MW,D,S,WC] 441 E Market St (at Vine, enter rear) 330/394-9483 *4pm-2:30am, from 2pm wknds*

The Funky Skunk [M,D,DS,K] 143 E Market St (at Park Ave) *9pm-close*

West Lafayette

RESTAURANTS

Lava Rock Grill at Unusual Junction [WC,GO] 56310 US Hwy 36 740/545-9772 *'50s-style diner in restored railroad station*

Yellow Springs

RESTAURANTS

Winds Cafe & Bakery [WC] 215 Xenia Ave (at Cory St) 937/767-1144 *lunch & dinner, Sun brunch, clsd Mon, full bar*

Youngstown

BARS

Mineshaft [M,NH] 1105 Poland Ave
330/207-6437

NIGHTCLUBS

Liquid Niteclub [MW,D,K] 1281 Salt Springs Rd 234/855-0351 *4pm-2:30am, from 8pm Sat-Sun*

Split Level/ Pulse [MW,D,DS,K] 169 S Four Mile Run Rd (at S Mahoning Ave) 330/318-9830

Utopia Video Nightclub [MW,D,DS] 876 E Midlothian Blvd (at Zedaker St) 330/781-9000 *5pm-close, clsd Mon*

CAFES

The Lemon Grove Cafe [F,BW,E] 122 W Federal Plaza W (at Hazel St) 330/744-7683 *7am-2am, from 11am wknds, events, movies, art, food served, also bar*

OKLAHOMA

Bartlesville

CRUISY AREAS

Johnstone Park [AYOR]

Grand Lake

ACCOMMODATIONS

Southern Oaks Resort & Spa [GF,SW,NS,GO] 2 miles S of Hwy 28/ 82 Junction, Langley 918/782-9346, 866/452-5307 *19 cabins on 30 acres*

RESTAURANTS

The Artichoke Restaurant & Bar 35896 S Hwy 82, Langley 918/782-9855 *5pm-10pm, clsd Sun-Mon*

Frosty & Edna's Cafe Highway 28, Langley 918/782-9123 *6am-9:30pm*

Lighthouse Supper Club Highway 85 & Main, Ketchum 918/782-3316 *5pm-9pm,, clsd Sun-Tue*

Lawton

CRUISY AREAS

The Strip [AYOR] Fort Sill Blvd, near Cache Rd *by car*

Oklahoma • *USA*

Oklahoma City

■INFO LINES & SERVICES

AA Live & Let Live 3405 N Villa
405/947-3834 *8pm Mon*

■ACCOMMODATIONS

➤**Habana Inn** [★MW,SW,NS,WC] 2200
NW 39th St (at Youngs)
405/528-2221, 800/988-2221
(reservations only) *gay resort, also 3
bars, restaurant, gift shop*

Hawthorn Suites [GF,SW,WI] 1600 NW
Expy (Richmond Square)
405/840-1440, 800/527-1133

Waterford Marriott [GF,SW,NS,WI]
6300 Waterford Blvd (at Pennsylvania)
405/848-4782 *also restaurant & bar*

■BARS

Alibi's [GS,NH,TG,GO] 1200 N
Pennsylvania (at NW 11th)
405/605-3795 *noon -2am*

The Boom [MW,NH,F,K,DS,WI,WC] 2218
NW 39th St (at Pennsylvania)
405/601-7200 *4pm-2am, from 11am
Sun, clsd Mon*

Edna's [GF,NH,F] 5137 N Classen Blvd
(at NW 51st) 405/840-3339 *2pm-
2am, from noon wknds, dive bar*

➤**The Finishline** [MW,NH,D,CW,WC] at
Habana Inn **405/525-2900** *noon-
2am, poolside bar*

Hi-Lo Club [MW,NH,D,E,DS] 1221 NW
50th St (btwn Western & Classen)
405/843-1722 *noon-2am, live bands*

KA's [W,NH,K,WI,WC] 2024 NW 11th (at
Pennsylvania) **405/525-3734** *3pm-
close, from 5pm Mon, clsd Tue, beer bar*

➤**The Ledo** [MW,F,K,NS,WC] at Habana
Inn **405/525-0730** *4pm-10:30pm, till
2am Fri-Sat, martini lounge*

Partners 4 Club [W,NH,D,E,K,WC] 2805
NW 36th St (at May Ave)
405/602-2030

Partners Too [MW,D,WC] 2807 NW
36th St (at May Ave) **405/942-2199**
open Wed-Sat

Phoenix Rising [M,NH,D,CW,B,L,GO]
2120 NW 39th St (at Pennsylvania Ave)
405/601-3711 *4pm-2am, from 2pm
Sun, patio*

Tramps [M,D,S,WI,WC] 2201 NW 39th St
(at Barnes) **405/521-9888** *noon-2am,
from 10am wknds*

■NIGHTCLUBS

➤**The Copa** [★MW,D,E,DS,K,S,WC] at
Habana Inn **405/525-0730** *9pm-2am,
clsd Mon, male dancers Fri-Sat*

The Park [★M,D,S,V,WC] 2125 NW 39th
St (at Pennsylvania) **405/528-4690**
*5pm-2am, from 3pm Sun (free buffet),
patio, cruisy*

Wreck Room [★MW,D,DS,S,YC] 2127
NW 39th St (at Pennsylvania)
405/525-7610 *10pm-close Fri-Sat
only, [18+] after 1am*

■CAFES

The Red Cup [F,E,NS,WI] 3122 N
Classen Blvd (at NW 30th St)
405/525-3430 *7am-5pm, till 8pm Th-
Fri, from 9am wknds, vegetarian*

■RESTAURANTS

Bricktown Brewery Restaurant 1 N
Oklahoma Ave (at Sheridan)
405/232-2739 *11am-10pm, till
midnight Sat, from noon Sun, full bar*

Cheever's Cafe [R] 2409 N Hudson Ave
(at NW 23rd) **405/525-7007** *11am-
9:30pm, 5pm-10:30pm Sat*

Earl's Rib Palace 216 Johnny Bench
Dr, Ste BBQ (in Bricktown)
405/272-9898 *11am-9pm, till 10pm
Fri-Sat, noon-8pm Sun*

➤**Gusher's** [WC] at Habana Inn
405/525-0730 *11am-10:30pm, from
9am wknds, till 3:30am Fri-Sat (after-
hours brkfst)*

Iguana Bar & Grill 9 NW 9th St (at N
Santa Fe Ave) **405/606-7172** *lunch &
dinner, Mexican*

Ingrid's Kitchen 3701 N Youngs (btwn
Penn & May, on NW 36th)
405/946-8444 *7am-8pm,10am-2pm
Sun, German/ American bakery & deli*

Pops 660 W Hwy 66, Arcadia
405/928-7677 *brkfst, lunch & dinner,
diner fare, look for the 66-foot tall soda
bottle*

Rococo Restaurant & Fine Wine
2824 N Pennsylvania (at NW 27th St)
405/528-2824 *lunch Mon-Fri, dinner
nightly, Sun jazz brunch, full bar*

Someplace Else Deli & Bakery [★] 2310 N Western Ave **405/524-0887** *7am-6:30pm, 9:30am-4pm Sat, clsd Sun*

Sushi Neko 4318 N Western (btwn 42nd & 43rd) **405/528-8862** *11am-11pm, clsd Sun*

Ted's Cafe Escondido 8324 S Western Ave (at 84th St) **405/635-8337** *lunch & dinner, Tex-Mex*

■ ENTERTAINMENT & RECREATION

First Friday Gallery Walk from 28th at N Walker to 30th at N Dewey **405/525-2688** *open tour of Paseo Arts District galleries, first Fri-Sat*

■ BOOKSTORES

Full Circle Bookstore [F] 50 Penn Pl, 1900 NW Expwy (in NE corner of 1st level) **405/842-2900, 800/683-7323** *10am-9pm, noon-5pm Sun, also cafe & coffee bar*

■ RETAIL SHOPS

➤**Jungle Red** [WC] at Habana Inn **405/524-5733** *novelties, leather, gifts*

■ PUBLICATIONS

Oklahoma Gazette **405/528-6000** *"Metro OKC's independent weekly"*

■ MEN'S SERVICES

➤**MegaMates** **405/524-3838** *Call to hook up with HOT local men. FREE to listen & respond to ads. Use FREE code DAMRON. MegaMates.com.*

■ EROTICA

Christie's Toy Box 7914 N MacArthur **405/720-2453** *multiple locations in OKC*

Naughty & Nice 3121 SW 29th St (at I-44) **405/681-5044** *24hrs*

■ CRUISY AREAS

Trosper Park [AYOR] *beware cops (!)*

Tulsa

■ INFO LINES & SERVICES

Dennis R Neill Equality Center [WC] 621 E 4th St (at Kenosha) **918/743-4297** *3pm-9pm, clsd Sun, also Pride store*

Gay/ Lesbian AA 2545 S Yale Ave (at Community of Hope) **918/627-2224** *5:30pm Sat*

■ ACCOMMODATIONS

The Mayo Hotel [GF,F,WI,WC] 115 W 5th St **918/582-6296**

Tulsa Hyatt [GF,F,SW,WI,WC] 100 E Second St (at 2nd St) **918/582-9000, 800/980-6429**

■ BARS

Bamboo Lounge [M,NH,D,K,DS,WC] 7204 E Pine **918/836-8700** *noon-2am*

Club 209 [GS,E,K] 209 N Boulder Ave (at Brady) **918/584-9944** *7pm-2am, clsd Mon-Wed*

End Up [M,S] 5336 E Admiral Pl **918/836-0915** *4pm-2am, from noon Tue*

New Age Renegade [MW,NH,K,C,S] 1649 S Main St (at 17th) **918/585-3405** *4pm-2am, patio*

Tulsa Eagle [★M,NH,K,L,WI,WC] 1338 E 3rd (at Peoria) **918/592-1188** *2pm-2am*

The Yellow Brick Road [MW,NH,WC] 2630 E 15th St (at Harvard) **918/293-0304** *1pm-2am*

■ NIGHTCLUBS

Club Majestic [MW,D,DS,TG,YC,Wi,WC,GO] 124 N Boston (at Brady) **918/584-9494** *9pm-2am Th-Sun*

■ CAFES

Gypsy's Coffee House [E,WI] 303 N Cincinnati Ave **918/295-2181** *7am-10pm, till 2am Fri-Sat, from 10am Sat-Sun*

■ RESTAURANTS

Cancun International [BW,WC] 705 S Lewis Ave (at 11th) **918/583-8089** *11am-9pm, from 10am Sat-Sun, clsd Wed*

Eloté [WC] 514 S Boston Ave **918/582-1403** *11am-10pm, till 2pm Mon, clsd Sun, fresh Mexican & full bar*

James E McNellie's Public House [WC] 409 E 1st St **918/382-7468** *11am-2am, great burgers & full bar*

Oklahoma • *USA*

White Lion Pub 6927 S Canton Ave (off 71st) **918/491-6533** *4pm-10pm, clsd Sun-Mon, British-style pub*

Wild Fork [WC] 1820 Utica Square **918/742-0712** *7am-10pm, clsd Sun*

■ENTERTAINMENT & RECREATION

Gilcrease Museum 1400 N Gilcrease Museum Rd **918/596-2700, 888/655-2278** *one of the best collections of Native American & cowboy art in the US*

Philbrook Museum of Art 2727 S Rockford Rd (1 block E of Peoria, at end of 27th St) **918/324-7941** *clsd Mon, Italian villa built in the '20s oil boom complete w/ kitschy lighted dance flr, the gardens are a must in spring & summer*

■PUBLICATIONS

Urban Tulsa Weekly **918/592-5550** *"Tulsa Metro's only independent newsweekly"*

■MEN'S SERVICES

➤**MegaMates** **918/663-2700** *Call to hook up with HOT local men. FREE to listen & respond to ads. Use FREE code DAMRON. MegaMates.com.*

■EROTICA

Midtown Superstore 319 E 3rd St (at Elgin) **918/584-3112** *24hrs*

OREGON

Ashland

■INFO LINES & SERVICES

Gay/ Lesbian AA **541/732-1850**

■ACCOMMODATIONS

The Arden Forest Inn [GS,NS,SW,WI,WC,GO] 261 W Hersey St (at N Main) **541/488-1496, 800/460-3912** *full brkfst*

Ashland Creek Inn [GF,NS,GO] 70 Water St **541/482-3315** *gourmet brkfst*

Country Willows B&B Inn [GF,SW,NS,WI,WC] 1313 Clay St (at Siskiyou Blvd) **541/488-1590, 800/945-5697** *full brkfst*

Lithia Springs Resort [GS,NS,WI] 2165 W Jackson Rd (at N Main) **541/482-7128, 800/482-7128**

Romeo Inn B&B [GF,SW,NS,WI] 295 Idaho St **800/915-8899** *full brkfst, jacuzzi*

■RESTAURANTS

The Black Sheep Pub & Restaurant [E,WI] 51 N Main St (on the Plaza) **541/482-6414** *11:30am-1am*

Greenleaf Restaurant [BW] 49 N Main St (on The Plaza) **541/482-2808** *8am-8pm, creekside dining*

■BOOKSTORES

Bloomsbury Books 290 E Main St (btwn 1st & 2nd) **541/488-0029** *8:30am-9pm, 10am-6pm Sun*

■RETAIL SHOPS

Travel Essentials 252 E Main St **541/482-7383, 800/258-0758** *10am-5:30pm, 11am-5pm Sun, luggage, books, accessories*

■CRUISY AREAS

Keno Rock Quarry *take Dead Indian Memorial Rd past Howard Prairie Lake to mile marker 18, turn right at Keno Rd, when you see pile of gravel on your left, turn right into quarry*

Bend

■ACCOMMODATIONS

Dawson House Lodge [GF,NS,WI] 109455 Hwy 97 N, Chemult **541/365-2232, 888/281-8375** *rustic inn w/ modern amenities, near Crater Lake*

■CRUISY AREAS

Drake Park [AYOR] Riverside Dr *clsd winter*

Sawyer Park [AYOR] *evenings*

Eugene

■INFO LINES & SERVICES

Gay/ Lesbian AA 1166 Oak St (at First Christian Church) **541/342-4113** *7pm Th, Fri & Sat & 5pm Sun*

■ACCOMMODATIONS

C'est La Vie Inn [GF,NS,WI] 1006 Taylor St (at W 10th) **541/302-3014, 866/302-3014** *full brkfst*

Valley River Inn [GF,SW,NS,WI,WC]
1000 Valley River Wy 541/743-1000,
800/543-8266

■ NIGHTCLUBS

Diablo's Downtown Lounge [GF,D,E,K]
959 Pearl St 541/343-2346 *1pm-
2:30am, from 3pm wknds*

■ CAFES

Eugene Coffee Company [GO] 240 E
17th St 541/344-0002 *7am-6pm*

■ RESTAURANTS

Glenwood Restaurant 1340 Alder St
(at 13th Ave) 541/687-0355 *7am-
9pm*

Keystone Cafe 395 W 5th Ave (at
Lawrence) 541/342-2075 *7am-3pm,
popular brkfst*

■ ENTERTAINMENT & RECREATION

**Glassbar Island Nude Beach/
Willamette River Beach** [GS] on the
Coast Fork (Franklin Blvd and I-5) *nude
beach, also hiking & biking, www.glass-
barisland.org for details*

■ EROTICA

Exclusively Adult 1166 South A St (at
10th St), Springfield 541/726-6969
8pm-midnight, 24hrs Th-Sun

■ CRUISY AREAS

Skinner Butte Park [AYOR]

Idleyld Park

■ ACCOMMODATIONS

**Umpqua's Last Resort Wilderness
RV Park & Campground** [GS,WI,GO]
115 Elk Ridge Ln 541/498-2500

Jacksonville

■ ACCOMMODATIONS

The TouVelle House [GF,SW,NS,WI] 455
N Oregon St (at E St) 541/899-8938,
800/846-8422 *1916 Craftsman*

Klamath Falls

■ ACCOMMODATIONS

Crystal Wood Lodge [GF,NS,WI,GO]
38625 Westside Road (at Hwy 140)
541/381-2322, 866/381-2322

■ CRUISY AREAS

Haglestein Park [AYOR] Hwy 97 (about
10 miles N of town, past Klamath Lake)

Moore Park [AYOR] *summers*

Medford

■ EROTICA

Castle Megastore 1601 Riverside
541/608-9540

■ CRUISY AREAS

Jackson County Sports Park [AYOR]

Touvelle Park [AYOR] along Rogue
River

Ontario

■ CRUISY AREAS

Ontario State Park [AYOR] on the
Snake River

Portland

see also Vancouver, Washington

■ INFO LINES & SERVICES

Live & Let Live Club 1210 SE 7th Ave
503/238-6091 *12-step meetings*

Q Center [WI] 4115 N Mississippi Ave
(at N Mason St) 503/234-7837 *LGBTQ
community center*

■ ACCOMMODATIONS

The Ace Hotel [GS,NS,WI,WC] 1022 SW
Stark (at 11th) 503/228-2277 *hip
hotel for "cultural influencers on a
budget"*

Hotel deLuxe [GF,NS,WI] 729 SW 15th
Ave (at SW Morrison) 503/219-2094,
866/895-2094

Hotel Monaco Portland [GF,WI] 506
SW Washington (at 5th Ave)
503/222-0001, 866/861-9514 *also
restaurant, gym*

Hotel Vintage Plaza [★GF,WI,WC] 422
SW Broadway (at SW Washington)
503/228-1212, 800/263-2305
upscale, also restaurant

Inn at Northrup Station [GF] 2025
NW Northrup St (at NW 21st)
503/224-0543, 800/224-1180 *cute,
colorful boutique hotel*

Jupiter Hotel [GF,NS,WI,WC] 800 E
Burnside 503/230-9200,
877/800-0004

The Lion & the Rose [GS,NS,WI,GO] 1810 NE 15th Ave (at NE Schuyler) **503/287-9245, 800/955-1647** *in 1906 Queen Anne mansion*

The Mark Spencer Hotel [GF,NS,WI] 409 SW Eleventh Ave (near Stark) **503/224-3293, 800/548-3934**

McMenamins Crystal Hotel [GS,SW,WI] 303 SW 12th Ave (at Stark) **503/972-2670, 855/205-3930** *former bathouse, also restaurant & bar*

The Nines [GF,WI,WC] 525 SW Morrison St **877/229-9995** *great art, rooftop deck & bar with vew of the west side*

Portland's White House B&B [GS,NS,WI,GO] 1914 NE 22nd Ave (at NE Hancock St) **503/287-7131, 800/272-7131** *in 1911 Greek Revival mansion*

Riverplace Hotel [GF] 1510 SW Harbor Way **503/228-3233** *restaurant & bar*

■ BARS

Boxxes [★M,D,K,V,WI,WC] 1035 SW 11th Ave (at SW 11th) **503/226-4171** *5pm-close, also Brig [MW,D], also Red Cap Garage*

CC Slaughter's [★M,D,CW,F,K,V,WI,WC] 219 NW Davis St (at 3rd) **503/248-9135, 888/348-9135** *3pm-2am, also martini lounge, Bear Night 4th Fri*

Chopsticks Express II [GS,F,K,YC,WC] 2651 E Burnside St (at NE 26th Ave) **503/234-6171** *noon-2am*

Crush [★GS,F,WI,WC] 1400 SE Morrison (at SE 14th) **503/235-8150** *4pm-2am, clsd Mon, wine & martini bar*

Darcelle XV [GS,F,C,DS,S,WC] 208 NW 3rd Ave (at NW Davis St) **503/222-5338** *6pm-11pm, till 2am Fri-Sat, clsd Sun-Tue*

Eagle Portland [M,B,L,N,WC] 835 N Lombard Ave (at N Albina Ave) **503/283-9734** *2pm-2:30am*

Fox & Hounds [★M,WC] 217 NW 2nd Ave (btwn Everett & Davis) **503/243-5530** *11am-2am, also restaurant, brunch wknds*

JOQ's Tavern [M,NH,F,WC] 2512 NE Broadway (at NE 25th Ave) **503/287-4210** *1pm-2am*

Moonstar [GS] 7410 NE Martin Luther King Jr Blvd (at NE Lombard St) **503/285-1230** *11am-1:30am*

Rotture [GF,E] 315 SE 3rd Ave (at SE Pine) **503/234-5683** *9pm-2:30am, live music venue*

Scandals [M,NH,K,E,F,WC,GO] 1125 SW Stark St (at SW 12th) **503/227-5887** *noon-2am, friendly bar*

Shaker and Vine [GS,NS] 2929 SE Powell Blvd (at SE 29th) **503/231-8466** *1pm-9pm, till 11pm Th, till midnight Fri-Sat, "Portland's first rock 'n' roll wine shop," retail & lounge*

Silverado [★M,D,F,K,S,WC,GO] 318 SW 3rd Ave (at SW Oak St) **503/224-4493** *9am-2:30am, strippers*

Starky's [★M,NH,F,WC] 2913 SE Stark St (at SE 29th Ave) **503/230-7980** *11am-2am, also restaurant, Sun brunch, patio*

Vault Martini Bar [GS,F,WC] 226 NW 12th Ave (btwn 12th & Davis Sts) **503/224-4909** *4pm-1am, till 2am Th-Sat, 1pm-10pm Sun, full menu*

■ NIGHTCLUBS

Casey's [M,D,K] 610 NW Couch St (at 6th) **503/505-9468** *11am-2:30am*

Embers [★M,D,F,DS,WC] 110 NW Broadway (at NW Couch St) **503/222-3082** *11am-2am, also restaurant*

Escape [MW,D,DS,V] 333 SW Park (btwn SW Oak & SW Stark) **503/227-0830** *10:30pm-close Fri-Sat only, Portland's only all-ages gay club*

Holocene [GS,D,E,DS] 1001 SE Morrison (at SE 10th) **503/239-7639** *many gay theme nights*

Under Wonder Lounge [GS,F,TG,DS,NS,GO] 128 NE Russell **503/284-8686** *5pm-midnight, open show nights only*

■ CAFES

Blend [WI,WC] 2710 N Killingsworth (at Greeley) **503/473-8616** *7am-6pm, 8am-5pm Sun*

Cup & Saucer Cafe [★F,NS,BW,WC] 3566 SE Hawthorne Blvd (at SE 36th) **503/236-6001** *7am-9pm, full menu, some veggie*

Elephant's Delicatessen [WC] 115 NW 22nd Ave (at NW Davis) 503/299-6304 *7am-7:30pm, 9:30am-6:30pm Sun*

Marco's Cafe & Espresso Bar [F,BW,WC] 7910 SW 35th (at Multnomah Blvd), Multnomah 503/245-0199 *7am-9pm, from 8am Sat, 8am-2pm Sun*

Pix Pâtisserie [BW,WC] 3402 SE Division St (at SE 34th) 503/232-4407 *2pm-midnight, noon-2am Fri-Sat, dessert*

Three Friends Coffeehouse [WI,WC] 201 SE 12th Ave (at Ash) 503/236-6411 *7am-10pm, from 9am Sun*

Voodoo Doughnut 22 SW 3rd Ave 503/241-4704 *24hrs*

■RESTAURANTS

Andina 1314 NW Glisan St (at 13th Ave) 503/228-9535 *lunch, dinner & tapas, Peruvian, full bar*

Aura Restaurant & Lounge [D,WC] 1022 W Burnside St (btwn SW 10th & 11th) 503/597-2872 *5pm-midnight, till 2:30am Fri-Sat, clsd Sun-Tue, also bar*

Bastas Trattoria [WC] 410 NW 21st (at Flanders) 503/274-1572 *dinner nightly, northern Italian, full bar till late*

Berbati's Pan [WC] 19 SW 2nd Ave (btwn Ankeny & Ankeny) 503/226-2122 *11am-2am, from 3pm Sun-Mon, Greek, full bar*

Besaw's [WC] 2301 NW Savier (at NW 23rd) 503/228-2619 *7am-10pm Tue-Fri, from 8am Sat, 8am-3pm Sun-Mon, American*

Bijou Cafe [★WI,WC] 132 SW 3rd Ave (at Pine St) 503/222-3187 *7am-2pm, from 8am wknds*

Bluehour [WC] 250 NW 13th Ave (at NW Everett St) 503/226-3394 *lunch Sun-Fri, dinner nightly, Sun brunch, extensive wine list*

Bread & Ink Cafe [★WI,WC] 3610 SE Hawthorne Blvd (at 36th) 503/239-4756 *brkfst, lunch & dinner, packed for brunch on Sun, full bar*

Dingo's Mexican Grill [★GO,WC] 4612 SE Hawthorne Blvd (at SE 46th) 503/233-3996 *noon-10pm, till 11pm Th, till 9pm Sun*

Dot's Cafe [★WC] 2521 SE Clinton (at 26th) 503/235-0203 *noon-2am, full bar*

Equinox [WC] 830 N Shaver St (at Mississippi) 503/460-3333 *dinner, brunch wknds, clsd Mon, int'l, patio*

Esparza's Tex-Mex Cafe [★WC] 2725 SE Ankeny St (at 28th) 503/234-7909 *11:30am-10pm, funky*

Farm Cafe [WC] 503/736-3276 *5pm-11pm, Northwest cuisine*

Fish Grotto [★WC] 1035 SW Stark (at SW 11th Ave, at Boxxes) 503/226-4171 *5pm-10pm, till 9pm Sun-Mon, full bar*

Genie's Cafe [WC] 1101 SE Division St (at 12th) 503/445-9777 *8am-3pm, brunch, house-infused vodkas*

Gypsy Restaurant & Lounge [K,WC] 625 NW 21st (btwn Hoyt & Irving) 503/796-1859 *4pm-2:30am, clsd Sun-Mon, full bar, inexpensive*

Hobo's [P,WC] 120 NW 3rd Ave (btwn Davis & Couch) 503/224-3285 *4pm-2:30am*

Masu [WI,WC] 406 SW 13th Ave (at Burnside) 503/221-6278 *lunch Mon-Th, dinner nightly, sushi*

Melt Bistro & Bar 716 NW 21st Ave (at Johnson) 503/295-4944 *11am-10pm, clsd Sun, sandwiches & more*

Mint [GO,WC] 816 N Russell St 503/284-5518 *5pm-10pm, till 11pm Fri-Sat, clsd Sun-Mon, fusion food, also 820 Lounge*

Montage [★WC] 301 SE Morrison (at 3rd) 503/234-1324 *lunch Tue-Fri, dinner till 2am, till 4am Fri-Sat, Louisiana-style cookin', full bar*

Nicholas' [WC] 318 SE Grand (btwn Oak & Pine) 503/235-5123 *11am-9pm, from noon Sun, Middle Eastern*

Nostrana [WC] 1401 SE Morrison 503/234-2427 *lunch Mon-Fri, dinner nightly; fresh, local, wood-fired Italian*

Old Town Pizza [WC] 226 NW Davis (at NW 3rd) 503/222-9999 *11:30am-11pm, above Shanghai Tunnels, supposedly home to 100-year-old ghost*

Oregon • USA

Old Wives Tales [★BW,E,WC] 1300 E Burnside St (at 13th) 503/238-0470 *8am-9pm, till 10pm Fri-Sat, multi-ethnic vegetarian*

Oven & Shaker 1134 NW Everett St 503/241-1600 *11:30am-midnight*

Paley's Place 1204 NW 21st Ave (at NW Northrup St) 503/243-2403 *dinner nightly, Northwest cuisine*

Paradox Cafe [★WC] 3439 SE Belmont St (at SE 35th) 503/232-7508 *brkfst, lunch & dinner, vegetarian diner, killer Reuben*

Pour [WC] 2755 NE Broadway (at NE 28th) 503/288-7687 *4:30pm-11pm, till close Fri-Sat, clsd Sun, wine bar & bistro*

The Roxy [★WI,WC] 1121 SW Stark St (btwn 11th & 12th) 503/223-9160 *24hrs, clsd Mon, retro American diner*

Santa Fe Taqueria [★E,WC] 831 NW 23rd (at Kearney) 503/220-0406 *11am-midnight*

Saucebox [D,WC,GO] 214 SW Broadway (at Burnside) 503/241-3393 *5pm-close, pan-Asian, full bar*

Tasty n Sons 3808 N Williams 503/241-1600 *9am-10pm, till 11pm Fri-Sat*

Vita Cafe [WC] 3023 NE Alberta St (btwn 30th & 31st) 503/335-8233 *brkfst, lunch & dinner, mostly vegetarian/vegan*

West Cafe [E,WI,WC] 1201 SW Jefferson St (12th Ave) 503/227-8189 *lunch Mon-Fri, dinner nightly, Sun brunch, "comfort food w/ a twist"*

Yakuza Lounge [WC] 5411 NE 30th Ave (at Killingsworth) 503/450-0893 *5pm-close, clsd Mon-Tue, Japanese, full bar*

■ENTERTAINMENT & RECREATION

Gay Skate 1 SE Spokane St (at Oaks Park Way, at Oaks Rink) 503/233-5777 *7pm-9pm 3rd Mon only*

Out Dancing [MW] 975 SE Sandy Blvd (at SE Ankeny St & SE 9th Ave) 503/236-5129 *LGBT dance lessons*

Sauvie's Island Beach 25 miles NW (off US 30) *follow Reeder Rd to the Collins beach area, park at the farthest end of the road, then follow path to beach; also "Rooster Rock," 22 miles E on Columbia River*

■BOOKSTORES

CounterMedia 927 SW Oak (btwn 9th & 10th) 503/226-8141 *11am-7pm, noon-6pm Sun, alternative comics, vintage gay books/ periodicals/ erotica*

Laughing Horse Bookstore [WC] 12 NE 10th Ave (near Burnside) 503/236-2893 *11am-7pm, clsd Sun, alternative/ progressive*

Powell's Books [★WC] 1005 W Burnside St (at 10th) 503/228-4651, 800/878-7323 *9am-11pm, huge mon & used bookstore, cafe, readings*

■RETAIL SHOPS

Hip Chicks Do Wine 4510 SE 23rd Ave (SE Holgate & 26th) 503/234-3790 *11am-6pm*

UnderU4men 800 SW Broadway St (at Washington) 503/274-2555 *10am-7pm, till 9pm Fri, 11am-6pm Sun, designer underwear & in-store underwear models*

■GYMS & HEALTH CLUBS

Common Ground Wellness Center [GF,R] 5010 NE 33rd Ave (at Alberta St) 503/238-1065 *10am-11pm, wellness center, public hot tubs, call for men's & trans nights*

■MEN'S CLUBS

Hawks PDX 234 SE Grand Ave 503/946-8659

Steam Portland [MO,PC,GO] 2885 NE Sandy Blvd 503/736-9999 *24hrs*

■MEN'S SERVICES

►**MegaMates** 503/299-9911 *Call to hook up with HOT local men. FREE to listen & respond to ads. Use FREE code DAMRON. MegaMates.com.*

■EROTICA

Fantasy for Adults 1512 W Burnside (near 15th) 503/295-6969

Fat Cobra Video 5940 N Interstate Ave 503/247-3425

Spartacus Leathers 300 SW 12th Ave (at Burnside) 503/224-2604

Taboo Video 237 SE MLK, Jr Blvd (at Pine) 503/239-1678 *24hrs*

■CRUISY AREAS

Kelly Point [AYOR] on Marine Dr *follow trail to left of parking lot*

Salem

■NIGHTCLUBS

Southside Speakeasy [GS,NH,D,F,K,DS,WI,GO] 3529 Fairview Industrial Dr SE (at Madrona) 503/362-1139 *11am-2am, from 3:30pm wknds*

■RESTAURANTS

Davinci's 180 High St SE 504/399-1413 *dinner only, clsd Sun, full bar*

Word Of Mouth 503/930-4285 *7am-3pm*

■EROTICA

Bob's Adult Bookstore 3815 State St (at Lancaster) 503/363-3846

■CRUISY AREAS

Bush Park [AYOR] 12th & State Sts *days only*

Sauvie Island

■ENTERTAINMENT & RECREATION

Collins Beach [GS,N,AYOR] take Hwy 30 N from Portland, turn onto "Sauvie Island Bridge" (then take Gillihan Rd to Reeder Rd) *get a parking permit before you go (available at general store at base of Sauvie Island Bridge)*

Silverton

■ACCOMMODATIONS

The Oregon Garden Resort [GF,F,SW,WI] 895 W Main St 800/966-6490 *boutique-style resort*

PENNSYLVANIA

Abington

■BARS

Kitchen Bar [GF,D,F,E] 1482 Old York Rd 215/576-9766 *noon-2am, from 8am wknds*

■RESTAURANTS

Vintage Bar & Restaurant [WC] 1116 Old York Rd 215/887-8500 *11am-2am*

Allentown

see also Bethlehem

■ACCOMMODATIONS

Grim's Manor B&B [MW,NS,GO] 10 Kern Rd, Kutztown 610/683-7089

■BARS

Candida's [MW,NH,D,F,K] 247 N 12th St (at Chew) 610/434-3071 *4pm-2am, from 2pm Fri-Sun*

Stonewall, Moose Lounge Bar & Grille [★M,D,F,E,K,DS,S,V] 28 N 10th St (at Hamilton) 610/432-0215 *7pm-2am, clsd Sun- Mon*

■MEN'S SERVICES

➤**MegaMates** 484/244-0144 *Call to hook up with HOT local men. FREE to listen & respond to ads. Use FREE code DAMRON. MegaMates.com.*

■EROTICA

Adult World 880 S West End Blvd/ Rte 309, Quakerstown 215/538-1522

■CRUISY AREAS

Union Terrace Park [AYOR] Union & St Elmo's Sts

Upper Macungie Park [AYOR] Rte 100 (1 mile N of the I-78 exit)

Altoona

■NIGHTCLUBS

Escapade [MW,D,GO] 2523 Union Ave, Rte 36 814/946-8195 *8pm-2am*

■EROTICA

Adult World Old Rte 220 (Bellwood exit, off I-99) 814/742-7781

Pennsylvania • *USA*

Beaver Falls

■ EROTICA
Video Hobby Land 7211 Big Beaver Blvd (on Rte 18) **724/847-3777**

Berwick

■ CRUISY AREAS
Test Track Park [AYOR] S Eaton St (off Rte 11)

Bethlehem

■ NIGHTCLUBS
Diamonz [W,D,F,E,K,WC] 1913 W Broad St (at Pennsylvania Ave) **610/865-1028** *7pm-2am, from 5pm Fri-Sat*

■ EROTICA
Green Door Video 1162 Pembroke Rd **610/865-5855** *24hrs; also Cupid's Treasures 861 Stefko Blvd, 610/868-6616*

Bristol

■ EROTICA
Bristol News World 576 Bristol Pike/ Rte 13 N **215/785-4770**

■ CRUISY AREAS
Silver Lake Park [AYOR]

Bryn Mawr

■ RETAIL SHOPS
TLA Video 761 Lancaster Ave **610/520-1222** *10am-11pm, extensive LGBT titles*

Butler

■ NIGHTCLUBS
M&J's Lounge [MW,NH,18+,PC,BYOB] 124 Mercer St **724/496-8955** *9pm-midnight Th, 9:30pm-3am Fri-Sat*

■ CRUISY AREAS
Moraine State Park [AYOR] Bear Run area (south shore)

Edinboro

■ CRUISY AREAS
Lakeside Commons [AYOR] Rte 6 N (behind the mall overlooking the lake), Waterford *days*

Elizabeth

■ EROTICA
51 Video & Books – Adult Mart 931 Hayden (Rte 51) **412/384-6383** *24hrs*

Erie

■ NIGHTCLUBS
Craze Nightclub [GS,D,K,DS] 1607 Raspberry St (at 16th) **814/456-3027** *9pm-2am, from 5pm Wed, clsd Tue & Th, [18+] Mon*

The Zone [MW,D,B,F,DS] 133 W 18th St (at Peach) **814/452-0125** *8pm-2am, from 4pm Wed*

■ RESTAURANTS
La Bella [BYOB,GO] 802 W 18th St **814/456-2244** *5pm-9pm, clsd Sun-Tue*

Pie in the Sky Cafe [BYOB,R,WC] 463 W 8th St (at Walnut) **814/459-8638** *lunch & dinner, clsd Sun-Mon*

■ RETAIL SHOPS
Ink Assassins Tattoos & Piercings 2601 Peach St **814/455-6752** *noon-10pm, till 6pm Sun*

■ PUBLICATIONS
Erie Gay News **814/456-9833** *covers news & events in the Erie, Cleveland, Pittsburgh, Buffalo & Chautauqua County (NY) region*

Gay People's Chronicle **216/916-9338** *Ohio's largest bi-weekly LGBT newspaper w/ extensive listings*

■ EROTICA
Eastern Adult Books – Adult Mart 1313 State St (btwn 13th & 14th) **814/459-7014**

Modern News 1113 State St (at 12th) **814/453-6932**

■ CRUISY AREAS
Glenwood Park [AYOR] park on the hill (overlooking the zoo)

Gettysburg

■ACCOMMODATIONS

Battlefield B&B [GS,WI,WC,GO] 2264 Emmitsburg Rd (at Ridge Rd) **717/334-8804, 888/766-3897** *full brkfst, Civil War home*

The Beechmont Inn B&B [GF,NS,WI,WC] 315 Broadway, Hanover **717/632-3013, 800/553-7009**

Sheppard Mansion B&B [GS,NS,WI] 117 Frederick St (at High St), Hanover **717/633-8075, 877/762-6746** *also restaurant & bar*

Gibson

■ACCOMMODATIONS

Hillside Campgrounds [★MO,D,SW,N,WI,21+GO] Creek Rd, 3 miles off I-81, at exit 219 **570/756-2007** *seasonal, campground, cabins, disco Fri-Sat*

Greensburg

■NIGHTCLUBS

Longbada Lounge [MW,D,K,DS,WC] 108 W Pittsburgh St (at Pennsylvania Ave) **724/837-6614** *9pm-2am, clsd Sun-Mon, patio*

■CRUISY AREAS

Harrison Ave [AYOR] off Otterman St

Harrisburg

■INFO LINES & SERVICES

LGBT Community Center Coalition of Central PA 1306 N 3rd St **717/920-9534**

■BARS

Bar 704 [M,NH,OC,WC] 704 N 3rd St **717/234-4226** *4pm-2am*

The Brownstone Lounge [MW,NH,F,WC] 412 Forster St (btwn 3rd & 6th) **717/234-7009** *11am-2am, from 5pm wknds*

■NIGHTCLUBS

Stallions [★M,D,E,K,DS,S,V,WC] 706 N 3rd St (enter rear) **717/232-3060** *7pm-2am*

■CRUISY AREAS

Riverfront Park [AYOR] Front & State Sts

Johnstown

■NIGHTCLUBS

Lucille's [MW,D,K,DS,S] 520 Washington St (near Central Park) **814/539-4448** *6pm-2am, clsd Sun-Mon*

■CRUISY AREAS

Central Park [AYOR]

Lancaster

■ACCOMMODATIONS

Cameron Estate Inn [GS,F,NS,WC,GO] 1855 Mansion Ln, Mount Joy **717/492-0111, 888/422-6376**

Lancaster Arts Hotel [GF,F,WC] 300 Harrisburg Ave **717/299-3000, 866/720-2787**

■BARS

Dad's Bar & Grill [GS,NH,F,K] 168 S Main St, Manheim **717/665-1960** *4pm-2am, from 11am Fri*

Tally Ho [MW,D,K,DS,YC] 201 W Orange St (at Water) **717/299-0661** *8pm-2am*

■RESTAURANTS

The Loft above Tally Ho bar **717/299-0661** *lunch & dinner, clsd Sun, contemporary American/ French*

■EROTICA

The Den 53 N Prince St **717/299-1779**

■CRUISY AREAS

Lancaster County Park [AYOR]

Long's Park [AYOR] Rte 30 at Harrisburg Pike

Lebanon

■EROTICA

Hobbeze Lebanon Adult Gifts 1604 E Cumberland St/ Rte 422 (at 15th Ave) **717/273-6398**

■CRUISY AREAS

Union Canal Tunnel Park [AYOR]

Liverpool

■EROTICA

Adult Depot [GO] 64 Old Trail Rd (near Rte 11 & 104 Jct) **717/444-3894** *all-male theater*

Pennsylvania • *USA*

Milford

■ACCOMMODATIONS

Hotel Fauchere [GF,NS,WI,WC] 401 Broad St (at Catharine St) **570/409-1212** *historic boutique hotel, also restaurant & bar*

Montgomery

■EROTICA

Adult Playtime Boutique 737 Rte 15 (top of the mountain, near the rest area)) **570/547-2663**

New Hope

see also Lambertville & Sergeantsville, New Jersey

■ACCOMMODATIONS

Ash Mill Farm B&B [GF,NS,WI] 5358 York Rd (at Rte 202), Holicong **215/794-5373**

The Lexington House [★GS,SW,NS,GO] 6171 Upper York Rd **215/794-0811** *1749 country home, full brkfst*

The Wishing Well Guesthouse [GS,NS,GO] 144 Old York Rd **215/862-8819**

■BARS

Bob Eagans [GS,C,F] 6426 Lower York Rd (at the Nevermore Hotel) **215/862-5225** *cabaret, dinner served, also hotel*

Havana [GS,FE,K] 105 S Main St **215/862-9897** *noon-2am*

■RESTAURANTS

Eagle Diner [WC] 6522 Lower York Rd **215/862-5575** *24hrs*

Karla's 5 W Mechanic St (at Main) **215/862-2612** *noon-11pm, till midnight Fri-Sat, from 11am Sun, full bar till 2am*

Wildflowers 8 W Mechanic St **215/862-2241** *seasonal, noon-9pm, full bar*

■EROTICA

Grownups [GO] 2 E Mechanic St (at Main) **215/862-9304**

Le Chateau Exotique 27 W Mechanic St **215/862-3810** *fetishwear*

New Milford

■ACCOMMODATIONS

Oneida Campground & Lodge [M,D,SW,N,WI,GO] **570/465-7011** *seasonal*

Norristown

■BARS

Beagle Tavern [GS,F,K,C] 1003 E Main St **610/272-3133** *11am-2am, more gay Wed & Fri*

Philadelphia

■INFO LINES & SERVICES

William Way LGBT Community Center 1315 Spruce St (at Juniper) **215/732-2220** *11am-10pm, noon-5pm wknds*

■ACCOMMODATIONS

Alexander Inn [GS,NS,WI,GO] Spruce (at 12th St) **215/923-3535, 877/253-9466**

The Gables B&B [GS,NS,WI,GO] 4520 Chester Ave **215/662-1918**

The Independent Hotel [GS,WI,WC] 1234 Locust St (at 13th) **215/772-1440**

Latham Hotel [GF,WI,WC] 135 S 17th St (at Walnut) **215/563-7474, 877/528-4261**

Morris House Hotel [GF,NS,WI] 225 S 8th St **215/922-2446**

Palomar Philadelphia [GF,WI,WC] 117 S 17th St **215/563-5006, 888/725-1778**

Uncles Upstairs Inn [M,NS,GO] 1220 Locust St (at 12th) **215/546-6660**

■BARS

Bike Stop [M,D,B,L,K] 204-206 S Quince St (btwn 11th & 12th) **215/627-1662** *4pm-2am, from 2pm wknds, cruisy*

iCandy [M,D] 254 S 12th St (btwn Locust & Spruce) **267/324-3500** *4pm-2am*

Khyber Pass Pub [GF,F,E,WC] 56 S 2nd St (btwn Market & Chestnut) **215/238-5888** *11am-2am*

L'Etage [GS,D,C] 624 S 6th St (at Bainbridge) **215/592-0656** 7:30pm-1am, till 2am Fri-Sat, clsd Mon, also crepe restaurant downstairs

North Third [GS,F] 801 N 3rd (at Brown) **215/413-3666** 4pm-2am, from 10am wknd brunch

Stir Lounge [MW,NH,D,V] 1705 Chancellor St (at Rittenhouse Sq btwn Walnut & Spruce) **215/732-2700** 4pm-2am

Tabu Lounge & Sports Bar [GS,F,K] 200 S 12th St **215/964 -9675** noon-2amFood For Thought

Tavern on Camac [MW,D,C,P] 243 S Camac St (at Spruce) **215/545-0900** 4pm-2am, also restaurant

U-Bar [M,NH] 1220 Locust St (at 12th) **215/546-6660** 11am-2am

Venture Inn [MW,NH,F] 255 S Camac (at Spruce) **215/545-8731** 11am-2am

The Westbury [MW,NH,F,WC,GO] 261 S 13th St (at Spruce) **215/546-5170** 4pm-2am. from 11am wknds

Woody's [M,D,CW,F,K,S,WI,YC,WC] 202 S 13th St (at Walnut) **215/545-1893** 4pm-2am, Latin Th

■NIGHTCLUBS

Bob & Barbara's Lounge [GS,E,DS] 1509 South St **215/545-4511** 3pm-2am, from 6pm Sun, [DS] Th, live jazz Fri-Sat

Shampoo [GS,D,A] 417 N 8th St (at Willow) **215/922-7500** 9pm-2am, clsd Mon-Tue & Th, more gay Fri

Voyeur [M,D,K,C,DS,PC] 1221 St James St (off 13th & Locust) **215/735-5772** 1am-3am, from 9pm wknds

■CAFES

10th Street Pour House [WC] 262 S 10th St (at Spruce) **215/922-5626** 6am-2pm, popular brunch wknds

B2 Cafe [WI] 1500 E Passyunk Ave **215/271-5520** great vegan soft serve ice cream

Capogiro 119 S 13th St (at Sansom) **215/351-0900** 7:30am-11:30pm, till 1am Fri-Sat, gelato

Capriccio 110 N 16th St (at Benjamin Franklin Pkwy) **215/735-9797** 6:30am-7pm, 8am-8pm wknds

Cosi 1128 Walnut St **215/413-1608** 7am-11pm

Green Line Cafe [F,E] 4239 Baltimore Ave (at 43rd) **215/222-3431** 7am-11pm, 8am-8pm Sun

■RESTAURANTS

13th Street Pizza 209 S 13th St (at Chancellor St) **215/546-4453** 11am-4am, popular late night

Alfa 1709 Walnut St (at 17th) **215/751-0201** 5pm-2am, also bar

Bar Ferdinand 1030 N 2nd St great tapas & wine

Cantina Feliz [WC] 424 S Bethlehem Pike, Fort Washington **215/646-1320** 11am-9pm, from 4pm Sat-Sun, till 10pm Fri- Sat

The Continental 138 Market St (at 2nd) **215/923-6069** lunch, dinner, wknd brunch, also bar until 2am

Honey's [BYOB] 800 N 4th St **215/925-1150** 7am-4pm, till 5pm wknds

Knock 226 S 12th St **215/925-1166** lunch & dinner, Sun brunch, American, also bar

Liberties 705 N 2nd St (at Fairmount) **215/238-0660** lunch & dinner, full bar till 2am

Lolita [BYOB] 106 S 13th St (at Sansom) **215/546-7100** 5pm-10pm, upscale Mexican

Mercato [BYOB] 1216 Spruce St **215/985-2962** dinner, Italian

Midtown II [TG] 122 S 11th St **215/627-6452** 24hrs, diner, popular late night

Mixto 1141 Pine St **215/592-0363** lunch & dinner, brkfst wknds, Latin American

My Thai 2200 South St (at 22nd) **215/985-1878** 5pm-10pm, till 11pm Fri-Sat, full bar

New Harmony 135 N 9th St (at Cherry) **215/627-4520** 11am-11pm, vegan/Chinese

Paesano's 1017 S 9th St **215/440-0371** 11am-7pm, great sandwiches

Sabrina's 910 Christian St **215/574-1599** *8am-10pm, till 8pm Tue-Th, till 4pm Sun-Mon*

El Vez 121 S 13th St (at Sansom) **215/928-9800** *lunch Mon-Sat, dinner nightly, Sun brunch, full bar*

■ENTERTAINMENT & RECREATION

The Walt Whitman House 328 Mickle Blvd, Camden, NJ **856/964-5383** *the last home of America's great & controversial poet, just across the Delaware River*

■BOOKSTORES

Giovanni's Room [★] 345 S 12th St (at Pine) **215/923-2960** *11:30am-7pm, from 1pm Sun, legendary LGBT bookstore*

■RETAIL SHOPS

Philadelphia AIDS Thrift 710 S 5th St **215/922-3186** *11am-8pm, till 9pm Fri-Sat, till 7pm Sun*

■PUBLICATIONS

PGN (Philadelphia Gay News) **215/625-8501** *LGBT newspaper w/ extensive listings*

■GYMS & HEALTH CLUBS

12th St Gym [SW] 204 S 12th St (btwn Locust & Walnut) **215/985-4092**

■MEN'S CLUBS

Club Body Center [NS,WI,PC] 1220 Chancellor St (at 12th & Walnut) **215/735-7671** *24hrs*

Philly Jacks [MO,18+,PC] 1318 Walnut St (btw 13th & Broad) **215/618-1519** *4 sex parties per month, club only open during parties; call for dates*

Sansom Street Gym [★MO,V,PC] 2020 Sansom St **267/330-0151** *24hrs*

■MEN'S SERVICES

➤MegaMates **215/877-3337** *Call to hook up with HOT local men. FREE to listen & respond to ads. Use FREE code DAMRON. MegaMates.com.*

■EROTICA

Adonis Cinema Complex [★] 2026 Sansom St (at 20th) **215/557-9319** *24hrs*

Condom Kingdom 437 South St (at 5th) **215/829-1668** *safer sex materials & toys*

Danny's 133 S 13th St (at Walnut) **215/925-5041** *24hrs*

Fantasy Island Adult Books 7363 State Rd **215/332-5454**

Passional Boutique 317 South St **215/829-4986, 877/826-7738** *noon-10pm*

Sexploratorium 317 South St (across from TLA theater) **215/923-1398** *noon-10pm*

Pittsburgh

■INFO LINES & SERVICES

AA Gay/ Lesbian **412/471-7472** *call for times & location*

Gay/ Lesbian Community Center 210 Grant St **412/422-0114** *9am-9pm, noon-6pm Sun*

■ACCOMMODATIONS

Arbors B&B [MO,NS,WI,GO] 745 Maginn St **412/231-4643**

Camp Davis [MW,D,SW] 311 Red Brush Rd, Boyers **724/637-2402** *1 hour from Pittsburgh, cabins & campsites, variety of events*

The Inn on Negley [GF,NS,WI,WC] 703 S Negley Ave (at Elmer St) **412/661-0631**

The Inn on the Mexican War Streets [MW,F,NS,WI,GO] 604 W North Ave **412/231-6544**

Morning Glory Inn B&B [GF,WI] 2119 Sarah St **412/431-1707**

The Parador Inn [GF,WI,GO] 939 Western Ave **412/231-4800, 877/540-1443**

The Priory [GF,NS,WI,WC] 614 Pressley St (near Cedar Ave) **412/231-3338, 866/377-4679**

■BARS

5801 [★MW,V,WC] 5801 Ellsworth Ave (at Maryland) **412/661-5600** *4pm-2am, from 2pm Sun, also restaurant*

The Backdraft Bar & Grill [GS,F,E,K] 3049 Churchview Ave **412/885-1239** *11am-2am, till midnight Sun*

Blue Moon Bar & Lounge [M,NH,TG,S] 5115 Butler St (in Lawrenceville) 412/781-1119 *5pm-2am, 4pm-1am Mon*

Cattivo [W,D,DS,K,F] 146 44th St 412/687-2157 *4pm-2am Wed-Sun, clsd Mon-Tue*

Cruze Bar [MW,D,E,GO] 1600 Smallman St (at 16th St) 412/471-1400 *4pm-2am, clsd Mon*

Images [M,K,S,V] 965 Liberty Ave (at 10th St) 412/391-9990 *2pm-2am, go-go boys*

Leather Central [★M,D,L,F,V] 1226 Herron Ave (downstairs) 412/682-6839 *9pm-2am Fri-Sat, 6pm-11pm Sun*

PTown [MW,D,S,WI] 4740 Baum Blvd 412/621-0111 *6pm-2am*

Real Luck Cafe [MW,NH,F,S,WC,GO] 1519 Penn Ave (at 16th) 412/471-7832 *4pm-2am*

Remedy [GS,NH,D,MR] 5121 Butler St, Lawrenceville 412/781-6771 *4pm-2am, from 12:30pm Sun, also restaurant upstairs*

Spin Bartini/ Ultra Lounge [GS,E,WC] 5744 Ellsworth Ave, Shadyside 412/362-7746 *4pm-2am*

There Ultra Lounge [MW,K,WC] 931 Liberty Ave (at Smithfield) 412/642-4435 *3:30pm-2am, from 7:30pm Sat-Sun*

■**NIGHTCLUBS**

1226 on Herron [MW,D] 1226 Herron Ave (at Liberty) 412/682-6839 *6pm-2am, clsd Mon-Wed, leather bar Fri-Sat lower level*

941 Saloon [MW,D,K] 941 Liberty Ave (at Smithfield St, 2nd flr) 412/281-5222 *2pm-2am*

The Link [MW,D,F,E,DS,S] 91 Wendel Rd, Herminie 724/446-7717 *7pm-2am, clsd Mon, patio*

■**CAFES**

Square Cafe [E,GO] 1137 S Braddock Ave 412/244-8002 *7am-3pm, from 8am Sun*

Zeke's Coffee 6012 Penn Ave 724/201-1671 *9am-5pm, till 2pm Mon, till 8pm Th, clsd Sun*

■**RESTAURANTS**

Abay 130 S Highland Ave (at Baum Blvd) 412/661-9736 *lunch & dinner, clsd Mon, Ethiopian, plenty veggie*

Capri 6001 Penn Ave (at Highland Ave) 412/363-1250 *11am-midnight, 6pm-2am Th-Sat*

Dinette 5996 Penn Cir S 412/362-0202 *dinner only, clsd Sun-Mon, plates to share, starters & thin-crust pizzas*

Dish 128 S 17th St (at Sarah) 412/390-2012 *5pm-2am, clsd Sun, Italian, also bar*

Double Wide Grill 2339 E Carson St (at S 24th St) 412/390-1111 *lunch & dinner, wknd brunch, BBQ, plenty veggie/ vegan*

Eleven 1150 Smallman St (at 11th) 412/201-5656 *lunch & dinner, Sun brunch*

Harris Grill 5747 Ellsworth Ave 412/362-5273 *dinner nightly, wknd brunch, full bar*

Kaya 2000 Smallman St (at 20th) 412/261-6565 *lunch & dinner, Latin/ Caribbean, plenty veggie*

NOLA On the Square [E] 24 Market Sq 412/471-9100 *11am-11pm, clsd Sun*

OTB Bicycle Cafe 2518 East Carson St (at S 26th) 412/381-3698 *11am-10pm, burgers, plenty veggie, also bar*

Pamela's Diner [★GO] 60 21st St 412/281-6366 *7am-3pm, from 8am Sun, also 5 other locations in Pittsburgh*

Point Brugge Cafe 401 Hastings (at Reynolds) 412/441-3334 *lunch & dinner, Sun brunch, clsd Mon, Belgian/ European*

Primanti Brothers [★] 46 18th St 412/263-2142 *Pittsburgh's iconic sandwich shop, many locations*

Quiet Storm [WI,WC] 5430 Penn Ave (at Graham St) 412/661-9355 *9am-9pm, 10am-4pm Sat, clsd Sun & Tue, vegetarian/ vegan*

Red Oak Cafe 3610 Forbes Ave (at Lothrop) 412/621-2221 *7am-7pm, till 5pm Fri, clsd wknds*

Pennsylvania • *USA*

Spoon 134 S Highland Ave
412/362-6001 *fresh "farm to table" menu, also lounge*

Zenith [WC] 86 S 26th St
412/481-4833 *11am-9pm, Sun brunch, clsd Mon-Wed, vegetarian/ vegan, also antiques store*

ENTERTAINMENT & RECREATION

Andy Warhol Museum 117 Sandusky St (at General Robinson)
412/237-8300 *10am-5pm, till 10pm Fri, clsd Mon, is it soup or is it art? see for yourself*

Burgh Bits & Bites Food Tour
412/209-3370, 800/979-3370 *explore the vivid history & culinary delights of the Steel City*

Pittsburgh Public Market 2100 Smallman St **412/281-4505** *the goodness of locally grown produce, fresh-baked goods, handmade crafts*

RETAIL SHOPS

Slacker [WC] 1321 E Carson St (btwn 13th & 14th) **412/381-3911** *noon-9pm, 11am-6pm Sun, magazines, clothing, leather*

Who New? [GO] 5156 Butler St
412/781-0588 *noon-6pm, clsd Mon-Tue, open Sun by chance, vintage modern design*

MEN'S CLUBS

Club Pittsburgh [★WI,PC] 1139 Penn Ave (enter side) **412/471-6790** *24hrs*

MEN'S SERVICES

➤**MegaMates** 412/937-9999 *Call to hook up with HOT local men. FREE to listen & respond to ads. Use FREE code DAMRON. MegaMates.com.*

EROTICA

Adult Mart 346 Blvd of the Allies
412/261-9119 *24hrs*

Monroeville News - Adult Mart
2735 Stroschein Rd (off Rte 22), Monroeville **412/372-5477** *24hrs, 13 miles from Pittsburgh*

CRUISY AREAS

Schenley Park [AYOR]

Poconos

ACCOMMODATIONS

Frog Hollow [MW,GO] 3535 High Crest Rd, Canadensis **570/595-2032** *secluded 1920s cottage*

Rainbow Mountain Resort
[MW,D,TG,E,K,SW,WI,GO] **570/223-8484** *also restaurant & bar, DJ Fri-Sat*

The Woods Campground [MW,SW,18+] 845 Vaughn Acres Ln, Lehighton
610/377-9577

Reading

BARS

The Peanut Bar & Restaurant
[GF,NS,WI] 332 Penn St **610/376-8500, 800/515-8500** *11am-11pm, till midnight Fri-Sat, clsd Sun, a Reading landmark!*

The Red Star
[M,NH,D,L,MR,TG,DS,OC,GO] 11 S 10th St (at Penn St) **610/375-4116** *9pm-2am, clsd Sun-Tue*

RESTAURANTS

Judy's On Cherry 332 Cherry St
610/374-8511 *lunch Tue-Fri, dinner Tue-Sat, clsd Sun-Mon, Mediterranean*

The Ugly Oyster [E] 21 S 5th St (at Cherry) **610/373-6791** *11:30am-10pm, from noon Sat, clsd Sun, traditional Irish pub (bar open till 2am)*

CRUISY AREAS

Mt Penn [AYOR] *btwn pagoda & fire tower & surrounding woodlands*

Scranton

BARS

Twelve Penny Saloon
[MW,NH,L,TG,F,K,DS,WC,GO] 3501 Birney Ave, Moosic **570/941-0444** *6pm-2am, from 3pm wknds*

CRUISY AREAS

Court House Square [AYOR]

Shippensburg

EROTICA

The Lion's Den Adult Superstore
8071 Oldc Scotland Rd (Penn exit 24, off I-81) **717/530-8032** *24hrs*

State College

■ ACCOMMODATIONS
The Atherton Hotel [GF,WI,WC] 125 S Atherton St (at College Ave) 814/231-2100, 800/832-0132

■ BARS
Chumley's [★M,NH,WC] 100 W College 814/238-4446 *5pm-2am, from 6pm Sun*

■ NIGHTCLUBS
Indigo [GS,D,V,YC] 112 W College Ave 814/234-1031 *9pm-2am, clsd Mon-Wed, "Alternative" night Sun*

■ CRUISY AREAS
The Wall [AYOR] 100 blk of College Ave

Sunbury

■ BARS
CC's [MW,D,K,DS] 555 Klinger Rd 570/286-6022 *7pm-2am Th-Sat, clsd Sun-Wed*

■ CRUISY AREAS
Market St & Park [AYOR] downtown

Uniontown

■ BARS
Eddie's Tavern [GF,F,K] 200 Francis St 724/438-9563 *11am-midnight, try the wings*

■ NIGHTCLUBS
Club 231 [M,NH,D,TG,K,DS,GO] 231 Pittsburgh St/ Rte 51 (at Fulton) 724/430-1477 *9pm-close*

■ CRUISY AREAS
Dunlap Creek Park [AYOR]

West Chester

■ CRUISY AREAS
Court House Wall [AYOR] *late nights*

Wilkes-Barre

■ INFO LINES & SERVICES
NEPA Rainbow Alliance Resource Center [WI] 67 Public Square, 5th flr, Edwardsville 570/763-9877

■ NIGHTCLUBS
Twist [M,D,MR,K,DS,WC] 1170 Hwy 315 (in Fox Ridge Plaza) 570/970-7503 *8pm-2am, from 6pm Sun, patio*

■ EROTICA
Cinema 309 [AYOR] Rte 309 (Blackman St exit, off I-81) 570/822-2694 *about a half mile on Route 309*

■ CRUISY AREAS
Nesbitt Park [AYOR] Susquehanna River (N of Pierce St bridge), Kingston

Williamsport

■ CRUISY AREAS
Scenic Overlook [AYOR] 3 miles S, on Rte 15 N

York

■ ACCOMMODATIONS
Yorktowne Hotel [GF,F,WI,WC] 48 E Market St 717/848-1111

■ NIGHTCLUBS
Altland's Ranch [MW,CW,D,K] 8505 Orchard Rd, Spring Grove 717/225-4479 *8pm-2am Fri-Sat only*

■ EROTICA
Cupid's Connection Adult Boutique 244 N George St (at North) 717/846-5029

RHODE ISLAND

Coventry

■ RESTAURANTS
Indigo Lounge & Pizzeria [E] 599 Tiogue Ave 401/615-9600 *4pm-10pm, till 1am wknds, live music*

Newport

■ INFO LINES & SERVICES
Sobriety First 135 Pelham St (at Channing Memorial Church) 401/438-8860 *8pm Fri*

■ ACCOMMODATIONS
Architect's Inn [GF,NS,WI,GO] 2 Sunnyside Pl 401/845-2547, 877/466-2547 *fireplaces, near beach, shops & restaurants*

Rhode Island • USA

Francis Malbone House Inn
[GF,NS,WI,WC] 392 Thames St (at Memorial Blvd) **401/846-0392, 800/846-0392**

Hilltop Inn [GF,NS,WI,GO] 2 Kay St **800/846-0392**

Hydrangea House Inn [★GS,NS,WI,GO]
16 Bellevue Ave **401/846-4435, 800/945-4667** *full brkfst, near beach*

The Spring Seasons Inn [GF,NS] 86 Spring St (btwn Mary St & Touro) **401/849-0004, 877/294-0004** *full brkfst*

■RESTAURANTS

Donick's Restaurant & Ice Cream Spa [BYOB,GO] 16 Broadway **401/835-5183** *6am-2am*

Whitehorse Tavern [NS] 26 Marlborough St (at Farewell) **401/849-3600** *lunch & dinner, Sun brunch, upscale dining, patio*

■EROTICA

Newport Video 228 JT Connell Hwy **401/847-4480** *arcade*

North Kingstown

■EROTICA

Amazing.net Video Store 6774 Post Rd/ Rte 1 **401/885-0209**

Providence

■INFO LINES & SERVICES

Brothers in Sobriety 372 Wayland Ave (at Community Church) **401/438-8860, 800/439-8860** *7:30pm Sat*

■ACCOMMODATIONS

Edgewood Manor [GF,NS,WI] 232 Norwood Ave (at Broad) **401/781-0099** *1905 Greek Revival mansion*

Hotel Dolce Villa [GS,NS] 63 De Pasquale Square (at Atwells) **401/383-7031**

The Hotel Providence [GS,F,WI,NS] 139 Mathewson **401/861-8000, 800/861-8990**

NYLO Hotel [GS,WI,WC] 400 Knight St, Warwick **401/734-4460** *also restaurant & bar*

Renaissance Providence Hotel
[GS,F,NS,WI,WC] 5 Avenue of the Arts (at Francis) **401/919-5000, 800/468-3571**

■BARS

Alleycat [MW,NH,V,GO] 17 Snow St (at Washington) **401/272-6369** *3pm-1am, till 2am Fri-Sat*

Deville's Cafe [MW,F,GO] 345 S Water St **401/383-8883** *4pm-midnight, till 1am Fri-Sat, clsd Mon*

The Stable [MW,NH,V,WC] 125 Washington (at Mathewson) **401/272-6950** *2pm-1am, till 2am Fri-Sat, from noon Sat-Sun*

■NIGHTCLUBS

Dark Lady [M,D,K,DS,V] 17 Snow St **401/272-6369** *9pm-1am, till 2am Fri-Sat, theme nights*

Hush RI [MO,S,18+] 257 Allens Ave (beside The Gay Mega-Plex) **401/862-4050** *8pm-1am, till 2am Fri-Sat, clsd Mon-, nude male dancers*

Mirabar [M,D,S,WC] 15 Elbow St **401/331-6761** *3pm-1am, till 2am Fri-Sat, male dancers*

Platforms Dance Club [GS,D,18+] 165 Poe St **401/781-3121** *gay night Sat, Salsa Sun*

■CAFES

Coffee Exchange 207 Wickenden St **401/273-1198** *6:30am-11pm, deck*

Nicks on Broadway 500 Broadway **401/421-0286** *lunch & dinner Wed-Sat, Sun brunch, clsd Mon-Tue*

Pastiche Fine Desserts 92 Spruce St **401/861-5190** *8:30am-11pm, 10am-10pm Sun*

White Electric Coffee 711 Westminster **401/453-3007** *7am-6:30pm*

■RESTAURANTS

Al Forno [★] 577 S Main St **401/273-9760** *dinner only, clsd Sun-Mon*

Blaze Restaurant [GO] 776 Hope St **401/277-2529** *lunch & dinner, clsd Mon*

Bravo Brasserie 123 Empire St
401/490-5112 *lunch Tue-Sat, dinner
nightly, Sun brunch*

Cafe' Paragon / Viva
234 Thayer St **401/331-6200** *11am-
1am, European Bistro/Café style atmosphere with a full bar*

Caffe Dolce Vita 59 DePasquale Plaza
(at Spruce St) **401/331-8240** *8am-
1am, till 2am wknds, wknd brunch,
authentic Italian cafe, patio*

Camille's 71 Bradford St (at Atwell's
Ave) **401/751-4812** *lunch & dinner,
clsd Sun, full bar*

CAV 14 Imperial Pl **401/751-9164**
11am-10pm, till 1am Fri, wknd brunch

Don José Tequilas Mexican 351
Atwells Ave **401/454-8951** *11:30-
11pm, from 3pm-10pm Mon-Wed, till
1am Fri-Sat*

Fellini Pizzeria [★GO] 166 Wickenden
St **401/751-6737**

Julian's [BW] 318 Broadway (at Vinton)
401/861-1770 *lunch & dinner*

Kartabar
284 Thayer St **401/331-8111**
*11:30am-1am, mixed-Mediterranean,
with some American classic*

Local 121 121 Washington St (at
Matthewson St) **401/274-2121** *lunch
Tue-Sat, dinner nightly,Sun brunch*

Mill's Tavern 101 N Main St
401/272-3331 *Mon-Fri happy hour
oysters , dinner nightly*

■**ENTERTAINMENT &
RECREATION**

Cable Car Cinema & Cafe 204 S Main
St **401/272-3970** *art-house flicks &
free popcorn refills*

WaterFire Waterplace Park
401/272-3111 *May-Oct only, bonfire
installations along the Providence River
at sunset*

■**BOOKSTORES**

Books on the Square 471 Angell St (at
Wayland) **401/331-9097,
888/669-9660** *9am-9pm, 10am-6pm
Sun, some LGBT*

■**PUBLICATIONS**

Get RI Magazine 401/226-9033
GLBT magazine

➤**Metroline 860/231-8845,
800/233-8334** *covers CT, RI & MA*

Options 401/724-5428 *LGBT
community magazine*

■**MEN'S CLUBS**

Club Body Center [WI,PC] 257
Weybosset St, 2nd flr (at Richmond)
401/274-0298 *24hrs*

Gay Mega-Plex [PC,WC,GO] 257 Allens
Ave (S of Public St) **401/780-8769**
24hrs

■**MEN'S SERVICES**

➤**MegaMates 401/738-7788** *Call to
hook up with HOT local men. FREE to
listen & respond to ads. Use FREE code
DAMRON. MegaMates.com.*

■**EROTICA**

Adult Video News 255 Allens Ave (at
Bay) **401/785-1324** *arcade*

Mister Sister 268 Wickenden St
401/421-6969 *fetishwear, sex toys,
classes*

■**CRUISY AREAS**

State House Circle Road [AYOR]
nights

Warwick

■**CRUISY AREAS**

Salter Grove Park [AYOR] Narragansett
Pkwy (off Post Rd)

Westerly

■**CRUISY AREAS**

Misquamicut State Beach [AYOR] go
left before the bridge (at Fenway Beach)

SOUTH CAROLINA

Aiken

■NIGHTCLUBS

Marlboro Station [MW,D,S] 141 Marlboro St NE **803/644-6485** *10pm-close Fri-Sun*

Blacksburg

■EROTICA

BedTyme Stories 145 Simper Rd (I-85, exit 100) **864/839-0007**

Bowman

■EROTICA

The Lion's Den Adult Superstore 2269 Homestead Rd (exit 159, off I-26) **803/829-1781** *24hrs*

Charleston

■INFO LINES & SERVICES

Acceptance Group (Gay AA) 45 Moultrie St (at St Barnabus Lutheran Church) **843/723-9633** (AA#) *7pm Mon, Th & Sat*

■ACCOMMODATIONS

A B&B @ 4 Unity Alley [GS,NS] 4 Unity Alley **843/577-6660** *18th-c warehouse, full brkfst*

Aloft Charleston Airport & Convention Center [GF,SW,WI,WC] 4875 Tanger Outlet Blvd (at International Blvd), N Charleston **843/566-7300, 877/462-5638**

Charleston Place [GF,F] 205 Meeting St **843/722-4900, 888/635-2350**

■BARS

Dudley's on Ann [M,NH,K,18+,GO] 42 Ann St (at King St) **843/577-6779** *4pm-2am*

■NIGHTCLUBS

Club Pantheon [M,D,MR,E,C,DS,18+,GO] 28 Ann St (at King) **843/577-2582** *10pm-2am Fri-Sun only*

Club Patrick's [MW,D,TG,E,K,S,WC] 1377 Ashley River Rd/ Hwy 61 **843/571-3435** *6pm-2am, patio bar*

Deja Vu II [W,D,F,E,DS,K,S,PC,WC,GO] 4628 Spruill Ave **843/554-5959** *5pm-close Th, from 10pm Fri-Sat*

■CAFES

Bear E Patch [WC] 1980-A Ashley River Rd **843/766-6490** *7am-9pm, 8am-8pm Sat, clsd Sun*

■RESTAURANTS

82 Queen 82 Queen St **843/723-7591, 800/849-0082** *lunch & dinner, Sun brunch, Lowcountry cuisine*

Fat Hen [★E,BW] 3140 Maybank Hwy, St Johns Island **843/559-9090** *dinner nightly, Sun brunch, French bistro, seafood*

Fig [WC] 232 Meeting St (near Hasell) **843/805-5900** *5:30pm-10:30pm, till 11pm Fri-Sat, clsd Sun, local ingredients*

High Cotton 199 E Bay St **843/724-3815** *dinner nightly, lunch Sat, Sun brunch, Southern cuisine, full bar*

Hominy Grill **843/937-0930** *brkfst, lunch & dinner, wknd brunch*

Joe Pasta 428 King St (at John) **843/965-5252** *11:30am-11pm, till midnight Fri-Sat, also full bar*

Mama Q's Kitchen [BW,WC,GO] 3157 Maybank Hwy #E, St Johns Island **843/559-0071** *11:30am-9pm, till 2pm Tue*

Melvin's Legendary Bar-B-Que 538 Folly Rd **843/762-0511** *10:45am-9:30pm, clsd Sun*

■ENTERTAINMENT & RECREATION

Historic Charleston Foundation 40 E Bay St **843/723-1623** *call for info on city walking tours (March-April only)*

■CRUISY AREAS

Folly Beach [AYOR] western tip of island (make a right at the island's only traffic light & drive all the way to county park)

West Ashley Park [AYOR]

Myrtle Beach • South Carolina

Columbia

■INFO LINES & SERVICES

The Harriet Hancock GLBT Community Center 1108 Woodrow St (at Millwood) **803/771-7713** *community info, resources, HIV programs & more*

Primary Purpose Gay/ Lesbian AA 5220 Clemson (in the house behind St Martin's Church) **803/254-5301(AA#)** *6:30 Tue, 7pm Fri & Sun*

■ACCOMMODATIONS

Holiday Inn Express [GF,SW] 1011 Clemson Frontage Rd **803/419-3558**

■BARS

Art Bar [GS,D,K] 1211 Park St **803/929-0198** *8pm-2am*

Capital Club [M,NH,P,PC,WC] 1002 Gervais St **803/256-6464** *5pm-2am*

■NIGHTCLUBS

PTS 1109 [MW,D,MR,TG,S,WI,PC,GO] 1109 Assembly St (at Gervais St) **803/253-8900** *5pm-2am, till 6am Fri, till 3am Sat-Sun*

■RESTAURANTS

Dianne's On Devine 2400 Devine St **803/254-3535** *dinner only, clsd Sun, upscale Italian*

Garibaldi's of Columbia 2013 Greene St **803/771-8888** *dinner nightly, full bar*

■MEN'S SERVICES

➤**MegaMates 803/939-0666** *Call to hook up with HOT local men. FREE to listen & respond to ads. Use FREE code DAMRON. MegaMates.com.*

■EROTICA

Video Magic 5445 Two Notch Rd **803/786-8125**

■CRUISY AREAS

Senate Street [AYOR] near the university

Greenville

■ACCOMMODATIONS

Walnut Lane Inn [GF,WI] 110 Ridge Rd (at Groce Rd), Lyman **864/949-7230** *full brkfst, mention Damron at booking for discount*

■BOOKSTORES

Out of Bounds 21 S Pleasantburg Dr **864/239-0106** *2pm- 8pm, till 6pm Sun, from 11am Fri-Sat*

■MEN'S SERVICES

➤**MegaMates 864/421-0400** *Call to hook up with HOT local men. FREE to listen & respond to ads. Use FREE code DAMRON. MegaMates.com.*

Hilton Head

■ACCOMMODATIONS

Sonesta Resort Hilton Head Island [GF,F] 130 Shipyard Dr **843/842-2400, 800/334-1881**

■BARS

Club Vibe [MW,NH,TG,F] 32 Palmetto Bay Rd #D-2 (at Sea Pines Cir) **843/341-6933** *5pm-3am, from 8pm Sat, clsd Sun*

■CRUISY AREAS

Coligny Circle Beach [AYOR] S of the Holiday Inn (at the end of Pope Ave)

Pinckney State Park [AYOR] Hwy 278 *days*

Lake Wylie

■NIGHTCLUBS

The Rainbow In [MW,D,K,DS,PC] 4376 Charlotte Hwy **803/831-0093** *9pm-3am, clsd Sun*

Leesville

■EROTICA

The Lion's Den Adult Superstore 2662 Ben Franklin (exit 139, off I-20) **803/657-5921** *24hrs*

Myrtle Beach

■BARS

Club Pulse [MW,D,F,K,DS,WC,GO] 803 Main St **843/315-0019** *5pm-4am*

South Carolina • *USA*

■RESTAURANTS

Carolina Roadhouse 4617 N Kings Hwy 843/497-9911 *11am-10pm*

Mr Fish 3401 N Kings Hwy 843/839-3474 *11am-9:30pm, full bar*

Sticky Fingers Smokehouse [WI,WC] 2461 Coastal Grand Cir 843/839-7427 *a chain, but a good one*

■RETAIL SHOPS

Kilgor Trouts Music & More 512 8th Ave N 843/445-2800

■EROTICA

X-citement Video 3106 Hwy 17 S 843/272-0744 *24hrs*

■CRUISY AREAS

Huntington Beach State Park [AYOR] Hwy 17 S *Mon-Fri*

Hurl Rock Park [AYOR] at 21st Ave S (south end)

Rock Hill

■BARS

Hideaway [MW,NH,K,DS,PC] 405 Baskins Rd 803/328-6630 *9pm-2am Th-Sat*

Spartanburg

■NIGHTCLUBS

Club Chameleon [M,D,DS] 995 Asheville Hwy 864/699-9160 *8pm-midnight, till 3am Fri-Sat, clsd Sun-Tue*

Club South 29 [M,D] 9112 Greenville Hwy (off I-85 exit 66 or I-26 exit 21a) 864/574-6087 *9pm-4am Fri-Sat only*

■MEN'S SERVICES

➤**MegaMates** 864/541-0522 *Call to hook up with HOT local men. FREE to listen & respond to ads. Use FREE code DAMRON. MegaMates.com.*

SOUTH DAKOTA

Murdo

■ACCOMMODATIONS

Iversen Inn [GF,WI,GO] 108 E 5th St (on I-90 Business Loop) 605/669-2452

Pierre

■CRUISY AREAS

LaFramboise Island [AYOR] off the causeway

Rapid City

■INFO LINES & SERVICES

The Black Hills Center for Equality 1102 West Rapid St (at Omaha St) 605/348-3244 *call for hours, clsd Sun, LGBT resource center*

■ACCOMMODATIONS

Camp Michael B&B [M,NS,GO] 1103 12th St 605/209-3503

Salem

■ACCOMMODATIONS

Camp America [GF,SW,NS,WI,GO] 25495 US 81 605/425-9085 *35 miles W of Sioux Falls*

Sioux Falls

■INFO LINES & SERVICES

The Center for Equality 406 S 2nd Ave #102 605/331-1153 *support groups, counseling, library & more*

■BARS

Toppers [MW,K] 1213 N Cliff Ave 605/339-7686 *4pm-close, clsd Sun*

■NIGHTCLUBS

Club David [GS,D,K,DS] 214 W 10th St (btwn Main & Dakota) 605/274-0700 *4:30pm-2am, also restaurant*

■EROTICA

Romantix Adult Superstore 311 N Dakota Ave (btwn 6th & 7th) 605/332-9316

■CRUISY AREAS

Sherman Park [AYOR] Kiwanis (btwn 12th & 26th Sts)

Spearfish

■CAFES

The Bay Leaf Cafe 126 W Hudson St 605/642-5462 *lunch & dinner, plenty veggie, espresso bar*

TENNESSEE

Bucksnort

■EROTICA
Miranda's [GO] 4970 Hwy 230
931/729-2006

Chattanooga

■BARS
Chuck's II [MW,NH,D] 27-1/2 W Main
St (at Market) **423/265-5405** *6pm-1am, till 3am Fri-Sat, patio*

■NIGHTCLUBS
Alan Gold's [★MW,D,F,DS,YC,WC] 1100
McCallie Ave (at National)
423/629-8080 *4:30pm-3am*

Images [MW,D,F,DS,WC] 6005 Lee Hwy **423/855-8210** *5pm-3am Th-Sun, restaurant*

■PUBLICATIONS
Out & About Newspaper
615/596-6210 *LGBT newspaper for Nashville, Knoxville, Chattanooga & Atlanta*

■MEN'S SERVICES
➤**MegaMates** 423/535-9900 *Call to hook up with HOT local men. FREE to listen & respond to ads. Use FREE code DAMRON. MegaMates.com.*

■EROTICA
Miranda's [GO] 2025 Broadway
423/266-5956

Clarksville

■EROTICA
Miranda's [GO] 19 Crossland Ave
931/648-0365

■CRUISY AREAS
Fairground Park [AYOR]

Clifton

■ACCOMMODATIONS
Bear Inn Resort [GS,WI,GO] 2250 Billy
Nance Hwy **931/676-5552**

Gatlinburg

■ACCOMMODATIONS
Big Creek Outdoors [GS,WC] 5019 Rag
Mtn Rd, Hartford **423/487-5742,
423/487-3490** *cabins, camping*

**Christopher Place, An Intimate
Resort** [GS,SW,NS,WC] 1500 Pinnacles
Wy, Newport **423/623-6555,
800/595-9441** *full brkfst*

Mountain Vista Cabins [MW,NS,WI]
1805 Shady Grove Rd (at Old Birds
Creek Rd), Sevierville **865/712-9897**
hot tub

Stonecreek Cabins [GS,NS,GO]
865/429-0400 *private Smoky Mtn cabins*

Greeneville

■ACCOMMODATIONS
Timberfell Lodge [MO,F,SW,N,NS,GO]
2240 Van Hill Rd (exit 36, off I-81)
423/234-0833, 800/437-0118 *also
camping & RV hookups, full brkfst, hot tub*

Jackson

■EROTICA
Miranda's 186 Providence Rd, Denmark
731/424-7226

■CRUISY AREAS
Muse Park [AYOR]

Johnson City

■ACCOMMODATIONS
Safe Haven Farm [GF,NS] 336 Stanley
Hollow Rd, Roan Mountain
423/725-4262 *cabins, creekside
privacy, fireplace, legally ordained minister*

■NIGHTCLUBS
New Beginnings [★M,D,F,DS,WC] 2910
N Bristol Hwy **423/282-4446** *9pm-2am, from 8pm Fri-Sat, clsd Sun-Mon*

■RETAIL SHOPS
My Secret Closet 2910 N Bristol Hwy
(inside New Beginnings)
423/282-4446 *10pm-3am Fri-Sat
only, pride gifts*

Kingsport

■CRUISY AREAS
Sullivan St [AYOR] *near library*

Tennessee • *USA*

Knoxville

■INFO LINES & SERVICES

AA Gay/ Lesbian 2931 Kingston Pike (at Unitarian Church) **865/522-9667 (AA#)** *7pm Th*

■BARS

Club Exile [M,D,F,DS,WI,,WC,GO] 4928 Homberg Dr (at Kingston Pike) **865/919-7490** *5pm-3am, from 11am Sun*

■NIGHTCLUBS

Club XYZ [MW,D,DS,K] 1215 N Central **865/637-4999** *5:30pm-3am, from 9pm Sun, from 7pm Sun*

The Edge Knox [MW,D,F,K,DS,WC] 7211 Kingston Pike SW (at Cheshire Dr) **865/602-2094** *5pm-3am*

■MEN'S SERVICES

►**MegaMates 865/291-0999** *Call to hook up with HOT local men. FREE to listen & respond to ads. Use FREE code DAMRON. MegaMates.com.*

■EROTICA

Town & Country News 6927 Clinton Hwy **865/947-9153**

West Knoxville News 5011 Kingston Pike **865/588-1972**

■CRUISY AREAS

The Block [AYOR] 100 Northview Dr (in Bearden area W of UT) *10pm-5am every night, hottest Fri-Sat after bars close*

Downtown [AYOR] btwn post office & library

IC King Park [AYOR] off Alcoa Hwy

Sharps Ridge [AYOR] off N Broadway

The Square [AYOR] intersection of Church, Market, Walnut & Union Sts

Memphis

■INFO LINES & SERVICES

AA Intergroup 1835 Union Ave #302 (at McLean) **901/726-6750**

Memphis Gay/ Lesbian Community Center 892 S Cooper (at Nelson) **901/278-6422** *2pm-9pm Mon-Fri*

■ACCOMMODATIONS

Madison Hotel [GF,SW,NS] 79 Madison Ave (at Center Ln) **901/333-1200**

Talbot Heirs Guesthouse [GF,NS] 99 S 2nd St (btwn Union & Peabody Pl) **901/527-9772, 800/955-3956** *suites w/ kitchens, funky decor*

■BARS

Dru's Place [W,NH,D,K,DS,BYOB] 1474 Madison (at McNeil) **901/275-8082** *11am-midnight, till 3am Fri-Sat, from noon Sun, beer & set-ups only*

Mollie Fontaine Lounge [GS,F] 679 Adams Ave (at Orleans) **901/524-1886** *5pm-2am, clsd Sun-Tue*

P&H Cafe [GS,F,E,K,BW,WC] 1532 Madison (at Adeline) **901/726-0906** *3pm-3am, from 5pm Sat, clsd Sun, dive bar*

Pumping Station [M,D,WC] 1382 Poplar (at Cleveland) **901/272-7600** *4pm-3am, from 3pm wknds, courtyard*

■NIGHTCLUBS

901 Complex [MW,D,MR-AF,DS, 18+,BYOB] 136 Webster Ave (at S 2nd St) **901/522-8455** *from 10pm Fri-Sat only*

■CAFES

Java Cabana [E,WI,WC] 2170 Young Ave (at Cooper) **901/272-7210** *6:30am-10pm, 9am-midnight Fri-Sat, noon-10pm Sun, clsd Mon, also art gallery*

Otherlands Coffee Bar [★F,E,WI,WC] 641 S Cooper (at Central) **901/278-4994** *7am-8pm, live music till 11pm Fri-Sat, also gift shop*

■RESTAURANTS

Automatic Slim's Tonga Club [WC] 83 S 2nd St (at Union) **901/525-7948** *lunch & dinner, Sun brunch, Caribbean & Southwestern, full bar*

Cafe Eclectic 603 N McLean Blvd (at Faxon Ave) **901/725-1718** *6am-10pm, 9am-3pm Sun; also Harbortown location*

Cafe Society [WC] 212 N Evergreen St (at Poplar) **901/722-2177** *lunch Mon-Fri, dinner nightly, full bar*

India Palace 1720 Poplar Ave (at Lemaster St) **901/278-1199** *lunch & dinner*

Leonard's Pit Barbecue 5465 Fox Plaza Dr (at Mt Moriah Rd) **901/360-1963** *11am-9pm, till 2:30pm Sun-Wed, Elvis ordered the pork sandwich at the original Leonard's (now closed), but the food is just as good here!*

Molly's La Casita 2006 Madison Ave (at N Morrison St) **901/726-1873** *lunch & dinner, Mexican*

Restaurant Iris [WC] 2146 Monroe Ave (at Cooper) **901/590-2828** *dinner Mon-Sat, French/ Creole, upscale*

RP Tracks 3547 Walker Ave (at Brister) **901/327-1471** *lunch & dinner, open till 3am, burgers, some veggie*

Saigon Le 51 N Cleveland (at Jefferson) **901/276-5326** *11am-9pm, clsd Sun, pan-Asian*

Tsunami [WC] 928 S Cooper (at Young) **901/274-2556** *dinner only, Pacific rim cuisine*

■ENTERTAINMENT & RECREATION

Center for Southern Folklore [F] 119 S Main St (at Peabody Pl) **901/525-3655** *11am-5pm, clsd Sun, open later for shows, live music, gallery, also cybercafe*

Graceland 3734 Elvis Presley Blvd **901/332-3322, 800/238-2000** *no visit to Memphis would be complete w/out a trip to see The King*

Memphis Rock 'N Roll Tours **901/359-3102** *historical tour of Memphis music scene*

■RETAIL SHOPS

Inz & Outz [WC] 553 S Cooper (at Peabody) **901/728-6535** *10am-8pm, noon-6pm Sun, pride items, books*

■MEN'S SERVICES

►**MegaMates** **901/888-0888** *Call to hook up with HOT local men. FREE to listen & respond to ads. Use FREE code DAMRON. MegaMates.com.*

■EROTICA

Cherokee Books 2947 Lamar **901/744-7494**

Getwell Books 1275 Getwell (at Park) **901/454-7765**

Paris Theater 2432 Summer Ave (at Hollywood) **901/323-2665**

Romantix Adult Superstore 2220 E Brooks Rd **901/396-9050**

Romantix Airport Books 2214 Brooks Rd E (at Airways) **901/345-0657**

Nashville

■INFO LINES & SERVICES

AA Gay/ Lesbian **615/831-1050** *call for info*

■ACCOMMODATIONS

The Big Bungalow B&B [GF,E,NS,WI] 618 Fatherland St (at 7th) **615/256-8375** *full brkfst, live music, massage available*

Hutton Hotel [GF,WI,WC] 1808 West End Ave (at 19th Ave) **615/340-9333**

Top O' Woodland Historic B&B Inn [GF,NS] 1603 Woodland St (at 16th) **615/228-3868, 888/228-3868**

Whispering Oaks Retreat Center [M,SW,N] **931/709-1192**

■BARS

Blue Gene's [M,B,K,WI] 1715 Church St (at 17th) **615/329-3508** *4pm-3am, from 3pm wknds, clsd Mon*

Canvas Lounge [M,D,K] 1707 Church St **615/320-8656** *4pm-3am*

The Patterson House [GS,F] 1711 Division St **615/636-7724** *5pm-3am, great speakeasy vibe*

Purple Heys [MW,NH,F,WC] 1401 4th Ave S (at Rains) **615/244-4433** *11am-3am*

Stirrup Nashville [M,NH,MR,F,WC] 1529 4th Ave S (at Mallory) **615/782-0043** *noon-3am, patio*

The Stone Fox [GS,F,E] 712 51st Ave N **615/953-1811** *5pm-3am, from 11am wknds*

Trax [M,NH,K,WI] 1501 2nd Ave S (at Carney) **615/742-8856** *noon-3am*

Tribe/ Suzy Wong's House of Yum [★MW,F,E,V,WC,GO] 1517 Church St (at 15th Ave S) **615/329-2912** *4pm-midnight, till 2am wknds, upscale, full restaurant*

Tennessee • *USA*

■NIGHTCLUBS

Bluebird Cafe [GF,E] 4104 Hillsboro Pike (nr Warfield Dr) **615/383-1461** *live country music venue*

Play Dance Bar [M,D,MR,TG,E,DS,18+,WC] 1519 Church St (at 16th Ave) **615/322-9627** *9pm-3am Wed-Sun*

Vibe [M,D,MR-L,DS,BYOB] 1713 Church St (at 17th & 18th) **615/329-3838** *afterhours bar, patio*

■CAFES

Bongo Java [E] 2007 Belmont Blvd **615/385-5282** *7am-11pm, from 8am wknds, coffeehouse, deck, also serves brkfst, lunch & dinner*

Fido [F] 1812 21st Ave S **615/777-3436** *7am-11pm, till midnight Fri-Sat, from 8am wknds, also full menu*

Grins Vegetarian Cafe 2421 Vanderbilt Pl (at 25th Ave) **615/322-8571** *7am-9pm, till 3pm Fri, clsd wknds*

■RESTAURANTS

Battered & Fried [WC] 1008 Woodland St (at S 10th) **615/226-9283** *lunch & dinner, seafood, bar, also Wave sushi bar*

Beyond the Edge 112 S 11th St **615/226-3343** *11am-2am, pizza & sandwiches, full bar*

Cafe Coco [E,BW] 210 Louise Ave (at State) **615/321-2626** *24hrs, patio*

Couva Calypso Cafe 2424 Elliston Pl **615/321-3878** *11am-9pm, 11:30am-8:30pm wknds, Caribbean*

Mad Donna's 1313 Woodland St (at 14th) **615/226-1617** *11am-10pm, till 11pm Sat, clsd Mon, also lounge, drag bingo Tue*

The Mad Platter [R,WC] 1239 6th Ave N (at Monroe) **615/242-2563** *lunch Mon-Fri, dinner Wed-Sun, eclectic, local & fresh*

Pancake Pantry 1796 21st Ave S (at Wedgewood Ave) **615/383-9333** *6am-3pm, till 4pm wknds, popular brkfst*

Rumours Wine & Art Bar [WC] 2304 12th Ave S (at Linden) **615/292-9400** *5pm-midnight, till 9pm Sun*

Sky Blue Coffeehouse & Bistro 700 Fatherland St (at S 7th St) **615/770-7097** *brkfst & lunch*

Sole Mio [WC] 311 3rd Ave S **615/256-4013** *11am-10pm, till 11pm Fri-Sat, clsd Mon, Italian*

The Standard at the Smith House [R,WC] 167 Rosa Parks Ave (at Charlotte) **615/254-1277** *dinner Tue-Sat, clsd Sun-Mon*

Watermark [WC] 507 12th Ave S (at Division) **615/254-2000** *dinner nightly, clsd Sun, seafood & more*

Yellow Porch [WC] 734 Thompson Ln (at Bransford Ave) **615/386-0260** *lunch & dinner, clsd Sun, fresh Southern cuisine*

■ENTERTAINMENT & RECREATION

NashTrash Tours [R] tours leave from the Farmers Market (900 8th Ave N) **615/226-7300, 800/342-2132** *campy tours of Nashville w/ the Jugg Sisters*

■PUBLICATIONS

Inside Out Nashville 615/831-1806 *LGBT newspaper & bar guide*

Out & About Newspaper 615/596-6210

■MEN'S SERVICES

➤**MegaMates** 615/777-0770 *Call to hook up with HOT local men. FREE to listen & respond to ads. Use FREE code DAMRON. MegaMates.com.*

■EROTICA

The Lion's Den Adult Superstore 2807 Nolensville Pike **615/254-8891** *24hrs*

Miranda's [GO] 822 5th Ave S **615/256-1310**

■CRUISY AREAS

J Percy Priest Dam [AYOR]

TEXAS

Abilene

■EROTICA

Midnight Video 3305 E Hwy 80 **325/672-2000** *more gay Wed*

■CRUISY AREAS

Kirby Park [AYOR]

Amarillo

■BARS

212 Club [MW,NH,D,DS,WC] 212 SW 6th Ave (at Harrison) **806/372-7997** *3pm-2am*

Kicked Back [MW,NH,K,GO] 521 SE 10th Ave (at Buchanan St) **806/371-3535** *3pm-2am, clsd Sun*

R&R [GF,NH,WC,GO] 701 S Georgia St **806/342-9000** *4pm-2am*

■RESTAURANTS

Furrbie's [GO] 210 W 6th Ave **806/220-0841** *11am-7pm, till 3pm Sat & Mon*

■EROTICA

Fantasy Gifts & Video 440 N Lakeside Dr **806/372-6500**

Arlington

see also Dallas & Fort Worth

■INFO LINES & SERVICES

Tarrant County Lesbian/ Gay Alliance **817/877-5544**

■NIGHTCLUBS

The 1851 Club [MW,D,K,DS,V,WC] 931 W Division **682/323-5315** *3pm-2am*

Austin

■INFO LINES & SERVICES

Lambda AA (Live & Let Live) [NS,WC] 6809 Guadalupe St (at Galano Club) **512/444-0071, 512/832-6767** (en español) *6:30pm & 8pm daily, 10am Sat, 11am Sun*

Q 3408 West Ave (2 blks W of Guadalupe & 34th) **512/420-8557** *2pm-10pm Tue-Sat, support & information for GBTQI men 18-29*

■ACCOMMODATIONS

Austin Folk House [GS,NS,WI,WC] 506 W 22nd St (at Nueces) **512/472-6700, 866/472-6700**

Brava House [GF,NS,WI] 1108 Blanco St (at W 12th) **512/478-5034, 866/892-5726** *close to downtown & 6th Street*

Crowne Plaza Hotel Austin [GF] 6121 North IH 35 **512/323-5466**

Hilton Garden Inn Austin Downtown [GF] 500 North IH 35 **512/480-8181**

Hotel Saint Cecilia [GF,SW,WC] 112 Academy Dr **512/852-2400**

Hotel San Jose [★GS,SW,NS,WC,GO] 1316 S Congress Ave **512/852-2350, 800/574-8897**

Kimber Modern [GS,WI,WO] 110 The Circle **512/912-1046**

Mt Gainor Inn B&B [GS,NS,WI] 2390 Prochnow Rd (at Mt Gainor Rd), Dripping Springs **512/858-0982, 888/644-0982**

Park Lane Guest House [GS,SW,WC,GO] 221 Park Ln (at Drakc) **512/447-7460, 800/492-8827** *full brkfst, also cottage*

Robin's Nest [GF,NS,WI] 1007 Stewart Cove **512/266-3413** *on Lake Travis*

■BARS

'Bout Time II [MW,NH,D,TG,K,WI,WC] 6607 I-35 N **512/419-9192** *2pm-3am*

Casino El Camino [GF,NH,F,WI,WC] 517 E 6th St (at Red River) **512/469-9330** *4pm-2am, psychedelic punk jazz lounge, great burgers*

Chain Drive [M,D,L,WC] 504 Willow St (at Red River) **512/480-9017** *6pm-2am, clsd Tue, cruisy*

Cheer Up Charlie's [MW,NH,E,F] 900 Red River *5pm-2am, live bands, shows, also vegan restaurant*

The Iron Bear [M,B] 121 W 8th St **512/482-8993** *3pm-2am*

■NIGHTCLUBS

404 [MW,D,WC] 404 Colorado **512/522-4044** *9pm-close Wed-Sat, from 5pm Sun*

The Basement [M,D,DS] 422 Congress (at 5th) *9pm-2am, till 3am wknds*

The Belmont [GF] 305 W 6th St **512/457-0300** *live music venue*

Oilcan Harry's [★M,D,K,S,DS,18+,WI,WC] 211 W 4th St (btwn Lavaca & Colorado) **512/320-8823** *2pm-2am, patio*

Rain [M,D,K,S,WC] 217-B W 4th St (at Colorado St) 512/494-1150 *4pm-close, from 3pm Fri-Sun*

■CAFES

Austin Java Cafe [F] 1608 Barton Springs Rd (at Kinney Ave) 512/482-9450 *7am-11pm, from 8am Sat-Sun; also 1206 Parkway, 512/476-1829 & 300 W 2nd St, 512/481-9400*

Bouldin Creek Coffeehouse [F] 1900 S 1st St 512/416-1601 *7am-midnight, from 9am wknds, vegetarian; occasional live music*

Joe's Bakery & Coffee Shop [WC] 2305 E 7th St (at Morelos & Northwestern) 512/472-0017 *6am-3pm, clsd Mon, Tex-Mex*

Spider House Patio Bar & Cafe [E] 2908 Fruth St (at West Dr) 512/480-9562 *10am-2am, patio*

■RESTAURANTS

Changos 3023 Guadalupe 512/480-8226 *taqueria, open all day*

Chez Nous [WC] 510 Neches St 512/473-2413 *lunch Tue-Fri, dinner nightly, clsd Mon*

Chuy's [WC] 1728 Barton Springs Rd 512/474-4452 *11am-10pm, till 11pm Fri-Sat, Tex-Mex, full bar*

Corazon at Castle Hill [WC] 1101 W 5th St (at Baylor) 512/476-0728 *lunch weekdays & dinner nightly, clsd Sun*

Eastside Cafe [BW,WC] 2113 Manor Rd (at Breeze Terrace) 512/476-5858 *11:30am-9:30pm, 10am-10pm wknds*

El Sol y La Luna [★E,WC,GO] 600 E 6th St (at Red River) 512/444-7770 *11am-10pm, 9am-1pm Fri-Sat, 9am-4pm Sun*

Fonda San Miguel 2330 W North Loop (at Hancock Rd) 512/459-4121 *dinner only, popular Sun brunch, Mexican, full bar*

Galaxy 1000 W Lynn 512/478-3434 *7am-10pm, quick, stylish & tasty*

Guero's [E] 1412 S Congress (at Elizabeth) 512/447-7688 *11am-11pm, from 8am wknds, great Mexican & people-watching, outdoor seating, live music outdoors on wknds*

Imperia [WC] 310 Colorado St 512/472-6770 *dinner only, upscale Asian, full bar*

Jo's Hot Coffee & Good Food [WC,GO] 1300 S Congress Ave (at James) 512/444-3800 *7am-9pm, till 10pm Sat; also 242 W 2nd St, 512/469-9003*

Kenichi [WC] 419 Colorado St 512/320-8883 *dinner nightly, Asian/sushi*

Mother's Cafe & Garden [★BW,WC] 4215 Duval St (at 43rd) 512/451-3994 *11:15am-10pm, from 10am wknds, vegetarian*

Mr Natural 1901 E Cesar Chavez St 512/477-5228 *8am-8pm, vegetarian/vegan*

Polvos [WC] 2004 S 1st St (at Johanna) 512/441-5446 *7am-11pm, Mexican, outdoor seating*

Santa Rita Cantina 1206 W 38th St 512/419-7482 *lunch & dinner, wknd brunch*

Threadgill's [E] 6416 N Lamar 512/451-5440 *10am-10pm, till 9pm Sun, great chicken-fried steak; also 301 W Riverside Dr, 512/472-9304*

Wink [WC] 1014 N Lamar Blvd 512/482-8868 *dinner nightly, clsd Sun, upscale, also wine bar*

■ENTERTAINMENT & RECREATION

Barton Springs [N] Barton Springs Rd (in Zilker Park) 512/867-3080 *natural swimming hole*

Bat Colony Congress Ave Bridge (at Barton Springs Dr) *colony of bats that flies out from under this bridge every evening March-Oct*

Capital City Men's Chorus 512/477-7464 *call for events*

■BOOKSTORES

Bookpeople 603 N Lamar Blvd (at 6th) 512/472-5050, 800/853-9757 *9am-11pm*

MonkeyWrench Books 110 E North Loop 512/407-6925 *11am-8pm, from noon wknds, independent, radical bookstore*

■RETAIL SHOPS

Tapelenders [GO] 1114 W 5th St #501 (at Baylor) **512/472-0844** *10am-10pm, till midnight Fri-Sat, LGBT*

■PUBLICATIONS

➤**Ambush Mag** 504/522-8049 *LGBT newspaper for the Gulf South (TX through FL)*

Austin Chronicle 512/454-5766 *has extensive online gay guide (check out www.austinchronicle.com)*

■GYMS & HEALTH CLUBS

Hyde Park Gym 4125 Guadalupe (at 41st St) **512/459-9174** *5am-10pm, 7am-7pm Sat, 8am-7pm Sun*

Milk + Honey Spa 204 Colorado St (at 2nd) **512/236-1115** *9am-9pm*

■MEN'S CLUBS

Midtowne Spa—Austin [PC] 5815 Airport Blvd (at Koenig) **512/302-9696** *24hrs, outdoor hot tub, sundeck*

■MEN'S SERVICES

➤**MegaMates** 512/480-8400 *Call to hook up with HOT local men. FREE to listen & respond to ads. Use FREE code DAMRON. MegaMates.com.*

■EROTICA

Adult Video Megaplexxx 7111 S Ih 35 **512/442-5430** *24hrs, arcade*

Forbidden Fruit 108 E North Loop **512/453-8090** *woman-owned & operated*

New Video 7901 S Ih 35 **512/280-1142** *24hrs, arcade*

■CRUISY AREAS

Hippie Hollow–Lake Travis [AYOR]

Beaumont

■BARS

Orleans Street Pub & Patio [MW,NH,D,K,DS] 650 Orleans St (at Forsythe) **409/835-4243** *7pm-2am, clsd Mon-Tue*

■MEN'S SERVICES

➤**MegaMates** 409/812-0333 *Call to hook up with HOT local men. FREE to listen & respond to ads. Use FREE code DAMRON. MegaMates.com.*

Bryan

■BARS

Revolution Cafe & Bar [GF,NH,TG,F,E,WI,WC] 211 B S Main St (at 27th) **979/823-4044** *6pm-2am, from 8pm Sun-Mon, from 4pm Fri*

■NIGHTCLUBS

Halo Bar [MW,D,K,DS,V,18+,WC] 121 N Main St (at William J Bryan Pkwy) **979/823-6174** *9:30pm-2am Th-Sat*

Corpus Christi

■INFO LINES & SERVICES

Clean & Serene AA 3026 S Staples (at MCC church) **361/992-8911, 866/672-7029** *8pm Fri*

■ACCOMMODATIONS

Anthony's By The Sea [GS,SW,WI,NS,WC,GO] 732 S Pearl St, Rockport **361/729-6100, 800/460-2557**

Port Aransas Inn [GS,SW,WI,WC] 1500 S 11th St (at Ave G), Port Aransas **361/749-5937**

■BARS

The Hidden Door [M,NH,D,DS,WC] 802 S Staples St (at Coleman) **361/882-5002** *noon-2am, patio, also the Loft piano bar Fri-Sun*

■NIGHTCLUBS

Triangle Niteclub [MW,D,DS] **361/903-0977** *5pm-2am, clsd Mon*

■MEN'S SERVICES

➤**MegaMates** 361/884-0884 *Call to hook up with HOT local men. FREE to listen & respond to ads. Use FREE code DAMRON. MegaMates.com.*

Dallas

see also Arlington, Fort Worth

■INFO LINES & SERVICES

John Thomas Gay/ Lesbian Community Center [WC] 2701 Reagan St (at Brown) **214/528-0144, 214/528-0022** *9am-9pm, till 5pm Sat, noon-5pm Sun*

Lambda AA 2438 Butler #106 **214/267-0222**

Texas • *USA*

■ACCOMMODATIONS

Bailey's Uptown Inn [GF,NS,WI] 2505 Worthington St (at Hibernia) **214/720-2258**

Hotel ZaZa [GF,SW] 2332 Leonard St (at State) **214/468-8399, 888/880-3244**

Lumen [GF,WI,WC] 6101 Hillcrest Ave **214/219-2400, 800/908-1140**

MCM Elegante' Hotel and Suites [GF,SW,WI] 2330 W Northwest Hwy **214/358-7846, 877/351-4477**

Palomar Dallas [GF] 5300 E Mockingbird Ln **214/520-7969, 888/253-9030**

■BARS

Alexandre's [GS,E,K,WC] 4026 Cedar Springs Rd (at Knight St) **214/559-0720** *9am-2pm, from 2pm Sun, live music*

Barbara's Pavillion [M,NH,K,WC] 325 Centre St **214/941-2145** *4pm-2am, from 2pm Sun, patio*

BJ's NXS [M,D,S,WC,GO] 3215 N Fitzhugh (at Travis) **214/526-9510** *6pm-2am from 4pm Sun-Mon, patio*

Dallas Eagle [M,B,L] 5740 Maple Ave (at Inwood Rd) **214/357-4375** *5pm-2am, from 4pm wknds, clsd Mon*

Grapevine [GS,WI,WC] 3902 Maple Ave (at Shelby) **214/522-8466** *3pm-2am, from 1pm Sun, classic dive bar*

The Hidden Door [M,NH,L,WC] 5025 Bowser Ave (at Mahanna) **214/526-0620** *7am-2am, from noon Sun, patio*

JR's Bar & Grill [★MW,F,E,V,YC,WI,WC] 3923 Cedar Springs Rd (at Throckmorton) **214/528-1004** *11am-2am, from noon Sun-Mon*

The Mining Co [★M,D,L] 3903 Cedar Springs Rd (at Reagan) **214/521-4204** *5pm-4am, clsd Mon-Wed*

Pekers [MW,NH,E,K,C,DS,WC] 2615 Oak Lawn Ave, Ste 101 (btwn Fairmount & Brown) **214/528-3333** *10am-2am*

Pub Pegasus [M,NH,WI,WC] 3326 N Fitzhugh Ave (at Travis) **214/559-4663** *noon-2am, patio*

Sue Ellen's [★W,D,E,WC] 3014 Throckmorton (at Cedar Springs) **214/559-0707** *5pm-2am, 2pm-close wknds, patio*

Tin Room [M,NH,WC] 2514 Hudnall St (at Maple Ave) **214/526-6365** *10am-2am, from noon Sun, patio*

Woody's [MW,K,V,WC] 4011 Cedar Springs Rd (btwn Douglas & Throckmorton) **214/520-6629** *2pm-2am, sports bar, patio*

Zippers [M,NH,S] 3333 N Fitzhugh (at Travis) **214/526-9519** *noon-2am*

■NIGHTCLUBS

The Brick/Joe's Dallas [MW,D,MR,DS] 2525 Wycliff Ave (btwn Maple & Tollway) **214/521-3154** *4pm-2am, till 4am Fri-Sat, from noon Sat-Sun*

Club Los Rieles [M,D,DS,MR-L] 600 S Riverfront (Industrial) Blvd **214/741-2125** *Latin club, wknds only*

Exklusive [MW,D,DS,MR-L] 4207 Maple Ave (at Knight St) **469/556-1395** *9pm-close Th-Sun*

Havana Bar & Grill [GS,D,MR-L,DS] 4006 Cedar Springs Rd (at Throckmorton) **214/526-9494** *grill 5pm-10pm, lounge from 10pm, clsd Mon*

Kaliente [M,D,MR-L,K,DS,WC] 4350 Maple Ave (at Hondo) **214/520-6676** *9pm-2am, clsd Tue, salsa & Tejano*

Panoptikon [GS,D] 3025 Main St (at Excuses) **214/741-1111** *monthly gothic/electro dance party*

Round-Up Saloon [★M,D,CW,K,WC] 3912 Cedar Springs Rd (at Throckmorton) **214/522-9611** *3pm-2am, from noon wknds*

Station 4 [★MW,D,C,DS,S,V,18+] 3911 Cedar Springs Rd (at Throckmorton) **214/526-7171** *9pm-4am Wed-Sun, also Rose Room cabaret, patio*

■CAFES

Buli [WI,WC] 3908 Cedar Springs Rd **214/528-5410** *7am-close*

Opening Bell Coffee [E,BW,WI] 1409 S Lamar St, Ste 012 **214/565-0383** *7am-10pm, from 9am wknds, till midnight wknds*

■RESTAURANTS

3025 Main/ Excuses Cafe [WI] 3025 Main St (in Deep Ellum) **214/741-1111** *11am-2am*

Dallas • Texas

Ali Baba Cafe 1901 Abrams Rd (near La Vista Dr) **214/823-8235** *lunch & dinner*

Bangkok Orchid [GO,BYOB,WC] 331 W Airport Fwy (at N Beltline), Irving **972/252-7770** *lunch & dinner, clsd Mon, ask for Danny*

Black-Eyed Pea [WC] 3857 Cedar Springs Rd (at Reagan) **214/521-4580** *11am-10pm*

Blue Mesa Grill 5100 Belt Line Rd (at Tollway), Addison **972/934-0165** *11am-10pm*

Bread Winners [WC] 3301 McKinney Ave **214/754-4940** *4pm-2am, from 10am wknds*

Cafe Brazil 3847 Cedar Springs Rd **214/461-8762** *open 24hrs*

Cosmic Cafe [E,BW,WI] 2912 Oak Lawn Ave **214/521-6157** *11am-10:30pm, till 11pm Fri-Sat, noon-10pm Sun, veggie, also yoga & meditation*

Cremona Bistro 2704 Worthington St (at Howell) **214/871-1115** *lunch weekdays & dinner nightly, Italian, full bar, patio*

Dish [E,WC] 4123 Cedar Springs Rd #110 **214/522-3474** *dinner & Sun brunch, full bar, patio*

Dream Cafe [BW,WI,WC] 2800 Routh St (in the Quadrangle) **214/954-0486** *7am-9pm, till 10pm Fri-Sat, brkfst served till 5pm*

Hattie's [WC] 418 N Bishop Ave **214/942-7400** *lunch daily, dinner Tue-Sun, Southern*

Hibiscus [WC] 2927 N Henderson Ave **214/827-2927** *dinner only, clsd Sun, steak & seafood*

Hunky's [★BW,WC,GO] 3940 Cedar Springs Rd (at Reagan) **214/522-1212** *11am-10pm, till 11pm Sat, from noon Sun, burgers & salads, patio*

Lucky's Cafe [WC] 3531 Oak Lawn **214/522-3500** *7am-10pm, classic comfort food, great brkfst*

Mario's [★] 5404 Lemmon Ave **214/599-9744** *11am-11pm, Mexican & Salvadorian*

Monica Aca y Alla [★TG,E,WC] 2914 Main St (at Malcolm X) **214/748-7140** *lunch Mon-Fri, dinner Tue-Sun, brunch wknds, Mexican, full bar*

Naga Kitchen & Bar 665 High Market St (Victory Park) **214/953-0023** *lunch Mon-Sat, dinner nightly, authentic Thai*

Stephan Pyles 1807 Ross Ave, Ste 200 **214/580-7000** *lunch Mon-Fri, dinner Mon-Sat, clsd Sun, Southwestern cuisine*

Taco Joint [WC] 911 N Peak St **214/826-8226** *6:30am-2pm, from 8am Sat, clsd Sun*

Thai Soon [WC] 101 S Coit, Ste 401 (at Belt Line) **972/234-6111** *lunch & dinner*

Ziziki's [WC] 4514 Travis St, #122 (in Travis Walk) **214/521-2233** *11am-10pm, Sun brunch, Greek & Italian, full bar*

■RETAIL SHOPS

Obscurities 4008 Cedar Springs **214/559-3706** *11am-9pm, 2pm-8pm Sun, clsd Mon, tattoo & piercing*

Tapelenders [GO] 3926 Cedar Springs Rd (at Throckmorton) **214/528-6344** *9am-midnight, LGBT*

Union Jack 3920 Cedar Springs Rd **214/528-9600** *men's clothing & underwear*

■PUBLICATIONS

Dallas Voice **214/754-8710** *LGBT newspaper*

■MEN'S CLUBS

Club Dallas [SW,PC,WI] 2616 Swiss Ave (at Good Latimer) **214/821-1990** *24hrs*

Midtowne Spa—Dallas [PC] 2509 Pacific Ave (at Hawkins) **214/821-8989** *24hrs, 3 flrs, rooftop sundeck*

■MEN'S SERVICES

▶**MegaMates** **214/615-0100** *Call to hook up with HOT local men. FREE to listen & respond to ads. Use FREE code DAMRON. MegaMates.com.*

Texas • *USA*

■EROTICA

Alternatives 1720 W Mockingbird Ln (at Hawes) 214/630-7071 *24hrs*

Amazing Superstore 11311 Harry Hines Blvd #603 972/243-2707

Leather Masters 3000 Main St 214/528-3865 *noon-10pm, clsd Sun-Mon*

Lido Theatre 7035 John Carpenter Fwy (at Mockinbird Ln) 214/630-7127

Mockingbird Video 708 W Mockingbird Ln (at I-35 & Halifax) 214/631-3003 *24hrs, bookstore w/ arcade*

Odyssey Video 11505 Anaheim Dr (at Forest Ln) 972/484-4999 *24hrs*

Paris Adult Book & Video Store 11118 Harry Hines Blvd 972/263-0774 *24hrs, bookstore w/ arcade*

■CRUISY AREAS

Reverchon Park [AYOR]

Tom Braniff Park [AYOR] off SH 114 (at Tom Braniff exit) *beware cops (!)*

Denison

■BARS

Good Time Lounge [MW,E,K,DS,PC] 2520 Hwy 91 N 903/463-6086 *7pm-2am Wed-Sun*

Denton

■NIGHTCLUBS

Mable Peabody's Beauty Parlor & Chainsaw Repair [MW,D,E,K,DS,WC,GO] 1125 E University Dr 940/566-9910 *4pm-2am*

El Paso

see also Ciudad Juárez, Mexico

■BARS

8 1/2 [M,S] 504 N Stanton St 915/351-0262 *4pm-2am*

Briar Patch [MW,NH,K] 508 N Stanton St (at Missouri) 915/577-9555 *2pm-2am, from noon wknds patio*

Chiquita's Bar [MW,NH,MR-L,WC] 310 E Missouri Ave (at Stanton) 915/351-0095 *2pm-2am*

Epic [W,NH,E] 510 N Stanton St (at Missouri) 915/566-0378 *live bands*

The Tool Box [M,NH] 506 N Stanton St (at Missouri) 915/351-1896 *2pm-2am, patio*

The Whatever Lounge [MW,D,MR-L,K,DS, WC] 701 E Paisano Dr (at Ochoa) *2pm-2am*

■RESTAURANTS

The Little Diner [BW,WC] 7209 7th St, Canutillo 915/877-2176 *11am-8pm, clsd Wed, true Texas fare*

■MEN'S SERVICES

➤**MegaMates** 915/541-8888 *Call to hook up with HOT local men. FREE to listen & respond to ads. Use FREE code DAMRON. MegaMates.com.*

■EROTICA

Venus 4828 Montana (near Reynolds) 915/565-2929

Eustace

■ACCOMMODATIONS

Captain's Quarters [GS] PO Box 577 75124 903/802-2771 *cabin rentals*

Circle J Ranch [M,18+,SW,N,WI,PC,GO] 903/479-4189 *campground (cabins, tents, RVs) 1 hour from Dallas*

Fort Worth

see also Arlington & Dallas

■INFO LINES & SERVICES

Tarrant County Lesbian/ Gay Alliance 817/877-5544 *info line & newsletter*

■ACCOMMODATIONS

Hotel Trinity InnSuites Hotel [GF,SW,NS,WI,WC] 2000 Beach St 817/534-4801, 800/989-3556

■BARS

Best Friends Club [MW,NH,D,F,K,DS] 2620 E Lancaster Ave 817/420-9220 *3pm-2am, clsd Mon*

Crossroads [M,NH] 515 S Jennings Ave (at Pennsylvania) 817/332-0071 *11am-2am, from noon Sun*

■NIGHTCLUBS

Rainbow Lounge [M,D,DS,WC] 651 S Jennings Ave (at Pennsylvania) 817/744-7723 *9am-2am*

■ MEN'S SERVICES

➤ **MegaMates** 817/282-2500 *Call to hook up with HOT local men. FREE to listen & respond to ads. Use FREE code DAMRON. MegaMates.com.*

■ CRUISY AREAS

Benbrook Dam [AYOR] *parking lot & woods*

Trinity Park [AYOR] *parking lot & woods*

Galveston

■ ACCOMMODATIONS

Hotel Galvez [GF,NS,WI] 2024 Seawall Blvd 409/765-7721, 877/999-3223

Lost Bayou Guesthouse B&B [GF,NS,WI] 1607 Ave L (at 16th) 409/770-0688 *1890 Victorian home survived hurricane of 1900*

■ BARS

3rd Coast Beach Bar [M,DS,S] 2416 Post Office St 409/765-6911 *4pm-2am, from 2pm wknds*

Pink Dolphin [M,K,BYOB] 1706 23rd St (at O Ave) 409/621-1808 *10am-midnight, strippers on wknds*

Robert's Lafitte [M,DS,WC] 2501 Q Ave (at 25th St) 409/765-9092 *7am-2am, from 10am Sun, [DS] wknds*

Stars Beach Club [MW,D,B,MR,K,DS] 3102 Seawall Blvd 409/497-4113 *noon-2am, theme nights*

■ CAFES

Mod Coffee & Tea House [F,E,BW,WI] 2126 Post Office St (at 22nd) 409/765-5659 *7am-10pm*

■ RESTAURANTS

Eat Cetera [BW,WC] 408 25th St 409/762-0803 *11am-7pm, clsd Sun*

Luigi's 2328 The Strand (at Tremont) 409/763-6500 *dinner only, clsd Sun*

Mosquito Cafe [WC] 628 14th St (at Winnie) 409/763-1010 *8am-9pm, 8am-9pm Sat, till 3pm Sun, clsd Mon*

The Spot [WC] 3204 Seawall Blvd (at 32nd St) 409/621-5237 *good burgers, great view, also Tiki Bar*

Star Drug Store [WC] 510 23rd St 409/766-7719 *9am-3pm, old-fashioned drug store & soda fountain*

■ CRUISY AREAS

The Dunes [AYOR] at East Beach off Hwy 87

Groesbeck

■ ACCOMMODATIONS

Rainbow Ranch Campground [MW,SW,NS,GO] 1662 LCR 800 254/729-8484, 888/875-7596 *on Lake Limestone*

Gun Barrel City

■ BARS

Garlow's [MW,D,DS] 308 E Main St 903/887-0853 *4pm-close*

Houston

■ INFO LINES & SERVICES

Gay & Lesbian Switchboard Houston 713/529-3211, 888/843-4564 *24hr crisis hotline*

Lambda AA Center [WC] 1201 W Clay (btwn Montrose & Waugh) 713/521-1243

■ ACCOMMODATIONS

Hotel Derek [GF] 2525 W Loop S (at Westheimer) 713/961-3000, 866/292-4100 *modern, chic hotel*

Hotel Sorella [GF] 800 W Sam Houston Pkwy N 713/973-1600, 866/842-0100

The Houstonian [GF,WC] 111 N Post Oak Ln (near Woodway Dr) 713/680-2626, 800/231-2759

Robin's Nest B&B Inn [GF,WI] 4104 Greeley St 713/528-5821, 800/622-8343

Sam Houston Hotel [GF,F,WI] 1117 Prairie St (at Fannin) 832/200-8800

Sycamore Heights B&B [GF,NS,WI,GO] 245 W 18th St 713/861-4117

■ BARS

13 The Heights Bar [MW] 1537 N Shepherd (at 16th St) 713/426-1313 *4pm-2am*

The 611 Club [★M,NH] 611 Hyde Park Blvd (at Stanford) 713/526-7070 *7am-2am, from noon Sun*

Texas • *USA*

Bayou City Bar & Grill [MW,F] 2409 Grant St (at Hyde Park Blvd) 713/522-2867 *4pm-2am, clsd Mon*

Blur [MW,D,18+] 710 Pacific St (at Crocker) **713/529-3447** *10pm-2am, clsd Mon-Tue*

Boom Boom Room [GF] 2518 Yale St 713/868-3740 *4pm-2am, clsd Sun-Mon, wine & panini bar*

Club 2020 [MW,D,MR,18+] 2020 Leeland **713/227-9667** *10pm-4am Sat, mostly African American, hip hop*

Cockpit Bar & Grill [GS,NH,K,WI,GO] 101 Airport Blvd **713/640-7139**

Crocker [MW,NH,K,WI] 2312 Crocker St 713/529-3355 *11am-2am*

The Eagle [M,D,E,S] 213 Milam St 713/236-8777 *9pm-5am Fri-Sat, 6pm-2am Sun*

EJ's [M,D,E,S] 2517 Ralph (at Westheimer) **713/527-9071** *10am-2am, patio*

George Country Sports Bar [M,NH,CW,GO] 617 Fairview (at Stanford) 713/528-8102 *7am-2am, from 10am Sun, sports bar, patio*

Guava Lamp [MW,K,V,WI,WC] 570 Waugh Dr **713/524-3359** *4pm-2am, from 2pm Sun*

JR's [★M,K,DS,S,V,WC] 808 Pacific (at Grant) **713/521-2519** *noon-2am, patio*

Meteor [M,DS,S,WC,GO] 2306 Genesee St (at Fairview) **713/521-0123** *4pm-2am*

Michael's Outpost [M,NH,E,OC] 1419 Richmond (at Mandell) **713/520-8446** *3pm-2am, from noon wknds*

Montrose Mining Co [★M,CW,L,WC] 808 Pacific St (at Grant) 713/529-7488 *4pm-2:30am, clsd Mon-Tue, patio*

Neon Boots [MW,CW,GO] 11410 Hempstead Hwy (in Esq Ballroom) 713/677-0288 *4pm-2am, from noon wknds, till midnight Sun*

Ripcord [M,L,WC] 715 Fairview (at Crocker) **713/521-2792** *1pm-2am, noon-3am Fri-Sat, popular after-hours*

TC's Show Bar [MW,NH,K,DS,TG] 817 Fairview (at Converse) 713/526-2625 *10am-2am*

Tony's Corner Pocket [MW,NH,K,S,WI] 817 W Dallas (btwn Arthur & Crosby) 713/571-7870 *noon-2am, large deck*

The Usual Pub [GS,NH,E,K,GO] 5519 Allen St **281/501-1478** *4pm-2am, from 3pm Sat, from noon Sun*

■NIGHTCLUBS

Crystal [M,D,DS,MR-L] 6680 Southwest Fwy (at Colorado) 713/278-2582 *9pm-3am Wed-Sun, Latino club, theme nights*

F Bar Houston [MW,D,E,K] 202 Tuam St 713/522-2227 *5pm-2am, from 9pm Sat, 3pm Sun, clsd Mon*

Numbers [GF,D,E,V,YC] 300 Westheimer (at Taft) **713/526-6551**

Ranch Hill Saloon [MW,NH,D,CW,K,DS,WC,GO] 24704 I-45 N, Spring **281/298-9035** *1pm-2am*

South Beach Nightclub [M,D,S] 810 Pacific **713/521-0107, 713/529-7623** *9pm-4am Fri-Sat*

Venus [MW,D,E,K] 2901 Fannin St 713/751-3185

Viviana's Nite Club [M,D,MR-L,DS] 4624 Dacoma St **713/681-4101** *9pm-5am, till 6am Sat, clsd Mon-Th*

■CAFES

Dirk's Coffee 4005 Montrose (btwn Richmond & W Alabama) 713/526-1319 *6am-6pm, 7am-5pm Sun*

Empire Cafe [WI,WC] 1732 Westheimer Rd **713/528-5282** *7:30am-10pm, till 11pm Fri-Sat*

Java Java Cafe [WC] 911 W 11th (at Shepherd) **713/880-5282** *7:30am-3pm*

The Path of Tea [WC] 2340 W Alabama St **713/252-4473** *10am-9pm, till 11pm Fri-Sat, 1pm-6pm Sun*

■RESTAURANTS

Aka 2390 W Alabama St 713/807-7875 *noon-11pm, sushi*

Argentina Cafe [WC] 3055 Sage Rd (at Hidalgo St) **713/622-8877** *9am-9pm, from 10am wknds*

Baba Yega's [WC] 2607 Grant (at Pacific) **713/522-0042** 11am-10pm, full bar, patio

Barnaby's Cafe [★BW,WC] 604 Fairview (btwn Stanford & Hopkins St) **713/522-0106** 11am-10pm, multiple locations

Beaver's 2310 Decatur (at Sawyer) **713/864-2328** 11am-10pm, till midnight Sat, clsd Mon, BBQ

Brasil [BW,WC] 2604 Dunlavy (at Westheimer) **713/528-1993** 7:30am-midnight

Chapultepec [WC] 813 Richmond (btwn Montrose & Main) **713/522-2365** 24hrs, Mexican

El Tiempo Cantina [WC] 1308 Montrose Blvd **713/807-8996** 11am-9pm, till 10pm Wed-Th, till 11pm Fri-Sat, Mexican seafood

House of Pies [★WC] 3112 Kirby Dr (btwn Richmond & Alabama) **713/528-3816** 24hrs

Hugo's [WC] 1600 Westheimer Rd (at Mandell) **713/524-7744** lunch & dinner, Mexican, popular brunch

Julia's Bistro [WC] 3722 Main St (at W Alabama) **713/807-0090** lunch Mon-Fri, dinner Mon-Sat, clsd Sun, Mexican

Kelley's Country Cookin' [WC] 8015 Park Pl (at Gulf Fwy) **713/645-6428** 6am-10pm, great brkfst

Mark's American Cuisine [WC] 1658 Westheimer Rd **713/523-3800** lunch Mon-Fri, dinner nightly, located in renovated 1920s church

Mo Mong 1201 Westheimer #B (at Montrose) **713/524-5664** 11am-10pm, clsd Sun, Vietnamese, full bar

Ninfa's [★] 2704 Navigation Blvd (at N Delano St) **713/228-1175** 11am-11pm, Mexican, full bar

Ruggles Green 2311 W Alabama **713/533-0777** 11am-10pm, organic & all-natural American

Sparrow Bar + Cookshop [GO] 3701 Travis St **713/524-6922** lunch & dinner Tue-Sat, also bar

▪ ENTERTAINMENT & RECREATION

After Hours - Queer Radio With Attitude KPFT 90.1 FM (also 89.5 Galveston) **713/526-4000, 713/526-5738** (request line) midnight-3am Sat/Sun, LGBT radio

Beer Can House 222 Malone St **713/926-6368** seasonal; 10am-2pm Wed-Fri; 50,000+ beer cans cover the building!

DiverseWorks Art Space 1117 East Fwy (I-10 at N Main) **713/223-8346, 713/335-3443** seasonal, some LGBT-themed art & performance

Orange Show Center for Visionary Art 2402 Munger St **713/926-6368** performance, music, public art

▪ RETAIL SHOPS

Black Hawk Leather 711 Fairview **713/532-8437, /** noon-8pm, 2pm-7pm Sun

The Chocolate Bar [WC] 1835 W Alabama St **713/520-8599** chocolate gifts & yummy desserts

Hollywood Super Center 2409 Grant St (at Crocker St) **713/527-8510** 10am-1am, till 3am Fri-Sat

▪ PUBLICATIONS

abOUT Magazine PO Box 130948, **713/396-2688**

OutSmart **713/520-7237** monthly LGBT newsmagazine

▪ GYMS & HEALTH CLUBS

Houston Gym [GF,GO] 1501 Durham Rd (at Washington & Eigel) **713/880-9191** 5am-10pm, 8am-8pm wknds

▪ MEN'S CLUBS

The Club Houston [★SW,PC] 2205 Fannin St (at Webster) **713/659-4998** 24hrs

Midtowne Spa—Houston [SW,PC] 3100 Fannin St (at Elgin) **713/522-2379** 24hrs

Texas • USA

■MEN'S SERVICES

➤MegaMates 713/225-5500 *Call to hook up with HOT local men. FREE to listen & respond to ads. Use FREE code DAMRON. MegaMates.com.*

■EROTICA

Eros 1207 [GO] 1207 Spencer Hwy (at Allen Genoa) 713/910-0220

Loveworks 25170 I-45 N, Spring 281/292-0070

Kilgore

■EROTICA

Texas Adult Video [GO] 1907 Industrial Blvd 903/986-2090

Lockhart

■ACCOMMODATIONS

Lazy J Paradise Campground & Park [MW,SW,WI] 270 Hidden Path (CR 303 and FM 2001) 210/863-9314 *campground w/ RV area catering to the LGBT community*

Longview

■NIGHTCLUBS

Rainbow Members Club (RMC) [MW,D,PC,WC] 203 S High (at Cotton) 903/753-9393 *5pm-2am Wed-Sat, from 3pm Sun*

■CRUISY AREAS

Hinsley Park [AYOR]

Teague Park [AYOR]

Lubbock

■INFO LINES & SERVICES

AA Lambda 4501 University Ave (at MCC) 806/792-5562 *8pm Fri*

■ACCOMMODATIONS

LaQuinta Inns & Suites North [GF,NS,WI,WC,GO] 5006 Auburn St (at Winston) 806/749-1600

■NIGHTCLUBS

Club Luxor [GS,D,K,DS,WC] 2211 4th St 806/744-3744 *9pm-2am Fri-Sun, more gay Fri & Sun*

Heaven Nightclub [GF,D,MR,DS,18+,YC] 1928 Buddy Holly Ave (at I-27) 806/762-4466 *9pm-3am Th-Sun*

■CRUISY AREAS

McKenzie Park [AYOR]

Marfa

■ACCOMMODATIONS

El Cosmico [GS,WI,GO] 802 S. Highland Ave 432/729-1950, 877/822-1950 *vintage trailer, yurt & teepee hotel & campground*

McAllen

see Rio Grande Valley

Odessa/ Midland

■EROTICA

B&L Adult Bookstore 5890 W University Blvd (at Mercury), W Odessa 432/381-6855

County Line 6947 Commerce, Odessa 432/552-0055 *24hrs*

Rio Grande Valley

■BARS

PBD's [M,D,DS,S,WC] 2908 N Ware Rd (at Daffodil), McAllen 956/682-8019 *8pm-2am, clsd Mon*

San Antonio

■INFO LINES & SERVICES

Lambda AA 319 Camden Rm #4 (Madison Square Presbyterian Church) 210/979-5939 *8:15pm daily*

■ACCOMMODATIONS

1908 Ayres Inn [GS,NS,WI,WC,GO] 124 W Woodlawn Ave (at N Main) 210/736-4232

Arbor House Suites B&B [GS,NS,WC,GO] 109 Arciniega (btwn S Alamo & S St Mary's) 210/472-2005, 888/272-6700

Brackenridge House [GF,SW,WI] 230 Madison (at Beauregard) 210/271-3442, 877/271-3442 *B&B in historic King William district*

Emily Morgan Hotel [GF,F,SW,WI] 705 E Houston St (at Ave E) 210/225-5100, 800/824-6674

Fiesta B&B [M,NS,WI,GO] 1823 Saunders Ave (at Trinity) 210/226-5548, 210/887-0074

Hotel Havana [GS,GO] 1015 Navarro St 210/222-2008

■**Bars**

2015 Place [M,NH,K] 2015 San Pedro (at Woodlawn) 210/733-3365 4pm-2am, patio, [K] Wed

The Annex [M,NH,WI,WC] 330 San Pedro Ave (at Euclid) 210/223-6957 2pm-2am, cruise bar

The Boss [M,NH] 1006 VFW Blvd (Jeffersonville) 210/550-2322, 210/449-8506 8pm-2am, dive bar

Electric Company [MW,D,S,18+] 820 San Pedro Ave (at W Laurel) 210/212-6635

Essence [M,NH,K,S] 1010 N Main Ave (at E Euclid) 210/223-5418 2pm-2am

The Flying Saucer [GF] 11255 Huebner Rd #212 (at I-10) 210/696-5080 11am-1am, till 2am Th-Sat, noon-midnight Sun, large beer selection

Mix [GF,E] 2423 N St Marys St 210/735-1313 5pm-2am, from 7:30pm Sat-Sun, dive bar

One-Oh-Six Off Broadway [M,NH,F] 106 Pershing St (at Broadway) 210/820-0906 noon-2am

Pegasus [M,K,L,S] 1402 N Main Ave (btwn Laurel & Evergreen) 210/299-4222 2pm-2am

Silver Dollar Saloon [MW,D,CW,K] 1818 N Main Ave (at Dewey) 210/227-2623 4pm-2am, clsd Mon

Sparky's Pub [M,NH] 1416 N Main Ave (at Evergreen) 210/320-5111 3pm-2am

■**Nightclubs**

The Bonham Exchange [★MW,D,V,18+,GO] 411 Bonham St (at 3rd/ Houston) 210/271-3811 4pm-2am, from 8pm Sat

Heat [M,D,S] 1500 N Main Ave (at Evergreen) 210/227-2600 9pm-2am, clsd Mon-Tue

The Industry [GS,D] 8021 Pinebrook Dr (at Callaghan) 210/366-3229 10pm-2am Th, from 8pm Fri-Sat

The Saint [M,D,DS,S,18+] 800 Lexington Ave 210/225-7330 4pm-3am

■**Cafes**

Candlelight Coffeehouse & Wine Bar [E,WI,WC] 3011 N St Mary's (at Rte 281) 210/738-0099 2pm-midnight, wknd brunch 10am-2pm, clsd Mon

■**Restaurants**

Chacho's [E,K,WC] 7870 Callaghan Rd (at I-10) 210/366-2023 24hrs, Mexican

Cool Cafe 12651 Vance Jackson 210/8775/5/20115001 brkfst, lunch & dinner, Mediterranean

Guenther House 129 E Guenther (at S Alamo St) 210/227-1061, 800/235-8186 7am-3pm, located in restored Pioneer Flour Mills founding family home

Lulu's Bakery & Cafe [WC] 918 N Main (at W Elmira) 210/222-9422 24hrs, Tex-Mex

Luther's Cafe [K,E,WC,GO] 1425 N Main Ave (at Evergreen) 210/223-7727 11am-3am, great burgers, live music

Madhatter's Tea House [BYOB,WI,WC] 320 Beauregard 210/212-4832 8am-9pm, till 3pm Sun, patio

El Mirador [BW,WC] 722 S St Mary's St (at Durango Blvd) 210/225-9444 6:30am-9pm, till 2pm Sun, patio

Taco Taco Cafe 145 E Hildebrand 210/822-9533 7am-2pm

WD Deli 3123 Broadway St 210/828-2322 10:30am-5pm, till 4pm Sat, clsd Sun

■**Retail Shops**

On Main/ Off Main 120 W Mistletoe Ave 210/737-2323 10am-6pm, till 5pm Sat, clsd Sun

ZEBRAZ.com 1608 N Main Ave (at E Park Ave) 210/472-2800, 800/788-4729 9am-midnight, till 10pm Sun-Tue, LGBT dept store

■**Men's Clubs**

Alternative Club Inc [SW,PC] 827 E Elmira St (at St Mary's) 210/223-2177 noon-9am, 24hrs wknds

Executive Health Club [PC] 402 Austin St (at Lamar) 210/299-1400

■MEN'S SERVICES

▶**MegaMates** 210/375-1155 *Call to hook up with HOT local men. FREE to listen & respond to ads. Use FREE code DAMRON. MegaMates.com.*

■EROTICA

Broadway News 2202 Broadway (at Appler St) 210/223-2034

Dreamers 2376 Austin Hwy (at Walzem) 210/653-3538 *24hrs*

Encore Video 1031 NE Loop 410 210/821-5345

■CRUISY AREAS

Please Note: All cruisy areas for San Antonio have been removed because the San Antonio Park Rangers aggressively police these areas.

Terrel

■EROTICA

Dreamers 6086 W Hwy 80 (Frontage Rd exit) 972/524-1449 *24hrs*

Tyler

■INFO LINES & SERVICES

Tyler Area Gays/ TAG 5701 Old Bullard Road #96 *events & LGBT resources*

■ACCOMMODATIONS

Cross Timber Ranch B&B [GS,SW,NS,WI,GO] 6271 FM 858 (at Hwy 64), Ben Wheeler 903/833-9000, 877/833-9002

■CRUISY AREAS

Bergfeld Park [AYOR]

Waco

■NIGHTCLUBS

Club Trix [MW,D,V,TG] 110 S 6th St 254/714-0767 *10pm-2am Th, 9pm-2am Fri-Sat*

■CRUISY AREAS

Midway Park [AYOR]

Webster

■BARS

Club Pride [MW,D] 229 E NASA Pkwy 281/557-4800 *9pm-2am Th-Sat*

Wichita Falls

■BARS

Krank It Karaoke Kafe [GF,D,K,18+,WC] 1400 N Scott Ave (at Old Iowa Park Rd) 940/761-9099 *8:30pm-2am, from 7pm Fri-Sat, clsd Mon-Tue*

Odds [MW,D,K,DS,18+,BW] 1205 Lamar St (at 12th) 940/322-2996 *4pm-2am, from 3pm Sun*

■CRUISY AREAS

Lucy Park [AYOR]

Wimberley

■ACCOMMODATIONS

Bella Vista [GS,SW,NS,GO] 2121 Hilltop 512/847-6425

UTAH

Bryce Canyon

■ACCOMMODATIONS

Hatch Station [GF,WI,WC] 177 S Main, Hatch 435/735-4015 *also restaurant, laundry & convenience store; safe oasis for LGBT travelers in S UT*

The Red Brick Inn of Panguitch B&B [GF,WI] 161 N 100 West (at 200 North), Panguitch 435/676-2141, 866/733-2745 *full brkfst*

■CAFES

Scoops from the Past [WI] 105 N Main St, Panguitch 435/676-8885 *noon-10pm, till 6pm Sun, retro ice cream parlor*

Logan

■CRUISY AREAS

Logan Canyon [AYOR] *Zanavoo loop*

Moab

■ACCOMMODATIONS

Mayor's House B&B [GF,SW,NS,WI,GO] 505 Rose Tree Ln (at 400 E) 435/259-6015, 888/791-2345 *hot tub, full brkfst*

Mt Peale Resort Inn, Lodge & Cabins [GS,NS,WI,GO] 1415 E Hwy 46 (at mile marker 14), Old La Sal 435/686-2284, 888/687-3253 *B&B & cabins, hot tub, lesbian-owned*

Red Cliffs Lodge [GF,SW,NS,WC] Hwy 128 (at mile marker 14) 435/259-2002, 866/812-2002 *resort, on Colorado River, hot tub*

Ogden

■MEN'S SERVICES

➤**MegaMates** 801/317-1111 *Call to hook up with HOT local men. FREE to listen & respond to ads. Use FREE code DAMRON. MegaMates.com.*

Park City

■RESTAURANTS

Loco Lizard Cantina [TG,WC] 1612 Ute Blvd (in Kimball Jct Shopping Ctr) 435/645-7000 *11am-10pm, till 11pm Fri-Sat, brunch wknds, Mexican, full bar*

■MEN'S SERVICES

➤**MegaMates** 435/608-0608 *Call to hook up with HOT local men. FREE to listen & respond to ads. Use FREE code DAMRON. MegaMates.com.*

Salt Lake City

■INFO LINES & SERVICES

Utah Pride Center 361 N 300 W, 1st flr 801/539-8800, 888/874-2743 *info, resource center, meetings, coffee shop, programs, youth activity center & much more*

■ACCOMMODATIONS

Anniversary Inn [GF] 460 S 1000 E (at 400) 801/363-4900, 800/324-4152 *elaborate, kitschy theme rms*

Hotel Monaco Salt Lake City [GF,F,WI,WC] 15 W 200 S (at S Main) 801/595-0000, 877/294-9710

Parrish Place [GF,NS,WI] 720 E Ashton Ave (at 700 E) 801/832-0970, 855/832-0970 *Victorian mansion, hot tub*

Peery Hotel [GF,F,NS,WI,WC] 110 W 300 S 801/521-4300, 800/331-0073

Under the Lindens [★M,NS,WI,GO] 128 S 1000 E (downtown) 801/355-9808 *mention Damron for discount*

■BARS

Club Try-Angles [M,NH,D,F,PC,GO] 251 W 900 S (at 300 W) 801/364-3203 *2pm-2am*

Jam [MW,NH,D,K,WI] 751 North 300 West (at Reed Ave) 801/891-1162 *5pm-2am, clsd Sun*

The Tavernacle Social Club [GF,F,K,P,NS,PC] 201 E 300 South (at 200 E) 801/519-8900 *5pm-close, from 8pm Sun-Mon, "Duelin' Pianos"*

The Trapp [MW,D,K,CW,WI,WC] 102 S 600 W (at 100 S) 801/531-8727 *11am-2am, patio*

■NIGHTCLUBS

Area 51 [GS,D] 451 South 400 West (at 400 S) 801/534-0819 *80s & goth theme nights Th-Sat only*

Fusion [M,D] 540 W 200 South (at Metro Bar) 9pm-2am Sat only

Hydrate SLC [★M,D] 579 W 200 S (at 600 W, at Club Sound) 801/328-0255 *9:30pm-2am Fri only*

Mixx [M,D,K] 615 W 100 South 801/575-6499 *9pm-2am Fri-Sat*

Pachanga at Karamba [M,D,MR-L] 1051 East 2100 South 801/696-0639 *9pm Sun only, gay Latin night*

■CAFES

Coffee Garden [WC] 878 E 900 S 801/355-3425 *6am-11pm*

■RESTAURANTS

Bambara 202 S Main St 801/363-5454 *lunch Mon-Fri, brkfst & dinner daily, upscale American*

Blue Plate Diner 2041 S 2100 E 801/463-1151 *7am-9pm, till 10pm Fri-Sat*

Cafe Trio Downtown 680 S 900 E 801/533-8746 *11am-10pm, Italian*

Cedars of Lebanon [WI,E] 152 E 200 South (at State St) 801/364-4096 *lunch & dinner, Lebanese, veggie/ vegan-friendly*

Citris Grill 2991 E 3300 South 801/466-1202

Finn's 1624 S 1100 East (at Logan) 801/467-4000 *7:30am-2:30pm*

Fresco Italian Cafe 1513 S 1500 East 801/486-1300 *dinner nightly, patio*

Himalayan Kitchen 360 S State St (at 400 S) 801/328-2077 *lunch & dinner, dinner only Sun, Indian/Himalayan, plenty veggie*

Utah • USA

Market St Grill [WC] 48 W Market St
801/322-4668 *11:30-9pm, from 9am Sun, fresh seafood, full bar*

The Med 420 E 3300 South
801/493-0100 *lunch & dinner, Mediterranean*

The Metropolitan [R] 173 W Broadway
801/364-3472 *lunch Mon-Fri, dinner nightly, clsd Sun, New American*

The New Yorker [WC] 60 W Market St
801/363-0166 *lunch Mon-Fri, dinner nightly, clsd Sun, fine dining, steak*

Off Trax [MW,WI] 259 W 900 S
801/364-4307 *7am-7pm, till 3pm Fri, brunch Sun, also from 1am-3am Fri-Sat nights*

Omar's Rawtopia 2148 Highland Dr
801/486-0332 *noon-8pm, till 9pm Fri-Sat, clsd Sun, raw food*

Red Iguana [★] 736 W North Temple
801/322-1489 *lunch & dinner, Mexican*

Sage's Cafe 234 W 900 S
801/322-3790 *lunch & dinner, brkfst wknds, clsd Mon-Tue, vegan/ vegetarian*

Stoneground 249 E 400 South
801/364-1368 *11am-11pm, 5pm-9pm Sun, pizza & more*

Vertical Diner [WC] 2280 S West Temple 801/484-8378 *10am-9pm, vegetarian diner*

Zest Kitchen & Bar 275 S 200 W
801/433-0589 *4pm-1am, till 11pm Tues, clsd Sun-Mon*

■ENTERTAINMENT & RECREATION

Lambda Hiking Club *hiking & other activities*

Plan B Theatre Company 138 West 300 South (at Rose Wagner Performing Arts Center, btwn W Temple & 200 West) 801/355-2787 *at least one LGBT-themed production each season*

Tower Theatre 876 E 900 South
801/321-0310 *alternative films, many LGBT movies*

■BOOKSTORES

Golden Braid Books [WI] 151 S 500 E
801/322-1162 *10am-9pm, till 6pm Sun, also Oasis Cafe, 8am-9pm, till 10pm wknds*

Weller Book Works 607 Trolley Sq
801/328-2586 *10am-9pm, noon-5pm Sun*

■RETAIL SHOPS

Cahoots [WC,GO] 878 E 900 S (at 900 E) 801/538-0606 *10am-9pm, unique gift shop*

■PUBLICATIONS

Q Salt Lake 801/649-6663, 800/806-7357 *bi-weekly LGBT newspaper*

■MEN'S SERVICES

➤**MegaMates** 801/595-0005 *Call to hook up with HOT local men. FREE to listen & respond to ads. Use FREE code DAMRON. MegaMates.com.*

■EROTICA

All For Love [TG,WC] 3072 S Main St (at 33rd St S) 801/487-8358 *clsd Sun, lingerie & S/M boutique*

Blue Boutique 1383 E 2100 South
801/485-2072 *also piercing*

Mischievous 559 S 300 W (at 6th St S)
801/530-3100 *clsd Sun*

■CRUISY AREAS

Memory Grove [AYOR] Canyon Rd (below the Capitol, on the E side)

Sugarhouse Park [AYOR] 21st S *also btwn 13th & 17th E*

Zion Nat'l Park

■ACCOMMODATIONS

Canyon Vista Lodge B&B [GF,NS] 2175 Zion Park Blvd (at Hwy 9), Springdale 435/772-3801

Red Rock Inn [GS,NS,WC,GO] 998 Zion Park Blvd, Springdale 435/772-3139 *cottages w/ views, full brkfst, hot tub*

■CAFES

Cafe Soleil [BW,GO] 205 Zion Nat'l Park Blvd 435/772-0505 *6am-8pm seasonal*

VERMONT
Statewide

■INFO LINES & SERVICES

Vermont Gay Tourism Association
see www.vermontgaytourism.com

Brattleboro

■ACCOMMODATIONS

Frog Meadow Farm [M,NS,WI,GO] 34
Upper Spring Hill Rd, Newfane
802/365-7242, 877/365-7242

Nutmeg Inn [GS,WI,WC,GO] 153 Rte 9
W, Wilmington 802/464-3907,
855/868-8634

■RESTAURANTS

Peter Havens [GO] 32 Elliot St (at
Main) 802/257-3333 6pm-10pm, clsd
Sun-Tue, cont'l

■BOOKSTORES

Everyone's Books [WC] 25 Elliot St
802/254-8160 9:30am-6pm, till 8pm
Fri, till 7pm Sat, 11am-5pm Sun

Burlington

■INFO LINES & SERVICES

R.U.1.2? Community Center 55 S
Champlain St # 12 802/860-RU12
(7812) drop-in & cybercenter, support
& advocacy, events

■ACCOMMODATIONS

The Black Bear Inn [GS,SW,NS,WI]
4010 Bolton Access Rd, Bolton Valley
802/434-2126, 800/395-6335 mtntop inn, full brkfst, hot tub

The Inn at Essex [GF,SW,WI,WC] 70
Essex Way, Essex 802/878-1100,
800/727-4295 culinary resort

One of a Kind B&B [NS,WI] 53
Lakeview Terrace 802/862-5576

■NIGHTCLUBS

Metronome/ Nectar's [GF,D,F,E] 188
Main St 802/658-4771,
802/865-4563

■CAFES

Muddy Waters [BW] 184 Main St
802/658-0466 9am-11pm

Radio Bean Coffeehouse [E] 8 N
Winooski Ave (at Pearl) 802/660-9346
8am-midnight, till 2am Th-Sat, 10am-
11pm Sun, cool bohemian coffeehouse

■RESTAURANTS

Bluebird Tavern [BW,GO] 86 St Paul St
802/540-1786 4pm-10pm Th-Sat,
5pm-9pm Tue-Wed, clsd Sun-Mon,
locally grown

Daily Planet 15 Center St (at College)
802/862-9647 4pm-close, also bar till
2am

Leunig's Bistro & Cafe [GO] 115
Church St 802/863-3759

Loretta's [GO] 44 Park St (near 5
Corners), Essex Junction
802/879-7777 lunch weekdays,
dinner nightly, clsd Sun-Mon, Italian

Shanty on the Shore 181 Battery St
802/864-0238 11am-9pm, seafood,
views of Lake Champlain

Silver Palace 1216 Williston Rd
802/864-0125 11:30am-9pm, 5pm-
9pm Sun, Chinese, full bar

■RETAIL SHOPS

Peace & Justice Store 60 Lake St (at
College St) 802/863-2345 10am-
6pm, limited hrs in winter, fair trade
retail store

■CRUISY AREAS

The Loop [AYOR] downtown Bank,
College & St Pauls Sts

Chester

■ACCOMMODATIONS

Chester House Inn [GS,NS,WI,WC,GO]
266 Main St 888/875-2205 inn circa
1780

Dorset

■CRUISY AREAS

Dorset Quarry [AYOR] on Rte 30 &
Kelly Rd

Jay Peak

■ACCOMMODATIONS

Phineas Swann B&B [GS,NS,WI,GO]
802/326-4306 restored Victorian on
Trout River, full brkfst

Vermont • USA

Killington

■ACCOMMODATIONS

Huntington House Inn [GF,WI,WC,GO] 19 Huntington Pl, Rochester **802/767-9140** *located on the park, restaurant & lounge*

The Inn of the Six Mountains [GF,SW,WI,WC] 2617 Killington Rd **802/422-4302, 800/228-4676** *full brkfst, jacuzzi*

Salt Ash Inn [GF,F,WI,SW,WC] 4758 Rte 100A (at Rte 100), Plymouth **802/672-3224**

Manchester

■ACCOMMODATIONS

Hill Farm Inn [GF,NS,WI] 458 Hill Farm Rd (at Historic Rte 7-A), Arlington **802/375-2269, 800/882-2545** *full brkfst*

■CAFES

Little Rooster Cafe Rte 7-A (at Hillvale Dr), Manchester Center **802/362-3496** *7am-2:30pm, clsd Wed (winters)*

■RESTAURANTS

Bistro Henry [R] 1942 Depot St (.5 mile E of Rte 7), Manchester Center **802/362-4982** *dinner only, clsd Mon, Mediterranean, also bar*

Chanteleer Rte 7-A N, E Dorset **802/362-1616** *call for hours, seasonal*

■BOOKSTORES

Northshire Bookstore 4869 Main St, Manchester Center **802/362-2200, 800/437-3700** *10am-7pm, till 9pm Fri-Sat*

Marshfield

■ACCOMMODATIONS

Marshfield Inn & Motel [GF,WI,NS,GO] 5630 US Rte 2 **802/426-3383**

Montpelier

■RESTAURANTS

Julio's [WI] 54 State **802/229-9348** *11:30am-10pm, till 11pm Fri-Sat, Mexican*

Sarducci's [WC] 3 Main St **802/223-0229** *11:30am-9:30pm, from 4:30pm Sun, Italian, full bar*

Wayside Restaurant [WC] 1873 Rte 302 **802/223-6611** *6:30am-9:30pm*

Plainfield

■ACCOMMODATIONS

Comstock House [GF,WI,GO] 1620 Middle Rd **802/272-2693** *overlooks Winooski River Valley, full brkfst*

Richmond

■RESTAURANTS

The Kitchen Table Bistro 1840 W Main St **802/434-8686** *5pm-9pm, clsd Sun-Mon, seasonal menu, local food*

Rutland

■ACCOMMODATIONS

Lilac Inn [WC] 53 Park St, Brandon **802/247-5463, 800/221-0720** *full brkfst*

Saxtons River

■ACCOMMODATIONS

The Saxtons River Inn [GF,NS,WI,GO] 27 Main St (at Academy Ave) **802/869-2110** *historic Victorian inn w/ charming pub & restaurant, located in quaint New England village*

St Johnsbury

■ACCOMMODATIONS

Comfort Inn & Suites [GF,SW,WI,WC] 703 US Rte 5 S (at I-91) **802/748-1500, 800/424-6423**

Fairbanks Inn [GF,SW,WI,WC] 401 Western Ave **802/748-5666**

■RESTAURANTS

Elements 98 Mill St **802/748-8400** *dinner, clsd Sun-Mon, local food*

Stowe

■ACCOMMODATIONS

Arbor Inn [GS,SW,NS,WI] 3214 Mountain Rd **802/253-4772, 800/543-1293** *full brkfst, hot tub*

Fitch Hill Inn [GS,WI,NS] 258 Fitch Hill Rd (at Rte 15/100), Hyde Park 802/888-3834, 800/639-2903 *full brkfst*

The Green Mountain Inn [GF,F,SW,NS,WI,WC] 18 Main St 802/253-7301, 800/253-7302

Northern Lights Lodge [GF,SW,WI,GO] 4441 Mountain Rd 802/253-8541, 800/448-4554 *full brkfst, hot tub, sauna*

The Old Stagecoach Inn [GF,NS,WI] 18 N Main St (at Stowe St), Waterbury 802/244-5056, 800/262-2206 *historic village inn, full brkfst, also full bar*

Timberholm Inn [GS,NS,WI] 452 Cottage Club Rd 802/253-7603, 800/753-7603 *full brkfst, hot tub*

Waterbury

■ACCOMMODATIONS

Grünberg Haus B&B & Cabins [GS,NS,WI] 94 Pine St, Rte 100 S 802/244-7726, 800/800-7760 *full brkfst, also cabins*

Moose Meadow Lodge [GS,NS,WI,GO] 607 Crossett Hill 802/244-5378

■RESTAURANTS

Cider House BBQ & Pub [GO] 1675 US Rte 2 802/244-8400 *noon-9pm, clsd Mon-Wed, full bar, patio*

Wells River

■ACCOMMODATIONS

The Gargoyle House [M,N,NS,WI,GO] 3351 Wallace Hill Rd (at US 302 & I-91) 802/429-2341

West Dover

■ACCOMMODATIONS

Deerhill Inn [GS,SW,NS,WI] 14 Valley View Rd 802/464-3100, 800/993-3379 *inn w/ restaurant*

Inn at Mount Snow [GF,NS,WI,GO] 401 Rte 100 802/464-8388

The Inn at Sawmill Farm [GS,NS,WC] 7 Crosstown Rd (at Rte 100) 802/464-8131, 800/493-1133

Windham

■ACCOMMODATIONS

A Stone Wall Inn [GS,NS,WI,GO] 578 Hitchcock Hill Rd 802/875-4238

Woodstock

■ACCOMMODATIONS

The Ardmore Inn [GF,NS,WI] 23 Pleasant St 802/457-3887 *1867 Greek Revival, full brkfst*

Deer Brook Inn [GF,NS,WI,GO] 4548 W Woodstock Rd 802/672-3713

The Woodstocker Inn B&B [GS,WI] 61 River St 802/457-3896

VIRGINIA

Alexandria

see also Washington, District of Columbia

■ACCOMMODATIONS

Crowne Plaza Old Town Alexandria [GF,WI] 901 N Fairfax St 703/683-6000

Lorien Hotel & Spa [GF,F,WC] 1600 King St 703/894-3434, 877/956-7436

Morrison House [GF] 116 S Alfred St 703/838-8000, 866/834-6628

Arlington

see also Washington, District of Columbia

■INFO LINES & SERVICES

Arlington Gay/ Lesbian Alliance *monthly meetings & outreach events (see: www.agla.org)*

■BARS

Freddie's Beach Bar & Restaurant [MW,F,E,K,DS,WC] 555 S 23rd St (at Fern St) 703/685-0555 *4pm-2am, from 11am Fri, fron 10an wknds for brunch, patio*

■CAFES

Java Shack [MW] 2507 N Franklin Rd (at Wilson Blvd & N Barton) 703/527-9556 *7am-8pm, 8am-6pm Sun*

■CRUISY AREAS

Seabee Memorial [AYOR] Memorial Dr

Virginia • *USA*

Bristol

■EROTICA

Exotic Illusions Adult Video 2003 W State St (at 20th St) **276/466-6909**

Cape Charles

■ACCOMMODATIONS

Cape Charles House B&B [GF,NS] 645 Tazewell Ave (at Fig) **757/331-4920** *1912 colonial revival home w/ antiques*

Sea Gate B&B [GF,WI,GO] 9 Tazewell Ave **757/331-2206** *full brkfst*

Charlottesville

■ACCOMMODATIONS

The Inn at Court Square [GF,NS] 410 E Jefferson St **434/295-2800, 866/466-2877**

■RESTAURANTS

Escafe [E,GO] 215 W Water St **434/295-8668** *lunch & dinner*

■EROTICA

Sneak Reviews Video 2244 Ivy Rd **434/979-4420**

■CRUISY AREAS

Chris Green Lake [AYOR] Rte 29 to Airport Rd

Danville

■CRUISY AREAS

Ballou Park [AYOR]

Hampton

■CAFES

The Java Junkies [F] 768 Settlers Landing Rd **757/722-6300** *7am-7pm, from 8am wknds, till 3pm Sun*

■CRUISY AREAS

Grandview Beach [AYOR] nude beach past rock mounds

Harrisonburg

■CAFES

Artful Dodger Coffeehouse [D,E,WC] 47 W Court Square **540/432-1179** *8:30am-2am, from 9:30am wknds, also bar*

Lynchburg

■CRUISY AREAS

Blackwater Creek area [AYOR]

Peaks View Park [AYOR]

Norfolk

■ACCOMMODATIONS

B&B at Historic Page House Inn [GF,NS,WI] 323 Fairfax Ave **757/625-5033, 800/599-7659** *1899 mansion*

Tazewell Hotel & Suites [GF,WI,WC] 245 Granby St (at Tazewell St) **757/623-6200**

■BARS

The Garage [M,NH,F,K,WC] 731 Granby St (at Brambleton) **757/623-0303** *4pm-2am*

Hershee Lounge & He Bar [W,D,F,E,WC] 6117 Sewells Pt Rd (at Norview) **757/853-9842** *4pm-2am, boys bar in the back*

■NIGHTCLUBS

The Wave [M,D,S,WC] 4107 Colley Ave (at 41st St) **757/440-5911** *10pm-2am, clsd Sun, Mon & Wed*

■RESTAURANTS

Charlie's Cafe [BW] 1800 Granby St (at 18th) **757/625-0824** *7am-2pm*

Tortilla West 508 Oropax St **757/440-3777** *dinner only, Sun brunch, open till 1am, Mexican, plenty veggie/ vegan*

■MEN'S SERVICES

►**MegaMates 757/498-3555** *Call to hook up with HOT local men. FREE to listen & respond to ads. Use FREE code DAMRON. MegaMates.com.*

■EROTICA

Leather & Lace 745 Battlefield Blvd N #104, Chesapeake **757/436-2525**

Petersburg

■EROTICA

Thriller Books 1919 E Washington (on Rte 36) **804/733-0064**

Richmond

■ACCOMMODATIONS

Omni Richmond Hotel [GF,SW,WI,WC]
100 S 12th St (at Cary St)
804/344-7000, 800/843-6664
views of city & James River

■BARS

Babes of Carytown
[MW,D,CW,DS,F,E,K,WC] 3166 W Cary St
(at Auburn) **804/355-9330** *11am-
2am, from noon Sat, 10am-8pm Sun*

Barcode [M,NH,F,K,WI] 6 E Grace St
(btwn 1st & Foushee Sts)
804/648-2040 *4pm-2am, from 3pm
wknds*

Godfrey's [MW,D,F,K,DS] 308 E Grace St
(btwn 3rd & 4th) **804/648-3957**
10pm-close, clsd Mon-Tue, brunch Sun

■NIGHTCLUBS

Club Colours [MW,D,MR-AF,F,S,WC] 536
N Harrison St (at Broad)
804/353-9776 *9pm-3am Sat*

■RESTAURANTS

Galaxy Diner 3109 W Cary St
804/213-0510 *11am-midnight, till
2am wknds, some veggie, full bar*

The Village 1001 W Grace
804/353-8204 *8am-2am, bar till 2am,
American*

■ENTERTAINMENT &
 RECREATION

Richmond Triangle Players 1300
Altamont Ave (at W Marshall St)
804/346-8113 *LGBT-themed plays,
films & cabaret*

Venture Richmond 804/788-6466
*tour the James River, lots of shops,
restaurants, etc*

■BOOKSTORES

Phoenix Rising [WC] 19 N Belmont
Ave **804/355-7939** *11am-7pm, clsd
Tue, LGBT*

■MEN'S SERVICES

►**MegaMates 804/675-1100** *Call to
hook up with HOT local men. FREE to
listen & respond to ads. Use FREE code
DAMRON. MegaMates.com.*

■EROTICA

Quality Books 8 S Crenshaw Ave
804/257-7146

■CRUISY AREAS

Deep Run Park [AYOR]

Forest Hill Park [AYOR] at 42nd St

Texas Beach/ North Bank Park
[AYOR] *also Great Shiplock Park*

Roanoke

■BARS

Backstreet Cafe [MW,NH,F] 356 Salem
Ave (off Jefferson) **540/345-1542**
7pm-2am, clsd Sun-Mon

Cuba Pete's [GF,NH,F,K,WC] 120 Church
Ave SW (at First St SW, inside Macado's)
540/342-7231 *11am-2am, more gay
wknds, also Macado's restaurant*

■RESTAURANTS

Metro Restaurant & Nighclub [D] 14
Campbell Ave SE *11:30am-midnight, till
2:30am Fri-Sat*

Shenandoah Valley

■ACCOMMODATIONS

Frog Hollow B&B [GS,GO] 492
Greenhouse Rd (at Rte 11), Lexington
540/463-5444 *full brkfst, hot tub*

The Olde Staunton Inn [GS,WI] 260 N
Lewis St, Staunton **540/886-0193,
866/653-3786** *B&B, hot tub*

Piney Hill B&B [GS,NS,GO] 1048 Piney
Hill Rd (at Mill Creek Crossroads), Luray
540/778-5261, 800/644-5261
country B&B, full brkfst, hot tub

Virginia Beach

■ACCOMMODATIONS

Capes Ocean Resort Hotel
[GF,SW,NS,WI,WC] 2001 Atlantic Ave (at
20th St) **757/428-5421,
877/956-5421** *oceanfront rooms,
private balconies*

Ocean Beach Club [GF,F,WC] 3401
Atlantic Ave (at 34th St)
800/245-1003

■BARS

Klub Ambush [MW,NH,D,F,K,DS,GO] 475
S Lynnhaven Rd (at Lynnhaven Pkwy)
757/498-4301 *5pm-2am*

Rainbow Cactus [M,D,CW,F,DS,WC] 3472 Holland Rd (at Diana Lee) **757/368-0441** *7pm-2am, clsd Mon-Tue*

■RESTAURANTS

Alexander's on the Bay 4536 Oceanview Ave **757/464-4999** *dinner only, seafood, upscale, Chesapeake Bay views*

■MEN'S SERVICES

➤**MegaMates 757/821-7373** *Call to hook up with HOT local men. FREE to listen & respond to ads. Use FREE code DAMRON. MegaMates.com.*

■EROTICA

Nancy's Nook 1301 Oceana Blvd **757/428-1498** *24hrs*

Washington

■ACCOMMODATIONS

Gay Street Inn [GF,NS,WI,GO] 160 Gay St **540/316-9220**

Waverly

■EROTICA

Country Bookstore 111 S County Dr (Rte 460) (at Rte 40) **804/834-1122**

WASHINGTON

Auburn

■CRUISY AREAS

Isaac Evans Park [AYOR] Green River Rd (off 104th Ave SE)

Bainbridge Island

■BOOKSTORES

Eagle Harbor Book Co 157 Winslow Wy E **206/842-5332** *9am-7pm, till 9pm Th, till 6pm Sat, 10am-6pm Sun*

Bellevue

see also Seattle

Bellingham

■BARS

Rumors [MW,D,WC] 1119 Railroad Ave (at Chestnut) **360/671-1846** *4pm-2am*

■CAFES

Tony's Coffee House [WC] 1101 Harris Ave (at 11th), Fairhaven **360/738-4710** *7am-6pm*

■RESTAURANTS

Bobby Lee's Pub & Eatery [GO,WC] 108 W Main St (Washington Ave), Everson **360/966-8838** *11am-2am, clsd Mon*

Skylark's Hidden Cafe [E] 1308 11th St (at McKenzie) **360/715-3642** *7am-midnight, outdoor seating, full bar, live jazz wknds*

■BOOKSTORES

Village Books 1200 11th St (at Harris) **360/671-2626** *10am-7:30pm, till 7pm Sun, new & used*

■EROTICA

Great Northern Bookstore 1308 Railroad Ave (at Holly) **360/733-1650**

■CRUISY AREAS

Teddy Bear Cove [AYOR]

Bender Creek

■ACCOMMODATIONS

Triangle Recreation Camp [MW,PC] PO Box 1226, Granite Falls 98252 *members-only camping on 80-acre nature conservancy; www.camptrc.org*

Bremerton

■INFO LINES & SERVICES

AA Gay/ Lesbian 700 Callahan Dr (at St Paul's Episcopal) **360/475-0775, 800/562-7455** *7:30pm Tue*

Centralia

■CRUISY AREAS

Fort Borst Park [AYOR] Harrison Ave

Edmonds

■CRUISY AREAS

Edmonds City Park [AYOR] by ferry dock

Everett

■INFO LINES & SERVICES

AA Gay/ Lesbian 2624 Rockefeller **425/252-2525** *7pm Sun*

MEN'S SERVICES
➤MegaMates 425/322-2200 Call to hook up with HOT local men. FREE to listen & respond to ads. Use FREE code DAMRON. MegaMates.com.

EROTICA
Airport Video 11732 Airport Rd (1 block W of Hwy 99, at 128th St) 425/290-7555 24hrs

CRUISY AREAS
Forest Park [AYOR] off 41st St

Glacier

ACCOMMODATIONS
Mt Baker B&B & Cabins [GS,NS,WI] 9434 Cornell Creek Rd 360/599-2299 modern chalet, hot tub

Issaquah

CRUISY AREAS
Sammamish State Park [AYOR] I-90 & SR 900

Kennewick

CRUISY AREAS
Columbia Park [AYOR] days only, cops & bashers after dark

Kent

MEN'S SERVICES
➤MegaMates 253/234-0700 Call to hook up with HOT local men. FREE to listen & respond to ads. Use FREE code DAMRON. MegaMates.com.

EROTICA
The Voyeur 604 Central Ave S 253/850-8428 videos, toys, clothing

La Conner

ACCOMMODATIONS
The Wild Iris [GF,NS,WI,WC,GO] 121 Maple Ave 360/466-1400, 800/477-1400

Long Beach Peninsula

ACCOMMODATIONS
Anthony's Home Court [GS,NS,WI,GO] 1310 Pacific Hwy N, Long Beach 360/642-2802, 888/787-2754 cabins & RV hookups

The Historic Sou'wester Lodge, Cabins & RV Park [GF,NS] Beach Access Rd (38th Pl), Seaview 360/642-2542 inexpensive suites, cabins w/ kitchens & vintage trailers

Mt Vernon

RESTAURANTS
Deli Next Door [WI,WC] 202 S 1st St (at Memorial Hwy) 360/336-3886 8am-9pm, 9pm-8pm Sun

CRUISY AREAS
Lions Park [AYOR] Freeway Dr (along the river)

Oak Harbor

CRUISY AREAS
Joseph Whidbey Park [AYOR] Swantown & Crosby

Olympia

INFO LINES & SERVICES
Free at Last AA 360/352-7344 call for info

ACCOMMODATIONS
Swantown Inn B&B [GF,NS,WI] 1431 11th Ave SE (at Central St) 360/753-9123, 877/753-9123

BARS
Hannah's [GS,NH,F] 123 5th Ave SW (at Columbia) 360/357-9890 11am-2am, till midnight Sun-Mon

NIGHTCLUBS
Jakes on 4th [MW,D,K] 311 E 4th 360/956-3247 10am-2am

CAFES
Darby's Cafe [GS,GO] 211 SE 5th Ave (at Washington) 360/357-6229 7am-2pm, 8am-2pm wknds, clsd Mon-Tue

RESTAURANTS
Saigon Rendez-Vous 117 5th Ave SW (btwn Columbia & Capitol Wy) 360/352-1989 Vietnamese, plenty veggie

Urban Onion [WC] 116 Legion Wy SE (at Capitol) 360/943-9242 11am-9pm, 4am-2am wknds, plenty veggie, also lounge

Washington • *USA*

■RETAIL SHOPS

Dumpster Values 302 4th (at Franklin)
360/705-3772 *10am-8pm
Sun, clothing, zines, records, toys*

■EROTICA

Desire Video 3200 Pacific Ave SE (off
I-5, at exit 107) **360/352-0820** *noon-
2am*

■CRUISY AREAS

Capitol Lake Marathon Park *take
5th Ave E to the parkway, follow signs to
park*

Pasco

■NIGHTCLUBS

Out & About Restaurant & Lounge
[MW,D,F,K,C,DS,WC] 327 W Lewis
509/543-3796, 877/388-3796
*6pm-2am, clsd Sun-Mon, 18+ Fri, also
restaurant*

Redmond

■CRUISY AREAS

Marymoor Park [AYOR] *days (cops
evenings)*

San Juan Islands

■ACCOMMODATIONS

Inn on Orcas Island [GF,NS,GO]
360/376-5227, 888/886-1661
waterfront, full brkfst

**Lopez Farm Cottages & Tent
Camping** [GS,NS] 555 Fisherman Bay
Rd, Lopez Island **360/468-3555,
800/440-3556** *hot tub, also camping*

■ENTERTAINMENT &
  RECREATION

**Western Prince Whale & Wildlife
Tours** 2 Spring St (at Front), Friday
Harbor **360/378-5315,
800/757-6722** *whale-watching &
wildlife tours April-Oct*

Seattle

■ACCOMMODATIONS

11th Avenue Inn [GF,NS,WI] 121 11th
Ave E (at Boren) **206/720-7161,
800/720-7161**

The Ace Hotel [GS,NS,WI,GO] 2423 1st
Ave (at Wall St) **206/448-4721**

Alexis Hotel [GF,WI,WC] 1007 1st Ave
(at Madison) **206/624-4844,
866/356-8894** *luxury hotel w/ Aveda
spa*

Bacon Mansion [GS,NS,WI,WC] 959
Broadway E (at E Prospect)
206/329-1864, 800/240-1864

Bed & Breakfast on Broadway
[GS,NS,WI] 722 Broadway Ave E (at
Aloha) **206/329-8933**

Gaslight Inn [★GS,SW,NS,WI,GO] 1727
15th Ave (at E Howell St)
206/325-3654 *B&B in Arts & Crafts
home*

Hotel 1000 [GF,WI] 1000 First Ave
206/957-1000, 877/315-1088

Hotel Monaco [GF,F,WI,WC] 1101 4th
Ave (at Spring St) **206/621-1770,
800/715-6513**

MarQueen Hotel [GS] 600 Queen Anne
Ave N (btwn Roy & Mercer)
206/282-7407, 888/445-3076 *in
Theater District, kitchenettes*

Sleeping Bulldog Bed & Breakfast
[GS,NS,WI,GO] 816 19th Ave S (at S
Dearborn St) **206/325-0202**

The Sorrento Hotel [GF,F,WI] 900
Madison St **206/622-6400, 800/426-
1265**

Washington • USA

■BARS

The Baltic Room [GS,E] 1207 Pine St (at Melrose) 206/625-4444 *9pm-2am, LGBT night Th*

The Bottleneck Lounge [GS,GO] 2328 Madison St (at John St) 206/323-1098 *4pm-2am, bar snacks*

The Can Can [GS,F,C] 93 Pike St #307 (in the Pike Place Market) 206/652-0832 *6pm-2am*

CC Attle's [★M,NH,F,V,WC] 1701 E Olive Way 206/323-4017 *noon-2am, patio, also Veranda Room & Men's Room*

Cha Cha Lounge & Bimbo's Cantina [GF,NH,GO] 1013 E Pike St (at 11th Ave) 206/322-0703 *5pm-2am, hipster lounge, big burritos*

Changes [M,NH,F,K,V,WC] 2103 N 45th St (at Meridian) 206/545-8363 *noon-2am*

The Crescent Lounge [GS,NH,K,WC] 1413 E Olive Wy (at Bellevue) *noon-2am, karaoke nightly*

►The Cuff [★M,D,CW,B,WIWC] 1533 13th Ave (at Pine) 206/323-1525 *2pm-2am, after-hours wknds, T-dance Sun, levi crowd, patio*

Diesel [M,NH,B,WC] 1413 14th Ave (at Madison) 206/322-1080 *2pm-2am, from noon wknds*

Double Header [GS,NH] 407 2nd Ave S Extension (at Washington) 206/464-9918 *10am-11pm, till 1am Fri-Sat*

Hula Hula [GF,K] 106 1st Ave N (at Denny) 206/284-5003 *4pm-close, tiki bar*

The Lobby Bar [M,F,E] 916 E Pike St (at Broadway) 206/328-6703 *3pm-midnight, till 2am Th-Sat*

Madison Pub [★M,NH,WI,WC] 1315 E Madison St (at 13th) 206/325-6537 *noon-2am*

OutWest [MW,NH,E,K] 5401 California Ave SW 206/937-1540 *4pm-midnight, till 2am Th-Sat*

Poco Wine Room [GS,F] 1408 E Pine St (at 14th Ave) 206/322-9463 *5pm-close*

Pony [M] 1221 E Madison St (at 13th Ave) 206/324-2854 *5pm-2am*

R Place [M,NH,D,F,K,S,V,WI] 619 E Pine St (at Boylston Ave) 206/322-8828 *4pm-2am, from 2pm wknds*

Rendezvous [GF,C,E] 2322 2nd Ave (at Battery) 206/441-5823 *4pm-2am, live shows, also restaurant*

The Seattle Eagle [M,L,WC] 314 E Pike St (at Bellevue) 206/621-7591 *2pm-2am, patio, rock 'n' roll, theme nights*

Temple Billiards [GF,F] 126 S Jackson 206/682-3242 *11am-2am, from 3pm wknds*

■NIGHTCLUBS

Contour [GF,D,F,E] 807 1st Ave (at Columbia) 206/447-7704 *3pm-2am, till 6am Fri-Sat, fire performances, also bar & restaurant*

Dimitriou's Jazz Alley [GF,F,E,NS,$] 2033 6th Ave (at Lenora) 206/441-9729 *call for events & reservations*

Neighbours Dance Club [★MW,D,YC,WC] 1509 Broadway (btwn Pike & Pine) 206/324-5358 *9pm-2am, till 3am Th, till 4am Fri-Sat, 2 flrs, also [18+] room Th-Sat*

Purr [M,F,K] 1518 11th Ave (at Pike St) 206/325-3112 *3pm-2am, till midnight Sun, cocktail lounge, Mexican-inspired food*

Re-bar [★GS,D,E,C] 1114 Howell (at Boren Ave) 206/233-9873 *10pm-2am, clsd Mon, DJ Wed-Sun*

Showbox [GF,E,$] 1426 1st Ave (at Pike) 206/628-3151 *live music venue*

■CAfES

The Allegro [WI] 4214 University Wy NE (at NE 42nd St) 206/633-3030 *7am-10:30pm*

Cafe Besalu 5909 24th Ave NW 206/789-1463 *7am-3pm, clsd Mon-Tue, great pastries*

Espresso Vivace [WI] 532 Broadway Ave 206/860-5869 *6am-11pm*

Fuel Coffee [WI] 610 19th Ave E 206/329-4700 *6am-9pm,*

Kaladi Brothers Coffee [WI] 511 E Pike St (at Summit) 206/388-1700 *6am-9pm, from 8am wknds*

Louisa's 2379 Eastlake Ave E 206/325-0081 *7am-9pm, till 10pm Fri-Sat, 8am-3pm Sun*

■RESTAURANTS

Al Boccalino 1 Yesler Wy (at Alaskan) 206/622-7688 *lunch Tue-Fri, dinner nightly, classy southern Italian*

Bamboo Garden 364 Roy St (at Mercer St) 206/282-6616 *11am-10pm, Chinese vegetarian & kosher*

Cafe Flora [BW,NS,WC] 2901 E Madison St 206/325-9100 *lunch, dinner, wknd brunch*

Campagne [R] 86 Pine St (at 1st) 206/728-2800 *dinner only, clsd Mon*

Canlis 2576 Aurora Ave N 206/283-3313 *dinner only, fancy seafood*

Dahlia Lounge 2001 4th Ave (at Virginia) 206/682-4142 *lunch Mon-Fri, dinner nightly, wknd brunch, full bar*

Dick's Drive In 115 Broadway E (at Denny) 206/323-1300 *10:30am-2am, excellent fries & shakes*

Flying Fish 300 Westlake Ave N 206/728-8595 *lunch Mon-Fri, dinner nightly, full bar*

Fresh Bistro 4725 42nd Ave SW (btwn Alaska St & Edmunds) 206/935-3733 *dinner Mon-Sat, lunch Wed-Fri, wknd brunch*

Glo's [★] 1621 E Olive Wy (at Summit Ave E) 206/324-2577 *7am-3pm, midnight -4pm wknds, brkfst only*

The Grill on Broadway [★] 314 Broadway E (at E Harrison) 206/328-7000 *11am-11pm, from 8am wknds, full bar*

Julia's [E] 300 Broadway E (at Thomas) 206/860-1818 *8am-11pm, till midnight Fri-Sat, full bar, [DS] Sat*

Kabul 2301 N 45th St 206/545-9000 *5pm-9:30pm, till 10pm Fri-Sat, Afghan*

Lola 2000 4th Ave (at Virginia) 206/441-1430 *6am-midnight, till 2am wknds, popular brunch*

Mama's Mexican Kitchen 2234 2nd Ave (in Belltown) 206/728-6262 *lunch & dinner, cheap & funky*

Paseo 4225 Fremont Ave N (at N 43rd St) 206/545-7440 *11am-9pm, clsd Sun-Mon, Cuban*

Queen City Grill [★WC] 2201 1st Ave (at Blanchard) 206/443-0975 *dinner only, fresh seafood, full bar*

Restaurant Zoe 2137 2nd Ave (at Blanchard) 206/256-2060 *dinner only*

Snappy Dragon 8917 Roosevelt Wy NE 206/528-5575 *11am-9:30pm, 4pm-9pm Sun, Chinese*

Spinasse 1531 14th Ave E 206/251-7673 *clsd Tue, traditional cuisine of the Piedmont region of Northern Italy*

Sunlight Cafe [BW,WC] 6403 Roosevelt Wy NE (at 64th) 206/522-9060 *8am-9pm, vegetarian*

Szmania's 3321 W McGraw St (in Magnolia Bluff) 206/284-7305 *dinner nightly, clsd Mon, full bar*

Tamarind Tree 1036 S Jackson St 206/860-1404 *10am-10pm, till midnight Fri-Sat, Vietnamese*

Teapot Vegetarian House 345 15th Ave E 206/325-1010 *11am-10pm, vegan*

Thaiger Room 206/632-9299 *11am-10pm, from noon wknds, Thai*

Wild Ginger Asian Restaurant & Triple Bar [★] 1401 3rd Ave (at Union) 206/623-4450 *lunch Mon-Sat, dinner nightly, bar till 1am*

Wild Mountain 1408 NW 85th St 206/297-9453 *8:30am-9pm, clsd Tue*

■ENTERTAINMENT & RECREATION

Alki Beach Park 1702 Alki Ave SW, West Seattle *popular on warm days*

Century Ballroom [MW,D,F] 915 E Pine, 2nd flr (at Broadway) 206/324-7263 *ballroom dancing; check schedule for gay nights*

Garage [★F,21+] 1130 Broadway 206/322-2296 *3pm-2am, way-cool pool hall, full bar, also bowling alley*

Northwest Lesbian & Gay History Museum Project 206/903-9517 *exhibits & publication*

Washington • *USA*

Richard Hugo House [C,WC] 1634 11th Ave 206/322-7030 *noon-6pm, till 5pm Sat, clsd Sun; Zine Archive & Publishing Project; open later for events; also cafe*

The Vera Project [GF] corner of Warren Ave N & Republican St (in Seattle Center) 206/956-8372 *queer-friendly all-ages music arts center*

■BOOKSTORES

Elliott Bay Book Company 1521 10th Ave 206/624-6600, 800/962-5311 *10am-10pm, till 11pm Fri-Sat, till 9pm Sun*

Left Bank Books 92 Pike St (at 1st Ave) 206/622-0195 *10am-7pm*

■RETAIL SHOPS

Broadway Market [★] 401 Broadway E (at Harrison & Republican) *mall full of funky, hip stores*

Lifelong Thrift 1002 E Seneca 206/328-8979 *all sales from donated items fund Lifelong AIDS*

Metropolis 7321 Greenwood Ave N 206/782-7002 *10am-7pm, till 6pm Sat, noon-5pm Sun, cards & gifts*

UnderU4men 709 Broadway E (at Roy) 206/324-6446 *11am-7pm, till 9pm Fri, designer underwear & swimwear & in-store models*

■PUBLICATIONS

SGN (Seattle Gay News) 206/324-4297 *weekly LGBT newspaper*

The Stranger 206/323-7101 *queer-positive alternative weekly*

■MEN'S CLUBS

Club Z [PC] 1117 Pike St (at Boren) 206/622-9958 *24hrs daily*

Steamworks [★WI,PC] 1520 Summit Ave (btwn Pike & Pine) 206/388-4818 *24hrs*

■MEN'S SERVICES

➤MegaMates 206/877-0877 *Call to hook up with HOT local men. FREE to listen & respond to ads. Use FREE code DAMRON. MegaMates.com.*

■EROTICA

Castle Megastore 206 Broadway Ave E 206/204-0126

The Crypt Off Broadway 1516 11th Ave (at E Pine) 206/325-3882

Fantasy Unlimited 2027 Westlake Ave (at 7th) 206/622-4669 *24hrs*

Hollywood Erotic Boutique 12706 Lake City Wy NE 206/363-0056

Taboo Video 1012 1st Ave 206/622-7399 *24hrs*

■CRUISY AREAS

Arboretum [AYOR] *days*

Green Lake Park [AYOR] 5500 blk of W Green Lake Wy (btwn putting course & aqua theater) *evenings*

Spokane

■INFO LINES & SERVICES

AA Gay/ Lesbian 1614 W Riverside 509/624-1442 *call for meeting times*

Inland Northwest LGBT Center 1522 N Washington #102 509/489-1914 *support groups, events, also art gallery*

■ACCOMMODATIONS

Montvale Hotel [GF,TG,F,NS,WI,GO] 1005 W First Ave (at Monroe) 509/747-1919, 866/668-8253 *luxury, boutique hotel*

■RESTAURANTS

Mizuna 214 N Howard 509/747-2004 *lunch Mon-Fri, dinner nightly, full bar*

■BOOKSTORES

Auntie's Bookstore [WC] 402 W Main Ave (at Washington) 509/838-0206 *9am-9pm, 11am-6pm Sun-Mon*

■MEN'S SERVICES

➤MegaMates 509/777-2100 *Call to hook up with HOT local men. FREE to listen & respond to ads. Use FREE code DAMRON. MegaMates.com.*

Suquamish

■INFO LINES & SERVICES

Kitsap Lesbian/ Gay AA 18732 Division Ave NE (at church) 360/475-0775, 800/562-7455 *7pm Sun*

Tacoma

■INFO LINES & SERVICES

AA Gay/ Lesbian 759 S 45th St (at MCC) **253/474-8897** *7:30pm Fri*

Rainbow Center 741 St Helens Ave **253/383-2318** *1pm-5pm Mon-Fri, till 4pm Sat, community & resource center*

■ACCOMMODATIONS

Chinaberry Hill [GF,NS,WI] 302 Tacoma Ave N **253/272-1282** *full brkfst, jacuzzis, bay views, fireplaces*

Hotel Murano [GF,WI,WC] 1320 Broadway Plaza (at S 15th) **253/238-8000, 866/986-8083** *restaurants & bars*

■BARS

Airport Bar & Grill [MW,NH] 5406 S Tacoma Wy (at 54th) **253/475-9730** *2pm-2am*

■NIGHTCLUBS

➤Club Silverstone [MW,NH,D,F,K] 739 1/2 St Helens Ave (at 9th) **253/404-0273** *11am-2am*

■CAFES

Shakabrah Java Cafe [WC] **253/572-2787** *7am-4pm, clsd Sun*

■MEN'S SERVICES

➤MegaMates 253/882-0882 *Call to hook up with HOT local men. FREE to listen & respond to ads. Use FREE code DAMRON. MegaMates.com.*

■EROTICA

Castle Megastore 6015 Tacoma Mall Blvd **253/471-0391**

■CRUISY AREAS

Wright Park [AYOR] 6th & G Sts

Vancouver

see also Portland, Oregon

■BARS

Tiger Lily [MW,F,K,E] 1109 Washington St (at W 12th St) **360/828-1245** *10am-2am, also restaurant*

■MEN'S SERVICES

➤MegaMates 360/433-6100 *Call to hook up with HOT local men. FREE to listen & respond to ads. Use FREE code DAMRON. MegaMates.com.*

Walla Walla

■CRUISY AREAS

Fort Walla Walla Park [AYOR]

Pioneer Park [AYOR]

Wenatchee

■CAFES

The Cellar Cafe [BW,GO] 249 N Mission St (at 5th) **509/662-1722** *9am-3pm Mon-Fri, patio*

■CRUISY AREAS

River Walk [AYOR] at 19th St

Whidbey Island

■ACCOMMODATIONS

Whidwood Inn [GS,NS,GO] **360/720-6228** *near historic Coupeville, hot tub*

Winthrop

■ACCOMMODATIONS

Chewuch Inn [GF,NS,WI,WC] 223 White Ave **509/996-3107, 800/747-3107** *E of N Cascades Mtns*

Yakima

■EROTICA

Yakima Magazine Center 1111 N 1st St **509/248-8598**

WEST VIRGINIA

Statewide

■PUBLICATIONS

Out 724/733-0828 *Pittsburgh's only LGBTQ newspaper since 1973! news, local events, classifieds & more for Western & Central PA, OH & WV*

Beckley

■EROTICA

Blue Moon Video 3427 Robert C Byrd Dr (at New River Dr) **304/255-1200**

Eccles Video 3517 Harper Rd, Harper **304/250-0068**

West Virginia • *USA*

Berkeley Springs

■EROTICA

Action Books & Video [AYOR] US 522
(7 miles S of town) **304/258-2529**
open till midnight, arcade

Bluefield

■CRUISY AREAS

East River Mountain Overlook [AYOR]
off Rte 460 (take lane nearest mtn &
turn off, go all the way up mtn)

Charleston

■ACCOMMODATIONS

Long Fork Campgrounds
[M,SW,N,WI,GO] 114 Long Fork Camp Rd
(at Charleston Rd), Walton
304/577-9347 *40 minutes from
Charleston, also bar on wknds*

■BARS

Broadway [M,D,DS] 210 Leon Sullivan
Wy (at Lee) **304/343-2162** *12:30pm-
3am*

■ENTERTAINMENT &
RECREATION

Living AIDS Memorial Garden corner
of Washington St E (at Sidney Ave)
304/346-0246

■BOOKSTORES

Taylor Books [WI] 226 Capitol St
304/342-1461 *7:30am-8pm, till 10pm
Fri, 9am-10pm Sat, till 3pm Sun, also
cafe*

■EROTICA

Bookmart Video 4100 Maccorkle Ave
SE (at 41st St SE) **304/925-9000**

Crazy Mitch's Adult Books 6721
Maccorkle Ave, St Albans
304/768-0947

■CRUISY AREAS

Coonskin Park [AYOR] Greenbriar St
(take Greenbriar St exit from I-77 heading from Beckley)

Daniel Boone Park [AYOR] Kanawha
Blvd (just N of Capitol) *evenings*

Fairmont

■CRUISY AREAS

Morris Park [AYOR] Pleasant Valley Rd

Follansbee

■BARS

Wild Coyote Saloon [MW,D,DS] 869
Main St **304/527-7191** *6pm-close*

Ghent

■EROTICA

The Lion's Den Adult Superstore 302
Odd Rd (exit 28 off I-77)
304/787-3333

Harpers Ferry

■ACCOMMODATIONS

Laurel Lodge [GF,NS,WI,GO] 844 Ridge
St **304/535-2886** *bungalow overlooking Potomac River gorge, full brkfst*

Huntington

■ACCOMMODATIONS

Pullman Plaza Hotel [GF,SW,NS,WI,WC]
1001 3rd Ave (at 10th St)
304/525-1001, 866/613-3611

■BARS

Club Deception [M,D,B,K,DS,PC,WC]
1037 7th Ave (at 11th St)
304/522-3146 *5pm-2am*

The Stonewall
[★MW,D,K,DS,18+,WC,GO] 820 7th Ave
(enter in alley) **304/523-2242** *8pm-
3am, clsd Mon-Tue*

■RESTAURANTS

Sharkey's [E,K] 410 10th St
304/523-3200 *4pm-2:30am, clsd Sun,
full bar*

■CRUISY AREAS

Rotary Park [AYOR] near 8th Ave &
29th St (off Rte 60 E, take 29th St exit)

Lewisburg

■CRUISY AREAS

Tuckwiller Park [AYOR] off Rte 60
(from I-64 take exit 161 & head E for 1
mile)

Logan

■CRUISY AREAS

Chief Logan State Park [AYOR]
daylight till 10pm

Lost River

■ACCOMMODATIONS

Guest House at Lost River [MW,F,SW,NS,WI,GO] 288 Settlers Valley Wy (at Mill Gap Rd) **304/897-5707** *full brkfst, hot tub, restaurant & bar*

■RESTAURANTS

Lost River Grill & Motel [WI] St Rd 259 **304/897-6482** *11:45am-9pm, 8am-10pm Sat, 4pm-9pm Mon, full bar*

Lost River Trading Post 295 E. Main St, Wardensville **304/874-3300** *12pm-7pm Fri, 10am-6pm Sat-Sun, antiques and cafe*

Martinsburg

■BARS

The Club [M,D,F,K] 5268 Williamsport Pike (Rte 11) **304/274-6080** *6pm-1am, till 3am Fri-Sat, clsd Sun-Tue*

Martinsburg

■EROTICA

Variety Books & Video 255 N Queen St (at Race) **304/263-4334** *24hrs*

■CRUISY AREAS

I-81 Rest Area 1/2 mile past exit 20 (in closed weigh station) *evenings*

Morgantown

■NIGHTCLUBS

Vice Versa [MW,D,K,DS,S,PC,18+,WC] 335 High St (enter rear) **304/292-2010** *8pm-3am Th-Sun*

■EROTICA

Adult Toy Boxxx Hartman Run Rd **304/296-3428** *bookstore w/ arcade*

■CRUISY AREAS

Cooper's Rock State Park [AYOR] 10 miles E of town (off I-68, take Cooper's State Park exit) *parking lot & woods*

Marilla Park [AYOR] E Brockway Ave (btwn Morgantown & Sabraton) *midday & evenings*

Parkersburg

■NIGHTCLUBS

The Otherside of the Nip n Cue [MW,D,K,DS] 1300 19th St **304/485-7752** *9pm Fri-Sat only*

■EROTICA

Pioneer Adult Books & Videos 6603 Emerson Ave **304/428-8604**

■CRUISY AREAS

Corning Boat Ramp [AYOR] Staunton Ave (off I-77)

Pliny

■EROTICA

Route 35 Adult Video & Books 1651 US Rte 35 N (near Buffalo) **304/937-4900** *24hrs*

Princeton

■EROTICA

Exotic Illusions Adult Bookstore 853 Frontage Rd/ Rte 460 (btwn Bluefield & Princeton) **304/487-2170** *24hrs*

Proctor

■ACCOMMODATIONS

Roseland Guest House & Campground [MO,F,SW,N,NS,GO] **304/455-3838** *222 secluded acres w/ campsites, theme wknds*

Wheeling

■EROTICA

Market St News 1437 Market St (at 14th St) **304/232-2414**

WISCONSIN

Algoma

■RETAIL SHOPS

The Flying Pig [GF,GO] N6975 Hwy 42 (at Tenth) **920/487-9902** *9am-6pm May-Oct, call for hrs off season, art gallery & coffee bar*

Wisconsin • USA

Appleton

■BARS

Rascals Bar & Grill [MW,F] 702 E Wisconsin Ave (at Lawe) 920/954-9262 5pm-2am, from noon Sun, fish-fry Fri, patio

Ravens [M,D,K,DS] 215 E College Ave 920/364-9599 8pm-2am, clsd Sun-Mon

■CAFES

Harmony Cafe [GS,E,YC] 233 E College Ave 920/734-2233 7am-9pm, till 10pm Th-Sat, 8am-6pm Sun, also educational & support groups

■MEN'S SERVICES

➤**MegaMates** 920/243-0043 Call to hook up with HOT local men. FREE to listen & respond to ads. Use FREE code DAMRON. MegaMates.com.

■EROTICA

Eldorado's 2545 S Memorial Dr (at Hwys 47 & 441) 920/830-0042

■CRUISY AREAS

Lutz Park [AYOR]

Ashland

■CRUISY AREAS

Prentice Park [AYOR]

Beloit

■BARS

Club Impulse [MW,D,K,DS] 132 W Grand Ave 608/361-0000 4pm-2am, till 2:30am Fri-Sat, from 7pm Sat

Eau Claire

■INFO LINES & SERVICES

LGBT Community Center of the Chippewa Valley 1305 Woodland Ave 715/552-5428 drop-in 7pm-10pm Fri, call for other hours, library & variety of events

■NIGHTCLUBS

Scooters [MW,D,K,DS,WC] 411 Galloway (at Farwell) 715/835-9959 3pm-2am

■EROTICA

Adult Video Unlimited 1518 Bellinger St 715/834-3393

Green Bay

■INFO LINES & SERVICES

Gay AA 920/432-2600 call for times & locations

■BARS

Napalese Lounge [M,NH,F,DS,WC] 1351 Cedar St 920/432-9646 11am-close, DJ Fri-Sat

Roundabout [MW] 1264 Main St 920/544-9544 2pm-2am

■NIGHTCLUBS

Club XS [MW,D] 1106 Main St 7pm-2am

The Shelter [MW,D,CW,B,L,TG,F,K,DS,V,GO] 730 N Quincy St (at 54302) 920/432-2662 4pm-2am, theme nights

■CAFES

Harmony Cafe [E] 1660 W Mason St 920/569-1593 7am-9pm, 10am-6pm Sun, shows, support groups

■PUBLICATIONS

Outbound/ Quest 920/655-0611, 800/578-3785 news & arts reviews for WI's LGBT community

■EROTICA

Lion's Den Adult Superstore 836 S Broadway (at 5th) 920/433-9640 24hrs

Hayward

■ACCOMMODATIONS

The Lake House [MW,SW,NS,WI,WC,GO] 5793 Division, Stone Lake 715/865-6803 full brkfst, lesbian-owned

Kenosha

see also Racine

■BARS

Club Icon [MW,D,K] 6305 120th Ave (on E Frontage road of I-94) 262/857-3240 7pm-2am, from 3pm Sun, clsd Mon

La Crosse

■ACCOMMODATIONS

Rainbow Ridge Farms B&B [GF,NS,WI] N 5732 Hauser Rd (at County S), Onalaska **608/783-8181, 888/347-2594**

■BARS

Chances R [MW,NH] 417 Jay St (at 4th) **608/782-5105** *3pm-close*

My Place [MW,NH,GO] 3201 South Ave (at East Ave) **608/788-9073** *3pm-close, from noon wknds*

Players [★MW,D,MR,TG,WC,GO] 300 S 4th St (at Jay St) **608/784-4200** *5pm-2am, from 3pm Fri-Sun, till 2:30am Fri-Sat*

■EROTICA

Pleasures [GS] 405 S 3rd **608/784-6350**

■CRUISY AREAS

Pettibone Park [AYOR] on the Mississippi River (off of North Beach, across from the Holiday Inn) *days only*

Madison

■INFO LINES & SERVICES

OutReach, Inc 600 Williamson St #P-1 **608/255-8582** *10am-7pm, noon-4pm Sat, clsd Sun*

■BARS

Five Nightclub [★MW,D,K,DS,V,TG] 5 Applegate Ct (btwn Fish Hatchery Rd & W Beltline Hwy) **608/277-9700, 877/648-9700** *4pm-2am, from 2pm Sun*

Green Bush [GF] 914 Regent St (at Park) **608/257-2874** *4pm-midnight, clsd Sun, also Sicilian restaurant*

Woof's [MW,NH,B,D,L,F] 114 King St (on Capitol Sq) **608/204-6222** *4pm-2am, from noon Sun*

■NIGHTCLUBS

Cardinal [GS,E,D] 418 E Wilson St (at S Franklin) **608/257-2473** *7pm-2am, from 4pm Fri*

IQ/ IndieQueer [MW,D] *weekly & monthly queer parties in Madison, check local listings for dates & info*

Plan B [MW,D,K] 924 Williamson St **608/257-5262** *4pm-2am, from 9pm Sun, clsd Mon*

Sotto [MW,D] 303 N Henry St **920/251-2753** *9pm-2am, clsd Sun-Mon*

■CAFES

Java Cat [F,WI] 3918 Monona Dr (at Cottage Grove Rd) **608/223-5553**

■RESTAURANTS

Fromagination 12 S Carroll (on Capital Sq) **608/255-2430** *9:30am-6pm, 9am-5pm Sat, clsd Sun*

La Hacienda [★] 515 S Park St **608/255-8227** *9am-3am, Mexican, popular & cruisy post-Club 5 spot*

Monty's Blue Plate Diner [BW,WC] 2089 Atwood Ave (at Winnebago) **608/244-8505** *7am-9pm, till 10pm wknds*

■PUBLICATIONS

Our Lives *LGBT publication,* www.ourlivesmadison.com

■EROTICA

Red Letter News 2528 E Washington (btwn North & Milwaukee) **608/241-9958**

■CRUISY AREAS

Burrows Park [AYOR]

Olin Park [AYOR] W shore of Lake Monona (parking lot near Sheraton) *afternoons*

Mazomanie

■CRUISY AREAS

Mazo Nude Beach [AYOR] Madison *30 miles NW on Hwy 4, then 14 miles N to Laws Dr, turn left & go 1/2 mile to gravel rd*

Milwaukee

■INFO LINES & SERVICES

AA Galano Club 315 W Court #201 (in LGBT Community Center) **414/276-6936**

Milwaukee LGBT Community Center [WI] 1110 N Market St, 2nd Fl **414/271-2656** *10am-10pm, from 6pm Sat, till 5pm Mon, clsd Sun*

Wisconsin • *USA*

■ACCOMMODATIONS

Ambassador Hotel [GS,WI,WC] 2308 W Wisconsin Ave (at N 24th) **414/345-5000, 888/322-3326**

The Brumder Mansion [GF,NS,WI] 3046 W Wisconsin Ave (at N 31st) **414/342-9767, 866/793-3676**

Hotel of the Arts/ Days Inn [GF,NS,WI] 1840 N 6th St (at Reservoir Ave) **414/265-5629**

The Iron Horse Hotel [GF] 500 W Florida St (at S 5th St) **888/543-4766** *friendly hotel geared toward motorcycle enthusiasts*

The Milwaukee Hilton [GF,F,SW,WI,WC] 509 W Wisconsin Ave (at 5th St) **414/271-7250, 800/445-8667**

■BARS

Art Bar [GS,E,WI,GO] 722 E Burleigh St (at Fratney) **414/372-7880** *3pm-2am, from 10am wknds*

Boom/ The Room [MW,NH,F,V,S] 625 S 2nd (at W Bruce) **414/277-5040** *5pm-2am, from 2pm wknds, patio, also martini bar*

D.I.X. [M,V] 739 S 1st St (at National) **414/231-9085** *4pm-2am, from noon Sun*

Fluid [M,NH,V] 819 S 2nd St (at W National) **414/643-5843** *5pm-close, from 3pm Fri, from 2pm wknds*

Hamburger Mary's Milwaukee [MW,F,DS,K] 2130 Kinnickinnic **414/988-9324** *11am-10pm, 10am-midnight wknds*

Harbor Room [M,L,F,V] 117 E Greenfield Ave (at S 1st St) **414/672-7988** *6am-2am*

Hybrid Lounge [M] 707 E Brady (at Van Buren) **414/810-1809** *4pm-close, from 10am Sat-Sun*

Kruz [M,L] 354 E National Ave (at S Water St) **414/272-5789** *3pm-close, patio, cruisy*

The Nomad [GF] 1401 E Brady St (at Warren) **414/224-8111** *2pm-2am, from noon wknds, soccer pub*

Taylor's [GS,NH,D,WC,GO] 795 N Jefferson St (at Wells) **414/271-2855** *4pm-close, patio*

This Is It [M,OC] 418 E Wells St (at Jefferson) **414/278-9192** *3pm-2am*

Two [GS] 718 E Burleigh St (at Fratney) | *7pm-close Wed-Sat*

Woody's [M,NH,WI] 1579 S 2nd St (at Lapham St) **414/672-0806** *4pm-close, from 2pm wknds, sports bar*

■NIGHTCLUBS

La Cage/ ETC/Montage Lounge [★M,D,S,V,YC,WC] 801 S 2nd St (at National) **414/383-8330** *6pm-close, from 10pm Fri-Sat*

■CAFES

Alterra Coffee Roasters [WI] 2211 N Prospect Ave (at North) **414/273-3753** *7am-6pm*

Bella Caffe 189 N Milwaukee St **414/273-5620** *6am-9pm, till 11pm Fri-Sat, 8am-6pm Sun*

Fuel Cafe [WI,WC] 818 E Center St **414/374-3835** *7am-10pm,from 8am wknds*

■RESTAURANTS

Beans & Barley 1901 E North Ave (at Oakland Ave) **414/278-7878** *8am-9pm, vegetarian cafe & deli*

Coquette Cafe [WC] 316 N Milwaukee St (btwn Buffalo & St Paul) **414/291-2655** *11am-10pm, till 11pm Fri, 5pm-11pm Sat, 11am-5pm Sun*

Crisp Pizza Bar & Lounge 1323 E Brady St **414/727-4217** *4pm-2am, from 11:30am wknds*

Harvey's [E] 1340 W Towne Sq Rd, Mequon **262/241-9589** *dinner nightly, cont'l*

Honeypie Cafe 2643 S Kinnickinnic Ave (at Potter) **414/489-7437** *10am-10pm, from 9am wknds, till 9pm Sun, homemade midwestern classics*

The Knick [★WC] 1030 E Juneau Ave (at Waverly) **414/272-0011** *11am-midnight, from 9am wknds, full bar*

La Perla 734 S 5th St (at National) **414/645-9888** *11am-10pm, till 11:30pm Fri-Sat, Mexican, also bar*

Lulu [E] 2261 & 2265 S Howell Ave **414/294-5858** *11am-10pm, also bar till late, live music wknds*

Meritage [WC] 5921 W Vliet St
414/479-0620 5pm-10pm, till 11pm
Fri-Sat, till 9pm Mon, clsd Sun

Range Line Inn [R] 2635 W Mequon
Rd, Mequon 262/242-0530 4:30pm-
10pm, clsd Sun-Mon

Ryan Braun's Graffito
102 N Water St 414/727-2888 5pm-
9pm, from 11am Fri-Sun, clsd Mon

Sanford Restaurant 1547 N Jackson
St 414/276-9608 dinner only, clsd
Sun, Milwaukee fine dining Euro-style

■ENTERTAINMENT & RECREATION

Boerner Botanical Gardens 9400
Boerner Dr (in Whitnall Park), Hales
Corners 414/525-5600,
414/525-5601 8am-dusk, 40-acre
garden & arboretum, garden clsd in
winter

Harley-Davidson Museum 400 Canal
St (at N 6th St) 877/287-2789

Mitchell Park Domes 524 S Layton
Blvd (27th St, at Pierce) 414/257-5611
botanical gardens

Off the Wall Theatre 127 E Wells St
414/327-3552 alternative theatre
group

■BOOKSTORES

OutWords Books, Gifts & Coffee
[WC] 2710 N Murray Ave (at Park Pl)
414/963-9089 11am-7pm, till 8pm
Fri-Sat, noon-6pm Sun, LGBT, pride items

Peoples' Books 804 E Center
414/962-0575 10am-6pm, clsd Sun

Woodland Pattern 720 E Locust St
414/263-5001 11am-8pm, noon-5pm
wknds, clsd Mon

■PUBLICATIONS

Quest/Outbound 920/655-0611,
800/578-3785 news & arts reviews
for WI's LGBT community

■MEN'S CLUBS

Midtowne Spa—Milwaukee [PC,WC]
315 S Water (at Florida)
414/278-8989 24hrs

■MEN'S SERVICES

➤**MegaMates** 414/342-2222 Call to
hook up with HOT local men. FREE to
listen & respond to ads. Use FREE code
DAMRON. MegaMates.com.

■EROTICA

Booked Solid 7035 W Greenfield Ave
(at 70th), West Allis 414/774-7210

■CRUISY AREAS

Juneau Park [AYOR] beware after
10pm

Oshkosh

■BARS

Deb's Spare Time [MW,NH,F,E,18+,GO]
1303 Harrison St (btwn Main & New
York) 920/235-6577 11am-2am, from
9am wknds

PJ's [MW,NH,D] 1601 Oregon St
920/385-0442 5pm-close Tue-Sat,
clsd Sun-Mon

■EROTICA

The Lion's Den Adult Superstore
1650 Plainview Dr (at Hwys 41 & 26)
920/235-9040 24hrs

Pure Pleasure 1212 Oshkosh Ave (off
Hwy 21) 920/235-9727

Supreme Lingerie & Gifts 1911 S
Washburn St 920/235-2012

Racine

■NIGHTCLUBS

JoDee's International [MW,D,E,K,DS,S]
2139 Racine St/ S Hwy 32 (at 22nd)
262/880-0058 9pm Fri-Sun only, park
in rear

Sheboygan

■BARS

The Blue Lite [MW,NH,D] 1029 N 8th St
(off Rte 143) 920/457-1636 7pm-
close, from 3pm Sun

Filibusters [MW.D] 434 Pennsylvania
Ave 920/287-3300 4pm-2am, from
1pm wknds, clsd Mon

Sturgeon Bay

■ACCOMMODATIONS

The Chadwick Inn [GF,NS,GO] 25 N 8th
Ave 920/743-2771

Wisconsin • *USA*

The Chanticleer Guest House
[★GS,SW,NS,WI,WC,GO] 4072 Cherry Rd
920/746-0334, 866/682-0384 *on*
70 acres

Superior

■BARS

The Flame [MW,D,E,K,DS,WI] 1612
Tower Ave **715/395-0101** *3pm-*
2:30am

The Main Club [M,D,L,E,WI,WC] 1217
Tower Ave (at 12th) **715/392-1756**
3pm-2am

Wausau

■NIGHTCLUBS

Oz [M,D,K,DS,V] 320 Washington
715/842-3225 *7pm-close*

Wisconsin Dells

■BARS

Captain Dix [MW,K] 4124 River Rd (at
Rainbow Valley Resort) **608/253-1818**
6pm-close, from 11am wknds, also
accommodations

WYOMING

Casper

■EROTICA

Emporium Video Exchange 1210 East
F St **307/265-9726**

■CRUISY AREAS

Morad Park [AYOR]

Cheyenne

see also Fort Collins, Colorado

■INFO LINES & SERVICES

**Wyoming Equality/ United Gays &
Lesbians of Wyoming 307/778-7645**
10am-2pm Mon-Fri, info, referrals &
newsletter, social activities

■BARS

Choice City Shots
[MW,NH,D,K,S,WC,GO] 124 LaPorte Ave
(at College), Fort Collins, CO
970/221-4333 *open 6:30pm*

■CRUISY AREAS

I-25 Rest Area Southbound [AYOR]
parking lot & woods, late nights

Lions Park [AYOR] *near skating pond*

Etna

■RETAIL SHOPS

Blue Fox Studio & Gallery [GO]
107452 N US Hwy 89 **307/883-3310**
open 7 days, hours vary, pottery, jewelry
& mask studio, local travel info

Evanston

■EROTICA

Romantix Adult Superstore 1939
Harrison Dr **307/789-0800**

Gillette

■CRUISY AREAS

Camplex Park [AYOR] Garner Lake Rd
(off I-90, Garner Lake Rd exit, go S 1
mile) *parking lot & woods*

Lander

■CRUISY AREAS

City Park 3rd St (at City Park Ave)

Laramie

■ACCOMMODATIONS

Cowgirl Horse Hotel [W] 32 Black Elk
Trail **307/745-8794** or **399-2502**
specializing in women travelers & their
horses, men welcome

■BOOKSTORES

The Second Story 105 Ivinson Ave
307/745-4423 *10am-6pm, clsd Sun,*
independent

■CRUISY AREAS

I-80 Rest Area [AYOR] Happy Jack Rd
(13 miles E, take Happy Jack Rd exit off
I-80) *afternoons, late evenings*

Rock Springs

■EROTICA

Exit 107 Video 1554 9th St (off I-80,
exit 107) **307/362-0700** *arcade*

Sheridan

■CRUISY AREAS

Sheridan Information Center [AYOR]
take 5th Ave exit off I-90 *parking lot &*
woods

Canada

Calgary

■INFO LINES & SERVICES

Calgary Outlink: Centre for Gender & Sexual Diversity 223 12th Ave SW (at the Old Y Centre) **403/234-8973** *11am-2pm Tues, 4pm-7pm Wed, 3pm-6pm Th, Community Cafe is the 2nd Fri of the month at 7pm*

Front Runners AA 1227 Kensington Close NW (at Hillhurst United Church) **403/777-1212** *8:30pm Wed & Sat*

■ACCOMMODATIONS

11th Street Lodging [GS,NS,WI,GO] **403/209-1800** *"no shoe" policy inside*

Calgary Westways Guest House [GS,NS,WI,GO] 216 25th Ave SW **403/229-1758, 866/846-7038** *full brkfst*

■BARS

The Back Lot [M,WC] 209 10th Ave SW (at 1st St SW) **403/265-5211** *2pm-2am, martini lounge, patio*

Ming [GF] 520 17th Ave SW **403/229-1986** *4pm-2am, martini lounge*

Texas Lounge [MO] 308 17th Ave SW (enter rear) **403/229-0911** *11am-2am*

■NIGHTCLUBS

Lolita's [GS,C] 1413 9th Ave SE **403/265-5739** *cabaret/ performance club, also restaurant*

Twisted Element [M,D,K,DS,S,WI] 1006 11th Ave SW **403/802-0230** *9pm-close, clsd Mon*

■CAFES

Caffe Beano [WC] 1613 9th St SW (at 17th Ave) **403/229-1232** *6am-midnight, from 7am wknds*

■RESTAURANTS

Halo 13226 Macleod Trail SE **403/271-4111** *lunch & dinner, steak, seafood & wine bar*

Melrose Cafe & Bar 730 17th Ave SW (at 7th St) **403/228-3566** *11am-2am, from 10am wknds, full bar till 2am, patio*

Thai Sa-On 351 10th Ave SW (at 4th) **403/264-3526** *lunch & dinner, clsd Sun*

■BOOKSTORES

Daily Globe News Shop 1004 17th Ave SW (at 10th St) **403/244-2060** *9am-10pm*

■PUBLICATIONS

Gay Calgary & Edmonton Magazine **888/543-6960** *monthly LGBT publication*

■MEN'S CLUBS

Goliath's Saunatel [F,PC] 308 17th Ave SW (enter rear) **403/229-0911** *24hrs, cocktails*

■CRUISY AREAS

North Glenmore Park [AYOR] S end of Crowchild *down the ravine*

Edmonton

■INFO LINES & SERVICES

AA Gay/ Lesbian 11355 Jasper Ave (at church) **780/424-5900** *7:30pm Mon; also 8pm Fri at 10804 119th St*

Pride Centre of Edmonton 10608 105 Ave **780/488-3234** *noon-9pm, 2pm-6:30pm Sat, clsd Sun-Mon*

■ACCOMMODATIONS

Labyrinth Lake Lodge [GS,NS,WI] **780/878-3301** *lodge on private lake, hot tubs*

Northern Lights B&B [MW,SW,NS,GO] **780/483-1572** *full brkfst*

■BARS

The Junction [MW,D,E,DS] 10242 106th St **780/756-5667** *4pm-close, theme nights, also restaurant*

Woody's Pub & Cafe [MW,NH,F,K] 11723 A Jasper (above Buddy's) **780/488-6557** *3pm-midnight, till 3am wknds*

■NIGHTCLUBS

Buddy's Nite Club [MW,D,DS] 11725-B Jasper **780/488-6636** *8pm-3am*

Flash [MW] 10018 105th St **780/969-9965** *9pm-3am Fri-Sat only*

■RESTAURANTS

Cafe de Ville [R] 10137 124th St
780/488-9188 *11:30am-10pm, till midnight Fri-Sat, 10am-2pm & 5pm-10pm Sun*

■RETAIL SHOPS

Divine Decadence 10441 82nd Ave (at 105th) 780/439-2977 *hip fashions, accessories*

■PUBLICATIONS

Gay Calgary & Edmonton Magazine Calgary 888/543-6960 *monthly LGBT publication*

■MEN'S CLUBS

Steamworks [WI] 11745 Jasper Ave (at 118th St) 780/451-5554 *24hrs*

Westerose

■ACCOMMODATIONS

Pine Trails Getaway [MW] RR1
780/586-0002

BRITISH COLUMBIA

Birken

■ACCOMMODATIONS

Birken Lakeside Resort [GF,SW,GO]
9179 Portage Rd 604/452-3255
cabins & campsites, hot tub, lesbian-owned

Chilliwack

■RESTAURANTS

Bravo Restaurant & Lounge [WC,GO]
46224 Yale Rd (at Nowell St)
604/792-7721 *5pm-close, clsd Sun-Tue, Pacific NW cuisine, martinis*

Gulf Islands

■INFO LINES & SERVICES

Gays & Lesbians of Salt Spring Island (GLOSSI) PO Box 644, Salt Spring Island V8K 2W2 250/537-7773

■ACCOMMODATIONS

Bellhouse Inn [GS,NS,WI] 29 Farmhouse Rd, Galiano Island 250/539-5667, 800/970-7464 *full brkfst*

Birdsong B&B [GS,WI] 153 Rourke Rd, Salt Spring Island 250/537-4608 *ocean & harbor views*

Fulford Dunderry Guest House [GF,NS,WI,GO] 2900 Fulford-Ganges Rd, Salt Spring Island 250/653-4860

Hummingbird Lodge B&B [GF,NS] 1597 Starbuck Ln (at Whalebone Dr), Gabriola 250/247-9300, 877/551-9383

Island Farmhouse B&B [GS,NS,GO] 185 Horel Rd W, Salt Spring Island 250/653-9898, 877/537-5912 *kids/ pets ok, lesbian-owned*

Kamloops

■CRUISY AREAS

Mission Flats Beach [AYOR] off Mission Flats Rd (15 miles W of town) *popular nude beach*

Okanagan County

■INFO LINES & SERVICES

Okanagan Rainbow Coalition 1476 Water St, Kelowna 250/860-8555 *24-hr recorded info, support groups, social events & dances*

■ACCOMMODATIONS

Eagles Nest B&B [M,NS,WI,GO] 15620 Commonage Rd (at Carrs Landing Rd), Kelowna 250/766-9350, 866/766-9350 *full brkfst, hot tub, overlooking Lake Okanagan*

Grapeseed Guesthouse & Gardens [MW,WI,GO] 607 Munson Mountain Rd, Penticton 250/809-9998

■CAFES

Bean Scene [WC] 274 Bernard Ave, Kelowna 250/763-1814 *6am-9pm, till 11pm Wed-Sat*

■RESTAURANTS

Greek House 3159 Woodsdale Rd, Kelowna 250/766-0090 *4pm-9pm, cont'l*

Prince George

■INFO LINES & SERVICES

GALA North 250/562-7124 *24-hr recorded info, call for drop-in hours & location*

■EROTICA

Doctor Love 1412 Patricia Blvd
250/614-1411

Surrey

■CRUISY AREAS
Green Timbers Park [AYOR] 144th St &
100th Ave

Tofino

■ACCOMMODATIONS
Beachwood [GF,NS,GO] 1368
Chesterman Beach Rd 250/725-4250
private apt, steps to the beach

BriMar B&B [GS] 1375 Thornberg
Crescent **250/725-3410,
800/714-9373** *on the beach, full
brkfst*

**Eagle Nook Wilderness Resort &
Spa** [GF] Ucluelet **800/760-2777**
*private log cabins, gourmet meals,
health spa*

■RESTAURANTS
Blue Heron [WC] 634 Campbell St
250/725-2043 *7am-10pm, full bar*

Vancouver

■INFO LINES & SERVICES
AA Gay/ Lesbian 604/434-3933

The Greater Vancouver Pride Line
604/684-6869 x290, 800/566-1170
7pm-10pm, info & support

QMUNITY: BC's Resource Centre
1170 Bute St (btwn Davie & Pendrell
Sts) **604/684-5307, 800/566-1170**

■ACCOMMODATIONS
Barclay House B&B [GS,NS,WI,GO]
1351 Barclay St (at Jervis)
604/605-1351, 800/971-1351 *full
brkfst*

Granville B&B [GF,WI] 5050 Granville
St (at 34th Ave) **604/739-9002,
866/739-9002**

L' Hermitage Hotel [GS,SW,WI] 788
Richards St (at Robson) **778/327-4100**

The Langtry [GS,NS,WI,GO] 968 Nicola
St (at Barclay) **604/687-7892,
800/699-7892**

The Listel Hotel [★GS,F,SW,NS,WI]
1300 Robson Street (at Jervis)
604/684-8461, 800/663-5491
boutique hotel, gym

Moda Hotel [GS,WI] 900 Seymour St
(at Smithe) **604/683-4251,
877/683-5522** *also 3 bars [M,S]*

Nelson House B&B [MW,WI,GO] 977
Broughton St (btwn Nelson & Barclay)
604/684-9793, 866/684-9793

"O Canada" House B&B [GS,WI,GO]
1114 Barclay St (at Thurlow)
604/688-0555, 877/688-1114 *full
brkfst*

Opus Hotel [GF,WC] 322 Davie St (at
Hamilton, Yaletown) **604/642-6787,
866/642-6787** *also bar and restaurant*

The West End Guest House
[GS,NS,GO] 1362 Haro St (at Broughton)
604/681-2889, 888/546-3327

■BARS
1181 [M] 1181 Davie St (at Bute)
604/687-3991 *4pm-close, upscale
cocktail lounge*

The Fountainhead Pub [MW,NH,TG]
1025 Davie St (at Burrard)
604/687-2222 *11am-midnight, till
2am Fri-Sat, wknd brunch, patio*

Guilt and Company [GS,F,E] 1
Alexander St (downstairs)
604/288-1704 *7pm-1am, infused
drinks and homemade beef jerky*

The Oasis [MW,NH,F,E,P] 1240 Thurlow
(at Davie) **604/685-1724** *5pm-close,
theme nights*

The PumpJack Pub [M,NH,L,WC] 1167
Davie St (off Bute) **604/685-3417**
1pm-1am, till 2am Fri-Sat

■NIGHTCLUBS
816 Granville/ The World [M,D] 816
Granville St *midnight-6am Fri-Sun*

Club 23 West [GS,D] 23 W Cordova (at
Carrall) **604/200-2923** *10pm-4am Fri-
Sat, call for events*

Five Sixty [GS,D,E] 560 Seymour St (at
Pender) **604/678-6322** *live bands, art
gallery*

Junction Pub [M,D,F,DS] 1138 Davie St
604/669-2013 *1pm-3am Fri-Sat,
from noon wknds*

Numbers [★M,D,K,V] 1042 Davie (btwn
Thurlow & Burrard) **604/685-4077**
*9pm-2am, till 4am Fri-Sat, 8pm-2am
Sun, cruisy*

British Columbia • CANADA

Shine [GF,D] 364 Water St (at Richards) 604/408-4321

Thickset [M,D,B] *monthly bear parties, check thickset.ca*

■ CAFES

Coming Home [GO] 753 6th St (at 8th Ave), New Westminster **604/544-5018** *9am--3pm, clsd Mon*

Delaney's 1105 Denman St **604/662-3344** *6am-9pm, from 6:30am wknds, coffee shop*

Rhizome Cafe [F] 317 E Broadway **604/872-3166** *11am-10pm, till midnight Fri-Sat, till 3pm Sun, clsd Mon*

Sweet Revenge [GO] 4160 Main St (at 26th) **604/879-7933** *7pm-midnight, till 1am Fri-Sat, patisserie*

Turk's Coffee Exchange [WI] 1276 Commercial Dr **604/255-5805** *6:30am-11pm*

■ RESTAURANTS

Bin 941 [★] 941 Davie St **604/683-1246** *5pm-2am, till midnight Sun, tiny tapas parlor*

Brioche 401 W Cordova (at Homer, in Gastown) **604/682-4037** *7am-8:30pm, 8am-7:30pm wknds*

Cafe Deux Soleils [MW,E] 2096 Commercial Dr **604/254-1195** *8am-midnight, till 5pm Sun, vegetarian*

Cascade Room 2616 Main St (at 10th) **604/709-8650** *5pm-1am, from noon-2am wknds*

Chill Winston 3 Alexander St **604/288-9575** *11am-1am, in Gastown*

The Dish [GO] 1068 Davie St **604/689-0208** *7am-10pm, 9am-9pm Sun, veggie fast food*

Elbow Room Cafe 560 Davie St (at Seymour) **604/685-3628** *8am-4pm, great brkfst*

Foundation Lounge 2301 Main St **604/708-0881** *noon-1am, till 2am wknds, vegetarian*

Glowbal Grill & Satay Bar 1079 Mainland St (Yaletown) **604/602-0835** *lunch, dinner, brunch wknds; also Afterglow Lounge*

Hamburger Mary's 1202 Davie St (at Bute) **604/687-1293** *8am-3am, till 4am Fri-Sat, till 2am Sun, full bar*

Havana [★] 1212 Commercial Dr **604/253-9119** *11am-11pm, Cuban fusion, full bar, patio*

Lickerish 903 Davie St (at Hornby) **604/696-0725** *5:30pm-midnight, till 1am Th-Sun, cocktail lounge*

Lift Bar & Grill 333 Menchions Mews **604/689-5438** *11:30am-midnight*

Lolita's 1326 Davie St (at Jervis) **604/696-9996** *4:30pm till late, wknd brunch, innovative Mexican, worth the wait*

Maenam 1938 W 4th Ave **604/730-5579** *lunch Tue-Sat, dinner 5pm-midnight, Thai*

Martini's Whole Wheat Pizza 151 W Broadway (btwn Cambie & Main) **604/873-0021** *11am-2am, from 2pm Sat, till 1am Sun, great pizza & full bar*

Miura Waffle Milk Bar 829 Davie St **604/687-2909** *9am-7pm, from 10am Sat, clsd Sun*

Naam [E,WC] 2724 W 4th St (at MacDonald) **604/738-7151** *24hrs, vegetarian*

Score [MW,NH] 1262 Davie St (at Jervis St) **604/632-1646** *11am-late, sports bar*

Seasons in the Park Cambie St & W 33rd Ave **604/874-8008** *from 11:30am, 10:30am Sun*

Tanpopo Sushi 1122 Denman (at Pendrell) **604/681-7777** *lunch & dinner, excellent, affordable sushi*

■ ENTERTAINMENT & RECREATION

Capilano Suspension Bridge 3735 Capilano Rd, N Vancouver **604/985-7474**

Cruisey T [MW,D,F,E,$] leaves from N foot of Denman St (at Harbor Cruises) **604/551-2628** *Sun (seasonal), 4-hour party cruise around Vancouver Harbour*

Rockwood Adventures 6578 Acorn Rd, Sechelt **604/741-0802**, **888/236-6606** *rain forest walks & city tours for all levels w/ free hotel pickup*

Sunset Beach Beach Ave, right in the West End (near Burrard St Bridge) *home of Vancouver AIDS memorial*

Vancouver Nature Adventures [$] 1251 Cardero St #2005 **604/684-4922, 800/528-3531** *orca-watching safari, guided kayaking day trip & beach BBQ*

Wreck Beach below UBC

■BOOKSTORES

Little Sister's [★WC] 1238 Davie St (btwn Bute & Jervis) **604/669-1753, 800/567-1662 (in Canada only)** *10am-11pm, LGBT*

People's Co-op Bookstore 1391 Commercial Dr (btwn Kitchener & Charles) **604/253-6442, 888/511-5556** *LGBT section*

■RETAIL SHOPS

Cupcakes 1116 Denman St (at Pendrell) **604/974-1300** *10am-9pm, till 10pm Fri-Sat; also at 2887 W Broadway*

Mintage 1714 Commercial Dr **604/646-8243** *vintage & future fashions*

Next Body Piercing 1068 Granville St (at Nelson) **604/684-6398** *noon-6pm, 11am-7pm Fri-Sat, also tattooing*

Top Drawers 1030 Denman St (at Comox) **604/684-4861** *men's underwear & swimwear*

■PUBLICATIONS

Xtra! West **604/684-9696** *LGBT newspaper*

■GYMS & HEALTH CLUBS

Fitness World 1214 Howe St (at Davie) **604/681-3232** *day passes*

Spartacus Gym 1522 Commercial Dr **604/254-6267**

■MEN'S CLUBS

Fahrenheit 212° [PC,WI] 1048 Davie St (at Burrard) **604/689-9719** *24hrs*

M2M [L,PC] 1210 Granville, downstairs (at Davie) **604/684-6011** *6pm-7am, 24hrs Fri-Mon*

Steamworks 123 W Pender St (at Beatty St) **604/974-0602** *24hrs*

■EROTICA

Love's Touch 1069 Davie St **604/681-7024**

■CRUISY AREAS

Central Park [AYOR] S side of the Boundary & Kingsway intersection *on the Vancouver/ Burnaby border*

Harbor Quay Promenade [AYOR] Port Alberni

Richmond Nature Park [AYOR] Richmond /

Stanley Park [AYOR] Lee's Trail

Wreck Beach [AYOR] below UBC

Victoria

■ACCOMMODATIONS

Albion Manor B&B [GS,NS,WI,WC,GO] 224 Superior St **250/389-0012, 877/389-0012** *full brkfst*

Ambrosia Historic B&B [GS,NS] 522 Quadra (at Humboldt) **250/380-7705, 877/262-7672** *3 blocks from Victoria's inner harbor*

Dashwood Manor Seaside B&B [GS,WI,GO] 1 Cook St **250/385-5517, 800/667-5517** *great views of the ocean*

Inn at Laurel Point [GF,F,SW,WI,WC] 680 Montreal St (at Quebec St) **250/386-8721, 800/663-7667**

Oak Bay Guest House [GF,NS] 1052 Newport Ave **250/598-3812** *1912 Tudor-style house, full brkfst, near beaches*

■BARS

Paparazzi [MW,D,K,DS,V,WC] 642 Johnson St (enter on Broad St) **250/388-0505** *1pm-2am, till midnight Sun*

■NIGHTCLUBS

Hush [GS,D] 1325 Government St (in basement) **250/385-0566** *9pm-2am, clsd Sun-Tue, more gay wknds*

■RESTAURANTS

Green Cuisine 560 Johnson St #5 (in Market Square) **250/385-1809** *10am-8pm, vegan, also juice bar, bakery*

British Columbia • CANADA

Rosie's Diner [WC,GO] 253 Cook St 250/384-6090 *8am-9pm, '50s & '60s music & videos*

Santiago's Cafe [GO] 660 Oswego St 250/388-7376 *11am-9pm, tapas bar, patio*

■ ENTERTAINMENT & RECREATION

Butchart Gardens 800 Benvenuto Ave, Brentwood Bay 250/652-5256, 866/652-4422

■ BOOKSTORES

Bolen Books 1644 Hillside Ave #111 (in shopping center) 250/595-4232 *8:30am-10pm, LGBT section*

■ RETAIL SHOPS

Oceanside Gifts [WC] 812 Wharf St, Ste 102 (across from Empress Hotel on the lower causeway) 250/380-1777 *10am-10pm, gifts from across Canada*

■ MEN'S CLUBS

Steamworks [MO,V] 582 Johnson St (at Gov't St, look for red alley) 250/383-6623 *6pm-2am, till 8am wknds*

■ CRUISY AREAS

Albert Head Beach [AYOR] Colwood

Beacon Hill Park [AYOR] Dallas Rd, near totem pole

Island View Beach [AYOR] Saanichton

Saxe Point Park [AYOR] take Esquimalt Rd to Fraser St, Esquimalt

Thetis Lake Park [AYOR] Highland Rd exit, toward Duncan (off Hwy 1) *look for parked cars & pathway to "Blowjob Hill"*

Whistler

■ ACCOMMODATIONS

Best Western Listel Whistler Hotel [GF,SW,NS,WI,WC] 4121 Village Green (at Whistler Way) 604/932-1133, 800/663-5472 *hotel w/ pool, sauna & outdoor hot tub*

Coast Blackcomb Suites at Whistler [GF,SW,NS,WC] 4899 Painted Cliff Rd 604/905-3400, 800/716-6199 *bar & restaurant*

Four Seasons Resort Whistler [GF,SW,NS,WC] 4591 Blackcomb Wy 604/935-3400, 800/268-6282 *luxury resort & spa*

Westin Whistler [GF,SW,NS,WI,WC] 4090 Whistler Wy 604/905-5000, 800/937-8461 *full-service resort hotel, full bar & restaurant*

■ RESTAURANTS

Araxi 4222 Village Square 604/932-4540 *lunch & dinner, local ingredients, also seafood bar & lounge*

The Bearfoot Bistro [R] 4121 Village Green 604/932-3433 *6pm-midnight, excellent wine cellar*

La Rua 4557 Blackcomb Blvd 604/932-5011 *6pm-close, clsd Tue*

Quattro 4319 Main St 604/905-4844 *dinner nightly, Italian*

Sachi Sushi 106-4359 Main St 604/935-5649 *lunch & dinner*

Southside Diner 2102 Lake Placid Rd (off Hwy 99) 604/966-0668 *7am-midnight, hosts occasional Gay Social*

Trattoria di Umberto [R] 4417 Sundial Pl 604/932-5858 *lunch & dinner*

■ ENTERTAINMENT & RECREATION

Ziptrek Ecotours PO Box 734 V0N 1B0 604/935-0001, 866/935-0001 *ziplines crisscross the Fitzsimmons Creek btwn Whistler & Blackcomb*

■ EROTICA

The Love Nest #102-4338 Main St 604/932-6906

■ CRUISY AREAS

Lost Lake *from the parking lot, walk 1 km counter-clockwise around the lake to Dick Dock*

White Rock

■ CRUISY AREAS

Marine Dr/ White Rock Beach [AYOR] walk E toward Crescent Beach

MANITOBA

Winnipeg

■INFO LINES & SERVICES

Rainbow Resource Centre 170 Scott St (at Wardlaw) **204/474-0212, 204/284-5208** *call for hrs, clsd wknds, also info line, many social/ support groups*

■BARS

Club 200 [MW,K,DS,S,WC] 190 Garry St (at St Mary Ave) **204/943-6045** *4pm-2am, 6pm-midnight Sun*

Fame [MW,D,DS,TG] 279 Garry St **204/414-9433**

■RESTAURANTS

Buccacino's Cucina Italiana [E] 155 Osborne St **204/452-8251** *11am-10pm, till 11pm Fri-Sat, from 10am Sun, full bar, patio*

Step'N Out [WC] 157 Provencher Blvd **204/956-7837** *5pm-9pm, clsd Sun-Mon*

■BOOKSTORES

McNally Robinson [WC] 1120 Grant Ave #4000 (in the mall) **204/475-0483, 800/561-1833** *9am-10pm, till 11pm Fri-Sat, noon-6pm Sun*

■PUBLICATIONS

Outwords 204/942-4599 *LGBT newspaper*

■MEN'S CLUBS

Adonis Spa [MO] 1060 Main St (at Burrows) **204/589-6133** *24hrs*

■EROTICA

Dominion News 262 Portage Ave (btwn Garry & Smith) **204/942-6563** *8am-7pm, till 9pm Fri-Sat Sat, noon-5pm Sun*

Love Nest 172 St Anne's Rd **204/254-0422** *also 1341 Main St, 204/589-4141; also Portage & Westwood, 204/837-6475*

■CRUISY AREAS

Assiniboine Ave [AYOR] parking lot (btwn Main & Smith Sts) *nights by car*

Assiniboine Park [AYOR] parking lot of central picnic area (1/4 km W of pavilion) *weekday afternoons*

Bonnycastle Park [AYOR]

Osborne St Village [AYOR]

NEW BRUNSWICK

Fredericton

■NIGHTCLUBS

boom! [MW,D,K] 474 Queen St **506/463-2666** *8pm-2am, 4pm-7pm Sun, clsd Mon-Wed*

■RESTAURANTS

Molly's Cafe 554 Queen St **506/457-9305** *9am-10pm, noon-midnight Fri-Sun, full bar, garden patio*

■EROTICA

Pleasures N' Treasures 558 Queen St **506/458-2048** *11am-10pm, till 11pm Th-Sat*

■CRUISY AREAS

The Green [AYOR]

Moncton

■ACCOMMODATIONS

Auberge Au Bois Dormant Inn [GF,NS,WI,GO] 67 rue John (at Birch) **506/855-6767** *affordable luxury inn, full brkfst*

■NIGHTCLUBS

Triangles [MW,NH,D,K] 234 St George St (at Archibald) **506/857-8779** *8pm-2am*

■RESTAURANTS

Calactus Cafe 125 Church St (at St George) **506/388-4833** *11am-10pm, vegetarian*

■EROTICA

X-Citement 651 Mountain Rd **506/388-2226**

■CRUISY AREAS

The Block [AYOR] Main St (btwn Highland & Fleet Sts)

Champlaine Place [AYOR]

New Brunswick • CANADA

St John

■ACCOMMODATIONS

Mahogany Manor [GS,NS,WC,GO] 220 Germain St **506/636-8000, 800/796-7755** *full brkfst*

■NIGHTCLUBS

Happinez Wine Bar [GF] 42 Princess St **506/634-7340** *4pm-midnight, till 2am Fri-Sat*

■RESTAURANTS

Opera Bistro 60 Prince William St **506/642-2822** *lunch & dinner*

■CRUISY AREAS

Rockwood Park [AYOR] at beach & on trails

NOVA SCOTIA

Annapolis Royal

■ACCOMMODATIONS

Bailey House B&B [GF,WI] 150 St George St (at Drury Ln) **902/532-1285, 877/532-1285**

King George Inn [MW,NS,WI,GO] **902/532-5286, 888/799-5464** *full brkfst*

Digby

■ACCOMMODATIONS

Harbourview Inn [GF,SW,NS,WI,WC,GO] 25 Harbourview Rd (at Hwy 1), Smith's Cove **902/245-5686, 877/449-0705** *century-old country inn*

Seawinds Motel [GF,NS] 90 Montague Row **902/245-2573**

Halifax

■ACCOMMODATIONS

Fresh Start B&B [GF,NS,WI] 2720 Gottingen St (at Black) **902/453-6616, 888/453-6616** *Victorian mansion, women-owned*

■BARS

Menz & Mollyz Bar [MW,NH,DS,K,P] 2182 Gottingen St, Level 2 (btw Cunard & Agricola) **902/446-6969** *4pm-2:30am*

Reflections Cabaret [MW,D,E,C,DS,WC] 5184 Sackville St (at Barrington) **902/422-2957** *10pm-4am, clsd Tue*

■CAFES

Coburg Coffee House [WI] 6085 Coburg Rd **902/429-2326** *7am-9pm*

The Daily Grind [F,WI] 5686 Spring Garden Rd (near South Park) **902/429-6397** *8am-6pm, noon-5pm Sun, also newsstand*

The Second Cup [F,WI] 5425 Spring Garden Rd **902/429-0883** *7am-11pm, till midnight Th-Sat, internet access*

Uncommon Grounds [WI] 1030 S Park St **902/404-3124** *7am-10pm*

■RESTAURANTS

Chives Canadian Bistro 1537 Barrington St **902/420-9626** *5pm-9:30pm*

Heartwood 6250 Quinpool Rd **902/425-2808** *11am-9pm, 10am-3pm Sun, vegetarian*

Tess [GO] 5687 Charles St **902/406-3133** *lunch & dinner, wknd brunch, clsd Mon*

■ENTERTAINMENT & RECREATION

The Khyber 1588 Barrington St **902/422-9668** *visual & performing arts center*

■BOOKSTORES

Atlantic News 5560 Morris St (at Queen) **902/429-5468** *8am-9pm, from 9am Sun*

Trident Booksellers & Cafe [WI] 1256 Hollis St (at Morris St) **902/423-7100** *8am-5:30pm, 10am-5pm Sun, used, popular cafe*

■RETAIL SHOPS

Venus Envy 1598 Barrington St **902/422-0004, 877/370-9288**

■PUBLICATIONS

Wayves PO Box 34090 Scotia Square B3J 3S1 **902/889-2229** *monthly magazine "for the rainbow community of Atlantic Canada"*

■MEN'S CLUBS

SeaDog's Sauna & Spa
[MO,V,18+,WI,PC,GO] 2199 Gottingen St (at Cunard St) **902/444-3647, 888/837-1388** *24hrs wknds, steam, darkroom, internet access*

■EROTICA

Night Magic Fashions 5268 Sackville St **902/420-9309** *clsd Sun*

X-Citement 6260 Quinpool Rd **902/492-0026**

■CRUISY AREAS

Citadel Hill [AYOR] *evenings*

Crystal Crescent Beach [N,AYOR] 45 minutes from Halifax *for nude beach, head S from parking lot; 20-minute walk*

Scotsburn

■ACCOMMODATIONS

The Mermaid & the Cow [MW,SW,GO] West Branch **902/351-2714** *cabin & campsites*

Tangier

■ACCOMMODATIONS

Spry Bay Campground & Cabins [GS,GO] 19867 Highway #7 **902/772-2554, 866/229-8014** *also restaurant & convenience store*

ONTARIO

Belleville

■CRUISY AREAS

Zwick's Park [AYOR]

Grand Valley

■ACCOMMODATIONS

Rainbow Ridge Resort [MW,F,SW,GO] Country Rd 109 (at Hwy 25 S) **519/928-3262** *trailers & tents, restaurant, day visitors welcome, seasonal*

Hamilton

■ACCOMMODATIONS

Cedars Campground [MW,D,SW,GO] 1039 5th Concession W Rd, Millgrove **905/659-3655, 905/659-7342** *seasonal, private campground, also bar, restaurant wknds*

■BARS

The Embassy Club [MW,D,TG,K,DS,V] 54 King St E (at Houston) **905/522-1100** *noon-3am, nightclub from 10pm wknds*

■MEN'S CLUBS

Central Spa [GO] 401 Main St W (at Poulette) **905/523-7636** *10am-midnight*

Karel's Steambaths [PC] 12 Holton Ave N (at King St) **905/549-9666**

■EROTICA

Stag Shop 58 Centennial Pkwy N **905/573-4242** *also 980 Upper James St, 905/385-3300*

■CRUISY AREAS

Jackson St [AYOR] from Catherine to City Hall

Kingston

■CRUISY AREAS

Little Cataraqui Conservation Area [AYOR] King St W

MacDonald Park [AYOR]

Kitchener

■NIGHTCLUBS

Club Renaissance [MW,D,F,DS] 24 Charles St W **519/570-2406, 877/635-2352** *9pm-3am, clsd Sun-Tue, also billiards lounge*

■EROTICA

Stag Shop 10 Manitou Dr **519/895-1228**

London

■ACCOMMODATIONS

Hilton Hotel [GF,SW,WI,WC] 300 King St **800/210-9336**

■BARS

Buck Wild Bar [M,D,DS,K,GO] 722 York St (at Central Spa) **519/438-2625** *8pm-close Th-Sat*

■NIGHTCLUBS

Club Lavish [GS,D,K] 238 Dundas St **519/667-1222** *9pm-2am, clsd Sun-Wed*

Ontario • CANADA

■RESTAURANTS

Blackfriars Bistro [★] 46 Blackfriars (2 blocks S of Oxford) 519/667-4930 *lunch & dinner, Sun brunch, full bar*

■MEN'S CLUBS

Central Spa [F] 722 York St (at rear, Complex 722) 519/438-2625 *10am-2am, 24hrs Fri-Sat, also bar*

■EROTICA

Stag Shop 1548 Dundas St E 519/453-7676 *also 371 Wellington Rd S, 519/668-3334*

Niagara Falls

■ACCOMMODATIONS

Absolute Elegance B&B [GS,NS,GO] 6023 Culp St (at Main & Ferry) 905/353-8522, 877/353-8522

Angels Hideaway [GS,NS] 4360 Simcoe St (at River Rd) 905/354-1119

Britaly B&B [GF,WI,GO] 57 The Promenade (at Charlotte & John), Niagara-on-the-Lake 905/468-8778

■CRUISY AREAS

Clifton Hill [AYOR]

Oshawa

■NIGHTCLUBS

Club 717 [MW,D,DS,K,WI] 717 Wilson Rd S #7 905/434-4297 *7pm-midnight, 9pm-2am Fri-Sat, clsd Mon-Wed*

■EROTICA

Forbidden Pleasures 1268 Simcoe St N 905/728-0834

Ottawa

■INFO LINES & SERVICES

Pink Triangle Services 251 Bank St #301 613/563-4818 *many groups & services, library, call for times*

■ACCOMMODATIONS

Ambiance B&B [GS,NS,WI,GO] 330 Nepean St 613/563-0421, 888/366-8772

Brookstreet [GF,SW] 525 Legget Dr 613/271-1800, 888/826-2220

Lord Elgin Hotel [GF,SW] 100 Elgin St 613/235-3333, 800/267-4298

Rideau Inn [GS,NS,GO] 177 Frank St 613/688-2753, 877/580-5015

■BARS

Centretown Pub [MW,D,V] 340 Somerset St W (at Bank) 613/594-0233 *2pm-2am; also Cell Block [L] & Silhouette Lounge [P] wknds*

The Lookout [MW,F,WC,GO] 41 York, 2nd flr (in Byward Market) 613/789-1624 *2pm-2am, from noon wknds, men's night Th*

Swizzles [MW,D,K,WI] 246 Queen St 613/232-4200 *11am-2am, from 7pm wknds, noon-10pm Tue, clsd Mon*

■NIGHTCLUBS

Lotus Lounge [GS,D] 129 Bank St 613/216-9661 *10pm-2am Fri, till 7am Sat*

Mercury Lounge [GS,D,E,F,WI] 56 Byward Market Sq (side door upstairs) 613/789-5324 *8pm-3am, clsd Sun-Tue, popular Wed Hump night party*

Zaphod Beeblebrox [GS,NH,D,S] 27 York 613/562-1010 *4pm-2am, live music*

■CAFES

Bridgehead Coffee [WI,GO] 366 Bank St (at Gilmour) 613/569-5600 *7am-9pm*

Raw Sugar Cafe [E] 692 Somerset W 613/216-2850 *vegan & gluten-free options*

■RESTAURANTS

Ahora Mexican Cuisine [GO] 307 Dalhousie St (below Sweet Art) 613/562-2081 *noon-10pm*

The Buzz 374 Bank St 613/565-9595 *dinner nightly, Sun brunch, also bar*

Johnny Farina [WC] 216 Elgin St 613/565-5155 *Italian*

Kinki [DJ,E] 41 York St 613/789-7559 *lunch & dinner, Asian fusion, full bar*

La Dolce Vita 180 Preston Street 613/233-6239 *gluten-free menu available*

Shanghai Restaurant [K] 651 Somerset St W (at Bronson Ave) 613/233-4001 *lunch Tue-Fri, dinner nightly, clsd Mon, also bar, DJ*

■BOOKSTORES

Mags & Fags 254 Elgin St (btwn Somerset & Cooper) **613/233-9651** *gay magazines*

■RETAIL SHOPS

Venus Envy 320 Lisgar St (at Bank St) **613/789-4646**

■PUBLICATIONS

Capital Xtra! 416/925-6665 *LGBT newspaper*

■MEN'S CLUBS

Central Spa [PC] 1069 Wellington St **613/722-8978**

Steamworks 487 Lewis (at Bank St) **613/230-8431** *24hrs*

■EROTICA

One in Ten 256 Bank St (2nd Fl) **613/563-0110** *noon-8pm. clsd Sun*

Wicked Wanda's 382 Bank St **613/820-6032**

Wilde's [WC] 367 Bank St (at Gilmour) **613/234-5512** *11am-7:30pm, till 9pm Fri, noon-5pm Sun*

■CRUISY AREAS

Elgin St [AYOR]

Remic Rapids Lookout [AYOR] *parking spot along Ottawa river*

St Catharines

■BARS

Envy [MW,D,GO] 127 Queenston St **905/682-7774** *theme nights*

Stratford

■RESTAURANTS

Down the Street [★] 30 Ontario St **519/273-5886** *11am-midnight, clsd Mon, bar till 1am*

Rundles [GO,WC] 9 Cobourg St **519/271-6442** *dinner Tue-Sun, lunch wknds*

■CRUISY AREAS

Shakespeare Memorial Gardens [AYOR]

Toronto

■INFO LINES & SERVICES

519 Church St Community Centre [WC] 519 Church St (on Cawthra Park) **416/392-6874** *9am-10pm, till 5pm wknds, LGBT info center & cafe*

AA Gay/ Lesbian 416/487-5591

Canadian Lesbian/ Gay Archives 34 Isabella **416/777-2755** *7:30pm-10pm Tue-Th & by appt*

■ACCOMMODATIONS

213 Carlton—Toronto Townhouse B&B [GS,NS,WI,GO] 416/323-8898, 877/500-0466

Bonnevue Manor B&B [GS,NS,WI] 33 Beaty Ave (at Queen St & Roncesvalles) **416/536-1455**

Drake Hotel [GF,NS] 1150 Queen St W (at Beaconsfield) **416/531-5042, 866/372-5386**

Dundonald House [M,NS,WI,GO] 35 Dundonald St (at Church) **416/961-9888, 800/260-7227**

The Gladstone Hotel [★GS,NS,WI] 1214 Queen St W (at Gladstone Ave) **416/531-4635**

Hazelton Hotel [GF,NS,WI] 118 Yorkville Ave (at Avenue Rd) **416/963-6300, 866/473-6301**

Hotel Le Germain [GF,WI,WC] 30 Mercer St (at Peter St) **416/345-9500, 866/345-9501**

■BARS

Andy Poolhall [GS,D] 489 College St (at Markham) **416/923-5300** *7pm-2am, clsd Sun-Mon*

Beaver Cafe [MW,D,F,GO] 1192 Queen St W (at Northcote Ave) **416/537-2768** *11am-2am, patio*

Bistro 422 [GS,F] 422 College St (at Bathurst St) **416/963-9416** *5pm-2am, dive bar*

The Black Eagle [M,B,L,F] 457 Church St (btwn Maitland & Alexander) **416/413-1219** *3pm-2am, heated rooftop patio*

Boutique Bar [MW] 506 Church St (at Maitland) **647/705-0006** *2:30pm-2am, patio*

Ontario • CANADA

The Cameron House [GS,E] 408 Queen St W (at Cameron St) 416/703-0811 4pm-close, also theater

Church [GS,D] 504 Church St (at Alexander) 647/352-5223 5pm-2:30am, clsd Sun-Tue

The Churchmouse & Firkin [MW,NH] 475 Church St (at Maitland) 416/927-1735 11am-2am, English pub, leather brunch 3rd Sun

Dakota Tavern [GF,CW,F] 249 Ossington Ave (at Dundas) 416/850-4579 6pm-2am, bluegrass brunch Sun

The Hair of the Dog [GS,NH,F] 425 Church St (at Wood) 416/964-2708 11am-2am, patio

The House on Parliament Pub [GS,NH,F] 456 Parliament St (at Carlton) 416/925-4074 11:30am-2am, patio

LeVack Block [GS,D,F] 88 Ossington Ave (at Humbert) 416/916-0571 5pm-close, from 11am wknds, clsd Mon

Melody Bar [GS,E,K] 1214 Queen St W (at Gladstone Hotel) 416/531-4635 clsd Mon, more gay Wed

O'Grady's [GS,F] 518 Church St (at Maitland) 416/323-2822 11am-2am, till 3am Fri-Sat, huge patio, bear night Fri

Pegasus [MW,NH] 489-B Church St (at Wellesley, upstairs) 416/927-8832 11am-2am

Pic Nic [GF,F] 747 Queen St E 647/435-5298 wine bar

The Raq [GS,D] 739 Queen St W, 2nd flr (at Palmerston) 416/504-9120 5pm-1am, from 4pm Th-Sun, clsd Mon

Remington's Men of Steel [M,S,WC,GO] 379 Yonge St (at Gerrard) 416/977-2160 5pm-2am, strip bar

Smiling Buddha [GS,C,YC] 961 College St (at Dovercourt) 416/516-2531 7:30pm-2am

Sneaky Dee's [GF,F,E] 431 College St (at Bathurst) 416/603-3090 11am-3am, from 9am Sun

WAYLA (What Are You Looking At) Lounge [GS,K] 996 Queen St E 406/901-5570 5pm-2am

Woody's/ Sailor [★M,NH,E,DS,V,18+,WC] 465-467 Church (at Maitland) 416/972-0887 1pm-2am

The Zipperz/Cellblock [M,D,C,DS] 72 Carlton St (at Cross St) 416/921-0066 noon-2am, Cellblock 10pm-2am Wed-Sun

■ NIGHTCLUBS

The Annex Wreck Room [GS,D,A,E] 794 Bathurst St (at Bloor) 416/536-0346 10pm-close, bands

AsianXpress (AX)Toronto [M,D,MR-A] bi-monthly, check out www.aznxp.com

Big Primpin' [MW,D] 1279 Queen St W (at Wrongbat) 10pm 1st Fri, monthly hip-hop, dancehall, R&B club, check local listings

The Comfort Zone [GS,D] 480 Spadina Ave (N of College) 416/763-9139 after-hours wknds only

El Convento Rico [★GS,D,MR-L,TG,DS] 750 College St (at Crawford) 416/588-7800 9pm-4am, clsd Mon-Th

Flash [MO,S,PC] 463 Church St 5pm-2am, sex club featuring male dancers

Fly Toronto [★M,D,S] 8 Gloucester St (2 streets N of Yonge & Wellesley) 416/410-5426, 416/925-6222 open Fri-Sat only

Goodhandy's [M,TG,S] 120 Church St, 2nd flr (at Richmond) 10pm-close, clsd Sun-Mon, trans-themed club

Guvernment [GF,D] 132 Queens Quay E (at Lower Jarvis) 416/869-0045 visiting big-name DJs

Lee's Palace/ Dance Cave [GS,D,E] 529 Bloor St (at Albany) 416/532-1598 dance cave Mon, Th-Sat

The Mod Club [GS,D] 722 College (at Crawford) 416/588-4663 10pm Fri-Sat

Pink Mafia alternative queer & straight events in hip locations, check www.pinkmafia.ca

Tattoo Rock Parlour [GS,D,E] 567 Queen St W (at Denison) 416/703-5488 10am-3am Fri-Sun

ODYSSEY

odysseymagazine.net

Ontario • CANADA

Wrongbar [GS,D] 1279 Queen St W (at Brock) **415/516-8677** *Big Primpin 1st Fri, check listing for other queer events*

■CAFES

Alternative Grounds 333 Roncesvalles Ave **416/534-5543** *7am-7pm*

Fuel Plus [GO] 471Church St **647/352-8807**

JetFuel [WI] 519 Parliament St **416/968-9982** *7am-8pm*

Timothy's [WI] 500 Church St (at Alexander) **416/925-8550** *7am-midnight, till 3:30am wknds, cruisy steps in summer*

■RESTAURANTS

Black Hoof 938 Dundas St W **416/551-8854** *6pm-midnight, clsd Tue-Wed, charcuterie & cheese, not for vegetarians!*

Byzantium [GO] 499 Church St (S of Wellesley) **416/922-3859** *5pm-11pm*

Cafe 668 885 Dundas St W **416/703-0668** *lunch & dinner, vegetarian*

Cafe Diplomatico [★] 594 College (at Clinton, in Little Italy) **416/534-4637** *8am-2am, clsd Mon, Italian*

Corner Cafe [WI] 1150 Queen St W (at Drake Hotel) **416/531-5042** *8am-6pm, till 9pm Wed-Th,till 11pm Fri-Sat, popular brkfst spot*

Easy Restaurant 1645 Queen St W **416/537-4893** *9am-5pm*

Fire on the East Side 6 Gloucester St (at Yonge) **416/960-3473** *noon-1am, 10am-midnight wknds, Southern comfort food, patio*

Flo's Diner [GO] 70 Yorkville Ave (near Bay St) **416/961-4333** *7:30am-4pm Mon till 9pm Tu-Fri, from 8am -9pm wknds*

Joy Bistro 884 Queen St E **416/465-8855** *noon-1am*

Kalendar 546 College St **416/923-4138** *10:30am-1am, patio*

La Hacienda 640 Queen St W (near Bathurst) **416/703-3377** *noon-1am, from 11am wknds*

Lee Restaurant 603 King S W **416/504-7867**

Nota Bene 180 Queen St W **416/977-6400** *lunch Mon-Fri, dinner nightly, clsd Sun, Mediterranean*

The Sister [E] 1554 Queen St W **416/532-2570** *4pm-2am, till midnight Sun-Wed, popular wknd brunch from 10am*

Smith 553 Church St (at Dundonald) **416/926-2501**

Supermarket 268 Augusta Ave (at College) **416/840-0501** *call for hours,Asian, also bar w/ DJs*

Urban Herbivore 64 Oxford St (at Augusta) **416/927-1231** *9am-7pm, vegetarian/vegan*

Wine Bar 9 Church St **416/504-9463** *noon-11pm, tapas*

■ENTERTAINMENT & RECREATION

AIDS Memorial in Cawthra Square Park

The Bata Shoe Museum 327 Bloor St W **416/979-7799** *10,000 shoes from over 4,500 years—including the platforms of Elton John & the pumps of Marilyn Monroe*

Buddies in Bad Times Theatre 12 Alexander St (at Yonge) **416/975-8555** *LGBT theater; also Tallulah's cabaret*

■BOOKSTORES

Glad Day Bookshop [★] 598-A Yonge St (at Wellesley) **416/961-4161** *10am-7pm, till 9pm Th-Sat, noon-6pm Sun, LGBT*

■RETAIL SHOPS

Out on the Street 551 Church St **416/967-2759, 800/263-5747** *10am-8pm, till 9pm Th-Sat, 11am-7pm Sun*

Take a Walk on the Wild Side 161 Gerrard St E (at Jarvis) **416/921-6112, 800/260-0102** *"hotel, boutique & club for crossdressers, transvestites, transexuals & other persons of gender"*

■PUBLICATIONS

➤Odyssey Magazine 323/874-8788 *dish on Toronto's club scene*

Xtra! 416/925-6665, 800/268-9872 *LGBT newspaper*

Charlottetown • Prince Edward Island

■MEN'S CLUBS

Central Spa 1610 Dundas St W (at Brock) **416/588-6191** *10am-midnight*

Spa Excess [★] 105 Carlton St (at Jarvis) **416/260-2363, 877/867-3301** *24hrs*

Steamworks [WI] 540 Church (at Wellesley, level 2) **416/925-1571** *24hrs*

■EROTICA

Come As You Are 701 Queen St W (at Bathurst) **416/504-7934** *co-op-owned sex store*

North Bound Leather [WC] 586 Yonge (W of Wellesley St) **416/972-1037** *toys & clothing*

Seduction 577 Yonge St **416/966-6969**

Stag Shop 239 Yonge St **416/368-3507** *also 532 Church St,* **416/323-0772**

■CRUISY AREAS

Balfour Park [AYOR]

Cawthra Park [AYOR] Church St *summer sunbathing*

Hanlan's Pt Beach [AYOR] Toronto Islands *summers*

High Park [AYOR]

Yonge Street Walkway [★AYOR]

Turkey Point

■ACCOMMODATIONS

The Point Tent & Trailer Resort [MO,L,SW,N,GO] 906 Charlotteville Rd #2, RR 1, Vittoria **519/426-7275** *on 50 acres*

Waterloo

■ACCOMMODATIONS

Colonial Creekside [GS,SW,WI,GO] 485 Bridge St W (at Lexington) **519/886-2726**

■RESTAURANTS

Ethel's Lounge 114 King St N (at Spring) **519/725-2361** *11:30am-2am, full bar, patio*

■EROTICA

Stag Shop 7 King St N **519/886-4500**

Windsor

■ACCOMMODATIONS

Windsor Inn on the River [GF,NS,WI] 3857 Riverside Dr E (at George Ave) **519/945-2110, 866/635-0055** *full brkfst*

■BARS

Phog [GF,F,E] 157 University Ave W (at Church St) **519/253-1605** *5pm-2am, from 8pm Sun-Mon, art & events*

Vermouth [GF] 333 Ouellette **519/977-6102** *5pm-2am, from 6pm Sat, clsd Sun-Mon, popular martini lounge*

■NIGHTCLUBS

Club 2012 [MW,D,DS,S] 1056 Wyandotte St E (at Langlois Ave) **519/791-0816** *7pm-2am, till 4am Sat, clsd Sun-Mon*

The Loop [GF,D,E,YC] 156 Chatham St W (at Ferry St) **519/253-3474** *10pm-2am, clsd Mon & Wed*

■CAFES

The Coffee Exchange [WI] 266 Ouellette **519/971-7424** *7am-11pm, 8am-midnight wknds*

■EROTICA

Stag Shop 2950 Dougall Ave **519/967-8798**

■CRUISY AREAS

Jackson Park [AYOR] area at Ouelette Overpass

River Front Park [AYOR] at foot of Ouelette St *evenings*

PRINCE EDWARD ISLAND

Charlottetown

■INFO LINES & SERVICES

Abegweit Rainbow Collective 375 University Avenue #2 (at Eden St, in AIDS PEI office) **902/894-5776, 877/380-5776** *24-hr info line, drop-in hrs 6:30pm-7:30pm Mon, monthly dances & other social activities*

■ACCOMMODATIONS

Evening Primrose [GF,NS,WI,GO] 114 Lord's Pond Rd, Albany **902/437-3134** *full brkfst, seasonal*

Ontario • *CANADA*

The Great George [GF,NS,WI,WC,GO] 58 Great George 902/892-0606, 800/361-1118

The Hotel on Pownal [GF,WI] 146 Pownal St 902/892-1217, 800/268-6261

Shipwright Inn Heritage B&B [GF,NS,WI] 51 Fitzroy St 902/368-1905, 888/306-9966 *full brkfst*

■ BARS

Baba's Lounge [GF,F,E] 81 University Ave 902/892-7377 *11am-11pm, till midnight Fri-Sat from 5pm Sun; also Cedars Lebanese restaurant*

■ ENTERTAINMENT & RECREATION

Blooming Point Blooming Point *nude beach*

■ BOOKSTORES

Book Mark 172 Queen St (in mall) 902/566-4888 *9am-8pm, till 9pm Th-Fri, till 5:30pm Sat, clsd Sun*

Hermanville

■ ACCOMMODATIONS

Johnson Shore Inn [GS,WC,GO] 9984 Rte 16 902/687-1340, 877/510-9669 *full brkfst, seasonal*

York

■ ACCOMMODATIONS

Little York B&B [GF,WI,GO] 775 Rte 25 902/569-0271, 800/953-6755 *full brkfst*

Stanhope Beach Resort [GF,SW,WI,WC,GO] 3445 Bayshore Rd 902/672-2701, 866/672-2701 *also restaurant & bar*

PROVINCE OF QUÉBEC

Hull

■ RESTAURANTS

Le Twist 88 Montcalm St, Gatineau 819/777-8886 *opens 11am daily, full bar*

■ CRUISY AREAS

Meech Lake Beach [AYOR]

Laurentides (Laurentian Mtns)

■ ACCOMMODATIONS

Havre du Parc Auberge [GS,F,GO] 2788 Rte 125 N, St-Donat 819/424-7686 *quiet lakeside inn for nature lovers, full brkfst*

Le Septentrion B&B [MW,SW,NS,WI,GO] 901 chemin St-Adolphe, Morin-Heights/ St-Sauveur 450/226-2665

Magog

■ ACCOMMODATIONS

Au Gîte du Cerf Argenté B&B [GS,NS,GO] 2984 chemin Georgeville Rd (off Hwy 10) 819/847-4264 *renovated century-old farmhouse*

Auberge aux Deux Pères [GF,SW,WI,GO] 680 chemin des Pères 819/769-3115, 514/616-3114

Montréal

Note: M°=Metro station

■ INFO LINES & SERVICES

AA Gay/ Lesbian 514/376-9230

Gay/ Lesbian Community Centre of Montréal 2075 rue Plessis #110 (at Ontario) 514/528-8424 *10am-5:30pm, 1pm-8pm Wed & Fri, clsd wknds*

Gay Line/ Gai Ecoute 514/866-5090 (English) *7pm-11pm*

The Village Tourism Information Center/ Gay Chamber of Commerce 1307 rue Ste-Catherine Est 514/522-1885, 888/595-8110 *10am-6pm, clsd wknds*

■ ACCOMMODATIONS

Alexandre Logan [GF,WI] 1631 rue Alexandre DeSève (at Logan) 514/598-0555, 866/895-0555

Alexandrie Hostel [GF,F,NS,WI,GO] 1750 Amherst (at Robin) 514/525-9420

Auberge le Pomerol [GF,F,NS,WI] 819 boul de Maisonneuve E (at St-Christophe) 800/361-6896

►**Aubergell B&B** [MO,F,NS,WI,GO] 1641 Amherst (at de Maisonneuve) 514/597-0878, 514/525-7744 *also full bar, rooftop terrace*

Aux Studios Montcalm—Guesthouse
[M,WI,GO] 1303 rue Montcalm (at Ste-Catherine St) 514/815-6195

B&B Le Cartier [GS,NS,WI,GO] 1219 rue Cartier (at Ste-Catherine Est) 514/917-1829, 877/524-0495 *private studio*

B&B Le Terra Nostra [GF,NS,WI] 277 rue Beatty (at Lasalle) 514/762-1223, 866/550-5235

BBV (B&B du Village) [M,WI] 1279 rue Montcalm (at Ste-Catherine) 514/522-4771, 888/228-8455

Les Bons Matins [MW,NS,WI] 1401 Argyle Ave 514/931-9167, 800/588-5280

Le Chasseur B&B [GS,GO] 1567 rue St-André (at Maisonneuve) 514/521-2238, 800/451-2238 *Victorian row house, summer terrace*

L' Escogriffe B&B [MO,WI,GO] 1264 rue Wolfe (at rue Ste-Catherine E) 877/523-6105

Le Gîte Nuzone B&B [M,N,WI,GO] 1729 rue St-Hubert (at Ontario) 514/524-5292

Hôtel Dorion [GS,WI] 1477 rue Dorion (at Maisonneuve) 514/523-2427, 877/523-5908

Hotel du Fort [GS,WC] 1390 rue du Fort (at Ste-Catherine) 514/938-8333, 800/565-6333

Hôtel Gouverneur Montréal Place Dupuis [GF,SW,WI] 1415 rue St-Hubert (at Maisonneuve) 888/910-1111

Hotel Lord Berri [GF,WC] 1199 rue Berri (at Ste-Catherine) 514/845-9236, 888/363-0363 *also Italian resto-bar*

Jade Blue B&B [GS,NS,WI] 1225 de Bullion St (at Ste-Catherine) 514/878-9843, 800/878-5048 *theme rooms, full brkfst*

L Hotel Montreal [GF,WI] 262 rue St-Jacques W (at St Nicolas) 514/985-0019, 877/553-0019 *also bar & lounge*

Loews Hotel Vogue [GF,WC] 1425 rue de la Montagne (near Ste-Catherine) 514/285-5555, 800/465-6654

La Loggia Art & Breakfast
[GS,NS,WI,GO] 1637 rue Amherst (at Maisonneuve) 514/524-2493, 866/520-2493 *in Gay Village, sundeck*

►Sir Montcalm B&B [M,NS,WI,GO] 1453 Montcalm (at Ste Catherine St) 514/522-7747

Le St-Christophe [MO,N,NS,WI,GO] 1597 rue St-Christophe (at Maisonneuve) 514/527-7836, 888/521-7836 *full brkfst*

Turquoise B&B [M,GO] 1576 rue Alexandre DeSève (at Maisonneuve) 514/523-9943, 877/707-1576 *shared baths*

■BARS

Bar Le Cocktail [MW,NH,K] 1669 Ste-Catherine Est (at Champlain) 514/597-0814 *11am-3am*

Bar Rocky [M,DS,OC] 1673 rue Ste-Catherine Est (at Papineau) 514/521-7865 *8am-3am*

Black Eagle Bar (Aigle Noir) [M,L,PC] 1315 Ste-Catherine Est (at Visitation) 514/529-0040 *8am-3am, theme nights*

Cabaret Mado [★MW,D,K,C,DS,WC] 1115 rue Ste-Catherine Est (at Amherst, below Le Campus) 514/525-7566 *11am-3am, theme nights, owned by the fabulous Mado!*

Le Campus [M,S] 1111 rue Ste-Catherine Est, 2nd flr (at Amherst) 514/526-3616 *3pm-3am, from 1pm wknds, nude dancers, ladies night Sun*

Citibar [GS,NH,E,TG] 1603 Ontario Est (at Champlain) 514/525-4251 *11am-3am*

Club Bolo [MW,D,CW,$] 2093 rue de la Visitation (at Association Sportive) 514/849-4777 *9:30pm-12:30am Fri, special events Sat, T-dance from 3:30pm Sun, also lessons*

Club Date Piano Bar [MW,NH,K,P,S] 1218 rue Ste-Catherine Est (at Beaudry) 514/521-1242 *8am-3am*

Le Drugstore [MW,D,K,F,E,S] 1366 rue Ste-Catherine Est (at Panêt) 514/524-1960 *10am-3am*

Foufounes Electriques [GF,D,E] 87 Ste-Catherine Est (at St-Laurent) 514/844-5539 *4pm-3am, patio*

Fun Spot [MW,NH,D,TG,K,DS,WI] 1151 rue Ontario Est (at Wolfe) 514/522-0416 *11am-3am, poker machines*

Le Gotha Lounge [M,NH,E] 1641 Amherst (at Maisonneuve) 514/526-1270 *4pm-3am*

Katakombes [M,YC] 1450 rue Ste-Catherine Est *4pm-3am*

Normandie [MW,NH,K] 1295 Amherst (at Ste-Catherine) 514/522-2766 *10am-3am, terrace, popular happy hour*

La Relaxe [M,NH] 1309 rue Ste-Catherine Est, 2nd flr (at Visitation) 514/523-0578 *noon-3am, open to the street—as the name implies, a good place to relax & people-watch*

Royal Phoenix [★MW,NH,D,F] 5788 St Laurent Blvd (at Bernard) 514/658-1622 *8am-3am, theme nights, terrace*

St-Sulpice [GS,K,WI] 1680 rue St-Denis (at Ontario) 514/844-9458 *11am-3am, till midnight Sun, terrace*

Le Stud [MO,D,F,B,L] 1812 rue Ste-Catherine Est (at Papineau) 514/598-8243 *10am-3am*

■NIGHTCLUBS

Apollon [M,D] 1450 rue Ste-Catherine Est *10pm-3am clsd Mon-Wed*

Circus After Hours [GS,D] 915 rue Ste-Catherine Est 514/844-3626 *2am-8am Th & Sun, 1am-10pm Fri-Sat*

Cirque du Boudoir [GS,D,E] 514/789-9068 *opulent quarterly theme parties*

Complexe Sky [★MW,D,SW,L,F,C,DS,S] 1474 rue Ste-Catherine Est 514/529-6969, 514/529-8989 *noon-3am*

Red Lite (After Hours) [★GF,D,$] 1755 rue de Lierre, Laval 450/967-3057 *Fri-Sun only 2am-10am*

Stéréo [★GS,E,$] 858 rue Ste-Catherine Est (at St-Andre) 514/658-2646 *after-hours Fri-Sun only*

Stock Bar [★MO,S] 1171 Ste-Catherine (at Montcalm) 514/842-1336 *shows start at 8pm nightly, nude dancers*

Unity II [★MW,D,S,YC] 1171 rue Ste-Catherine Est (at Montcalm) 514/523-2777 *9pm-close Fri-Sat only, great rooftoop terrace*

■CAFES

Cafe Santropol [WC] 3990 St-Urbain (at Duluth) 514/842-3110 *11:30am-10pm, from 9am during summer, unique sandwiches*

Cafe Titanic [★WI] 445 St-Pierre (in Old Montréal) 514/849-0894 *8am-4:30pm, clsd wknds, salads & soups*

Kilo 6744 rue Hutchison 514/270-3024, 877/270-3024 *9am-5pm, clsd wknds*

■RESTAURANTS

L' Anecdote [GO] 801 rue Rachel Est (at St-Hubert) 514/526-7967 *7:30am-10pm, from 9am wknds*

Après le Jour [BYOB,WC] 901 rue Rachel Est (at St-Andre) 514/527-4141 *5pm-9pm, clsd Mon*

Au Pain Perdu 4489 rue de la Roche 514/527-2900 *7am-3pm, charming brunch spot in renovated garage*

Bangkok [WC] 1616 rue Ste-Catherine Ouest 514/935-2178 *9am-9pm*

Beauty's [★] 93 Mont-Royal Ouest 514/849-8883 *7am-3pm, 8am-4pm wknds, diner/ Jewish deli, worth the wait*

La Binerie 367 Mt-Royal 514/285-9078 *6am-8pm, 8am-3pm wknds*

Le Cagibi [E] 5490 boul St-Laurent 514/509-1199 *9am-1am, from 10:30am wknds, 6pm-midnight Mon, vegetarian*

La Colombe [BYOB] 554 Duluth Est 514/849-8844 *5:30pm-midnight, clsd Sun-Mon, French*

Commensal [BW,GO] 1720 rue St-Denis (at Ontario) 514/845-2627 *11am-10:30pm, till 11pm Fri-Sat, vegetarian*

Ella Grill [GO] 1237 Amherst 514/523-5553 *upscale Mediterranean/Greek*

L' Exception 1200 rue St-Hubert (at Réné-Lévèsque) 514/282-1282 *11am-8pm, fill 10pm Sat, terrace*

L' Express [★R,WC] 3927 rue St-Denis (at Duluth) 514/845-5333 *8am-2am, from 10am Sat-Sun, French bistro & bar, great pâté*

Fantasie [GO] 1355 rue Ste-Catherine Est 514/523-3466 *dinner only, sushi*

La Strega [WC] 1477 rue Ste-Catherine Est 514/523-6000 *11am-midnight, from 5pm wknds, inexpensive Italian*

Le Nouveau Palais 281 rue Bernard W 514/273-1180 *open till 3am wknds, clsd Mon, old school diner*

La Paryse [MW,GO] 302 rue Ontario Est (near Sanguinet) 514/842-2040 *11am-11pm, clsd Mon, '50s-style diner*

Le Planète [BW] 1451 rue Ste-Catherine Est (at Plessis) 514/528-6953 *5pm-10:30pm, brunch only Sun*

Resto du Village [WI,GO] 1310 rue Wolfe 514/524-5404 *24hrs, "cuisine Canadienne"*

Saloon Cafe [★] 1333 rue Ste-Catherine Est (at Panêt) 514/522-1333 *dinner nightly, lunch wknds only, big dishes & even bigger drinks*

Schwartz's Deli 3895 boul St-Laurent 514/842-4813 *8am-12:30am, till 1:30am Fri, till 2:30am Sat*

Thai Grill 5101 boul St-Laurent (at Laurier) 514/270-5566 *one of Montréal's best Thai eateries*

■ENTERTAINMENT & RECREATION

Ça Roule 27 rue de la Commune Est 514/866-0633, 877/866-0633 *join the beautiful people skating up & & biking down Ste-Catherine*

Prince Arthur Est at boul St-Laurent, not far from Sherbrooke Métro station *closed-off street w/ tons of outdoor restaurants & cafés—it's touristy but oh-so-European*

■RETAIL SHOPS

Cuir Mont-Royal 826-A Mont Royal Est (at St-Hubert) 514/527-0238, 888/333-8283 *leather, fetish*

Priape [★] 1311 Ste-Catherine Est (at Visitation) 514 /521–8451, 800/461–6969 *clubwear, leather, books, toys & more*

Screaming Eagle 1424 boul St-Laurent 514/849–2843 *leather shop*

■PUBLICATIONS

2B 514/521–3973 *English-language LGBT publication covering Québec*

Fugues 514/848–1854, 888/848–1854 *glossy LGBT bar/ entertainment guide*

■MEN'S CLUBS

Le 5018 Sauna [V] 5018 boul St-Laurent (at St-Joseph) 514/277–3555 *24hrs, hot tub*

Colonial Bath 3963 av Coloniale (at Napoléon) 514/285–0132 *noon-midnight, from 7am Sun*

GI Joe 1166 Ste-Catherine Est (at Montcalm) 514/528–3326 *24hrs*

L' Oasis [★V,PC] 1390 Ste-Catherine Est (at Plessis) 514/521–0785 *24hrs, hot tub*

Sauna 1286 [V] 1286 chemin de Chambly (at Breggs), Longueuil 450/677–1286 *24hrs*

Sauna 456 456 rue de la Gauchetière Ouest (at Metro Square) 514/871–8465

Sauna Centre-Ville [★V,WI] 1465 rue Ste-Catherine Est (at Plessis) 514/524–3486 *24hrs*

Sauna Pont-Viau [V] 1–A rue de Nevers (at boul de Prairies), Laval 450/663–3386 *24hrs*

Sauna St-Hubert [V] 6527 rue St-Hubert (at Beaubien) 514/277–0176 *24hrs Th-Sun*

■EROTICA

La Capoterie 2061 St-Denis 514/845–0027

Il Bolero 6846 St-Hubert (btwn St-Zotique & Bélanger) 514/270–6065 *fetish & clubwear emporium, ask about monthly fetish party*

■CRUISY AREAS

Angrignon Park [AYOR]

De Maisonneuve Park [AYOR]

Parc Mont-Royal [AYOR] Park Ave *summer nights*

Québec City

■ACCOMMODATIONS

ALT Hotel Québec [GF,NS,WI,WC] 1200 av Germain des Prés (at Laurier Blvd), Sainte-Foy 418/658–1224, 800/463–5253 *restaurant*

Asselline de Ronval [GS,WI,GO] 354 rue Richelieu 418/524–3588, 418/580–6694

Auberge Place D'Armes [GF,NS,WI] 24 rue Ste-Anne (at St-Louis) 418/694–9485, 866/333–9485

Le Château du Faubourg [GF,NS,GO] 429A rue St-Jean (at Claire Fontaine) 418/524–2902 *B&B in château, also beauty salon*

Dans les Bras de Morphée [GF,SW,WI,GO] 225 chemin Royal, St-Jean-De-L'lle d'Orléans 418/829–3792, 866/220–4061 *full brkfst, near beach, shared baths*

Domaine de l' Arc-en-Ciel [MO,SW,18+] 1878 rang 5 Ouest (exit 266, off Rte 20), Joly 418/728–5522 *camping, full brkfst, also bar & restaurant*

Gite TerreCiel [GS,WI,GO] 113 rue Sainte Anne, Baie-Saint-Paul 418/435–0149

Hotel Le Clos Saint-Louis [GS,NS,WI] 69 St-Louis (at St-Ursule) 418/694–1311, 800/461–1311

Hôtel Le Germain Dominion 1912 [GF,WI,WC] 126 rue St-Pierre (at Marché Finlay) 418/692–2224, 888/833–5253 *boutique hotel in city's 1st skyscraper*

Hôtel-Motel Le Voyageur [GS,SW,WI] 2250 boul Ste-Anne (at Estimauville) 418/661–7701, 800/463–5568 *restaurant & bar*

Le Moulin de St-Laurent Chalets [GS,SW,NS] 754 chemin Royal, St Laurent, Ile d' Orleans 418/829–3888, 888/629–3888 *cottages, also restaurant*

Bars

Bar Le Drague [★M,NH,D,F,K,C,DS,WC] 815 rue St-Augustin (at St-Jean) 418/649-7212 *10am-3am, terrace*

Bar St Matthew's [MW,NH] 889 côte Ste-Geneviève (at St-Gabriel) 418/524-5000 *11am-3am, patio*

ForHom [MO,OC,PC] 221 rue St-Jean (entrance at 225) 418/522-4918 *5pm-1am, till 3am Fri-Sat, good place for quiet conversation*

Restaurants

Le Commensal 860 rue St-Jean 418/647-3733 *11am-9pm, till 10pm Th-Sat, vegetarian/ vegan*

Le Hobbit 700 rue St-Jean (at Ste-Geneviève) 418/647-2677 *9am-10pm*

La Piazzetta 707 rue St-Jean 418/529-7489 *11am-10:30pm*

Le Poisson d'Avril 115 quai St-André (at St-Thomas) 418/692-1010, 877/692-1010 *5pm-close, name is French for "April Fools"*

Vertige 540 Ave Duluth E 514/842-4443 *5pm-10pm, till 11pm Fri-Sat, clsd Sun-Mon*

Entertainment & Recreation

Fairmont Le Château Frontenac 1 rue des Carrières 418/692-3861, 800/257-7544 *this hotel disguised as a castle remains the symbol of Québec, come & enjoy the view from outside*

Ice Hotel /Hôtel de Glace [GF] 75, Montée de l'Auberge, Pavillon Ukiuk, Sainte-Catherine-de-la-Jacques-Cartier 418/875-4522, 877/505-0423 *sometimes getting put on ice isn't a bad thing—check it out before it melts away, 9 km E of Québec City in Montmorency Falls Park (Jan-March only)*

Publications

2B 514/521-3873 *English-language LGBT publication covering Québec*

Men's Clubs

Bloc 225 [PC] 225 St-Jean (at Turnbull) 418/523-2562, 877/523-2562 *24hrs*

Sauna Backboys [V] 264 rue de la Couronne (at Prince Edward) 418/521-6686, 877/523-6686 *24hrs*

Sauna/ Hotel Hippocampe [★V] 31 rue McMahon (at Ste-Angèle) 418/692-1521, 888/388-1521 *24hrs, bar, also small hotel*

Erotica

Importation André Dubois [TG,WC] 46 côte de la Montagne (at Frontenac Castle) 418/692-0264

Cruisy Areas

Rue St-Denis [AYOR]

St-Alphonse-de-Granby

Accommodations

Bain de Nature [MO,SW,N,GO] 127 rue Lussier 450/375-4765 *B&B & free-form camping, beautiful small lake, all meals included, hot tub, day visitors welcome*

St-François-du-Lac

Accommodations

Domaine Emeraude [MO,F,SW,N,GO] 450/568-3634 *seasonal, cabins, camping, RV spots & rental condos, also restaurant & bar*

St-Georges-de-Beauce

Bars

Le Planet [GS,NH] 8450 Blvd Lacroix 418/228-1322 *2pm-3am, till 10pm Sun, clsd Mon-Tue*

St-Hubert

Men's Clubs

3481 Sauna [MO] 3481 Montee St-Hubert 450/462-3481 *24hrs*

Ste-Julienne

Accommodations

Camping de la Fierté [MO,SW,N,18+] 2905 Montée Hamilton 450/834-2888 *theme wknds summers, tent & RV spots, cabin, also bar/ restaurant/ rec hall*

Province of Québec • CANADA

Ste-Marthe

■ACCOMMODATIONS

Camping Plein Bois [MO,D,SW,N,WI,GO] 550 chemin St-Henri **450/459-4646, 888/459-4646** *seasonal, DJ Fri-Sat, also restaurant & bar, volleyball, 350 campsites & 200 trailer sites*

SASKATCHEWAN

Provincewide

■PUBLICATIONS

Perceptions **306/244-1930** *covers the Canadian prairies*

Ravenscrag

■ACCOMMODATIONS

Spring Valley Guest Ranch [★GS,F,NS,GO] **306/295-4124** *1913 character home, also cabin, full brkfst*

Regina

■INFO LINES & SERVICES

The Gay & Lesbian Community of Regina 2070 Broad St (at Victoria) **306/569-1995** *7am-3pm*

■NIGHTCLUBS

The OUTside [MW,D] 2070 Broad St (at Victoria, at Gay Center) **306/569-1995** *7pm-3am*

■RESTAURANTS

Abstractions Cafe [E] 2161 Rose St **306/352-5374** *9am-6pm, from 11am Sat, clsd Sun*

The Creek in Cathedral Bistro 3414 13th Ave **306/352-4448** *lunch & dinner, clsd Sun*

■CRUISY AREAS

Douglas Park [AYOR]

Wascana Park [AYOR] at College Dr & Lorne St

Saskatoon

■INFO LINES & SERVICES

Avenue Community Centre 201-320 21st St W **306/665-1224, 800/358-1833** *10am-5pm, till 9pm Wed-Fri,4:30pm-9:30pm Sat,*

Circle of Choice Gay/ Lesbian AA 505 10th St E (at Grace Westminster United Church) **306/665-6727** *8pm Wed*

■NIGHTCLUBS

302 Lounge [MW,D] 302 Pacific Ave **306/665-6863** *7am-2am, till 3am Fri-Sat, clsd Sun-Tue*

Diva's [MW,D,DS,K,WI,PC] 220 3rd Ave S #110 (alley entrance) **306/665-0100** *8pm-2am, till 5am Sat,, clsd Mon-Tue*

■RESTAURANTS

2nd Ave Grill 10-123 2nd Ave S **306/244-9899** *11am-10pm, till 11pm Fri-Sat*

The Berry Barn 830 Valley Rd **306/978-9797** *open daily, seasonal, home-style eatery w/ views of river*

The Ivy Dining & Lounge 24th St E & Ontario Ave **306/384-4444** *lunch & dinner Mon-Fri, dinner only Sat-Sun*

Prairie Ink 3130 8th St E **306/955-3579** *9am-10pm, till 11pm Fri-Sat, till 6pm Sun, also bookstore*

■ENTERTAINMENT & RECREATION

AKA Gallery 424 20th St W **306/652-0044** *noon-6pm, till 4pm Sat, clsd Sun-Mon, contemporary art & performance*

■BOOKSTORES

Turning the Tide 525 11th St E **306/955-3070** *noon-8pm, till 10pm Th-Sat, Saskatoon's alternative bookstore*

■CRUISY AREAS

Lakewood Park [AYOR] *nights*

Caribbean

BAHAMAS

Nassau

■NIGHTCLUBS

Club Waterloo [GF,D,F,E,SW] E Bay St (1/2 mile E of Paradise Island Bridge) **242/393-7324** *4pm-close, indoor/outdoor complex*

BARBADOS

Bridgetown

■RESTAURANTS

The Waterfront Cafe [E] The Careenage **246/427-0093** *10am-midnight, clsd Sun, also bar*

BRITISH VIRGIN ISLANDS

Tortola

■ACCOMMODATIONS

Fort Recovery Villa Beach Resort [GF,SW,WC] Road Town, Tortola **284/495-4467, 800/367-8455 (wait for ring)** *grand home on beach & private beachfront villas*

DOMINICAN REPUBLIC

Puerto Plata

■ACCOMMODATIONS

Tropix Hotel [GF,SW,GO] **809/571-2291** *garden setting near center of town & beach, full brkfst*

Santiago

■BARS

Monaco Bar [MW,D] 40 Av 27 de Febrero, Santo Domingo **809/226-1589**

Santo Domingo

■ACCOMMODATIONS

Caribe Colonial Hotel [GF,WI] Isabel Catolica 159 **809/688-7799** *boutique hotel*

Foreigners Club Hotel [MW,NS,WI,WC,GO] 102 Calle Canela (at Estrelleta) **809/689-3017**

Hotel Aida [GF] Calle El Conde 464 **809/685-7692** *near gay bars*

■BARS

Bar Friends [M,AYOR] 10 Calle Povorin **809/689-7572** *buggarones (hustlers)*

Click [W,K] 3 Vicente Celestino Duarte (Zona Colonial) **829/449-5154**

Colonial Bar & Disco [M,D,K] 109 Mella Ave (nr Calle Arzobispo Nouel) **809/205-1970** *open Th-Sun*

Esedeku [MW,F] **809/869-6322** *8pm-close, from 5pm Sun, clsd Mon*

Fogoo Discotec [M,D,DS] 67 Calle Arzobispo Nouel (btw Espaillat & Santome) **809/205-1970**

Jay Dee's [M,NH,S,V] Jose Reyes 10, Zona Colonial **809/335-5905**

■NIGHTCLUBS

Pure Disco Club [GS,D] 365 George Washington Ave (at Hotel Meliá) **809/221-6666** *open till 6am, no shorts or flip flops*

Sunev Bar & Lounge [M,D] 203 Calle 19 de Marzo (nr Calle El Conde) **809/221-5167** *9pm-midnight, till 2am Fri-Sat from 6am Sun, clsd Mon-Tue*

■RESTAURANTS

El Conuco 152 Casimiro de Moya (behind Jaragua Hotel) **809/686-0129** *touristy local landmark*

Green Light Cuisine 20 Heriberto Pieter, Naco **809/732-7719** *sandwiches & salads, fresh & light*

Mamajuana 451 Avenida Roberto Pastoriza **809/547-1019**

Onno's Bar 157 Calle Hostos (at El Conde) **809/689-1183** *DJ on the wknds*

■ENTERTAINMENT & RECREATION

Parque Duarte Calle Duarte (at Calle Padre Billini) *Th-Sun nights, this park is the gathering place for young gay Dominicans*

Dominican Republic • CARIBBEAN

■MEN'S CLUBS
Apolo Spa 108 Calle Arzobispo Noue (btw 19 de Marzo & Calle Duarte) **829/787-2010**

■EROTICA
Cine Lido [AYOR] 342Avenida Mella **809/682-8082** *6:30pm-10:30pm*

■CRUISY AREAS
Avenida el Conde [AYOR] *pedestrian mall*

DUTCH & FRENCH WEST INDIES

Aruba

■ACCOMMODATIONS
Little David Guest House [M,SW,N,GO] Seroe Blanco 56L, Oranjestad **297/583-8288**

■BARS
Jimmy's Place [★MW,NH,D,F] Windstraat 32, Oranjestad **297/582-2550** *5pm-2am, till 4am Fri-Sat, from 8pm Mon*

The Paddock [GS,NH,F] LG Smith Blvd #13, Oranjestad **297/583-2334, 297/583-2606** *10am-2am*

■RESTAURANTS
Cafe the Plaza Seaport Marketplace, Oranjestad **297/583-8826** *8am-1am, patio*

■CRUISY AREAS
Eagle Beach [AYOR] btwn La Quinta Resort & Dutch Village Hotel, Oranjestad *afternoons*

Barbados

■ACCOMMODATIONS
Gemini House B&B [GF,WI] 70 Plover Court, Inch Marlow, Christ Church **246/428-7221**

Inchcape Seaside Villas [GF,WI] **246/428-7006**

Curaçao

■INFO LINES & SERVICES
Pink House Charlottestraat 6, Willemstad **5999/462-6616** *LGBT community center, health & rights organization; also events*

■ACCOMMODATIONS
The Avila Beach Hotel [GF] 130 Penstraat, Willemstad **800/747-8162**

Floris Suite Hotel [M,SW,WI,WC,GO] Piscadera Bay **5999/462-6111, 800/411-0170**

Kura Hulanda [GF] Langestraat 8, Willemstad **888/264-3106 , 5999/434-7700** *also Jacob's Bar*

Papagayo Beach Resort [GF] Willemstad **800/652-2962 (from US), 5999/747-4333**

■BARS
Grand Cafe De Heeren [GS,E] Zuikertuintjeweg 1 **5999/736-0491** *9am-1am, till 2:30am Th-Fri, clsd Sun, also restaurant*

Mundo Bizarro [GF,E] Nieuwestraat 12 (in the Pietermaai quarter) **5999/461-6767** *weird & wonderful eatery & café*

Rainbow Lounge [MW] at Floris Suite Hotel, Piscadera Bay **5999/462-6111** *5pm-midnight*

■NIGHTCLUBS
Bermuda Disco [GF,D] Scharlooweg 72-76 (at the Waaigat, behind the movies), Willemstad **5999/461-4685** *10pm-4am, popular Fri-Sat*

Cabana Beach [GF,D] at Seaquarium Beach **599/946-5158** *open Wed-Sat, also restaurant*

Tu Tu Tango [GF] Plasa Mundo Merced, Punda **5999/465-4633** *11pm-4am, more gay Fri, also restaurant*

■RESTAURANTS
Mambo Beach [GF] Bapor Kibra, Seaquarium Beach **5999/461-8999** *9am-midnight, till 4am Sat, full bar, more gay Sat*

O Mundo Zuikertuintje Shopping Mall, Willemstad *lunch & dinner, also gay party 2nd Sat*

■ENTERTAINMENT & RECREATION
Cas Abao Beach [GF] *popular local beach*

Dolphin Academy Curaçao Sea Aquarium, Bapor Kibra z/n (east of Willemstad, at Sea Aquarium Park) **5999/465-8900, 5999/465-8300** *swim w/ dolphins!*

Jan Thiel Beach
good people-watching

Museum Kura Hulanda Klipstraat 9, Willemstad **5999/434-7765** *African history & culture, Antillean art*

Saba

■ACCOMMODATIONS

Juliana's Hotel [GS,SW,WI] Dutch West Indies, Windwardside **599/416-2269, 866/783-3319**

Shearwater Resort [GF,SW,WI,GO] Cliff Side (Booby Hill) **589/416-2498**

■RESTAURANTS

Rainforest Restaurant Windwardside (Dutch WI) **599/416-3888** *brkfst, lunch & dinner, full bar*

Restaurant Eden The Road (Windwardside), Windwardside **599/416-2539** *5:30pm-9:30pm*

St Barthelemy

■ACCOMMODATIONS

Hotel le Village St-Jean [GF,SW] St-Jean Hill **590-590/27-61-39, 800/651-8366** *hotel & cottages*

Hotel Normandie [GF,WI] Quartier Lorient **590-590/27-61-66**

Hotel St-Barth Isle De France [GF,F] Plage des Flamands **508/528-7727, 800/421-3396** *ultraluxe hotel*

■NIGHTCLUBS

Le Sélect [GF] Gustavia **590-590/27-86-87** *more gay after 11pm*

■RESTAURANTS

Le Grain de Sel Grand Saline Beach **590/524-605** *lunch & dinner, clsd Mon, relaxing setting, ideal before & after sunbathing*

■ENTERTAINMENT & RECREATION

Anse Gouverneur St-Jean Beach [N]

Anse Grande Saline Beach [N] *gay section on the left side of Saline*

Orient Beach [N] *gay beach*

St Maarten

■ACCOMMODATIONS

Blue Ocean Villas [GF] **352/505-2805** *private villa rentals*

Holland House [GF] 43 Front St, Philipsburg **599/542-2572** *on the beach, restaurant, bar*

■RESTAURANTS

Cheri's Cafe [★D,E,WC] Rhine Rd #45 (Maho Reef) **599/54-53-361** *11am-1:30am, clsd Tue, full bar, live music, touristy*

St Martin

■ACCOMMODATIONS

Villa Rainbow [MO,SW,NS,WI,GO] Pic Paradis **590/690-766-235** *stone villa w/ view of Caribbean*

■BARS

Tantra [GS] Rhine Road, Maho Bay, Marigot (at the Marina Royale) **599/545-2861** *11pm-close Wed, Fri-Sat*

■NIGHTCLUBS

Eros [M,D] Rue Victor Maurasse, Marigot **590/690-881-930** *spectacular view from top of the club*

■RESTAURANTS

L' Escapade [R] 94 Blvd de Grand Case **590-590/87-75-04** *French*

Le Pressoir 30 Blvd de Grand Case **590-590/87-76-62** *dinner nightly, clsd Sun*

■ENTERTAINMENT & RECREATION

Orient Beach [GF,N] on the northeast side of the island

■CRUISY AREAS

Cupecoy Beach [AYOR] park at established lot w/ blue & white "Cupecoy Beach" sign (near French border) *gay beach, take a friend & avoid if beach is secluded*

JAMAICA

Montego Bay

■ACCOMMODATIONS

Half Moon [GF,SW] **877/956-625, 866/648-6951** *upscale resort*

Negril

■ACCOMMODATIONS
Seagrape Villas [GS] The Cliffs, West End Rd 831/625-1255 (US#)

Ocho Rios

■ACCOMMODATIONS
Golden Clouds Villa [GF,SW,WC,GO] North Coast Rd, Oracabessa 941/922-9191, 888/625-6007 *private estate, full brkfst, fully staffed*

Port Antonio

■ACCOMMODATIONS
Hotel Mocking Bird Hill [GF,F,SW,WC,GO] 876/993-7267, 876/993-7134

Westmoreland

■ACCOMMODATIONS
Moun Tambrin Retreat [GS,F,SW,NS] set in the mtns 28 miles from Montego Bay 876/437-4353

MARTINIQUE

Les Trois Ilets

■ACCOMMODATIONS
Le Carbet B&tB [MW,N,GO] 18 rue des Alamandas (in Anse Mitan district) 596/596-66-0331

PUERTO RICO

Please Note: For those with rusty or no Spanish, "carretera" means "highway" and "calle" means "street."

Baja Sucia

■ENTERTAINMENT & RECREATION
Playa Sucia/ La Playuela S of Cabo Rojo Nat'l Wildlife Refuge, Guanica *beautiful, secluded beach*

Bayamon

■BARS
Start Night Club [MW,DS] 31 Ongay St (behind Clendo lab) 787/536-3593 *open Th-Sat*

Boqueron

■BARS
El Schamar Bar [GS,DS] at corner of Muñoz Rivera & Jose de Diego 787/851-0542 *11am-midnight, also hotel*

Sunset Sunrise [GS,OC] 65 Calle Barbosa 787/255-1478 *10am-close*

■RESTAURANTS
The Fish Net & Roberto's Villa Playera Calle de Diego 787/254-3163 *best seafood in town*

Camuy

■BARS
Distortion [MW,D,SW] Carr 119 Norte, KM 7.6 (Barrio Membrio) 787/614-3404 *10pm Sat only*

Ceiba

■ACCOMMODATIONS
Ceiba Country Inn [GF,WI,GO] Carretera 977 787/885-0471, 888/560-2816 *dramatic ocean views*

Guanica

■ENTERTAINMENT & RECREATION
Gilligan's Island take Rd 333 to Copamarina Resort, then take ferry to island 787/821-5706 (ferry info) *beautiful beach located in a biosphere on Southern coast of PR*

Ponce

■BARS
Wejele's Cafe [MW,NH] 8 Leon St 787/603-8095 *9pm-3am Wed-Sat*

Rincon

■ACCOMMODATIONS
Horned Dorset Primavera Hotel [GS,SW] Apartado 1132 800/633-1857

Lemontree Oceanfront Cottages
[GS,NS,WI,WC] Carr 429, km 4.1 (at Carr 115) **787/823-6452, 888/418-8733**

San Juan

■INFO LINES & SERVICES

Centro Communitario LGBTT/ LGBT Community Center 37 Calle Mayaguez **787/294-9850** *1pm-10pm, clsd wknds,, resources, events, AIDS testing; also cyber cafe*

■ACCOMMODATIONS

Andalucia Guesthouse & Vacation Rentals [M,WI,GO] 2011 McLeary Ave (at San Miguel St, Ocean Park) **787/309-3373**

Casa del Caribe Guest House [GF,NS,WI] Calle Caribe 57, Condado (at Magdalena) **787/722-7139, 877/722-7139**

La Concha [GS] 1077 Ashford Ave, Condado **787/721-7500** *retro urban showcase & architectural landmark*

Coqui del Mar Guesthouse [GF,GO] 2218 Calle General del Valle (at General Patton, Ocean Park) **787/220-4204**

Hotel El Convento [GF,SW,WI] Calle Cristo 100, Old San Juan (btwn Caleta de las Monjas & Calle Sol) **787/723-9020, 800/468-2779**

Miramar Hotel [GF,WI] 606 Ave Ponce de Leon (at Miramar) **787/977-1000** *also restaurant & bar*

Numero Uno on the Beach [GS,SW,WC] Calle Santa Ana 1, Ocean Park (near Calle Italia) **787/726-5010, 866/726-5010** *also Pamela's restaurant & bar*

The San Juan Water & Beach Club Hotel [GF,SW,NS,WI,WC] 2 Tartak St (Isla Verde), Carolina **787/728-3666, 888/265-6699** *boutique hotel on beach, restaurant & lounge*

■BARS

Angelu's Cafe [W,NH] Calle Eleanor Roosevelt 239, Hato Rey *clsd Sun-Mon*

Atlantic Beach Bar & Hotel [GS] 1 Calle Vendig, Condado **787/721-6900** *10am-2am, great beach location*

Batucada [GS,NH,K] 15 Ave Carlos Chardon, Hato Rey **787/993-1291** *sports bar & grill*

Splash [★M] Av Condado 6 (in Condado, next to the San Juan Marriot) **787/721-7145** *1pm-close, near beach*

SX [M,D,S] 1204 Ponce de Leon (at RH Todd Ave) *stripper bar*

Tia Maria's [MW,NH] 326 Ave Jose de Diego, Parada 22 (at Ponce de León), Santurce **787/724-4011** *noon-2am, also liquor shop*

■NIGHTCLUBS

Circo Bar [★M,D,K,DS] Calle Condado 650, Parada 18, Santurce **787/725-9676** *9pm-5am,beware of the neighborhood*

Kenny's Country Club [M,D] take PR-1 toward Caguas (23.6 KM) *9:30pm Sat only, 15 min outside of San Juan*

■CAFES

Cafe Berlin [★] Calle San Francisco 407, Plaza Colón, Old San Juan (btwn Calles Norzagary & O'Donnel) **787/722-5205** *11am-11pm, espresso bar*

Kasalta Bakery 1966 McLeary Ave (at Teniente Matta) **787/727-7340** *6am-10pm, bakery & deli*

■RESTAURANTS

Aguaviva [WC] 364 Calle La Fortaleza, Old San Juan (at Calle O'Donnell) **787/722-0665** *dinner nightly, fresh seafood & ceviche*

Ajili Mojili 1052 Ashford Ave, Condado (at Aguadilla) **787/725-9195** *local specialties, live music, great ambiance*

Al Dente 309 Calle Recinto S, Old San Juan **787/723-7303** *lunch & dinner, clsd Sun, Italian, also wine bar*

Bebo's Cafe 1600 Calle Loiza (at Del Parque) **787/268-5087** *cheap & delicious, cafeteria-style Puerto Rican favorites*

Cafe Puerto Rico 208 O'Donnell, Old San Juan **787/724-2281** *noon-11pm, great mofongo, patio*

Puerto Rico • CARIBBEAN

La Casita Blanca 351 Calle Tapia (off Ave Eduardo Conde, near Laguna Los Corozas) 787/726-5501 *11am-4pm, till 6pm Th, till 9pm Fri-Sat, amazing local cuisine, best reached by car, no English spoken, beware of neighborhood*

Dieguito & Markito's [K] Kiosk 44 in Luquillo 787/355-0875 *2pm-9pm, open late wknds, also bar*

Dragonfly 364 S Fortaleza St, Old San Juan (across from Parrot Club) 787/977-3886 *opens 5:30pm daily, full bar*

Fleria 1754 Calle Loiza, Santurce 787/268-0010 *lunch & dinner, clsd Sun-Mon, Greek*

El Jibarito Calle Sol 280 787/725-8375 *Puerto Rican/ criolla, also bar*

Oceano Restaurant & Lounge 2 Calle Vendig, Condado 787/724-6400 *great location on the beach, Sun gay party*

The Parrot Club [E] Calle Fortaleza 363, Old San Juan (btwn Plaza Colón & Callejón de la Capilla) 787/725-7370 *lunch & dinner, chic Nuevo Latino bistro & bar*

Perla 1077 Ashford Ave, at La Concha Resort, Condado 787/721-7500 *enjoy an upscale dining experience inside a gigantic conch shell*

Pura Vida [WI] 1853 McLeary Ave, Condado (at Calle Atlantic Pl) 787/728-8119 *noon-10pm, vegetarian*

Vidy's Cafe [K] Ave Universidad 104 (Rio Piedras) 787/767-3062 *10am-1am, plenty veggie*

■ENTERTAINMENT & RECREATION

Atlantic Beach in front of Atlantic Beach Hotel *very gay-friendly beach*

Nuyorican Cafe San Francisco 312 (by El Callejon) 787/977-1276, 787/366-5074 *live music & arts venue*

Ocean Park Beach E of Condado *adult-oriented (less kids)*

La Placita/ Plaza del Mercado Santurce *open-air market by day, street-party by night; lots of bars & restaurants*

■PUBLICATIONS

Conexion G 787/607-3939 *LGBT paper, in Spanish*

■GYMS & HEALTH CLUBS

Muscle Factory Avenida Ashford (at Vendig, Condado) 787/721-0717

■CRUISY AREAS

Parque Central [AYOR] at Interstate PR-1 & PR-2 *popular evenings*

La Playita [AYOR] Av Muñoz Rivera (in front of capitol bldg in Old San Juan) *afternoons*

Scenic Overlook [AYOR] off Muñoz Rivera Dr *observation parking area near capitol bldg*

Las Uvas [AYOR] E of Condado (at Ocean Park Beach, W of Calle Yardley Pl) *mixed gay/ straight by day, cruisy by night*

Vieques Island

■ACCOMMODATIONS

Bravo! [GS,SW,GO] North Shore Rd (at Lighthouse) 787/741-1128

Casa de Amistad [GS,SW,WI,GO] 27 Benitez Castano 787/741-3758

Crow's Nest Inn [GF,SW,NS] 787/741-0033, 877/276-9763 *restaurant*

Inn on the Blue Horizon [GF,SW,F,NS,WI] 787/741-3318

TRINIDAD & TOBAGO

Tobago

■ACCOMMODATIONS

Grafton Beach Resort [GF,F,SW] 868/639-0191, 888/790-5264

Kariwak Village Hotel & Holistic Haven [GF,F,SW,WI,WC] Store Bay Local Rd, Crown Point 868/639-8442, 868/639-8545 *holistic hotel*

US VIRGIN ISLANDS

St Croix

■ACCOMMODATIONS

King Christian Hotel [GF,F,SW] 59 Kings Wharf, Christiansted 340/773-6330, 800/524-2012 *also restaurant*

The Palms at Pelican Cove [MW,F,SW]
4126 La Grande Princesse
340/778-8920, 888/790-5264
beachfront resort

Sand Castle on the Beach
[★MW,SW,WI,GO] 127 Smithfield,
Frederiksted 340/772-1205,
800/524-2018 *gay resort (from rooms
to beachfront villas), also restaurant &
bar*

St John

■ACCOMMODATIONS
Gallows Point Suite Resort
[GF,F,SW,WC] Cruz Bay 340/776-6434,
800/323-7229 *beachfront resort*

Hillcrest Guest House [GF,NS,WI]
340/776-6774, 340/998-8388

St John Inn [GF,SW,NS,WI]
800/666-7688, 340/693-8688

■RESTAURANTS
Asolare Rte 20, Cruz Bay
340/779-4747 *5:30pm-9:30pm,
Asian/ French fusion, hip & elegant*

■ENTERTAINMENT &
RECREATION
Salomon Bay *20-minute hike on
Salomon Beach Trail*

St Thomas

■ACCOMMODATIONS
Hotel 1829 [GF,F,SW] Government Hill
340/776-1829, 800/524-2002

Magen's Point Resort [GF,SW,WC]
6200 Magen's Bay Rd 340/777-6000,
877/850-4465

Pavilions & Pools Hotel [GF,SW] 6400
Estate Smith Bay 340/775-6110,
800/524-2001 *1-bdrm villas each w/
own private swimming pool*

■RESTAURANTS
Mafolie Hotel & Restaurant 7091
Estate Mafolie 340/774-2790 *great
place for lunch w/ a view*

Oceana Restaurant & Wine Bar
Historic Pointe at Villa Olga
340/774-4262 *on the water's edge*

Virgilio's 18 Dronningens Gade
340/776-4920 *great Italian, full bar*

■ENTERTAINMENT &
RECREATION
Beach at Emerald Beach Resort up
hill (near airport runway) *walking
distance from cruise ship dock*

Little Magens Beach *gay nude beach,
near main beach at Magens Bay*

Morning Star Beach *popular gay
beach*

Mexico

MEXICO

Please Note: Mexican cities are
often divided into districts or
"Colonias," which we abbreviate as
"Col." Please use these when giving
addresses for directions.

Acapulco

■ACCOMMODATIONS
Casa Condesa [M,SW] Bella Vista 125
52-744/484-1616, 800/816-4817
(US & Canada) *full brkfst*

Hotel Boca Chica [GF,F,SW] Punta
Caletilla (Fraccionamiento las Playas)
800/337-4685

Hotel Encanto [GF,F,SW,WI] Jacques
Cousteau 51 (Fraccionamiento Brisas
Marques) 52-744/446-7101

Las Brisas [GF,SW,WC] Carretera
Escenica 5255 52-744/469-6900,
866/221-2961 (US#) *luxury resort,*

■BARS
Picante [★GS,D,S,AYOR,$] Privada Piedra
Picuda 16 (behind Demas)
52-744/484-2209 *9pm-5am, popular
male dancers, hustlers*

■NIGHTCLUBS
Baby 'O [GS,D] 52-744/484-7474
10:30pm-5am, till midnight Sun

Cabaré-Tito Beach [MW,D] Privada de
Piedra Picuda 17 PA (nr Torres Gemelas)
52-744/1-24-89-29 *6pm-3am, from
4pm Th-Sat*

Demas Factory/ Pink [★MO,D,S,$] Ave
de los Deportes #10
52-744/484-1800 *10:30pm-3am*

Acapulco • MEXICO

Relax [★MW,D,DS,S,V,YC] Calle Lomas de Mar 4 (Zona Dorada) 52-744/482-0421 *10pm-late, clsd Mon-Wed, [DS,S] wknds*

■RESTAURANTS

100% Natural Av Costera Miguel Alemán 200 (near Acapulco Plaza) 52-744/485-3982 *24hrs, fast (healthy) food, plenty veggie*

Becco al Mare 52-744/446-7402 *lunch & dinner, Italian, nice views*

Beto's Restaurant [MW] Av Costera Miguel Alemán 99 (at Condesa Beach) 52-744/484-0473 *11am-midnight, full bar, seafood, palapas*

El Cabrito Av Costera Miguel Alemán 1480 (near Convention Center) 52-744/484-7711 *2pm-midnight, till 11pm Sun*

Carlos & Charlie's [E] Blvd de las Naciones #1813 (in La Isla Shopping Village) 52-744/462-2104 *lunch & dinner*

Kookaburra 3 Fracc (at Marina Las Brisas) 52-744/446-6039 *lunch & dinner, int'l, expensive*

La Cabaña de Caleta Playa Caleta Lado Oriente s/n (Fracc. las Playas) 52-744/469-8553, 52-744/469-7919 *9am-9pm, seafood, right on Playa Caleta, great magaritas*

La Tortuga [GO] Calle Lomas del Mar 5 52-744/484-6985 *noon-midnight, clsd Mon, full bar, patio*

Shu 52-744/462-2001 *Japanese*

Su Casa Angel & Shelly Av Anahuac 110 52-744/484-1261, 52-744/484-4350

Suntory de Acapulco Costera Miguel Alemán 36 52-744/484-8088 *2pm-midnight, Japanese, gardens*

El Zorrito's Av Costera Miguel Alemán (at Anton de Alaminos) 52-744/485-3735 *traditional Mexican, several locations along Costera, some all night*

■CRUISY AREAS

Playa Condesa & Beto's Beach near Hotel Fiesta Americana *cruisy by the rocks, at sundown*

Plaza Alvarez/ Zócalo [AYOR] *hustlers (chichifos)*

San Diego Fort [AYOR] along the Costera

Aguascalientes

■NIGHTCLUBS

Mandiles [MW,D] Av Lopez Mateos Poniente 730 W (btwn Agucate & Chabacano) 52-449/153-281 *10pm-3am Fri-Sat only*

■CRUISY AREAS

Plaza Principal [AYOR]

Cabo San Lucas

■ACCOMMODATIONS

Cabo Villas Beach Resort [GF,SW] Callejon del Pescador s/n (Col. El Medano) 52-624/143-9199 *resort on Medano Beach*

Solmar Suites [GF,SW] Av Solmar 1 800/344-3349, 310/459-9861 (US#) *oceanfront suites at southernmost tip*

■NIGHTCLUBS

Las Varitas [GF,D,E] Calle Vallentin Gomez Farias (at Camino Viejo a San Jose) 52-624/143-9999 *9pm-3am, clsd Mon, rock 'n' roll bar*

■RESTAURANTS

Mi Casa [R] Av Cabo San Lucas (at Lazarus Cardenas) 52-624/143-1933 *clsd Sun, lunch & dinner, great chicken mole*

Cancún

see also Cozumel & Playa del Carmen

■ACCOMMODATIONS

Rancho Sak Ol [GF] Puerto Morelos 52-998/871-0181 *beachfront palapa-style B&B, 30 minutes from Cancún*

■BARS

Picante Bar [★M,D,DS,S,YC] Av Tulúm 20, Centro (E of Av Uxmal, next to Plaza Galerías) *9pm-5am, hustlers, [DS,S] Wed-Sat*

Risky Times [GS,AYOR] Av Tulúm (at Av Coba) **52-998/884-7503** *24hrs, rowdy after-hours, best after 4am*

■NIGHTCLUBS

Karamba [★MW,D,K,DS,S] Av Tulúm 9 (Azucenas 2nd flr, SM 22) **52-998/884-0032** *10:30pm-close, clsd Mon, go-go boys Fri*

Sexy's Club [M,D,$] Av Tulum Plaza Safa Planta Alta **52-998/280-3943** *10pm-8am, clsd Mon-Tue*

■RESTAURANTS

100% Natural Sunyaxchen 62 **52-998/884-0102** *healthy fast food*

Perico's Av Yaxhilan 61 **52-998/884-3152** *noon-1am, traditional Mexican served up w/ huge theatrical flare*

■ENTERTAINMENT & RECREATION

Chichén Itza *the must-see Mayan ruin 125 miles from Cancún*

Playa Delfines in the Hotel Zone (next to Hilton's beach) *gay beach*

■CRUISY AREAS

Avenida Tulúm [AYOR] Centro *take a stroll & take your pick, late*

El Mirador (Ruinas del Rei) [AYOR] next to Hilton Hotel (near the lighthouse)

Parque de las Palapas [AYOR] opposite Cinema Blanquita *near the Cine Blanquita*

Playa Delfines [AYOR] at S end of hotel zone *afternoons, beware cops (!) back in the bushes*

Chihuahua

■ACCOMMODATIONS

Hacienda Huiyochi [MW] Copper Canyon **51-1/625-121-8101**

Ciudad Juárez

see also El Paso, Texas, USA

■BARS

Bananas [S,AYOR] Ramon Corona & Ignacio Pena **52-656/222-5557** *till 2am, nude dancers, beware hustlers outside*

Club La Escondida [GS,NH] Calle Ignacio de la Peña 366 W

Club Olímpico [★M,NH,P] Av Lerdo 210 S (city center) **52-656/612-5742** *noon-2am*

■NIGHTCLUBS

G&G Disco [M,D,S,V,$] Av Lincoln 1252, Córdoba-Américas *9pm-3am, strippers wknds*

■MEN'S CLUBS

Baños Roma Calle Ignacio Mejía 881 E (at Calle Constitución) **52-656/612-7732** *9am-9pm*

■CRUISY AREAS

Plaza de la Constitución [AYOR] Plaza Hidalgo

Copala

■ACCOMMODATIONS

La Caracola [GS,SW,WI] Antelmo Ventura 68 (2 1/2 hrs from Acapulco) **52-741/101-3047**

Cordoba

■BARS

Salon Bar El Metro [MW,D] Av 7 no. 117-C (btwn Calles 1 & 3)

■CRUISY AREAS

Mercado Juárez [AYOR] btwn Calles 7 & 9

Sidewalk Cafes [AYOR] El Portal Zevallos

Cozumel

see also Cancún & Playa del Carmen

■ACCOMMODATIONS

Flamingo Hotel [GF] Calle 6 Norte #81 (at Ave 5) **954/351-9236, 800/806-1601**

Cuernavaca

■ACCOMMODATIONS

Casa del Angel [GS,NS,GO] Calle Clavel 18, Col. Satelite (at Begonia) **52-777/512-6775**

Las Mañanitas [GF,SW] Ricardo Linares 107 **52-777/312-8982** & **314-1466, 888/413-9199** (US only)

La Nuestra [GS,SW,NS,WI,GO] Calle Mesalina 18 (at Calle Neptuno) **52-777/315-2272, 404/806-9694**

Cuernavaca • MEXICO

■BARS

Barecito [MW,F,GO] Comonfort 17 (at Morrow) 52-777/314-1425

La Casa del Dictador [M,D] Jacarandas 4 (at Av Emiliano Zapata) 52-777/317-3186, 52-777/317-2377 *wknds only, garden*

■NIGHTCLUBS

Oxygen [M,D,F,E,DS,S,V,18+,YC] Av Vincente Guerrero 1303 (near Sam's Club) 52-777/317-2714 *10pm-close, Fri-Sat only*

■RESTAURANTS

La India Bonita Dwight Morrow 15 (btwn Morelos & Matamoros) 52-777/312-5021 *9am-9pm, till 5pm Sun-Mon*

La Maga [E] Calle Morrow #9 Altos 52-777/310-0432 *clsd Sun, popular lunch buffet, plenty veggie*

Marco Polo Calle Hidalgo 30 (in front of cathedral, 2nd flr) 52-777/312-3484, 52-777/318-4032 *1pm-close, Italian (pasta & pizza), overlooking cathedral*

■ENTERTAINMENT & RECREATION

Diego Rivera Murals Plaza de Museo (in Cuauhnáhuac Regional Museum)

■MEN'S CLUBS

Banos San Carlos Amado Nervo 111 (Col. Carolina) 52-777/317-2796 *6am-8am, clsd Sun*

Tepoz Spa [MO,18+,SW] Carretera San Andres de la Cal #69 (next to Gallaecia), Tepoztlan, Morelos 739/395-8457 *11am-9:30pm Sat-Sun only, also apt rental*

■CRUISY AREAS

Mercado [AYOR] *Sun*

Plaza Morelos [AYOR]

Zócalo [AYOR] *also adjacent bar, Fri-Sat only*

Ensenada

■NIGHTCLUBS

Sublime [M,D] Plaza Blanca , 3rd Fl 52-646/128-8798 *9pm-close*

■RESTAURANTS

Casamar [★] Blvd Costero 987 52-646/174-0417 *8am-10:30pm, seafood, also bar*

Guadalajara

■ACCOMMODATIONS

Casa Alebrijes Hotel [M,WI,GO] Libertad 1016, Zona Centro 52-33/3614-5232 *boutique hotel in historic center, two blocks from gay nightlife area*

Casa de las Flores B&B [GF,WI] Santos Degollado 175, Tlaquepaque 52-33/3659-3186, 888/582-4896 *15 minutes from Guadalajara*

Casa Rayon [GS,WI,GO] Calle Rayon 179 (at Lopez Cotilla) 619/798-0568 (US#)

Casa Venezuela [GS,NS,WI,GO] Calle Venezuela 459 (at Col. Americana) 52-33/3826-6590 *B&B in 100-year-old colonial house, full brkfst*

Escape B&B [MO,WI] Enrique Gonzalez Martinez 446 52-33/1596-6017

Hostel Lit [GF,WI] Degollado 413 52-33/1200-5505

Hotel San Francisco [GF,F] Degollado 267 52-33/3613-3256

Old Guadalajara B&B [GS,NS,GO] Belén 236 (Centro Histórico) 52-33/3613-9958

Orchid House B&B [GS,GO] Juan de Ojeda 75 (at Ave La Paz) 52-33/3335-19 21

La Perla B&B [GS,NS,WI,GO] Prado 128, Col. Americana (Vallarta y Lopez Cotilla) 52-33/3825-1948

La Villa del Ensueño [GS,NS] Florida St 305, Tlaquepaque 52-33/3635-8792

■BARS

Arizona's Bar Saloon [MO,B,DS,S] Av La Paz 1985 (at Av Chapultepec, Zona Rosa) 52-33/3826-3743 *11pm-3am, clsd Mon*

California's [M] Pedro Moreno 652 (at 8 de Julio, Col. Centro) 52-33/3614-3221 *6pm-3am, Mexican cantina bar*

Caudillos Bar [★M,D,F,YC] Calle Prisciliano Sánchez 305, Centro (at Ocampo) **52-33/3613-5445** *5pm-3am, dancing from 9pm, friendly bar, also restaurant*

El Ciervo [M,D] 20 de Noviembre 797 (at Los Angeles, Sector Reforma) **52-33/3619-6765** *cruisy*

Club YeYe [MW,V,F] Prisciliano Sánchez 395 (Zona Centro) **52-33/1337-5253** *5pm-3am, chic video lounge*

Condado [MO,CW] Colon 434 (btwn Leandro Valle & Nueva Galicia) *6pm-3am Wed-Sun*

Dona Diabla [GS,E] Colon 530 *7pm-3am Wed-Sun*

Equilibrio Restaurant & Bar Ocampo 293 (at Miguel Blanco)

Maskaras [MW,NH,F,E] Calle Maestranza 238 (at Prisciliano Sánchez) **52-33/3614-8103** *noon-3am, colorful atmosphere, live music*

La Minerva [M,K,S] 8 de Julio #73 **52-33/3613-5167** *theme nights*

Voltio [MO,L,B,S] Mexicaltzingo 1521 (Av Enrique Diaz de Leon) *theme nights*

■NIGHTCLUBS

7 Sins [M,D] Pedro Moreno 532 (at Donato Guerra, Zona Centro) **52-33/3658-0713**

Babel [M,D] Morelos 741 *Fri-Sat only*

Black Cherry Grand [M,D] Popocatepetl 40 (at Adolfo Lopez Mateos Sur) **52-33/3647-9024** *10pm-5am Sat only*

El Botanero [M,D,F,K,DS,YC,$] Calle Javier Mina 1348 (at Calle 54, Sector Libertad) **52-33/3643-0545** *6pm-3am, till 1am Sun, clsd Mon-Tue, T-dance Sun*

Circus [★MW,D,E,DS] Galeana 277 (at Prisciliano Sánchez, Centro Histórico) **52-33/3613-0299** *9pm-5am*

Mónica's [★M,D,DS,S,YC,$] Av Álvaro Obregón 1713 (btwn Calles 68 & 70, Sector Libertad; no sign, look for canopy under a big palm tree) **52-33/3643-9544** *9pm-5am, clsd Mon-Tue, packed after midnight, [DS,S] wknds, take a taxi to & from*

Om Club [M,D] Ocampo 270 **52-33/3121-9547** *9am-4pm Th-Sat, 5pm-10pm Sun*

Velvett [MW,D] **52-33/3830-4165** *9pm-5am*

■CAFES

Dolce Veele [MW,WI] Enrique González Martínez 177 **52-33/1523-9593** *4pm-1am*

Queer Nation López Cotilla 611 *5pm-midnight, clsd Sun, souvenirs*

Vida Caffe [MW] Av Hidalgo 907 **52-33/1181-1834** *4:30pm-close*

■RESTAURANTS

Sanborns [WI] Av 16 de Septiembre 127 **52-33/3613-6264** *many locations*

■PUBLICATIONS

GAYGDL *online magazine at* www.gaygdl.com

Urbana Revista *gay lifestyle magazine w/ bars & clubs for Guadalajara & Puerto Vallarta*

■GYMS & HEALTH CLUBS

Renacer Day Spa [★MO] Amado Nervo 106 (Col. Ladrón de Guevara) **52-33/3616-4441 or 4442** *noon-9pm, European-style day spa*

■MEN'S CLUBS

La Academia [★PC] Prisciliano Sánchez 484 (btwn Donato Guerra & Enrique González Martínez) **52-33/3124-1154**

Baños Guadalajara Federalismo Sur #634 **52-33/3826-4149** *open till 8pm, till 3pm Sun, bar, popular afternoons*

Baños La Fuente Calle Manuel Acuña #1107 (btwn Nicolas Romero & Gregoria Davila) **52-33/3826-3618** *clsd Sun*

Banos Santa Terecita Andres Teram #462 (btwn Manuel Acuna & Herrara y Cairo Sts, Colonia Santa Terecita) **52-33/3825-1464** *open daily, popular evenings, till 3pm Sun, four steam rooms*

Riilax [MO] Venustiano Carranza 313 (at Angulo) **52-33/3331-1062**

Guadalajara • MEXICO

■EROTICA
Bite Garibaldi #1389-B
52-33/1661-4016

■CRUISY AREAS
Parque Revolución [AYOR] Av Juárez at
Av Federalismo

Plaza Tapatía [AYOR] near Degollado
Theater *days*

Isla Mujeres

■ACCOMMODATIONS
Casa Sirena [GF,GO] Av Miguel Hidalgo,
Centro (at Bravo y Allende)

La Paz

■ACCOMMODATIONS
La Casa Mexicana Inn [GS,NS,WI,WC]
Calle Nicolas Bravo 106 (btwn Madero &
Mutualista) 52-612/125-2748 *open
Nov-June*

Hotel Mediterrane [GS,F,NS,WI,GO]
Allende 36 (at Malecón)
52-612/125-1195 *sundeck, also bar
& restaurant*

■BARS
Cafe La Pazta [GS,NH,YC,GO] Allende
36 (at Hotel Mediterrane)
52-612/125-1195 *7am-11pm*

■NIGHTCLUBS
Las Varitas [GF,D,E] Calle Independencia
111 (at Malecón) 52-612/123-1590
9pm-3am, clsd Mon, rock 'n' roll bar

■CRUISY AREAS
Malecón (Seawall) [AYOR] *afternoon
& early evening*

León

■BARS
G*bar [M,YC] Madero 226 (at Gante,
Centro Histórico) 52-477/740-8863
6pm-2am, café-bar w/ terrace

■NIGHTCLUBS
La Madame [M,D,DS] Blvd A López
Mateos 1709 Oriente (in front of Torre
Banamex) 52-477/763-3086 *10pm-
3am, clsd Mon-Wed, go-go boys*

Nation [GS,D] 52-477/716-3695

Manzanillo

■ACCOMMODATIONS
Las Hadas [GF,SW] Av Vista Hermosa
s/n (Fracc. Península de Santiago)
52-314/331-0101, 888/559-4329
great resort & location

Red Tree Melaque Inn
[GF,SW,NS,WI,GO] Primaveras 32 (30
miles N of Manzanillo), Melaque-Villa
Obregon 52-315/355-8917,
480/389-5786 (US) *bungalows, near
ocean*

■CRUISY AREAS
Santiago Beach [AYOR]

Mazatlán

■ACCOMMODATIONS
El Cid Resort [GF,SW] 866/306-6113,
52-669/913-3333

Hotel Los Sábalos [GF,SW] Av Playa
Gaviotas 100 (Zona Dorada)
52-669/983-5333, 800/528-8760
(US#) *resort, also popular Joe's Oyster
Bar*

Old Mazatlan Inn [GF,SW,WI,GO]
52-520/366-8487, 866/385-2945

The Pueblo Bonito Emerald Bay
[GF,SW] Ave Ernesto Coppel Compaña
201 52-669/989-0525,
800/990-8250 *also piano bar*

■BARS
La Alemana [GS] Calle Zaragoza 16 (at
Benito Juarez & Serdan) *sports bar*

Pepe Toro [★M,D,DS,S] Av de las Garzas
18 (1 block W of Av Camarón Sábalo,
Zona Dorada) 52-669/914-4176
9:30pm-4am, clsd Mon-Th

Vitrolas Bar [MW,F,K,DS,S] Heriberto
Frías 1608 (in Centro Historico)
52-669/985-2221 *3pm-1am, clsd
Mon, lunch menu, [DS,S] Sun*

■RESTAURANTS
Panamá Restaurant & Pastelería
[GS] at Avs de las Garzas & Camarón
Sábalo (Zona Dorada)
52-669/913-6977

Roca Mar [★] Av del Mar (at Calle Isla
de Lobos, Zona Costera)
52-669/981-6008 *till 2am, seafood,
full bar*

■MEN'S CLUBS

Baños Juan Carlos [AYOR] Calle Genaro Estrada 712 (btwn Benito Juarez & Arquiles Serdan) **52-669/981-7205** *sleazy, busy after 5pm, closes early*

Mérida

■ACCOMMODATIONS

Angeles de Mérida [GF,SW,NS] Calle 74-A, #494-A (at Calle 57 & Calle 59) **52-999/923-8163** *restored 18th-c home, full brkfst, spa services available*

Los Arcos B&B [GF,SW,GO] Calle 66 **52-999/928-0214**

Casa Ana B&B [GF,SW,NS] Calle 52 #469 (btwn 51 & 53) **52-999/924-0005**

La Casa Lorenzo [GF,SW,WI,GO] Calle 41 #516 A (btwn 62 & 64) **52-999/139-0423 , 866/515-4105**

Casa San Juan B&B [GS,NS,WC,GO] 545-A Calle 62 (btwn Calle 69 & Calle 71) **52-999/986-2937, 866/979-6753**

Casa Santiago B&B [GS,SW,NS,WI,WC,GO] Calle 63 #562 (btwn Calles 70 & 72) **52-999/928-9375**

Gran Hotel [GF,F] Calle 60 #496 (nr Parque Cepeda Peraza) **52-999/924-7730 & 923-6963**

Las Arecas Guesthouse [GF,GO] Calle 59 #541 (btwn Calle 66 & Calle 68) **52-999/928-3626** *guesthouse, full brkfst*

Posada Santiago Guesthouse [GS,SW,NS,WI,WC,GO] Calle 57 No 552 (between Calle 66 & 68, Centro Historico) **52-999/928-4258**

■BARS

El Establo [★GF,D,F] Calle 60 #482 (btwn Calle 56 & 58) **52-999/ 924-2289** *popular w/ tourists & locals*

■NIGHTCLUBS

Angeluz [M,D] *all taxi drivers know where it is located, near Pride Disco*

Pride Disco [M,D,S] Calle 67 (200 meters del Puente de Ulman), Anillo Periferico **52-999/946-4401** *south of town, take a taxi*

Scalibur [M,D,S] **52-999/108-2046** *from 11pm, also wknd T-dance from 2pm, difficult to find but worth the ride*

■RESTAURANTS

Cafe La Habana Calle 59 #511-A (at Calle 62) **52-999/928-6502** *24hrs, also bar & café*

Cafeteria Pop [BW] Calle 57 (btwn Calle 60 & 62) **52-999/928-6163** *brkfst, lunch & "light dinner"*

La Bella Época Calle 60 #447 (upstairs in the Hotel del Parque) **52-99/928-1928** *4pm-1am, Yucatécan, try for a balcony table*

■MEN'S CLUBS

La Banana Azul [M,WI,NS,GO] 514 Calle 70 (btwn 65 & 67, 3 blocks from Parque Santiago) **52-999/923-3957** *steam room, massage, gym, friendly*

■CRUISY AREAS

Calle 60 [AYOR] btwn the Zócalo & Santa Lucia park

Santa Lucia Park [AYOR] *late afternoons & evenings*

Zócalo [AYOR] near corner of Calle 60 & 61

Mexico City

Note: M°=Metro station

Note: Mexico City is divided into "Zonas" (ie, Zona Rosa) & "Colonias" (abbreviated here as "Col."). Remember to use these when giving addresses to taxi drivers.

■INFO LINES & SERVICES

Cálamo (LGBT AA) Av de Chapultepec 465, desd 202 (Col. Juárez) **52-55/5574-1210** *8pm Mon-Fri, 7pm Sat, 6pm Sun*

Centro Cultural de la Diversidad Sexual Colima 267 (Col. Roma Norte) **52-55/5514-2565, 52-55/1450-9511** *Mexico City's LGBT center, also cafe*

Jovenes La Villa AA Calle 521 #248 (nr Ave 510) **52-55/2603-7696**

Mexico City • MEXICO

■ACCOMMODATIONS

Best Western Majestic Hotel [GF,WC] Ave Madero 73, Col. Centro **52-55/5521-8600** *on the Zócalo Plaza, rooftop restaurant*

Condesa Haus [GF,WI,GO] Cuernavaca 142 (at Campeche) **52-55/5256-2494, 310/622 4825 (US)**

Downtown México [GF] 30 Isabel la Catolica **52-55/5130-6830**

Hostal Central Historico Regina [GF,F,WI] 5 de Febrero #53 (Col. Centro) **52-55/5709-4192**

Hotel Casa Blanca [GF,F,SW] Lafragua 7 (Col. Tabacalera) **52-55/5096-4500, 800/905-2905** *also restaurant & bar*

Hotel Gillow [GF,F,WI] Isabel la Católica 17 (Col. Centro) **52-55/5518-1440, 52-55/5510-2636**

Hotel Principado [GF] Londres 42 (Col Juarez) **52-55/5533-2944**

El Patio 77 [GF,WI] Icazbalceta 77 (Col. San Rafael) **52-55/5455-0332, 52-55/5592-8452** *eco-friendly B&B*

The Red Tree House [GF,GO] Culiacan 6 (at Avenida Amsterdam) **52-55/5584-3829** *stylish B&B*

W Mexico City [★GF,WI] Campos Eliseos 252 **52-55/9138-1800** *in trendy Polanco, 2 restaurants & bar*

■BARS

42 Bar Amberes 4 (Zona Rosa) **52-55/5208-0352**

Bar Lili [MW,NH] Calle 65 #7 (Col. Puebla) **52-55/4551-0414**

Black Out [GS] Amberes 11 (Zona Rosa) **52-55/5511-9247** *upscale lounge, also restaurant*

Boy Bar [M] Amberes 14 (Zona Rosa) **52-55/5511-3915, 52-55/5207-5591** *10pm-close Fri-Sat only*

Cafeína [GF,D] Nuevo Leon 73 (in Condesa) **52-55/5212-0090** *7pm-4am, 6pm-10pm Sun, co-owned by Diego Luna of Y Tu Mama También fame*

El Celo [M,NH,D,F,S,$] Calle Londres 104 (Zona Rosa) **52-55/5514-4766** *5pm-close, clsd Mon*

Enigma [MW,D,S,$] Calle Morelia 111, Col. Roma (4 blocks from M° Niños Héroes, Zona Rosa) **52-55/5207-7367** *9pm-3:30am, 6pm-2am Sun, clsd Mon, go-go boys*

La Gayta/ Pussy Bar [MW,NH,YC] Amberes 18 (Zona Rosa) **52-551/055-5873**

Lipstick [GS,DS,V] Amberes 1 (at Paseo de la Reforma, Zona Rosa) **52-55/5514-4920** *clsd Sun-Wed, lounge, more gay Fri-Sat*

El Marrakech Salón [MW,NH] Republica de Cuba 18 (Col. Centro)

Oasis [M,DS,$] República de Cuba 2 (Centro Historico) **52-55/5511-9740** *3pm-1am, till 3am Fri-Sat*

Papi Fun Bar [MW,NH,YC] Amberes 18 (Zona Rosa) **52-55/5208-3755**

Pride Restbar Alfonso Reyes 281 (Col. Condessa) **52-55/5516-2368**

El Taller/ El Almacen [MO,D,B,L,S,V] Av Florencia 37-A, Zona Rosa (basement, no sign so look for big nuts & bolts above door) **52-55/5207-0727** *5pm-3am, clsd Mon, cruisy leather/ levi crowd, also sex shop*

Tom's Leather Bar [★M,B,L,S,V,$] Av Insurgentes 357 (Col. Condesa) **55-84/5564-0728** *9pm-4am, clsd Mon*

Viena Bar [★M] República de Cuba 3 (Centro Historico) **52-55/5512-0929** *11am-11pm, clsd Mon-Tue, beer bar*

■NIGHTCLUBS

Butterflies [★MW,D,DS,S,$] Calle Izazaga 9 (at Av Lazaro Cárdenas S, Centro Historico) **52-55/5761-1861** *9pm-3am, till 4:30am Fri-Sat, clsd Mon, 2 flrs, lavish drag shows Fri-Sat*

Cabaré-Tito Fusion [MW,18+] Londres 77 (Zona Rosa) **52-55/5511-1613** *open 4pm, clsd Mon-Tue, drag shows Th*

Cabaré-Tito Neón [MW,D,DS,S] Calle Londres 161, Local 20-A, Plaza del Angel (Zona Rosa) **52-55/5514-9455** *6pm-close*

Club 24 [M,D] Santa María La Ribera # 24 Del Cuauhtémoc **52-55/2198-2580** *9am-4am Fri-Sat only*

Envy [GS,D] Av Las Palmas 500 (Sierra Gamon)

Hibrido [MW,D,S] Calle Londres 161, Plaza del Angel, 2nd flr (Zona Rosa) **52-55/5511-1197** *Th-Sun*

Ken Club [M,D] Medellín 65, Roma Norte (at Ixchel) **52-55/4612-1755** *Th & Sat only*

Liverpool 100 [M,D] Liverpool 100 (Col. Juarez) **52-55/5208-4507** *9pm-close Wed, Fri-Sat only*

Living [★M,D,DS,S] Bucareli 144 (Col. Juarez) **55-55/5512-7281** *10pm-close Fri-Sat only, theme nights*

Nicho [MO,B] Calle Londres 182 *open 8pm, clsd Sun*

■CAFES

B Gay B Proud [F] Amberes 12-B (Zona Rosa)

Coffee Station Londres 167-A (Zona Rosa) **52-55/5525-2705** *clsd Mon-Tue*

■RESTAURANTS

12:30 Amberes 13 (Zona Rosa) **52-55/5514-5971** *popular before-clubbing hangout*

La Antigua Cortesana Chiapas 173-A (Col. Roma) **52-55/5584-4678** *1pm-11pm, till midnight Fri-Sat, till 7pm Sun, popular Mexican cuisine, also bar*

Cafe 22 [E] Montes de Oca 22 (Col. Condesa) **52-55/5212-1533** *6pm-2am, Mexican & Italian, also shows*

El Cardenal Calle de Palma 23 **52-55/5521-8815** *incredible pastries*

Casa Merlos Victoriano Zepeda 80 (at Observatoria) **52-55/5277-4360** *traditional poblano food, definitely try the molé*

Cote Sud Orizaba 87 (Col. Roma) **52-55/5219-2981** *8am-11pm, till midnight Fri, 10am-6pm Sun, French/tapas*

Fonda San Ángel Plaza San Jacinto 3, Col. San Ángel (across from Bazar San Ángel) **52-55/5550-1641 & 1942** *popular after 7pm Fri-Sat, classic Mexican dishes*

Ixchel Medellín 65, Roma Norte **52-55/5208-4055**

Ligaya Nuevo Leon 68 (in Condesa) **52-55/5286-6268** *nouvelle Mexican, dinner nightly, outdoor seating*

La Nueva Opera [P] Ave Cinco de Mayo 10 (Centro Historico) **52-55/5512-8959** *1pm-midnight, clsd Sun, legendary cantina since Pancho Villa fired a bullet into the ceiling*

Sanborns Madera 4 (in Casa de los Azulejos) **52-55/5518-6676** *often cruisy, especially in magazine/ newsstand section*

Xel-Ha **52-55/5553-5968** *traditional cuisine of the Yucatan*

■ENTERTAINMENT & RECREATION

El Hábito [S] Madrid 13 (Coyacán District) **52-55/5659-1139** *avant-garde theater & bar*

Museo de Arte Carrillo Gil Av Revolución 1608 (Col San Angel) **52-55/5550-6260, 52-55/5550-3983** *10am-6pm, clsd Mon, contemporary art*

Museo de Frida Kahlo Calle Londres 247 (Coyacán) **52-55/5554-5999** *10am-5:45pm, clsd Mon, also garden & café*

Museo Templo Mayor Calle Seminario 8 (at República de Guatemala, enter on plaza, near Cathedral) **52-55/4040-5600** *9am-5pm, clsd Mon, artifacts from the central Aztec temple at Tenochtitlán*

■BOOKSTORES

El Armario Abierto Agustin Melgar 25 (Col. Condesa) **52-55/5286-0895** *Mexico's only bookstore specializing in sexuality, some LGBT titles*

■RETAIL SHOPS

Rainbowland Estrasburgo 31 (Zona Rosa) **52-55/5525-9066**

Roshell Lorenzo Boturini 440 **52-55/5768-1317** *drag emporium, hair styling, also monthly shows & events*

■PUBLICATIONS

Ser Gay **52-55/1450-9511** *quarterly magazine, covers all Mexico nightlife*

Mexico City • MEXICO

■GYMS & HEALTH CLUBS

Club San Francisco [M] Calle Rio Pánuco 207 (Col. Cuauhtémoc) 52-55/5525-0936

QI Amsterdam 317 (in Condesa) 52-55/5574-5095 gym w/ spa

■MEN'S CLUBS

Baños Finisterre [AYOR] Manuel Maria Contreras 11, Col. San Rafael (4 blocks W of M° San Cosme) 52-55/5555-3543 traditional bathhouse where men go, hang out & get a massage; not "anything goes" like in US or Europe

Baños San Juan [F,AYOR] Calle López 120 (N of M° Salto de Agua, in Centro Historico) 52-55/5521-3376 also salon

Baños Señorial [AYOR] Calle Isabel la Católica 92 (Centro Historico) 52-55/5709-0732, 52-55/5709-3120

La Casita I [AYOR,18+] Viaducto Miguel Alemán 72, Col. Algarín (near Bolivar— no sign/ number on door) 52-55/5519-8842 24hrs, gym equipment, porn shop

La Casita II [AYOR,18+] Insurgentes S 228 (Col. Roma) 52-55/5514-4639, 52-55/5514-4591 24hrs

So Do Me [★] 52-55/5250-6653 noon-10pm, till 1am Fri, 24hrs wknds

La Toalla Obregon [AYOR,18+] Álvaro Obregón 259 (Col. Roma) 52-55/5511-0686 24hrs

La Toalla Valley [AYOR,18+] Cda. Sánchez Azcona 1724 (Col. del Valle) 52-55/5534-9399 7am-11pm

■CRUISY AREAS

Alameda Central [AYOR] W side of park (Centro Historico) afternoons & early evenings, dangerous later

Bosque de Chapultepec [AYOR] either side of gate to monument (Zona Rosa) afternoons

Zona Rosa [AYOR] nights, anywhere & everywhere, but especially Calle Florencia btwn Reforma & Liverpool, also Calles Génova, Hamburgo & Londres

Monterrey

■ACCOMMODATIONS

Holiday Inn Monterrey Centro [GF,SW] Av Padre Mier 194 N (at Garibaldi, Centro) 52-81/8228-6000 also restaurant, near Zona Rosa

■BARS

Akbal [GS] Abasolo 870B, 2nd flr, Casa del Maíz 52-81/1257-2986 more gay Sun

Casa de Lola [M,D,K] 52-81/8343-6210 Th-Sat only

■NIGHTCLUBS

Baby Shower [MW,D,S,V] Ocampo 433 Puente (btwn Rayon & Aldama Centro) 52-81/8881-5632 9pm-close, clsd Mon-Tue

Bizù Disco [M,DS] 1355 Miguel Hidalgo y Costilla 52-81/8994-4676

Parking [M,D] Allende 120 Ote (btwn Juarez & Guerrero) 52-81/8343-2624 10pm-close Wed-Sat

Vongole & Between Bar [M,DS] 2121 Eugenio Garza Sada Ave 52-81/8358-7035

■MEN'S CLUBS

Baños Orientales Calle Hidalgo 310 Oriente, Guadalupe 52-81/8367-2843 8am-10pm, till 3pm Sun, hustlers

Sparta Sauna Gym 107 Álvaro Obregón 52-81/8342-2770 noon-midnight, clsd Sun

STIC Baños de Vapor & Spa Av de los Héroes 47 (at Av Francisco I Madero) 52-81/8375-7690 6am-10pm, till 2pm Sun

■CRUISY AREAS

Avenida Juárez [AYOR] btwn Calle Matamoros & Calle Padre Mier (Centro) part of "El Circuito," hustlers

Plaza Hidalgo [AYOR] Zona Rosa late afternoons & early evenings

Morelia

■ACCOMMODATIONS

Hotel de la Soledad [GF,WI] Ignacio Zaragoza 90 52-443/312-1888 in converted convent, also restaurant & bar

BARS

Beered [M,B] Vicente Barrozo 44 (at Félix Ireta) **52-44/3155-1481**

NIGHTCLUBS

Con la Rojas [M,D,$] Calle Aldama 343 (Centro) **52-443/312-1578** *10pm-2:30am, clsd Sun-Tue*

Mamá no lo sabe [M,K] Aldama 116 (at García Obeso) **52-44/3189-9447** *10pm-3am*

RESTAURANTS

Fonda Las Mercedes [★] Calle Leon Guzmán 47 **52-443/312-6113 & 313-3222** *inside beautiful colonial home*

MEN'S CLUBS

Baños Mintzicuri Calle Vasco de Quiroga 227 (enter through the Hotel Mintzicuri) **52-443/312-0664** *gay area through door marked "Ruso General"*

Baños Valladolid Eduardo Ruiz 605 **52-44/3312-9985** *7am-8pm, till 2pm Sun*

EROTICA

Cine Arcadia Eduardo Ruiz 870

CRUISY AREAS

Escalinatas de Santa María [AYOR]

Oaxaca

ACCOMMODATIONS

Casa Adobe B&B [GS,WI,GO] Independencia 801 (at Matamoros), Tlalixtac de Cabrera **52-951/517-7268** *15 minutes from center of Oaxaca*

Casa Colonial [GF,WI,WC] Calle Miguel Negrete 105 (Division Poniente) **52-951/516-5280**

La Casa de Don Pablo Hostel [GS,NS] Melchor Ocampo 412, Centro (at Rayon St) **52-951/516-8384**

Casa Machaya Oaxaca B&B [GF] Sierra Nevada 164, Col. Loma Linda **52/951-1328203**

Casa Sol Zipolite [M,SW,WI,GO] 6 Arco Iris, Col. Arroyo Tres **52-95/8100-0462** *300 meters from famous Playa Zipolite*

Posada Arigalan [GS,WI] **52-958/111-5801, 956/280-2165 (US)**

NIGHTCLUBS

Club Privado 502 (aka El Número) [GS,D,K,PC,$] Calle Porfirio Díaz 502 (Centro, ring to enter) *10pm-close, clsd Sun-Tue*

La Costa [M,D,S] Av 16 de Septiembre #517 (Col. Cinco Señores) **52-951/511-2908** *wknds only 9pm-close*

Elefante [GS,D] 20 de Noviembre **52-951/164-8637**

Gavana Dance Club [GS] Calzada Porfirio Díaz #216 (Col. Reforma) *9pm-close Th-Sat*

CAFES

B Proud [WI] Morelos 1107-A *open 9am & 4pm Sun*

RESTAURANTS

El Asador Vasco [★] Portal de Flores 10-A (Centro) **52-951/514-4755** *great views & authentic Oaxacan cuisine (can you say ¡mole!)*

Casa Crespo Allende 107 **52-951/516-0918** *lunch & dinner, also cooking classes*

MEN'S CLUBS

Baños del Jardin Melchor Ocampo 509 **52-951/516-5668**

Banos La Fuente [MO] 20 de Noviembre #1021 (near Periferico) **52-958/516-5668** *open till 8pm, 2 steam rms, friendly*

Baños La Fuente Calle 20 de Noviembre **52-951/516-5668**

CRUISY AREAS

Parque Alemeda & Zócalo [AYOR] *early evenings*

Playa del Carmen

see also Cancún & Cozumel

ACCOMMODATIONS

Acanto Boutique Hotel [GF,SW,NS,WI,GO] 16th St N (btwn 5th Ave & the beach) **631/882-1986**

Aventura Mexicana Hotel [GF,SW,N] Av 10 (at Calle 24) **52-984/873-1876, 800/455-3417**

Hotel Copa Cabana [GS,WI,WC] 5ta Av Norte 52-984/873-0218

Luna Blue Hotel & Bar [GS,WI] Calle 26 (at 5th Av) 415/839-8541

Reina Roja Hotel [GS,SW,WI] 22 Street (btwn 5th & 10th Ave) 52-984/877-3800

■NIGHTCLUBS

Playa 69 [M,D,GO] Av 5 (btwn Calle 4 & Calle 6, ground flr) 9pm-4am wknds, cruisy

Playa Palms [GS,SW] 1st Avenue Bis (btwn 12 & 14th N St) 52-984/803-3908, 888/676-4431

■RESTAURANTS

100% Natural Av 5 (btwn 10th & 12th) 52-984/73-2242 vegetarian

Puebla

■BARS

La Cigarra [M,S,V] Ave 5 Poniente 538 (at Calle 7, Centro) 52-222/246-6356 6pm-3am, beer bar

Franco's Bule Bar [M,E,DS,S] 5 Oriente 402 (Los Sapos) 52-222/232-3409 10pm-3am, till 6am Th-Sat, clsd Mon-Tue

Mono [GS,D,F] Avenia Juarez 2505 (Colonia La Paz) small bar in front, dance club in back

■NIGHTCLUBS

Cabaré-Tito VIP [MW,D,DS,S] Av Juarez 2309 Local B (Colonia La Paz), Mexico City 9pm-close wknds only, theme nights

Garotos [GF,D,$] 22 Orient E 602 (close to Blvd 5 de Mayo, Xenenetla) 52-222/242-4232 9pm-3am Fri-Sat only

■MEN'S CLUBS

Baños Las Termas Av 5 de Mayo 2810, Centro 52-222/232-9562 8am-8pm, open later wknds, till 3pm Sun, clsd Mon, popular afternoons

■CRUISY AREAS

Zócalo/ Main Park [AYOR] at cathedral late evenings

Puerto Vallarta

■INFO LINES & SERVICES

Community Center GLBT SETAC 427 Constitucion (at Manuel M Diéguez) 52-322/224-1974 AA meetings, movie nights, HIV testing & Spanish classes

■ACCOMMODATIONS

Abbey Hotel [MO,SW] Pulpito 138 (at Olas Altas) 52-322/222-4488 also restaurant & lounge

Blue Chairs Beach Resort [★MW,SW,WI,WC] 52-322/222-5040 , 888/302-3662

Boana Torre Malibu Condo Hotel [GS,F,SW,GO] Calle Amapas 325 52-322/222-0999, 52-322/222-6695 near gay beach

Casa Cúpula [MW,SW,NS,WI,WC,GO] Callejon de la Igualdad 129, Col. Amapas 52-322/223-2484, 866/352-2511

Casa de las Flores [GO] Calle Santa Barbara #359 503 /314-444(US), 52-3222/120-5242

Casa Fantasía [GS,SW,NS,WC,GO] Pinot Suarez 203, Col. Emiliano Zapata (near the Rio Cuale) 52-322/223-2444 B&B made up of 3 haciendas, terrace

Hotel Emperador [GS,WI] Amapas 114 52-322/222-1767 , 800/523-1158 located right on "Los muertos" beach

Hotel Mercurio [MW,SW,WI,GO] 52-322/222-4793, 866/388-2689 gay/ lesbian hotel in Vallarta's Gayborhood, 1 1/2 blocks from beach

The San Franciscan Resort & Gym [GS,SW,WI] Calle Pilitas #213 (at Playa Los Muertos) 52-322/222-6473 x0

Villa Safari Condo [GS,SW,NS,GO] Francisca Rodriguez 203 269/469-0468 (US #)

Villas David B&B [MO,SW,NS,WI,GO] Calle Galeana 348 (at Calle Miramar) 877/832-3315 (US#), 52-322/223-0315

■BARS

Los Amigos Bar [MW,NH] Calle Venustiano Carranza 237 (upstairs, next to Paco's Ranch) 52-322/222-7802 6pm-4am, Mexican cantina, patio

Anonimo [M,NH] Rodolfo Gomez 157 *4pm-2am*

Apaches [★GS,F,GO] Olas Altas 439 (at Rodriguez) 52-322/222-4004 *5pm-2am, till 1am Sun-Mon, classy cocktail bar, martinis & margaritas, tapas*

Divas [MW,NH] 388 Francisco L Madero (E of Insurgentes) 52-322/135-0336 *2pm-2am*

Frida [GS,B,F,GO] 301-A Insurgentes (at Venustiano Carranza) 52-322/222-3668 *1pm-2am, from 7pm Mon-Tue, Mexican cantina, more gay later in evening*

Garbo [M,E,P,GO,18+] Pulpito 142 (at Olas Altas) 52-322/223-5753 *6pm-2am, upscale martini lounge, live music*

Hot Frida's [GS,F] 155 Francisca Rodriguez 2nd fl (at Olas Altas) 52-322/181-4556 *clsd Wed*

La Noche [MW] Lázaro Cárdenas 257 (Zona Romantica) 52-322/222-3364 *7pm-2am*

The Palm/ Viva [M,D,C] Olas Altas 508 (at Rodolfo Gomez) 52-322/223-4818 *4pm-4am*

Reinas [M,NH] Lazaro Cardenas 361 52-322/125-9532 *5pm-2am*

Sama [MW,NH,18+] Olas Altas 510 (at Rodolfo Gomez) 52-322/223-3182 *4:30pm-2am, small martini bar w/ sidewalk seating*

Wet Dreams [MO,S] Lazaro Cardenas 312 (Col Emiliano Zapata) 52-322/222-8112 *8pm-2am, strippers*

■NIGHTCLUBS

Antropology [M,S] 101 Morelos (Plaza Rio) *9pm-4am, stripper bar*

Antropology [MO,DS,S,YC,$] Calle Morelos 101, Plaza Río (at Plaza Río Cuale) 52-322/306-1058 *9pm-4am*

CC Slaughter's [M,D] Lazaro Cardenas 254 Emiliano (Zapata) 52-322/222-3412

Club Enter [M,D] Venustiano Carranza 212 52-322/123 -077 *10pm-6am Th-Sun*

Club Mañana [M,D] Venustiano Carranza #290 (at Col Emiliano Zapata) *10pm-6am, clsd Sun-Tue*

Eros [M,D,DS,S] 1994 Francisco Medina Ascencio 52-322/111-4243

No Borders [MW,NH] 221 Libertad 52-322/136-8775 *1pm-2am, rooftop patio*

Paco's Ranch [★M,D,DS,GO,$] 237 Ignacio Vallarta 52-322/222-1899 *10pm-6am, also rooftop terrace*

■CAFES

A Page in the Sun 179 Plaza Lázaro Cárdenas (in Zona Romantica) 52-322/222-3608 *7am-11pm, coffee shop & English bookstore*

Cafe San Angel [F] Olas Altas 449 (at Francisco Rodreguez) 52-322/223-1273 *7am-1am*

The Coffee Cup [GO] Rodolfo Gómez 146-A (at Olas Altas) 52-322/222-8584 *7am-10pm, clsd Sun in summer*

Uncommon Grounds Buddha Lounge [F] Lazaro Cardenas 625 52-322/223-3834 *5pm-close, clsd Mon-Tue, also aromatherapy & gifts*

Xcodiva Rodolfo Gomez 118 52-322/113-0352 *artisanal chocolate*

■RESTAURANTS

El Arrayan [GO] Allende #344 (at El Centro) 52-322/222-7195 *6pm-11pm, clsd Tue*

The Blue Shrimp Olas Altas 366 (Zona Romantica) 52-322/222-4246 *11am-midnight*

El Brujo [★] Venustiano Carranza 510 (at Naranjo) 52-322/223-3026 *1pm-9:30pm, clsd Mon, Mexican/ seafood, worth the wait*

Cafe Bohemio [MW,GO] Rodolfo Gómez 127 (at Olas Altas) 44-322/134-2436 *5pm-2am, clsd Sun, open-air cafe, late-evening happy hour*

Cafe de Olla [★] Calle Basilio Badillo 168 52-322/223-1626 *10am-11pm, clsd Tue, Mexican, wait list an hour*

Cafe des Artistes [★R] Calle Guadalupe Sánchez 740 (at Leona Vicario) 52-322/222-3228 *6pm-11:30pm, upscale French w/ a Mexican twist*

Puerto Vallarta • MEXICO

Chez Elena [GO] Matamoros 520, Centro (at Los Quatro Vientos Hotel) **52-322/222-0161** *6pm-11pm, seasonal, garden restaurant, also rooftop bar*

Daiquiri Dick's [★] Olas Altas 314 (on Playa Los Muertos) **310/697-3799** *8:30am-1:30pm & 5:30pm-11pm, clsd Tue & clsd Sept*

De Santos [E] 2483 Francisco Medina Ascencio **52-322/221-3090** *5pm-4am*

El Dorado Pulpito 102, Playa de los Muertos **52-322/222-4124** *beach club & restaurant, evening shows*

Le Bistro Jazz Cafe [GO] Isla Rio Cuale 16-A (on the island, at the East Bridge) **52-322/222-0283** *9am-midnight, clsd Sun*

Lido Beach Club Malecon 1 Esq Abedul Col Emiliano Zapata **813/855-0190** *10am-6pm*

Memo's Casa de los Hotcakes [★] Calle Basilio Badillo 289 **52-322/222-6272** *8am-2pm, long lines for cheap & good brkfst*

Mezzogiorno Ristorante Italiano Avenida del Pacifico 33 (North Beach Bucerias Nayarit) **52-329/298-0350** *6pm-11pm (clsd Mon off-season)*

El Mole de Jovita 220B Basillo Badillo *3pm-10pm, clsd Sun, authentic mole*

La Palapa Pulpito 103, Col Emiliano Zapata **52-322/222-5225** *brkfst, lunch & dinner, beachside dining*

La Piazzetta Rodolfo Gomez #143 (at Olas Atlas, Romantic Zone) **52-322/222-0650** *4pm-11pm, Italian*

Planeta Vegetariano Iturbide 270 (Centro) **52-322/222-3073** *8am-10pm, clsd Sun, buffet-style*

Red Cabbage [GO] Calle Rivera del Rio 204-A (at Basilio Badillo) **52-322/223-0411** *5pm-11pm, on Rio Cuale w/ great kitschy decor*

The Swedes/ Crows Nest Bar [MW,GO] Púlpito 154 (at Olas Altas) **52-322/223-2353** *4pm-2am, Swedish/ European, also bar upstairs*

Trio [★E] Guerrero 264 (Centro) **52-322/222-2196** *6pm-midnight, clsd Sun*

■ENTERTAINMENT & RECREATION

Boana Tours Calle Amapas 325 (at Casa Boana Torre Malibu) **52-322/222-0999, 52-322/222-6695** *horseback tours daily*

Diana's Cruise the Bay Tour [MW,F] meet at Los Muertos pier *9:30am-5pm Th, open bar*

Ocean Friendly [GF] Paseo del Marlin 510-103, Col. Aralias **52-322/225-3774, 044-322/294-0385 (cell)** *whale-watching tours, Dec 15-March 31*

Playa Los Muertos/ Playa del Sol [★] S of Rio Cuale *the gay beach, now spans "Blue Chairs" & "Green Chairs"*

■PUBLICATIONS

Gay PV 52-322/113-0224 *great gay magazine for PV*

Urbana Revista 52-333/844-6471 *gay lifestyle magazine*

■GYMS & HEALTH CLUBS

Acqua Day Spa & Gym Calle Constitución 450 (F Rodriguez) **52-322/223-5270** *7am-9pm, till 5pm Sat, clsd Sun*

■MEN'S CLUBS

Spartacus Spa Ignacio L Vallarta 264 **52-322/178-4299** *3pm-midnight*

Vallarta Cora [★F] Calle Pilitas 174 (at Vallarta Cora hotel) **52-322/222-6234** *3pm-11pm, poolside bar, jacuzzi, also hotel*

■EROTICA

The Closet Lazaro Cardenas 230 **52-322/223-3030** *noon-9pm*

■CRUISY AREAS

Malecón (Seawall) [AYOR] facing Calle Morelos (esp near benches across from Presidencia Municipal at Iturbide) *evenings*

Playa Los Muertos [AYOR] near green chairs at The Beach Café & further S by the rocks *afternoons*

Plaza Caracol Mall [AYOR]

Querétaro

■NIGHTCLUBS

Con la Rojas [M,D,$] Ave Constituyentes Pte 42A (Centro) **52-442/212-4795** *10pm-2:30am, clsd Sun-Wed*

■CRUISY AREAS

Alameda Parque [AYOR]

El Jardín Guerrero [AYOR] 3 blks from Centro Historico

Plaza de Armas [AYOR]

Zócalo/ Obregón Plaza [AYOR]

San Jose del Cabo

■ACCOMMODATIONS

El Encanto Inn [GF,SW] 210/858-6649, 52-614/142-0388

One & Only Palmilla [GF,SW] Apartado Postal 52, 23400 **52-624/146-7000, 866/829-2977 (US#)** *upscale resort*

■RESTAURANTS

Voila Bistro & Catering [★] 1705 Comonfort (Plaza Paulina) **52-624/130-7569** *noon-10pm, from 4pm Sun, Mexican w/ French twist, full bar, patio*

San Miguel de Allende

■ACCOMMODATIONS

Casa de Sierra Nevada [GF,SW] Calle Hospicio 35 (Centro) **52-415/152-7040, 800/701-1561 (US#)**

Casa Schuck Boutique B&B [GF,SW,WI] Garita 3, Centro **52-415/152-6618, 937/684-4092**

Dos Casas [GF] Calle Quebrada 101 (Guanajuato) **52-415/154-4073**

Las Terrazas San Miguel [GS,NS,WI,GO] Santo Domingo 3 **52-415/152-5028, 707/534-1833 (US#)** *4 rental homes*

■RESTAURANTS

La Azotea Umaran 6 **52-415/152-4977** *delicious tapas & drinks*

Mezzanine Bistro [GO] Cuna de Allende 11 (at Hotel Vista Hermosa) **52-415/152-2799**

Tepic

■MEN'S CLUBS

Banos America Jesus Garcia #37 (Fraccionamiento Simancas) **52-311/213-3747** *6am-10pm, till 3pm Sun, two steam rms, bar, popular afternoons*

Tijuana

■BARS

DF [M,NH,OC] Plaza Santa Cecilia 781 (btwn 1st Str & Ave Revolución) *open late*

Gay Bar Endless Summer [M] Km 29.5 Carretera Libre Ensenada-Tijuana, Rosarito **52/611-006-832** *10:30am-2am, 5pm-5am Fri-Sat, 2pm-2am Sun, clsd Mon*

Luna Sol Lounge [GS,GO] Av Pacifico 640, Playas de Tijuana **52-664/609-4977** *2pm-midnight, beach bar*

El Ranchero Bar [★M,NH,D,F,AYOR] Plaza Santa Cecilia 769 (btwn Calles 1, 2, Revolución & Constitución) **52-664/685-2800** *1pm-late, cruisy cantina, hustlers, use caution in bathrooms*

El Taurino Bar [M,NH,S] Av Niños Héroes 189 (at Calles 1 & Constitución) **52-664/685-2478** *3pm-2am, till 5am Fri-Sat, cruisy, hustlers*

Villa Garcia [M,D] Plaza Santa Cecilia 751 (next to El Ranchero) *10am-late, small dance flr, cruisy*

■NIGHTCLUBS

Club Fusion [M,D,K,DS] Calle Larroque 213 **52-664/345-8817** *8pm-3am Fri-Sun*

Extasis [★M,D,S,$] Larroque 213 (in Plaza Viva Tijuana, next to the border) **52-664/682-8339** *8pm-late, clsd Mon-Wed, go-go boys, more women Th*

Mike's Disco [MW,D,DS,V,18+] Av Revolución 1220 (at Calle 6A) **52-664/685-3534** *8pm-5am, till 3am Th, clsd Wed*

Premier [M,S] Av Revolución (btwn 1st & Coahuila) *7pm-3am, clsd Mon-Tue*

Sin Tabu [GS] Av Sanchez Taboada 10291-7 **52-664/681-8138**

Tijuana • *MEXICO*

Terraza 9 [GF,D] Calle 5a (at Av Revolución) **52-664/685-3534** *5pm-2am, till 5am Fri-Sat, clsd Mon*

■CAFES

D'Luna Cafe Calle 8 #8380 **52-664/321-9735**

■MEN'S CLUBS

Banos Vica [GS] Gustavo Díaz Ordaz 1535 **52-664/622-0386**

Todos Santos

■ACCOMMODATIONS

The Todos Santos Inn [GS,SW,NS,GO] Calle Legaspi #33 (Topete) **52-612/145-0040** *colonial inn w/ bar*

Tulúm

■ACCOMMODATIONS

Adonis Tulum Riviera Maya Gay Resort & Spa [M,SW] Carretera Tulum Boca Paila Km 3.8 **800/233-5162, 52-984/871-1000**

Casa de las Olas [GF,WI] 10.6km Tulum Beach Rd **52-984/807-3909**

EcoTulum Resorts & Spa [GF,WI] Carretera Tulum Ruinas Km 5 **54-115/5918-6400, 877/301-4666**

Om Tulum [GF,WI] Caraterra Ruinas Punta -Allen Km 9.5 **521-98/4114-0538**

Posada Luna del Sur [GF] Calle Luna Sur 5 **52-984/871-2984**

Veracruz

■ACCOMMODATIONS

Hotel Villa del Mar [GF,SW] Blvd Miguel Ávila Camacho 2431 (across street from Playa del Mar beach) **52-229/989-6500**

■ENTERTAINMENT & RECREATION

San Juan de Ulua Fortress *9am-4:30pm, clsd Mon, impressive early colonial-era floating fortress*

Veracruz Aquarium Blvd Avila Camacho (at Xicolencat) **52-229/932-7984** *10am-7pm, one of the largest & best in the world; don't miss it!*

■MEN'S CLUBS

Baños El Edén [AYOR] Miguel Hidalgo 1113 (Centro) **52-229/932-3360** *buy tickets at rear counter of music store*

■CRUISY AREAS

Plaza de Armas/ Zócalo [AYOR]

Waterfront & Av República [AYOR]

Zacatecas

■ACCOMMODATIONS

Quinta Real Zacatecas [GF] Av Ignacio Rayón 434 (Col. Centro) **52-492/1105-1010, 866/621-9288** *5-star hotel built into grandstand of bullfighting ring*

■CRUISY AREAS

Av Juárez [AYOR] E from Av Hidalgo for 2 blks

Zihuatanejo

■ACCOMMODATIONS

Hotel Las Palmas [GF,SW] Calle de Aeropuerto (at lot 5) **52-755/557-0634, 888/527-7256**

■NIGHTCLUBS

Mydori Disco Bar [MW,D,DS,S] Calle La Laja s/n (Col. Centro) **52-755/104-5670** *8pm-4am*

Tequila Town [★GF,K,V] Cuauhtemoc 3 (Col Centro) **52-755/553-8587** *8pm-4am, more gay after 11pm*

Central America

COSTA RICA

Alajuela

■BARS

Rick's Bar & Restaurant [MW] 500 mts Este Casino Fiesta, carretera Heredia, en Río Segundo de Alajuela **506-2/441-3213** *6pm-close, from 4pm Sun*

Chirripó Nat'l Park

■ACCOMMODATIONS

Monte Azul [GS,F,GO] Contiguo al puente de Chucuyo, Chimirol **506/2742-5222**

Dominical

■ACCOMMODATIONS

Paradise Costa Rica [GS,SW,NS,GO] Escaleras (at San Martin Sur) **800/708-4552** *vacation villas*

Guanacaste

■ACCOMMODATIONS

Villa Decary [GF,GO] Nuevo Arenal, 5717 Tilaran **506-2/694-4330, 800/556-0505 (from US & Canada)** *former coffee farm overlooking Lake Arenal*

Manuel Antonio, Quepos

■ACCOMMODATIONS

Casa Antonio [MW,GO] Enter at Arboleda Hotel **506/8639-1085**

Casa de Frutas [GS,GO] **506-8/825-3257 (cell), 800/936-9622** *luxury villa in Tulemar Gardens*

Casa Mono Titi [GF,SW,NS,WI,GO] in the hills **800/282-3680** *vacation home, near beaches & bars*

Casa Romano [GS,SW,WI,WC,GO] **404/290-6919** *near gay beach*

Casitas Eclipse [GS] KM 5 Manuel Antonio Rd **506-2/777-0408** *detached casitas*

Costa Verde [GS,SW,GO] **506-2/777-0584, 866/854-7958 (from US & Canada)**

Gaia Hotel & Reserve [GF,SW,WI,GO] km 2.7 Carretera Quepos a Manuel Antonio **506-2/777-9797, 800/226-2515** *boutique hotel, surrounded by wildlife refuge, full brkfst*

Hotel Parador [GF,SW,WI] **506-2/777-1414, 877/506-1414** *large luxury resort*

Hotel Villa Roca [M,SW,NS,GO] **506-2/777-1349**

Las Aguas Resort [M,SW,WI,GO] **813/784-7930 (US#), 506-2/296-1880**

La Mansion Inn [GS,F,SW,GO] **506-2/777-3489, 800/360-2071**

La Posada [GF,SW,GO] **506-2/777-1446**

Si Como No [GF,SW,WC] **506-2/777-0777, 888/742-6667** *25-acre wildlife refuge, also spa*

■BARS

Tutu/ Gato Negro [★GS] KM 5 Manuel Antonio Rd (at Casitas Eclipse) **506-2/777-0408**

■NIGHTCLUBS

Liquid Lounge [M,D,DS] **506-2/777-5158** *9pm-3am Tue & Th-Sun*

■RESTAURANTS

El Barba Roja [★] Carretera al Parque Nacional **506-2/777-0331** *7am-10pm, from 4pm Mon, American, great sunset location*

El Gran Escape & Fish Head Bar Quepos Centro **506-2/777-0395** *brkfst, lunch, dinner, clsd Tue, seafood, full bar*

La Hacienda Restaurante [E] Plaza Yara **506-2/777-3473** *10:30am-10:30pm*

Rico Tico [★E] in Hotel Si Como No *brkfst, lunch & dinner, Tex/ Mex, includes use of pool bar*

■ENTERTAINMENT & RECREATION

La Playita N end of Playa Espadilla (w/ a steep hike over rocks) *the gay beach (impassable 2 hours before & after high tide)*

Osa Peninsula

■ACCOMMODATIONS

Blue Osa Yoga Sanctuary & Spa [GS,SW,NS,WI,GO] **506/8704-7006** *all meals included*

Pavones

■ACCOMMODATIONS

Casa Siempre Domingo B & B [GS,SW,WI,GO] **506/2776-2185**

Playa Sámara

■ACCOMMODATIONS

Casitas LazDivaz B&B [GF,WI,WC,GO] **506/2656-0295**

Puerto Viejo

■ACCOMMODATIONS

Banana Azul [M,WI,GO] 200 meters N of Perla Negra Hotel **506-2/750-2035, 506-2/351-4582 (cell)**

■RESTAURANTS

Koki Beach Restaurant Bar & Lounge [WI] Main St (town center across from water) **506/8305-0747** *5pm-11pm, clsd Mon, Latin fusion cuisine*

Puntarenas

■ACCOMMODATIONS

Villa Caletas [GS,F,SW] Garabito **506/2630-3000** *a luxury boutique hotel, 1 hour from San Jose airport*

■CRUISY AREAS

Beach [AYOR]

San José

■ACCOMMODATIONS

Colours Oasis Resort [MW,F,E,SW,WI,GO] El Triangulo Noroeste, Blvd Rohrmoser (200 meters before end of blvd) **506-2/296-1880, 866/517-4390 (US & Canada)** *full brkfst*

Hotel El Mirador [M,SW] Bello Horizonte, Escazú **506/2289-3981**

Hotel Kekoldi [GS,WI,GO] Av 9 (btwn Calles 5 & 7, Barrio Amón) **506-2/248-0804, 786/221-9011 (from US)**

Secret Garden B&B [GS,WI,GO] **506-2/290-3890**

■BARS

Bar Al Despiste [GS,K] in front of Mudanzas Mundiales (W of Universal Zapote) **506-2/234-5956** *6pm-2am, 5pm-10pm Sun, clsd Mon*

Buenas Vibraciones [MW,GO] Ave 14 (btw Calle 7 & 9, in Paseo de los Estudiantes) **506-2/223-4573**

Casa Vieja [MW,F] 400 metros al este de la capilla religiosa de Montserrat, Alajuela **506/2440-8525** *6pm-2am, noon-midnight Sun*

Zona Rosa [MW,D,K] 250m norte del Correo Central

■NIGHTCLUBS

La Avispa [MW,D] 834 Calle 1 (pink house btwn Avs 8 & 10) **506-2/223-5343** *8pm-2am, popular T-dance till 7pm Sun, clsd Mon-Wed*

Azotea [GS,D] Uruca, de Capris 300 Norte (Plaza Rohrmoser) **506-2/220-2506**

El Bochinche [MW,D,V] Calle 11 (btwn Avs 10 & 12, Paseo de los Estudiantes), San Pedro **506-2/221-0500** *7pm-2am, till 5pm Fri-Sat, clsd Sun-Tue, also full restaurant, Mexican, dancing/DJ after 10pm*

Club Energy [MW,D,F] Paseo Colon (near 30th, by Pizza Hut) **506/2223-7594** *from 7:30pm Th-Sun, also restaurant*

Club Oh! [GS,D] Calle 2 (btwn Avs 14 & 16) **506-22/221-9341** *9pm-close Fri-Sat, take taxi to avoid bad area*

Club Oh [M,D] Calle 2 (btwn Ave 14 & 16) **506-2/221-9341** *9pm-2am Fri-Sat*

Puchos [M,DS,S] Calle 11 & Av 8 (knock to enter) **506-2/256-1147, 506-2/222-7967** *8pm-2:30am, clsd Sun*

■RESTAURANTS

Ankara [E] San José de la Montaña (Heredia, San Antonio de Belén, S of church) **50/8326 6646** *clsd Mon-Tue, live music*

Cafe Mundo [GO] Av 9 & Calle 15 (200 meters E of parking lot for INS, Barrio Amón) **506-2/222-6190** *11am-11pm, 5pm-midnight Sat, clsd Sun, garden seating, bar*

La Cocina de Leña [R] in El Pueblo complex **506-2/255-1360** *11am-11pm, 5 minutes from downtown*

Machu Picchu Calle 32 (btwn Aves 1 & 3) **506-2/283-3679** *Peruvian*

Mirador Ram Luna from center of Aserrí, go 4 kilometers on the road toward Tabarca, Aserrí **506-2/230-3060** *dinner nightly, lunch & dinner wknds, clsd Mon, hillside restaurant w/ amazing views*

Olio [★] Escalante, Bario California (N of Baselman's, San Pedro/ Los Yoses) **506-2/281-0541** *lunch & dinner, clsd Sun, Spanish, also full bar*

Vishnu Vegetarian Restaurant [★] Av 1 (btwn Calles 3 & 1) **506-2/256-6063** *8am-9:30pm*

■ENTERTAINMENT & RECREATION

Gay Tours Costa Rica 309-2200 Coronado **506-2/305-8044** *daily events & excursions*

Mercado Central/ Central Market Central Avenida (btwn Calles 6 & 8) *bustling market selling food, clothing, souvenirs & more*

■MEN'S CLUBS

Oasis Spa [MO] Avenida 4 (at Calle 20) **506/8824-8511, 506/8648-9504** *professional massage*

Paris Sauna corner of Calle 7 & Av 7 (1 block from Morazan Park) **506-2/258-7254** *noon-2am, till 4am Fri-Sat*

Sauna Hispalis [★V] Av 2 #1762 (E of the Plaza de la Democracia, btwn Calles 17 & 19) **506-2/256-9540** *noon-1am, [N] Wed*

■CRUISY AREAS

Parque La Sabana [AYOR] next to Municipal Stadium (btwn airport & San José) *evenings & wknds*

Parque Nacional [AYOR] N of Av 1 (btwn Calles 15 & 19)

Plaza de la Cultura [★AYOR] in front of the Nat'l Theater (btwn Calles 3 & 5) *late afternoons & early evenings*

San Ramon

■ACCOMMODATIONS

Angel Valley Farm B&B [GS,NS,WI,WC] 200m N & 300m E of Iglesia de Los Angeles (at Autopista to Arenal Volcano) **506-2/456-4084, 910/805-0149 (US#)** *full brkfst*

Santa Clara

■ACCOMMODATIONS

Tree Houses Hotel Costa Rica [GS,NS,GO] **506-2/475-6507** *private treehouses in canopy of trees on wildlife refuge*

Tamarindo

■ACCOMMODATIONS

Cala Luna Hotel & Villas [GF,SW] Playa Langosta (at Playa Tamarindo) **506-2/653-0214, 800/503-5202**

Hotel Sueño del Mar [GF,SW,NS,WI] Playa Langosta **506-2/653-0284** *private hacienda on the beach, full brkfst*

South America

ARGENTINA

Buenos Aires

■INFO LINES & SERVICES

Comunidad Homosexual Argentina Tomas Liberti 1080 **54-11/4361-6382**

Pink Point Avenida de Mayo 1370, 10th flr (at Palacio Barolo) **54-1/4382-8227** *LGBT tourist info*

■ACCOMMODATIONS

1555 Malabia House [GF,WI] Malabia 1555, Palermo Viejo (at Honduras) **54-11/4833-2410**

Bayres B&B [M,GO] Av Córdoba 5842 (in Palermo) **54-11/4772-3877**

The Cocker [GF,WI,GO] Av Juan de Garay 458 (at Defensa) **54-1/4362-8451**

Don Sancho Youth Hostel [GS,WI] Constitucion 4062 (at Boedo) **54-11/4923-1422** *full brkfst, some shared baths, hot tub*

Faena Hotel & Universe [GS,WI] 445 Martha Salotti St **54-11/4010-9000** *luxury hotel, live shows at The Universe*

Home Hotel [GF,WI,SW] Honduras 5860 **54-11/4778-1008** *boutique hotel*

Hotel Axel [MW,F,WI] Venezuela 649 **54-11/4136-9393** *luxury gay hotel, pool parties*

Argentina • SOUTH AMERICA

Hotel Intercontinental Buenos Aires
[GF,WI] Moreno 809 **888/424-6835**
(US#), 54-11/4340-7100

Hotel Vitrum [GF] 5641 Gorriti
54-1/4776-5030 *stylish boutique hotel*

Lugar Gay B&B [MO,WI,GO] Defensa
1120 **54-11/4300-4747**

Palermo Viejo B&B [GS,NS,WI,GO]
Niceto Vega 4629 (at Av Scalabrini
Ortiz) **54-11/4773-6012** *near shopping & gay nightlife*

Solar Soler B&B [GF,NS] Soler 5676 (at
Bonpland) **54-11/4776-3065**

Telmho Hotel Boutique [GF,WI] 1086
Defensa St (at Humberto Primo)
54-11/4116-5467

■BARS

Bach Bar [MW,E,K,V] Antonio Cabrera
4390 **54-11/5184-0137**

Bulnes Class [MW,D] Bulnes 1250
(Palermo) **54-11/4861-7492** *from 7pm Th & 11pm Fri-Sat*

Cero Consecuencia [MW] Cabrera
3769 *10pm-close, clsd Mon-Tue*

Flux Bar [MW,D] Marcelo T de Alvear
980 (at 9 de Julio) **54-11/5252-0258**
7pm-close, from 8pm wknds, clsd Sun

Inside [M,F,E,S,OC] Bartolomé Mitre
1571 **54-11/4372-5439** *[S] wknds*

Kadu [MO,L,18+] Sánchez de
Bustamante 1633 *9pm-4am Wed & Fri-Sun, leather/ fetish bar, theme nights w/ strict dress code & entry times*

KM Zero [MW,D,DS,S,V] Av Santa Fe
2516 **54-11/4822-7530**

Mundo Bizarro [GF,F] 1222 Serrano
54-11/4773-1967 *1950s American-style cocktail lounge*

Shangay [M,D] Guemes 151 (Ramos
Mejia) **54-1/5151-5788**

Sitges [★MW] Córdoba 4119
54-11/4861-3763 *10:30pm-4am, till 6am Fri-Sat, clsd Mon-Tue*

Tom's [MO] Viamonte 638, in basement
54-11/4322-4404 *dark room*

Zoom [M,L,B$] Uriburu 1018
54-11/4827-4828 *noon-3am, maze, lounge, cruisy*

■NIGHTCLUBS

Ambar La Fox [MW,D] Av Federico
Lacroze 3455 (at Alvarez Thomas, at El
Teatro) *Sat only, young, alternative mixed crowd*

Amerika [M,D] Gascón 1040 (at
Cordoba) **54-11/4865-4416** *dark-room*

Angel's Viamonte 2168 *midnight-7am Th-Sat*

Bahrein [GS,D,F] Lavalle 345 *6pm-7am Wed & Fri, from 10pm Sat, from midnight Tue*

Club 69 [GS,D,DS] Niceto Vega 5510
(btwn Humboldt & Fitzroy, Palermo)
54-1/4779-9396 *11:30pm Th only, over-the-top theme parties*

Club Namunkura [MW,D,TG] Niceto
Vega 5699 (Palermo, at Club M) *1st Fri only*

Cocoliche [GS,D] Rivadavia 878

Contramano [MO,D,B] Rodriguez Peña
1082 (at Av Santa Fe) *midnight-close, from 7pm Sun, clsd Mon-Tue, hustlers*

Fiesta Dorothy [MW,D] Alsina 940
(near Plaza de Mayo, at Palacio Alsina)
54-11/4334-0097,
54-11/4334-0098 *huge dance bi-monthly dance party*

Fiesta Eyeliner [MW,D,A,DS] Sarmiento
1272 (at Salon Real) *monthly queer/ alternative dance party, check web for dates*

Fiesta Oliver [MW,D] Cordoba 543 (at
Sub Club) *1am Fri only (Fri night)*

Fiesta Plop [MW,D] Av Federico Lacroze
3455 (at Alvarez Thomas, at El Teatro)
Fri only, young, alternative mixed crowd

Fiesta Puerca [M,D] Federico Lacroze
(at Alvarez Thomas)

Glam [★M,D] Cabrera 3046
54-11/4963-2521 *midnight-close wknds, darkroom, patio*

Human [M,D] Av Costanera Norte
Rafael Obligado (at Av Sarmiento, at
Mandalay Complex) *midnight Fri only, huge dance party*

Juana [MW,D] 775 Av 44
54-1/557-6807 *from 11:30pm Fri-Sat only*

Pacha [GF,D] Av Costanera y Pampa **54–11/4788–4280**

Rheo [M,D] Marcelino Freyre S/N, Arco 17 (at Crobar) **54–1/3430–2711** *midnight Sat only*

Sub Club [MW,D] Cordoba 543 *Fri-Sat only*

■CAFES

Gout Cafe [GO] Juncal 2124 **54–11/4825–8330** *sandwiches, pastries*

Pride Cafe [E] Balcarce 869 (in San Telmo) **54–11/4300–6435** *10am-10pm, live show Th night*

Pure Vida Reconquista 516 (btwn Tucuman & Lavalle) **54–11/4393–0093** *8:30am-7pm, 10am-5:30pm Sat, clsd Sun, juice bar, food served, plenty veggie*

■RESTAURANTS

Arevalito Arevalo 1478 **54–11/4776–4252** *9am-midnight, vegetarian*

Bio Humbolt 2192 (Palermo Viejo) **54–11/4774–3880** *lunch & dinner, vegetarian, organic market*

La Cabana [★] Alicia Moreau de Justo 380 **54–11/4314–3710** *brkfst, lunch & dinner, upscale steak house*

Casa Cruz 1658 Uriarte **54–11/4833–1112** *8:30pm-3am, later Fri-Sat, upscale, trendy restaurant, also bar*

Cumana [★] Rodriguez Pena 1149 (at Arenales) **54–11/4813–9207** *regional cuisine*

El Palacio de la Papa Frita [★] Lavalle 735 (at Maipu) **54–11/4393–5849** *also Av Corrientes 1612, 11/4374–8063*

Filo San Martin 975 **54–11/4311–0312, 54–11/4311–1871** *8pm-close*

Lobby Nicaragua 5944 **54–11/4770–9335** *8am-1am, till 8pm Sun-Mon, wine bar, cafe & restaurant*

Mark's Deli & Coffeehouse [★] El Salvador 4107 (in Palermo) **54–11/4832–6244**

Milion [★] Parana 1048 **54–11/4815–9925** *swank lounge/restaurant spread over 3-flr mansion, garden*

Naturaleza Sabia Balcarce 958 (at Carlos Calvo) **54–11/4300–6454** *clsd Mon, vegetarian*

Rave [★] Gorriti 5092 **54–11/4833–7832**

Sucre Sucre 676 **54–11/4782–9082** *upscale contemporary*

Verde Llama Jorge Newbery 3623 **54–11/4554–7467** *11am-6pm, till midnight Th-Sat, organic vegetarian cafe*

■ENTERTAINMENT & RECREATION

Casa Brandon [F] Luis Maria Drago 236 (at Lavalleja) **54–11/4858–0610** *LGBT events, dance parties, poetry readings, art & more*

Espanol al Sur [GF,GO] Pichincha 1031 #2 (at Carlos Calvo) **54–11/4942–9582, 54–11/6449–5447** *Spanish language & tango classes*

La Marshall [★] Maipu 444 **54–11/4912–9043** *8:30pm Wed, exclusively gay tango lessons*

Museo Evita Peron Lafinur 2988 (in Palermo) **54–11/4807–9433** *2pm-7:30pm, clsd Mon*

Out & About Pub Crawl [MW] **54–911/3036–1361** *make new friends on a tour of the local gay bars*

Private Gay Tours *custom gay tours of Buenos Aires*

■BOOKSTORES

Otras Letras Soler 4796, Palermo **54–1/2060–2942** *2pm-8pm, from 3pm Sat, clsd Sun, LGBT books & culture*

■PUBLICATIONS

Actitud www.agmagazine.info

G-Maps Buenos Aires Franklin 1463, Florida Oeste **54–11/4730–0729** *free pocket-size gay map of Buenos Aires*

The Ronda *gay pocket guide w/ local listings (www.theronda.com.ar)*

Argentina • SOUTH AMERICA

■MEN'S CLUBS

A Full Spa [MO,V,GO] Viamonte 1770
(at Av Callao) **54-11/4371-7263**
noon-3am, 24hrs wknds

Energy Spa [MO] Bravard 1105 (at Av
Angel Gallardo, Villa Crespo)
54-1/4854-5625

Grupo Los Fiesteros [MO] *bi-weekly
sex parties, grupolosfiesteros.com.ar*

Homo Sapiens [MO] Gascon 956
54-11/4862-6519

Nagasaki [MO] Aguero 427
54-1/4866-6335

Sauna Unikus Av Pueyrredón 1180
(near Calle Mansilla)
54-1/4961-7792

■EROTICA

American Top Video Av Cabildo 2230
(Galeria Las Vegas) **54-11/4781-5343**
clsd Sun

Box Laprida 1423 (at Santa Fe) *2pm-
6am*

Cine ABC Esmeralda 506 (at the
Microcentro)

Eden Av Santa Fe 1833 (gal Bozzini, B
Norte)

Emporium [M] Cerrito 842 (btwn
Marcelo T Alvear & Santa Fe) *sex store,
also dark room, cruisy*

Ideal Suipacha 378

Multicine Lavalle 750

■CRUISY AREAS

Avenida Santa Fe [AYOR] btwn Callao
& Coronel Diaz

Bosques de Palermo [AYOR] Figueroa
Alcorta & Dorrego St

Plaza Las Heras [AYOR] Coronel Dias &
Av Las Heras

BRAZIL

Rio de Janeiro

Note: M°=Metro station

■INFO LINES & SERVICES

Grupo Arco-Iris Rio de Janeiro Rua
do Senado 230 **55-21/2222-7286**
*1pm-7pm, till 11pm Sat, clsd Sun, LGBT
community center*

Rainbow Kiosk/ Quiosque [★MW,DS]
Atlantic Av (in front of Copacabana
Palace Hotel) **55-21/2275-1641**

■ACCOMMODATIONS

Casa Cool Beans [GS,SW,WI,GO] Rua
Laurinda Santos Lobo 136
55-21/2262-0552

Casa Dois Gatos [M,SW,WI,GO] Rua
Rosalina Terra 6, Cabo Frio
561/282-0023, 55-22/2645-5806
free transportation from Rio airport

Ipanema Plaza [GS,SW] Rua Farme
Amoedo (at Rua Prudente de Morais)
55-21/3687-2000 *near gay beach,
rooftop pool, also restaurant*

MyRioCondo.com [GS,WI,GO] 3150
Avenida Atlantica, Apt 901
(Copacabana) **215/847-2397 (US#)**

Rio Penthouse [GF]
55-21/2541-3882 *beachfront apts &
penthouse suites*

■BARS

Melt [GF,F,E] Rua Rita Ludolf 47
55-21/2249-9309 *lounge, also
restaurant*

TV Bar [M,NH] Av Nossa Senhora de
Copacabana 1417 **55-21/2267-1663**
*10pm-5am, 9pm-3am Sun, clsd Mon-
Wed*

■NIGHTCLUBS

Boite 1140 [MW,D,DS] 1140 Rua
Capitao Menezes **55-21/7830-8867**
11pm-5am Th-Sun

Le Boy [★MW,D,S,YC] Rua Raul
Pompeia 102 (Copacabana)
55-21/2513-4993 *11pm-close, clsd
Mon, also sauna*

Casa da Matriz [GS,D,18+] Rua Henrique de Novaes 107 54-11/2226-9691, 54-11/2266-1014 *11pm-close, clsd Tue*

Cine Ideal [GS,D] Rua da Carioca 64 55-21/2252-3460 *huge club w/ visting big-name DJs*

La Cueva [M,D,B,L] Rua Miguel Lemos 51 (Copacabana) 55-21/2267-1364

Fosfobox [GS,D] Rua Siqueira Campos 143 55-21/2548-7498 *open Th-Sun, underground techno*

Galeria Cafe [GS,D] Rua Teixeira de Melo 31 (Ipanema) 55-21/2523-8250 *10:30pm-close, clsd Sun-Tue, also gallery*

Papa G [MW,D,DS] 42 Almerinda Freitas 55-21/2450-1253

Turma OK [M,DS] 43 Rua do Resende 55-21/2210-0965

Up Turn [MW,D,F] 2000 Av das Americas 55-21/3387-7957 *patio*

The Week [GF,D] 154 Rua Sacadura Cabral 55-21/2253-1020

■CAFES

Cafeína Rua Farme de Amoedo 43 (Ipanema) 55-21/2521-2194 *8am-11:30pm*

Copa Cafe Av Atlantica 3056 55-21/2235-2947

Expresso Carioca Rua Farme de Amoedo 76 55-21/2267-8604

■RESTAURANTS

Bar d'Hotel Av Delfim Moreira 696 (2nd flr, inside Marina All Suites Hotel, Leblon) 55-21/2172-1112 *Mediterranean, food served all day, bar till late, see & be seen*

Boox Rua Br Torre 368 (in Ipanema) 55-21/2522-3730 *upscale restaurant & nightclub*

Cafe del Mar [GF] Av Atlantica 1910 55-21/7857-8681 *upscale lounge*

Caroline Cafe 10 Rua JJ Seabra 55-21/2540-0705 *steak & burgers, full bar*

Gringo Cafe Rua Barao da Torre 240 55-21/3813-3972 *American classics*

Maxim's Av Atlantica 1850 55-21/2255-7444

Pizzaria Guanabara 1228 Ave Ataulfo de Paiva, Leblon 55-21/2294-0797

To Nem Ai [MW] Rua Farme de Amoedo 57 55-21/2247-8403 *popular bar w/ outdoor seating*

Via Sete 55-21/2512-8100 *noon-midnight, plenty veggie*

Zero Zero [★GS,D,F] Av Padre Leonel Franca 240 (inside planetarium) 55-21/2540-8041 *gay night Sun, upscale restaurant & nightclub*

■ENTERTAINMENT & RECREATION

Copacabana Beach at Rua Rodolfo Dantas *gay across from Copacabana Palace Hotel*

Farme de Amoedo/ Farme Gay Beach across from Rua Farme de Amoedo *see & be seen at this popular gay beach*

Ipanema Beach E of Rua Farme Amoedo

■PUBLICATIONS

Rio For Partiers 55-21/2523-9857 *great guide book*

■MEN'S CLUBS

Bonsucesso Sauna Rua Bonsucesso 252 55-21/2260-9385 *1pm-10pm, till 11pm wknds*

Club 117 Rua Cándido Mendes 117 (Gloria) 55-21/2252-0160 *clsd Mon, large sauna, steam, escorts*

Club 29 Rua Professor Alfredo Gomes 29 55-21/2286-6380 *1pm-4am, bathhouse, cybercafe*

Copacabana Sauna [B] Rua Dias da Rocha 83 55-21/2235-5563 *popular w/ bears*

Estação Rua Tonelero 217 (Copacabana) 55-21/2547-9953 *3pm-close*

Gaylígola [M,V] Rua Ubaldino do Amaral 50 (downtown) 55-21/9259-5625, 55-21/2224-6144

Brazil • SOUTH AMERICA

Nuovo Spazio [DS,18+] Rua Santo Amaro 18 (at Rua Catete) **55-21/2222-7319** *3pm-midnight, clsd Sun, also bar, theme nights*

Point 202 Rua Siqueira Campos 202 **55-21/3816-1757** *3pm-1am, also bar, massage, shows*

Projeto SB Rua 19 de Fevereiro 162 (M° Botafogo) **55-21/2244-4263, 55-21/2541-8698** *also internet cafe*

Rio G Spa Rua Teixeira de Melo 16 (at Prudente de Moraes) **55-21/2523-5092** *3pm-midnight, also bar, darkroom, massage*

Studio 64 [MO] Rua Redentor 64 **55-21/2523-5670, 55-21/2513-4229**

Termas Catete [MO,V] Rua Correia Dutra 34 **55-21/2265-5478** *darkrooms, cabins*

Termas Kabalk [MO,V] Rua Santa Luiza 459 (near Varnhagem Square) **55-21/2252-6210** *3pm-11pm, bar, darkroom, very clean*

Termas Leblon [MO] Rua Barao da Torre 522 (at Rua Garcia d'Avila, Ipanema) **55-21/2287-3762** *sauna, mature crowd*

■EROTICA

Cinema Iris Rua Caroica 49 **55-21/262-1729** *historic adult theater*

■CRUISY AREAS

Avenida Copacabana & Av Atlantica

Barra Beach *across street from beach; look for flags & go past building into woods*

CHILE

Santiago

Note: M°=Metro station

■INFO LINES & SERVICES

Acciongay - Corporacion Chilena de Prevencion del SIDA San Ignacio 165 **56-32/672-0000, 56-32/755-285** *AIDS info, testing & workshops*

■ACCOMMODATIONS

The Aubrey Hotel [GF] Constitución 299-317, Bellavista **56-2/940-2800** *hip boutique hotel*

Casa Moro [MW,GO] Corte Suprema 177 (at Padre Gomez Vidaurre) **56-2/2696-9499** *full brkfst*

Hotel Maury [M] Tarapaca 1112 **56-2/672-5859**

Lastarria Hotel [GF] Coronel Santiago Bueras 188 **56-2/840-3700** *luxury boutique hotel*

Le Reve Hotel [GF] Orrego Luco 023, Providencia **56-2/757-6000, 56-2/757-6011** *luxury boutique hotel*

■BARS

Bar 105 Bombero Nuñez 105 **56-2/403-2990** *9pm-late Th-Sat*

Bar de Willy [MW,E,S] Av 11 de Septiembre 2214 (Común Providencia) **56-2/381-1806** *10pm-4am, till 5am wknds, strippers on 1st flr*

El Closet [MW,K] Santa Filomena 138 (at Bombero Nuñez)

Farinelli [F,E,DS,S] Bombero Nuñez 68 (Recoleta) **56-2/732-8966** *5pm-2am, also hotel*

Pub Friend's [MW,E,DS] Bombero Nuñez 365 (at Dominica, barrio Bellavista) **56-2/777-3979** *9:30pm-4am, till 5am Fri-Sat*

Vox Populi [M,F] Ernesto Pinto Lagarrigue 364 (Bellavista) **56-2/671-1267** *9:30pm-3am, clsd Sun-Mon, also restaurant, garden patio*

■NIGHTCLUBS

Blondie [GS,D,A] Alameda 2879, loc 104 **56-2/681-7793** *theme nights*

Bokhara Discoteque [★M,D,F,DS,S] Pio Nono 430 (at Constitución, barrio Bellavista) **56-2/732-1050, 56-2/735-1271** *10pm-6am, till 7am wknds, darkroom*

Bunker [MW,D,F,E] Bombero Nuñez 159 (Bellavista) **56-2/738-2301, 56-2/738-2314** *11pm-close Fri-Sat*

Club Ignorancia Ernesto Pinto Lagarrigue 282 **56-2/8216-3857**

Club Principe [M,D] Pio Nono 398 **56-2/777-6381**

Fausto [M,D,DS] Av Sta Maria 832
56-2/777-1041

Nueva Cero [M,D,DS] Euclides 1204 par
2 Gran Avenida

■**CAFES**

Tavelli [★] Andrés de Fuenzalida 34
(Providencia) 56-2/231-5830
8:30am-10pm, from 9:30am Sat

■**RESTAURANTS**

Ali Baba 102 Santa Filomena (Barrio
Bellavista, Recoleta) 56-2/732-7036
Middle Eastern

Capricho Español [MW] Purisima 65
(barrio Bellavista) 56-2/777-7674
dinner only, Spanish, full bar

La Pizza Nostra Av Providencia 1975 &
Pedro de Valdivia 56-2/231-8941
Italian

Santo Remedio [D] 152 Roman Diaz,
Providencia 56-2/235-0984 6:30pm-
close, from 10:30pm wknds, global
cuisine, full bar

El Toro Loreto 33 56-2/737-5937
noon-midnight

■**MEN'S CLUBS**

Baños 282 Bellavista 282
56-2/777-1709

Banos Metro [MO,V] Almirante Montt
471 56-2/633-1321 1pm-midnight,
also cafe, darkroom

Sauna Mi Tiempo [V] Bombero Nuñez
230 56-2/735-3949 2pm-midnight,
24hrs wknds, cafe, darkroom

■**EROTICA**

Japi Jane Luis Thayer Ojeda 059,
Oficina 11 56-2/234-4917 11am-
8pm, till 4pm Sat, clsd Sun

Sex Shop Amsterdam

Sex Shop Multivariedades Paseo Las
Palmas 2225, Local 111

■**CRUISY AREAS**

Paseo Las Palmas [AYOR] in
Providencia neighborhood

Plaza de Armas [AYOR]

Europe

AUSTRIA

Vienna

■**INFO LINES & SERVICES**

Gay & Lesbian AA 43-1/799-5599,
43-665/490-5603 (English)

Hosi Zentrum Heumuhlgasse 14
43-1/216-6604 LGBT political organization, groups & events, cafe, news
magazine

Rosa Lila Villa Linke Wienzeile 102
(near Hofmühlgasse, U4-Pilgramgasse)
43-1/586-8150 (women),
43-1/585-4343 (men) LGBT center,
staffed 5pm-8pm Mon, Wed, Fri, info,
gay city maps, also meeting place for
various groups, also cafe-bar

■**ACCOMMODATIONS**

Altstadt [GF,WI] Kirchengasse 41
43-1/522-6666

Arcotel Wimberger [GF] Neubaugürtel
34-36 (at Goldschlagstr)
43-1/521-650 4-star hotel, restaurant & bar on premises

Art Hotel [GF] Brandmayergasse 7-9
43-1/544-5108 modern, art-filled
hotel

Boutique Hotel Stadthalle [GS]
Hackengasse 20 43-1/982-4272 eco-
friendly boutique hotel

Designapartment Vienna [GF,WI,GO]
Glockengasse 25/9 43-650/592-8941

Gay At Home [MW,GO]
43-1/586-1200 rental apts around
Vienna

Le Méridien Wien [GF,SW] Opernring
13-15 43-1/588-900,
800/543-4300 sauna, hot tub, also
restaurant & bar

Pension Wild [M,F,GO] Lange Gasse 10
(off Lerchenfelder Str) 43-1/406-5174

Das Tyrol [GF] Mariahilfer Str 15
43-1/587-5415 small luxury hotel

Austria • EUROPE

■Bars

Alte Lampe [★M,P,OC] Heumühlgasse 13 (at Rechte Weinzeile, U4-Kettenbrückengasse) 43-1/587-3454 8pm-1am, clsd Mon-Tue, piano bar wknds, Vienna's oldest gay bar

Cafe Cheri [M,F] Franzensg 2 43-650/208-1471 10pm-4am, also cafe

Cafe Savoy [★MW,F] Linke Wienzeile 36 (at Köstlergasse) 43-1/581-1557 8am-2am, upscale cafe-bar

Eagle Bar [★M,LV] Blümelgasse 1 (at Gumpendorfer Str, U3-Neubaugasse) 43-1/587-2661 9pm-4am, darkroom, also sex shop

Felixx [MW,F,WI] Gumpendorferstr 5 43-1/920-4714 7pm-3am, from 10am Sat, 7pm-1am Sun

Goldener Spiegel [★M,F,YC] Linke Wienzeile 46 (enter on Stiegengasse, U4-Kettenbrückengasse) 43-1/586-6608 7pm-2am, hustlers

Losch [MO,L] Fünfhuasgasse 1 (at Sechshauserstr) 43-1/895-9979 from 10pm Fri-Sat, also Sun in winter, call for events, leather/ uniform/ fetish club, strict dress code, 3 flrs

Mango Bar [★M,YC,GO] Laimgrubengasse 3 (U4-Kettenbrückengasse) 43-1/920-4714 9pm-4am

Merandy Lounge [MW,D] Mollardgasse 17 7pm-2am Th, 8pm-6am Fri-Sat

Peter's Operncafé Hartauer [GS,F] Riemergasse 9 (at Singer) 43-1/512-8981 6pm-2am, clsd Sun-Mon, terrace

Red Carpet [MW,D,YC] Magdalenenstr 2 43-1/676-782-2966 theme nights

Schik [MW,WI] Schikanedergasse 5 7pm-2am, till 4am Fri-Sat, clsd Sun

Sling [M,L] Kettenbrückengasse 4 (at Grüngasse, U4-Kettenbrückengasse) 43-1/586-2362 3pm-4am, darkroom, private rooms, sling, erotic shop, "piss cinema"

Studio 67 [GS,D] Gumpendorferstr 67 43-1/966-7182 10am-4am Th-Sat, upscale lounge & dance club

Le Swing [M,TG,V,$] Hannovergasse 5 (at Wallensteinstr) 43-1/332-1670 gay 9pm-2am Tue only for Transnight, also sauna

Village Bar [★M,YC] Stiegengasse 8 (near Naschmarkt) 43-1/676-3848977 8pm-3am

Wiener Freiheit [MW,D,TG,F,V] Schönbrunner Str 25 (U4-Kettenbrückengasse) 43-1/931-9111 8pm-midnight, clsd Sun-Mon, 3 flrs, disco 10pm-4am Fri-Sat

X Bar [M] Mariahilfer Str 45 (enter on Stiegengasse, U3-Neubaugasse) 43-1/009-2251 4pm-4am, 6pm-midnight Sun

■Nightclubs

BallCanCan [MW,D] Schwarzenberg Platz 10 (at Ost Klub) monthly queer Balkan club

Heaven Gay Night [★M,D,TG,S,YC] 43-1/523-3063 10pm-6am Sat

Inside Bar [M,D,V] Schikanedergasse 12 43-1/581-2184 8pm-4am

Meat Market [MW,D] queer electro dance party, check local listings

Pitbull [M,D,B,L] Zieglergasse 26 (at Club Pi) 10pm 2nd Fri only

Queer Beat [M,D] Landstr Hauptstr 38 (at the Viper Room) 2nd & 4th Sat only

Up! [M,D] Mariahilfer Str 3 (at Lutz Club) 2nd Fri only, uplifing house music

Why Not? [M,D,S,V] Tiefer Graben 22 (at Wipplinger, U-Schottentor) 43-1/925-3024 10pm-close Fri-Sat & before public holidays, darkroom

■Cafes

Bakul Margaretenstr 58 9am-2am, also guesthouse

Cafe Berg [★MW,F,YC] Berggasse 8 (at Wasagasse, U2-Schottentor) 43-1/319-5720 10am-1am, cafe-bar

Cafe Central Herrengasse 14 (at Strauchgasse) 43-1/533-3763 7:30am-10pm, from 10am Sun & public holidays, "world's most famous coffee-house"

Cafe Raimann [M] Schönbrunner Straße 285 43-1/813-5767 8am-2am, till midnight Sat, clsd wknds & holidays

Cafe Rifugio [M] Schönbrunner Str 10
43-699/1138-0250 *10am-10pm*

Cafe Standard Margaretenstr 63
43-1/581-0586 *8am-midnight, from 11am wknds*

Cafe Stein [GF,F] Währinger Str 6-8 (near U-Schottentor) **43-1/319-7241** *7am-1am, from 9am Sun, internet access, terrace*

Das Möbel Burggasse 10 (Spittelberg) **43-1/524-9497** *10am-1am, trendy, internet, also art gallery*

Point of Sale [WI] Schleifmuhlgasse 12 **43-1/941-6397** *7am-1am, cafe & deli, also vegan items, also bar*

SMart Cafe [GS,F] Kostlergasse 9 **43-1/585-7165** *6pm-2am, till 4am Fri-Sat, clsd Sun-Mon, S/M & fetish cafe*

■ **RESTAURANTS**

Andino [GS,E] Münzwardeingasse 2 (U4-Pilgramgasse) **43-1/587-6125** *11am-2am, from 10am Sat, 11am-midnight Sun, Latin American, full bar*

Aux Gazelles Rahlgasse 5 **43-1/585-6645** *French/ Moroccan restaurant 6pm-midnight; Arabian-style lounge, cafe & deli 11am-2am; also Turkish steam baths noon-10pm*

Bin Im Leo [BW] Servitengasse 14 **43-1/391-7763** *4pm-midnight, from noon wknds, plenty veggie*

Cafe-Restaurant Willendorf [MW] Linke Wienzeile 102 (near Hofmuhlgasse, U4-Pilgramgasse) **43-1/587-1789** *6pm-2am, food served till midnight, plenty veggie, full bar, terrace*

Halle Museumsquartier 1 **43-1/523-7001** *10am-2am, modern bistro, artsy crowd*

Kantine Porzellangasse 19 **43-1/319-5918** *6pm-2am, Thai*

Motto [★R] Schönbrunner Str 30 (enter on Rüdigergasse) **43-1/587-0672** *6pm-2am, till 4am Fri-Sat, trendy, also bar, patio*

Santo Spirito [E] Kumpfgasse 7 **43-1/512-9998** *6pm-11pm, bar till 2am, classical music*

Schon Schön Lindengasse 53 (Ecke Andreagasse) *lunch & dinner, fashionable restaurant, also bar; also clothing & hair salon*

Sly & Arny Lothringerstrasse 22 **43-1/405-0458** *lunch Mon-Fri, dinner nightly, bar till late*

Stöger Ramperstorffergasse 63 **43-1/544-7596** *11am-midnight, clsd Sun, from 5pm Mon, Viennese*

Zum Roten Elefanten Gumpendorferstrasse 3 **43-1/966-8008** *lunch & dinner, open late Fri-Sat, clsd Sun (lunch only in summer)*

■ **ENTERTAINMENT & RECREATION**

Haus der Musik/ House of Music [F] Seilerstätte 30 **43-1/516-4810** *10am-10pm, interactive museum of sound, also cafe*

Kunsthistorisches Museum Maria Theresien-Platz (enter Heldenplatz) **43-1/525-240** *10am-6pm, till 9pm Th, clsd Mon, not to be missed*

■ **BOOKSTORES**

American Discount Rechte Wienzeile 5 (at Paniglgasse) **43-1/587-5772** *9:30am-6:30pm, till 5pm Sat, clsd Sun, int'l magazines & books; also Neubaugasse 39, 43-1/523-37-07*

Löwenherz Berggasse 8 (next to Cafe Berg, enter on Wasagasse, U2-Schottentor) **43-1/317-2982** *10am-7pm, till 8pm Fri, till 6pm Sat, clsd Sun, LGBT, large selection of English titles*

■ **PUBLICATIONS**

Vienna Gay Guide **43-1/789-1000** *city map & guide*

Xtra *ww.xtra-news.at*

■ **MEN'S CLUBS**

Apollo City Sauna [SW,V] Wimbergergasse 34 **43-699/811-65200** *bar, darkroom, gym equipment*

Hard On [MO,L] Hamburgerstr 4 **43-1/0681108-55105** *fetish club; hangout for LMC (Leather & Motorbike Community)*

Austria • *EUROPE*

Kaiserbründl [F,V,SW] Weihburggasse 18-20 (at Grünangergasse, U1-Stephansplatz) **43-1/513-3293** *2pm-midnight, till 2am Fri-Sat, 3 flrs, 2 bars, darkroom maze, gym equipment*

Kino Labyrinth [M,TG,V] Favoritenstr 164 **43-1/920-4088** *[MO] Wed, gay & [TG] Fri, darkrooms, cabins, huge cruising area*

Sauna Frisco [F,V] Schönbrunner Str 28 **43-1/920-2488** *3pm-midnight, 24hrs wknds, private rooms, full bar*

Sport Sauna [★F,V,YC] Lange Gasse 10 (at Pension Wild, U2-Lerchenfelderstr) **43-1/406-7156** *3pm-1am, 24hrs wknds, bar, gym equipment*

■EROTICA

Art-X Percostr 3 **43-1/25804-4413** *erotic supermarket, clsd Sun*

Man for Man [V] Hamburgerstr 8 (at Rechte Wienzeile, U-Kettenbrückengasse) **43-1/585-2064** *books, toys, videos, DVDs, private rooms*

Sexworld XXL Store [GS,V] Mariahilfer Str 49 **43-1/587-6656** *clsd Sun, cabins, darkroom, cruisy, special gay section*

Spartacus XXL Store Mariahilfer Str 49 (enter through Sexworld) **43-1/587-6656** *clsd Sun, toys, leather, books, videos, DVDs*

Tiberius [WC] Lindengasse 2 (at Stiftgasse, U3-Neubaugasse) **43-1/522-0474** *clsd Sun, designer fetish-wear*

Wiscot Center Lerchenfelder Gürtel 45 **43-1/402-7822**

■CRUISY AREAS

Rathauspark [AYOR] *evenings only*

Schweizer Garten [AYOR] next to Südbahnhof

CZECH REPUBLIC

PRAGUE (PRAHA)

Note: M°=Metro station

Prague is divided into 10 city districts: Praha−1, Praha−2, etc.

Praha — Overview

■ACCOMMODATIONS

Apartments in Prague [GS,WI,WC] **420/775-588-508, 303/800-0858**

■ENTERTAINMENT & RECREATION

Letna Park & Beer Garden *great view of the city*

Praha — 1

■ACCOMMODATIONS

Buddha Bar Hotel [GS,WI] Jakubská 649/8 **420 /221-776-300** *small sexy hotel*

Gay Hotel Prague [M,WI] Jecna 12 **420/602-455-127** *also bar/ cafe*

Hotel Leonardo [GS,F,WI] Karolïny Svetle 27 **420 /239-009-239** *great location*

Hotel Metropol [GS] Narodni 33 (at Na Perstyne) **420/246-022-100**

The ICON Boutique Hotel [★GS,F,WI,WC] V Jame 6 (at Vodickova) **420/221-634-100**

The Palace Road Hotel Prague [GS,WI] Nerudova 7 (at Malostranske Namesti) **420/257-531-941**

■BARS

Café Bar Flirt [M,D,B,F,K] Martinská 5/419 **420/224-248-592** *cafe open 10am-2am, bar open 10pm-2am Fri-Sat, bears meet 7pm Wed*

Friends Bar [★M,NH,D,V,WI] Bartolomejská 11 **420/226-211-920** *7pm-6am*

K.U. Bar [GS,D,E] Rytirská 13 (at Perlová, near Oldtown Square) **420/724-695-910** *7pm-4am, upscale & trendy*

Kafirna U Ceského Pána [★M,F] Kozí 13, Stare Mesto **420/222-328-283** *1pm-11pm, small bar popular w/ locals*

Loca Cafe Bar [MW,D,F] Smetanovo nabrezi24 **420/6049-01188** *5pm-2am, till 3am Wed-Th, 4am Fri-Sat*

U Rudolfa [M,BW,OC] Mezibranská 3 **420/605-872-492** *2pm-2am, from 4pm wknds*

◼NIGHTCLUBS

Escape Club [MO,D,F,S,$] V Jame 8 (off Wenceslas Square) **420/774-873-411** *9pm-4am, go-go boys, also hustlers*

Stage [M,D,F,K] Stepanska 23 (at Reznicka) **420/252-548-683** *cafe/ restaurant from 4pm, nightclub opens 9pm; karaoke Tue*

◼CAFES

Cafe Cafe [WI] Rytirská 10 (at Perlová, near Oldtown Square) **420/224-210-597** *10am-11pm*

Cafe Erra [F] Konviktská 11 **420/222-220-568** *10am-midnight, salads, sandwiches & entrées*

Cafe Louvre [GS,F,NS] Národni 22 (M° Narodni Trida) **420/224-930-949** *9am-11:30pm, the favorite hangout of Albert Einstein & Franz Kafka*

Cafe Muzeum [★] Mezibranska 19 **420/222-221-312** *10am-11pm, from 1pm wknds*

Q Cafe Opatovická 166/12 **420/776-856-361** *noon-midnight*

◼RESTAURANTS

Campanulla Cafe Restaurant Velkoprevorske namesti 4 **420/257-217-736** *set in the beautiful garden of The Grand Priory of Bohemia Palace*

Farrango Dusni 15 **420/224-815-996** *4pm-midnight, clsd Sun, Thai*

Lehka Hlava Borsov 2/280 **420/222-220-665** *noon-11:30pm, vegetarian*

Maitrea Tynska 6/1064 (nr Old Town Square) **420/221-711-631** *noon-11:30pm, vegetarian*

Noi [GO] Ujezd 19 **420/257-311-411** *11am-1am, Thai*

Petrinské Terasy [GO] Seminarská Zahrada 393, Malá Strana **420/257-320-688** *noon-11pm, in a former monastery, great view*

Restaurant Dlouhá Dlouhá 23 (basement) **420/222-329-853** *11am-11pm*

Staromestska Restaurace Staromestske namesti 19 **420/224-213-015** *11am-midnight, local Czech specialties*

◼ENTERTAINMENT & RECREATION

NoD Gallery/ Roxy Dlouhá 33 *experimental theater, dance & performance; also cafe & live music venue*

Sex Machines Museum Melantrichova 18 **420/227-186-260** *10am-11pm*

◼BOOKSTORES

Globe [E,F] Patrossova 6 **420/224-934-203** *English-language bookstore*

◼MEN'S CLUBS

Sauna Babylonia [★WI] Martinská 6 (at Na Perstyne) **420/224-232-304** *2pm-3am, gym equipment, bar*

◼EROTICA

Erotic City Zitna 43 **420/737-221-264**

Praha—2

◼ACCOMMODATIONS

Balbin Penzion [GF,WI] Balbinova 26 (near Wenceslas Square) **420/222-250-660**

Heaven Accommodations [★] Gorazdova 11 (at Trojanova) **420/602-455-127** *also bar/ cafe, erotica store*

Prague Saints [MW,GO] Polska 32 (office location) (at Trebizkeho, at Saints Bar) **420/775-152-041,** **420/775-152-042** *apts in gay Vinohrady district*

◼BARS

Angels Cafe [MW,WI] Vinohradská 30 *6pm-midnight, from 2pm Sat, 11am-10pm Sun, cafe & lounge*

Club Strelec [M,B] Anglicka 2 **420/224-941-446** *5pm-2am, till midnight Sun, more bears on Wed & Sat*

Czech Republic • *EUROPE*

Fan Fan Club [M,K,L] Dittrichova 5 (at Trojanova) **420/776-360-698** *5pm-2am, Czech leathermen every 3rd Sat*

FenoMan Club [M,D,F,WI] Blanická 28 (at Vinohradska) **420/603-740-263** *5pm-5am, till 9am Wed, Fri-Sat*

JampaDampa [★W,D,K] V Tunich 10 (at Zitna) **420/603-260-678** *6pm-2am, till 4am Wed, 6pm-6am Fri-Sat, clsd Sun-Mon*

Klub 21 [MW,F,YC] Rimska 21 **420/222-364-720** *7pm-close, clsd Sun, cellar bar/ gallery, mostly Czechs*

Saints [MW] Polska 32 (at Trebizkeho) **420/222-250-326** *7pm-2am, till 4am wknds*

■NIGHTCLUBS

Lollypop [M,D] Belehradska 120, Vinohrady (at Radost FX) **420/224-254-776, 420/603-193-711** *huge, bi-monthly gay party*

On [MW,D,V] Vinohradska 40 (at Blanicka) **420/222-520-630, 420/776-360-698 (cell)** *noon-5am, 3 levels, darkroom*

Termix [★MW,D,K] Trebizskeho 4 (at Vinohrada) **420/222-710-462** *10pm-5am, clsd Sun-Tue*

■RESTAURANTS

Celebrity Cafe Vinohradska 40 (in Vinohrady) **420/222-511-343** *8am-2am, noon-3am Sat, noon-midnight Sun, also bar*

Céleste Restaurant & Bar Rasalnovo nabrezi 1981/80 (at Dancing House) **420/2219-84160** *lunch & dinner, clsd Sun, French dining with great views of the river*

Radost FX Belehradska 120, Vinohrady **420/224-254-776, 420/603-193-711** *fabulous wknd brunch, vegetarian cafe, also nightclub [GF] w/ popular bi-monthly gay party Lollypop*

Sahara Cafe & Lounge [E] Namesti Miru 6 **420/222-514-987** *11am-midnight*

■MEN'S CLUBS

Sauna Marco [★V] Lublanská 17, Vinohrady (at Wenzigova) **420/224-262-833** *2pm-3am, also bar, small but popular*

■EROTICA

Heaven [★] Gorazdova 11 **420/224-912-282** *cinema, toys, magazines, DVDs, darkroom, also bar & accommodations*

Praha—3

■BARS

Club Temple [★M,DS,S,AYOR] Seifertova 3 (at Pribenicka) **420/222-710-773** *8pm-4am, hustlers, also sex shop, rent boys & hotel: aslo Little Temple bar noon-10pm*

Latimerie Club Cafe [MW,DS] Slezska 74 (at Nitranska) **420/224-252-049** *4pm-close, from 6pm wknds*

Piano Bar [MW,F,OC] Milesovská 10 (at Ondrickova) **420/775-727-496** *5pm-close, mostly Czech*

■CAFES

Blaze Husitska 43 **420/777-102-028** *5pm-close, live music, art & more*

■RESTAURANTS

Restaurant Mozaika [NS] Nitranská 13 **420/224-253-011** *contemporary take on international cuisine*

■ENTERTAINMENT & RECREATION

TV Tower Mahlerovy sady 1 **420/724-251-286** *get a bird's-eye view of the city from the top of this tower*

■MEN'S CLUBS

Alcatraz [MO,L,V,S] Borivojova 58 (off Seifertova, in Zizhkov) **420/222-711-458** *9pm-6am, clsd Mon, S/M club, theme nights*

Praha—5

■ACCOMMODATIONS

Andel's Hotel [GF] Stroupeznickeho 21 (at Pizenska) **420/296-889-688** *restaurant & bar*

■MEN'S CLUBS

Drake's [F,WI] Zborovska 50 (at Petrinska) **420/257-326-828** *24hrs, full bat, darkroom, maze, sex shop*

Praha—6

■CRUISY AREAS

Sarka Lake [AYOR] by metro to Dejvicka & tram 26 to end station *nude bathing, summers*

Praha—7

■NIGHTCLUBS

OMG/ Oh My Gay Party [M,D] U Pruhonu 3 (at Mecca) *3rd Sat only*

■CAFES

Duhova Cajovna [MW,F,WI] Milada Horáková 73 (at Ovenecka) **420/775-269-699** *3pm-midnight, "Rainbow Tearoom"*

Praha—8

■ACCOMMODATIONS

Hotel Villa Mansland Prague [M,F,SW,WI,GO] Stepnicná 9, Liben (at Na Malem Klinu) **420/286-884-405, 420/777-839-733**

■MEN'S CLUBS

Sauna David [WI] Sokolovská 44, Karlin (at Vitkova) **420/222-317-869** *9am-11pm, from 11am wknds*

Sauna Labyrint [★MO] Pernerova 4 (at Peckova) *2pm-7am, sauna, steam room, dark room, also bar*

Praha—10

■ACCOMMODATIONS

Arco Guest House [M,WI,GO] Donská 176/13 **420/271-740-734**

Rainbow-Inn Prague [MO,SW,WI,GO] Zernovská 1195/2 (at Prubezna) **420/776-496-877**

Ron's Rainbow Guest House [GS,WI,GO] Bulharska 4 (at Finská) **420/271-725-664, 420/731-165-022** (cell)

■MEN'S CLUBS

Sauna Bonbon Cernomorska 6 (at Charkovska) **420/777-146-068** *3pm-1am, till 2am Fri-Sun*

Praha—11

■CRUISY AREAS

Seberak Lake [AYOR] *from endstation in Seberak, go to opposite side of lake to nude beach, summers*

DENMARK

Copenhagen

■INFO LINES & SERVICES

Kafe Knud Skindergade 21 **45/3332-5861** *4pm 10pm Tue & Th only, HIV resource center, cafe open Tue & Th only*

Sabaah Onkel Dannys Plads 1 *community center for LGBT ethnic minorities*

Wonderful Copenhagen Convention & Visitors Bureau Vesterbrogade 4A **45/7022-2442** (tourist info)

■ACCOMMODATIONS

Carstens Guesthouse [MW,WI,GO] Christians Brygge 28, 5th flr **45/3314-9107, 45/4050-9107** (cell) *B&B, hostel & apts, 5 minutes from gay area*

Copenhagen Admiral Hotel [GF,WI] Toldbodgade 24-28 **45/3374-1414** *great views*

First Hotel Kong Frederik [GF] Vester Voldgade 25 **45/3312-5902**

First Hotel Skt. Petri [GF,F,WI,WC] Krystalgade 22 **45/3345-9100**

First Hotel Twentyseven [GF] Løngangstræde 27 **45/7027-5627**

Hotel Fox [GS,NS] Jarmers Plads 3 **45/3395-7755, 45/3313-3000** *artistic rooms, central location, roof terrace; also lounge & restaurant*

Hotel Kong Arthur [GF] Norre Sogade 11 **45/3311-1212**

Hotel Windsor [M,GO] Frederiksborggade 30, 1360 **45/3311-0830** *near gay scene, shared baths*

Denmark • EUROPE

Radisson Blu Royal Hotel [GF] Hammerichsgade 1 45/3342-6000

The Square [GF] Rådhuspladsen 14 45/3338-1200

■BARS

Amigo Bar [MW,NH,K] Schønbergsgade 4, Frederiksberg 45 5/3321-4915 10pm-6am

Cafe Intime [GF,P] Allegade 25, Frederiksberg 45/3834-1958 6pm-2am, cafe-bar

Can-Can [M,NH] Mikkel Bryggers Gade 11 45/3311-5010 2pm-2am, till 5am Fri-Sat

Centralhjørnet [M,WI] Kattesundet 18 45/3311-8549 noon-2am

Cosy Bar [★M] Studiestræde 24 (in Latin Quarter) 45/3312-7427 10pm-6am, till 8am Fri-Sat

Heaven [★MW,F] Radhuspladsen 75 45/3333-0806 10am-2am, till 5am wknds, bar/ cafe by day, nightclub late [MO]

Masken [★MW,F,WI] Studiestræde 33 45/3391-0937 2pm-3am, till 5am Fri-Sat

Men's Bar [MO,L] Teglgårdsstræde 3 45/3312-7303 3pm-2am, popular brunch 1st Sun

Never Mind [M] Nørre Voldgade 2 45/3311-8886 10pm-6am

Oscar Bar Cafe [★M,F,WI] Radhuspladsen 77 45/3312-0999 noon-2am, great happy hour

■NIGHTCLUBS

Bear Aware [M,D] bear parties, check local listings for dates

Christopher Club [MW,D] Knabrostræde 3 midnight-5am Fri-Sat only

SLM (Scandinavian Leather Men)Copenhagen [MO,L,PC] 17-C Lavendelstraede (in back building) 45/3332-0601 10pm-close Fri-Sat, strict dress code; also 4pm-10pm 2nd Sun (no dress code)

■CAFES

Jernbanecafeen [WI] 7am-2am, patio

■RESTAURANTS

Jailhouse Restaurant & Bar [★M,B,F] Studiestræde 12 45/3315-2255 3pm-2am, till 5am Fri-Sat

Laekkerier Borgergade 17F 8:30am-5pm, till 10pm Th, from 10am wknds, organic take-out

Luna's Diner Vesterbrogade 42 45/3322-4757 10am-midnight, till 1am Fri-Sat

Tight Hyskenstraede 10 45/3311-0900 5pm-10pm, from noon wknds, Canadian, French & Australian

■ENTERTAINMENT & RECREATION

Amager Strandpark beach 5 km from city center

Bellevue Beach mostly gay beach, left end is nude

Kifak Staldgade 8 venue for LGBT special events

Tisvildeleje Beach N of the city (take S-train to Hillerød, then local train to beach) gay beach

Warehouse 9 Bygning 66 (enter from parking lot in front of Oksnehallen, in the meatpacking district) 45/3322-2847 queer art, music, performance & more

■PUBLICATIONS

Out & About 45/4093-1977

■MEN'S CLUBS

Amigo Sauna [★V] Studiestræde 31 45/3315-2028 sauna, steam, tanning, cabins, mazes

Body Bio [M,TG,V] Kingosgade 7 cabins, sauna, cruisy; mostly gay men, but open to all genders

Copenhagen Gay Center [V] Istedgade 34-36 (behind erotica shop) 45/33-220-300 2-flr sauna, tanning

■EROTICA

EP-video Kattesundet 10 45/3311-6406

Men's Shop Viktoriagade 24 45/3325-4475 magazines, books, toys, leather/ rubber gear, videos

CRUISY AREAS

Ørstedsparken [AYOR] btwn Nørre voldgade & Nørre farimagsgade *mainly at night*

Utterslev Mose [AYOR] off hwy toward Farum

Zigøjnerpladsen (Gypsy Square) [AYOR] near Arillerivej & Lossepladsvej

ENGLAND

LONDON

London is divided into 6 regions:
London—Overview
London—Central
London—West
London—North
London—East
London—South

London—Overview

NIGHTCLUBS

Exilio [MW,D,MR-L] 44–(0)79/5698–3230 *9:30pm-2:30am twice a month on Sat, call for location*

Torture Garden 44–020/7700–1441 *the worlds largest fetish/ body art club; visit www.torturegarden.com for events*

PUBLICATIONS

Boyz 44–020/7025–6100 *newspaper w/ extensive club & event listings*

Gay Times 44–020/7424–7400 *glorious gay glossy*

London—Central

London—Central includes Soho, Covent Garden, Bloomsbury, Mayfair, Westminster, Pimlico & Belgravia

ACCOMMODATIONS

Dover Hotel [GF,WI] 42/44 Belgrave Rd 44–020/7821–9085

Fitz B&B [MW,NS,WI,GO] 15 Colville Place (btwn Charlotte & Whitfield) 44–(0)78/3437–2866

George Hotel [GF] 58–60 Cartwright Gardens (N of Russell Square) 44–020/7387–8777

Hazlitt's [GF,WI] 6 Frith St (Soho Sq) 44–020/7434–1771

Lincoln House [GS,WI,WC] 33 Gloucester Pl, Marble Arch (at Baker St) 44–20/7486–7630 *B&B, full brkfst*

Marble Arch Inn [GF] 49-50 Upper Berkeley St 44–020/7723–7888

Z Hotel [GS,WI] 17 Moor St 44–020/3551–3700 *great Soho location*

BARS

The Admiral Duncan [★MW,NH,TG] 54 Old Compton St (Soho) 44–020/7437–5300 *pub hours*

Bar Soho [GS] 23-25 Old Compton St (at Frith St) 44–020/7439–0439 *noon-1am, till 3am Fri-Sat, from 2pm Sun*

Circa [M,D] 62 Frith St 44–020/7734–6826 *4pm-1am*

City of Quebec [M,NH,OC] 12 Old Quebec St (at Marble Arch) 44–020/7629–6159 *pub hours*

Compton's of Soho [★M,F,WC] 51-53 Old Compton St (at Dean St) 44–020/7479–7961 *noon-midnight, till 10:30pm Sun, cruisy*

Dog & Duck [GS,NH,F] 18 Bateman St (at Frith St) 44–020/7494–0697 *10am-11:30pm*

Duke of Wellington [GS,F] 77 Wardour (Soho) 44–020/7439–1274 *pub hours*

The Edge [★MW,D,F,WC] 11 Soho Square (at Oxford St) 44–020/7439–1313 *3pm-1am, till 3am Fri-Sat, till 11:30pm Sun*

The Escape [★M,D,V] 10-A Brewer St (at Rupert) 44–020/7734–3040 *5pm-3am, clsd Sun-Mon, theme nights*

Freedom Bar [MW,D,F,YC] 66 Wardour St (off Old Compton St) 44–020/7734–0071 *4pm-3am, from 2pm Fri-Sat, 2pm-11:30pm Sun*

Friendly Society [MW,YC] 79 Wardour St (the basement at Old Compton, enter Tisbury Ct) 44–020/7434–3805 *4pm-11pm, till 10:30pm Sun*

G-A-Y Bar [MW,F,V] 30 Old Compton St (at Frith) 44–020/7494–2756 *noon-midnight*

England • EUROPE

Green Carnation [★MW,D,F] 4-5 Greek St (Soho Sq) 44-020/8123-4267 *4pm-2am, inspired by the time & life of Oscar Wilde*

Halfway to Heaven [M,NH,K,C,OC,GO] 7 Duncannon St (at Charing Cross, West End) 44-020/7321-2791 *noon-11pm, clsd Sun*

King's Arms Soho [M,NH,B,F,K,V] 23 Poland St (at Noel, Soho) 44-020/7734-5907 *noon-11pm, till 1am Fri-Sat, 1pm-midnight Sun, popular bear hangout*

Ku Bar/ Ku Klub [MW,K,YC,WI] 30 Lisle St (Leicester Sq) 44-020/7437-4303 *noon-3am, till 10:30pm Sun, also Soho bar at 25 Frith St*

Madam JoJo's [M,E,C] 8-10 Brewer St (at Rupert) 44-020/7734-3040 *Tranny Shack Wed*

The New Bloomsbury Set [GS] 76 Marchmont St (at Tavistock Pl) 44-020/7383-3084 *4pm-11pm, 2pm-10:30pm Sun*

Note: "Pub hours" usually means 11am-11pm Mon-Sat and noon-3pm & 7pm-10:30pm Sun

The Retro Bar [MW,NH,D,K] 2 George Ct (at Strand) 44-020/7321-2811 *pub hours*

Rupert Street [★MW,F,WC] 50 Rupert St (off Brewer) 44-020/7292-7141 *pub hours, upscale "fashiony-types"*

Star at Night [MW,D,F,E] 22 Great Chapel St (at Hollen St) 44-020/7494-2488 *6pm-11:30pm, clsd Sun-Mon*

Vault 139 [M] 139-143 Whitfield St (Warren St) 44-020/7388-5500 *4pm-1am, from 1pm Sun, theme nights/dress codes*

The Village Soho [★M,F,18+,YC] 81 Wardour St (at Old Compton) 44-020/7478-0530 *4pm-1am, till 11:30pm Sun*

The Yard [★M,F,E,YC,WC] 57 Rupert St (off Brewer) 44-020/7437-2652, 871/426-2243 *pub hours*

■NIGHTCLUBS

G-A-Y Club [★M,D,E,YC,$] Under the Arches, Villers St (at Heaven) 44-020/7734-6963 *11pm-3am*

Heaven [★M,D] 9 The Arches (off Villiers St) 44-020/7930-2020 *the mother of all London gay clubs, call for hours/ events*

KU Bar Frith St [M,D] 25 Frith St (at Old Compton St, Soho) 44-020/7287-7986 *noon-11pm, till midnight wknds, 3 floors*

Room Service [M,D] 12-13 Greek St (at Miabella) *10pm Th only*

The Shadow Lounge [M,D,PC] 5-7 Brewer St (Soho) 44-020/7317-9270 *10pm-3am, clsd Sun*

■CAFES

Balans Cafe [★MW] 34 Old Compton St 44-020/7439-3309 *24hrs, terrace*

Caffe Nero 43 Frith St 44-020/7434-3887 *cruisy cafe*

Flat White 17 Berwick St 44-020/7734-0370 *8am-7pm, 9am-6pm wknds, Australian-style cafe*

LJ Coffee House 3 Winnett St (at Rupert) 44-020/7434-1174 *7:30am-7pm, 10am-8pm Sat, from 1pm Sun, cozy cafe, lovely street views*

Milk Bar [WC] 3 Bateman St 44-020/7287-4796 *8am-7pm, till 5pm wknds*

■RESTAURANTS

Cha Cha Moon 15-21 Ganton St 44-020/7297-9800 *noon-11pm, till 10pm Sun, inexpensive Chinese*

Food for Thought [BYOB] 31 Neal St, downstairs (Covent Garden) 44-020/7836-0239 *noon-8:30pm, till 5:30pm Sun, vegetarian*

The Gay Hussar [WC] 2 Greek St (on Soho Square) 44-020/7437-0973 *lunch & dinner, clsd Sun, Hungarian*

Mildred's [★] 45 Lexington 44-020/7494-1634 *noon-11pm, clsd Sun*

Randall & Aubin 16 Brewer St (at Walkers Court) 44-020/7287-4447 *noon-11pm, casual French, good people-watching*

Wagamama Noodle Bar [NS] 10-A Lexington St 44-020/7292-0990 *noon-11pm, Japanese; many locations throughout city*

■BOOKSTORES

Gay's the Word 66 Marchmont St (near Russell Sq Underground) **44-020/7278-7654** *10am-6:30pm, 2pm-6pm Sun*

■RETAIL SHOPS

Prowler Soho [★] 5-7 Brewer St (behind Village Soho bar) **44-020/7734-4031** *11am-10pm, noon-8pm Sun, large gay dept store*

■GYMS & HEALTH CLUBS

Soho Athletic Club [★M] 12 Macklin St (at Drury Ln, Covent Garden) **44-020/7242-1290**

Sweatbox [GO] 1-2 Ramilies St, Soho **44-020/3214-6014** *gym & sauna*

■MEN'S CLUBS

The Sauna Bar Covent Garden [F] 29 Endell St (at Betterton) **44-020/7836-2236** *also bar*

Saunabar Portsea [MO] 2 Portsea Pl (at Connaught St, Marble Arch) **44-020/7402-3385**

■EROTICA

Clone Zone Soho 64 Old Compton St (at Whitcomb) **44-020/7287-1619**

London—West

London—West includes Earl's Court, Kensington, Chelsea & Bayswater

■ACCOMMODATIONS

Cardiff Hotel [GF,WI] 5, 7, 9 Norfolk Sq (Hyde Park) **44-020/7723-9068** *B&B hotel in 3 Victorian townhouses, some share baths*

Millennium Bailey's Hotel [GF] 140 Gloucester Rd (at Old Brompton Rd, Kensington) **44-020/7373-6000** *also restaurant & bar*

Myhotel Chelsea [GF] 35 Ixworth Place (at Elystan St, Chelsea) **44-020/7225-7500, 44-020/7637-2000**

Parkwood Hotel [GF,NS] 4 Stanhope Pl (Marble Arch) **44-020/7402-2241** *full brkfst*

■BARS

Queen's Head [M,NH,F,OC] 27 Tryon St (btwn King's Rd & Sloane Ave, Chelsea) **44-020/7589-0262** *pub hours, professional crowd*

Richmond Arms [MW,D,K,C,DS] 20 The Square (at Princes, Richmond) **44-020/8940-2118** *pub hours, professional crowd*

Ted's Place [M,D,TG,K,DS,V,PC] 305-A North End Rd (at Lillie Rd, Earl's Ct) **44-020/7385-9359** *7pm-midnight, men-only Mon-Wed & Fri, TV/TG from 8pm Th & 6pm Sun, darkroom, cruisy*

West Five (W5) [MW,C,P] 6 Popes Ln (South Ealing) **44-020/8579-3266** *7pm-close, clsd Mon-Tue*

■RESTAURANTS

The Churchill Arms 119 Kensington Church St **44-020/7727-4242** *inexpensive, fantastic Thai, also pub*

The Gate 51 Queen Caroline St, Hammersmith *lunch & dinner, clsd Sun, vegetarian*

Star of India 154 Old Brompton Rd **44-020/737-2901** *lunch & dinner, upscale*

■ENTERTAINMENT & RECREATION

Walking Tour of Gay SOHO 56 Old Compton St (at Admiral Duncan Pub) **44-020/7437-6063** *2pm Sun*

■RETAIL SHOPS

Adonis Art Gallery 1b Coleherne Rd **44-020/3417-0238** *gay art*

Clone Zone [GO] 266 Old Brompton Rd (Earl's Court) **44-020/7373-0598** *11:30am-8pm, 11am-6pm Sun; also Soho location, 64 Old Compton St*

London—North

London—North includes Paddington, Regents Park, Camden, St Pancras & Islington

■ACCOMMODATIONS

Ambassadors Bloomsbury [GF,WI,WC] 12 Upper Woburn Pl (at Euston Rd, Bloomsbury) **44-020/7693-5400**

Ossian Guesthouse [GF] 20 Ossian Rd (at Mt Pleasant Villas, Crouch Hill) 44–020/8340–4331

The Royal Park Hotel [GF,WI] 3 Westbourne Terr (Hyde Park) 44–020/7479–6600

■BARS

The Black Cap [★MW,D,TG,F,K,C] 171 Camden High St (Camden Town) 44–020/7485–0538 *noon-2am, till-3am Fri-Sat*

G-A-Y Late [M] 5 Goslett Yard (Camden Town) *11pm-3am*

The George Music Bar [M,TG,K,C,GO] 114 Twickenham Rd (Isleworth) 44–020/8560–1456 *5pm-close, from noon wknds, cabaret*

King William IV (KW) [★MW,F] 77 Hampstead High St (Hampstead) 44–020/7435–5747 *pub hours, beer garden*

■NIGHTCLUBS

Central Station [★MW,D,TG,F,C,DS,S,V,WI] 37 Wharfdale Rd (King's Cross) 44–020/7278–3294 *noon-1pm, complex includes B&B, terrace*

Club Kali [★MW,D,MR-A,TG,E,$] 1 Dartmouth Park Hill (at The Dome) 44–020/7272–8153 *Dome #) 10pm-3am 3rd Fri, South Asian music*

Dream Bags Jaquar Shoes [MW,D] 32-36 Kingsland Rd 44–020/7729–5830 *noon-1am, jam-packed club in a former shoe shop*

East Bloc [M,D] 217 City Rd (at Shepherdess Walk, Old Street) 44–020/7253–0367 *10pm-4am, till 6am Fri-Sat, clsd Mon-Wed, electro dance club in funky basement space*

Egg [GS,D] 200 York Way (Kings Cross) 44–020/7871–1111 *10pm-6am Sat, until late afternoon Sun*

Habibi London [MW,D] 99-100 Turnmills (Farringdon) *10:30pm last Fri only, Middle Eastern*

■RESTAURANTS

Manna [R] 4 Erskine Rd (at Ainger Rd, Camden) 44–020/7722–8028 *lunch Tue-Sun, dinner nightly, vegetarian*

Providores and Tapa Room 109 Marylebone High St (at New Cavendish St) 44–020/7935–6175 *lunch & dinner, Asian fusion*

■ENTERTAINMENT & RECREATION

Rosemary Branch Theatre [GS,F] 2 Shepperton Rd 44–020/7704–2730 (bar), 44–020/7704–6665 (theatre) *also restaurant & bar, many gay-themed plays*

■MEN'S CLUBS

Pants [MO,V] 37 Wharfdale Rd (King's Cross, at the Underground Club (below Central Station bar)) 44–020/7278–3294 *1pm-6pm, clsd Wed & Sun*

Paradise Spa 17 Crouch Hill 44–020/7263–9675 *1pm-11pm*

Underground Club [★MO] 37 Wharfdale Rd (King's Cross), below Central Station bar) 44–020/7278–3294 *sex parties, theme nights, check web for events*

■EROTICA

Regulation 17a St Albans Pl (Islington Green) 44–020/7226–0665 *fetish gear & toys "made to measure"*

■CRUISY AREAS

Clapham Common [AYOR] *west side of the common near to the south circular road in the wooded area*

Earls Court Graveyard *summers,watch out for the bobbies*

Hampstead Heath [★AYOR]

Highgate Hill *take Archway Tube male sun bathing area at the Highgate Ponds*

London—East

London—East includes City, Tower, Clerkenwell & Shoreditch

■ACCOMMODATIONS

Andaz Liverpool Street [GS,F] 40 Liverpool St (near Bishopsgate, at Liverpool Street Station) 44–020/7961–1234

The Hoxton [GF,NS,WI] 81 Great Eastern St 44–020/7550–1000

■BARS

Bar Music Hall [GF,D,E,F] 134 Curtain Rd (Shoreditch) 44–020/7729–7216 *11am-midnight, till 3am Fri-Sat*

Bethnal Green Working Men's Club [MW,DS,C,TG] 42-44 Pollard Row (at Squirries St, Bethnal Green) 44–020/7739–7170 *performance art & cabaret*

BJ's White Swan [M,D,TG,F,WC] 556 Commercial Rd (near Bromley St) 44–020/7780–9870 *9pm-close, from 6pm Sun, clsd Mon*

Dalston Superstore [GS,NH,F,D,WI] 117 Kingsland High St (at Sandringham Rd) 44–020/7254 2273 *noon-2am*

Joiners Arms [M,E] 116 Hackney Rd 44–020/7739–9854 *5pm-2am, till 4am Fri-Sat, theme nights, live bands*

The Macbeth [GS,E,WI] 70 Hoxton St (at Crondall St, Old St) 44–020/ 7749–0600 *8pm-1am*

The Old Ship [MW,NH,C,WC] 17 Barnes St (Stepney) 44–020/7790–4082 *from 4pm Mon, from 7pm Wed-Sat, from 6pm Sun, clsd Tue*

■NIGHTCLUBS

Backstreet [MO,L,PC] Wentworth Mews, Burdett Rd (at Mile End Rd, Bow) 44–020/8980–8557, 44–020/8980–7880 *10pm-2am, till 3am Fri-Sat, till 1am Sun, clsd Mon-Wed, strict leather/ rubber dress code*

Kaos at Stunners [GS,TG,D,PC] 566 Cable St (at Butcher Row, Cable St Studios, Limehouse) *monthy parties, check www.kaoslondon.com*

Pelucas y Tacones [MW,D,A] 6 Shoreditch High St (at Concrete/ Pizza East) *9pm-2am 2nd Sat only*

Unskinny Bop [W,D,E] 42-44 Pollard Row (Bethnal Green Club) *9pm 3rd Sat only*

Urban Desi [MW,D,MR-A] 18-20 Houndsditch (at Dukes) *11pm-5am 2nd Sat, South Asian*

Way Out Club [MW,D,TG,S,PC,$] 14 New London St (at Gilt Bar, corner of Crutched Friers and Seething Ln) 44–(0)20/7264–1910 *9pm-4am Sat only, TV/TS & their friends*

■CAFES

Pogo Cafe 76 Clarence Rd 44–020/8533–1214 *12:30pm-9pm, from 11am Sun, vegan, volunteer-run, queer social space*

■RESTAURANTS

Bistrotheque 23-27 Waderson St 44–020/8983–7900 *expensive & glamorous, also cabaret shows after dinner*

Bonds Restaurant & Bar 5 Threadneedle St 44–020/7657–8090 *lunch & dinner Mon-Fri, just bar service & snacks wknds, space formerly a bank lobby*

Cafe Spice Namaste 16 Prescott St 44–020/7488–9242 *lunch Mon-Fri, dinner nightly, clsd Sun, Indian*

Canteen 2 Crispin Pl (Spitalfields) 44–(0)84/5686–1122 *place to be for brkfst*

Hoxton Square Bar & Kitchen [E] 2-4 Hoxton Square 44–020/9613–1171 *great dark spot for brkfst*

Les Trois Garçons [R] 1 Club Row (at Bethnal, Shoreditch) 44–020/7613–1924 *6pm-midnight, clsd Sun*

Lounge Lover [R,WC] 44–020/7012–1234 *fancy cuisine in a posh lounge*

Royal Oak 73 Columbia Rd (at Hackney Rd, Old St) 44–020/7729–2220 *4pm-11pm, from noon Fri-Sun*

Saf 63-97 Barkers Building, High Street (in Kensington, at Wholefoods Market) 44–020/7368–4555 *lunch & dinner, also bar till midnight, upscale vegan/ raw food*

■MEN'S CLUBS

Chariots Limehouse [F,V] 574 Commercial Rd (near Limehouse tube) 44–020/7247–5333 *24hrs*

Chariots Shoreditch [★SW,F,V] 1 Fairchild St (Shoreditch) 44–020/7247–5333

E15 Club 6 Leytonstone Rd 44–020/8555–5455 *9am-10pm*

■EROTICA

Expectations 75 Great Eastern St (Shoreditch) 44-020/7739-0292 *rubber store*

London—South

London—South includes Southwark, Lambeth, Kennington, Vauxhall, Battersea, Lewisham & Greenwich

■ACCOMMODATIONS

Griffin House [MW,WI,GO] 22 Stockwell Green 44-020/7096-3332 *2 rental apts near Vauxhall Gay Village & West End*

■BARS

Bar Code [M,D,E,YC] 69 Goding St, Arch 69, Albert Embankment (Vauxhall) 44-020/7582-4180 *7pm-4am Th, 8pm-9am Fri-Sat, 8pm-3am Sun*

Battersea Barge [GF,F,E,C,GO] Riverside Walk Nine Elms Ln (Vauxhall) 44-020/7498-0004 *call for events, cabaret, comedy on the Thames River!*

The Cambria [GS,E,F] 40 Kemerton Rd (Denmark Hill) 44-020/7737-3676 *upmarket eclectic pub, beautiful back garden*

The Eagle London [M,L] 349 Kennington Ln (Vauxhall) 44-020/7793-0903 *9pm-close, from 8pm Sun*

George & Dragon [MW,C] 2 Blackheath Hill (Greenwich) 44-020/8691-3764 *6pm-2am, till 4am Fri-Sat,*

Kazbar [MW,TG,V] 50 Clapham High St (Clapham) 44-020/7622-0070 *5pm-midnight, till 1am Fri-Sat, from 1pm Sun*

The Little Apple [MW,D,TG,F,WC] 98 Kennington Ln 44-020/7735-2039 *noon-midnight, till 3am Sat, terrace*

Prince of Greenwich [M,NH,F,DS] 72 Royal Hill (Greenwich) *4pm-11pm, from noon Fri-Sat*

The Star & Garter [MW,K,WI,WC] 227 High St (Bromley) 44-020/8466-7733 *pub hours*

The Two Brewers [MW,D,K,C] 114 Clapham High St (Clapham) 44-020/7819-9539

■NIGHTCLUBS

Black Sheep Bar [GS,D,A] 68 High St (at S Norwood Hill, Croydon) 44-020/8680-2233

Bootylicious [MW,MR] 1 Nine Elms (at Club Colosseum) *11pm 3rd Sat, popular black gay club*

Fire [GS,D,$] 47B S Lambeth Rd (Vauxhall) 44-020/3242-0040 *after-hours, Sat mornings & Sun afternoons*

Hard On [MW,D,PC] 66 Albert Embankment (at Union, in Vauxhall) 44-020/7533 402 985 *3rd Sat only, fetish party, large play area with equipment*

The Hoist [M,L] Railway Arch 47b&tc, S Lambeth Rd (Vauxhall) 44-020/7735-9972 *S/M club w/ strict dress code, theme nights*

Horse Meat Disco [MW,D,TG] 349 Kennington Ln (at the Eagle) 44-020/7793-0903 *8pm Sun only, popular queer dance party*

Onyx [M,D] 65 Albert Embankment (Vauxhall) *London's hottest Friday night party*

Popstarz [★MW,D,$] 100 Tinworth St (at Hidden bar, Vauxhall) 44-020/7240-1900 *10pm-6am Fri, 4 rooms*

Royal Vauxhall Tavern [M,D,TG,F,WC] 372 Kennington Ln (Vauxhall) 44-020/7820-1222 *8pm-late, 9pm-3am Fri-Sat, 2pm-midnight Sun*

Union Club [M,D] 66 Albert Embankment (Vauxhall) 44-020/7278-3294 *cruise mazes, dark corners, popular last Fri & 3rd Sat*

XXL [MO,D,B] 1 Invicta Plaza (South Bank, at Pulse) 44-(0)78/7261-0981 *10pm-6am Sat, till 3am Wed, "one club fits all"*

■CAFES

Glow Lounge [WI] 6 Cavendish Parade (Clapham Common S Side) 44-020/8673-4471 *noon-11pm, 9:30am-1am Fri-Sat, 10am-7pm Sun*

▪ENTERTAINMENT & RECREATION

Oval Theatre Cafe Bar [F] 52-54 Kennington Oval 44-020/7582-0080 *6pm-11pm Tue-Sat (cafe), inquire about current theatre & art*

▪GYMS & HEALTH CLUBS

Paris Gymnasium [MO] 73 Goding St (behind Vauxhall Tavern, Vauxhall) **44-020/7735-8989**

▪MEN'S CLUBS

Chariots Streatham 292 Streatham High Rd (at Babington Rd, enter rear) 44-020/8696-0929 *24hrs wknds*

Chariots Vauxhall [F,WI] Rail Arches 63-64 (Albert Embankment) 44-020/7247-5333 *24hrs wknds*

Chariots Waterloo [WI] 101 Lower Marsh (at Waterloo Rd) 44-020/7401-8484 *24hrs*

The Locker Room [V] 8 Cleaver St (Kennington) 44-020/7735-6064 *24hrs wknds*

Pleasuredrome [F,V,NS] 124 Cornwall Rd (at Alaska St, Waterloo) 44-020/7633-9194 *24hrs*

Steamworks [V] 309 New Cross Rd 44-020/8694-0606 *24hrs wknds*

▪CRUISY AREAS

Hyde Park [AYOR] *Southeast corner of Hyde Park in the Rose Garden*

FRANCE

PARIS

Note: M°=Métro station

Paris is divided by arrondissements (city districts); 01=1st arrondissement, 02=2nd arrondissement, etc

Paris—Overview

Note: When phoning Paris from the US, dial the country code + the city code + the local phone number

▪INFO LINES & SERVICES

Centre Gai et Lesbien 63 rue Beaubourg 33-1/4357-2147 *drop-in evenings, many groups/ events*

Gay AA 7 rue Auguste Vacquerie (at St George's Anglican) 33-1/4634-5965 *7:30pm Tue, see calendar for other times*

▪ACCOMMODATIONS

Gay Accommodation Paris [GO] 271, rue du Faubourg Saint Antoine 33-1/4348-1382 *studios for rent in central Paris*

▪PUBLICATIONS

Têtu 33-1/5680-2080 *stylish & intelligent LGBT monthly (en français)*

Paris—01

▪ACCOMMODATIONS

Hotel Louvre Richelieu [GS,NS,WI] 51 rue de Richelieu (M° Palais-Royal) 33-1/4297-4620

Hotel Louvre Saint-Honoré [GS,WI,WC] 141 rue Saint-Honoré (at rue du Louvre) 33-1/4296-2323

▪BARS

Le Banana Cafe [★MW,D,E,P,S,YC,WC] 13-15 rue de la Ferronnerie (near rue St-Denis, M° Châtelet) 33-1/4233-3531 *6pm-dawn, go-go boys Th-Sat terrace*

Bar du Kent'z [M] 2-4 rue Vauvilliers (M° Chatelet-Les Halles) 33-1/4221-0116 *1920s style cocktail lounge*

Le Tropic Cafe [MW,D,TG,F,YC,WC] 66 rue des Lombards (M° Châtelet) 33-1/4013-9262 *4pm-5am, tapas, terrace*

Wolf [M,B,V] 37 rue des Lombards (M° Châtelet) 33-1/4028-0252 *5pm-2am*

▪NIGHTCLUBS

Le Club 18 [★M,D,YC,PC,$] 18 rue du Beaujolais (at rue Vivienne, M° Palais-Royal) 33-1/4297-5213 *Wed, Fri-Sat only*

Le Klub [GS,E,MR,$] 14 rue St-Denis (at rue des Lombards, M° Châtelet) 33-1/4508-9625 *8pm-11pm, till 6am Fri-Sat, clsd Wed & Sun, rock & electro*

▪RESTAURANTS

L' Amazonial [MW,C,DS,WC] 3 rue Ste-Opportune (at rue Ferronnerie, M° Châtelet) 33-1/4233-5313 *lunch & dinner, brunch wknds, Brazilian/ int'l, heated terrace*

Au Diable des Lombards 64 rue des Lombards (at rue St-Denis, M° Châtelet) **33-1/4233-8184** *8am-1am, American, full bar, terrace*

Marc Mitonne [E,C] 60 rue de l'Arbre-Sec (M° Les Halles) **33-1/4261-5316** *6pm-2am, clsd Sun-Mon*

La Poule au Pot 9 rue Vauvilliers (M° Les Halles) **33-1/4236-3296** *7pm-5am, clsd Mon & Aug, bistro, French*

Le Velvet 43 rue Saint Honore *Thai restaurant & small gay bar*

■**ENTERTAINMENT & RECREATION**

Forum des Halles 101 Porte Berger (M° Châtelet-Les Halles) **33-1/4476-9656** *underground sports/ entertainment complex w/ museums, theater, shops, clubs, cafes & more*

■**GYMS & HEALTH CLUBS**

Club Med Gym [GS] 147 rue St-Honoré (M° Louvre) **33-1/4020-0303** *day passes available, many locations throughout city*

■**MEN'S CLUBS**

The Hole Next [MO] 87 rue St Honoré (at rue du Roule, M° Chatelet-Les Halles)

Til't [V] 41 rue Ste-Anne (near av de l'Opera, M° Pyramides) **33-1/4296-0743** *noon-7am, bar*

Le Transfert [MO] 3 rue de la Sourdiere (M° Tuileries) *10:30pm-daybreak, open 4pm-10pm some wknds*

■**EROTICA**

Boxxman 2 rue de la Cossonnerie (M° Châtelet) **33-1/4221-4702** *videos, toys & fetish gear, also sex club, internet access*

■**CRUISY AREAS**

Quai des Tuileries [AYOR] on bank of The Seine (M° Louvre) *aka Tata Beach*

Paris—02

■**BARS**

Alex's [M,NH,OC] 2 rue de Marivaux (at boul des Italiens) **33-1/4296-4079** *6pm-close, friendly neighborhood bar, snacks served*

L' Impact [MO,N,V] 18 rue Grenéta (M° Châtelet) **33-1/4221-9424** *8pm-3am, 10pm-6am Fri-Sat, from 3pm Sun, 100% naked, backroom, theme nights, free brkfst wknds*

■**NIGHTCLUBS**

Chez Carmen [GS,D] 53 rue Vivienne *after hours club*

Rex Club [GF,D,E,$] 5 blvd Poissonière (M° Bonne Nouvelle) **33-1/4236-1096** *call for events, clsd August*

■**CAFES**

Stuart Friendly [F] 16 rue Marie Stuart **33-1/4233-2400** *noon-11pm, till midnight Fri-Sat, till 5:30pm Sun, "straight-friendly" cafe*

■**RESTAURANTS**

Le Lezard Cafe 32 rue Etienne Marcel **33-1/4233-2273** *full bar, terrace year round*

Le Loup Blanc [★MW] 42 rue Tiquetonne (M° Etienne-Marcel) **33-1/4013-0835** *7:30pm-midnight, till 1am Sat, also brunch 11am-4:30pm Sun*

■**RETAIL SHOPS**

Galerie au Bonheur du Jour 11 rue Chabanais **33-1/4296-5864** *2:30pm-7:30pm, clsd Sun-Mon, gay art*

■**MEN'S CLUBS**

Euro Men's Club [V,SW,OC] 10 rue St-Marc (M° Bourse) **33-1/4233-9263** *1pm-9pm*

Paris—03

■**ACCOMMODATIONS**

►**Absolu Living** [MW,GO] 236 rue St Martin **33-1/4454-9700** *fully furnished apts in central Paris, short & long-term stays*

Adorable Apartment in Paris [★GF,NS,GO] (M° Rambuteau) **415/287-0306 (US#)**

Hôtel du Vieux Saule [GF] 6 rue de Picardie **33-1/4272-0114**

Hotel Jules & Jim [GS,GO] 11 rue des Gravilliers **33-1/4454-1313**

■BARS

Le CUD Club [★M,D,YC] 12 rue des Haudriettes **33-1/4277-4412** *11pm-6am, till 7am wknds*

Le Dépôt [MO,D,S,YC,$] 10 rue aux Ours (btwn bd de Sébastopol & rue St-Martin, M° Rambuteau) **33-1/4454-9696** *2pm-8am, huge cruise bar on 3 flrs, big backroom*

Le Duplex [MW,NH,S,WI] 25 rue Michel-Le-Comte (at rue Beaubourg, M° Rambuteau) **33-1/4272-8086** *8pm-2am, till 4am Fri-Sat*

One Way [M,NH,B,L,F,V,OC] 28 rue Charlot (at rue des 4 Fils, M° République) **33-1/4887-4610** *5pm-2am, cruisy, darkroom, tapas*

Snax Kfé [M,F] 182 rue Saint Martin (M° Rambuteau) **33-1/4027-8933** *10am-2am, from 3:30pm Sat, clsd Sun*

Le Tango/ La Boite à Frissons [★MW,F] 13 rue au Maire (M° Arts-et-Métiers) **33-1/4272-1778** *10:30pm-5am, clsd Mon*

■RESTAURANTS

La Fontaine Gourmande 11 rue Charlot **33-1/4278-7240** *lunch Tue-Fri & dinner Tue-Sun, French*

■MEN'S CLUBS

The Glove [L] 34 rue Charlot (M° St-Sebastien-Froissard) **33-1/4887-3136** *from 10:30pm, 4:30pm-9pm Sun, clsd Mon-Wed, leather/ rubber/ uniform, also bar, brkfst wknds*

Sun City [SW] 62 Blvd de Sébastopol (M° Rambuteau) **33-1/4274-3141** *noon-6am, cruise bar & sauna, swimming, gym, private cabins*

■EROTICA

Rex 42 rue de Poitou (at rue Charlot, M° St-Sébastien-Froissard) **33-1/4277-5857** *1pm-8pm, clsd Sun, leather & S/M accessories*

Paris—04

■ACCOMMODATIONS

Historic Rentals [GF,NS,WI]
800/537-5408 (US#) *1-bdrm apt*

Hôtel Beaubourg [GS,WI] 11 rue Simon le Franc (btwn rue Beaubourg & rue du Temple, M° Hôtel-de-Ville)
33-1/4274-3424 *next to Centre Pompidou*

Hôtel de la Bretonnerie [GF] 22 rue Ste-Croix-de-la-Bretonnerie (M° Hôtel-de-Ville) **33-1/4887-7763**

Hôtel du Vieux Marais [GF,WI] 8 rue du Plâtre (M° Hôtel-de-Ville)
33-1/4278-4722 *centrally located*

Paris At Home [MW,WI,GO]
33-06/1991-5828 *B&B & apts*

■BARS

Au Mange Disque [M] 15 rue de la Reynie (at Boule de Sebastopol)
33-1/4804-7817 *11am-2am, from 5pm Sun-Mon*

Bears' Den [MO,D,B,V] 6 rue des Lombards (at rue St-Martin, M° Hôtel-de-Ville) **33-1/4271-0820** *4pm-2am, till 4am Fri-Sat, T-dance Sun, darkroom, terrace*

Le Carrefour [M,NH] 8 rue des Archives (at rue de la Verrerie)
33-1/4029-9005 *6am-2am, good location & terrace*

Cox [★M,D,V] 15 rue des Archives (at rue Ste-Croix-de-la-Bretonnerie, M° Hôtel-de-Ville) **33-1/4272-0800**
5:30pm-2am, from 4:30pm Fri-Sun, terrace

Dandy's Cafe [M] 9 rue Nicolas Flamel **33-1/4271-4582** *2pm-2am*

L' Enchanteur [MW,K] 15 rue Michel Lecomte (M° Rambuteau)
33-1/4804-0238 *6pm-6am, clsd Mon*

Le Feeling [MW,NH,YC] 43 rue Ste-Croix-de-la-Bretonnerie (M° Hôtel-de-Ville) **33-1/4804-7003** *3pm-2am*

Les Filles de Paris [GS,D,E,C,K] 57 rue Quincampoix **33-1/4271-7220**
10pm-5am Wed-Sat, also restaurant from 7pm, clsd Sun-Mon, burlesque & drag shows

Le Freedj [MW,D] 35 rue Ste-Croix-de-la-Bretonnerie (at rue du Temple, M° Hôtel-de-Ville) **33-1/4029-4440**
6pm-4am

Full Metal [M,L] 40 rue des Blancs-Manteaux (M° Rambuteau)
33-1/4272-3005 *5pm-4am, till 6am Fri-Sat, from 3pm Sun, well-stocked "hard backroom bar," theme parties, dress code*

Gossip Cafe [MW,F] 16 rue des Lombards (at bd de Sébastopol, M° Châtelet) **33-1/4271-3683** *2pm-6am*

L' Imprevu Cafe [M,NH,F] 9 rue Quincampoix **33-1/4278-2350** *3pm-2am, from 1pm Sun, low key cafe/ bar*

Les Jacasses [★W] 5 rue des Ecouffes (M° St Paul) **33-1/4271-1551** *5pm-2am*

Krash [★MO,L,V] 12 rue Simon Lefranc (at rue du Renard, M° Rambuteau)
33-1/5041-1326 *3pm-5am, till 7am Fri-Sat, sex bar*

Le Mic-Man [M,NH,V] 24 rue Geoffroy-l'Angevin (at rue Beaubourg, M° Rambuteau) **33-1/4274-3980** *noon-2am, open later wknds, friendly bar w/ cruisy cave downstairs*

Morgan Bar [MW,D,WI] 25 rue du Roi de Sicile **33-1/4277-0666**

L' Oiseau Bariolé [MW] 16 rue Saint-Croix-de-la-Bretonnerie (M° Hotel de Ville) **33-1/4272-3712** *5pm-close, quiet*

Okawa [★GS,F,C,P,YC] 40 rue Vieille du Temple (at rue Ste-Croix-de-la-Bretonnerie, M° Hôtel-de-Ville)
33-1/4804-3069 *10am-2am, till 4am Fri-Sat, trendy cafe-bar in 12th- & 13th-c caves*

L' Open Cafe [★MW,F] 17 rue des Archives (at rue Ste-Croix-de-la-Bretonnerie, M° Hôtel-de-Ville) *11am-2am, till 4am Fri-Sat, sidewalk cafe-bar*

La Perle [GS] 78 rue Vieille du Temple **33-1/4272-6993** *Parisian hipster dive bar*

Le Pur Bar/ Titi's Bar [MW,NH] 12 rue de Plâtre (btwn rue du Temple & rue des Archives, M° Hôtel-de-Ville).
33-1/4887-0259 *5pm-2am, cafe-bar*

Quetzal [★M,NH,S,WI] 10 rue de la Verrerie (at rue des Archives, M° Hôtel-de-Ville) **33-1/4887-9907** *5pm-5am, cruise bar, darkroom, terrace*

Le Raidd [M,D,S] 23 rue du Temple (M° Hotel de ville) **33-1/4277-0488** *5pm-5am*

Secteur X [MO] 49 rue des Blancs-Manteaux (at rue du Temple, M° Rambuteau) **33-1-09/5039-5085** *5pm-2am, cruisy, back room*

Sly Bar [M,NH,D] 22 rue des Lombards **33-1/8253-2781**

Les Souffleurs [MW,D,YC] 7 rue de la Verrerie (M° Hôtel-de-Ville) **33-1/6421-8133** *artsy, younger crowd*

Le Spyce [★M,D] 23 rue Ste Croix de la Bretonnerie *6pm-close*

Le Voulez-Vous [MW,F] 18 rue du Temple (M° Hôtel-de-Ville) **33-1/4459-3857** *11am-2am, lounge & restaurant, terrace*

Yono [M,D,E,F] 37 rue Vieille du Temple **33-1/4274-3165** *6pm-2am, 4:30pm-11pm Sun, clsd Mon, cozy basement bar*

Ze Baar [M,NH,F] 41 rue des Blancs Manteaux (at rue du Temple) **33-1/4271-7508** *5pm-2am, also restaurant*

▪CAFES

La Fronde 33 rue des Archives **33-1/4272-2734**

Jul's Cafe 20 rue du Plâtre **33-1/4271-3039** *5pm-2am, also bar*

Le Kofi du Marais [MW] 54 rue Ste-Croix-de-la-Bretonnerie (M° Hôtel de Ville) **33-1/4887-4871** *7pm-midnight, clsd Sun*

▪RESTAURANTS

4 Pat [D] 4 rue St Merri **33-1/4277-2545** *noon-2am, Italian menu*

Les Agités 15 rue de la Reynie (at Boule de Sebastopol) **33-1/8389-5309** *7pm-2am, clsd Sun-Mon*

L' Alimentari 6 Rue des Ecouffes **33-1/4277-2459** *very good small trattoria*

Le Chant des Voyelles 4 rue des Lombards (M° Châtelet) **33-1/4277-7707** *lunch & dinner, traditional French, terrace*

Etamine Cafe 13 rue des Ecouffes (at rue des Rosiers, M° Hotel de Ville) **33-1/4478-0962** *noon-midnight, clsd Mon, also bar*

Le Gai Moulin [MW] 10 rue St-Merri (at rue du Temple, M° Hôtel-de-Ville) **33-1/4887-0600** *noon-midnight*

HD Diner 6-8 Square Ste-Croix de la Bretonnerie **33-1/4277-6934** *11am-midnight, 50's style diner*

La Pas-Sage-Oblige 29 rue du Bourg-Tibourg (M° Hôtel-de-Ville) **33-1/4041-9503** *lunch & dinner, vegetarian*

Les Piétons 8 rue des Lombards (M° Châtelet) **33-1/4887-8287** *noon-2am, Spanish/ tapas, also bar*

Who's 14 rue Saint Merri (M° Rambuteau) **33-1/4272-7597** *noon-6am*

Woo Bar 3 rue Pierre au Lard (M° Rambuteau) **33-1/4272-7597** *noon-6am*

▪ENTERTAINMENT & RECREATION

Gay Beach E end of Ile St-Louis *sunbathing*

▪BOOKSTORES

Les Mots à la Bouche 6 rue Ste-Croix-de-la-Bretonnerie (near rue du Vieille du Temple, M° Hôtel-de-Ville) **33-1/4278-8830** *11am-11pm, 1pm-9pm Sun, LGBT, English titles*

▪RETAIL SHOPS

Bow 5 rue St Merri **33-1/4278-0189** *menswear*

Boy'z Bazaar Collections 5 rue Ste-Croix-de-la-Bretonnerie (at rue Vieille du Temple, M° Hôtel-de-Ville) **33-1/4271-9400** *noon-8:30pm, till 10pm Fri-Sat, clubwear to drag to leather*

Sweetman 17 blvd de Raspail **33-8/4277-1137** *10:30am-7pm, clsd Sun, men's underwear & more*

∎EROTICA

BMC Store 21 rue des Lombards **33-1/4027-9809** *videos, DVDs, toys*

IEM Marais 16 rue Ste-Croix-de-la-Bretonnerie (M° Hôtel-de-Ville) **33-1/4274-0161** *leather, latex, uniforms & fetish gear*

Menstore 8 Square Ste-Croix de la Bretonnerie **33-1/4454-5115**

RoB Paris 8 Square Ste-Croix de la Bretonnerie **33-1/4454-5116** *clsd Sun, leather/ fetish*

∎CRUISY AREAS

Square du Pont de Sully [AYOR] at the end of Ile St-Louis (M° Sully-Morland) *along the side paths at night*

Paris—05

∎RESTAURANTS

Le Petit Prince [★] 12 rue de Lanneau (M° Maubert-Mutualité) **33-1/4354-7726** *7:30pm-midnight, French*

∎ENTERTAINMENT & RECREATION

Open-Air Sculpture Museum Quai Saint-Bernard *along the Seine btwn the Jardin des Plantes & the Institut du Monde Arabe*

Paris—06

∎ACCOMMODATIONS

The Hotel Luxembourg Parc [GS] 42 rue de Vaugirard **33-1/5310-3650**

Paris—07

∎CRUISY AREAS

Champs de Mars [AYOR] (M° Pont-de-l'Alma)

Paris—08

∎ACCOMMODATIONS

François 1er [GF,WI] 7 rue Magellan **33-1/4723-4404** *boutique hotel near les Champs-Elysées, also bar*

∎BARS

Le Day Off [MW,NH,F] 10 rue de l'Isly (M° Gare-St-Lazare) **33-1/4522-8790**

∎NIGHTCLUBS

Escualita [M,D,TG] 128 rue de la Boetie (at Club "MadaM") *midnight Sun only, fabulous tranny dance party, all are welcome*

Le Queen [★GS,D,TG,DS,YC,$] 102 av des Champs-Élysées (btwn rue Washington & rue de Berri, M° Georges-V) **33-8/5389-0890** *midnight-dawn, more gay Sun*

∎MEN'S CLUBS

Steel Club [S,V] 23 rue de Penthièvre (off Champs d'Elysées, M° Miromesnil) **33-1/4561-9028** *noon-1am, maze, theme nights, also bar*

∎EROTICA

Vidéovision 62 rue de Rome (M° Europe) **33-1/4522-5735** *clsd Sun*

Paris—09

∎ACCOMMODATIONS

The Grand [GF,WI] 2 rue Scribe **33-1/4007-3232, 888/424-6835 (US#)** *ultraluxe art deco hotel*

∎BARS

Mec Zone [M,L,V] 27 rue Turgot (M° Anvers) **33-1/4082-9418** *9pm-5am, 2pm-6am wknds, cruisy, theme nights, darkroom*

Rosa Bonheur [GF] 1 rue Botzaris **33-1/4200-0045** *more gay Sun, arrive before 6pm to avoid the line*

∎NIGHTCLUBS

Blacks Blancs Beurs/ KELMA T-Dance [M,D,MR] 11 Place Pigalle (at Folies Pigalle) **33-1/4205-7300** (info-line) *10pm-5am Sun only, R&B & Arabic dance music, check www.kelma.org for location*

Folies Pigalle [GS,D,MR,$] 11 place Pigalle (M° Pigalle) **33-1/4878-5525, 33-1/4280-1203** (BBB info line) *midnight-dawn*

Glass [GS,D] 7 rue Frochot (in Pigalle) **33-9/8072-9883** *7pm-2am, popular with locals Mon*

■Men's Clubs

IDM [★V,WI] 4 rue du Faubourg-Montmartre (at bd St-Martin, M° Grand-Blvds) 33-1/4523-1003 *full gym, jacuzzi, bar*

Paris—10

■Bars

Cafe Moustache [M,NH,F,B,V] 138 rue du Faubourg St-Martin (at bd de Magenta, M° Gare-de-l'Est) 33-1/4607-7270 *4pm-2am, dark-room, patio*

■Men's Clubs

Key West Sauna [★SW] 141 rue Lafayette (M° Gare-du-Nord) 33-1/4526-3174 *noon-1am, till 2am Fri-Sat*

■Erotica

Concorde 27 Blvd de Magenta 33-1/4249-1172 *also at 6 rue du Dahomey*

■Cruisy Areas

Canal St-Martin Jean-Jaurès [AYOR] (M° Jaurès) *on the quais btwn the Jean-Jaurès & Louis-Blanc bridges*

Paris—11

■Accommodations

Le 20 Prieure Hotel [GS,WI] 20 rue du Grand Prieuré 33-1/4700-7414

Le General Hotel [GF,WI,WC] 5/7 rue Rampon 33-1/4700-4157

HI Matic [GF,WI,WC, GO] 71 rue de Charonne *a new urban eco-lodging concept*

Hôtel Beaumarchais [GS,WI] 3 rue Oberkampf (btwn bd Beaumarchais & bd Voltaire, M° Filles-du-Calvaire) 33-1/5336-8686

■Bars

Le Bataclan [GF,E] 50 blvd Voltaire (at Bataclan club, M° Saint Ambroise) 33-1/4314-0030 *live music venue, more gay for the Follivores & Crazyvores*

Follivores/ Crazyvores [MW,D] 50 blvd Voltaire (M° Saint Ambroise) 33-1/4314-0030 *monthly sing-along dance parties; Follivores is 1960s-1990s French pop, Crazyvores is English-speaking; kitsch factor very high!*

In Out [GS,D,YC] 241 rue du Fbg St Antoine 33-9/5241-0037 *5pm-2am, clsd Sun*

■Nightclubs

Les Disquaires [GS,D,E] 6 rue des Taillandiers (M° Bastille) 33-1/4021-9460 *dance bar, live bands*

Scream [M,D,18+] 18 rue du Faubourg-du-Temple (M° République, at Gibus Club) 33-1/4700-7888 *Sat only*

■Cafes

Cannibale Café [WI] 93 Rue Jean-Pierre Timbaud 33-1/4929-0040 *an old-fashioned Parisian café in Belleville*

Le Pause Cafe [F] 41 rue de Charonne 33-1/4806-8033 *8am-2am, 9am-8pm Sun*

■Restaurants

Le Tabarin [MW,P] 3 rue Amelot 33-1/4807-1522 *lunch Sun-Fri, dinner Sun-Sat, full bar*

■Entertainment & Recreation

L' ArtiShow 3 cite Souzy 33-1/4002-1803 *cabaret, also lunch & dinner served*

■Bookstores

Violette & Co [GO] 102 rue de Charonne (at boulevard Voltaire, M° Charonne) 33-1/4372-1607 *11am-8pm, 2pm-7pm Sun, clsd Mon, LGBT & feminist, English titles & art shows*

■Men's Clubs

Boys Video Club 8 rue de Nice (M° Charonne) 33-9/5392-5586 *11am-2am, gloryholes, video rooms, bar*

Bunker [V] 150 rue St-Maur (M° Goncourt) 33-1/5336-7887 *4pm-2am, till 3:30am Fri, till 4:30am Sat, till 1am Sun*

France • EUROPE

Entre Deux Eaux [MO] 45 rue de la Folie Mericourt (at rue Oberkampf) **33-1/4357-7646** *naked sex club for men, theme nights*

Paris—12

■GYMS & HEALTH CLUBS

Atlantide [GS,TG,V] 13 rue Parrot (M° Gare de Lyon) **33-1/4342-2243** *women & transgender welcome, cabins, tanning, also bar*

■CRUISY AREAS

Bois de Vincennes [AYOR]

Paris—13

■CRUISY AREAS

Quai d'Austerlitz [AYOR]

Les Sablières [AYOR] *along the quai d'Austerlitz, from library to blvds Perijheriques, at night only*

Paris—14

■ENTERTAINMENT & RECREATION

Friday Night Fever [GS] Place Raoul Dautry (btwn Montparnasse office tower & Montparnasse train station) *10pm-1am Fri (weather permitting), meet 9:30pm, rollerblading*

■GYMS & HEALTH CLUBS

Amphibi [GS,TG] 73 rue Hallé (at rue Bézout, M° Alesia) **33-1/4047-5090** *sauna where everyone is welcome: gay, straight, bisexual, transgendered*

■MEN'S CLUBS

Les Bains d' Odessa [MO,SW,WI] 5 rue d'Odessa **33-1/4047-8343** *noon-10pm, also bar*

Paris—15

■ACCOMMODATIONS

Platine Hotel [GS,WI,WC] 20 rue Ingénieur Robert Keller **33-1/4571-1515** *Marilyn Monroe and 50's theme*

■BARS

Mix [GS,D,$] 24 rue de l'Arrivée **33-1/5680-3737** *open Th & Sat only*

■NIGHTCLUBS

Le Red Light [GS,D] 34 rue du Depart (M° Montparnasse-Bienvenue) **33-1/4279-9453** *midnight-5am*

■MEN'S CLUBS

Le Steamer [MO] 5 rue du Dr Jacquemarie Clemenceau **33-1/4250-3649** *1pm-midnight, from 3pm wknds, also bar*

Paris—16

■ACCOMMODATIONS

Keppler [GF,WI] 10 rue Keppler **33-1/4720-6505** *near major tourist stops, also bar*

■CRUISY AREAS

Bois de Boulogne [AYOR] (M° Porte Dauphine)

Paris—17

■RESTAURANTS

Sans Gêne 112 rue Legendre **33-1/4627-6782** *5pm-2am, Sun brunch, clsd Mon, also bar*

■MEN'S CLUBS

King Sauna [★] 21 rue Bridaine (near place de Clichy, M° Rome) **33-1/4294-1910** *1pm-7am, bar*

Paris—18

■BARS

Karambole Cafe [GS,F] 10 rue Hegesippe Moreau (M° Place de Clichy or La Fourche) **33-1/4293-3068** *9am-2am, from 6pm Sat, clsd Sun, artsy cafe by day, DJs by night*

Le Tagada Bar [M,F] 40 rue Trois-Frères (M° Abesses) **33-1/4255-9556** *6pm-2am, clsd Mon*

■NIGHTCLUBS

Beardrop [MO,D,B] 75 rue des Martyrs (at Le Divan du Monde club) *monthly bear party*

■ENTERTAINMENT & RECREATION

Michou [F] 80 rue des Martyrs (at Blvd de Clichy, M° Pigalle) **33-1/4606-1604** *infamous drag cabaret, dinner show*

■MEN'S CLUBS

Sauna Mykonos 71 rue des Martyrs
33-1/4252-1546 *noon-11:30pm*

Paris—19

■CAFES

Cafe Cherie [GS,E,WI] 44 Blvd de la
Villette (M° Belleville)
33-1/4202-0205 *8am-2am, live
music & DJs starting at 10pm*

Paris—20

■ACCOMMODATIONS

Mama Shelter [GS,WI] 109 rue de
Bagnolet **33-1/ 4348-4848**

■ENTERTAINMENT &
RECREATION

Père Lachaise Cemetery bd de
Ménilmontant (M° Père-Lachaise)
*perhaps the world's most famous resting
place, where lie such notables as Chopin,
Oscar Wilde, Sarah Bernhardt, Isadora
Duncan, Gertrude Stein & Jim Morrison*

■MEN'S CLUBS

Le Riad [SW,V] 184 rue des Pyrénnès
(M° Gambetta) **33-1/4797-2552**

GERMANY

BERLIN

Berlin is divided into 5 regions:
Berlin—Overview
Berlin—Kreuzberg
Berlin—Prenzlauer Berg—Mitte
Berlin—Schöneberg-Tiergarten
Berlin—Outer

Berlin—Overview

■INFO LINES & SERVICES

Gay AA for English Speakers at
Mann-O-Meter **49-30/787-5188**
5pm Tue, also Gay AA 8pm Th

Mann-O-Meter Bülowstr 106 (at
Nollendorfplatz) **49-30/216-8008**
*5pm-10pm, gay center, cafe and B&B
referral service*

Sonntags Club Greifenhagener Str 28
(S/U-Schönhauser Allee)
49-30/449-7590 *info line 10am-
6pm, LGBT info, also cafe-bar open 5pm-
midnight*

■RESTAURANTS

Paris Bar Kantstrasse152
49-30/313-8052 *bistro & bar*

■ENTERTAINMENT &
RECREATION

Fritz Music Tour 49-30/3087-5633
*visit the haunts of David Bowie, Nina
Hagen, Iggy Pop & Rammstein, among
other popular musical acts*

The Jewish Museum Berlin Lindenstr
9-14 **49-30/2599-3300** *10am-8pm,
till 10pm Mon*

Schwules (Gay) Museum U6/U7
Mehringdamm 61 **49-30/6959-9050**
*2pm-6pm, till 7pm Sat, clsd Tue, guided
tours 5pm Sat (in German)*

■PUBLICATIONS

Blu 49-30/443-1980 *free monthly
gay magazine*

Siegessäule 49-30/235-5390 *free
monthly LGBT city magazine (in
German), awesome maps*

Berlin—Kreuzberg

■ACCOMMODATIONS

Hotel Transit [GF] Hagelberger Straße
53-54 **49-30/789-0470** *hotel in
restored 19th-c factory*

The Mövenpick Hotel [GF,F]
49-30/230-060 *convenient location,
space-agey bar*

■BARS

Barbie Bar [MW] Mehringdamm 77 (at
Kreuzbergstr) **49-30/6956-8610**
3pm-close, lounge, terrace

Bierhimmel [GS,YC] Oranienstr 183 (U-
Kottbusser Tor) **49-30/615-3122**
9am-3am, from 1pm wknds

Galander [GS] Grossbeerenstr 54 (nr
Mehringdamm) **49-30/2850-9030**
6pm-2am

Mobel Olfe [★MW]
Reichenbergerstrasse 177 (at Skalitzer)
49-30/2327-4690 *8pm-close Tue-
Sun*

Germany • *EUROPE*

Pork at Ficken 3000 [M,D,L,V,YC] Urbanstr 70 (at Hermannplatz) **49-30/6950-7335** *10pm Sun, cruisy, large darkroom*

Rauschgold [MW] Mehringdamm 62 (U-Mehringdamm) **49-30/7895-2668** *8pm-close*

Roses [★MW,TG,YC] Oranienstr 187 (at Kottbusser Tor) **49-30/615-6570** *10pm-close*

Sofia [MW] *open 9am, from 11am Sat & 8pm Sun*

■NIGHTCLUBS

SchwuZ (SchwulenZentrum) [★M,D,E,WC] Mehringdamm 61 (enter through Café Sundstroem) **49-30/629-088** *from 11pm Fri-Sat*

Serene Bar [MW,D] Schwiebusser Str 2 **49-30/6904-1580**

SO 36 [★GS,D,TG,S,V,YC,WC] Oranienstr 190 (at Kottbusser Tor) **49-30/6140-1306, 49-30/6140-1307** *theme nights, also live music venue*

■CAFES

Drama Mehringdamm 63 **49-30/6746-9562** *opens 2pm, also bar & terrace*

Melitta Sundström [MW,WC] Mehringdamm 61 (at Gneisenaustr, U-Mehringdamm) **49-30/692-4414** *10am-11pm, terrace, also gay bookstore*

Sudblock [★MW,E] Admiralstrasse 1-2 *10am-7pm*

■RESTAURANTS

Amrit Oranienstr 202 **49-30/612-5550** *noon-1am, Indian*

Kaiserstein Mehringdamm 80 **49-30/7889-5887** *9am-1am*

Little Otik [GO] Graefestrasse 71 **49-30/5036-2301** *7pm-11pm, clsd Sun-Tue*

Locus [★MW] Marheinekeplatz 4 **49-30/691-5637** *10am-1:30am, Mexican, full bar*

Restaurant Z Friesenstr 12 **49-30/692-2716** *5pm-1am, Greek/ Mediterranean*

■MEN'S CLUBS

Böse Buben Sachsendamm 76-77 **49-30/6270-5610** *4pm Wed, from 9pm Fri-Sat*

Triebwerk [M,L,V,WC] Urbanstr 64 (at Leinestr, U-Hermannplatz) **49-30/6950-5203** *10pm-close, cruise bar w/ darkroom*

■SEX CLUBS

Club Culture Houze [GS] Görlitzer Str 71 (off Skalitzer Str) **49-30/6170-9669** *gay male theme nights Mon, Th & Sun, open to all other nights*

Berlin—Prenzlauer Berg-Mitte

■ACCOMMODATIONS

Arte Luise Kunsthotel [GF] Luisenstr 19 (Mitte) **49-30/284-480** *near River Spree*

Le Moustache [M] Gartenstr 4 (at Rosenthaler Platz, U-Oranienburger Tor) **49-30/281-7777** *also Moustache Bar open 9pm-3am, clsd Sun-Tue*

Schall & Rauch Pension [MW] Gleimstr 23 (at Schönhauser Allee) **49-30/339-723** *also bar & restaurant*

■BARS

Bärenhöhle [M,B,BW,WI] Schönhauser Allee 90 **49-30/4473-6553** *4pm-6am, from 8pm Sat, from 6pm Sun*

Besenkammer Bar [MW] Rathausstr 1 (at Alexanderplatz, under the S-Bahn bridge) **49-30/242-4083** *24hrs, tiny "beer bar"*

Betty F*** [MW,NH] Mulackstrasse 13 (at Gormannstrasse)

Cafe Amsterdam [GS,TG,F,YC,WC] Gleimstr 24 (at Schönhauser Allee) **49-30/448-0792, 49-30/231-6796** *9am-3am, till 5am Fri-Sat, terrace, also pension*

Cocks [M] Greifenhagener Strasse 33 (at Wisbyer Str) **49-152/2941-6510** *10pm-close, from 8pm Wed & Sun, cruisy*

DarkRoom [MO,L] Rodenbergstr 23 (at Schönhauser Allee) **49-30/444-9321** *10pm-6am, uniform bar, darkroom, theme parties wknds*

Greifbar [MO,L,V] Wichertstr 10 (at Greifenhagener Str, S/U-Schönhauser Allee) **49-30/444-0828** *10pm-6am, darkroom*

Grosse Freiheit 114 [MO] Boxhagener Str 114 (in Friedrichshain) **49-30/2977-6713** *10pm-4am, clsd Mon, darkroom*

Marietta [MW] Stargarder Str 13 **49-30/4372-0646** *10am-2am, till 4am Sat-Sun*

Perle [MW] Sredzkistrasse 64 *7pm-close, clsd Sun-Mon*

Privatleben [MW] Rhinowerstr 12 (at Gleimstra) **49-30/4320-5851** *from 6pm, small friendly bar*

Reingold [GS,F,E,GO] Novalisstr 11 (U-Oranienburger Str) **49-30/4985-3450** *from 7pm, clsd Sun-Mon, more gay Th*

Sanatorium 23 [GS] Frankfurter Allee 23 **49-30/4202-1193** *from 3pm, cafe/ bar, also guesthouse*

Schoppenstube [M,D] Schönhauser Allee 44 (at Eberswalder Str) **49-30/442-8204** *9pm-close, from 10pm Fri-Sun, clsd Mon, terrace*

Sharon Stonewall [MW,WI] Kleinen Präsidentenstr 3 (at Hackeschen Market) **49-30/2408-5502** *8pm-2am, till 4:30am Fri-Sat, clsd Mon*

Stahlrohr [MO] Paul Robeson Strasse 50 **49-70/803-7691** *10pm-close, sex parties*

Zum Schmutzigen Hobby/ Nina's Bar [MW,D,DS,TG,V] Revalerstrasse 99 *6pm-close*

■NIGHTCLUBS

Berghain [★MW,D,E] Am Wrietzener Bahnhof (off Strasse der Pariser Kommune, near Ostbahnhof station) **49-30/2936-0210** *converted power station is now dance club*

Chantals House of Shame [MW,D] *11pm Th*

GMF [M,D,DS] Alexanderstrasse 7 (at Week End, U-Alexanderplatz) **49-30/2809-5396** *Sun only 11pm-close*

Irrenhouse [MW,D,DS,TG] Am Friedrichshain 33 (at Geburtstagsklub) *3rd Sat, Nina Queer's monthly drag party*

KitKat Club [GS,D,C] Kopenickerstrasse 76 (enter on Bruckenstrasse) **49-30/2173-6841** *8pm-close Th, 11pm-8am Fri-Sat, also S/M club*

Klub International [M,D,$] Karl-Marx-Allee 33 (at Kino International, U-Schillingstr) **49-30/2475-6011** *11pm-close 1st Sat*

Spy Club [MW,D] Friedrichstr/ Unter den Linden (at Cookies) **49-30/2809-5396** *last Sat only*

■CAFES

Anna Blume Kollwitzstrasse 83 **49-30/4404-8749** *8am-2am, great brkfst*

Café Berger [★WI] Senefelderstr 4 (btwn Helmholtzplatz & Kollwitz area) **49-30/4320-5851** *10am-7pm*

November [MW] Husemannstr 15 (at Sredzkistr) **49-30/442-8425** *10am-2am, cafe-bar, terrace, brkfst buffet wknds*

■RESTAURANTS

Anda Lucia Savignyplatz 2 **49-30/5471-0271** *6pm-10pm, tapas bar*

The Kosher Classroom Auguststrasse 11-13 **49-30/3300-6070** *traditional Jewish cuisine, vegan meals and specialties from the sea*

Rice Queen Danziger Str 13 (U-Eberswalder Str) **49-30/4404-5800** *5pm-11pm, from 2pm wknds, Asian fusion*

Schall & Rauch Wirtshaus [MW] Gleimstr 23 (at Schönhauser Allee) **49-30/443-3970** *10am-close*

Thüringer Stuben Stargarder Str 28 (at Dunckerstr, S/U-Schönhauser Allee) **49-30/4463-3339** *4pm-1am, from noon Sun, full bar*

■MEN'S CLUBS

Gate Sauna [F,V,WI] Hannah Arendtstrasse 6 (U-Mohrenstr) **49-30/229-9430** *24hrs wknds, also bar*

Lab.oratory [MO] Am Wrietzener Bahnhof (downstairs at Berghain nightclub) *hardcore sex club*

Treibhaus Sauna [F,V,YC] Schönhauser Allee 132 (U-Eberswalder Str) **49-30/448-4503** *24hrs wknds, also bar*

■EROTICA

Blackstyle Seelower Str 5 (S/U-Schönhauser Allee) **49-30/4468-8595** *clsd Sun, latex & rubber wear*

Duplexx Schönhauser Allee 131 (U-Eberswalder Str) **49-30/4849-4200** *videos, cruisy*

Leathers [V] Schliemannstr 38 (U-Eberswalder Str) **49-30/442-7786** *noon-8pm*

XXL Schönhauser Alle 98 **49-30/3289-8222** *large cruising cinema*

■CRUISY AREAS

Volkspark Friedrichshain [AYOR] (at Märchenbrunnen, in Friedrichshain)

Berlin—Schöneberg-Tiergarten

■ACCOMMODATIONS

Arco Hotel [GS,WC,GO] Geisbergstr 30 (at Ansbacherstr, U-Wittenbergplatz) **49-30/235-1480** *centrally located*

Art-Hotel Connection [MO,L,WI,WC,GO] Fuggerstr 33 (corner Welser Str, near U-Wittenbergplatz) **49-30/2102-18800** *also special "fantasy" apt for kink & S/M types*

Axel Hotel Berlin [M,WI] Lietzenburger Str 13/15 **49-30/2100-2893**

Bananas Berlin [M,WI,GO] Geisbergstr 41 **49-30/2196-1768** *central location in a quiet area*

Berlin B&B [MW,WI,GO] *apt rentals, 2 locations*

Hotel California [GF] Kurfürstendamm 35 (at Knesebeckstr, U-Uhlandstr) **49-30/880-120** *cafe/bar*

Hotel Hansablick [GF,WI] Flotowstr 6 (at Bachstr, off Str des 17 Juni) **49-30/390-4800**

Hotel Zu Hause [GS,WI,GO] Kleistrasse 35 (at Eisenacher Str) **49-(0)30/2362-6522**

RoB Play 'n Stay Leather Apartments [MO,GO] Fuggerstr 19 (behind RoB Berlin shop) **49-30/2196-7400** *in the heart of Berlin's gay scene, playroom*

Tom's Hotel [M] Motzstr 19 (at Eisenacherstr, U-Nollendorfplatz) **49-30/2196-6604**

■BARS

Ajpnia eV [MO] Eisenacher Str 23 (U-Eisenacher Str) **49-30/2191-8881** *sex parties*

Blond [GS,F,WI] Eisenacher Str 3a (at Fuggerstr, U-Nollendorfplatz) **49-30/6640-3947** *10am-2am*

Blue Boy Bar [M,V] Eisenacher Str 3a (at Fuggerstr, U-Nollendorfplatz) **49-30/218-7498** *24hrs, ring bell, hustlers; also Fugger-Eck [GS,NH], 1pm-6am, clsd Sun, terrace*

Bull [★MO,L,V] Kleistr 35 (at Eisenacherstr, U-Nollendorfplatz) **49-30/9608-5760** *24hrs, darkroom, very cruisy*

CDL [MO] Hohenstauffenstr 58 **49-30/3266-7855** *open 7pm, from 9pm Fri-Sat, from 3pm Sun, sex club*

Eldorado [M,F,E] Motzstr 20 (U-Nollendorfplatz) **49-30/8431-6901** *24hrs, terrace*

Green Door [GS] Winterfeldstr 50 **49-30/152-515** *6pm-3am, till 4am Fri-Sat, cute decor*

Hafen [★M,TG,S,YC] Motzstr 19 (at Eisenacher Str, U-Nollendorfplatz) **49-30/211-4118** *8pm-close*

HarDie's Kneipe [M,NH,F,OC] Ansbacherstr 29 (in Wittenberplatz) **49-30/2363-9841** *noon-midnight, till 2am wknds*

Heile Welt [★MW] Motzstrasse 5 **49-30/2191-7507** *6pm-4am*

Incognito [MW,TG] Hohenstauffenstr 53 (off Luther Str, U-Viktoria Luise Platz) **49-30/2191-6300** *6pm-4am*

Kumpelnest 3000 [GF,D,TG,YC] Lützowstr 23 (at Potsdamer Str, U-Kurfürstenstr) **49-30/261-6918** *5pm-5am, till 8am Fri-Sat, popular wknds*

Mutschmann's [MO,L] Martin-Luther-Str 19 (at Motzstr, U-Nollendorfplatz) **49–30/2191–9640** *10pm-close, from 11pm Fri-Sat, clsd Sun-Mon, darkroom*

Neues Ufer [MW,OC] Haupstrasse 157 (U-Bahn Kleistpark) **49–30/7895–7900** *11am-2am, clsd wknds, city's oldest gay bar*

New Action [★MO,L] Kleiststr 35 (at Eisenacherstr, U-Nollendorfplatz) *10pm-5am, till 7am Fri-Sat, from 5pm Sun, fetish/ cruise bar*

Pinocchio Musikcafe [M] Fuggerstr 3 (at Schönhauser Allee, U-Nollendorfplatz) **49–30/2362–0333** *2pm-2am, till 4am wknds*

Prinz Knecht [★M] Fuggerstr 33 (U-Nollendorfplatz) **49–30/236–27444** *3pm-2am*

Reizbar [M] Motzstr 30 (Kalckreuthstr) **49–30/2363–7981** *9pm-close, from 8pm Tue, clsd Mon*

Scheune [★MO,L,V] Motzstr 25 (at Nollendorfplatz) **49–30/213–8580** *9pm-7am, till 9am Fri-Sat, uniform bar, theme nights*

Storks [M,F] Kleiststrasse 7 **49–30/2362–4700** *10pm-late, 24hrs wknds*

Tabasco [M,F,AYOR] Fuggerstr 3 (at Schönhauser Allee, U-Nollendorfplatz) **49–30/214–2636** *6pm-6am, 24hrs wknds, hustlers*

Tom's Bar [★MO,L,V] Motzstr 19 (at Eisenacherstr, U-Nollendorfplatz) **49–30/213–4570** *10pm-6am, open later Fri-Sat, very cruisy, downstairs maze*

Tramps [M,NH,B,L] Eisenacher Str 6 (atFuggerstr) *24hrs*

Vielharmonie [M,F] **49–30/3064–7302** *6pm-close*

Woof [M,B] Fuggerstr 37 (at Ansbacherstr) **49–30/2360–7870** *10pm-4am, 9pm-2am Sun*

■NIGHTCLUBS

Connection [★MO,D,L,V,$] Fuggerstr 33 (at Art-Hotel Connection) **49–30/218–1432** *11pm-close Fri-Sat only, cruisy, darkroom; also sex shop & cinema*

Propaganda [M,D,DS] Nollendorfplatz 5 (at Goya Theater) *2nd Sat only*

■CAFES

Cafe Berio [★WC] Maaßenstr 7 (at Winterfeldtstr, U-Nollendorfstr) **49–30/216–1946** *7am-midnight, from 8am wknds, brkfast all day, terrace, also bar*

Cafe Savigny Grolmanstr 53–54 (at Savignyplatz) **49–30/4470–8386** *9am-midnight, full bar, terrace*

■RESTAURANTS

Café des Artistes Fuggerstr 35 **49–30/2363–5249** *noon-midnight, great food & nice staff*

Diodata Goltzstrasse 51 **49–30/2191–7884** *11am-11pm, 10am-3pm Sun, Viennese*

Fritz & Co Wittenbergplatz *organic snack bar, look for the rainbow flags*

Gnadenbrot Martin-Luther-Str 20a **49–30/2196–1786** *3pm-1am, cheap & good*

Hamburger Mary's [DS,K,WC,GO] Lietzenburger Str 15 (in theAxel Hotel) **49–30/2100–2895** *brkfst & dinner, full bar*

More [★] Motzstrasse 28 (at Martin-Lutherstrasse) **49–30/2363–5702** *9am-midnight*

Sissi Motzstr 34 **49–30/2101–8101** *great Austrian food, terrace & location*

■ENTERTAINMENT & RECREATION

Xenon Kino Kolonnenstr 5-6 **49–30/7800–1530** *gay & lesbian cinema*

■BOOKSTORES

Bruno's [GO] Bülowstrasse 106 (U-Nollendorfplatz) **49–30/6150–0385**

Prinz Eisenherz Buchladen [WC] Lietzenburger Str 9 A (at Welserstr) **49–30/313–9936** *10am-8pm, clsd Sun, LGBT books, magazines, DVDs "in all languages"*

■MEN'S CLUBS

Apollo Sauna [F,V] Kurfürstenstr 101 (in Charlottenburg, U-Wittenbergplatz) **49–30/213–2424**

■EROTICA

Beate Uhse International
Joachimstaler Str 4 (at Kantstr, at Erotic Museum) **49-30/886-0666**

City Men Fuggerstr 26
49-30/218-2959

The Jaxx Club [V] Motzstr 19 (U-Nollendorfplatz) **49-30/213-8103**

Mazeworld Kurfürstenstr 79 (at Keithstr) **49-30/4405-0540** *noon-5am*

Pool Berlin [V] Schaperstr 11 (at Joachimsthaler Str, in Wilmersdorf, U-Kurfürstendamm) **49-30/214-1989** *clsd Sun, gay emporium*

RoB Berlin Fuggerstr 19
49-30/2196-7400 *clsd Sun, leather/fetish shop*

■CRUISY AREAS

Tiergarten [AYOR] along Str de 17 Juni (near the Siegessäule monument)

Berlin—Outer

■ACCOMMODATIONS

Charlottenburger Hof [GF,F] Stuttgarter Platz 14 (at Wilmersdorfer Str) **49-30/329-070** *also bar*

Romantik Hotel Kronprinz Berlin [GF,WC] Kronprinzendamm 1 (at Kurfürstendamm, in Halensee) **49-30/896-030**

■BARS

Himmelreich [MW] Simon Dach Str 36 (off Warschauer Str, in Friedrichshain, U-Frankfurter Tor) **49-30/2936-9292** *from 7pm Mon-Fri, 2pm-close wknds*

Monster Ronsons [★MW,K] Warschauerstr 34 **49-30/8975-1327** *7pm-4am*

Silver Future [MW] Weserstr 206 (Neukölln) **49-30/7563-4987** *2pm-2am, till 3am Th-Sat*

■NIGHTCLUBS

Die Busche [★MW,D,S,$] Warschauer Platz 18 **49-30/296-0800** *10pm-5am, till 7am Fri-Sat, clsd Tue & Th, terrace*

■CAFES

Schrader's [GO] Malplaquetstr 16b (at Utrechter Str, Wedding) **49-30/4508-2663** *also bar*

■RESTAURANTS

Cafe Rix Karl-Marx-Str 141 (in Neükölln) **49-30/686-9020** *9am-midnight, till 1am Fri-Sat, Mediterranean, also bar*

Kurhaus Korsakow Grunbergerstrasse 81 (in Friedrichshain)
49-30/5473-7786 *5pm-close, from 9am wknds, clsd Mon*

■CRUISY AREAS

Volkspark Wilmersdorf [AYOR]

IRELAND

Dublin

■INFO LINES & SERVICES

AA 105 Capel St (at Outhouse)
353-1/873-4999 *6pm Tue & 7:45pm Fri*

Gay Switchboard Dublin
353-1/872-1055 *6:30pm-9:30pm, 4pm-6pm wknds*

Outhouse 105 Capel St
353-1/873-4999 *LGBT community center, cafe, library, meetings*

■ACCOMMODATIONS

The Arlington Hotel Temple Bar [GS] 16 Lord Edward St **353-1/670-8777** *conveniently located with restaurant & bar*

The Clarence [GF,WI,WC] 6-8 Wellington Quay **353-1/407-0800** *owned by Bono & The Edge of U2*

The Dylan [★GS] Eastmoreland Place **353-1/660-3000** *restaurant & bar*

Fitzwilliam Hotel [GF] St Stephen's Green **353-1/478-7000**

Inn On the Liffey [MW,WI,GO] 21 Upper Ormond Quay **353-1/677-0828**

The Merchant House [GS,WI,GO] 8 Eustace St (Temple Bar Area)
353-1/633-4477 *free access to Basic Instincts Cruise Zone*

Waterloo House [GS,F] 8-10 Waterloo Rd **353-1/660-1888** *restaurant & bar*

◼BARS

Bears Upstairs [M,B] Capel St (at Jack Nealon's Pub) 1st Sat 9pm

The Dragon [MW,D] 64-45 S Great Georges St 353-1/478-1590 8pm-3am, clsd Sun, Tue & Wed

Front Lounge [★MW,D,TG,K] 33 Parliament St 353-1/670-4112 noon-11:30pm, till 2am Sat

The George aka Bridies [★MW,D,K,DS,E] 89 S Great George St 353-1/478-2983 2pm-2:30am, till 11:30pm Mon-Tue, till 1am Sun

Honeypot & Bears Upstairs [M,B] check www.dublinbears.ie for events

Panti Bar [MW,D,F,DS,WC] 7-8 Capel St 353-1/874-0710 5pm-close, theme nights

◼NIGHTCLUBS

Mother [MW,D] Exchange St (at Copper Alley, Arlington Hotel) 10:30pm Sat only

Nimhneach [GS] fetish & BDSM party, strict dress code, see www.nimhneach.ie for dates & location

Prhomo [MW,D] 6 Wicklow St (at Base Ba) 10:30pm Th only

◼CAFES

3Fe 54 Middle Abbey St (Twisted Pepper Bldg) 353-1/661-9329 10am-7pm, noon-6pm Sun, run by barista champion

Irish Film Institute Bar & Restaurant 6 Eustace St (in Temple Bar) 353-1/679-5744 lunch & dinner, next to independent cinema

Lovinspoon Cafe 13 N Frederick St 353-1/804-7604 7am-6pm, clsd Sun (except summers)

◼RESTAURANTS

Brasserie Sixty6 [WI] 66 S Great Georges St 353-1/400-5878 lunch, dinner, brkfst wknds

La Cave 28 S Anne St 353-1/679-4409 12:30pm-close, from 6pm Sun, French

The Chameleon 1 Lower Fownes St 353-1/671-0362 5pm-11pm, from 3pm Sun, clsd Mon, Indonesian

Cornucopia 19 Wicklow 353-1/677-7583 8:30am-9pm, till 10:30pm Sat, from noon Sun, affordable vegetarian

DavyByrnes 21 Duke St 353-1/677-5217 11am-11pm, famous pub frequented by James Joyce

L' Ecrivain [P,R] 109A Lower Baggot St 353-1/661-1919 lunch Mon-Fri, dinner Mon-Sat, clsd Sun

Eden 7 South William St 353-1/670-6887 lunch & dinner, wknd brunch, patio dining

F.X. Buckley 2 Crow St 353-1/671-1248 5:30pm-close, steak & seafood

Fire Restaurant Mansion House, Dawson St 353-1/676-7200 5:30pm-close, noon-3pm jazz lunch Sat, clsd Sun

Gruel 68A Dame St 353-1/670-7119 lunch & dinner

Odessa [★DS] 14 Dame Court 353-1/670-7634 also nightclub

Shack 24 E Essex St 353-1/679-0043 lunch & dinner

Town Bar & Grill 21 Kildare St 353-1/662-4800 lunch & dinner, clsd Sun-Mon, modern Irish brasserie

Trocadero 4 Saint Andrew St 353-1/677-5545 5pm-midnight, clsd Sun

The Winding Stair Restaurant [YC] 40 Lower Ormond Quay 353-1/872-7320 lunch & dinner, Irish, also bookshop

◼ENTERTAINMENT & RECREATION

Irish Queer Archive 2 Kildare St (National Library of Ireland)

◼BOOKSTORES

Chapters Bookstore Ivy House, Parnell St 353-1/872-3297

The Winding Stair Bookshop 40 Lower Ormond Quay 353-1/872-7320 10am-6pm, till 7pm Th-Sat, from noon Sun, also restaurant

■PUBLICATIONS

GCN (Gay Community News) Unit 2 Scarlet Row, Essex St W, Temple Bar, 8 353–1/675–5025 *monthly LGBT newspaper, many resources*

■MEN'S CLUBS

The Boilerhouse [★F,V] 12 Crane Ln 353–1/677–3130 *noon-6am, 24hrs wknds*

The Dock Sauna [WI] 21 Upper Ormond Quay (at the Inn On the Liffey) 353–1/677 0828 *10am-4am, 24hrs wknds; also gay B&B*

ITALY

Rome

Note: M°=Metro station

■INFO LINES & SERVICES

Circolo di Cultura Omosessual Mario Mieli Via Efeso 2a (M° San Paolo) 800/110–611 *4pm-7pm Mon-Fri, switchboard, meetings & discussion groups*

Gay Help Line 800/713–713 *4pm-8pm, clsd Sun*

■ACCOMMODATIONS

2nd Floor B&B [MW,WI,GO] via San Giovanni in Laterano 10 39–06/9604–9256 *in the heart of Rome's gaylife*

58 Le Real de Luxe [GS,NS,WI,WC] Via Cavour 58, 4th flr (near Colosseum) 39–06/482–3566, 0039/347–182–9387 (cell) *B&B inn a few steps from Colosseum*

Albergo Del Sole al Pantheon [GF] Piazza della Rotonda 63 39–06/678–0441

Ares Rooms [GF] Via Domenichino 7 39–06/474–4525, 39–340/278–1248 (cell) *some shared baths*

B&B In And Out Rome [GS,NS,WI,WC,GO] Via Arco del Monte (at Viale Trastevere) 39–339/784–0653

Best Place [MW,R] Via Turati 13 39–329/213–2320

Claridge Hotel [GF] Via Liegi 62 39–06/845–441 *near Borghese park, gym w/ sauna & Turkish bath*

Daphne Veneto [GF,NS] Via di San Basilio 55 39–06/8745–0086 *cozy inn in heart of historical Rome; also Daphne Trevi at Via degli Avignonesi 20*

Discover Roma [MW] Via Castelfidardo 50 39–06/4470–3154

Domus Valeria B&B [MW,WI,GO] Via del Babuino 96, Apt 14 (Spanish Square) 39–339/232–6540

Franklin [GF] Via Rodi 29 39–06/3903–0165 *music-themed hotel w/ CD library*

Gayopen B&B [GS,GO] Via dello Statuto 44, Apt 18 (at Via Merulana, Piazza Vittorio) 39–06/482–0013 *full brkfst*

Hotel Altavilla [GF] Via Principe Amedeo 9 39–06/474–1186

Hotel Edera [GF,WI] Via A Poliziano 75 39–06/7045–3888

Hotel Labelle [MW] Via Cavour 310 39–06/679–4750 *near the Roman Forum*

Hotel Malu [GF,WI] Via Principe Amedeo 85/a 39–06/9603–1250 *near Termini Station*

Hotel Scott House [GF] Via Gioberti 30 39–06/446–5379

Hotel Welcome Piram [MW] Via Amendola 7 39–06/4890–1248 *hot tubs*

Nicolas Inn [GF,NS,WI] Via Cavour 295 (at Via dei Serpenti) 39–06/9761–8483, 39–338/937–8387 *near the Colosseum & Roman Forum*

Pensione Ottaviano [GF] Via Ottaviano 6 39–06/3973–8138 *in quiet area near St Peter's Square, hostel*

The Rainbow B&B [MW,WI] Viale Giulio Cesare 151 39–06/347–507–0344 (cell), 39–06/348–3343689

Relais Conte di Cavour de Luxe B&B [GF,WI] Via Farini 16 (at Via Cavour) 39–06/482–1638 *great location*

Relais le Clarisse [GS,NS,WI,GO] Via Cardinale Merry del Val 20 (at Viale Trastevere) **39-06/5833-4437** *on historic site in central Rome*

Scalinata di Spagna [GS,NS,WI] Piazza Trinità dei Monti 17 (M° Piazza di Spagna) **39-06/6994-0896, 39-06/679-3006 (booking #)** *roof garden*

Valadier [GF,WI] Via della Fontanella 15 **39-06/361-1998** *2 restaurants & piano bar*

■Bars

Coming Out [★MW,D,TG,F,E,K,V,GO] Via San Giovanni in Laterano 8 (near Colosseum) **39-06/700-9871** *7:30pm-2am*

Garbo [MW,F,GO] Vicolo di Santa Margherita 1a (in Trastevere, Tram 8) **39-06/581-2766, 39-34/9815-1446** *10pm-3am, clsd Mon, cocktail bar*

Gate/ Frequency [MO,D,NS,V] Via Tuscolana, 378/380 **39-06/7840-335, 39-340/693-9719** *10pm-3am, till 4am Fri-Sat, sex club, naked bear parties*

Il Giardino dei Ciliegi [MW,F,E] Via dei Fienaroli 4 **39-06/580-3423** *5pm-2am, from 1pm Sun, tea salon & bar*

Hangar [★M,D,L,S,V,YC] Via In Selci 69 (M° Cavour) **39-06/488-1397** *10:30pm-2am, clsd Tue, cruisy, dark room*

Skyline [M,L,F,S,V,PC] Via Pontremoli 36 **39-06/700-9431** *10:30pm-3am, till 4am Fri-Sat, clsd Mon, 2-floor American bar, backroom, darkroom, monthly sex parties*

■Nightclubs

L' Alibi [★MW,D,S,YC] Via di Monte Testaccio 40-44 (M° Piramide) **39-06/574-3448** *11pm-4am, clsd Mon-Tue, theme nights, rooftop garden in summer*

Amigdala [MW,D] Via delle Conce 14 (at Rising Love) *Sat only, check site for dates,www.amigdalaqueer.it*

Il Diavolo Dentro [M,L,N] Largo Itri 23-24 **39-392/490-7271** *11pm-5am Fri-Sat, 6pm-3am Sun, clsd Mon-Th & month of August*

Frutta e Verdura [MW,D] Via Placido Zurla 68-70 (in Casilina) **39-347/244-6721 (English), 39-348/879-7063 (Italian)** *4:30am-10am Sun & public holiday evenings, darkroom*

Gorgeous [M,D] Via del Commercio 36 (at Alpheus) **39-06/574-7826** *11pm-5am Sat*

Muccassassina [★MW,D,S,YC,$] via di Portonaccio 212 (at Qube) **39-06/541-3985** *10:30pm-5am Fri only (Sept-June)*

■Cafes

Oppio Caffè [★MW,F,E] Via delle Terme di Tito 72 **39-06/474-5262, 39-347/510-8594 (cell)** *brkfst, lunch & dinner, open 24hrs in Aug, full bar, terrace w/ great view*

■Restaurants

Asino Cotto Ristorante [R,GO] Via dei Vascellari 38 (in Travestere, Tram 8) **39-06/589-8985** *lunch & dinner, clsd Mon, creative gourmet Mediterranean*

La Carbonara Via Panisperna 214 **39-06/482-5176** *lunch & dinner, clsd Sun, classic Roman cuisine since 1906*

Città in Fiore [MW] Via Cavour 269 **39-06/482-4874** *lunch Th-Mon, dinner nightly, Chinese*

Ditirambo Piazza della Cancelleria 74-75 (near Campo dei Fiori) **39-06/687-1626**

La Focaccia Via della Pace 11 **39-06/6880-3312** *11am-2am, pizza*

Gelateria San Crispino Via Panetteria 42 (near Trevi Fountain) **39-06/679-3924** *noon-12:30am, till 1:30am Fri-Sat, clsd Tue, gelato!*

Mater Matuta [★] Via Milano 47 (basement) **39-06/4782-5746** *lunch Mon-Fri, dinner nightly, also wine bar*

Osteria del Pegno [WC] Vicolo Montevecchio 8 (Plaza Navona) **39-06/6880-7025** *lunch & dinner, clsd Wed winter, large pizza selection*

Ristorante da Dino Via dei Mille 10 (at Piazza Indipendenza) **39-06/491-425** *clsd Wed*

La Taverna di Edoardo II [MW,WC]
Vicolo Margana 14 39-06/6994-2419
7:30pm-midnight, clsd Tue, full bar

■ENTERTAINMENT & RECREATION

Gay Village 39-06/753-8396 *gay summer festival*

■RETAIL SHOPS

Hydra II [L] Via Urbana 139
39-06/489-7773 *leather, vinyl, club-wear, western, vintage & more*

Souvenir Rainbow via San Giovanni in Laterano 26 39-06/7720-4593 *9am-9pm, gay gifts*

■GYMS & HEALTH CLUBS

Roman Sport Center [GS] Via del Galoppatoio 33 39-06/320-1667

■MEN'S CLUBS

Apollion Sauna [V] Via Mecenate 59a (at Via Carlo Botta, M° Piazza Vittorio) 39-06/482-5389 *gym equipment, bar*

EMC-Europa Multiclub [V,YC,SW,PC] Via Aureliana 40 (M° Repubblica)
39-06/482-3650 *1pm-midnight, 24hrs wknds, fountain whirlpool, gym & bar*

Gate [MO] 39-392/795-9441 *theme nights, bear parties*

K Sex Club [L,V,PC] Via Amato Amati 6-8 (at Via Dulceri), Casilina
39-06/2170-1268,
39-349/587-6731 *10pm-4am, S/M club & bar, maze, darkroom*

Mediterraneo Sauna [F,V,PC] Via Pasquale Villari 3 (btwn Via Merulana & Via Labicana, M° Manzoni)
39-06/7720-5934 *3 flrs, full bar, jacuzzi, maze*

■EROTICA

Alcova Piazza Sforza Cesarini 27 (at Corso Vittorio Emanuele II)
39-06/686-4118 *fetish shop*

■CRUISY AREAS

Colosseo Quadrato [AYOR] (near Palazzo della Civiltà del Lavoro park)

Monte Caprino Park [AYOR] Capidoglio Hill

Villa Borghese [AYOR] (in front of the Architecture Academy)

■TRAVEL AGENTS

Through Eternity Tours Italy [GO] Via Astura 2/B 39-06/700-9336 *walking tours of Rome, get 10% off by using the code "Damron10"*

NETHERLANDS

AMSTERDAM

Amsterdam is divided into 5 regions:
Amsterdam—Overview
Amsterdam—Centrum
Amsterdam—Jordaan
Amsterdam—Rembrandtplein
Amsterdam—Outer

Amsterdam—Overview

■INFO LINES & SERVICES

COC-Amsterdam Rozenstraat 14 (at Prinsengracht, in the Jordaan)
31-20/626-3087 *info line 10am-5pm, also cafe 8pm-11:30pm Wed-Fri*

Gay/ Lesbian Switchboard
31-20/623-6565 *noon-10pm, 4pm-8pm wknds, English spoken*

Pink Point Westermarkt
(Raadhuisstraat & Keizersgracht, in the Jordaan by Homomonument)
31-20/428-1070 *10am-6pm; info on Homomonument & general LGBT info; friendly volunteers; souvenirs & gifts*

■NIGHTCLUBS

Fuckin' Pop Queers/ Ultrasexi/ Multisexi [MW,D,TG,A] *monthly queer dance parties at different clubs around the city*

Rapido/ Celebrate [M,D] *popular monthly dance parties, check clubrapido.com for dates & locations*

UNK [MW,D] Admiraal de Ruijterweg 56 B (at Club 8) 31-20/685-1703 *4th Sat only, electro/ queer dance party*

■ENTERTAINMENT & RECREATION

The Anne Frank House Prinsengracht 263-267 (in the Jordaan)
31-20/556-7105 (recorded info),
31-20/556-7100 *the final hiding place of Amsterdam's most famous resident*

Boom Chicago Leidseplein 12 (Leidseplein Theater) 31–20/423–0101 (tickets) *English-language improv comedy; distributes free Boom! guide*

Gay and Lesbian History Walks 31–20/628–689–775 *mention Damron & you get 10% off*

MacBike Stationsplein 12 (next to Centraal Station) 31–20/620–0985 *rental bikes & map for self-guided tour of Amsterdam's gay points of interest, also 4 other locations*

The van Gogh Museum [WC] Paulus Potterstr 7 (on the Museumplein) 31–20/570–5200 *under renovations, check www.vangoghmuseum.nl for updates*

■PUBLICATIONS

Gay News Amsterdam 31–20/679–1556 *bilingual paper, extensive listings*

Gay & Night 31–20/788–1360 *free monthly bilingual entertainment paper w/ club listings*

Amsterdam—Centrum

■ACCOMMODATIONS

Amsterdam B&B Barangay [GS,NS,WI,GO] 31–6/2504–5432 *near tourist attractions*

Amsterdam Central B&B [MW,WI,GO] Oudebrugsteeg 6-II (at Warmoesstraat) 31–62/445–7593 *in 16th-c guesthouse, also apts, full brkfst*

Anco Hotel-Bar [MO,L,N,NS,WI,GO] OZ Voorburgwal 55 (across from the Oude Kerk) 31–20/624–1126 *1640 canal house, also bar*

Crowne Plaza Amsterdam City Centre [GF,F,SW,WI,WC] NZ Voorburgwal 5 31–20/620–0500, 877/227–6963 (US#)

Hotel The Exchange [GS,WI,WC] Damrak 50 31–20/523–0088

Mauro Mansion [GS] Geldersekade 16 (at OZ Kolk)

NH City Centre Hotel [GF,WI,WC] Spuistraat 288–292 31–20/420–4545

NH Grand Hotel Krasnapolsky [GF,WI,WC] Dam 9 (at Warmoesstraat) 31–20/554–9111

Palace B&B [GS,NS,WI,GO] Spuistraat 224 31–6/3169–3878 *1794 bldg w/ indoor garden*

Victoria Hotel Amsterdam [GF,SW,WI,NS,WC] Damrak 1-5 (opposite Centraal Station) 31–20/623–4255, 800/777–1700 (US#)

Winston Hotel [GF] Warmoesstraat 129 31–20/623–1380 *hipster hotel w/ alt-rock bar & decor*

■BARS

Argos [★MO,L] Warmoesstraat 95 (at Oudekerksplein) 31–20/622–6595 *10pm-3am, till 4am Fri-Sat, popular darkroom, strict dress code, theme nights*

De Barderij [M,NH,OC] Zeedijk 14 (at OZ Kolk) 31–20/420–5132 *noon–1am, till 3am Fri-Sat, large brown café*

Boys Club 21 [MO,S] Spuistraat 21 31–20/622–8828 *noon-2am, boys' house (escorts) w/ full bar & live strip shows*

Cafe Mandje [GS] Zeedijk 63 (at Stormsteeg) 31–20/622–5375 *originally opened in 1927 as Amsterdam's first gay bar by dyke-on-bike Bet van Beeren*

Cozy Bar [M,NH,D] Sint Jacobsstraat 8 31–20/420–8321

The Cuckoo's Nest [MO,L,V,18+] NZ Kolk 6 (at NZ Voorburgwal) 31–20/627–1752 *1pm-1am, till 2am Fri-Sat, cruisy, large play cellar*

Dirty Dick's [MO,L] Warmoesstraat 86 (at Oudebrugsteeg) 31–20/627–8634 *4pm-3am, till 4am Fri-Sat, very cruisy, darkroom*

De Engel Next Door [M] Zeedijk 23-25 (at OZ Kolk) 31–20/427–6381 *1pm-1am, till 3am Fri-Sat, clsd Mon-Tue*

De Engel van Amsterdam [M] Zeedijk 21 (at OZ Kolk) 31–20/427–6381 *1pm-1am, till 3am Fri-Sat, patio*

Getto [★MW,F,K] Warmoesstraat 51 (at Niezel) 31–20/421–5151 *4pm-1am, from 7pm Tue, 1pm-midnight Sun, clsd Mon, also restaurant*

Prik [★MW,F] Spuistraat 109 31–20/320–0002 *4pm-1am, till 3am Fri-Sat, patio*

Queen's Head [M,DS,S] Zeedijk 20 (off Nieuwmarkt) 31-20/420-2475 *4pm-1am, till 3am Fri-Sat, bingo Tue*

The Web [★M0,B,L,F,V] St Jacobsstraat 6 (btwn Nieuwendijk & NZ Voorburgwal) 31-20/623-6758 *1pm-1am, till 2am Fri-Sat, darkroom, [B] Sat, rooftop patio*

■NIGHTCLUBS

Bear-Necessity [M,D,B] Singel 460 (at Odeon Theater) *Sat bi-monthly party*

Club Fuxxx [★M0,D,S,V] Warmoesstraat 96 31-20/456-45-879 *11pm-4am, till 5am Fri-Sat, cruisy darkroom*

Club Stereo [GS,D,E] Jonge Roelensteeg 4 (at Kalvertstraat) 31-20/770-4037 *7pm-1am, till 3am Fri-Sat*

■CAFES

Dampkring Haarlemmerstraat 44 31-20/638-0705 *smoking coffeeshop*

Gary's Late Night [★] TT Vasumweg 260 31-20/637-3643 *noon-3am, till 4am Fri-Sat, fresh muffins & bagels*

Puccini Bomboni [★] Staalstraat 17 31-20/626-5474 *If you love chocolate, do we have a cafe for you!*

■RESTAURANTS

Cafe de Jaren [GS,YC] Nieuwe Doelenstraat 20-22 31-20/625-5771 *10am-1am, full bar, terrace*

Cafe de Schutter Voetboogstraat 13-15 (upstairs) 31-20/622-4608 *noon-1am, till 3am Fri-Sat, popular local hangout, plenty veggie, full bar, terrace*

Cafe Latei [WI] Zeedijk 143 (in Red Light District) 31-20/625-7485 *8am-5pm, from 9am Sat, from 11am Sun, Indian food*

Greenwoods Singel 103 (near Dam Square) 31-20/623-7071 *English-style brkfst & tea snacks*

Hemelse Modder [★WC,G0] Oude Waal 11 31-20/624-3203 *6pm-10pm, popular w/ lesbians & gay men, full bar*

Japans Restaurant An Weteringschans 76 (at Vijzerstraat) 31-20/624-4672 *lunch & dinner, clsd Sun-Mon, Japanese, full bar, patio, cash only*

Krua Thai [WC] Staalstraat 22 31-20/622-9533 *5pm-10:30pm*

Het Land van Walem [WC,G0] Keizersgracht 449 31-20/625-3544 *lunch & dinner, int'l, local crowd, canalside terrace*

Maoz Muntplein 1 31-20/420-7435 *11am-1am, till 3am wknds, vegetarian*

't Sluisje [★MW,TG,DS] Torensteeg 1 31-20/624-0813 *6pm-close, clsd Mon-Tue, steak house, full bar, drag shows nightly, cash only*

Song Kwae Kloveniersburgwal 14 (near Nieuwmarkt & Chinatown) 31-20/624-2568 *1pm-10:30pm, Thai, full bar, terrace*

■BOOKSTORES

The American Book Center [WC] Spui 12 31-20/625-5537 *10am-8pm, till 9pm Th, 11am-6:30pm Sun, large LGBT section*

Boekhandel Vrolijk Gay & Lesbian Bookshop [★] Paleisstraat 135 (at Spuistraat, near Dam Square) 31-20/623-5142 *11am-6pm, 10am-5pm Sat, from 1pm Sun*

■RETAIL SHOPS

Gays & Gadgets Spuistraat 44 31-20/330-1461 *gifts, gadgets, clothing, cards*

Magic Mushroom Spuistraat 249 31-20/427-5765 *11am-7pm, till 8pm Fri-Sat, "smartshop": magic mushrooms & more; also Singel 524*

Sissy Boy Kalverstraat 199 31-20/638-9305 *French & Dutch designers duke it out on the racks*

■GYMS & HEALTH CLUBS

Splash Looiersgracht 26-30 31-20/624-8404 *gym & wellness center*

■EROTICA

4men Spuistraat 21 31-20/625-8797 *cinema, darkroom, all-day ticket, private cabin, large sexshop*

Adonis [V] Warmoesstraat 92 31-20/627-2959 *10am-1am, till 3am wknds*

Alfa Blue Nieuwendijk 26
31–20/627-1664 *porn store & video theater*

Black Body [WC] Spuistraat 44
31–20/626-2553 *clsd Sun, rubber clothing specialists, also leather, toys, DVDs & more*

Christine Le Duc Spui 6
31–20/624-8265

Condomerie Het Gulden Vlies
Warmoesstraat 141 **31–20/627-4174** *11am-6pm, clsd Sun, condoms in every size or color or configuration*

DeMask Zeedijk 64 **31–20/423-3090** *11am-7pm, clsd Sun, rubber & leather clothing*

Drake's of LA [★] Damrak 61
31–20/627-9544 *videos & magazines, video cabins, cinema upstairs*

Mr B [WC] Warmoesstraat 89
31–20/788-3060 *leather & rubber, also tattoo & piercing*

RoB Accessories Warmoesstraat 71
31–20/428-3000 *leather, rubber, toys*

Le Salon Nieuwendijk 20-22 (near the Spui) **31–20/622-6565** *sex supermarket, cinema*

Amsterdam—Jordaan

■ACCOMMODATIONS

Chic and Basic Amsterdam [GF,NS,WI]
Herengracht 13-19 (at Brouwersgr)
31–20/522-2345 *"the quiet hotel," full brkfst*

The Dylan [GF,WI] Keizersgracht 384 (at Runstraat) **31–20/530-2010** *also restaurant*

Hotel Acacia [GF,WI] Lindengracht 251 (at Lijnbaansgr) **31–20/622-1460** *"homey hotel in heart of Jordaan*

Hotel Pulitzer [GF,F,WI] Prinsengracht 315-331 (at Reestraat)
31–20/523-5235

Hotel Rembrandt Centrum [GS]
Herengracht 255 (at Hartenstraat)
31–20/622-1727 *canalside hotel near Dam Square*

Maes B&B [★GS,NS,WI,GO] Herenstraat 26 (at Keizersgr) **31–20/427-5165** *renovated 18th-c home btwn 2 canals*

Marnixkade Canalview Apartments
[MW,NS,WI,GO] **31–6/1012-1296**

Sunhead of 1617 [GS,NS,WI,GO]
Herengracht 152 (at Leliegracht & Raadshuisstraat) **31–20/626-1809** *full brkfst*

■BARS

Cafe de Gijs [GF,TG] Lindengracht 249 (at Lijnbaansgr) **31–20/638-0740,** **31–6/2537-3674** *4pm-1am, 1st Wed of month social gathering for transvestites & transsexuals, from 6pm*

■NIGHTCLUBS

Jet Lounge [★GS,D,E] Groen van Prinstererstraat 41 (3 blks W of Westerpark) **31–20/684-1126** *6pm-1am, till 3am Fri-Sat, clsd Sun-Mon*

de Trut [★MW,D,YC] Bilderdijkstraat 165 (at Kinkerstraat) **31–20/612-3524** *10pm-3am Sun only, hip underground party in legalized squat, doors close when it's full (btwn 11:30pm-midnight) so come early*

■CAFES

Cafe 't Smalle Egelantiersgracht 12
31–20/623-9617 *10am-1am, till 2am wknds, brown cafe, full bar, outdoor seating*

Lab111 [E] Arie Biemondstrat 111
31–20/616-9994 *noon-1am, till 3am Fri-Sat*

■RESTAURANTS

Bojo [★] Lange Leidsedwarsstraat 49-51 (near Leidseplein)
31–20/622-7434 *11am-9pm, from 4:30pm wknds, Indonesian*

De Bolhoed Prinsengracht 60 (at Tuinstr) **31–20/626-1803** *vegetarian/ vegan*

Burger's Patio 2e Tuindwarsstr 12
31–20/623-6854 *6pm-1am, Italian, plenty veggie*

Foodism Nassaukade 122 (at Hugo de Grootstraat) **31–20/486-8137** *5pm-10pm, good Mediterranean food; funky & fun*

Freud [E] Spaarndammerstraat 424
31–20/688-5548 *lunch & dinner, clsd Sun-Mon*

Netherlands • EUROPE

Granada [E] Leidsekruisstraat 13
31–20/625–1073 *5pm-close, Spanish, tapas, also bar*

De Vliegende Schotel Nieuwe
Leliestraat 162 **31–20/625–2041**
4pm-11:30p, vegetarian/ vegan

■**ENTERTAINMENT &
RECREATION**

Homomonument Westermarkt
(Raadhuisstraat/Keizersgracht) *moving
sculptural tribute to lesbians & gays
killed by Nazis*

■**RETAIL SHOPS**

Dare to Wear Buiten Oranjestraat 15
31–20/686–8679 *piercing, jewelry &
accessories*

House of Tattoos Haarlemmerdijk
130c **31–20/330–9046** *11am-6pm,
from 1pm Sun, great tattoos, great
people*

■**SEX CLUBS**

Sameplace [GS,TG,D] Nassaukade 120
31–20/475–1981 *[MO] Mon night
only, theme nights, darkroom*

Amsterdam— Rembrandtplein

■**ACCOMMODATIONS**

Amsterdam House [GF] 's
Gravelandseveer 7 (at
Kloveniersburgwal) **31–20/626–2577
(office), 31–20/624–6607 (hotel)**
hotel, apts & houseboats

Dikker & Thijs Fenice Hotel [GF]
Prinsengracht 444 (at Leidsestraat)
31–20/620–1212 *great location,
restaurant & bar*

Eden Hotel [GF,WI,WC] Amstel 144
31–20/530–7878 *3-star hotel overlooking Amstel River, brasserie*

Hotel Amistad & Apts
[★M,NS,WI,WC,GO] Kerkstraat 42 (at
Leidsestraat) **31–20/624–8074**

Hotel de l'Europe [GF,SW,WI] Nieuwe
Doelenstraat 2-8 **31–20/531–1777**
grand hotel on the River Amstel

Hotel Monopole [GF] Amstel 60 (at
Kloveniersburgwal) **31–20/624–6271**
also Cafe Rouge

Hotel Orlando [GF,GO] Prinsengracht
1099 (at Amstel River)
31–20/638–6915

Hotel The Golden Bear
[★MW,B,OC,WI,GO] Kerkstraat 37 (at
Leidsestraat) **31–20/624–4785**

Hotel Waterfront [GF] Singel 458 (at
Koningsplein) **31–20/421–6621**

ITC Hotel [MW,WI,GO] Prinsengracht
1051 (at Utrechtsestraat)
31–20/623–0230, 31–20/623–1711
*18th-c canal house, great location, also
bar & lounge*

Seven Bridges [★GF] Reguliersgracht
31 (at KeizersGracht) **31–20/623–1329**
*small & so elegant, canalside, view of 7
bridges (surprise!), brkfst brought to you*

■**BARS**

Amstel Fifty Four [M,NH] Amstel 54
(at Kloveniersburgwal)
31–20/623–4254 *5pm-1am, till 3am
Fri-Sat, classic brown cafe gone gay*

Cafe Dwarsliggertje [M,NH]
Reguliersdwarsstraat 105 *2pm-1am, till
3am wknds*

Cafe Mon Ami [M,NH,OC] Amstelstraat
34 (at Amstel) **31–20/626–2243**
5pm-1am, till 3am Fri-Sat, clsd Mon

Cafe Rouge [M,NH] Amstel 60 (at
Kloveniersburgwal) **31–20/420–9881**
4pm-1am, till 3am wknds

Chez Rene [MW,GO] Amstel 50 (at
Kloveniersburgwal) **31–20/420–3388**
8pm-3am, till 4am Fri-Sat

Het Dwarsliggertje Cafe [M,NH]
Reguliersdwarsstraat 105
31–61/677–8599 *3pm-1am, till 3am
Fri-Sat*

Entre Nous [MW,NH] Halvemaansteeg
14 (at Reguliersbreestr)
31–20/623–1700 *9pm-3am, till 4am
Fri-Sat*

Eve [★GS,D,F,YC] Reguliersdwarsstraat
44 (at Geelvinckssteeg)
31–20/689–7070 *4pm-1am, till 3am
Fri-Sat, also restaurant*

Habibi Ana [MW,MR,E] Lange
Leidsedwarsstraat 93
31–06/2192–1686 *7pm-1am, till 3am
Fri-Sat, clsd Mon-Tue, Arabian clientele,
Arabian & int'l music, bellydancing
shows wknds*

Hot Spot Cafe [M,NH] Amstel 102 (at Bakkersstr) **31–20/622–8335** *9pm-3am, from 8pm Fri-Sun*

Lellebel [★M,NH,TG,F,K,DS] Utrechtsestraat 4 **31–20/427–5139** *8pm-3am, till 4am Fri-Sat, drag bar, very trans-friendly*

Ludwig [M,D] Reguliersdwarsstraat 37 (at St Jorisstraat) **31–20/625–3661** *7pm-1am, till 3am Fri-Sat, clsd Mon-Tue, terrace*

Mankind [MW,F,WI] Weteringstraat 60 (at Weteringschans) **31–20/638–4755** *noon-11pm, clsd Sun, cafe-bar, canal-side terrace*

Le Montmartre [★M,NH,YC] Halvemaansteeg 17 (at Reguliersbreestr) **31–20/625–5565** *5pm-1am, till 4am Fri-Sat, very Dutch*

Music Box [MO,AYOR] Paardenstraat 9 (near Rembrandtplein) **31–20/620–4110** *9pm-2am, till 3am Fri-Sat, clsd Mon, hustlers*

Reality [M,NH,MR-L] Reguliersdwarsstraat 129 **31–20/639–3012** *8pm-3am, till 4am Fri-Sat, Surinamese*

Soho [★MW,D,YC] Reguliersdwarsstraat 36 (at St Jorisstraat) **31–20/422–3312** *5pm-3am, till 4am Fri-Sat, British pub 1st flr, lounge upstairs, happy hour 10pm-11pm*

Spijker [★MO,NH,L,V] Kerkstraat 4 (at Leidsegracht) **31–20/341–7366** *4pm-1am, till 3am Fri-Sat, darkroom*

Taboo [MW,NH] Reguliersdwarsstraat 45 **31–20/775–3963** *5pm-3am, from 4pm wknds*

Het Wapen van Londen [★M,YC] Amstel 14 (at Vijzelstraat) **31–6/1539–5317** *4pm-1am, till 2am Fri-Sat, clsd Mon, cafe-bar, terrace*

◼NIGHTCLUBS

Church [MO,D] Kerkstraat 52 (at Leidsestraat) *clsd Mon, theme nights w/ dress code, open to all on Th for Blue party*

Club Roque [MW,D] Amstel 178 (at Wagenstraat) *11pm-5am, clsd Sun-Tue*

F*cking Pop Queers [M,D] Korte Leidsedwarsstraat 18 (at Jimmy Woo) *2nd Sat*

Studio 80 [GS,D] Rembrandtplein 17 (at Amstelstraat) **31–20/521–8333** *9pm-5am Th-Sat*

◼CAFES

Betty, Too Reguliersdwarsstraat 29 (at Leidsestraat) *10am-1am, occasional gay events*

Happy Feelings Kerkstr 51 **31–20/423–1936** *smoking coffeeshop*

Lunchroom [GO] Reguliersdwarsstraat 31 (at Koningsplein) **31–20/622–9958** *10am-7pm, terrace open in summer*

The Other Side [M,GO] Reguliersdwarsstr 6 (at Koningsplein) **31–72/625–5141** *11am-1am, gay smoking coffeeshop*

◼RESTAURANTS

Garlic Queen [R] Reguliersdwarsstr 27 **31–20/422–6426** *6pm-close, clsd Mon-Tue, even the desserts are made w/ garlic!*

Golden Temple [NS] Utrechtsestr 126 **31–20/626–8560** *5pm-9:30pm, vegetarian & vegan*

De Huyschkaemer Utrechtsestraat 137 **31–20/627–0575** *noon-1am, till 3am wknds*

Rose's Cantina [★] Reguliersdwarsstr 40 (near Rembrandtplein) **31–20/625–9797** *5pm-11pm, Tex-Mex, full bar*

Saturnino [GO] Reguliersdwarsstr 5 **31–20/639–0102** *noon-midnight, Italian, full bar*

◼MEN'S CLUBS

Thermos [★SW,F,WI] Raamstraat 33 (at Raamplein) **31–20/623–9158** *noon-8am, cruisy sauna on 5 flrs, also bar & cafe*

◼EROTICA

B1 Cinema Reguliersbreestraat 4 **31–20/623–9546** *9am-midnight, from noon Sun*

The Bronx Kerkstraat 53-55 (near Leidseplein) **31–20/623–1548** *huge gay shop for sex supplies & cinema*

Amsterdam—Outer

■ACCOMMODATIONS

Amsterdam B&B [GF,NS,WI,GO] Roeterstraat 18 (at Nieuwe Achtergracht) **31–20/624–0174** *powered by green energy*

Between Art & Kitsch [GF,WI] Ruysdaelkade 75-2 (at Daniel Stalpertstraat) **31–20/679–0485** *near museums*

Blue Moon B&B [GS,WI,GO] Weteringschans 123A (at Weteringstraat) **31–20/428–8800**

The Collector B&B [GF,WI,GO] De Lairessestr 46 hs (in museum area) **31–6/1101–0105 (cell), 31–20/673–6779** *full brkfst*

Conscious Hotel Vondelpark [GS,WI,WC] Overtoom 519 **31–20/820–3333**

Freeland Hotel [GF,WI,GO] Marnixstraat 386 (at Leidsegracht) **31–20/622–7511** *full brkfst*

Hemp Hotel Frederiksplein 15 (at Achtergracht) **31–20/625–4425** *only in Amsterdam: sleep on a hemp mattress, eat a hemp roll for brkfst or drink hemp beer in the Hemp Temple bar*

Hotel Arena [★GF,WI] Gravesandestraat 51 (at Mauritskade) **31–20/850–2400** *hotel in former orphanage, popular nightclub in restored chapel*

Hotel Kap [GS,GO] Den Texstraat 5 **31–20/624–5908** *bikes available to rent, also self-catering apt*

Hotel Rembrandt [GF,NS] Plantage Middenlaan 17 (at Plantage Parklaan) **31–20/627–2714** *beautiful brkfst rm w/ 17th-c art, near Rembrandtplein*

Lloyd Hotel [★GF,F,WI] Oostelijke Handelskade 34 **31–20/561–3636, 31–20/561–3604** *hip hotel for all budgets in cool Eastern Harbor area*

NL Hotel [GS,WI,GO] Nassaukade 368 (at B Toussaintstraat) **31–20/689–0030**

Prinsen Hotel [GF] Vondelstraat 36-38 (near Leidseplein) **31–20/616–2323**

■NIGHTCLUBS

Melkweg [GS,E] Lijnbaansgracht 234 (at Leidseplein) **31–20/531–8181** *popular live-music venue, also restaurant/ cafe, cinema, theater*

■RESTAURANTS

De Peper Overtoom 301 **31–20/412–2954** *7pm-close Sun, Tue & Th-Fri, sliding scale, volunteer-run vegan cafe, also monthly queer parties*

De Waaghals Frans Halsstraat 29 **31–20/679–9609** *5pm-9:30pm, vegetarian*

■CRUISY AREAS

Oosterpark [AYOR] at Linnaeusstr (behind the Tropenmuseum)

Sarphatipark [AYOR] *near baseball field*

Vondelpark [AYOR] at Vondelstr *in the rose garden*

Westerpark [AYOR] *at night, N of lake*

SCOTLAND

Edinburgh

■INFO LINES & SERVICES

The Edinburgh LGBT Centre [WI] 58A & 60 Broughton St **44–0131/556–9471**

The Edinburgh LGBT Centre [WI] 58A & 60 Broughton St **44–0131/556–9471**

LGBT Centre for Health & Wellbeing 9 Howe St **44–0131/523–1100**

■ACCOMMODATIONS

94DR [GS,WI,GO] 94 Dalkeith Rd **44–131/662–9286** *guesthouse central location*

Alva House [M,NS,GO] 45 Alva Pl **44–0845/257–1475** *near gay bars & nightlife*

Ardmor House [★MW,NS,WC,GO] 74 Pilrig St (at Leith Walk) **44–0131/554–4944** *Victorian in city center near gay life*

Averon Guest House [GF,NS] 44 Gilmore Pl **44–0131/229–9932** *comfortable guesthouse in city center*

Ayden Guest House [GS,NS,WI,GO] 70 Pilrig St **44-0131/554-2187** *in-house chef cooks fabulous brkfst*

Garlands [GS,NS,WI,GO] 48 Pilrig St (off Leith Walk) **44-0131/554-4205** *Georgian town house, full brkfst*

Sheraton Grand Hotel and Spa [GF,SW] 1 Festival Sq **44-131/229-9131**

Tigerlily [GF,WI] 125 George St **44-131/225-5005**

Village Apartments [MO,GO] 5 Broughton Market **44-0131/556-5094**

The Witchery by the Castle [GF] Castlehill (The Royal Mile) **44-0131/225.5613** *theatrical suites at the gates of Edinburgh castle*

■BARS

The Auld Hoose [GS,NH,F] 23-25 St Leonards St **44-0131/668-2934** *noon-1am, from 12:30pm Sun*

Cafe Habana [MW,WI] 22 Greenside Pl **44-0131/558-1270** *1pm-1am, theme nights, popular pre-clubbing*

Cafe Nom de Plume [F] 60 Broughton St **44-0131/478-1372** *11am-11pm, till 1am Fri-Sat*

CC Bloom's [M,S,D,GO] 23 Greenside Pl (at Leith Walk) **44-0131/556-9331** *6pm-3am, from 7pm Sun, theme nights*

Elbow [GS] 133-135 E Claremont St **44-0131/556-5662** *11am-1pm*

Woodland Creatures [GS,F,E] 260 - 262 Leith Walk **44-0131/629-5509** *11am-1pm*

Newtown Bar [MW,D,F,WI] 26-B Dublin St **44-0131/538-7775** *noon-1am, till 2am Fri-Sat*

Planet [★MW,F,WI] 6 Baxter's Pl (at Leith Walk) **44-0131/556-5551** *4pm-1am*

The Regent [M,F,WI] 2 Montrose Terrace **44-0131/661-8198** *noon-1am, from 12:30pm Sun*

The Street [GS,D,F,WI] 2 Picardy Pl **44-0131/556-4272** *noon-1am, patio*

Theatre Royal Bar [GF,F] 25-27 Greenside Pl **44-0131/557-2142** *noon-midnight*

■NIGHTCLUBS

GHQ [M,D] 4 Picardy Pl **44-0131/550-1780** *9pm-3am, fashionable gay crowd, theme nights*

■CAFES

Cafe Lucia 13-29 Nicolson St (next to Edinburgh Festival Theatre) **44-0131/662-1112** *10am-10pm*

Filmhouse Cafe [BW] 88 Lothian Rd **44-0131/229-5932, 44-0131/228-2688 (cinema)** *10am-11:30pm, till 12:30am Fri-Sat, also cinema*

■RESTAURANTS

Blue Moon [★MW,F,GO] 1 Barony St **44-0131/556-2788** *11am-midnight, from 10am wknds*

Henderson's [BW] 94 Hanover St **44-0131/225.2131** *organic vegetarian, also deli & cafe*

Tower Restaurant & Terrace [WC] National Museum of Scotland, Chambers St (at George IV Brigde) **44-0131/225-3003** *lunch & dinner, panoramic views of Edinburgh's castle & historic skyline*

Valvona & Crolla [★] 19 Elm Row **44-0131/556-6066** *clsd Sun, oldest Italian deli in Scotland*

■ENTERTAINMENT & RECREATION

Black Kilt Tours [GO] 125b Grange Loan **44-786/416-5362**

■BOOKSTORES

Bobbie's Bookshop 220 Morrison St **44-0131/538-7069** *10am-5pm, clsd Sun*

Word Power Books 43-45 W Nicolson St **44-0131/662-9112** *10am-6pm, noon-5pm Sun, independent & radical, events*

■RETAIL SHOPS

Q Store 5 Barony St **44-0131/477-4756**

■NATIONAL PUBLICATIONS

ScotsGay **44-0131/539-0666**

■ **MEN'S CLUBS**

No 18 18 Albert Pl
44-0131/553-3222 *noon-10pm, till
11pm Fri-Sun, sauna club*

Steamworks [WI] 5 Broughton Market
(btwn Barony & Dublin)
44-0131/477-3567 *11am-11pm,
cafe/labyrinth*

■ **EROTICA**

Adult Conceptions 8 Drummond St
44-0131/557-9413 *10am-9pm, from
noon Sun, toys, clothing & videos*

Fem 2 Dom 25 Easter Rd
44-0131/623-6969 *10am-9pm, from
noon Sun, toys, clothing & videos*

SPAIN

Barcelona

Note: M°=Metro station

■ **INFO LINES & SERVICES**

Casal Lambda Verdaguer y Callis 10
(M° Drassanes) **34/93-319-5550**
*5pm-9pm, community center & cafe,
archives & library, also publish magazine*

Col-Lectiu Gai de Barcelona (CGB)
34/934-534-125 *staffed 7pm-9pm
Mon-Sat, also publishess Info Gai*

Coordinadora Gai Lesbiana Vicant
d'Hongria 156, E-08014
34/900-601-601 *7pm-9pm Mon-Fri,
6pm-8pm Sat*

■ **ACCOMMODATIONS**

Agua Alegre [GS] c/ Roger de Lluria 47
(M° Catalunya) **34/93-487-8032**

Barcelona City Centre [M,WI,GO]
34/653-900-039 *in Eixample District*

California Hotel [GS] Rauric 14 (at
Ferran, M° Liceu) **34/93-317-7766**

Casa de Billy Barcelona [GS,NS,WI,GO]
Rambla Catalunya 85, Piso 5, Puerta 1
(at Mallorca) **34/93-426-3048** *shared
baths, full brkfst*

Catalonia Diagonal Centro
[GF,F,WI,WC] Balmes 142-146
34/93-415-9090

Catalonia Portal de l'Àngel
[GF,SW,WI] Avenida Portal de L'Angel 17
34/93-318-4141

Central Town Rooms & Apartments
[M,WC,GO] Ronda San Pau 51
34/93-442-7057, 24/670-260-298
guesthouse

Éos [MW,GO] Gran Via de los Corts
Catalanes 575 (M° Universitat)
34/93-451-8772, 34/617-931-439
B&B in gay district

Fashion House [MW] Bruc 13 Principal
34/63-790-4044 *shared baths*

GayStay BCN [M,WI,GO] C / Piquer 15,
Pral 3 (at Carrer de Mata)
34/676-145-909

HCC Regente [GF,SW,WI,WC] Rambla de
Catalunya 76 **34/93-487-5989**

HCC Taber [GF,WI] Arago 256
34/93-487-3887

Hostal Absolut Centro [M,GO]
Casanova 72 (at Balmes)
34/649-550-238 *hostel, some shared
baths*

Hostal Baires [GF] **34/93-319-7774**
in Barrio Gótico

Hostal Que Tal [M] Mallorca 290 (at
Bruch) **34/93-459-2366**

Hotel Axel [MW,SW,WI,WC] Aribau 33
(at Consell de Cent) **34/93-323-9393**
full brkfst, rooftop bar

Hotel Catalonia Fira [GF,SW,WI] Av.
Gran Via N 50 (Plaza Europa)
34/93-236-0000 *new 4-star hotel in
the heart of old Barcelona*

Hotel Colon [GF] Avenida Catedral 7
34/93-301-1404

Hotel Majestic Barcelona [GF,SW,WC]
Paseo de Gracia 68 (in city center)
34/93-488-1717 *5-star hotel, rooftop
pool*

Room Mate Emma [GF,WI] Carrer
Rosselló 205 **34/932-385-606**

■ **BARS**

Aire/ Sala Diana [GS,D,F,S,YC] Valencia
236 (btwn Enriq. Granados & c/ Balmes)
34/93-451-8462

Al Maximo [MW,NH] Assaonadora 25

Átame [M,E,DS] Consell de Cent 257 (at
M° Universidad) **34/93-454-9273**
7pm-2:30am

Bacon Bear Bar [M,B] Casanova 64
(M° Urgell) *6pm-3am, theme nights*

El Balcon des Aquiles [M,NH] Lleo 9 *7pm-3am*

Bar Plata [M] Consejo de Ciento 233 (at Urgell) *5pm-3am*

La Base [M,L,N] Carme 27 34/933-017-396 *10pm-3am, till 5am Fri-Sat, leather & fetish, naked party Wed & Sat*

Berlin Dark [M,L] Pasage Prunera 18 (at de la Font Honrada) *10pm-3am Tue-Sun, also Berlin Day 5pm-9pm Mon-Fri*

BimBamBum [M,D] Casanova 48 *11pm-3am, clsd Mon-Tue*

Black Bull [M] Muntaner 64 34/934-515 -104 *8pm-2:30am*

Butch Bear Barcelona [M,B] Diputació 206 (btwn Muntaner & Ariba) *10pm-3am Ih-Sat*

El Cangrejo [MW,D] Villarroel 86 *10:30pm-3am, clsd Mon-Tue*

La Chapelle [M] Muntaner 65 *cafe by day*

Chiringuito GayLorenzo [M] Ed Dulce Deseo de Lorenzo (Playa de la Mar Bella) *summer beach bar*

La Cueva [MW,DS] Calàbria 91 *open 4pm, clsd Mon*

Dacksy [MW,D] Consell de Cent 247 34/934-519-925 *5pm-3am, trendy cocktail lounge*

Lust [MW] Casanova 75 (at Consell de Cent) *9pm-2:30am, clsd Mon, pre-clubbing bar*

La Madame [★GS,D] Ronda Sant Pere 19-21 (M° Urquinaona) 34/93-426-8444 *from midnight Sun only*

Moeem [MW] Muntaner 11 34/659-229-033 *6pm-3am, cheap drinks*

Museum Cafe & Club [M] Sepulveda 178 (at Urgell) *6:30pm-3am*

Museum Retro [M] Urgell 106 *11:30pm-3am Fri-Sat*

New Chaps [M,L,S,V] Av Diagonal 365 (M° Diagonal) 34/93-215-5365 *9pm-3am, till 3:30am Fri-Sat, from 7pm Sun, darkroom*

Nightberry [MO,S] Diputación 161 (M° Urgell) 34/934-543-805 *6pm-2:30am, till 3am Fri-Sat, darkroom & cabins*

People Lounge [M,E,F] Villarroel 71 (M° Urgell) 34/93-451-5986 *7pm-3am*

Punto BCN [★M,WC] Muntaner 63-65 (at Y Aragón, Metro, M° Universitat) 34-93/451-9152 *6pm-2:30am, upscale cafe-bar*

SkyBar [MW] Aribau 33 (at Hotel Axel) 34/93-323-9393 *open to non-guests 9pm-1:30am Wed*

Zelig [GS,D,F] 34/93-441-5622 *7pm-2am, till 3am wknds, clsd Mon*

■NIGHTCLUBS

Arena Classic [★M,D,S,V,YC,$] Diputació 233 (at Balmes, M° Universitat) 34/93-487-8342 *12:30am-5am Fri-Sat only, Spanish music*

Arena Dandy/ VIP [M,D,S,V,YC,$] Gran Via 593 (at Balmes, M° Universitat) 34/93-487-8342 *1am-6am Fri-Sat*

Arena Sala Madre [★M,D,F,S,V,YC,$] Balmes 32 (at Diputació, M° Universitat) 34/93-487-8342 *12:30am-5am, clsd Mon (except in Aug), darkroom*

Bitch@Priviledge [M,D] Calle de Tarragona 141-147 *12:30am Sat only*

Bubbleboys [M] *10pm-3am Th-Sat, gay pole-dance bar*

Centrik Weekend Bar [M] Aribau 30 *11pm-3am Fri-Sat*

Martin's [MO,D,L,S,V] C/ de Béjar 87 34/934-265-332 *midnight-5am Sat only, small backroom*

Metro [★M,D,L,DS,V,YC,$] Sepulveda 185 (M° Universitat) 34/93-323-5227 *midnight-5am, from 1am Mon*

Souvenir Barcelona [★GS,D] Noi del Sucre 75 (Viladecans) *after-hours club 6am-1pm Sat-Sun & holidays*

■CAFES

La Concha del Barrio Chino [GS,D,TG] Guardia 14 (M° Liceu) 34/93-302-4118 *4pm-3am*

Spain • EUROPE

▉RESTAURANTS

7 Portes Passeig d'Isabel II, 14
34/93-319-3033, 34/93-319-2950
1pm-1am, Catalan

El Berro Diputació 180
34/933-236-956 *7am-3am, from
9am wknds, inexpensive diner-style
restaurant, also bar*

Botafumeiro [R] El Gran de Gràcia 81
34/93-218-4230, 34/93-217-9642
1pm-1am, Galician seafood, full bar

Castro [S] Casanova 85 (Mº Urgell)
34/93-323-6784 *1pm-4pm & 9pm-
midnight, clsd Sun, Catalan, full bar*

dDivine [MW,DS,R] Balmes 24 (Mº
Universitat) **34/93-317-2248**
*9:30pm-1am, clsd Sun-Tue, dinner show
hosted by "Divine"*

Eterna [MW,DS] Consell de Cent 127-
129 (at Villarroel) **34/93-424-2526**
*1pm-4pm Mon-Fri, 9:30pm-midnight
Th-Sat, clsd Sun*

La Flauta Magica [WC] c/ de Banys
Vells 18 (Mº Jaume I)
34/93-268-4694 *dinner nightly,
vegetarian/ organic*

Iurantia [R] Casanova 42 (Mº Urgell)
34/93-454-7887 *lunch Mon-Fri,
dinner Mon-Sat, clsd Sun, pizzeria*

Little Italy [E] Carrer del Rec 30 (near
Passeig del Born) **34/93-319-7973**
1pm-4pm & 9pm-midnight, live jazz

Madrid-Barcelona [★] Carrer d'Arago
282 (Mº Passeig de Gracia)
34/93-215-7027 *lunch & dinner, clsd
Sun*

Marquette Diputació 172 (Mº
Universitat) **34/93-162-3905** *6pm-
3am*

Sazzerak 34/93-451-1138 *full bar*

Tafino Consejo de Ciento 193 *1pm-
4pm Mon-Fri, 8:30pm-midnight Tue-Sat*

Tu Sabes 34/615-999-282 *7pm-
midnight Th, 9pm-3am Fri-Sat*

La Veronica Rambla de Raval 2-4
34/93-329-3303 *1pm-1am, clsd
Mon, popular pizzeria*

▉ENTERTAINMENT & RECREATION

Chernobyl Beach take the Metro to
Sant Roc *popular gay beach*

Mar Bella *popular gay beach*

Museu Picasso Montcada 15-23
34/93-256-3000 *early Picasso works*

Parc Guell Mount Tibidado *mosiacs &
sculpture by Gaudi*

Sant Sebastián *popular gay beach*

▉BOOKSTORES

Antinous [WC] Josep Anselm Clavé 6
(btwn Las Ramblas & Ample, Mº
Drassanes) **34/93-301-9070** *LGBT,
books & gifts, also cafe*

Cómplices Cervantes 2 (at Avinyó, Mº
Liceu) **34/93-412-7283** *10:30am-
8:30pm, from noon Sat, clsd Sun, LGBT,
Spanish & English titles*

Nosotr@s Casanova 56 (Mº Urgell)
34/93-451-5134 *LGBT*

▉RETAIL SHOPS

Ovlas C/ d'Aribau 31
34/93-268-7691 *clothing, also cafe*

▉PUBLICATIONS

Gay Barcelona Av Roma 152
34/93-454-9100 *monthly gay magazine*

▉MEN'S CLUBS

Bruch C/ Pau Clarís 87
34/93-487-4814 *11am-10pm*

Buenos Aires Urgell 114 (at Consell de
Cent) **34/93-323-8199** *24hrs*

Casanova [★F,V] Casanova 57 (at
Diputació, Mº Universitat)
34/93-323-7860, 34/65-016-5078
24hrs, gym equipment, also bar

Condal [F,V,SW] Espolsasacs 1 (at Carrer
Condal, Mº Catalunya)
34/93-317-6817 *24hrs*

Corinto [★F,V] Pelayo 62 (at Rambla,
Mº Catalunya) **34/93-318-6422**
24hrs wknds

Galilea Sauna [F,V,WI] Calabria 59 (Mº
Rocafort) **34/93-426-7905** *24hrs
wknds*

Neron Urgell 185 **34/934-511-0 28**

Open Mind Arago 130
34/934-510-479 *11pm-4am, till 7am Fri-Sat, clsd Mon-Tue, cruising, fetish and SM club*

Sauna Barcelona [V,SW,WI] Tuset 1 (at Av Diagonal) **34/93-200-7716** *24hrs wknds*

Thermas [SW] Diputación 46 (at Entenza, M° Rocafort)
34/93-325-9346 *24hrs, hustlers*

Trash Calle de la Mare de Déu del Remei 11 *10pm-3am, midnight-6am Fri-Sat, 7pm-2am Sun, clsd Mon-Tue, fetish club and playground*

■EROTICA

Blue Star [GS] Av Roma 153 (Edificio Torre Catalunya) **34/93-452-5890**

Boyberry Calàbria 96 (M° Rocafort) **34/93-426-2312**

Erotic Museum of Barcelona Ramblas 96 **34/93-318-9865**

Harmony Love **34/93-405-3300**

Kitsch Muntaner 17-19 (at Gran Vía) **34/93-453-2052**

Nostromo Diputació 208 (downstairs, M° Universitat) **34/93-451-3323** *video cabins, darkroom*

Sestienda Rauric 11 (at Farran, M° Liceu) **34/93-318-8676** *clsd Sun*

Skorpius Gran Vía 384-390 **34/93-423-4040**

Zeus Gay Shop Riera Alta 20 (M° Sant Antoni) **34/93-442-9795** *clsd Sun*

■CRUISY AREAS

Parc de Montjuïc [AYOR] btwn Avs del Estadio & Rius y Taulet *behind the archaeology museum, by the cascade*

Parc Sagrada Familia [AYOR]

Playa de la Mar Bella [AYOR] *on the beach & in the park*

Las Ramblas [AYOR]

Madrid

Note: M°=Metro station

■INFO LINES & SERVICES

COGAM (Colectivo de Lesbianas, Gays, Transexuales, y Bisexuales de Madrid) Puebla 9 (Bajo)
34/91-522-4517 *LGBT center, groups, library, also cafe-bar*

■ACCOMMODATIONS

Camino de Soto [GS,SW,WI,GO] Puente de la Reine 18, Soto del Real **34-66/744-1351**

Chueca Pension [MW,WI] Gravina 4 **34/91-523-1473** *hostel*

Hostal CasaChueca [MW,WI,GO] Calle San Bartolomé 4 (at San Marcos) **34/91-523-8127**

Hostal La Fontana [MW,WI] Valverde 6, 1° (M° Gran Vía) **34/91-521-8449, 34/91-523-1561**

Hostal la Zona [M,WI,GO] Calle Valverde 7, 1 & 2 (at Gran Vía) **34/91-521-9904** *full brkfst, private balconies*

Hostal Odesa [★M,WI] Calle Hortaleza 38, 3rd flr (at Perez Galdos) **34/91-521-0338, 34/91-521-5901**

Hostal Puerta del Sol [M,WI,WC,GO] Plaza Puerta del Sol 14, 4° (at Calle de Alcalá, M° Sol) **34/91-522-5126** *centrally located*

Hotel Catalonia Gaudí [GF,F,WI] Gran Vía 7-9 (at Alcalá) **34/91-531-2222** *4-star hotel in the heart of the city*

Hotel Urban Madrid [GF,SW,WI] Carrera de San Jerónimo 34 **34/91-787-7770** *upscale hotel w/ 3 restaurants*

Pensión Madrid House [GS,WI,GO] Barbieri 1 **34/651-387 535** *one block from Chueca Square*

■BARS

El 51 [★M] Hortaleza 51 (in Chueca) **34/91-521-2564** *6pm-3am, from 4pm wknds, upscale cocktail lounge*

A Noite [M,D,DS,S,V] Hortaleza 43 (M° Chueca) **34/91-531-0715** *9pm-6am, darkroom, hustlers*

Spain • *EUROPE*

Ambienta2 [MW,D,DS,E] 22 San Bartolome (at Figueroa) **34/606-939592** *6pm-2am, till 2:30am wknds, from noon Sun, theme nights*

The Angel [M,D,B] Calle Infantas 9 (at Hortaleza) **34/68-779-1452** *noon-5:30am, till 6am Fri-Sat, clsd Mon-Tue*

Attack Fun SX Bar [M,V] Calle de Lavapiés 12 (at Plaza Tirso de Molina) **34-91/115-4290** *9pm-late, clsd Mon, sex club, darkroom, naked & underwear nights*

Bar Lio [MW,K,DS,TG] Pelayo 58 *7pm-2am*

Bear's Bar [★MO,B,L,V] Calle Pelayo 4 (M° Chueca, ring to enter) **34/91-521-7358** *6pm-2:30am, till 3:30am wknds, clsd Mon, darkroom, cruisy*

Bebop [M,NH,F] Plaza de Chueca 9 **34/9152-19873** *11am-3am, cafe/ bar*

Black & White (Blanco y Negro) [★M,D,S] Libertad 34 (at Gravina, M° Chueca) **34/91-531-1141** *8pm-5am, hustlers*

The Cage [M,L] San Marcos 11 **34/911-234-567** *3pm-2am, from 5pm Sat-Sun*

Copper [MO,D,L,N] Calle San Vincente Ferrer 34 (M° Tribunal) *2pm-3am, till 3:30am Fri-Sat, dress code, sling, darkroom*

Cruising [★M,D,L,V,YC] Calle de Pérez Galdós 5 (M° Chueca) **34/91-521-5143** *9pm-close, till 3:30am Fri-Sat, hustlers*

Eagle Madrid [M,L,F,V,N,PC] Calle Pelayo 30 (M° Chueca) **34/91-524-1627** *2pm-close, from 3pm wknds, theme nights, darkroom*

Enfrente [M,B,L] Infantas 12 (M° Gran Vía) **34/68-779-1462** *8pm-3am, DJs Th & Sun*

Fu3l [M,B] San Marcos 16 (at Barbieri) *7pm-3:30am*

Fulanita de Tal [W,D] Calle del Conde de Xiquena 2 (at Prim)

Gris [★MW,E] *10pm-3am, from 9pm Th-Sat, clsd Sun-Mon, reduced drink prices until 11:30pm*

Hot Bar [M,B,L,V] Infantas 9 (M° Chueca, ring to enter) *1pm-3am, cruising in the basement*

Leather [MO,D,L,S,V,OC] Pelayo 42 (at Gravina, M° Chueca) **34/91-308-1462** *7pm-3pm [S] Th-Sat, darkroom*

Liquid [M,D,V] Calle Barbieri 7 (M° Banco) **34/91-532-7428** *9pm-close, good place to start the night*

LL [★M,D,S,DS,V] Pelayo 11 (M° Chueca) **34/91-523-3121** *5pm-close*

Museo Chicote [★GS,F,E] Calle Gran Via 12 **34/915-326-737** *9pm-3am*

The Paso [★M,V] Calle Costanilla de los Capuchinos 1 (M° Gran Vía) **34/91-522-0888** *6pm-close*

Picardias Pub [M,NH,S,V,OC] Calle de Pérez Galdós 8 (M° Chueca) *7pm-3am, darkroom*

Rick's [★M,D,YC] Calle del Clavel 8 (at Infantas, M° Gran Vía, ring to enter) **34/91-531-9186** *11pm-6am, open later Fri-Sat, 9pm-2am Sun*

Rimmel [M,NH,V,YC] Calle de Luis de Góngora 2 (M° Chueca) *7pm-3am, darkroom, hustlers*

El Rincón Guay [MW,NH,F,WI] Embajadores 62 (Lavapiés quarter) **34/914-68-37-00** *9am-2am*

Sacha's [MW,D,DS] Plaza de Chueca 1 (M° Chueca) *8pm-3am, terrace*

Sixta [GS,GO] Calatrava 15 (M° La Latina) **34/913-663-018** *10pm-2am, 3pm-midnight Sun, clsd Mon-Wed, packed on Sun afternoon*

Studio 54 Madrid [MW,D,S] Barbieri 7 (btwn San Marcos & Infantas, M° Chueca) **34/615-126-807** *11:30pm-3:30am, clsd Mon-Tue*

Tántalo [M,WI] Libertad 14 **34/915-213-127** *6pm-2:30am*

Truco [★W,D] Calle de Gravina 10 (at Plaza de Chueca) **34/91-532-8921** *8pm-close, clsd Mon-Tue, dance bar, seasonal terrace*

Why Not [M,D] San Bartolomé 6 (M° Gran Vía) *9pm-3am, till 5am Fri-Sat*

◼ NIGHTCLUBS

Bangalá [MO,MR,V,YC,N] Escuadra 1 (M° Antón Martin/Lavapiés) *9pm-2:30am, darkroom*

Boite [GS,D] Calle Tetuan 27 (Plaza del Carmen) 34/91-522-9620 *check listings for gay club nights*

Dark Hole [GS,D] Pelayo 80-82 *1am - 6am Sat, gay goth club*

Delirio [M,D,S] Libertad 28 (at Figueroa) 34/91-531-1870 *11pm-5:30am, go-go boys Wed*

Griffin's [★M,D,DS,E] Marqués de Valdeiglesias 6 (M° Banco de España) 34/91-522-0999 *11pm-late*

Heaven Madrid [★GF] 34/91-535-4417 *12:30am-6am only, mixed metrosexual party*

Joy Eslava [★GS,D,DS,S] Arenal 11 (M° Sol) 34/91-366-3733 *11:30pm-6pm Sat only, fabulous crowd*

Long Play [MW,D] Plaza de Vázquez de Mella 2 *midnight-6am wknds only*

The Moon [GF,D] Aduana 21 34/91-522-3561 *after-hours club*

Ohm [★GS,D,S] Plaza de Callao 4 (at Sala Bash, M° Callao) 34/91-531-0132 *midnight-close Fri-Sat*

The Paw [M,N] Calatrava 29 (M° La Latina) 34/91-366-6093 *7pm-late, Sun, sex club, darkroom, slings*

Strong Center [M,D,L,S,V,$] Trujillos 7 (M° Santo Domingo) 34/91-541-5415 *7pm-3am, the main attraction is its enormous darkroom*

Tábata [MW,D,YC,$] Vergara 12 (next to Teatro Real, M° Opera) 34/91-547-9735 *11:30pm-late Wed-Sat*

Week-end [★MW,D,A,$] Plaza de Callao 4 (at Ohm Club) 34/91-541-3500 *midnight-6am Sun*

CAFES

El Apolo Barco 18 34/915-210-830 *8am-3pm & 6pm-2am, 10am-2am Sat, from 5pm Sun*

Cafe Acuarela [MW] Gravina 10 (M° Chueca) 34/91-522-2143, 34/91-570-6907 *3pm-3am, from 11am Sat-Sun, bohemian cafe-bar*

Cafe Figueroa [MW] Augusto Figueroa 17 (at Hortaleza, M° Chueca) 34/91-521-1673 *4pm-midnight, till 2:30am wknds, also bar*

Cafe la Troje [MW] Pelayo 26 (at Figueroa, M° Chueca) 34/91-531-0535 *5pm-2am, full bar*

D'Mystic [★GS,F] Gravina 5 (M° Pelayo) 34/91-308-2460 *9:30am-close, hip cafe-bar in Chueca area*

Mama Inés [★] Hortaleza 22 (M° Chueca) 34/91-523-2333 *10am-2am, sandwiches, pies*

XXX Cafe [M,F,C] Clavel 2 (M° Gran Vía) 34/91-532-8415 *1pm-1am, till 2:30am Fri-Sat*

RESTAURANTS

Al Natural Zorrilla 11 (M° Sevilla) 34/91-369-4709 *lunch & dinner, no dinner Sun, vegetarian*

Antigua Taqueria [GO] Calle Cabestreros 4 (in Lavapies area) 34/915-308-270 *11am-midnight, till 2am Fri-Sat, Tex-Mex*

El Armario [MW,S] San Bartolomé 7 (btwn Figueroa & San Marcos, M° Chueca) 34/91-532-8377

Artemisa [MW] Ventura de la Vega 4 (at Zorrilla) 34/91-429-5092 *vegetarian*

La Berenjena [GO] Calle Marqués de Toca,7 (in Lavapies area) 34/914-675-297 *8pm-2am, from 1:30pm wknds, till midnight Sun, clsd Mon*

La Berenjena [GO] Calle Marqués de Toca 7 (in Lavapies area) 34/914-675-297 *8pm-2am, from 1:30pm wknds, till midnight Sun, clsd Mon*

Botin 34/91-366-4217 *one of the oldest restaurants in the world*

Colby 34/91-521-2554 *9:30am-close, from 11:30am Sun*

Divina La Cocina [MW] Colmenares 13 (at San Marcos, M° Chueca) 34/91-531-3765 *lunch & dinner, elegant & trendy*

Spain • *EUROPE*

Ecocentro Esquilache 2, 4, y 6 (at Pablo Iglesias, Mº Ríos Rosas) **34/91–553–5502** *open till midnight, vegetarian, natural foods, also shop, herbalist school*

El Chambao Manuel Malasana 16 (at Calle de Monteleon) *tapas restaurant, also bar*

La Gastrocroqueteria de Chema Calle Segovia 17 **34/913-642-263** *dinner nightly from 9pm, lunch wknds from 2pm*

Gula Gula [★MW,E,DS,R] Gran Via 1 (Mº Gran Via) **34/91–522–8764** *lunch & dinner, buffet/ salad bar*

Marsot Pelayo 6 (Mº Chueca) **34/91–531–0726** *lunch & dinner*

Mercado de la Reina Calle Gran Vía 12 **34/915 –213–198** *9am-2am, hip and happening with high quality food*

Momo [NS,GO] Calle de la Libertad 8 **34/91–532–7162** *lunch & dinner, charming staff*

Paris Tokyo [GO] Plaza Vázquez de Mella 12 **34/915–216–128**

El Rincón de Pelayo [★MW] Pelayo 19 (Mº Chueca) **34/91–521–8407** *lunch & dinner*

Sama-Sama San Bartolomé 23 (Mº Chueca) **34/91–521–5547** *lunch & dinner, clsd Sun, Balinese decor*

Taberna el Olivar [GO] Calle Olivar 54 (in Lavapies area) *7pm-midnight, from 1pm Fri-Sun, clsd Tues*

Vegaviana Pelayo 35 **34/913–080–381** *lunch & dinner, clsd Sun-Mon, vegetarian*

■BOOKSTORES

A Different Life Pelayo 30 (Mº Chueca) **34/91–532–9652** *11am-10pm, LGBT, books, magazines, music, videos, sex shop downstairs*

Berkana Bookstore [WC] Hortaleza 64 **34/91–522–5599** *10:30am-9pm, from noon Sat-Sun, LGBT, ask for free gay map of Madrid*

■PUBLICATIONS

Shangay Express **34/91–445–1741** *free bi-weekly gay paper, also publishes Shanguide*

■GYMS & HEALTH CLUBS

Energy Gym [★] Hortaleza 19 (Mº Gran Vía, Chueca) **34/91–531–1029, 34/91–522–3073**

Gimnasio V35 Valverde 35 (Mº Gran Via) **34/91–523–9352**

Holiday Gym Princesa [SW] Serrano Jover 3 (Mº Argüelles) **34/91–547–4033** *central location*

■MEN'S CLUBS

Adán [V,SW] San Bernardo 38 (Mº Noviciado) **34/91–532–9138** *24hrs wknds, 3 flrs, darkroom, also bar, hustlers*

Alameda [SW] Alameda 20 (Mº Atocha) **34/91–429–8745** *1pm-11pm, darkroom, also bar*

Comendadoras [★OC,V] Plaza Comendadoras 9 (at Calle de Montserrat, Mº Noviciado) **34/91–532–8892** *24hrs, also bar*

Cristal [V,SW] Augusto Figueroa 17 (Mº Tribunal y Gran Via) **34/91–531–4489** *3pm-3am, also bar*

Men [V] Pelayo 25 (Mº Chueca) **34/91–531–2583** *3pm-8am, 24hrs wknds, also bar*

Octopus [M,V,SW] Churruca 10 (at Apodaca, Mº Tribunal/ Chueca) **34/91–183–2832** *3pm-midnight, darkroom, bar*

Odarko [MO,D] Loreto & Chicote 7 (at Ballesta, Mº Callao) **34/91–522–9251** *10pm-close, from 6pm Sun, "pervy & fetish sex club in Madrid"*

Paraíso [★SW,V] Norte 15 (at San Vicente F, Mº Noviciado) **34/91–522–4232, 34/91–531–9891** *noon-midnight, 24hrs wknds, gym equipment, also bar, darkroom*

Premium Sauna Calle Costanilla de los Ángeles 5 (enter Priora 2) **34/911–155–411** *3pm-11pm, from 3am wknds*

Sauna Center [D] Cuesta de Santo Domingo 1

Sauna Gran Via [M] Barco 6 **34/915–230–468**

Sauna Lavapiés Zurita 3 *24hrs*

Sauna Príncipe [F,V] Travesia de las Beatas 3 (Mº Ópera) **34/91-559-5353, 34/91-548-2218** *2pm-midnight, also bar, darkroom*

Sauna Puerta de Toledo 34/913-659-095 *2pm-11pm*

Xtrem Sex Club Valverde 3 (at del Desengaño 2) *6pm-3am, from 2pm Sun*

■EROTICA

Amantis Pelayo 46 34/91-702-0510

City Sex Store c/ Hortaleza, next to #18 (in Chueca) 34/91-181-2723 *open every day*

La Juguetería Travesia de San Mateo 12 34-91/308-7269

Play 34/91-523-0841 *10am-8pm*

SR [GO] Pelayo 7 (Mº Chueca) 34/91-523-1964 *clsd Sun, fetish, military, leather*

■CRUISY AREAS

Casa de Campo [AYOR] *at night on top of hill—travel along only road going up from lake*

El Corte Ingles [AYOR] Puerta del Sol *large department store, men's lounge on 3rd & 5th flrs*

Parque del Campo de las Naciones [AYOR] *by the bridge leading to the auditorium*

Parque El Retiro [AYOR] (Mº Atocha) *at night in garden around statue of fallen angel*

Plaza de Toros [AYOR] *car cruising at night*

Sitges

■ACCOMMODATIONS

Antonio's Guesthouse [MW,WI,GO] Passeig Vilanova 58 34/93-894-9207 *also apts*

Los Globos [MW,WI,WC,GO] Avda Ntra Sra de Montserrat 43 34/93-894-9374 *also bar*

Hotel Antemare [GF,SW] Verge de Montserrat 48-50 34/93-894-7000 *1 block from beach*

Hotel Liberty [★MW,NS,WI,WC,GO] Isla de Cuba 45 (at Artur Carbonell) 34/93-811-0872 *seasonal*

Hotel Renaixença [M] Illa de Cuba 13 , 08070 34/93-894-8375 *some shared baths, bar*

Hotel Romàntic [GS] Sant Isidre 33 34/93-894-8375 *full brkfst, some shared baths, seasonal, also bar*

Hotel Santa Maria [GS] Paseo de la Ribera 52 34/93-894-0999 *clean & modest, great restaurant*

Medium Sitges Park Hotel [GS,SW,WI,WC] Calle Jesus 16 34/938-940-205 *restaurant, bar & garden*

Parrot's Hotel [MW,WI] Joan Tarrida 16 34/93-894-1350 *also bar, restaurant & sauna*

Pensión Espalter [M] Espalter 11 34/938-942-863 *also sauna*

San Sebastian Playa [GF,SW,NS,WC] Port Alegre 53 305/538-9697 (US#), 866/376-7831 (in US) *also bar/restaurant*

Sitges Royal Rooms [M,WI,GO] 34/64-998-1148

■BARS

Azul [★M,NH,V] Sant Bonaventura 10 34/93-894-7634 *9pm-3am*

B-Side [★M,F,S,V] San Gaudencio 7 34/91-799-0926 *10pm-3:30am, cafe-bar, darkroom*

Bears' Bar [M,B,V] Bonaire 17 34/93-894-6296 *10pm-3am (Fri-Sat only off-season), also rooms to rent*

Dark/ DSB [M] Bonaire 14 *5pm-3am, sleek lounge*

El Horno [★M,B,L,F,V] Joan Tarrida Ferratges 6 34/93-894-0909 *5:30pm-3am, darkroom*

La Locacola [M] Bonaire 35 *7pm-close*

Man [★M,L] Bonaventura 19 *10pm-3:30am, nightly underwear parties except Th*

Mojito & Co [M] Plaza Industrial 1 *5pm-3am, breezy lounge w/ outdoor seating*

Parrot's Pub [★MW,S] Plaza Industria 2 (at Primero de Mayo) 34/93-894-7881 *5pm-close, seasonal, patio, also restaurant*

Ruby's Terrace [M,E,DS] Joan Tarrida Ferratges 14

El Seven [M,D,S,V] Calle Nou 7 *10pm-3am (wknds only off-season), clsd Nov, terrace, darkroom*

XXL [★M,D,L,V] Joan Tarrida Ferratges 7 *11pm-3:30am (wknds only off-season), darkroom*

■NIGHTCLUBS

L' Atlántida [M] *gay beach party from midnight on Tue (summers)*

Bourbon's [★M,D,V,YC] Sant Bonaventura 13 34/93-894-3347 *10:30pm-3:30am (Sat only off-season), darkroom*

El Candil [★M,D,V,YC] Carreta 9 34/93-894-1632 *seasonal, 10pm-3am, till 3:30am Fri-Sat, darkroom*

Comodín [M,D,DS] Tacó 4 34/93-894-1698 *10pm-3am, darkroom*

Le Male à Bar [MO,D,F,V] Centro Comercial Oasis 28 *11pm-late (only wknds in winter), underwear parties Mon & Wed*

Mediterraneo [★M,D,YC] Sant Bonaventura 6 34/93-894-3347 *11pm-3:30am, patio*

Orek's [★M,D,S,V] Bonaire 13 *10pm-3am (only Fri-Sat in winter), darkroom*

Organic [M,D,TG,S,$] Bonaire 15 34/93-894-2230 *opens 2:30am (wknds only off-season), singles party Th, darkroom*

Perfil [M,NH,D,DS,V] Espalter 7 34/656-376-791 (cell) *10:30pm-3am, darkroom, seasonal*

El Piano [MW,C,P] Bonaventura 37 34/93-814-6245 *10pm-3am*

Prinz [M,C,DS,S] Nou 4 34/93-894-6736 *11pm-3:30am*

Privilege [M,D] Bonaire 24 *11pm-3:30am, seasonal, darkroom*

Queenz [M,D,DS,C] Bonaire 17 *10pm-3:30am, seasonal*

Ricky's [GS] *midnight-6am, clsd Mon, more gay Fri*

Trailer [★M,D] Angel Vidal 36 *1am-6am, seasonal, foam parties in summer*

■CAFES

Cafe Al Fresco Carrer Major 33 34/93-811-3307 *9am-midnight*

Mont Roig Cafe [★WI] Marques de Montroig 11-13 34/93-894-8439 *9am-3am, patio, also full bar*

■RESTAURANTS

Air Coco [★R] Paseo Maritim 2 34/93-894-2445

Alma [MW,F] Tacó 16 34/93-894-6387 *8pm-close (clsd Tue-Wed off-season), French, terrace*

Beach House [GO] Sant Pau 34 34/93-894-9029 *brkfst & dinner, full bar*

El Celler Vell 34/93-811-1961 *dinner nightly, lunch Fri-Sun, clsd Wed*

Ma Maison [★MW] Bonaire 28 34/93-894-6054 *lunch & dinner, French, full bar, terrace*

Mezzanine Espalter 8 34/93-894-9940 *dinner only, French*

Pic Nic [WI] Paseo de la Ribera 34/93-811-0040 *in front of gay beach*

Sitthai Bonaire 29 34/938-111-6 58 *8pm-midnight, clsd Mon*

So Ca/ Southern California Sant Gaudenci 9 34/93-894-3046 *1pm-close, also bar*

El Trull [★MW] Mossèn Felix Clará 3 (off Major) 34/93-894-4705 *dinner only, clsd Wed, French/ int'l*

■ENTERTAINMENT & RECREATION

Gay Beach Party La Playa De La Bossa Rodona *midnight-6am Tue in season*

Gay Beach (Platja de la Bassa Rodona) *in front of Calipolis Hotel & Picnic cafe*

Playa De Las Balmins *turn left then pass a long beach strip & then climb a hill past a cemetery*

Playa del Muerto *exclusively gay beach 50 minutes walk from the center of Sitges, also beach bar*

■RETAIL SHOPS

Boyzone Sant Bonaventura 18 34/93-894-6466 *clubwear, swimwear*

Laguna Beach Shop Sant Josep 25 34/938-947-204 *10:30am-2pm, 5pm-9pm*

Oscar Marquès de Montroig 2 (at Plaza Industria) 34/93-894-1976 *designer clothing*

■MEN'S CLUBS

Parrots Sauna [MO] Joan Tarrida 16 34/93-894-1350

Sauna Sitges Espalter 11 34/93-894-2863 *4pm-10am, also bar & foam parties*

■EROTICA

The Mask 34/93-811-2214 *24hrs wknds*

■CRUISY AREAS

Espigon Beach [AYOR] *beware of cops!*

L' Estanyol Beach [AYOR] *nights, go right, past gay beach—beware of cops!*

Gay Beach [AYOR] La Playa De La Bossa Rodona *in front of Calipolis Hotel & Picnic cafe (beware of cops!)*

Playa del Muerto [AYOR] *in woods near Terramar Hotel, daytime (beware of cops!)*

Asia

JAPAN

Tokyo

■ACCOMMODATIONS

24 Kaikan [M,F,V] Shinjuku 2-13-1 81-3/3354-2424 *hotel & sauna; also Asakusa 2-29-16 (81-3/5827-2424) & Kita-Ueno 1-8-7 (81-3/3847-2424)*

Capitol Tokyu [GF] 10-3 Nagata-cho 2-chome (Chiyoda-ku) 81-3/3581-4511, 800/428-6598 *near the Diet*

Four Seasons Hotel [GF,SW,WC] 10-8 Sekiguchi 2-chome (Bunkyo-ku) 81-3/3943-2222 *surrounded by historic Japanese garden*

HI Tokyo Central Hostel [GF] 18F Central Plaza (1-1 Kagurakashi, Shinjuku-ku) 81-3/3235-1107 *11pm curfew*

Hotel Century Southern Tower [GF] 2-2-1 Yoyogi (Shibuya-ku) 81-3/5354-0111 *near gay district*

Hotel Sunroute Plaza Shinjuku [GF] 2-3-1 Yoyogi (Shibuya-ku) 81-3/3375-3211 *near gay district*

Keio Plaza Hotel [GF,SW] 2-2-1 Nishi Shinjuku 81-3/3344-0111 *restaurants & bars*

Park Hyatt [GF,SW] 3-7-1-2 Nishi Shinjuku 81-3/5322-1234 *luxury hotel featured in Lost in Translation; also restaurants & lounge*

Shinjuku Prince Hotel [GF,WI] 30-1 Kabuki-cho 1-chome (Shinjuku-ku) 81-3/3205-1111, 800/542-8686 (US)

Shinjuku Washington Hotel [GF] 3-2-9 Nishi-Shinjuku (Shinjuku-ku) 81-3/3343-3111

Tokyu Stay [GF] 5-9-8 Nishi Shinjuku 81-3/3370-1090 *great location*

■BARS

Advocates Cafe [★MW,YC] 1-F, Dai-7 Tenka Bldg (Shinjuku 2-18-1) 81-3/3358-3988 *6pm-4am, till 1am Sun, cafe-bar*

Alamas Cafe [MW,D] 1/F Garnet Bldg, Shinjuku 2-12-1 81-3/6457-4242 *6pm-2am, till 5am Fri-Sat, 3pm-midnight Sun*

The Annex [M,F,OC] 1/F Futami Bld (2-14-11 Shinjuku Ni-Cho) 81-3/3356-5029 *5pm-3am*

Arty Farty [★M,D,YC] 2F, #33 Kyutei Bldg (Shinjuku 2-11-7), Shinjuku 81-3/5362-9720 *6pm-5am, from 7pm Fri, from 5pm wknds, till 3am Sun*

Base [M,B,YC] 10-16 Maruyamacho (Shibuya) 81-3/5728-1233 *a warm den for young bears*

Bravo! [M] 2F Shinbashi 2-9-17 81-3/3503-8805 *6pm-midnight, clsd Sun*

DNA [GS,NH] 81-3/3341-4445 *3pm-5am*

Japan • ASIA

The Dock [★M,D] B1, Dai-2 Seiko Bldg (Shinjuku 2-18-5), Shinjuku-ku 81-3/3226-4006 *9pm-4am*

Fuji [M,K,OC] St Four Bldg, B104 (Shinjuku 2-12-16), Shinjuku-ku 81-3/3354-2707 *8pm-3am, till 5am wknds*

GB [★M] B1, Shinjuku Plaza Bldg (Shinjuku 2-12-3), Shinjuku-ku 81-3/3352-8972 *8pm-2am, till Fri-Sat*

Keivi [M,NH] 4F Yoshino Bldg, 17-10 Sakuragaoka 81-3/3496-0006 *6pm-midnight*

Kinsmen [MW] 2F Shinjuku 2-12-16 (near Shinjuku Sanchome Station) 81-3/3354-4949 *7pm-1am, till 3am Fri-Sat, clsd Mon*

Kusuo [M] 3F Sunflower Bldg (Shinjuku 2-17-1) 81-3/3354-5050 *8pm-4am, till 5am wknds*

Lamp Post [M,P] 201 Yamahara Heights (Shinjuku 2-12-15) 81-3/3354-0436 *7pm-3am*

Magnum [M,B,L] 3-11-12, B1 Nagatani Teikueito Bld, Shinjuku 81-3/3358-5245 *9pm-3am, from 8pm Sun-Mon, till 5am Fri-Sat*

Mango Mango [M] 81-3/3464-3884 *7pm-5am*

Monsoon [M] Shimazaki Bldg 6F (2-14-9 Shinjuku) 81-3/3354-0470 *3pm-6am, small, inexpensive bar*

Poplar [M,OC] B1 St Four Bldg (Shinjuku 2-12-16) 81-3/3350-6929 *6pm-2am*

Shibuya 246 [MO,WI,GO] 3/F Tozaki Bldg, 2-7-4 Dogen-zaka Shibuya 81-3/6277-5023 *6pm-2am, till midnight Sun*

Tac's Knot [MW] 2F, Rm 202 (Shinjuku 3-11-12) 81-3/3341-9404 *8pm-2am, also art exhibitions*

Town House [M,K] Ginza 6 Shinbashi, Bldg 1-11-15 (Minato-ku) 81-3/3289-8558 *6pm-midnight, from 4pm Sat, clsd Sun*

Usagi [M] on lock U facing block V, 5th Fl (up the narrow stairs) *great balcony*

Warai-Tei [M,B] 301 Nakae Bldg III, 2F (2-15-13 Shinjuku) 81-3/3226-0830 *8pm-1am, till 5am Fri-Sat, special welcome for hearing impaired gays*

Wordup Bar [M,D] 2-10-7 2F TOM Bld Shinjuku 81-3/3353-2466

■ NIGHTCLUBS

Agit [MW,K,GO] 81-3/3350-8083 *8pm-6am*

Arch [★MW,D,DS] B1F Hayakawa Bldg (Shinjuku 2-14-6) 81-3/3352-6297

Club Dragon [★MO,D,L,V] 2-14-4 Accord Bldg B1 (Exit C8,Shinjuku Sanchom) 81-3/3341-0606 *6pm-3am, till 5am Fri-Sat*

Club Zinc [MW] Shinjuku 2-14-6 (across from Shinjuku Park) 81-3/3352-6297 *8pm-4am*

Hijoguchi [GF,D] 1F (Shinjuku 2-12-16) 81-3/3341-5445 *8pm-5am, till 3am Sun*

Rehab Lounge [M,D] 81-3/3355-7833 *7pm-2am, till 3am Fri-Sat, popular happy hour 7pm-9pm*

Shangri-La [★M,D] 2-2-10, Shinkiba (at ageHa, Studio Coast) 81-3/5534-2525

Warehouse [GS,D] Fukao Bldg B 1-4-5 (exit 7 Azabu Juban station) 81-3/6230 0343 *large underground club host Red gay nights*

Word Up Bar [M,D] 2-10-7 2F Tom Bldg (Shinjyuku) 81-3/3353-2466 *11pm-close*

■ RESTAURANTS

Angkor Wat 1-38-13 Yoyogi (Shibuya-ku) 81-3/3370-3019 *lunch & dinner, Cambodian*

Ban Thai 1-23-14 Kabuki-cho, 3rd flr (Shinjuku) 81-3/3207-0068 *lunch & dinner*

Chin-ya 1-3-4 Asukusa 81-3/3841-0010 *lunch & dinner, serving shabu-shabu & sukiyaki since 1880*

Edogin [★] 4-5-1 Tsukiji (Chuo-ku) 81-3/3543-4401 *11am-9:30pm, till 8pm Sun, sushi*

Gonpachi 1-13-11 Nishi Azabu, 1F, 2F (Minato-ku) **81-3/5771-0170** *11:30am-5am, multiple locations*

Kakiden 3-37-11 Shinjuku, 8th flr **81-3/3352-5121** *lunch & dinner, upscale Japanese*

Kitchen Five 4-2-15 Nishi-Azabu (Minato-ku) **81-3/3409-8835** *6pm-9:45pm, Mediterranean*

Kozue [R] 3-7-1-2 Nishi Shinjuku (at the Park Hyatt) **81-3/5323-3460**

Las Chicas Jingumae 5-47-6 (off Shibuya), Shibuya-ku **81-3/3407-6865** *11:30am-11pm, English spoken*

Maisen 4-8-5 Jingu-mae (Shibuya-ku) **81-3/3470-0071** *specializes in tonkatsu*

Moti 3F Roppongi Hama Bldg (6-2-35 Roppongi) **81-3/3479-1939** *noon-10pm, Indian*

New York Grill [R] 3-7-1-2 Nishi Shinjuku (at Park Hyatt Hotel, 52nd flr) **81-3/5322-1234** *lunch & dinner*

The Pink Cow 1-3-18 Shibuya, Shibuya-ku (Villa Modernuna B-1, across from Aoyama Park Tower) **81-3/3406-5597** *5pm-late, clsd Mon*

Sasa-no-yuki 2-15-10 Negishi (Taito-ku) **81-3/3873-1145** *11am-9pm, clsd Mon, serving homemade tofu for 300 years*

Tenmatsu 1-6-1 Dogen-zaka (Shibuya-ku) **81-3/3462-2815** *tempura*

Teyandei 2-20-1 Nishi Azabu (Minato-ku) **81-3/3407-8127** *a cozy izakaya in a 2 story house on a quiet discrete street with more residences than businesses, also other locations*

Yuian 2-6-1 Nishi-Shinjuku 52nd Fl (in the Shinjuku Sumitomo Bldg) **81-3/3342-5671** \

■RETAIL SHOPS

Isetan Men's 3-14-1 Shinjyuku 1-11-15 **81-3/3352-1111** *popular place for men's fashion, cruisy*

■GYMS & HEALTH CLUBS

Gold's Gym Harajuku 6-31-17 Jingumae (Shibuya-ku) **81-3/5766-3131** *24 hrs, except Sun, many gay members*

Shinjuku Tipness Kaleido Bldg 5-7F (Nishi-Shinjuku 7-1), Shinjuku-ku **81-3/3368-3531** *many locations throughout city*

■MEN'S CLUBS

24 Kaikan [M,F,V] Shinjuku 2-13-1 **81-3/3354-2424** *24hrs, darkroom, sauna, restaurant, hotel; also Asakusa 2-29-16 & Kita-Ueno 1-8-7*

Babylon Tokyo [MO] Sendagaya Bldg 3F-5F (Sendagaya 5-30-9, near Yoyogi Station), Yoyogi **81-3/3359-7619** *3pm-1am, till 7am Fri-Sat, [N] Wed & Fri*

Gong 1 Yoyogi (Shibuya-ku) **81-3/3372-3955** *5pm-1am, from 3pm Sat-Sun*

HX [MO,YC] 1F, UI Bldg (Shinjuku 5-9-6) **81-3/3226-4448** *3pm-10am, 24hrs wknds*

Jinya 2-30-19 Toshima-ku (Ikebukuro) **81-3/3931-0186** *24hrs*

King of College 2F Sakagami Bldg (2-14-5, Shinjuku-ku) **81-3/3352-3930** *6am-10pm, rent boys*

Roppongi Inch 2F Nakanomachi Mansion (3-3-25 Roppongi exit 3) **81-3/3589-2102** *behind bar called Lost Angels*

Treff 4F Fukutomi Bldg (Akasaka 2-13-4) **81-3/5563-0523** *wknds naked*

■CRUISY AREAS

Hibiya Park [AYOR] near Yurakucho Station

Shin Kiba Park [AYOR] near Shin Kiba Station

Ueno Park near Tokyo Metropolitan Festival Hall

■TRAVEL AGENTS

Magnet Tours 2-11-14 Nishishinbash Bldg 2F (Minato-ku) **81-3/3500-4819** *tour operator in Japan to focus specifically on LGBT travelers*

Southeast Asia

THAILAND

Bangkok

■INFO LINES & SERVICES

Gay AA 12/3 Silom Rd (at the Coffee Society) **66-2/231-8300** *7pm Th*

■ACCOMMODATIONS

Baan Saladaeng [GF,WI] 69/2 Soi Saladaeng 3, Saladaeng Rd (Silom, Bangrak) **66-2/2636-3038** *upscale, near gay scene*

The Babylon Bangkok [MO,SW,WI] 34 Soi Nandha, Sathon Soi 1, S Sathon Rd **66-2/679-7984** *also spa & saunas, foam party last Sat*

Bangkok Rama Place, City Resort & Hotel [GF,SW,WI,WC,GO] 1546 Pattanakarn Rd (in Suan-Luang District) **66-2/722-6602-10** *full brkfst, also restaurant*

Best Comfort Residential Hotel [M,SW,WI] 49 Soi Sukhumvit 19 (Wattana) **66-2/651-1310** *residential hotel in the heart of Bangkok*

D&D Inn [GF,SW] 68-70 Khaosan Rd (Phranakorn) **66-2/629-0526**

Elephantstay [GS,GO] Royal Elephant Kraal & Village (74/1 M3 Tumbol Suanpik), Phra Nakhon Si Ayutthaya **66-81/668-7727, 66-87/116-3307** *live w/, care for & learn about elephants; near Lopburi River; 1 hour to Bangkok*

Furama Silom [GF,SW] 59 Silom Rd **66-2/237-0488** *also gym, restaurant & bar*

Heaven@4 Hotel [GS,WI] Sukhumvit Soi 4 **66-2/656-9450** *also bar*

Hotel de Moc [GF,SW,WI,WC] 78 Prajatipatai Rd, Pra-Nakorn **66-2/282-2831-3, 66-2/629-2100-5**

Lub d [GF] 4 Decho Rd (Silom, Bangrak) **66-2/634-7999**

Luxx [GF,WI] 6/11 Decho Rd **66-2/635-8800** *style-conscious, minimalist design hotel, full brkfst*

Old Bangkok Inn [GF,NS] 607 Pra Sumen Rd (at Rajdamnern Ave, in Pra Nakhon) **66-2/629-1787** *environmentally-friendly hotel*

Omyim Lodge [GS,NS,WI,GO] 72-74 Naratiwat Rd Silom **66-2/635-0169** *also restaurant*

Pinnacle Hotel [GS] 17 Soi Ngam Duphli, Rama 4 Rd, Sathorn **66-2/287-0111**

Regency Park Hotel [GF,SW] 12/3 Sukhumvit 22, Soi Sainamthip **66-2/259-7420** *located in heart of Bangkok, full brkfst*

Sheraton Grande Sukhumvit [GF,SW,WI,WC] 250 Sukhumvit Rd **66-2/649-8888**

Tarntawan Place Hotel [MW,WI,WC] 119/ 5-10 Surawong Rd **66-2/238-2620** *centrally located, modern amenities, bar & lounge*

Wow Bangkok [GF,WI] 3/16 Sukhumvit Soi 31 **66-2/260-3560**

■BARS

70's Bar [MW,D] 231/16 Sarasin (Chitlom) **66-2/253-4433** *retro lounge*

The Balcony Pub & Restaurant [★,M,F,K] 86-88 Silom Soi 4 (off Silom Rd) **66-2/235-5891** *5:30pm-close*

Balls Sports Bar [M,F] Duangthawee Plaza, 894 Soi Pratoochai, Surawong Rd **66-2/637-0078** *5pm-1am*

Bearbie Bar [M,B,K] 82 Silom Soi 4, 2nd flr **66-2/632-8446** *7:30pm-1am, till 2am Fri-Sat*

Bed Supperclub [GS,D,F] 26 Soi Sukhumvit 11, Sukhumvit Rd, Klongtoey-nua, Wattana **66-2/651-3537** *7:30pm-close*

Blue Club [M,D] 3161 Ramkhamhaeng Rd (btwn Soi 81 & 83, 2nd floor, above Duan Chai) **66-2/732-2360** *mostly Thai*

Club Cafe [M] 8/5 Silom Soi 2 (Bang Rak) **66-86/978-5221** *3pm-3am*

Club Love Remix [GS,D,F,YC] Ramkhamhaeng Soi 89/2 **66-2/378-4345, 66-1/987-4946** *also restaurant*

@**Diamond** [M,NH,F] 10/17 Silom Soi 2/1 **66-2/234-0459** *6pm-2am*

E-Male [M,C,DS] 62-64 Ramkhamhaeng, Soi 24 **66-2/319-6772**

Expresso [M] 8/10-11 Silom Rd, Soi 2 (Bang Rak) *relaxed café-bar*

Finallé [M,D,C] Ramkhamhaeng Soi 89/2 **66-1/503-5398** *9pm-2am*

G.O.D. [M,D] **66-2/632-8033** *11pm-5am, "guys on display"*

Golden Cock [M] 39/27 Soi Rajanakarindra 1, Surawong Rd (Bang Rak) **66-2/236-3859** *1pm-1am*

Golden Dome [MW,C] 252/5 Ratchadapisek Rd Soi 18 (Huay Khwang) **66-2/692-8202** *shows nightly at 5pm, 7pm & 9pm*

JJ Park [GS,F,E] 8/3 Silom Rd, Soi 2 (Bang Rak) **66-2/235-1227** *10:30pm-2am, live music*

Jupiter 2002 Men's Club [M,S] Thaniya Soi 2 (in Suriwonges Hotel) 0-81/617-2163 *8pm-1am*

Maxi's Bar & Restaurant [M] 38/1-2 Soi Pratoochai Suriwong Rd **66-2/2266-4225** *6pm-2am*

MTV Remix [GS,D] Ramkhamhaeng Soi 24 **66-2/319-8340**

One Night Only [M,D] Silom Soi 4, 74-1 **66-89/499-0303** *6pm-3am, small bar on the first floor, also lounge & outside area*

Tawan [★M,S] 2/2 Soi Thantawan, Silom Soi 6 (off Suriwong Rd) **66-2/634-5833** *8pm-1am, specializing in muscular go-go boys*

Telephone Pub & Restaurant [★MW,F,K,WI] 114/ 11 Silom Rd, Soi 4 **66-2/234-3279** *6pm-1am, Skype videophones on all the tables*

■NIGHTCLUBS

Disco Disco [M,D] 8/12-13 Silom Rd, Soi 2 (Bang Rak) **66-2/234-6151, 66-2/266-4029** *9pm-2am*

DJ Station [★MW,D] 8/6-8 Silom Rd, Soi 2 (Bang Rak) **66-02/266-4029** *10:30pm-2am*

Dream Boy [★M,S] 38/3-6 Duangthawee Plaza (at 38 Surawong Rd, Bang Rak) **66-2/233-2121** *8pm-2am, go-go boy shows nightly at 10:30pm & 12:30am*

G-Star [M,D] Ratchada Rd, Soi 8 (Din Daeng) **66-2/643-8792** *7pm-2am*

Happen [M,K] 8/14 Silom Soi 2 *8pm-late, busy after 11pm*

Ick [M,D,E] Ramkhamhaeng Soi 89/2 0-83/975-3778 *5pm-2am*

Pharaoh's Music Bar [GS,F,K] 104 Silom Soi 4 (above Sphinx) **66-2/234-7249** *7pm-2am*

X Boom [M,D,S] Soi Anuman Ratchathon, Suriwong, Bangkok *opens at 8pm, popular 'after-hours' place, go-go dancers*

■CAFES

Bug & Bee 18 Silom Rd, Suriyawong (Bang Rak) **66-2/233-8118** *24hrs*

Coffee Society [F,WI] 12/3 Silom Rd (Suriyawong, Bang Rak) **66-2/235-9784** *24hrs, also art gallery*

Dick's Cafe Bangkok 894/7-8 Soi Pratuchai (Duangthawee Plaza, off Surawong Rd) **66-2/637-0078** *11am-2am, European-style cafe*

■RESTAURANTS

Cabbages & Condoms 6 Soi 12 Sukhumvit Rd (at Birds & Bees Resort) **66-2/229-4611** *11am-10pm, Thai food w/ safe-sex education*

Coyote on Convent 1/2 Sivadon Bldg Convent (Silom Bangrak) **66-2/631-2325** *11am-midnight, Mexican*

Crêpes & Co 59/4 Langsuan Soi 1 (Ploenchit Rd, Lumpini) **66-2/653-3990** *9am-11pm, lounge, full bar*

Eat Me [E] Soi Pipat 2 (off Soi Convent) **66-2/238-0931** *3pm-1am, upscale, also gallery, live music*

Food Loft 1027 Ploenchit Rd, Lumpini, Pathumwan (Central Chisholm, 7th flr) **66-2/655-7777** *upscale int'l food*

Full Moon [GO] 144/2 Silom Soi 10 **66-2/634-0766** *Thai food*

Indigo 6 Convent Rd (off Silom Rd) **66-2/235-3268** *noon-1am, clsd Sun, patio, full bar, French*

Loy Nava Dinner Cruises [R] 37 Charoen Nakorn Rd, Klongsan **66-2/437-4932** *traditional Thai cuisine on rice barge on Chao Phraya River*

Mali [GO] 43 Sathorn Soi 1 **66-2/679-8693** *8am-11pm*

Mango Tree [★R] 37 Soi Tantawan (off Suriwong Rd) **66-2/236-2820** *traditional Thai food, live music nightly*

May Kaidee 111 Tanao Rd, Bang-lam-phu (behind Burger King) **66-9/137-3173** *9am-11pm, innovative vegetarian; also 33 Samen Rd*

O...Ho... [GO] 2/8 Soi Sri Bumphen **66-2/286-5292** *9am-midnight, Thai & Western menu*

Once Upon a Time 32 Soi Petchaburi 17, Pratunam **66-2/252-8629** *11am-11pm, Thai*

Sphinx [★M,K] 100 Silom Soi 4 **66-2/234-7249** *6pm-1am, Thai & Western, full bar, terrace*

Sweet Basil [★] 1 Srivieng Rd (Si Lom, Bang Rak) **66-02/234-1889** *11:30am-9pm, Vietnamese food*

■ENTERTAINMENT & RECREATION

Calypso Cabaret [MW,C,DS] 296 Phaya Thai Rd, Pathumwan (at Asia Hotel) **66-2/261-6355** *shows nightly at 8:15pm & 9:30pm*

Mambo [C] 59/28 Sathu-phararam 3 Rd **66-2/294-7381-2** *shows nightly at 7:15pm & 10pm*

■GYMS & HEALTH CLUBS

Hercules Health Club [M,F] 91/194 Siam Park City, Sukhapiban 2 Rd, Siam Park Ave (Bangkapi) **66-2/919-9603** *4pm-midnight; also restaurant & bar*

■MEN'S CLUBS

Adonis Massage [★] 44/11 Convent Rd (Silom) **66-2/236-7789** *1pm-11pm*

Albury Men's Club 66/2 Soi Sukhumvit 26 **66-2/255-8920** *1pm-11pm*

Aqua Spa Club [F] 11/5 Soi Sathorn 9 **66-2/286-5233** *2pm-midnight, massage, tarot readings*

Arena 2/F Silom Plaza **66-2/635-3645** *Thai massage*

Banana Club [F] 41/9 Sukhumvit Soi 11 **66-2/651-0002** *3 flrs, massage, also restaurant*

Body Club 4/24-25 Sukhumvit Soi 8 **66-89/171-9009** *noon-10pm*

Chakran [F,K,V,SW] 32 Soi Ari 4, Phaholyothin Soi 7, Phayathai **66-2/279-1359** *darkroom, gym, poolside bar*

Sauna Mania 35/2 Soi Pipat 2 (off Soi Convent, Silom) **66-2/817-4073** *3pm-2am, enter on 2nd flr*

V Club 7 [F] 32 Chakran Bldg, Soi Paholyothin 7 (Soi Ari 4) **66-02/279-3322** *2pm-midnight*

Australia

NEW SOUTH WALES

Sydney

■INFO LINES & SERVICES

The Gender Centre **61-2/9569-2366** *9am-4:30pm Mon-Fri, free services for transgender/ transsexual people & their partners/ friends/ families*

Lesbian & Gay Counselling Service **61-2/8594-9596, 1-800/18-4527** (outside Sydney) *5:30pm-10:30pm, info & support*

■ACCOMMODATIONS

Best Western Hotel Stellar [GS,WI] 4 Wentworth Ave (at Oxford St) **61-2/9264-9754** *kitchenette in each room, also cafe & bar*

Brickfield Hill B&B Inn [GS,WI,GO] 403 Riley St (at Foveaux), Surry Hills **61-2/9211-4886** *in gay district, near beaches*

Chelsea Guest House [GS,NS,GO] 49 Womerah Ave (at Oswald Ln), Darlinghurst **61-2/9380-5994** *Victorian w/ courtyard*

Governors on Fitzroy B&B [M,WI,GO]
64 Fitzroy St (at Bourke), Surry Hills
61-2/9331-4652 *3 blocks from Oxford St, full brkfst, hot tub, shared baths, garden*

Kirketon Boutique Hotel [GF,WI] 229
Darlinghurst Rd (at Farrell Ave)
**61-2/9332-2011, 800/332-920
(Australia only)** *also restaurant & bar*

Medusa [GF,WI] 267 Darlinghurst Rd (at Liverpool), Darlinghurst
61-2/9331-1000 *modern boutique hotel*

Nomads Westend [GF,NS,WI,WC] 412
Pitt St (at Goulburn St)
61-2/9211-4588, 1800/013-186
budget/ backpacker's accommodations

Pensione Hotel [GF,WI] 631-635
George St (at Goulburn St)
61-2/9265-8888, 800/885-886
close to the Capital theatre

Victoria Court Hotel Sydney [GF,WI]
122 Victoria St (at Orwell, Potts Point)
61-2/9357-3200, 1800/630-505 (in Australia)

■ BARS

Bar Cleveland/ Hershey Bar
[GS,D,F,YC] 433 Cleveland St (at Bourke), Surry Hills **61-2/9698-1908** *11am-4am, noon-midnight Sun, cocktail lounge, DJ*

The Beauchamp [★GS,NH,F,GO] 265
Oxford St (at S Dowling), Darlinghurst
61-2/9331-2575 *noon-2am*

Beresford Sundays [MW] 354 Bourke
St (at Albion St), Surry Hills
61-2/9357-1111 *from noon Sun, fun in the sun*

The Colombian [★MW,D] 117-123
Oxford St (at Crown St), Darlinghurst
61-2/9360-2151 *9am-6am, trendy pub & cocktail bar, 2 levels, theme nights*

The Flinders Hotel [MW,D,F,S,YC]
63-65 Flinders St (at Hill St),
Darlinghurst **61-2/9356-3622** *5pm-3am, clsd Sun-Mon*

Green Park Hotel [GS] 360 Victoria St
(at Liverpool), Darlinghurst
61-2/9380-5311 *10am-2am, noon-midnight Sun, very gay Sun, stylish bar*

The Imperial Hotel [MW,D,F,K,DS,S] 35
Erskineville Rd, Newtown
61-2/9519-9899

The Oxford [★MW,D,F,E] 134 Oxford St
(at Bourke St, Taylor Square),
Darlinghurst **61-2/8324-5200** *10am-close, 3 bars*

The Palms On Oxford [★M,D] 124
Oxford St (at Bourke St, Taylor Square),
Darlinghurst **61-2/9357-4166** *8pm-late, clsd Mon-Wed*

Phoenix Bar [GS,D,E,DS] 34 Oxford St
(at Exchange Hotel), Darlinghurst
61-2/9331-2956 *10am-5am, till 7am Fri-Sun, clsd Mon-Tue, sweaty down-stairs dance den, also 5 other bars in complex*

The Stonewall [★M,D,K,DS,S] 175
Oxford St (at Bourke), Darlinghurst
61-2/9360-1963 *noon-6am, from 9am wknds, 3 bars*

ZanziBar [GF,F] 323 King St (at Phillips
St), Newtown **62-2/9519-1511**

■ NIGHTCLUBS

ARQ [★M,D,DS,$] 16 Flinders St (at
Taylor Square), Darlinghurst
61-2/9380-8700 *9pm-late Th-Sun, clsd Mon-Wed, drag shows Th*

Home [★GF,D,$] Tenancy 101, Cockle
Bay Wharf (at Wheat Rd, Darling
Harbour) **61-2/9266-0600** *open Fri-Sun, hosts Homesexual (www.homesexual.com.au)*

The Midnight Shift [★M,D,V] 85
Oxford St (at Riley), Darlinghurst
61-2/9358-3848 *10pm-late Fri-Sat, also Saddle Bar*

Nevermind [GS,D] 163 Oxford St,
Darlinghurst *Fri-Sun only, cutting edge electronic music, theme nights*

Rising Day Club [M,D] 34 Oxford St (at
Phoenix bar), Darlinghurst *recovery club starts at 4am Sat-Sun*

Slide [MW,D,F,E,C] 41 Oxford St (at
Pelican) **61-2/8915-1899** *6pm-3am, 5pm-4am Fri, 7pm-4am Sat-Sun, clsd Mon-Tue*

Sly Fox [MW,D,K] 199 Enmore Rd,
Enmore **61-2/9557-1016**

■ CAFES

Fratelli Fresh Waterloo [★] 7 Danks St **61-2/9699-3161** *9am-6pm, 8am-4pm Sat, 10am-4pm Sun, Italian vegetarian*

Victoire 285 Darling St **61-2/9818-5529** *great bread*

Vinyl Lounge Cafe [MW,F] 17 Elizabeth Bay Rd, Elizabeth Bay **61-2/9326-9224** *7am-4pm, from 8am wknds, clsd Mon, light menu, plenty veggie, cash only*

■ RESTAURANTS

Bentley Restaurant & Bar 320 Crown St (Surry Hills) **61-2/9332-2344** *noon-late, clsd Sun- Mon, tapas & small plates, excellent wine*

Bertoni Casalinga 281 Darling St **61-2/9818-5845** *6am-6:30pm, Italian*

Bills Surry Hills 359 Crown St (Surry Hills) **61-2/9360-4762** *7am-10pm, great ricotta pancakes*

Billy Kwong [★R,WC] 3/355 Crown St (Surry Hills) **61-2/9332-3300** *sustainable local & organic Chinese from 6pm daily*

The Boathouse on Blackwattle Bay [R] End of Ferry Road (Glebe) **61-2/9518-9011** *lunch & dinner Tue-Sun, gourmet seafood, some veggie, great view*

Bright N Up [MW,DS] 77 Oxford St (at the Brighton Hotel), Darlinghurst **61-2/9361-3379** *4:30pm-midnight*

Chu Bay 312a Bourke St, Darlinghurst **61-2/9331-3386** *5:30pm-11pm, Vietnamese, some veggie*

Fu Manchu [NS] 249 Victoria St, Darlinghurst **61-2/9360-9424** *lunch & dinner, chic noodle bar, cash only*

Iku Wholefood Kitchen [NS] 25a Glebe Point Rd, Glebe **61-2/9692-8720, 800/732-962** *lunch & dinner, creative vegan/ macrobiotic fare, outdoor seating*

Kujin 41b Elizabeth Bay Rd, Elizabeth Bay **61-2/9331-6077** *lunch & dinner, clsd Mon, Japanese*

Pink Peppercorn [GO] 122 Oxford St (near Taylor Square), Darlinghurst **61-2/9360-9922** *6pm-late, clsd Mon, Laotian & Thai*

Queen Victoria Hotel/ Razors Bistro 167 Enmore Rd, Enmore **61-2/9517-9685**

Sean's Panorama 270 Campbell Parade, Bondi Beach **61-2/9365-4924** *open 6pm , from noon Sat-Sun, clsd Mon-Tue*

Thai Kanteen [★GO] 541 Military Rd (at Harbour St), Mosman **61-2/9960-3282** *dinner nightly, clsd Sun, modern Thai*

Thai Pothong [WC] 294 King St (Newtown) **61-2/9550-6277** *lunch & dinner, Thai*

■ ENTERTAINMENT & RECREATION

Bondi Beach Bondi Beach *Sydney's most popular beach, more gay at north end*

Lady Jane Beach/ Lady Bay Beach [M,N] Watsons Bay

Obelisk Beach [M,N] Middle Head Rd (at Chowder Bay Rd)

Sydney by Diva departs from Oxford Hotel (in Taylor Square), Darlinghurst **61-2/9310-0200** *tour Sydney w/ drag queen host*

Sydney Gay/ Lesbian Mardi Gras 94 Oxford St, Darlinghurst 2010 **61-2/9383-0900** *the wildest party under the rainbow on this planet (see www.mardigras.org.au)*

■ BOOKSTORES

The Bookshop Darlinghurst 207 Oxford St (near Darlinghurst Rd), Darlinghurst **61-2/9331-1103** *10am-10pm, Australia's oldest LGBT bookstore, staff happy to help w/ tourist info*

Gertrude & Alice 46 Hall St (Bondi Beach) **61-2/9130-5155** *secondhand books, also coffee shop*

■ RETAIL SHOPS

House of Priscilla 47 Oxford St, Darlinghurst **61-2/9286-3023** *wigs, costumes & more*

■PUBLICATIONS

DNA 61-2/9764-0200, 888/263-2624 (US #) *monthly gay men's magazine*

SX Weekly 61-2/9360-8934 *free gay/ lesbian weekly*

Sydney Star Observer 61-2/8263-0500 *weekly newspaper w/ club & event listings*

■GYMS & HEALTH CLUBS

City Gym 107-113 Crown St (at William St), E Sydney 61-2/9360-6247 *day passes available*

Gold's Gym Sydney 58 Kippax St (level 1), Surry Hills 61-2/9211-2799 *5:30am-9pm, 8am-6pm Sat, till 5pm Sun*

TBC Gym 122 Lang Rd, #2205A (The Entertainment Quarter), Moore Park 61-2/9357-7416

■MEN'S CLUBS

Bodyline Spa & Sauna [★V] 10 Taylor St, Darlinghurst 61-2/9360-1006 *11am-1am, till 5am Fri-Sat*

Bodyline Spa & Sauna [V] 45 Peel St, S Brisbane 61-2/3846-4633 *11am-1am, till 5am Fri-Sat*

Headquarters [V,NS,WI] 273 Crown St (at Goulburn, near Oxford), Darlinghurst 61-2/9331-6217 *24hrs wknds, 3pm-7pm Mon-Th, theme rooms, theme nights*

Kingsteam [F,WI] 38-42 Oxford St (next to Exchange Hotel), Darlinghurst 61-2/8250-1818 *24hrs*

Signal [V,WI] at Riley & Arnold Sts (upstairs), Darlinghurst 61-2/9331-8830

Sydney City Steam [F,WI,GO] 357 Sussex St (Darling Harbour) 61-2/9267-6766 *24hrs wknds*

■SEX CLUBS

Aarows [MW,TG,18+] 17 Bridge St (at Pitt St), Rydalmere 61-2/9638-0553 *24hrs*

■EROTICA

Gay Exchange 44 Park St 61-2/9267-6812

House of Fetish 288 Crown St, Darlinghurst 61-2/9380-9042 *clsd Mon-Tues*

Pleasure Chest 705 George St (at Ultimo Rd), Haymarket 61-2/9212-6440 *24hrs*

Sax Fetish [GO] 110a Oxford St (Taylor Square) 61-2/9331-6105

Toolshed 81 Oxford St, Darlinghurst 61-2/9332-2792

■CRUISY AREAS

Beare Park [AYOR] Ithaca Rd

Bondi Beach Pavilion [AYOR] Bondi Beach

Gunnamatta Park [AYOR] Cronulla

Lady Bay Beach [AYOR] at N tip of South Head, Cronulla

Loftus Oval [AYOR] Princes Hwy (Loftus), Cronulla *park*

Marks Park [AYOR] S end of Bondi Beach, Cronulla *head toward the cliffs, evenings*

Rushcutters Bay Park [AYOR] New Beach Rd

Sydney Park [AYOR] King St & Mitchell Rd, Newtown *behind Old Brick Works*

2014 Tours & Tour Operators

CRUISES

Men Only

SAILORdudes Admiraly Quay, ZH 3063EE Rotterdam, Netherlands **3165/133–1459** fun, affordable, active gay sailing holidays (clothing optional) for fit dudes • www.sailordudes.com

Mostly Men

Atlantis Events 9200 Sunset Blvd, Ste 500, West Hollywood, CA 90069 **310/859–8800, 800/628–5268** largest LGBT tour operator in the world • all-gay cruise, resort & tour vacations • www.atlantisevents.com

Pied Piper Tours 330 W 42nd St, Ste 1804, New York, NY 10036 **212/239–2412, 800/874–7312** gay group cruises • www.gaygroupcruises.com

Gay/Lesbian

Aquafest 4801 Woodway #100-W, Houston, TX 77056 **800/592–9058** LGBT groups mingle w/ mixed clientele on major cruise lines • www.aquafestcruises.com

Gayribbean Cruises Dallas, TX **877/560–8318** gay & lesbian group cruise organizer • fabulous destinations • annual Halloween cruise from Galveston, TX • www.gayribbeancruises.com

Port Yacht Charters 9 Belleview Ave, Port Washington, NY 11050 **516/883–0998, 877/DO-A-BOAT** custom charters worldwide, specializing in the Caribbean • commitment ceremonies • gourmet cuisine • www.portyachtcharters.com

R Family 5 Washington Ave, Nyack, NY 10960 **917/522–0985** family-friendly vacations designed especially for the LGBT community • www.rfamilyvacations.com

Rainbow Charters Kewalo Basin, Honolulu, HI 96814 **808/347–0235** gay & lesbian weddings • custom sailing cruises • whale-watching • snorkeling • sunset cruises • www.RainbowChartersHawaii.com

RSVP Vacations 800/328–7787 gay & lesbian cruise vacations • www.rsvpvacations.com

Sailing Affairs 58 E 1st St #6-B, New York City, NY 10003 **917/453–6425** gay sailboat charters, day trips, sunset sails & sailing vacations on 47-foot Beneteau • East Coast, Caribbean, Europe & Mediterranean • www.sailingaffairs.com

LUXURY TOURS

Men Only

Hanns Ebensten Travel, Inc 626 Josephine Parker Dr #206, Key West, FL 33040 **305/294–8174, 866/294–8174** worldwide adventures for the uncommon traveler • Peru, India, Morocco, South Africa, Greece, Turkey, Italy, Egypt & more • www.hetravel.com

Mostly Men

EuroPanache 410 Park Ave, 15th flr, New York City, NY 10022 **888/600–6777** unique, elite vacation experiences w/ an appealing mix of themes • www.europanache.com

Gay/Lesbian

DavidTravel 310 Dahlia Pl, Ste A, Corona del Mar, CA 92625-2821 **949/427–0199** small luxury group departures & customized travel for individuals & groups • milestone events, including honeymoons! • www.DavidTravel.com

Steele Luxury Travel New York City, NY 10011 **646/688-2274** unique & top-rated travel experiences to exotic destinations worldwide • www.steeletravel.com

GREAT OUTDOORS ADVENTURES

Men Only

Adventure Bound Expeditions 711 Walnut St, Boulder, CO 80302 **303/449-0990, 877/440-0990** outdoor adventure worldwide • hiking, kayaking, safaris, wildlife viewing • www.adventureboundmen.com

Mostly Men

Saltyboys gay & naturist sailing cruises • www.saltyboys.com

Scuba Scotty San Francisco, CA **760/974-6477** scuba instruction • local & exotic destinations • gay-owned • www.scubascotty.com

Touring Cairns Kewarra Beach, Cairns, QLD, Australia **61-7/0402-868080** rain forest tours in the Cairns hinterland • www.touringcairns.com.au

Gay/Lesbian

Alyson Adventures, Inc 626 Josephine Parker Dr #206, Key West, FL 33040 **305/296-9935, 800/825-9766** award-winning adventure travel & active vacations • hiking, biking & multi-sport activities • www.hetravel.com

Out in Alaska 1819 Dimond Dr, Anchorage, AK 99507 **907/339-0101** adventure travel throughout Alaska for LGBT travelers • your best bet for a fun & authentic Alaska vacation! • www.outinalaska.com

OutWest Global Adventures PO Box 2050, Red Lodge, MT 59068 **406/446-1533, 800/743-0458** specializing in gay/ lesbian active & adventure travel • worldwide • www.outwestadventures.com

Undersea Expeditions 758 Kapahulu Ave #100-1188, Honolulu, HI 96816 **858/270-2900, 800/669-0310** gay & lesbian scuba adventures worldwide • www.UnderseaX.com

Gay/Straight

GoNorth Alaska Adventure Travel Center 3713 South Lathrop St, Fairbanks, AK 99709 **907/479-7271, 855/236-7271** guided tours throughout Alaska & the Arctic • air taxis & transportation • www.GoNorth-Alaska.com

Himalayan High Treks 241 Dolores St, San Francisco, CA 94103 **415/551-1005, 800/455-8735** experience indigenous Buddhist & Hindu cultures • www.hightreks.com

Natural Habitat Adventures PO Box 3065, Boulder, CO 80307 **303/449-3711, 800/543-8917** up-close encounters w/ the world's most amazing wildlife in its natural habitat • www.nathab.com

Open Eye Tours PO Box 324, Makawao, HI 96768 **808/572-3483** customized private land tours of Maui & other islands • visit popular spots or places seldom seen, walking or not • sharing Maui's best-kept secrets since 1983 • www.openeyetours.com

Paddling South & Saddling South PO Box 827, Calistoga, CA 94515 **707/942-4550, 800/398-6200** horseback, mountain-biking & sea-kayak trips in Baja • also women-only trips • call for complete calendar • www.tourbaja.com

Puffin Fishing Charters PO Box 1169, Seward, AK 99664 **907/224-4653, 800/978-3346** guided charter fishing • almost 30 years of experience • halibut, salmon & rockfish on vessels custom-built for Alaskan waters • www.puffincharters.com

Voyageur North Outfitters 1829 E Sheridan, Ely, MN 55731 **218/365-3251,** **800/848-5530** canoe outfitting & trips • www.vnorth.com

SPIRITUAL/HEALTH VACATIONS

Gay/Lesbian

Spirit Journeys 134 River Rd, New Milford, NJ 97646 **201/483-3111, 800/754-1875** spiritual retreats, workshops & adventure trips throughout the US & abroad • www.spiritjourneys.com

THEMATIC TOURS

Mostly Men

Coda International Tours, Inc 12794 Forest Hill Blvd #1A, West Palm Beach, FL 33414 **561/791-9890, 888/677-2632** culturally focused travel programs • www.coda-tours.com

Hawaii Gay Tours Honolulu, HI 96821 **808/234-9260** experience Hawaii as the locals do • customizable tours • www.hawaiigaytours.com

Gay/Lesbian

Africa Outing 5 Alcyone Rd, Claremont, Capetown 7708, South Africa **27-21/671-4028** gay/ lesbian safaris & more • tours customized to your needs • www.afouting.com

Brazil Fiesta Visa Service 268 Bush St #3531, San Francisco, CA 94104 **415/986-1134, 800/200-0582** expedited Brazilian visa service • www.brazilfiesta.net

CM by Carlos Melia 630 5th Ave #2207, 10011 New York City **917/754-5515** boutique gay travel to Argentina, Uruguay & New York City • all services tested by me • "Been There Done That" • www.carlosmelia.com

Gay Bali Tours Jl. Braban No. 67, Seminyak, 80361 Bali, Indonesia **62-361/736-818, 62-361/788-6627** premier & professional tour operator permanently based in Bali • www.baligay.net

Go Pink China Beijing, China **86/1366-124-6689** adding queer elements to city tours & national trips in China • www.gopinkchina.com

Kuyay Travel Puerto Rosales 46, 5550000 Puerto Varas, Los Lagos, Chile **56-652/438-990, 56-97/519-3259** gay-owned/run travel planner & tour host in Patagonia • www.gaypatagonia.com

MexGay Vacations 355 S Grand Ave #2450, Los Angeles, CA 90071 **213/383-9491, 866/639-4299** specializing in gay travel to Mexico • www.mexgay.com

National Gay Pilots Association PO Box 1652, San Jose, CA 95109 **214/336-0873** several annual gatherings • call for more info • www.ngpa.org

Pacific Ocean Holidays Honolulu, HI **808/923-2400** Hawaii vacation packages • www.gayhawaiivacations.com

Planetdwellers Shop 47 Elizabeth Bay Rd, Elizabeth Bay, NSW 2011, Australia **61-2/8667-3336** LGBT tours of Australia • come to OZ! • www.planetdwellers.com.au

Toto Tours 1326 W Albion Ave #3W, Chicago, IL 60626 **773/274-8686, 800/565-1241** unique worldwide adventures for gay men, lesbians, their friends & adult family members • www.tototours.com

Venture Out 575 Pierce St #604, San Francisco, CA 94117 **415/626-5678, 888/431-6789** high-end, escorted, small-group tours for gay & lesbian travelers to countries around the world • www.venture-out.com

Tour Operators • Thematic Tours

Gay/Straight

Alaska Railroad 431 W 1st Ave, Anchorage, AK 99501 **907/265-2494, 800/544-0552 (reservations)** rail & tour packages • www.alaskarailroad.com

Aria Tours PO Box 159, Little Bridge St, Almonte, ON K0A 1A0, Canada **866/686-1288** luxury travel for opera & the arts • spectacular destinations in • www.ariatours.com

Brazil Ecojourneys Estrada Rozalia Paulina Ferreira 1132, Armação, 88063-555 Florianopolis, Brazil **55-48/3389-5619** lesbian-owned Brazil tour operator • www.brazilecojourneys.com

Ecotour Expeditions, Inc PO Box 128, Jamestown, RI 02835 **401/423-3377, 800/688-1822** small group boat tours of the Amazon & more • call for color catalog • www.naturetours.com

Heritage Tours Private Travel 121 W 27th St #1201, New York, NY 10001 **212/206-8400, 800/378-4555** custom private trips to Morocco, Spain, Portugal, Turkey, Southern & East Africa • www.HTprivatetravel.com

Holbrook Travel 3540 NW 13th St, Gainesville, FL 32609 **800/451-7111** natural history tours in Central America, South America & Africa • small groups • www.holbrooktravel.com

Lebtour.com 00961 Beirut, Lebanon **961-3/004-572** professional travel in Lebanon, Syria & Jordan • gay packages available • www.lebtour.com

Lima Tours Jr De la Union 1040, Lima, Peru **51-1/619-6900** personalized, gay-friendly tours to Peru • www.limatours.com.pe

New England Vacation Tours PO Box 560, West Dover, VT 05356 **802/464-2076, 800/742-7669** gay/ lesbian tours (including fall foliage) conducted by a mainstream tour operator • www.newenglandvacationtours.com

Pacha Tours 36 W 44th St # 1208, New York City, NY 10036 **800/722-4288** trips to Turkey, Spain, France & Greece • www.pachatours.com

Sublime Journeys Albrook Plaza, no. 31, Panama City, Panama **800/830-7142** progressive, diverse & extraordinary travel experiences in South & Central America • www.discoversublime.com

VIP Tours of New York 320 W 38th St, New York, NY 10018 **212/247-0366, 800/300-6203** private, custom-designed tours of New York • specializing in theater, architecture, gay life & more • groups from one to 100+ • www.viptoursny.com

Welcome Rajasthan Jaipur, Rajasthan 30216, India **91-141/220-5527 x107, 91-931/450-3423** tours & car rentals for Rajasthan, India • www.welcomerajasthan.com

Wild Rainbow African Safaris 308 Jones St, Ukiah, CA 95482 **800/423-1945** bespoke African safaris lead by Jody Cole • www.wildrainbowsafaris.com

CUSTOM TOURS

Gay/Straight

Costa Rica Experts 3166 N Lincoln Ave #424, Chicago, IL 60657 **773/935-1009, 800/827-9046** • www.costaricaexperts.com

Embassy Travel 927 N Kings Rd #311, West Hollywood, CA 90069 **323/650-0743** personalized tours to southern Africa & other worldwide destinations

Travel & Culture Dubai 201 Al Habbai Building (opposite Deira city center), Dubai, United Arab Emirates **971/5287-38211** tours, safaris & hotel reservations in Dubai • www.dubai.travel-culture.com

Travel & Culture Pakistan 702 Panorama Center Office Plaza, 75530 Karachi, Pakistan **92-321/242-4778** tours, safaris & hotel reservations in Pakistan • www.travel-culture.com

Travel & Culture Sri Lanka 07-1B, E Tower, World Trade Ctr, Colombo, Sri Lanka 94/777-864-479 tours, safaris & hotel reservations in Sri Lanka • www.srilanka.travel-culture.com

Various Tours

Mostly Men

Brand g Vacations 3333 Republic Ave, Minneapolis, MN 55426 952/405-9309, 800/433-4303 vacation experiences that reflect the dynamics & diversity of the LGBT community • www.brandgvacations.com

Detours Gay Travel 800/680-8066 boutique gay tour operator specializing in group adventures to the world's most exotic destinations • www.detourstravel.com

Source Events PO Box 530988, Miami, FL 33153 305/672-9779, 888/768-7238 specializing in all-gay Windstar cruises • luxury adventures around the world • www.sourceevents.com

Gay/Lesbian

Footprints 19 Madison Ave #300, Toronto, ON M5R 2S2, Canada 416/962-8111, 888/962-6211 custom-designed, private tours arranged to worldwide destinations • www.footprintstravel.com

Friends of Dorothy Travel® 1177 California St #B, San Francisco, CA 94108 415/864-1600, 800/640-4918 unique gay & lesbian adventures • individual & group arrangements • www.fodtravel.com

Out & About Travel 161 Federal St, Providence, RI 02903 800/842-4753 specializing in gay & lesbian tours, cruises, adventure travel, ski trips, honeymoons, customized packages & more • serving the GLBT community since 1999! • www.gaytravelpros.com

Zoom Vacations Chicago, IL 773/772-9666, 866/966-6822 takes gay group travel to the next level • experience the best of a destination w/ surprises, insider events & a sense of magic • www.zoomvacations.com

Events

January 2014

12-19: Arosa Gay Ski Week   *Arosa, Switzerland*
mostly men • 500 attendees • 41-21/566-7020 • **www.arosa-gayskiweek.com**

12-19: Aspen Gay Ski Week   *Aspen, CO*
LGBT • 5000+ attendees • 970/925-4123 • **www.gayskiweek.com**

12-Feb 2: Midsumma Festival   *Melbourne, Australia*
arts, culture & community • LGBTQ • 61-3/9415-9819 • **www.midsumma.org.au**

16-21: Sin City Shootout   *Las Vegas, NV*
LGBT athletes compete in softball, basketball, wrestling, body building & more • LGBT • 6,750 attendees • 909/227-1794 • **www.sincityshootout.com**

22-26: Winter Rendezvous   *Stowe, VT*
annual gay ski week • skiing, winter sports & entertainment • 587/445-7198 • **www.winterrendezvous.com**

26–Feb 2: WinterPRIDE: Whistler Gay Ski Week   *Whistler, BC, Canada*
annual gay/ lesbian ski week • parties for boys & girls! • top-notch DJs & venues •
popular destination 75 miles N of Vancouver • LGBT • 3,000+ attendees •
604/288-7218, 866/787-1966 • see ad in front color section •
www.gaywhistler.com

February 2014

7–March 2: Sydney Gay Mardi Gras   *Sydney, Australia*
extravagant season of festivities, arts & culture, culminating in the parade & world-
famous Mardi Gras party • 011-61-2/9383-0900 • **www.mardigras.org.au**

21–March 2: Telluride Gay Ski Week   *Telluride, CO*
214/695-2646 • **www.telluridegayskiweek.com**

March 2014

2–9: Lake Tahoe WinterFest Gay & Lesbian Ski Week   *Lake Tahoe, NV*
world-class skiing • gay comedy • Lake Tahoe dinner/dance cruise • LGBT • 800
attendees • **www.LakeTahoeWinterfest.com**

4: Mardi Gras   *New Orleans, LA*
mixed gay/ straight • 800/672-6124 • **www.neworleanscvb.com**

21–30: Winter Music Conference   *Miami, FL*
huge annual EDM conference • workshops, seminars, IDMA & of course dance
parties • mixed gay/ straight • 100,000 attendees • /954 •
www.WinterMusicConference.com

22–29: European Gay Ski Week   *Alpe d'Huez, France*
Europe's biggest gay winter sports & music festival • "the perfect winter holiday, in
a welcoming LGBT environment" • 44-020/7183 0823 (option 1) • **www.european-
gayskiweek.com**

25–30: OutBoard   *Steamboat Springs, CO*
annual lesbian/ gay snowboarding festival • 300+ attendees • 877/38-BOARD •
www.outboard.org

TBA: Chicago Takes Off   *Chicago, IL*
burlesque show to fight HIV/AIDS in the Chicagoland area • LGBT • 1400 attendees
• 773/989-9400 • **www.chicagotakesoff.org**

April 2014

13: AIDS Walk Miami   *Miami Beach, FL*
5K walk-a-thon fundraiser benefiting Care Resource • LGBT • 305/576-1234 •
www.aidswalkmiami.org

20–27: Philadelphia Black Gay Pride   *Philadelphia, PA*
a weekend of social & cultural activities • films, BBQ, spoken word, parties & more •
LGBT • 877/497-7247 • **www.phillyblackpride.org**

30: Queensday   *Amsterdam, Netherlands*
huge street festival to celebrate what was originally the birthday of the Queen
Mother • LGBT • **www.queensdayamsterdam.eu**

TBA: Boybutante Ball   *Athens, GA*
LGBT • 1000+ attendees • **www.boybutante.org**

May 2014

1-4: Equality Forum *Philadelphia, PA*
largest nat'l & int'l LGBT civil rights summit w/ panels, parties & special events •
215/732-3378 x116 • **www.equalityforum.com**

2-4: Blatino Oasis *Palm Springs, CA*
join Black, Blatino & Latino men and their friends from around the world for pool
parties, dance parties, erotic events, awards ceremonies, white party brunch & more!
• men only • **www.blatinooasis.com**

3: Down & Derby *Louisville, KY*
official LGBT event of the Kentucky Derby • LGBT • **www.louisvilledownand-derby.com**

5-18: Int'l Dublin Gay Theatre Festival *Dublin, Ireland*
353-87/657-3732 • **www.gaytheatre.ie**

8-11: Splash: Houston Black Gay Pride *Houston, TX*
LGBT • 832/443-1016 • **www.houstonsplash.com**

10-16: OutGames *Darwin, Australia*
gay sport & cultural festival • LGBT • 32 475/541 247 • **www.glisa.org**

12-14: Annual Gay Bowling Tournament *Tucson, AZ*
check site for local tournaments throughout the year • **www.igbo.org**

18: AIDS Walk New York *New York City, NY*
AIDS benefit • mixed gay/ straight • 212/807-9255 • **www.aidswalk.net**

18: Minnesota AIDS Walk *Minneapolis, MN*
enjoy a 10K walk from Minnehaha Park & raise money for MN AIDS Project • mixed
gay/ straight • 10,000 attendees • 612/373-2410 • **www.mnaidsproject.org**

**22-25: Int'l Association of Country Western Dance Clubs
Annual Convention** *Denver, CO*
also semi-annual conventions in March (Fort Lauderdale, FL) & October (San
Francisco, CA) • LGBT • 400-600 attendees • **www.outcountrydance.com**

22-26: Pensacola Memorial Day Weekend *Pensacola, FL*
many parties on beaches & in bars • LGBT • 35,000+ attendees • 850/433-9491 •
www.memorialweekendpensacola.com

23-June 8: Spoleto Festival USA *Charleston, SC*
one of the continent's premier avant-garde cultural arts festivals • 140+ performances of dance, theater & music from around the world • mixed gay/ straight •
843/579-3100 (tickets), 843/722-2764 (office) • **www.spoletousa.org**

June 2014

ongoing: LGBT Pride *Cross-country, USA*
celebrate yourself & attend one - or many - of the hundreds of Gay Pride parades
& festivities happening in cities around the world • **www.interpride.org**

ongoing: Music in the Mountains *Grass Valley, CA*
summer music festival • mixed gay/ straight • 530/265-6173 • **www.musicinthe-mountains.org**

ongoing: **National Queer Arts Festival**   *San Francisco, CA*
performances & exhibitions in the San Francisco Bay Area highlighting artists from
around the country • year-round events • LGBT • 415/935-5948 •
www.QueerCulturalCenter.org

1-7: **AIDS LifeCycle**   *San Francisco to Los Angeles, CA*
bike from San Francisco to Los Angeles to raise money for HIV/AIDS services •
415/581-7077 • **www.aidslifecycle.org**

1-8: **CMEN Spring Gathering**   *Whispering Oaks, TN*
swimming, parties, workshops & more with fellow gay male naturists • also West
Coast Gathering in August • men only • 400 attendees • 877/683-4781 •
www.mywhisperingoaks.org

3-9: **Gay Days Orlando**   *Orlando, FL*
including Gay Day at Disney • 7 days of parties & fun for boys & girls alike! • LGBT
• 407/896-8431 • **www.gaydays.com**

6-8: **PrideFest**   *Milwaukee, WI*
celebrate LGBT pride at Henry W Maier Festival Park • 414/272-3378 • www.pride-
fest.com

13-15: **Black Gay Pride**   *Memphis, TN*
LGBT • 901/522-8459 • **www.memphisblackpride.org**

15: **Unofficial Gay Day at Cedar Point**   *Sandusky, OH*
wear red to show your support on the unofficial Gay Day at this popular amuse-
ment park • mixed gay/ straight •

18-22: **South Carolina Black Pride**   *Columbia, SC*
• **www.southcarolinablackpride.com**

28-29: **San Francisco LGBT Pride Parade/ Celebration** *San Francisco, CA*
LGBT • 415/864-0831 • **www.sfpride.org**

29: **REACH Pride T-Dance**   *San Francisco, CA*
high energy music & fantastic DJs • mostly men • 600+ attendees • • www.grgr-
west.org/reach.html

TBA: **AIDS Walk Boston & 5K Run**   *Boston, MA*
mixed gay/ straight • 12,000 attendees • 617/424-9255 •
www.aidswalkboston.org

TBA: **Howl Festival**   *New York City, NY*
a cabaret from the underworld • outdoor murals • hip hop howl • all in Tompkins
Square Park • mixed gay/ straight • 212/243-3413 • **www.howlfestival.com**

TBA: **Idapalooza Fruit Jam**   *Dowelltown, TN*
queer music festival in backwoods TN • camping • vegetarian feasts •
615/597-4409 • **www.planetida.com**

TBA: **IGLFA World Championship**   *TBA, Worldwide*
Int'l Gay & Lesbian Football Association's annual soccer tournament •
www.iglfa.org

TBA: **Juneteenth Jamboree of New Plays**   *New York City, NY*
annual theater festival • new works about the African American experience & its
legacy • mixed gay/ straight • 212/964-1904 •
www.juneteenthlegacytheatre.com

TBA: Paris Circuit Party   *Paris, France*
gay culture festival • film • performance • political discussions • dance parties &
more • LGBT • www.pariscircuitparty.com

TBA: PDX Black Pride   *Portland, OR*
films, workshops, parties & more • LGBT • pflagpdx.org

TBA: UK Black Pride   *London, England*
44 020/8257 5358 • www.ukblackpride.org.uk

TBA: Windy City Black Pride   *Chicago, IL*
a weekend of parties, seminars & more • LGBT • 888/922-7244 • www.windycity-
blackpride.org

July 2014

2-6: At the Beach/ LA Black Pride Weekend   *Los Angeles, CA*
celebrate a weekend of diversity & LGBT-QS/SGL pride at the beach & across Los
Angeles • LGBT • 323/285-4225 • www.atbla.com

3-6: Int'l Gay Square Dance Clubs Convention   *Salt Lake City, UT*
303/722-5476 • www.iagsdc.org

8-12: Black & White Men Together Convention   *Milwaukee, WI*
mostly men • 100+ attendees • 800/NA4-BWMT • www.nabwmt.org

11-13: GaymerCon   *San Francisco, CA*
gaming & geek lifestyle convention w/ a focus on LGBT culture • www.gaymer-
con.org

12-13: Ride for AIDS Chicago   *Chicago, IL*
2-day bike ride to fight HIV/ AIDS in the Chicagoland area • LGBT • 500 attendees •
773/989-9400 • www.rideforaids.org

13-20: IMEN Gathering   *near Baltimore, MD*
all-inclusive summer camp for gay men • party naked w/ 300 guys for an entire
week • theme parties, pool parties & great food • airport transportation to/from
BWI • 603/841-5636 • www.imengonude.org

14: Joining Hearts   *Atlanta, GA*
at Piedmont Park Pool • open bar, catered hors d'oeuvres, live entertainment, dancing under the stars & a grand finale fireworks spectacular • 100% donated to beneficiaries • 678/318-1446 • www.joininghearts.org

21: AIDS Walk San Francisco   *San Francisco, CA*
mixed gay/ straight • 27,000+ attendees • 415/615-9255 • www.aidswalk.net

26: Crape Myrtle Festival   *Raleigh-Durham, Chapel Hill, NC*
yearlong fundraising events for HIV/LGBT concerns culminating in a grand gala the
last Saturday of July • mixed gay/ straight • 500+ attendees • 919/656-4205 •
www.crapemyrtlefest.org

TBA: Charlotte Black Gay Pride   *Charlotte, NC*
art & performances, community forums, dance parties & more • 704/953-8813 •
www.cbgp.org

TBA: EuroPride 2014   *Oslo, Norway*
parties, politics, performance & more • there is something for everyone at this
massive celebration of gay pride • www.europride.info

TBA: Gaylaxicon *Boston, MA*
LGBT science fiction, fantasy, horror & gaming convention •
www.gaylacticnetwork.org

TBA: Hotter Than July Weekend *Detroit, MI*
the Midwest's oldest black same-gender-loving pride celebration • LGBT •
888/755-9165 • blackpridesociety.org

TBA: Miami Beach Bruthaz *Miami, FL*
lifestyle event for same-gender-loving men & women • hip hop party • rooftop
pool party • fashion show & more! • mostly men • miamibeachbruthaz.com

TBA: Triangle Black Pride *Raleigh-Durham, Chapel Hill, NC*
celebrate & honor the diversity of the African American LGBTQ community in the
Triangle • 919/233-2044 • triangleblackpride.org

August 2014

1-25: Edinburgh Fringe Festival *Edinburgh, Scotland*
the largest arts festival in the world • dance, theater, music, comedy, events & more
• mixed gay/ straight • 44-131/226-0026 • www.edfringe.com

6-9: Rendezvous 2014 *Medicine Bow Nat'l Forest, WY*
5-day camping festival to celebrate LGBT pride • 400+ attendees • 307/778-7645 •
www.wyomingequality.org

8-10: Fire Island Black Out (FIBO) *Fire Island, NY*
3-day beach event for the LGBT community & friends • all are invited to attend &
enjoy, regardless of race, gender or orientation • LGBT • 215/751-0808 •
www.fireislandblackout.com

9-16: Gay Games 2014 *Cleveland, OH*
8 days of sports, cultural events, arts & ceremonies • LGBT • 49-221/925 2607 •
www.gg9cle.com

14-17: Tropical Heat *Key West, FL*
naked pool party • dungeon & fetish party • 4 days of HOT male events! • men only
• www.tropicalheatkw.com

16-22: Provincetown Carnival *Provincetown, MA*
508/487-2313 • www.ptown.org

22-27: National Gay Softball World Series *Dallas, TX*
LGBT • 412/362-1247 • www.gaysoftballworldseries.com

24-31: 'Camp' Camp *Porter, ME*
summer camp for LGBT adults • sports, pottery, theater, yoga & more • LGBT •
347/453-5257 • www.campcamp.com

27-Sept 1: Atlanta Black Pride Weekend *Atlanta, GA*
celebrate Black Pride over Labor Day weekend in Atlanta • LGBT • 678/799-8526 •
www.inthelifeatlanta.org

27-Sept 1: Southern Decadence *New Orleans, LA*
mostly men • 504/522-8049 • www.southerndecadence.com

27-Sept 9: CMEN West Coast Gathering *Malibu, CA*
swimming, parties, workshops & more with fellow gay male naturists • also Spring
Gathering near Nashville, TN in June • men only • 400 attendees • 877/683-4781 •
www.cmen.info

29-Sept 1: Splash Days *Austin, TX*
weekend of music, dance, unity & lake parties in Austin over Labor Day Wknd •
www.splashdays.com

30-Sept 6: Gay Ski Week QT *Queenstown, New Zealand*
64 21/033-6270 • www.gayskiweekqt.com

TBA: AIDS Walk Colorado *Denver, CO*
303/962-5302 • www.aidswalkcolorado.org

TBA: Black Pride NYC *New York City, NY*
multicultural LGBT festival w/ a wide array of entertainment, forums, workshops &
events • LGBT • www.nycblackpride.com

TBA: Blackout: Oakland Black & Brown Pride *Oakland, CA*
celebrate w/ a weekend of conferences, awards ceremonies & parties •
510/621-3553 • www.oaklandpride.org

TBA: GNI (Gay Naturist Int'l) Gathering *Poconos, PA*
weeklong gathering of gay nudists • price includes food, beverages, lodging &
entertainment • workshops • men only • 800 attendees • 954/567-2700 •
www.gaynaturists.org

TBA: Inferno Dominican Republic *Punta Cana, Dominican Republic*
the premier Labor Day pride celebration • deluxe, all-inclusive accommodations •
LGBT • 305/891-7536 • www.infernodr.com

TBA: Northalsted Market Days *Chicago, IL*
a good ol' summer block party on Main St of Boys' Town, USA • LGBT •
773/883-0500 • www.northalsted.com

TBA: St Louis Black Pride *St Louis, MO*
314/531-2284 • www.st-louisblackpride.org

September 2014

2-8: Gay Days Las Vegas *Orlando, FL*
including Gay Day at Disney • 7 days of parties & fun for boys & girls alike! • LGBT
• 407/896-8431 • www.gaydays.com

21: Out in the Park *Springfield, MA*
unofficial gay day at Six Flags New England • wear red to show your support •
LGBT • 1000+ attendees • www.outinthepark.info

TBA: Braking the Cycle *Boston, MA to New York City, NY*
3-day fully-supported bike ride from Boston to New York • benefiting the HIV/AIDS
related services of the LGBT Community Center in NYC • mixed gay/ straight •
212/989-1111 • www.brakingthecycle.com

TBA: Get Wet Weekend *Curaçao, Netherlands Antilles, Caribbean*
discover the Caribbean Dutch Paradise of Curaçao! • gay/ lesbian • 599/9510-6479,
599/9510-6499 • www.gaycuracao.com

TBA: Out On The Mountain *Valencia, CA*
gay day at Six Flags Magic Mountain • LGBT • www.outonthemountain.com

TBA: Pink Season *Hong Kong, China*
2-month festival featuring speakers, plays, dance parties, pageants & more • LGBT •
www.pinkseason.hk

TBA: Seattle AIDS Walk *Seattle, WA*
mixed gay/ straight • 4000+ attendees • 206/957-1606 •
www.SeattleAIDSWalk.org

October 2014

1-6: Dallas Black Pride *Dallas, TX*
LGBT • 214/440-9300 • **dfwpridemovement.org**

3-5: Gay Days Anaheim *Anaheim, CA*
"join 30,000 GLBT mouseketeers as we turn the happiest place in earth into the
gayest!" • **www.GayDaysAnaheim.com**

5: Castro Street Fair *San Francisco, CA*
performance, arts & community groups street fair • co-founded by Harvey Milk •
800/853-5950 • **www.castrostreetfair.org**

11: National Coming Out Day *Cross-country, USA*
check local listings for events in your area or visit www.hrc.com/ncop •
202/628-4160, 800/777-4723 • **www.hrc.org/comingout**

16-19: Sundance Stompede *San Francisco, CA*
San Francisco's annual country/ western dance weekend • LGBT • 415/820-1403 •
www.stompede.com

16-19: World Gay Rodeo Finals *Fort Worth, TX*
check w/ local chapters for events throughout the year in your area •
303/766-5630 • **www.igra.com**

17-26: Fantasy Fest *Key West, FL*
10 days of parties, costume contests, street fairs, masquerade balls & parades •
70,000 attendees • 305/296-1817 • **www.fantasyfest.com**

19: AIDS Walk LA *Los Angeles, CA*
annual AIDS fundraiser in West Hollywood • mixed gay/ straight • 213/201-9255 •
www.aidswalk.net

19-28: Fantasia Fair *Provincetown, MA*
a weeklong celebration of gender diversity • workshops, fashion show, cabaret,
banquets & more • **www.fantasiafair.org**

TBA: Glasgay! *Glasgow, Scotland*
UK's largest lesbian & gay multi-arts festival • 44-141/552-7575 •
www.glasgay.com

TBA: AIDS Walk Atlanta & 5k Run *Atlanta, GA*
mixed gay/ straight • 10,000+ attendees • 404/876-9255 •
www.aidswalkatlanta.com

TBA: Black Pride *Nashville, TN*
gay/ lesbian • 615/974-2832, 800/845-4266x269 • **www.brothersunited.com**

TBA: Taiwan LGBT Pride *Taipei, Taiwan*
• **www.twpride.org**

November 2014

1-2: Greater Palm Springs Pride *Palm Springs, CA*
free entertainment, dance parties, lots of people & a parade on Sunday •
760/416-8711 • **www.PSPride.org**

TBA: Transgender Film Festival   *San Francisco, CA*
films that promote the visibility of transgender & gender variant people •
www.trannyfest.com

December 2014

15-18: Utah Gay & Lesbian Ski Week   *Salt Lake City, UT*
ski at Alta, Snowbird, Solitude, Brighton, Snow Basin & The Canyons •
877/429-6368 • www.gayskiing.org

31: Mummer's Strut   *Philadelphia, PA*
big New Year's Eve party • followed by New Year's Day Parade • mixed gay/ straight
• $40-50 • 215/336-3050 • www.mummers.com

TBA: Holly Folly   *Provincetown, MA*
lesbian/ gay holiday celebration • fabulous parties • holiday concert • open houses
• 1st wknd in December • www.ptown.org

TBA: IAGLBC Annual Bridge Tournament   *Palm Springs, CA*
Int'l Association of Gay & Lesbian Bridge Clubs • www.GayBridge.org

FILM FESTIVALS

January 2014

20-26: Zinegoak   *Bilbao, Spain*
LGBT film & performing arts festival • 34-94/415-6258 • www.zinegoak.com

30-Feb 8: Reelout Queer Film & Video Festival   *Kingston, ON, Canada*
celebrating the best of queer independent film & video • 613/549-7335 •
www.reelout.com

February 2014

13-23: Mardi Gras Film Festival   *Sydney, Australia*
Sydney film festival corresponds with massive Mardi Gras event • 61-2/9332-4938
• www.queerscreen.com.au

March 2014

13-24: Melbourne Queer Film Festival   *Melbourne, Australia*
613/9662-4147 • www.mqff.com.au

20-30: London Lesbian & Gay Film Festival   *London, England*
grab your tickets for the largest LGBT film fest in Europe • 44 (0)20/7928-3232 •
www.llgff.org.uk

TBA: Outfest Fusion LGBT People of Color Film Festival *Los Angeles, CA*
213/480-7088 • www.outfest.org

April 2014

3-12: Boston LGBT Film Festival   *Boston, MA*
617/369-3300 • www.bostonlgbtfilmfest.org

13-17: QFest   *St Louis, MO*
314/289-4152 • www.cinemastlouis.org/qfest

25-May 4: Miami Gay & Lesbian Film Festival   *Miami, FL*
305/751-6305 • www.MGLFF.com

TBA: Brisbane Queer Film Festival   *Brisbane, Australia*
61 7/3358 8600 • www.bqff.com.au

TBA: Out in Africa   *Cape Town, South Africa*
the only film festival of its kind on the African continent • three 10-day festivals
throughout the year • also August & October • also in Johannesburg • 27 21/461
40 27 • www.oia.co.za

May 2014

22-June 1: Inside Out:
Toronto LGBT Film & Video Festival   *Toronto, ON, Canada*
416/977-6847 • www.insideout.ca

23-31: Fairy Tales Int'l LGBT Film Festival   *Calgary, AB, Canada*
403/244-1956 • www.fairytalesfilmfest.com

29-June 11: Out Takes LGBT Film Festival   *Wellington, New Zealand*
week-long festival in Auckland, Wellington & Christchurch • 64-4/972-6775 •
www.outtakes.org.nz

30-June 1: FilmOut San Diego   *San Diego, CA*
LGBT film festival • 619/512-5157 • www.filmoutsandiego.com

30-June 7: Connecticut Gay & Lesbian Film Festival   *Hartford, CT*
gay & lesbian film festival at Cinestudio • 860/586-1136 • www.outfilmct.org

TBA: Translations: Transgender Film Festival   *Seattle, WA*
206/323-4874 • www.threedollarbillcinema.org

June 2014

1-15: Honolulu Rainbow Film Festival   *Honolulu, HI*
808/675-8428 • www.hglcf.org

3-13: Rio Gay Film Festival   *Rio de Janeiro, Brazil*
LGBT • www.riofgc.com

7-14: TLVFest: The Tel Aviv LGBT Film Festival   *Tel Aviv, Israel*
films will also show in Jerusalem & Haifa • 972-52/2767404 • www.tlvfest.com

18-22: Provincetown Int'l Film Festival   *Provincetown, MA*
mixed gay/ straight • 508/487-3456 • www.ptownfilmfest.org

19-29: Frameline: San Francisco Int'l
LGBT Film Festival   *San Francisco, CA*
get your tickets early for a slew of films about us • LGBT • 65,000+ attendees •
415/703-8650 • see ad in front color section • www.frameline.org

TBA: Identities Queer Film Festival   *Vienna, Austria*
43-1/524-6274 • www.identities.at/index/en/

TBA: Mix Milano Int'l LGBT Film Festival   *Milan, Italy*
• www.cinemagaylesbico.com

July 2014

10-20: Outfest Los Angeles LGBT Film Festival   *Los Angeles, CA*
Los Angeles' lesbian/ gay film & video festival in mid-July • 213/480-7088 •
www.outfest.org

TBA: Mostra Lambda Barcelona   *Barcelona, Spain*
LGBT film festival • www.cinemalambda.com

TBA: Philadelphia QFest   *Philadelphia, PA*
267/765-9800 • www.qfest.com

TBA: Tokyo Int'l Lesbian & Gay Film Festival   *Tokyo, Japan*
• www.tokyo-lgff.org

August 2014

5-10: Flickers: Rhode Island Int'l Film Festival   *Providence, RI*
don't miss the Gay & Lesbian Film Fest • mixed gay/ straight • 401/861-4445 •
www.film-festival.org

TBA: Birmingham Shout   *Birmingham, AL*
LGBT film festival • 205/324-0888 • www.bhamshout.com

TBA: Gaze Dublin Int'l LGBT Film Festival   *Dublin, Ireland*
0872/709700 • www.gaze.ie

TBA: North Carolina Gay & Lesbian Film Festival   *Durham, NC*
919/560-3030 (box office), 919/560-3040 • festivals.carolinatheatre.org/ncglff

TBA: Vancouver Queer Film & Video Festival   *Vancouver, BC, Canada*
LGBT • 604/844-1615 • www.queerfilmfestival.ca

September 2014

12-14: Q Film Festival   *Long Beach, CA*
showcasing films of interest to the queer community • 562/434-4455 •
www.qfilmslongbeach.com

TBA: Fresno Reel Pride   *Fresno, CA*
annual lesbian & gay film festival in central California • 559/999-7971 •
www.reelpride.com

TBA: Hong Kong Lesbian/ Gay Film Festival   *Hong Kong, China*
LGBT • 852/2311 8081 • www.hklgff.hk

TBA: NewFest: New York LGBT Film Festival   *New York City, NY*
646/290-8136 • www.newfest.org

TBA: Outflix   *Memphis, TN*
LGBT film festival • www.outflixfestival.org

TBA: Queer Lisbon   *Lisbon, Portugal*
Portugal's only LGBT film festival • 351 91/335-8603 • www.queerlisboa.pt

October 2014

2-9: Out on Film   *Atlanta, GA*
LGBT • 678/237-7206 • www.outonfilm.org

10-19: Reel Q Int'l Lesbian & Gay Film Festival   *Pittsburgh, PA*
412/422-6776 • www.plgfs.org

10-19: Southwest Gay & Lesbian Film Festival   *Albuquerque, NM*
also in Santa Fe, NM • 505/243-1870 • www.swglff.com

14-19: Hamburg Int'l Lesbian & Gay Film Festival   *Hamburg, Germany*
49-40/348-0670 • www.lsf-hamburg.de

16-26: Barcelona Int'l LGTIB Film Festival   *Barcelona, Spain*
gay/ lesbian • 973/664-421 • www.barcelonafilmfestival.org

16-26: Seattle Lesbian & Gay Film Festival   *Seattle, WA*
206/323-4274 • www.threedollarbillcinema.org

TBA: Cheries-Cheris:
Paris Gay, Lesbian & Trans Film Festival   *Paris, France*
• www.cheries-cheris.com

TBA: Madrid LGBT Film Festival   *Madrid, Spain*
34-91/593-0540 • www.lesgaicinemad.com

TBA: Milwaukee LGBT Film/ Video Festival   *Milwaukee, WI*
414/229-4758 • www4.uwm.edu/psoa/film/lgbtfilmfestival/

TBA: Mix   *Copenhagen, Denmark*
45/2843-4217 • www.mixcopenhagen.dk

TBA: Polari   *Austin, TX*
512/302-9889 • www.polarifest.com

TBA: Portland Lesbian & Gay Film Festival   *Portland, OR*
• www.plgff.org

TBA: Q Cinema   *Fort Worth, TX*
annual celebration of LGBT-themed movies • 817/723-4358 • www.qcinema.org

TBA: Reel Affirmations:
The Nation's LGBT Film Festival   *Washington, DC*
lesbian/ gay films • 202/349-7358 • www.reelaffirmations.org

TBA: Sacramento Int'l Gay & Lesbian Film Festival   *Sacramento, CA*
916/304-3456 • www.siglff.org

TBA: Tampa Bay Int'l Gay & Lesbian Film Festival   *Tampa Bay, FL*
813/879-4220 • www.tiglff.com

November 2014

6-13: Reeling: Chicago Lesbian & Gay Int'l Film Fest   *Chicago, IL*
773/293-1447 • www.reelingfilmfestival.org

7-10: Long Island Gay & Lesbian Film Festival   *Huntington, NY*
• www.liglff.org

TBA: image+nation: Montréal Int'l
LGBT Film Festival   *Montréal, QC, Canada*
LGBT • 514/285-4467 • www.image-nation.org

TBA: Mezipatra   *Prague & Brno, Czech Republic*
Czech LGBT film festival • www.mezipatra.cz

★ ★ ★ ★ ★ ★ ★ ★ ★ ★ ★ ★ ★ ★

LIKE TO WATCH?

COME SEE US IN SEATTLE

Keeping audiences entertained since 1996, Three Dollar Bill Cinema promotes and produces LGBT film events throughout the year, including free outdoor movies every summer, our Spring Film Series of vintage queer classics, the Seattle Lesbian & Gay Film Festival in October, and other unique events every month!

three dollar bill cinema

Check out our website or find us on Facebook to see what's happening on your next visit to Seattle.

www.threedollarbillcinema.org

TBA: Mix: New York Lesbian & Gay
   Experimental Film Fest   *New York City, NY*
   film, videos, installations & media performances • write for info • 212/742-8880 •
   www.mixnyc.org

LEATHER, FETISH & BEARS

January 2014

16-20: La Fiesta de Los Osos   *Tucson, AZ*
   a winter bear gathering in the warmth of the desert sun • men only •
   520/310-3485 • www.fiesta.botop.com

17-20: Mid-Atlantic Leather Weekend   *Washington, DC*
   LGBT • 703/863-7295 • www.leatherweekend.com

23-25: Southwest Leather Conference   *Phoenix, AZ*
   workshops, vendors & fetish ball • MASTER/slave, Bootblack & Daddy/boy contests •
   LGBT • www.southwestleather.org

26-Feb 2: Beef Dip: Int'l Bear Week   *Puerto Vallarta, Mexico*
   beach parties, pool parties & hot DJs • local tours • booze cruise • bring sunscreen!
   • men only • 416/922-1018 • www.beefdip.com

February 2014

21-23: SNOWBOUND Leather Weekend   *Provincetown, MA*
   get outta the cold and into the heat! hot weekend of leather parties, demos & more
   • 800/330-9413 • www.matesleatherweekend.com/snowbound

26-March 2: Fetish Pride Italy   *Rome, Italy*
   hot weekend of fetish parties, exhibitions, film festival & more • men only •
   www.fetishpride.it

TBA: West Coast Rubber Weekend   *Palm Springs, CA*
   hot weekend dedicated to rubber, spandex, dive gear, BDSM • men only •
   760/880-7470 • www.westcoastrubber.com

March 2014

14-23: Washington State Leather Pride Week   *Seattle, WA*
   • www.wsmlo.org

27-30: Sugarbear Weekend   *Montréal, QC, Canada*
   Quebecois bear party with lots of maple syrup • men only •
   www.sugarbearweekend.com

April 2014

4-6: Rubbout   *Vancouver, BC, Canada*
   annual party weekend of rubber & fetish for men • men only • 604/345-1357 •
   www.rubbout.com

11-13: Leather Leadership Conference   *Philadelphia, PA*
   join us to develop & strengthen problem-solving & camaraderie in the leather
   community • LGBT • www.leatherleadership.org

16-22: Easter 2014 Berlin   *Berlin, Germany*
annual leather & fetish weekend • German Mr Leather contest • 49 30/215 0099 •
www.blf.de

May 2014

1-5: Phurfest   *Phoenix, AZ*
let the fur fly in Phoenix • 602/370-3260 • **www.phurfest.org**

2-3: Mr LeatherMan Italy   *Rome, Italy*
hot weekend of leather events culminating in the election of Mr LeatherMan Italy •
men only • **www.lcroma.com**

7-12: Beach Bear Weekend   *Fort Lauderdale, FL*
get to the beach for a long weekend of dance parties, cocktails and great food • oh,
and bears! • **www.beachbearweekend.com**

16-18: Northwest Leather Celebration (NWLC)   *San Jose, CA*
host of the NW regional Master/slave contest • LGBT • **www.northwestleathercel-
ebration.com**

23-26: Bear Pride   *Chicago, IL*
1000+ attendees • 312/590-4485 • **www.bearpride.org**

23-26: International Mr Bootblack Contest   *Chicago, IL*
contest takes place during International Mr Leather weekend • 800/545-6753 •
www.imrl.com

23-26: International Mr Leather   *Chicago, IL*
weekend of leather events, capped by contest Sunday, Black & Blue Ball on Monday
• 800/545-6753 • **www.imrl.com**

June 2014

8-15: Southern HiBearnation   *Melbourne, Australia*
a week of furry fun down under, culminating in the Mr Australasia Bear Contest,
bringing bears from Australia, New Zealand, Southeast Asia, the South Pacific &
beyond • 500+ attendees • 0409/360-031 • **www.southernhibearnation.com**

19-22: Southeast Leatherfest   *Atlanta, GA*
LGBT • **www.seleatherfest.com**

TBA: Bear Arabia Trip   *Lebanon, Jordan, and Syria*
visit Lebanon, Jordan & Syria with the bears of Arabia • also in Sept or Oct • 961
3/004572 • **www.beararabia.org**

TBA: Folsom Street East   *New York City, NY*
New York City's answer to the famous San Francisco fetish street fair • LGBT •
www.folsomstreeteast.org

July 2014

11-13: Thunder in the Mountains   *Denver, CO*
weekend of pansexual leather events & seminars • kinky comedy revue • talent
show • LGBT • 800+ attendees • 303/698-1207 •
www.thunderinthemountains.com

12-20: Bear Week Provincetown   *Provincetown, MA*
come to Provincetown for a relaxing week of parties & events • men only •
www.ptownbears.org

25-27: International Deaf Leather   *Providence, RI*
weekend of events, including Mr & Ms Deaf Leather Contest • **www.international-aldeafleather.org**

25-27: Mobile Bleather Weekend   *Mobile, AL*
3-day party with bear/ levi/ leather guys from the Gulf Coast & beyond •
www.mobilebleatherweekend.com

27: Up Your Alley Fair   *San Francisco, CA*
local SM/ leather street fair held in Dore Alley, South-of-Market • thousands of
local kinky men & women attend • 415/777-3247 • **www.folsomstreetevents.org**

TBA: TransCampOUT   *Walton, WV*
presentations • games • auctions • outdoor dungeon • swimming • trans-oriented
• everyone welcome regardless of sexual orientation or gender identity • LGBT •
971/295-6106 • **www.transcampout.org**

August 2014

3-10: Toronto Leather Pride Week   *Toronto, ON, Canada*
hot parties all week • Mr Leather Toronto, Ms Leather Toronto & Bootblack Toronto
competitions • Leather Ball on Sat • mixed gay/ straight • 416/515-1910 •
www.torontoleatherpride.ca

8-10: Southeast Black & Blue   *Atlanta, GA*
SE Leather Sir, Leather Boy & Bootblack contests • also Mr SE Rubber contest •
www.southeastlsb.com

9-11: Rocky Mountain Olympus Leather   *Salt Lake City, UT*
leather competition • participants from Utah, Colorado, Wyoming, Idaho &
Montana • mixed gay/ straight • 200 attendees • 415/409-9447 • **www.rocky-mountainolympus.com**

28-Sept 1: International LeatherSIR/ Leatherboy   *Dallas, TX*
also Int'l Community BootBlack • check website for regional contest info •
214/395-8460 • **www.ILSb-ICBB.com**

TBA: Lazy Bear Weekend   *Russian River, CA*
no contests, no pageants, no frills—just fur! • FUNdraiser benefits AIDS charities in
Northern California & beyond • mostly men • **www.lazybearweekend.com**

September 2014

13-14: Folsom Europe   *Berlin, Germany*
49 30/23 62 86 32 • **www.folsomeurope.info**

21: Folsom Street Fair   *San Francisco, CA*
huge SM/ leather street fair, topping a week of kinky events • LGBT • thousands of
local & visiting kinky men & women attendees • 415/777-3247 • see ad in front
color section • **www.folsomstreetevents.org**

TBA: Oktobearfest   *Munich, Germany*
join the Munich bears • 49-176/6312-7540 • **www.oktobearfest.de**

October 2014

2-5: Mates Leather Weekend   *Provincetown, MA*
the hottest leather event in New England • 800/330-9413 • www.matesleather-weekend.com

TBA: Bear Bust   *Orlando, FL*
hot bear weekend at Parliament House Resort • men only • www.bearbust.org

TBA: Leather Pride Amsterdam   *Amsterdam, Netherlands*
weekend of hot leather events • men only • info@leatherpride.nl

TBA: OctobearFest   *Denver, CO*
1st or 2nd wknd in Oct • men only • www.octobearfest.org

TBA: Pantheon of Leather   *Atlanta, GA*
annual leather/ SM/ fetish community service awards & int'l Mr & Ms Olympus Leather • mixed gay/ straight • www.TheLeatherJournal.com/pantheon

November 2014

7-9: Mr Int'l Rubber & Rubber Blowout   *Chicago, IL*
largest rubber event in US • market, parties • men only • www.MIRubber.com

27-30: Bear Pride Week   *Cologne, Germany*
49-221/5481-9259 • www.bearscologne.de

TBA: Santa Clara County Leather Weekend   *San Jose, CA*
leather fellowship in the San Jose area • LGBT • www.SCCLeather.org

CONFERENCES & RETREATS

January 2014

29-Feb 2: Creating Change Conference   *Houston, TX*
for lesbians, gays, bisexuals, transgender people & allies seeking positive & enduring political & social change • 2500+ attendees • 617/492-6393 • www.creatingchange.org

March 2014

21-23: Together We Can   *Detroit, MI*
annual LGBT substance abuse conference • 248/838-9905 • www.twcdetroit.com

May 2014

15-18: Saints & Sinners   *New Orleans, LA*
LGBT writers & readers gather for a hot weekend of readings, panels & performance • 300 attendees • $100 • 504/581-1144 • www.sasfest.com

June 2014

TBA: Lambda Literary Awards   *New York City, NY*
the Lammies are the Oscars of LGBT writing & publishing • LGBT • 323/366-2104 • www.lambdaliterary.org

July 2014

TBA: NGLCC Conference   *TBA, USA*
anual gathering of Nat'l Gay & Lesbian Chamber of Commerce • 202/234-9181 •
www.nglcc.org

August 2014

14-17: Gender Odyssey   *Seattle, WA*
4 days of panels, workshops & meetings • entertainment & art • focus on transmen,
transwomen & families with transgender children & teens • open to all •
206/306-8383 • **www.genderodyssey.org**

TBA: Nat'l Lesbian & Gay Journalists Assoc Convention   *TBA, USA*
workshops • keynote speakers • entertainment • 202/588-9888 x10 •
www.nlgja.org

September 2014

1-7: Southern Comfort Conference   *Atlanta, GA*
entertainers & leaders from the entire spectrum of the transgender community
offering 5 days of learning, networking & fun • 910/443-3659 • **www.sccatl.org**

October 2014

2-4: National LGBT MBA Conference   *San Francisco, CA*
career fair & discussions of sexual orientation, gender & leadership in the workplace
by MBA students & out Fortune 500 company leaders • LGBT • 800+ attendees •
www.reachingoutmba.org

November 2014

TBA: Transgender Leadership Summit   *TBA, USA*
join transgender activists to help create a unified voice to advance the movement
for transgender equality • 200+ attendees • 415/865-0176 • **www.transgender-
lawcenter.org**

SPIRITUAL

February 2014

14-17: PantheaCon   *San Jose, CA*
pagan convention • mixed gay/ straight • 510/653-3244 • **www.pantheacon.com**

June 2014

15-22: Pagan Spirit Gathering   *Earlville, IL*
summer solstice celebration • primitive camping • workshops • rituals • advance
registration required • mixed gay/ straight • 608/924-2216 • **www.circlesanctu-
ary.org/psg**

August 2014

TBA: BC Witchcamp *near Vancouver, BC, Canada*
  weeklong Wiccan intensive at Evans Lake • mixed gay/ straight • 250/598-9229 •
  www.bcwitchcamp.ca

THE CIRCUIT

January 2014

26-Feb 2: WinterPRIDE: Whistler Gay Ski Week *Whistler, BC, Canada*
  annual gay/lesbian ski week • top-notch DJs & venues • popular destination 75
  miles N of Vancouver • LGBT • 3,000+ attendees • 604/288-7218, 866/787-1966 •
  www.gaywhistler.com

March 2014

5-10: Winter Party Festival *Miami Beach, FL*
  celebration & fundraiser for the LGBT community • 10,000 attendees •
  305/571-1924 • **www.winterparty.org**

22: The Black Party *New York City, NY*
  also BPX: Black Party Expo • www.blackpartyexpo.com • LGBT • $100 •
  212/674-8541 • **www.saintatlarge.com**

April 2014

4-6: Cherry Weekend *Washington, DC*
  703/389-1238 • **www.cherryfund.org**

25-28: White Party *Palm Springs, CA*
  spectacular live performances • top-notch talent • cutting-edge lighting & special
  effects • mostly men • 30,000 attendees • 323/782-9924 •
  www.jeffreysanker.com

May 2014

9-12: Purple Party *Dallas, TX*
  a weekend of dance parties & social events benefiting AIDS Services of Dallas •
  www.dallaspurpleparty.org

22-27: Sizzle South Beach 2014 *Miami, FL*
  Miami's original circuit event • 305/938-9612 • **www.sizzlesouthbeach.com**

July 2014

TBA: San Diego Pride Parties *San Diego, CA*
  a weekend of hot parties w/ big name DJs, including the Zoo Party at the world-
  famous San Diego Zoo • mostly men • 800-4,000 attendees • $75-100 •
  619/770-8322 • **www.billhardtpresents.com**

TBA: Summer Camp *Provincetown, MA*
  celebrate the week of the 4th at the longest running circuit celebration in New
  England • 508/487-9601 • **www.davidflower.com**

August 2014

6-17: Circuit _Barcelona, Spain_
water park events • club nights • pool parties • films, discussions & more • gay/
lesbian • **www.circuitfestival.net**

20-24: XLSior Int'l Gay Festival _Mykonos, Greece_
5 days of hot events, including the beach party at Elia beach in Mykonos, Greece •
mostly men • **www.xlsiorfestival.com**

31: Elysium Pool Party _Mykonos, Greece_
huge, int'l gay party • 30/22890-23952 • **www.mykonos-accommodation.com**

September 2014

20: Aftershock: Folsom Street Fair _San Francisco, CA_
DJ Abel keeps the leather crowd going • 4am Sunday morning/ Saturday night,
after Magnitude • mostly men • **www.TheDISCOSF.com**

20: Magnitude _San Francisco, CA_
the official, hottest dance & play party of the Folsom Street Fair • mostly men •
415/777-3247 • see ad in front color section •
www.folsomstreetevents.org/magnitude

21: REAL BAD _San Francisco, CA_
"Be Bad... Do Good" • annual fundraiser immediately following the Folsom Street
Fair • proceeds go directly to beneficiaries • mostly men • see ad in front color
section • **www.realbad.org**

October 2014

8-14: Black & Blue Festival _Montréal, QC, Canada_
North America's biggest & most innovative dance event & cultural festival • mostly
men • 25,000+ attendees • $60-100+ • 514/875-7026 • **www.bbcm.org**

23-26: Halloween New Orleans _New Orleans, LA_
mostly men • 5,000+ attendees • /310 • **www.halloweenneworleans.com**

November 2014

19-30: White Party Week _Miami Beach, FL_
6 days of festivities capped by the annual White Party at Vizcaya • benefitting Care
Resource • LGBT • 305/576-1234 • **www.whiteparty.org**

December 2014

31: Metropolis New Year's Eve 2014 _San Francisco, CA_
12-hour dance marathon • largest gay New Year's party in San Francisco • mostly
men • **www.guspresents.com**

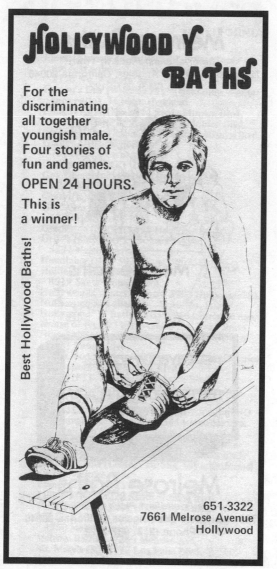

COME WEST

AT THE DOUBLE R MIAMI, FLORIDA

1001 N.E. 2nd AVE., MIAMI, FLORIDA / 374-9444

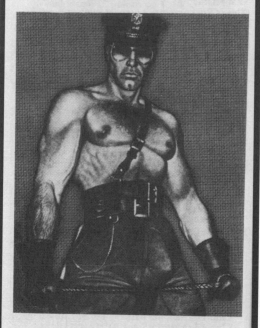

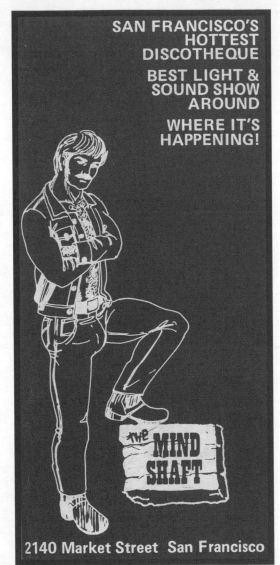

SAN FRANCISCO'S
HOTTEST
DISCOTHEQUE

BEST LIGHT &
SOUND SHOW
AROUND

WHERE IT'S
HAPPENING!

THE MIND SHAFT

2140 Market Street San Francisco

AFTER DARK
BOOKSHOP & FILM GALLERY
1067 Peachtree Street

ANIMALS

THE PALACE OF MALE BURLESQUE AND BIZARRE ENTERTAINMENT

Rear of 1055 Peachtree Street

(404) 885-9400

ATLANTA, GEORGIA

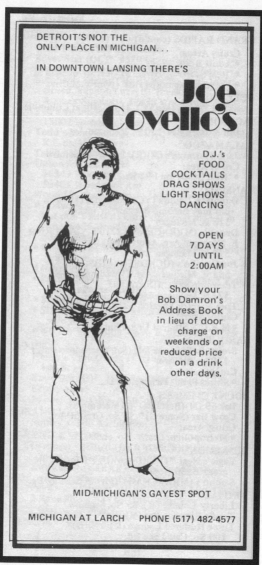

DETROIT'S NOT THE
ONLY PLACE IN MICHIGAN...

IN DOWNTOWN LANSING THERE'S

Joe Covello's

D.J.'s
FOOD
COCKTAILS
DRAG SHOWS
LIGHT SHOWS
DANCING

OPEN
7 DAYS
UNTIL
2:00AM

Show your
Bob Damron's
Address Book
in lieu of door
charge on
weekends or
reduced price
on a drink
other days.

MID-MICHIGAN'S GAYEST SPOT

MICHIGAN AT LARCH   PHONE (517) 482-4577

"His Master's Boots"

PHOTO COURTESY OF MATHEW OF GLENDALE

THE BOOT CAMP

**1010 Bryant
San Francisco**

A Disco Experience!

The Capital Corral in Raleigh is a western bar. It's also the home of "Glitter Gulch" - the hottest disco in North Carolina. An unusual combination? Come see how well it works!

**The Capital Corral
313 W. Hargett St.
Raleigh, N.C. 27601
(919) 755-9599**

Near the downtown Holiday Inn

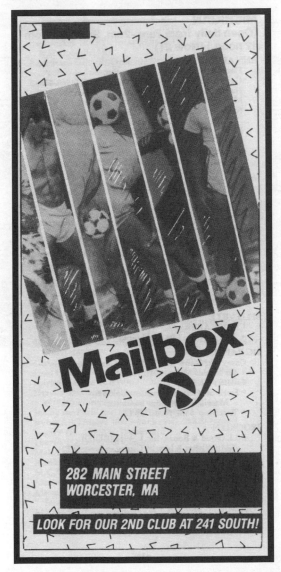